1995

BRITISH DESIGN AND ART DIRECTION

The 33rd Annual of the
Best in British and International
Advertising and Design

THE DESIGNERS AND ART DIRECTORS ASSOCIATION
OF THE UNITED KINGDOM

Cover Design
JOHN GORHAM

Annual Design
LEWIS MOBERLY

Implementation
PEARTREE DESIGN ASSOCIATES

Jury Photographers
ANITA CORBIN
JOHN O'GRADY

Annual Co-ordination and Editing
BEVERLEY PARKER

Printed in Hong Kong by
TOPPAN PRINTING COMPANY LIMITED

All book trade enquiries for Europe and all direct mail enquiries to:
Internos Books, 12 Percy Street, London W1P 9FB, England, UK.

USA and Canadian book trade rights:
Rizzoli International Publications Inc,
300 Park Avenue South, New York, NY 10010, USA.

International trade sales:
Hearst Books International,
105, Madison Avenue, New York, NY 10016, USA.

ISBN Number 1873968 752

CONTENTS

ANTHONY SIMONDS-GOODING

1995
CHAIRMAN'S STATEMENT

The diligence of our President and her Executive has been remarkable – many meetings, early meetings, late meetings, long meetings – they have all been attended. I would suggest that an important measure of health of an organisation is the support it receives from its leadership – in which case D&AD is healthy.

The look of D&AD's output has improved immeasurably – our literature, stationery, promotional material, annual – and is now designed to a system, that will avoid yearly interference and discontinuity.

The Festival Exhibition at The Saatchi Gallery was outstanding. The President's Lectures really have come into their own. When we started these three years ago, an audience of 100 was considered excellent. Now ten times that number is to be expected.

The new Director, David Kester, has played himself in. With an organisation as idiosyncratic as ours, the wicket is often sticky, but his energy and enthusiasm throughout the year has been a delight. His early runs have been scored particularly in the areas of sponsorship and fund-raising. I wish him growing success in the coming years, along with the 1996 President, Graham Fink and his new Executive Committee.

On a somewhat sadder note, The School of Communication Arts has been disbanded. However, I am delighted to report that John Gillard remains as a consultant to us on education matters. We are working on a challenging new education programme, which will begin to emerge through 1996.

Finally, my thanks to all the staff at D&AD, without whom nothing – well, not much. Thank you all.

ANTHONY SIMONDS-GOODING · Chairman, D&AD

MARY LEWIS

1995
PRESIDENT'S STATEMENT

An eventful year. The creative communities steeped in debate. And D&AD, as it has been for 33 years, the forum.

Be banned or damned was given a good airing. 'Yobbish Advertising' challenged 'Shock of the New'. Club 18 – 30, applauded by the advertising jury and nominated for a silver award, fell foul of the industry's self regulatory body CAP.

D&AD's own advertising for the Festival of Excellence hit the headlines too, dramatising another popular industry debate 'Is it Art?' Tony Kaye, advertising's Pied Piper put this myth to rest, (or did he?) with his spellbinding performance at the President's Lectures.

In design, problem solvers were challenged by stylists, but both participated in a bumper crop of awards, proving that relevance and excellence are the keys to the door.

As President I set myself the goal of raising the profile of design within the Association.

Unlike advertising, design is highly fragmented. Historically D&AD has treated both alike, too often resulting in compromise for design.

This year's design jury was specially tailored to acknowledge the design difference. And jurors participated in a more generous spirit.

More designers attended the Awards Ceremony than ever before, and saw, for the first time, the design awards animated. Hopefully the days of dingy stills are gone. By bringing design to life we can now dine with dignity.

Ruby Wax as presenter charmed and captivated us. The President's Award was an important first for product design. Another first was the Special Award for Outstanding Contribution to Education – a fitting tribute to John Gillard.

The awards are the highlight of the D&AD year and rightly so. They symbolise creative excellence, the life blood of our industry. Establishing the value of this with our client community is equally important – hence the Festival of Excellence.

The Saatchi Gallery provided a stunning backdrop to this year's event which hosted the first ever public exhibition of 'The Cream of British Design & Advertising'.

The President's Lectures attracted record audiences. They embraced those on the periphery of our profession as well as at the peak. Sell out speakers included Peter Blake, Sir Richard Rogers, Xavier Mariscal, Oliviero Toscani and Michael Wolff. Tony Kaye sang a song and Maurice Saatchi told a fairy story. Saul Bass lived his legend. A heady mix. My heartfelt thanks to them all.

Back at base, D&AD is stronger than ever. Gone are the days when the Executive Committee came and went and never saw the fruits of their labours. With a three year term, we have a new found continuity.

The Copy Book introduces the first of a Mastercraft Series. Our Newsletter is relaunched. We have a new identity, rationalised under The British Design and Art Direction banner. A focused confident Association now has a corresponding image.

None of this would have been possible without the inspiring leadership of our Chairman Anthony Simonds-Gooding, the support of the hard working and early to rise Executive and the D&AD Secretariat.

A special thank you to Beverley Parker who has a unique understanding of D&AD culture, and stage manages the awards and the annual with seasonal cool. And finally to my colleagues at Lewis Moberly who worked so hard behind the scenes.

The most enjoyable aspect of my Presidency has been the interaction between design and advertising. Our visually literate consumer is demanding more from both. We are strengthened by our unity and so is D&AD.

MARY LEWIS · President, D&AD

PAST PRESIDENTS

1994
ADRIAN HOLMES

1993
AZIZ CAMI

1992
TIM DELANEY

1991
MARTIN LAMBIE-NAIRN

1990
RON BROWN

1989
JOHN HEGARTY

1988
GERT DUMBAR

1987
JEREMY SINCLAIR

1986
JOHN McCONNELL

1985
ALLEN THOMAS

1984
RODNEY FITCH CBE

1983
TONY BRIGNULL

1982
MARCELLO MINALE

1981
MARTIN BOASE

1980
LORD SNOWDON

1979
ARTHUR PARSONS

1978
MICHAEL RAND

1977
JOHN SALMON

1976
ALAN PARKER

1975
DAVID ABBOTT

1974
ALAN FLETCHER

1973
PETER MAYLE

1972
MICHAEL WOLFF

1969-71
EDWARD BOOTH-CLIBBORN

1968
DENNIS HACKETT

1963-67
EDWARD BOOTH-CLIBBORN

1962
JOHN COMMANDER

RICHARD SEYMOUR · DICK POWELL

1995
PRESIDENT'S AWARD

PAST RECIPIENTS

1994
JOHN HEGARTY
1993
JOHN GORHAM
1992
NEIL GODFREY
1991
ABRAM GAMES
1990
RIDLEY SCOTT
1989
SIR TERENCE CONRAN
1988
FRANK LOWE
1987
MARCELLO MINALE
BRIAN TATTERSFIELD
1986
DAVID ABBOTT
1985
JOHN McCONNELL
1984
BOB BROOKS
1983
BILL BERNBACH
1982
JOHN WEBSTER
1981
HAROLD EVANS
1980
ALAN PARKER
1979
JOHN SALMON
1978
JEREMY BULLMORE
1977
ALAN FLETCHER
COLIN FORBES
1976
COLIN MILWARD

I first worked with them in 1985 a year after we both formed our own consultancies. I am sure they will forgive me when I recall waiting to meet them for the first time at Lewis Moberly. They were late and I was anxious. 'Call their office and see if they have left' I said to my secretary 'And why are those bikers sitting in the meeting room?' She replied that they had left, had indeed arrived, and the 'bikers' were Richard Seymour and Dick Powell.

In a business where team spirit too often means team formula and management levels numb creativity, these two are hands on and knee deep. They still do it. There is to quote Richard Seymour, 'a big dollop of Dick and Rich in most of what they do'.

They work uniquely as a creative team. In the same space, about four feet apart, rapidly exchanging ideas across the pad. They draw, think and persuade. Highly articulate they are as uncompromising with their clients as they are with their standards.

Blueprint's Editorial Director Dejan Sudjic pragmatically describes them as 'best known for big bikes'. But they are also Britain's most high profile product design group Seymour Powell, with a world wide reputation.

They built their brand physically by first moulding their name in Casio watches. From there on they never looked back. An impressive client list includes Tefal, Clairol, Yamaha and Racal.

Not shy to mention styling, they made it their mission. They share a passion for motorbikes which they design and ride. They stress a product's persona not what it's made of.

There the similarities end but not at the expense of their individuality. Pentagram Design partner Daniel Weil, describes them pithily as 'each filling their own space'.

The culture they create in their small company and the passion for what they do is critical to their success. They literally rode through the 80's avoiding stock market mergers and global networks and are all the stronger for it.

Their biographies are wonderfully rich. Not only with their design achievements, but forays into film production, book design, teaching, advertising, television and radio. Another clue to their success.

The design community nick names them 'Batman and Robin'. Chairman of Lowe Howard-Spink, Adrian Holmes, dubs them the 'Lennon & McCartney of design in the 90's.' Their client Petr-Karel Korous, Managing Director of MUZ says, with reference to their highly acclaimed work on Scorpion 'they are simply the best'.

Product design is the unsung hero of UK design. Alive and well and too often abroad. These two are actively raising the profile. They live and breathe what they do and it shows.

I pay formal tribute to their single minded pursuit of excellence and informal tribute to their intelligence, wit, generosity, energy and of course style. Long may they ride

MARY LEWIS · President, D&AD

BILLY MAWHINNEY

1995
FESTIVAL OF EXCELLENCE

Undoubtedly, for an Ulsterman such as myself, the hardest bit about organising the 3rd Festival of Excellence was telling my mum I wouldn't be back home in County Down for the 12th July holiday. She wasn't altogether happy but didn't feel quite so bad when I explained we were having our own festival. A gathering of notable speakers, banging their drums and parading their views – and all very kindly sponsored by those nice Orange men and women.

She almost came over.

As it turned out our own Conference and Exhibition created a few moments of controversy and the heat was most definitely on the entire Festival team during those scorching days of July. Everyone, however, responded magnificently, led by Festival Director, Di Robson, and our own David Kester. Both of them could not have worked harder and were ably supported by an equally dedicated back room team from D&AD. Our membership owes them all a great debt of thanks and a great deal more support next year as they continue to build on the process that Anthony Simonds-Gooding started so well, only three years ago.

Yes there were delays, and 'melt-downs' on the day, but everyone who walked into the Gallery couldn't fail to be impressed by the exhibition. For probably the first time we displayed our creative excellence in a truly excellent way, putting both Design and Advertising on the same pedestal.

Thankfully our esteemed speakers were too gentlemanly and professional to let any 'melt-downs' put them off, so they too have our deepest thanks.

We must also thank Orange, The Guardian, Capital Radio, Creative Review and Campaign for their sponsorship and the IPA, AA, Design Council, ISBA and the CBI for their tremendous support. The Partners, Lewis Moberly, Met Studios, S P Lintas, Simons Palmer Denton Clemmow and Johnson, all gave their time and talent unstintingly in our celebration of the Cream of British Design and Advertising.

Over the three weeks we had thousands of visitors from the Business Community, Design and Advertising, as well as Students and Tutors who all recognise the fact that creativity makes a difference, and that the most successful we can make the Festival the better for all of us.

We're already looking at a more suitable date for the Festival in D&AD's calendar. One that will suit everyone better and help balance our year both financially and socially. We're also looking at the highly successful President's Lectures which may be a better guide to the conferencing.

So while my mum looks forward to joining the discussion about the dates for next year's conference we should all look forward to D&AD's continuing obsession with creative excellence and next year's drum banging.

BILLY MAWHINNEY · Festival Chairman

1995
FRIENDS OF D&AD

Abbott Mead Vickers.BBDO
Adam Rawles
Advertising Association
Banks Hoggins O'Shea
Bartle Bogle Hegarty
Basten Greenhill Andrews
BMP DDB Needham
BSB Dorland
Burkitt Weinreich Bryant & Clients
Carter Wong
Coley Porter Bell
Collett Dickenson Pearce
Design Bridge
Design House
DMB&B
Duckworth Finn Grubb Waters
Euro RSCG Wnek Gosper
GGT
Howell Henry Chaldecott Lury & Partners
Institute of Practitioners in Advertising
J Walter Thompson
Jones Knowles Ritchie
Kevin Morley Marketing
Laing Henry
Leagas Delaney
Leo Burnett
Lewis Moberly
Little Leighton
Lowe Howard-Spink
Mars Confectionery
News International
Ogilvy & Mather
Pearl Assurance
Publicis
Reay Keating Hamer
Reed Design Consultant
Roose & Partners
Saatchi & Saatchi
Seymour Powell
Silk Pearce
Simons Palmer Denton Clemmow and Johnson
S P Lintas
The Four Hundred
The Partners
WCRS
Williams & Phoa
Young & Rubicam

1995
SPONSORS OF D&AD

ABSA
Adplates
Beck's
Benson & Hedges, Gallagher
Bowater
British Airways
Campaign
Capital Radio
Creative Review
CTD
Design Council
Dorothy Perkins
EMI Classics
Framestore
GGT for the Big Issue
Kendall Tarrant
Mercury Communications
More O'Ferrall
National Westminster Bank
Orange
Pearce Signs
Philippe Wrigley Design
Real Time Studio
Royle Print
Rushes
The Guardian
The James McNaughton Paper Group
The Tape Gallery
Thrislington Cubicles
Time Out
Touche Ross
Typographic Circle
Vauxhall

PAST RECIPIENTS OF GOLD AWARDS

1995 NO GOLD AWARDS PRESENTED

1994 IAIN GREENWAY, MARK CHAUDOIR, JASON HARRINGTON, MAYLIN LEE, TIM PLATT, IANE WYATT, STEVE BURRELL, PENNY DELMON

1993 LARRY FREY, ALEX PROYAS, STACY WALL, ANTHONY MICHAEL, STEPHANIE NASH, TERESA ROVIRAS, LARRY SHIU, DEAN TURNEY, FRANCIS WEE, TONY MEEUWISSEN

1992 NO GOLD AWARDS PRESENTED

1991 PAUL ELLIMAN, PETER MILES

1990 ROGER WOODBURN

1989 NO GOLD AWARDS PRESENTED

1988 ALAN STANTON, PAUL WILLIAMS, LESLIE DEKTOR, VERONICA NASH, MARK SHARP, MARY LEWIS, KATHY MILLER

1987 GERT DUMBAR, MICHEL DE BOER, RUHI HAMID

1986 DAVID BAILEY, ALAN PAGE, JEREMY PEMBERTON, NICK THIRKELL

1985 PAUL LEEVES, ALAN TILBY, PETER GATLEY, JOHN PALLANT, KEN CARROLL, MIKE DEMPSEY

1984 ANDY ARGHYROU, AXEL CHALDECOTT, CHRIS O'SHEA, JOHN HEGARTY, BARBARA NOKES, RICHARD SLOGGETT, STEVE HENRY

1983 TIM DELANEY, GRIFF RHYS-JONES, ROB KITCHEN, MARTIN LAMBIE-NAIRN, BERNARD LODGE, IAN POTTER, MEL SMITH

1982 GERT DUMBAR, DAVID PELHAM, JOHN WEBSTER

1981 MIKE COZENS, JOHN HORTON, SIMON LANGTON, JOHN McCONNELL, DAVID MYERSCOUGH-JONES, KEN TURNER, GRAHAM WATSON

1980 DAVID HORRY, PAUL WEILAND, PETER WINDETT

1979 MIKE COZENS, PAT GAVIN, ALAN WALDIE

1978 GUY GLADWELL, TONY HERTZ

1977 NEIL GODFREY, BOB ISHERWOOD, RALPH STEADMAN

1976 DAVID DRIVER, TERRY LOVELOCK

1975 COLIN CRAIG, JOHN KRISH, DANE KEITH WILSON

1974 GEORGE DUNNING, ALAN FLETCHER, NEIL GODFREY, ALAN PARKER

1973 NANCY FOUTS, DAVID HILLMAN, HUGH HUDSON

1972 DON McCULLIN, TONY MEEUWISSEN, SARAH MOON, ALAN PARKER

1971 JOHN HEGARTY, PETER PHILIPS, CHARLES SAATCHI, PETER WEBB

1970 MICHAEL RAND

1969 MICHAEL RAND

1968 NO GOLD AWARDS PRESENTED

1967 HARRY PECCINOTTI

1966 NO GOLD AWARDS PRESENTED

1965 ROBERT BROWNJOHN

1964 NO GOLD AWARDS PRESENTED

1963 GEOFFREY JONES

1995

EXECUTIVE COMMITTEE

JAY POND-JONES · GGT

MARY LEWIS · Lewis Moberly

BILLY MAWHINNEY · Ammirati & Puris/Lintas

NANCY WILLIAMS · Williams & Phoa

STEVE HOOPER · Bartle Bogle Hegarty

IAN LOGAN · The Ian Logan Design Company

PETER GATLEY · BMP DDB Needham

STEVE GIBBONS · The Partners

GRAHAM FINK · Paul Weiland Film Company

1995
ADMINISTRATION

President · MARY LEWIS · Lewis Moberly

President Elect · GRAHAM FINK · Paul Weiland Film Company

Chairman · ANTHONY SIMONDS-GOODING · Ammirati & Puris/Lintas

Director · DAVID KESTER · British Design and Art Direction

Honorary Treasurer · KEN HOMMEL · Lewis Moberly

HEAD OFFICE: 9 Graphite Square, Vauxhall Walk, London SE11 5EE

AWARDS

GOLD AWARD

SILVER AWARD

NOMINATION

ANDREW ROSS · Designer

KATHRYN FLETT · Arena

1995
DESIGN JURY

AZIZ CAMI · The Partners

DAVE WATERS · Duckworth Finn Grubb Waters

JOHN GORSE · Bartle Bogle Hegarty

VINCE FROST · Vince Frost Design

LIONEL HATCH · The Chase

MARK FARROW · Farrow

MICHAEL JOHNSON · Johnson Banks

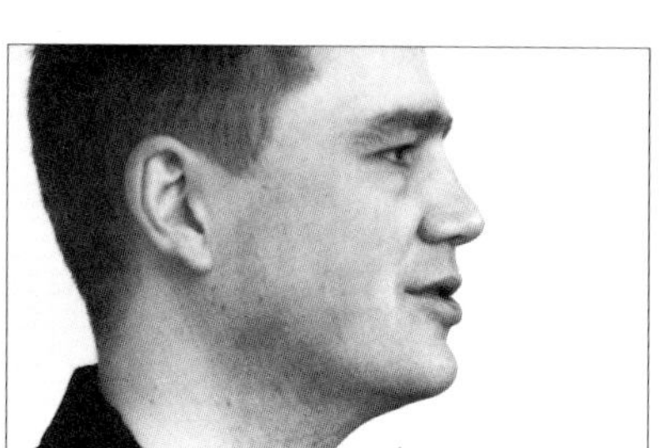
SEAN PERKINS · Designer

DAVID STUART · The Partners

PAULA SCHER · Pentagram Design, NY

STEVE BURRELL · BBC Bristol

CHRIS BRADLEY · Smith & Milton Original

NANCY WILLIAMS · Williams & Phoa

JOHN RUSHWORTH · Pentagram Design

BRIGID McMULLEN · The Work Room

BARBRO OHLSON · Persona

MARTIN McLOUGHLIN · Four IV Design Consultants

JOHN BLACKBURN · Blackburn's

ANN MARSHALL · Lewis Moberly

STEVE DAVIES · Davies Hall

FEN

GARY MARSHALL · Bean MC

1995
ADVERTISING JURY

JASON GORMLEY · BMP DDB Needham

ROGER KENNEDY · Saatchi & Saatchi

TONY KAYE · Tony Kaye Films

PETER MATTHEWS · S P Lintas

TREVOR ROBINSON · H H C L & Partners

JOHN MERRIMAN · Mustoe Merriman Herring Levy

NIGEL ROSE · Euro RSCG Wnek Gosper

TIM HEARN · Bates Dorland

MALCOLM VENVILLE · Photographer

NICK WOOTTON · J Walter Thompson

MANDIE FLETCHER · Fletcher Sanderson Films

WALTER CAMPBELL · Abbott Mead Vickers.BBDO

DANIEL BARBER · Rose Hackney Barber Productions

TREVOR BEATTIE · TBWA

PETER GODDARD · Poppy Films

NICK WELCH · S P Lintas

MICK BROWNFIELD · Illustrator

JOHN O'DONNELL · Propaganda

ROBERT SAVILLE · GGT

MARTIN LAMBIE-NAIRN · Lambie-Nairn & Company

JEREMY CLARKE · Copywriter

ANDY McKAY · Simons Palmer Denton Clemmow & Johnson

MATTHEW KEMSLEY · Bartle Bogle Hegarty

HELEN LANGRIDGE · Helen Langridge Associates

FRANK BUDGEN . Paul Weiland Film Company

JOHN PALLANT · Saatchi & Saatchi

WILL AWDRY · Leagas Delaney

ROONEY CARRUTHERS · WCRS

BRUCE CROUCH · Bartle Bogle Hegarty

PETER GATLEY · BMP DDB Needham

KEVIN THOMAS · Lowe Howard-Spink

NOT PICTURED

ALAN MIDGLEY · FCB

JOHN DEAN · Butterfield Day Devito Hockney

1995

PRODUCT DESIGN JURY

RODNEY KINSMAN · OMK Design

JOHN STODDARD · Ideo

PETER TENNANT · Pentagram Design

1995
ENVIRONMENTAL DESIGN JURY

MARTYN BULLOCK · Red Jacket

LOUISE HOSKER · Hosker Moore & Kent

JOHN HARVEY · Din Associates

JEANNE GIORDANO · MTA/NY

RODNEY FITCH · Rodney Fitch & Company

SIR MICHAEL HOPKINS · Michael Hopkins & Partners

1995

PRESS ADVERTISING

SILVER AWARD
for the Most Outstanding Newspaper Campaign

Art Director
WALTER CAMPBELL

Copywriter
TOM CARTY

Photographer
TONY KAYE

Typographer
ASHLEY PAYNE

Agency
ABBOTT MEAD VICKERS.BBDO LIMITED

Advertising Manager
TIM PATTEN

Client
BRITISH TELECOMMUNICATIONS

Joe Tear, England Manager. On July 19th 2026, he'll want to videophone his Dad from Canada, to celebrate England's first World Cup win since 1966.

In the future more people will need more numbers. Adding one digit to all existing numbers will solve the problem. Area codes starting '0' will start '01'. This happens on Phoneday, 16 April, 1995. For futher details call BT free on 0800 01 01 01.

PHONEDAY

Simone Hurley, Conceptual Artist. On May 14th 2013, The Tate Gallery will want to call her and set up an exhibition of her virtual reality sculptures.

In the future more people will need more numbers. Adding one digit to all existing numbers will solve the problem. Area codes starting '0' will start '01'. This happens on Phoneday, 16 April, 1995. For further details call BT free on 0800 01 01 01.

PHONEDAY

Marlene Keeton, Session Musician. On October 15th 2012, Cliff Richard's manager will want to fax her the sheet music she'll be playing on Cliff's new single.

In the future more people will need more numbers. Adding one digit to all existing numbers will solve the problem. Area codes starting '0' will start '01'. This happens on Phoneday, 16 April, 1995. For further details call BT free on 0800 01 01 01.

PHONEDAY

Sarah Brady, Eco Warrior. On October 28th 2017, she'll want to fax the world press with an agreement that ends the destruction of the rain forests.

In the future more people will need more numbers. Adding one digit to all existing numbers will solve the problem. Area codes starting '0' will start '01'. This happens on Phoneday, 16 April, 1995. For further details call BT free on 0800 01 01 01.

PHONEDAY

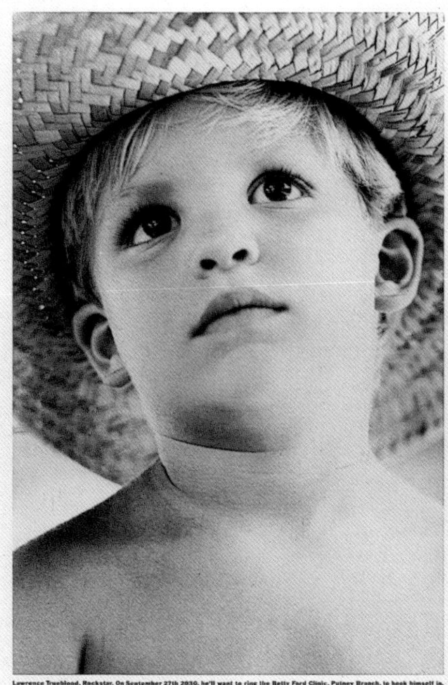

Lawrence Trueblood, Rockstar. On September 27th 2030, he'll want to ring the Betty Ford Clinic, Putney Branch, to book himself in.

In the future more people will need more numbers. Adding one digit to all existing numbers will solve the problem. Area codes starting '0' will start '01'. This happens on Phoneday, 16 April, 1995. For further details call BT free on 0800 01 01 01.

PHONEDAY

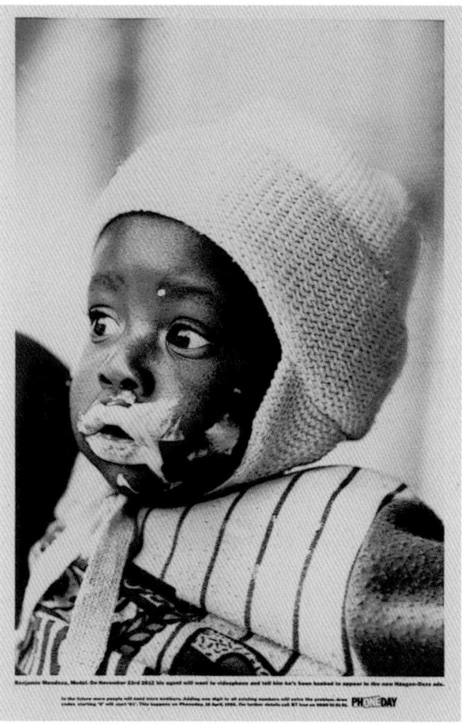
Benjamin Mendoza, Model. On November 23rd 2012 his agent will want to videophone and tell him he's been booked to appear in the new Häagen-Dazs ads.
PHONEDAY

Wayne Martin, MP. On February 23rd 2031, the Prime Minister will want to videophone him about his proposal to make the use of cannabis illegal again.
PHONEDAY

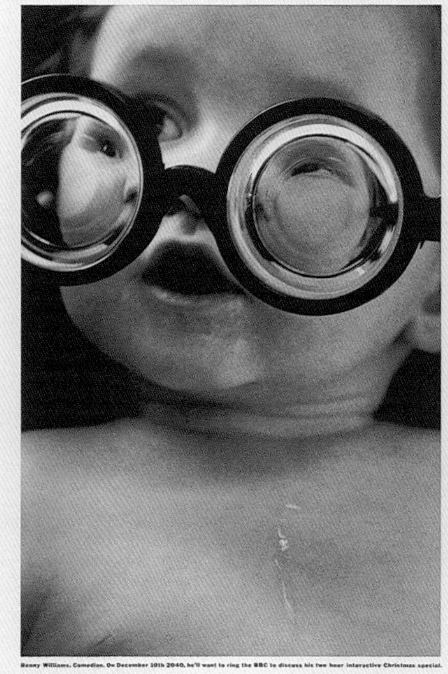
Benny Williams, Comedian. On December 10th 2040, he'll want to ring the BBC to discuss his two hour interactive Christmas special.
PHONEDAY

Angela Jeffries, Agony Aunt. On March 18th 2024, a nervous woman will want to call her radio chat show for advice on her husband's pregnancy.
PHONEDAY

THE DIAL-A-CAB
ANNUAL GENERAL MEETING.

Dial-a-Cab

The Metropole Hotel, 225 Edgware Road, London W2. Sunday November 28th at 11.30 am.

SILVER AWARD
for the Most
Outstanding Trade and
Professional Magazine
Advertisement

Art Directors
RICHARD FLINTHAM
PAUL SHEARER

Copywriters
ROB JACK
ANDY McLEOD

Photographer
MALCOLM VENVILLE

Typographer
ANDY DYMOCK

Agency
DUCKWORTH FINN
GRUBB WATERS

Client
DIAL-A-CAB

SILVER AWARD NOMINATION
for the Most Outstanding Black and White Consumer Magazine Advertisement

Art Director
SCOTT BAIN

Copywriter
GARY DAWSON

Illustrator
SCOTT BAIN

Typographer
DAVE JENNER

Agency
DAWSON BAIN

Marketing Executive
TEENA-MARIE

Client
'INTO YOU' BODY PIERCING

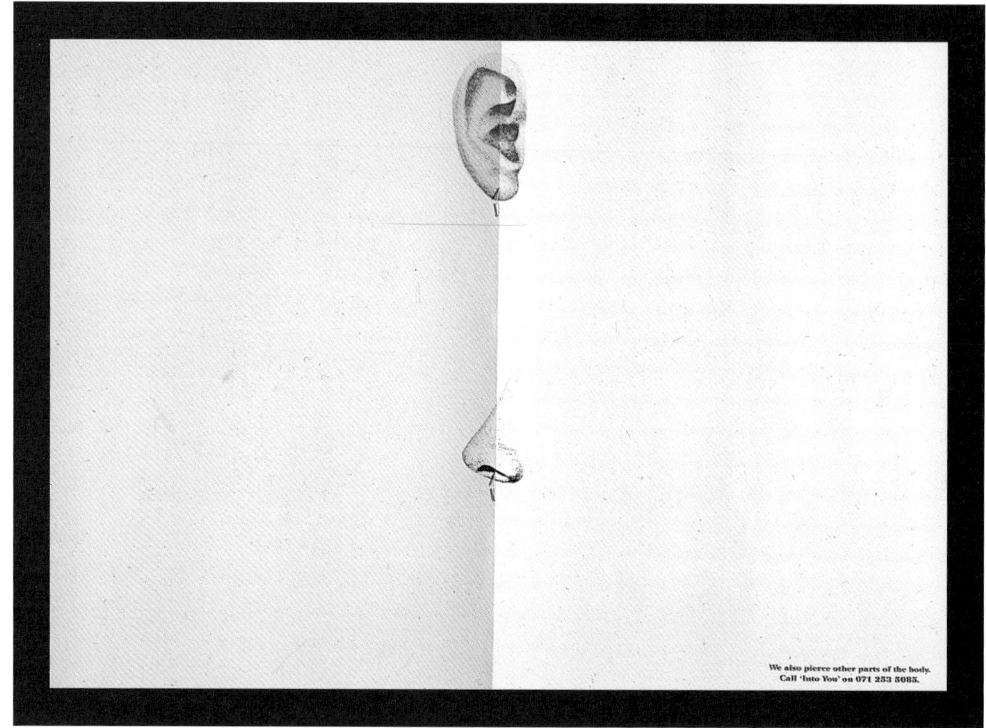

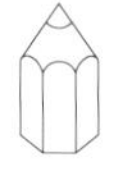

SILVER AWARD NOMINATION
for the Most Outstanding Colour Consumer Magazine Advertisement

Art Director
ANDY McKAY

Copywriter
GILES MONTGOMERY

Photographers
NORBET SCHANER
SEAMUS RYAN

Typographer
JOHN TISDALL

Agency
SIMONS PALMER DENTON CLEMMOW & JOHNSON

Advertising Manager
TONY HILL

Client
NIKE UK LIMITED

SILVER AWARD NOMINATION
for the Most Outstanding Black and White Newspaper Advertisement

Art Director
JEREMY CARR

Copywriter
JEREMY CRAIGEN

Illustrator
JEREMY CARR

Typographer
KEVIN CLARKE

Agency
BMP DDB NEEDHAM

Client
VAG UK LIMITED

**Volkswagen's free 24-hour breakdown service.
(Artist's impression.)**

Our On Call service really does exist
Believe us.
We offer national 24-hour roadside assistance, 365 days a year.
In the slim chance that we can't fix your car, we'll find some other means of getting you home.
And if that doesn't suit you, we'll even put you up for the night in a hotel.
All with a little help from our friends at the RAC.
To qualify for On Call, all you need to do is have your Volkswagen regularly serviced at a Volkswagen dealer. Something you probably do already.
But is all this really necessary?
Isn't this, after all, a Volkswagen we're talking about?
Well, we like to think that even if a Volkswagen does stop working, it doesn't stop being reliable.
And you never know. You could run out of petrol. You could lose your keys.
You could um er

On Call

SILVER AWARD NOMINATION
for the Most Outstanding Newspaper Campaign

Art Directors
ADAM HUNT
BEN NOTT

Copywriters
BEN NOTT
ADAM HUNT

Photographer
DIEDERIK KRATZ

Illustrator
FOLKERT DATEMA

Typographer
PAUL BENNELL

Agency
PMSvW/Y&R, AMSTERDAM

Chairman
RICHARD CRAM

Client
KADU SURFWEAR

Art Director
PAUL BENNELL

Photographer
SIMON HARSENT

Agency
ANDROMEDA

Art Directors
PAUL BENNELL
BEN NOTT

Copywriters
BEN NOTT
PAUL BENNELL

Photographer
SIMON HARSENT

Agency
ANDROMEDA

GEORGIES

We are looking at the exterior of the shop.

ROBERT:
Georgies, brought to you in association with the Snapple Beverage Corporation, makers of delicious fruit juice drinks and iced teas.

We cut to interior of the shop.

CUSTOMER:
Excuse me.

GEORGIE:
Welcome to Georgies. The biggest little shop in London.

ROBERT:
Hey Georgie where do you keep the Snapple?

Georgie points.

Camera bumps fridge.

ROBERT:
Why don't you carry all the flavours?

GEORGIE:
No Room. Yes please?

Camera pans around, jostles with customers.

CUSTOMER:
(Geoffrey)
Excuse me.

ROBERT:
(Wildtrack only)
Pardon me. Oops...sorry.

CUSTOMER:
(Karen)
Excuse me.

We cut to exterior of shop.

Pan up to Snapple logo on awning.

GEORGIE:
So come to Georgies, 78b Log Acre, Covent Garden, because biggest isn't always best.

SUPER:
Made from some of the best stuff on earth.

SILVER AWARD NOMINATION
for the Most Outstanding Mixed Media Campaign

Director
MARK STORY

Copywriter
GEOFF SMITH

Art Director
SIMON MORRIS

Creative Directors
CHRIS O'SHEA
KEN HOGGINS

Producer
LUCINDA WALLOP

Executive Producers
LISA BRYER
CAROL HEYWOOD

Agency Producer
SUSIE STOCK

Editor
IAN WEIL

Lighting Cameraman
DAVID WALSH

Production Company
COWBOY FILMS

Agency
BANKS HOGGINS O'SHEA

International Marketing Director
JUNE BLOCKLIN

Client
SNAPPLE BEVERAGE CORPORATION

Art Director
SIMON MORRIS

Copywriter
GEOFF SMITH

Photographer
STEVE CAVALIER

Typographer
ANDY DYMOCK

IN ASSOCIATION WITH Snapple BEVERAGES
MADE FROM SOME OF THE BEST STUFF ON EARTH
The Dave that's the 'D' and the John that's the 'J' say...
Eat at DJ's
FOR A BETTER CLASS OF SANDWICH. AND DRINK.
THIS IS WHERE WE ARE...
66 Leather Lane, EC1.
...AND THIS IS A DELICIOUS FRUITY DRINK.
(AVAILABLE IN A RANGE OF FLAVOURS.)

IN ASSOCIATION WITH Snapple BEVERAGES
MADE FROM SOME OF THE BEST STUFF ON EARTH
IT COSTAS LESS AT...
145 Tottenham Lane, Crouch End N8.
COSTAS
MINI-MARKET
WE SELL
and other stuff like milk, bread, potatoes, etc...

IN ASSOCIATION WITH Snapple BEVERAGES
MADE FROM SOME OF THE BEST STUFF ON EARTH
Out of milk?
Bread?
Snapple?
KWALITIES
215 Tooting High Street.
The Konvenience Store with a Kapital 'K'.

SILVER AWARD NOMINATION
for the Most Outstanding Mixed Media Campaign

Director
JOE PUBLIC

Copywriter
HUGH TODD

Art Director
ADAM SCHOLES

Creative Directors
JOHN DEAN
SIMON GREEN

Producer
CHRIS STEVENSON

Agency Producer
PATRICK MURPHY

Editor
MARK RICHARDS

Lighting Cameraman
SIMON RICHARDS

Music Composer/Arranger
SERGE GAINSBOURG

Production Company
STARK FILMS

Agency
BUTTERFIELD DAY DEVITO HOCKNEY

Managing Director
JOHN WARR

Client
WARR'S HARLEY DAVIDSON

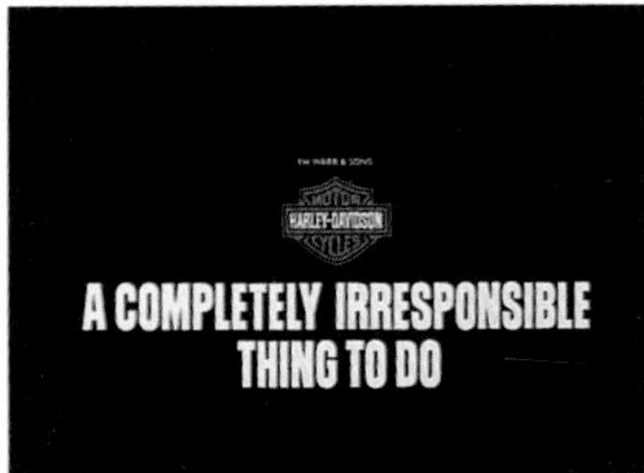

WIFE

Open on a woman standing on a street corner at night.

SFX:
Cars swishing by.
She talks to camera (positively):

What with things being so tight at the moment, my husband persuaded me to take a second job...I couldn't get the hang of it to begin with, but I'm improving......one good thing though, the hours are flexible and I do get to meet people. Some of them are a bit strange though.......I do get a bit exhausted sometimes 'cos I have to concentrate so hard. But like he says...we need every penny we can get.

MUSIC:
Brigitte Bardot, 'Harley Davidson'.

Cut to her husband standing proudly next to a brand spanking new Harley Davidson motorbike outside Warr's Harley Davidson shop.

Super logo and line:

Harley Davidson - A Completely Irresponsible Thing To Do.

Reprise to his wife leaning into a car window

'Hundred pounds, alright?'. She smiles at the camera and gets into the car.

EX-WIFE

Open on a woman with a baby and push-chair and two other children.

SFX
Natural.

She talks to camera:...Me ex-husband's missed a few payments lately. But he's finding it difficult...what with the way things are at the moment...I know he cares about us...'course he does...he's got three kids, hasn't he? I know he'll send some money when he's got some... I'm sure he will.

SFX:
Dog barks off camera.

Cut to her husband standing proudly next to a brand spanking new Harley Davidson motorbike outside Warr's Harley Davidson shop.

Super logo and line:

Harley Davidson - A Completely Irresponsible Thing To Do.

Reprise to ex-wife and kids.

'...oh for God's sake, will you shut up...' (Looking as if towards dog off camera.)

GRANDAD

Open on an old man with the support of a zimmer frame, in a suburban front room.

He talks to camera (understandingly):

I suppose my son's right......I don't really need an electric wheelchair right now......it would've got me out of the house a bit more - and I could have had a pint with my mates......but like he says...I can wait.

MUSIC:
Brigitte Bardot, 'Harley Davidson'.

Cut to his son standing proudly next to a brand spanking new Harley Davidson motorbike outside Warr's Harley Davidson shop.

Super logo and line:

Harley Davidson - A Completely Irresponsible Thing To Do.

Reprise to old man sitting by gas fire. The fire goes out. He attempts to stand up.

Art Director
ADAM SCHOLES

Copywriter
HUGH TODD

Photographer
EUGENIO FRANCHI

Typographer
ANDY BIRD

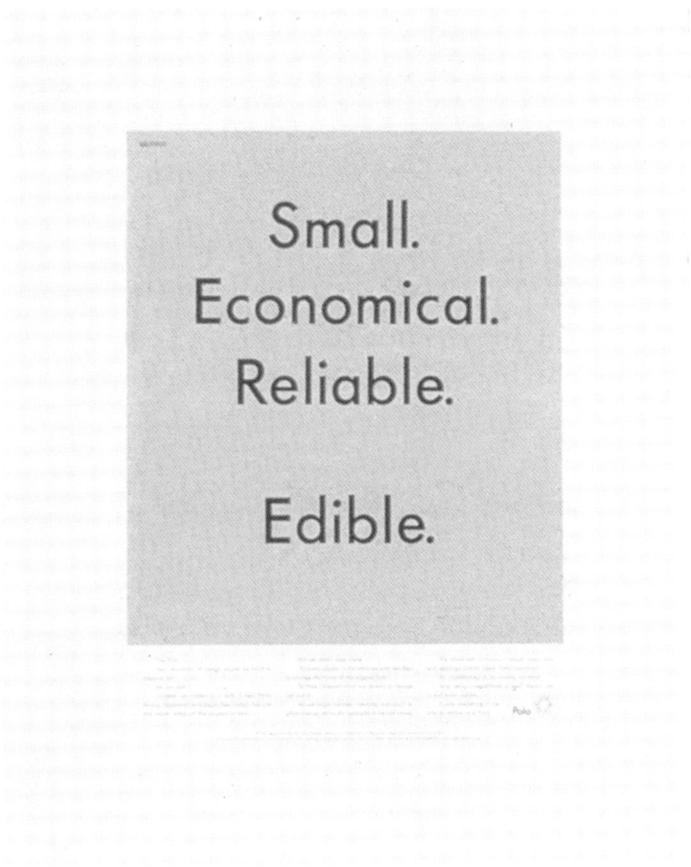

Small.
Economical.
Reliable.

Edible.

Consumer Magazines
Black & White

Art Director
DAVID MACKERSEY

Copywriters
SIGGI HALLING
TREVOR DE SILVA

Typographer
JOANNE CHEVLIN

Agency
J. WALTER
THOMPSON

Managing Director
DAVID HARRIS

Client
ROWNTREE PLC

Consumer Magazines
Black & White

Art Director
ANDRE COHEN

Copywriter
DAVID NOBAY

Creative Director
DAVID NOBAY

Typographer
ANDRE COHEN

Agency
COHN & WELLS,
SAN FRANCISCO

Marketing Executive
BERT JENSSENS

Client
NEO GRAPHICS

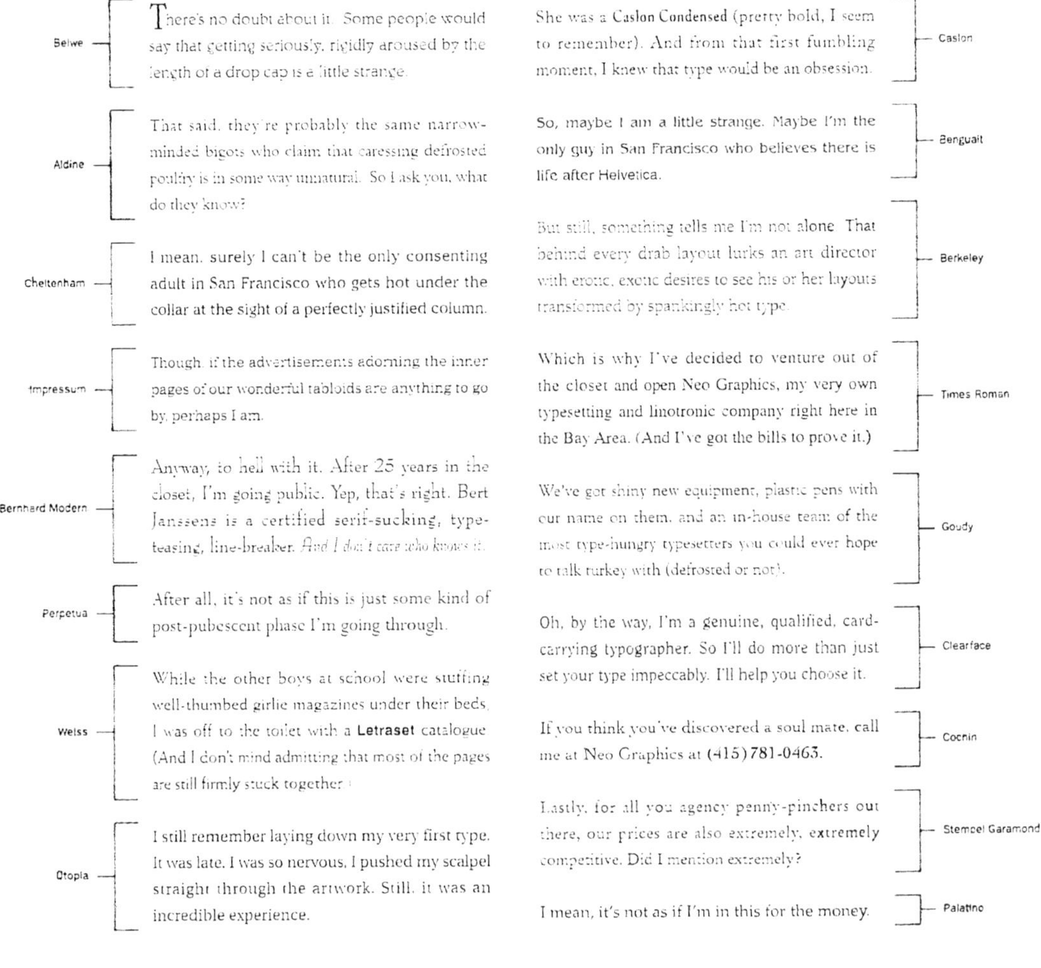

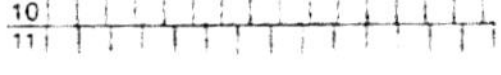

40 Gold Street, San Francisco, CA 94133 Tel: 415.781.0463 Fax: 415.781.0112

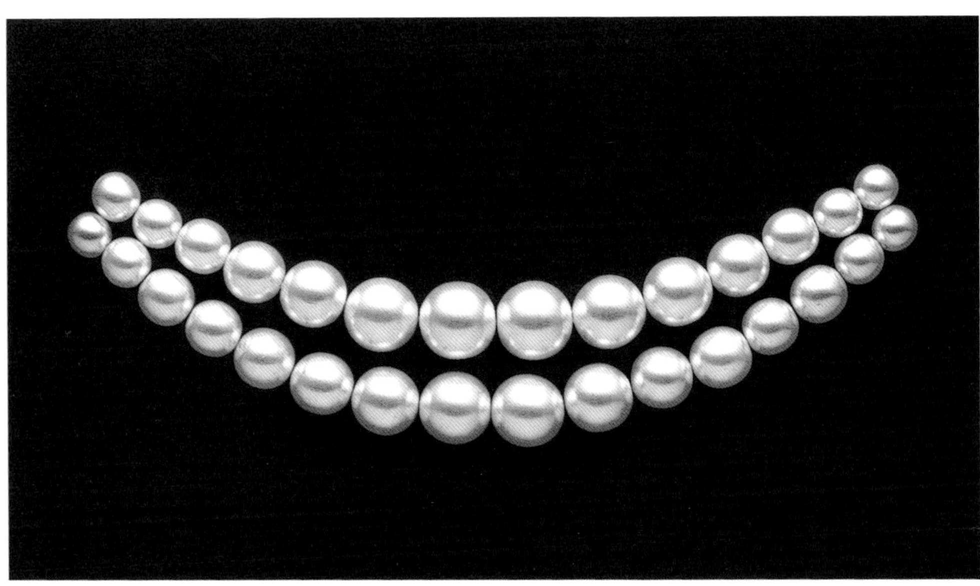

Consumer Magazines
Colour

Art Director
MIKE KEANE

Copywriter
TONY VEAZEY

Photographer
DAVID STEWART

Agency
BROADBENT
CHEETHAM VEAZEY

Managing Director
RICHARD AUSTIN

Client
KINGFISHER
TOOTHPASTE

Consumer Magazines
Colour

Art Director
MAX LANDRAK

Copywriter
LYNETTE CHIANG

Photographer
STEPHEN STEWART

Modelmaker
JUSTIN ROBSON

Agency
BOO ADVERTISING

Marketing Manager
MATTHEW SUTTLE

Client
FLICK
PEST CONTROL

Flick
PEST CONTROL

Consumer Magazines
Colour

Art Director
RUSSELL RAMSEY

Copywriter
JOHN O'KEEFFE

Photographer
DAVID STEWART

Typographer
MATTHEW KEMSLEY

Agency
BARTLE BOGLE
HEGARTY

Senior Marketing Manager
BRENDA JONES

Client
SONY UK LIMITED

Consumer Magazines
Colour

Art Director
MIKE WELLS

Copywriter
TIM RILEY

Photographer
TIF HUNTER

Typographer
MATTHEW KEMSLEY

Agency
BARTLE BOGLE
HEGARTY

Marketing Executive
MIKE DOWELL

Client
THE WHITBREAD
BEER COMPANY

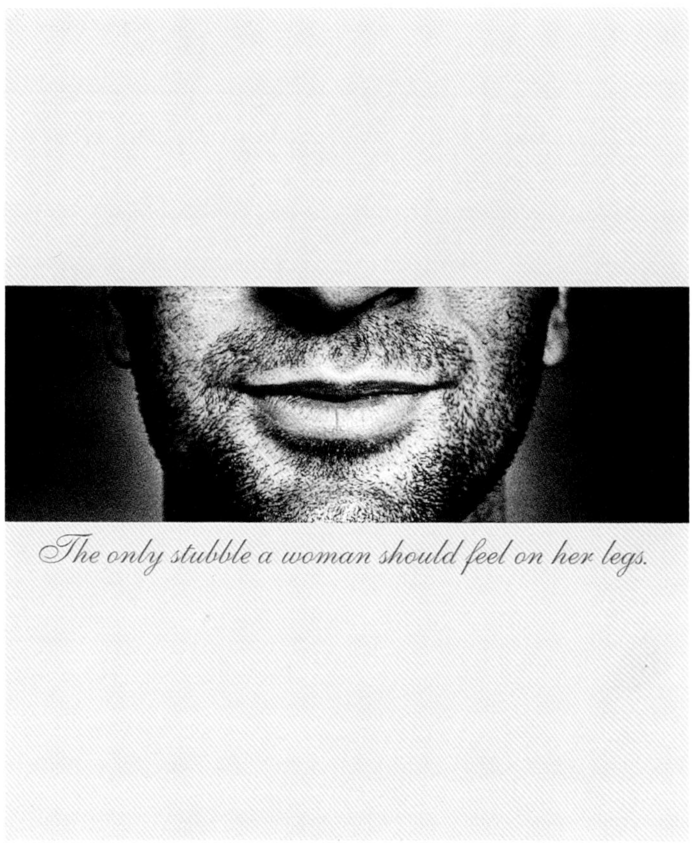

Leg waxing from £9 at Supershape Aromena, 55 Golborne Road, London W10 5NR Telephone: 0181 960 1888.

Consumer Magazines
Colour

Art Director
WAYNE HANSON

Copywriter
SUE HIGGS

Photographer
PHILIP LEE HARVEY

Typographer
JASVIR GARCHA

Agency
LOWE
HOWARD-SPINK

Marketing Executive
OLGA

Client
SUPERSHAPE
AROMENA

Consumer Magazines
Colour

Art Director
GRAEME NORWAYS

Copywriter
EWAN PATERSON

Photographer
ANNIE LEIBOVITZ

Typographer
BARRY BRAND

Agency
YOUNG & RUBICAM

Director of Communications
DR GIAN CARLO
ROCCO

Client
PIRELLI

Consumer Magazines
Colour

Art Director
T. J. RHINE

Copywriter
SHAWN PRESTON

Photographer
JAN WOOD

Illustrator
BARRY MARLER

Typographer
CHARLIE FISHER

Agency
THE INTEGER GROUP

Account Executive
PETER BURRIDGE

Client
COORS ARTIC ICE

Consumer Magazines
Colour

Art Director
JOHN PACE

Copywriter
MATTHEW BULL

Photographer
BARRY WHITE

Typographer
MICHAEL IPP

Agency
OGILVY & MATHER
RIGHTFORD SEARLE
TRIPP & MAKIN

Marketing Executive
BRYAN GIBSON

Client
DUNLOP TYRES

It was centuries of hatred.

It was years of bloodshed.

It was less than a minute on the evening news.

Understanding comes with TIME.

Consumer Magazines
Colour

Art Director
BOB BARRIE

Copywriter
DEAN BUCKHORN

Photographer
DAVID BURNETT

Agency
FALLON McELLIGOTT

Consumer Marketing Director
KEN GODSHALL

Assistant Consumer Marketing Director
HALA MAKOWSKA

Client
TIME MAGAZINE

In an era of tabloid journalism,

we believe the truth to be

sensational enough.

Understanding comes with TIME.

Consumer Magazines
Colour

Art Director
BOB BARRIE

Copywriter
DEAN BUCKHORN

Photographer
MARK SHAW

Agency
FALLON McELLIGOTT

Consumer Marketing Director
KEN GODSHALL

Assistant Consumer Marketing Director
HALA MAKOWSKA

Client
TIME MAGAZINE

Consumer Magazines
Colour

Art Director
BRETT WILD

Copywriter
ALISTAIR KING

Photographer
BARRY WHITE

Typographer
BRETT WILD

Agency
OGILVY & MATHER
RIGHTFORD SEARLE
TRIPP & MAKIN

Marketing Executive
RUSSELL HANLY

Client
VOLKSWAGEN,
SOUTH AFRICA

**The VW Bus.
Take away
its handsome exterior,
and what
have you got?**

Use a coin to scratch away the VW Bus.

True, the VW Bus has class. It's smart, sophisticated and altogether chic. But it's not just a pretty face.

Because under its skin, as you may know, are more proven safety features than any other vehicle in its class.

After all, what's the point of having dashing good looks, if you don't have inner strength?

Starting at design stage, all the way through production, safety is central to the VW Bus. And judging by the results of SABS crash tests, our engineers have excelled themselves. Allow us to reveal more.

Throughout the Bus, you will find safety engineering unique to Volkswagen.

At the front, body deformation zones have been built in to soak up much of the impact of a frontal collision. Along the base of the Bus, a yoke frame does the same.

Around the sides, safety cell reinforcements cradle and cocoon passengers in side, top, front and rear collisions. Because entry is reserved in a VW Bus.

Inside, there's more to feel secure about.

On impact, the steering wheel folds away from the driver's head, the safety belts keep a tight grip and the doors hold fast, thanks to anti-burst locks.

But only if the worst comes to the worst.

Active safety features like dual circuit, front/rear split brakes have been installed, to help prevent accidents altogether.

Of all the vehicles in its class, only the Volkswagen Bus has been SABS tested and approved to meet passenger vehicle safety regulations.

Few other manufacturers offer such safety features.

Which is why few would ever bare themselves as we have.

But then again, isn't that what you'd expect from Volkswagen?

**The VW Bus.
Take away
its handsome exterior,
and what
have you got?**

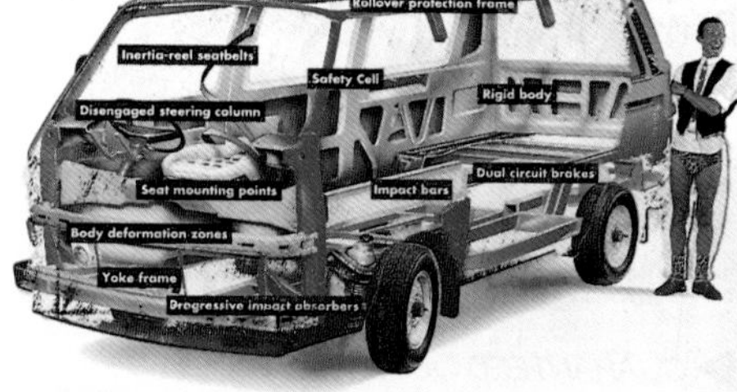

Use a coin to scratch away the VW Bus.

True, the VW Bus has class. It's smart, sophisticated and altogether chic. But it's not just a pretty face.

Because under its skin, as you may know, are more proven safety features than any other vehicle in its class.

After all, what's the point of having dashing good looks, if you don't have inner strength?

Starting at design stage, all the way through production, safety is central to the VW Bus. And judging by the results of SABS crash tests, our engineers have excelled themselves. Allow us to reveal more.

Throughout the Bus, you will find safety engineering unique to Volkswagen.

At the front, body deformation zones have been built in to soak up much of the impact of a frontal collision. Along the base of the Bus, a yoke frame does the same.

Around the sides, safety cell reinforcements cradle and cocoon passengers in side, top, front and rear collisions. Because entry is reserved in a VW Bus.

Inside, there's more to feel secure about.

On impact, the steering wheel folds away from the driver's head, the safety belts keep a tight grip and the doors hold fast, thanks to anti-burst locks.

But only if the worst comes to the worst.

Active safety features like dual circuit, front/rear split brakes have been installed, to help prevent accidents altogether.

Of all the vehicles in its class, only the Volkswagen Bus has been SABS tested and approved to meet passenger vehicle safety regulations.

Few other manufacturers offer such safety features.

Which is why few would ever bare themselves as we have.

But then again, isn't that what you'd expect from Volkswagen?

Consumer Magazines
Colour

Art Director
ANDY SMART

Copywriter
ROGER BECKETT

Photographer
EUGENE RICHARDS

Typographer
MATTHEW KEMSLEY

Agency
BARTLE BOGLE
HEGARTY

Consumer Marketing Manager
SCHUBANKER RAY

Client
LEVI STRAUSS UK
LIMITED

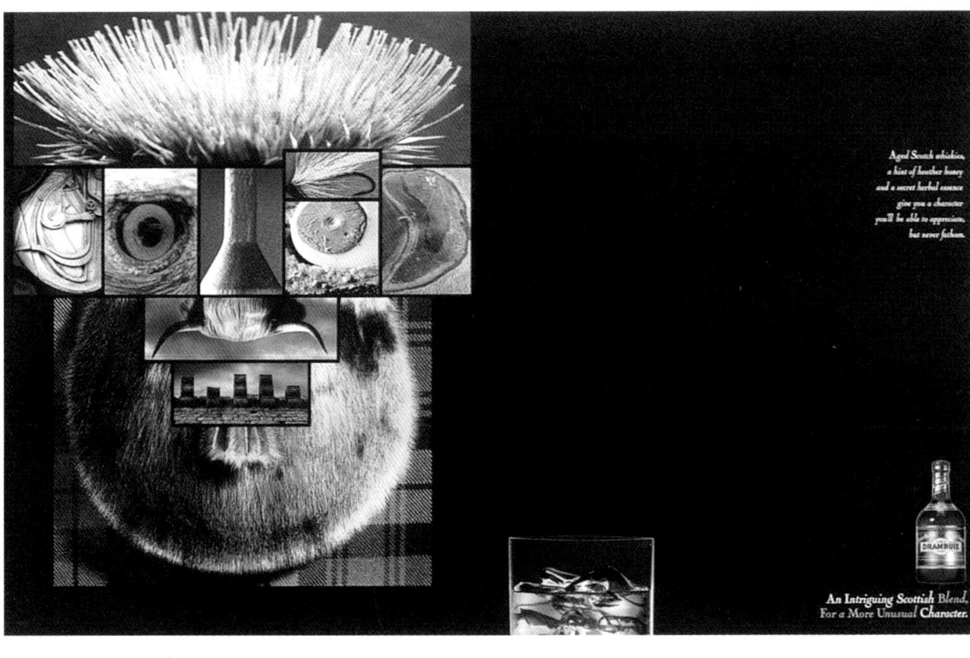

Consumer Magazines
Colour

Art Director
GUY MOORE

Copywriter
TONY MALCOLM

Photographer
JOHN CLARIDGE

Typographer
JOHN TISDALL

Agency
SIMONS PALMER
DENTON CLEMMOW
& JOHNSON

Brand Manager
LORAINE MORRIS

Client
IDV

Consumer Magazines
Colour

Art Director
MIKE WELLS

Copywriter
TIM RILEY

Photographer
TIF HUNTER

Typographer
MATTHEW KEMSLEY

Agency
BARTLE BOGLE
HEGARTY

Marketing Executive
MIKE DOWELL

Client
THE WHITBREAD
BEER COMPANY

Consumer Magazines
Colour

Art Director
MIKE WELLS

Copywriter
TIM RILEY

Photographer
TIF HUNTER

Typographer
MATTHEW KEMSLEY

Agency
BARTLE BOGLE
HEGARTY

Marketing Executive
MIKE DOWELL

Client
THE WHITBREAD
BEER COMPANY

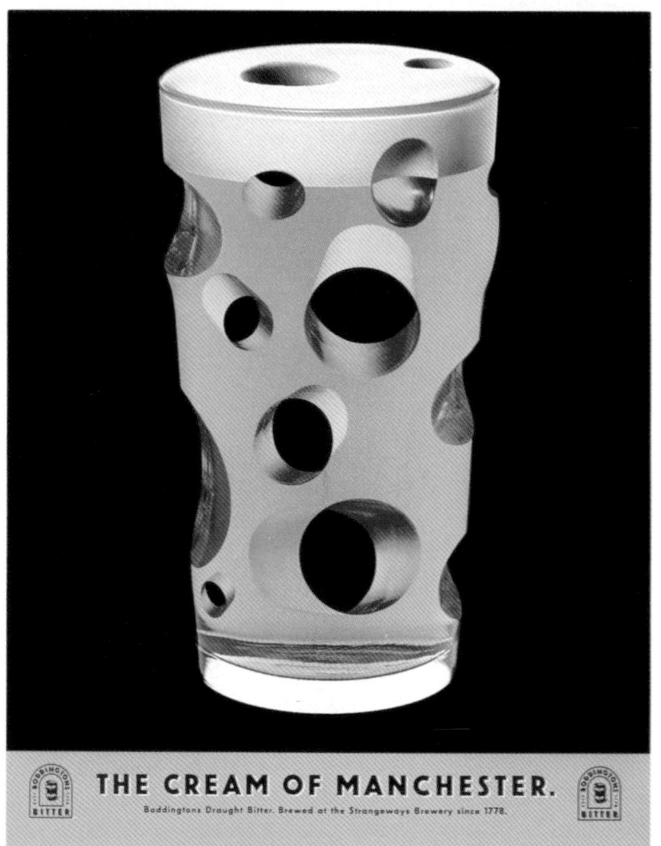

Fast relief from itchy feet.

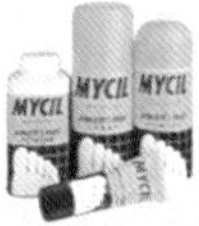

Consumer Magazines
Colour

Art Director
TONY DAVIDSON

Copywriter
KIM PAPWORTH

Photographer
NICK RIGG

Typographer
KEVIN CLARKE

Agency
BMP DDB NEEDHAM

Client
CROOKES
HEALTHCARE

Small.
Economical.
Reliable.

Edible.

Polo

Newspapers
Black & White

Art Director
DAVID MACKERSEY

Copywriters
SIGGI HALLING
TREVOR DE SILVA

Typographer
JOANNE CHEVLIN

Agency
J. WALTER
THOMPSON

Managing Director
DAVID HARRIS

Client
ROWNTREE PLC

Newspapers
Black & White

Art Director
STEVE DUNN

Copywriter
TONY BARRY

Photographer
JAKE CHEESAM

Typographer
SIMON WARDEN

Agency
LOWE
HOWARD-SPINK

Communications Director
IAN DICKENS

Client
OLYMPUS CAMERAS

"Take one more shot of me and I'm going to cross that street, jump over that fence, run through that wood, swim that river, climb to the top of that mountain and ram that camera right down your throat."

Whoever said the camera never lies was, to put it bluntly, lying. And there's no bigger liar than the Olympus Superzoom.

Its 35-120mm lens tells the massive whopper that you're right in the thick of the action when you're actually a safe distance away.

And when, like the charming Ms Bernhard here, your subject is more likely to respond with something stronger than "cheese" you'll find the Superzoom's other features come in handy.

For instance, a high speed recording action captures any fast moves. And when that mouth starts, it really motors.

By re-distributing the camera's weight we have also improved its balance and minimised any camera-shake. So your hand remains steady even if your pulse isn't.

But if you do get near enough to enjoy a filthy look, the flash makes sure it won't be coming from a pair of red eyes.

In fact, no less than four different flash modes adjust automatically as you get further and further away from your subject.

Throw in an ultra compact, lightweight and weatherproof design and we think you'll agree it makes quite a neat little package. Which, to be frank, is more than you'll have if Ms Bernhard were ever to get hold of you.

OLYMPUS SUPERZOOM 120

Newspapers
Black & White

Art Director
WALTER CAMPBELL

Copywriter
TOM CARTY

Photographer
TONY KAYE

Typographer
ASHLEY PAYNE

Agency
ABBOTT MEAD
VICKERS.BBDO
LIMITED

Advertising Manager
TIM PATTEN

Client
BRITISH
TELECOMMUNICATIONS

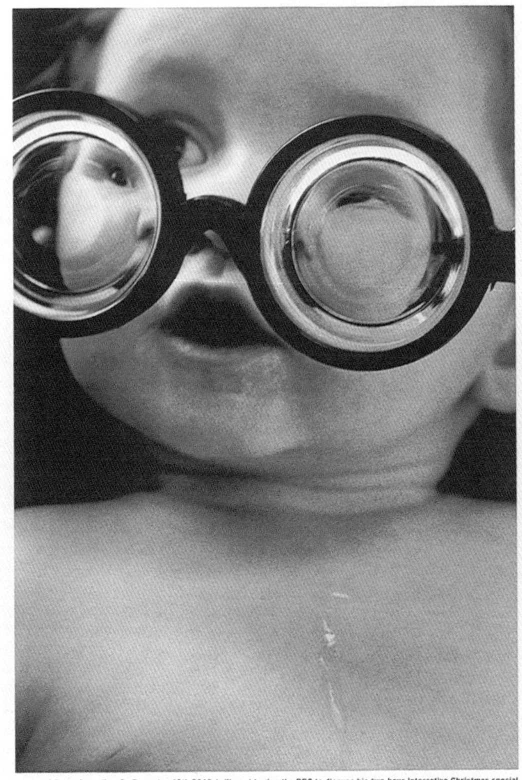

Newspapers
Black & White

Art Director
WALTER CAMPBELL

Copywriter
TOM CARTY

Photographer
TONY KAYE

Typographer
ASHLEY PAYNE

Agency
ABBOTT MEAD
VICKERS.BBDO
LIMITED

Advertising Manager
TIM PATTEN

Client
BRITISH
TELECOMMUNICATIONS

Newspapers
Black & White

Art Director
BIL BUNGAY

Copywriter
PAT HOLDEN

Typographer
TIVY DAVIES

Agency
TBWA

Marketing Executives
DES WILSON
ALASDAIR RITCHIE

Client
SHRC

WHAT DO YOU MEAN YOU DON'T AGREE WITH SUNDAY SHOPPING?

WHEN DID YOU BUY THIS NEWSPAPER?

THE SUNDAY SHOPPING LAWS ARE PAST THEIR SELL BY DATE.

Newspapers
Colour

Art Director
WALTER CAMPBELL

Copywriter
TOM CARTY

Photographer
TONY KAYE

Typographer
ASHLEY PAYNE

Agency
ABBOTT MEAD
VICKERS.BBDO
LIMITED

Advertising Manager
TIM PATTEN

Client
BRITISH
TELECOMMUNICATIONS

Newspapers
Colour

Art Director
MIKE WELLS

Copywriter
TIM RILEY

Photographer
TIF HUNTER

Typographer
MATTHEW KEMSLEY

Agency
BARTLE BOGLE
HEGARTY

Marketing Executive
MIKE DOWELL

Client
THE WHITBREAD
BEER COMPANY

Newspapers
Colour

Art Director
MIKE WELLS

Copywriter
TIM RILEY

Photographer
TIF HUNTER

Typographer
MATTHEW KEMSLEY

Agency
BARTLE BOGLE
HEGARTY

Marketing Executive
MIKE DOWELL

Client
THE WHITBREAD
BEER COMPANY

Newspapers
Colour

Art Director
GRAEME NORWAYS

Copywriter
EWAN PATERSON

Photographer
ANNIE LEIBOVITZ

Typographer
BARRY BRAND

Agency
YOUNG & RUBICAM

Director of Communications
DR GIAN CARLO ROCCO

Client
PIRELLI

A proud Parks is seen showing off his tasteful little number in prime pork, honey, spices and lemon juice. The whole ensemble set off perfectly, in the designer's own words, by 'some rather cunning herbs'. The creation was inspired by Tobago, or more accurately, the utter lack of a decent sausage when Parks set up home there. For a dedicated bangerphile, this was quite intolerable. But fortunately, while the digestive juices were starved,

the creative ones flowed. Fashion took a back seat to the frying pan as Parks perfected his recipe. The end result after three years work? The award-winning Famous Porkinson. Now available in three styles, Banger, Chipolata and Sausage Roll, at Harrods and well-known supermarkets. And also, ready-to-eat, at any number of appropriately fashionable restaurants, clubs and bars.

PORKINSON BANGER

The first sausage from an internationally renowned photographer.

After photographing the designs of Dior, Chanel & Shuji Tojo for forty five years, Norman Parkinson decided to model a creation of his own.

Campaigns
Newspaper

Art Director
BILL GALLACHER

Copywriter
RICHARD MYERS

Photographer
ALISTAIR MORRISON

Typographer
ROGER KENNEDY

Agency
SAATCHI & SAATCHI

Marketing Controller
GARRY SMITH

Client
PORK FARMS BOWYERS

A gentleman's true desires are not always readily apparent. After all, who would have imagined that Norman Parkinson, the royal family's favourite photographer and confidant of the rich and glamorous, would have a consuming passion for something as, well, humble as sausages? But he did. So much so that he decided to create his own. He agonised over the recipe for three years, settling finally on a combination of

lean pork, honey, spices, herbs and lemon juice. Unselfishly, he didn't keep his sausage to himself. As a consequence, the far-from-humble, award-winning Famous Porkinson is now available as Chipolata, Banger, and Sausage Roll at Harrods Food Hall and well-known supermarkets. And, ready to eat, at a number of notable establishments such as the Cumberland Hotel.

PORKINSON BANGER

The first sausage from an internationally renowned photographer.

As some of the world's most beautiful women would quickly discover, photographer Norman Parkinson usually had one thing on his mind. The perfect chipolata.

Photographer
NORMAN PARKINSON

Without doubt, certain things lie deep in an Englishman's psyche. There's fair play. Driving on the left. Losing at cricket. But above all, there's the longing for a decent sausage. Take the photographer, Norman Parkinson, when he set up home in Tobago. It was paradise, until the inevitable happened. 'I grew homesick for a good banger,' Parks explained. So he created his own, with prime lean pork, honey, spices, lemon juice

and 'some rather cunning herbs.' Which is how one Englishman's triumph over adversity became the benchmark for bangers, and indeed, chipolatas and sausage rolls. And why the award-winning Famous Porkinson can be found gracing the shelves at Harrods Food Hall and well-known supermarkets, and gracing the tables at such notable places as the Cumberland Hotel.

PORKINSON BANGER

The first sausage from an internationally renowned photographer.

White, palm fringed beaches. Cloudless blue Caribbean skies. Scantily clad girls. Is it any wonder an Englishman's thoughts turned to sausages?

Photographer
NORMAN PARKINSON

Campaigns
Newspaper

Art Director
SIMON MORRIS

Copywriter
GEOFF SMITH

Photographer
STEVE CAVALIER

Typographer
ANDY DYMOCK

Agency
BANKS HOGGINS O'SHEA

Managing Director
B. J. CUNNINGHAM

Client
THE ENLIGHTENED TOBACCO COMPANY

Enlightened Tobacco Company Plc:

TAKE AN ACTIVE PART IN CANCER RESEARCH. SMOKE OUR CIGARETTES.

Every time you smoke a cigarette you are increasing your chances of developing lung cancer.

No surprise there. Until, that is, you consider that the above statement is made by a tobacco company.

As you will no doubt be aware, it is far more usual for cigarette manufacturers to avoid any discussions on the health risks involved.

'No comment' is the most detailed statement you can typically expect from an industry spokesperson.

The same does not apply to the Enlightened Tobacco Company. We are the only tobacco company to openly admit that smoking is the major cause of lung cancer.

But that's not enough.

As far as we're concerned, if we're willing to accept the association, we should also be willing to accept some of the responsibility.

That's why we give 10% of our pre-tax profits to non-vivisection cancer charities.

Before you all breathe a sigh of relief, however, our contribution should be put into perspective.

Over the last few decades, billions of pounds have been poured into cancer research. There is still no cure. Neither is there likely to be one in the foreseeable future.

Besides, even if a miracle cure for lung cancer was found, you'd still have to hope for an equally miraculous cure for emphysema, bronchitis, laryngeal cancer and heart disease.

The best way to avoid developing any of these smoking-related illnesses is obvious. Give up.

And that's another surprising statement to be made by a tobacco company.

Do we really want our customers to stop smoking?

If that were the case, Death as a brand would not have much of a life.

That's clearly absurd.

We make cigarettes and we want you, as a smoker, to buy them. That's why both Death and Death Lights are made from the finest blends of luxury Virginia tobacco.

In fact, the only real difference between Death and other cigarettes is that we make no attempt to disguise any of the dangers.

Take our name for example. It leaves no doubt as to the consequences you face by smoking. That's simply not true of other brand names.

It is hard to think of many that don't project an image of

something expensive, stylish, sophisticated or exotic.

The same can be said of their advertising campaigns.

Despite all the stringent guidelines that apply, or perhaps because of them, cigarette advertisements are now so subtle that they rarely contain any reference to cigarettes whatsoever.

Ironically, there is often just one way to tell what is actually being advertised.

And that is the health warning at the bottom.

But unless they decide to ban tobacco, the Government health warning remains just that. A warning.

You have every right to ignore the risks and continue to smoke if you choose.

No doubt there will always be people who say that you are wasting your money on cigarettes.

Buy Death however, and you'll be able to answer, quite truthfully, that you are not.

After all, 10% of the money we make is going to cancer research.

DEATH 13mg TAR 1.0mg NICOTINE
DEATH LIGHTS 7mg TAR 0.7mg NICOTINE

PROTECT CHILDREN: DON'T MAKE THEM BREATHE YOUR SMOKE
Health Department's Chief Medical Officers

Enlightened Tobacco Company Plc:

13.5 MILLION SMOKERS WILL ADMIT IT'S BAD FOR THEM. ONLY ONE TOBACCO COMPANY WILL.

DEATH 13mg TAR 1.0mg NICOTINE
DEATH LIGHTS 7mg TAR 0.7mg NICOTINE

SMOKING KILLS
Health Departments' Chief Medical Officers

Enlightened Tobacco Company Plc:

THEY'RE EVERY BIT AS GOOD AS OTHER CIGARETTES. AND EVERY BIT AS BAD.

DEATH 13mg TAR 1.0mg NICOTINE
DEATH LIGHTS 7mg TAR 0.7mg NICOTINE

SMOKING CAUSES HEART DISEASES
Health Departments' Chief Medical Officers

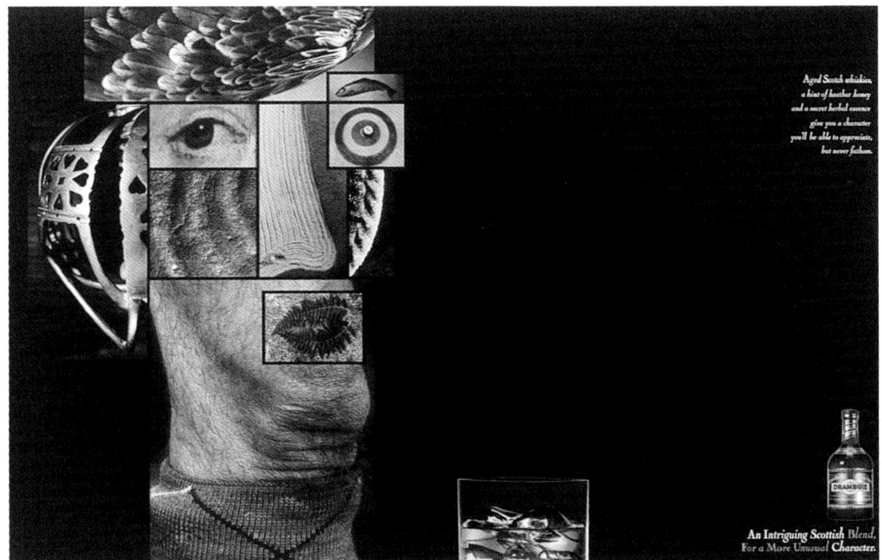

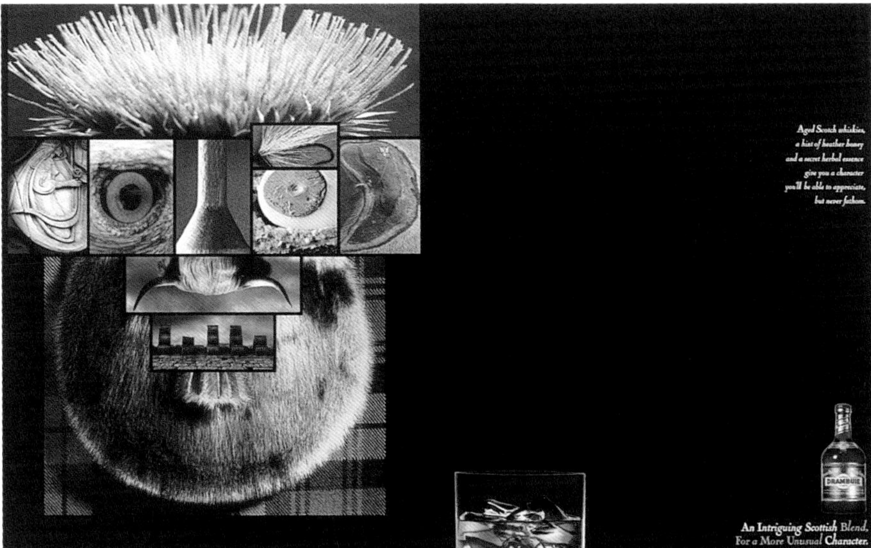

Campaigns
Consumer Magazines

Art Director
GUY MOORE

Copywriter
TONY MALCOLM

Photographer
JOHN CLARIDGE

Typographer
JOHN TISDALL

Agency
SIMONS PALMER
DENTON CLEMMOW
& JOHNSON

Brand Manager
LORAINE MORRIS

Client
IDV

Campaigns
Consumer Magazines

Art Directors
MARTIN GALTON
DAVE DYE
DAVE BEVERLEY

Copywriters
DAVE HIEATT
TONY BARRY
ROB BURLEIGH

Photographers
THE DOUGLAS BROTHERS
JOHN CLARIDGE

Typographer
MARTIN GALTON

Agency
LEAGAS DELANEY

Senior Vice President, Marketing Communications
TOM HARRINGTON

Client
ADIDAS AG

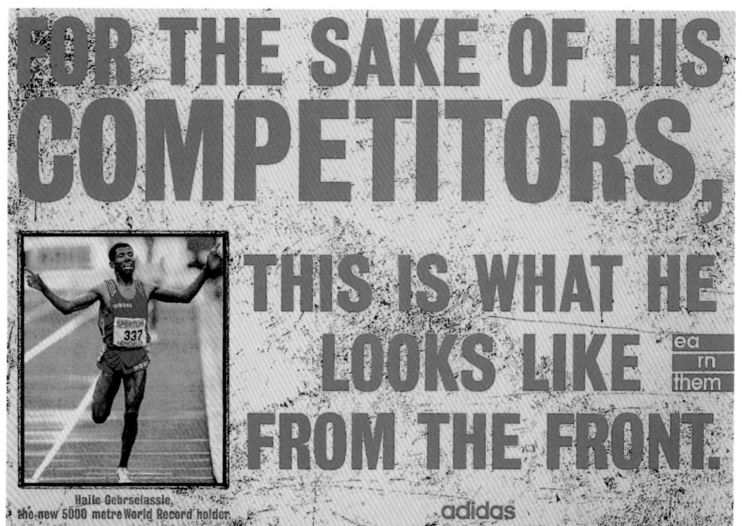

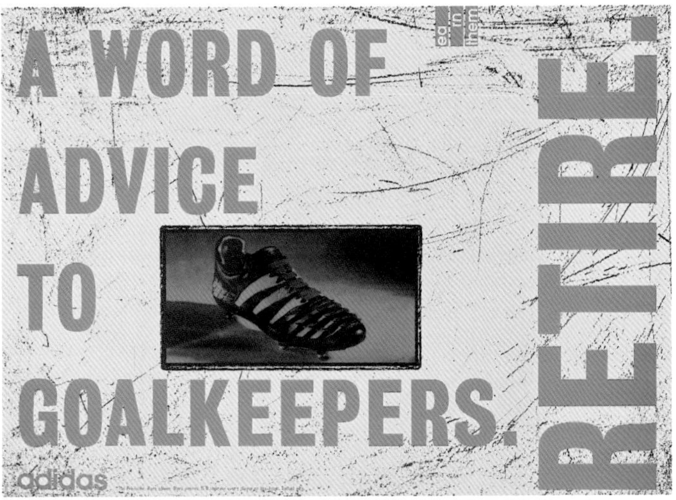
A WORD OF
ADVICE
TO
GOALKEEPERS.
RETIRE.
ea
rn
them
adidas

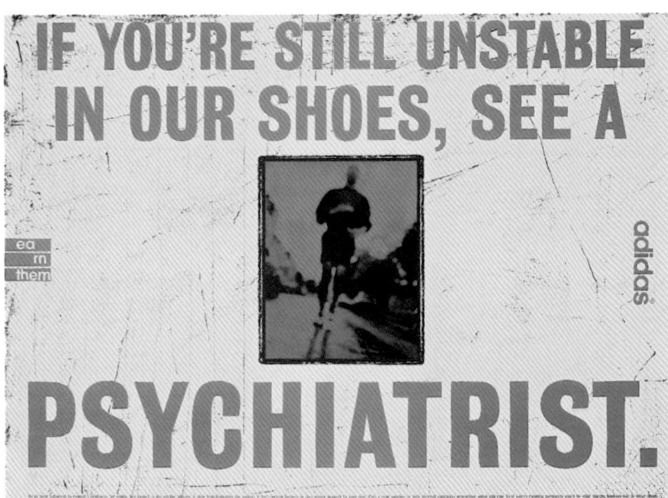
IF YOU'RE STILL UNSTABLE
IN OUR SHOES, SEE A
PSYCHIATRIST.
ea
rn
them
adidas

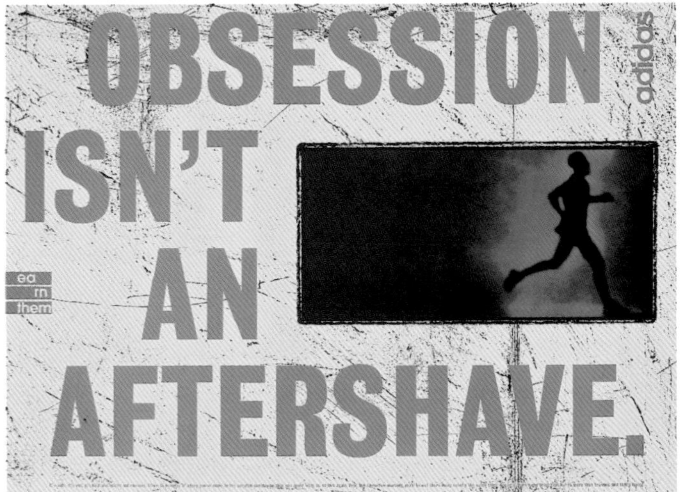
OBSESSION
ISN'T
AN
AFTERSHAVE.
ea
rn
them
adidas

Trade & Professional Magazines
Single Black & White or Colour

Art Director
DAVID MACKERSEY

Copywriters
SIGGI HALLING
TREVOR DE SILVA

Typographer
JOANNE CHEVLIN

Agency
J. WALTER THOMPSON

Managing Director
DAVID HARRIS

Client
ROWNTREE PLC

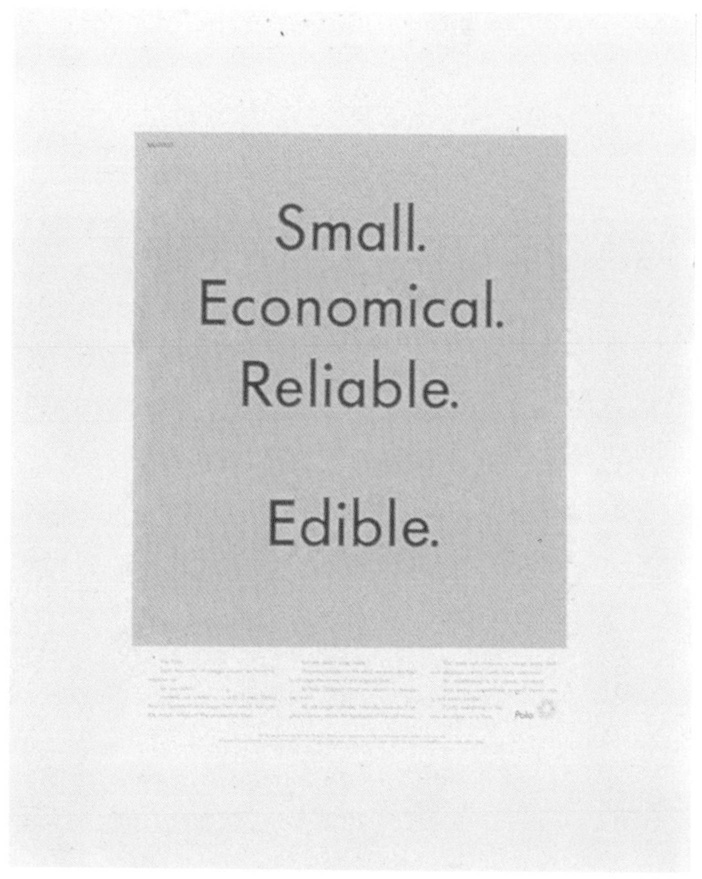

Trade & Professional Magazines
Single Black & White or Colour

Art Director
PAUL BRAZIER

Copywriter
PETER SOUTER

Photographer
MIKE PARSONS

Typographer
JOE HOZA

Agency
ABBOTT MEAD VICKERS.BBDO LIMITED

Awards & Editorial Manager
BEVERLEY PARKER

Client
BRITISH DESIGN AND ART DIRECTION

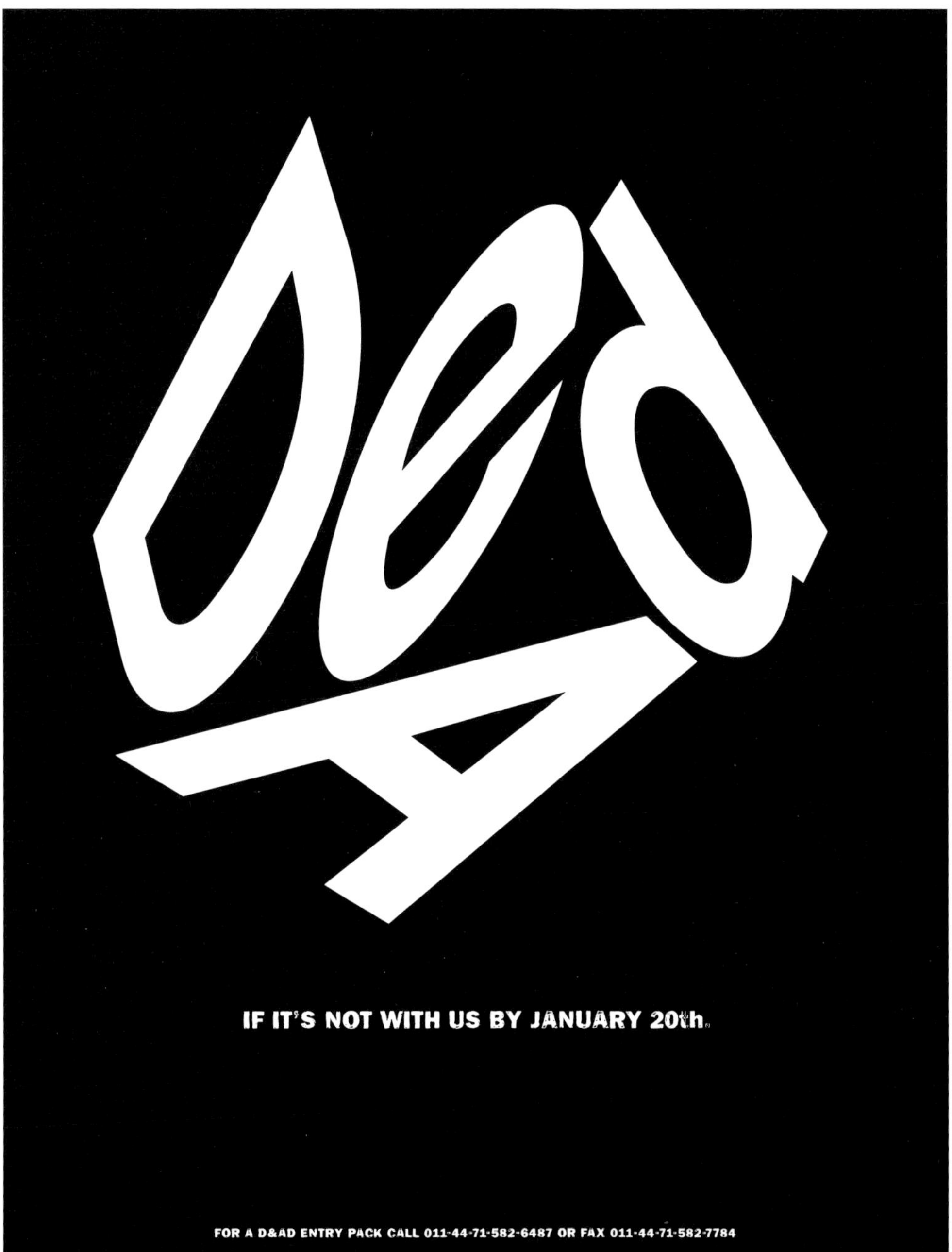

Trade & Professional Magazines Single Black & White or Colour

Art Directors
PAUL BRAZIER
PAUL BRIGINSHAW

Copywriters
PETER SOUTER
MALCOLM DUFFY

Typographer
JOE HOZA

Agency
ABBOTT MEAD VICKERS.BBDO LIMITED

Awards & Editorial Manager
BEVERLEY PARKER

Client
BRITISH DESIGN AND ART DIRECTION

Trade & Professional Magazines Campaign Black & White or Colour

Art Directors
TOMMIE PINNOW
PIT HOFMANN

Copywriter
HERMANN VASKE

Photographer
JOE SEDELMAIER

Agency
HERMANN VASKE

Associate Editor
MICHAEL WEINZETTL

Client
WALTER LURZER

Illustrators
TONY KAYE
JOHN HEGARTY

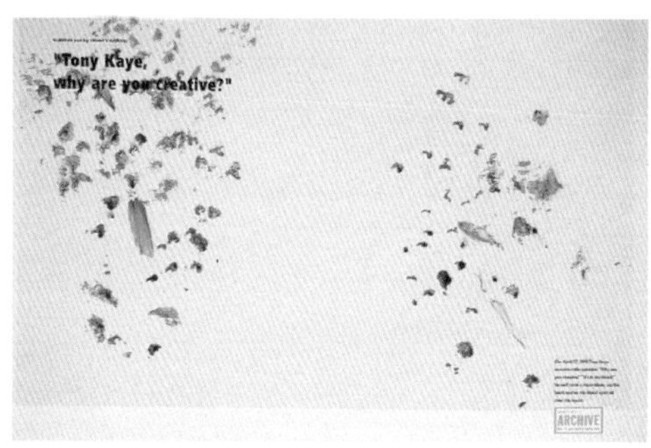

Photographer
JERRY DELLA FEMINA

Illustrator
TONY SCOTT

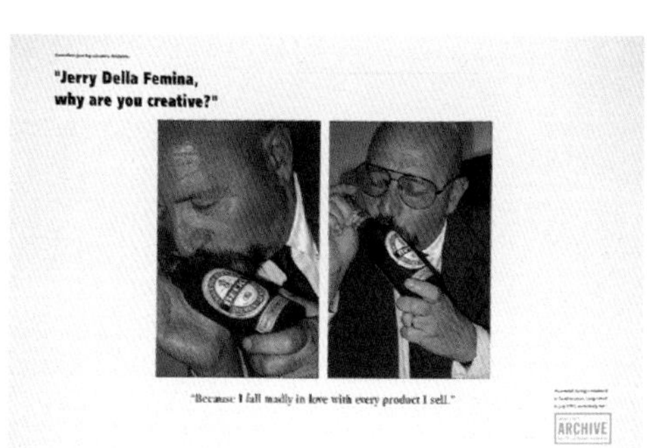

Trade & Professional Magazines Campaign Black & White or Colour

Art Director
DAVE DYE

Copywriter
GILES MONTGOMERY

Typographer
JOHN TISDALL

Agency
SIMONS PALMER DENTON CLEMMOW & JOHNSON

Marketing Manager
TOBY CONSTANTINE

Client
NEWS INTERNATIONAL

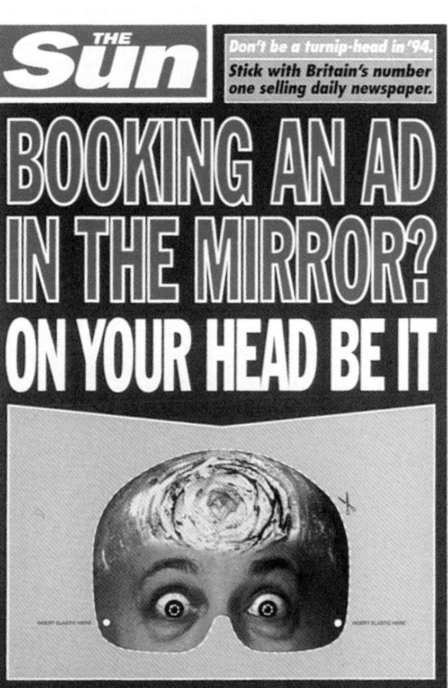

Sausage
Art Director
TIGER SAVAGE

Copywriter
PAUL SILBURN

Photographer
JOHN CLARIDGE

Turnip
Art Director
GUY MOORE

Copywriter
TONY MALCOLM

1995

ADVERTISING CRAFTS

Sponsored by Adplates

SILVER AWARD
for the Most Outstanding Typography Individual

Director
JONATHAN BARNBROOK

Copywriter
ADRIAN JEFFERY

Art Director
LINDSEY REDDING

Creative Directors
SIMON SCOTT
ANDREW LINDSAY

Producer
YVONNE CHALK

Agency Producer
TIM MAGUIRE

Editor
JON HOLLIS

Music Composers/Arrangers
LOGORHYTHM

Animators
SARAH LEWIS
JONATHAN BARNBROOK

Production Company
TONY KAYE FILMS

Agency
FAULDS ADVERTISING

Account Group Director
TOM GILL

Head of Presentation
PETER GOURD

Client
BBC RADIO SCOTLAND

FOGGIE BUMMER

VIDEO:
As we hear the gripping radio article we see the words appear on screen. The words help to dramatise the action.

MVO1:
An exercise I often do is write words like 'BOMBAIZE' and 'FORFOUGHEN' and words like that up on the board, you see. And they think things like, a foggie bummer, what's a foggie bummer? Then we'll ask one another, you see, and...

MVO 2:
What is a foggie bummer?

MVO 1:
Foggie bummer means a bumble bee! (laughs)

MVO 2:
I was away to say you could have got us struck off air then!

MVO 1:
Oh no no no! It's not that bad!

CAPTION:
Mix up caption which reads,

Re-discover the power of the spoken word.

Silence.

SFX:
Music ident.

VIDEO:
Mix to end frame. We see the BBC Scotland logo and tuning device which demonstrates where to find the signal.

CAPTION:
UK National Station of the Year.

TRUE ROMANCE

As we hear the radio article, we see the words appear on the screen. The words help to dramatise the action.

SPEAKER:
These are the...these are the things that life is made of. I wanted to see what the Atlantic was like, you can only see it by going there. But much more importantly, I wanted to see what I was like on the Atlantic.

What's wrong with romance?

It brings light into life. Into your own life and into other peoples' lives.

God forbid that we were all practical pragmatists.

Silence.

Mix up caption which reads:

Re-discover the power of the spoken word.

Mix to end frame. We see the BBC Scotland logo and tuning device which demonstrates where to find the signal.

CAPTION:
UK National Station of the Year.

TARTAN TOYBOYS

As we hear the radio article, we see the words appear on the screen. The words help to dramatise the action.

MUM:
I'm looking forward to seeing the Tartan Toyboys.

DAUGHTER:
What do you think they're going to be like, though?

MUM:
Well, I hope they're going to have long legs and wee bums and broad shoulders, and I hope they're going to wear kilts. I'll be terribly disappointed if they don't have kilts on (laughs). I'll be equally disappointed if they don't have them off before the night's over.

Silence.

Mix up caption which reads:

Re-discover the power of the spoken word.

Mix to end frame. We see the BBC Scotland logo and tuning device which demonstrates where to find the signal.

CAPTION:
UK National Station of the Year.

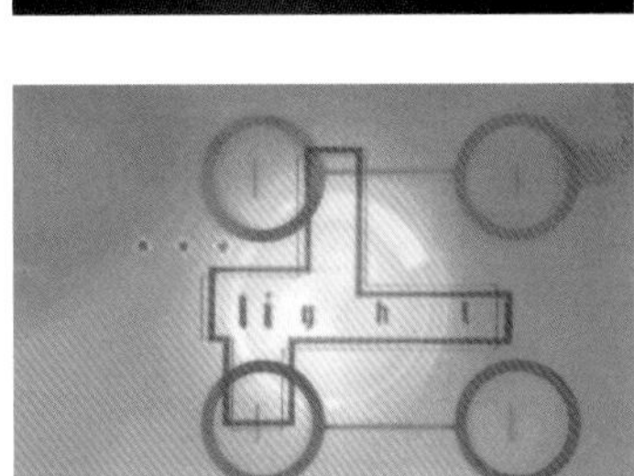

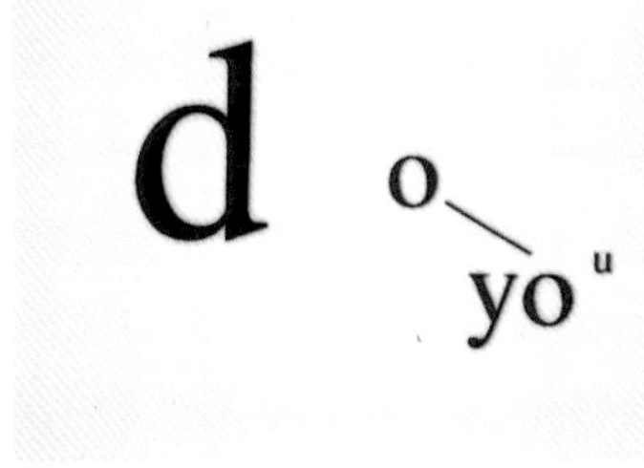

SILVER AWARD
for the Most Outstanding Typography Campaign

Director
JONATHAN BARNBROOK

Copywriter
ADRIAN JEFFERY

Art Director
LINDSEY REDDING

Creative Directors
SIMON SCOTT
ANDREW LINDSAY

Producer
YVONNE CHALK

Agency Producer
TIM MAGUIRE

Editor
JON HOLLIS

Music Composer/Arranger
LOGORHYTHM

Production Company
TONY KAYE FILMS

Agency
FAULDS ADVERTISING

Account Group Director
TOM GILL

Head of Presentation
PETER GOURD

Client
BBC RADIO SCOTLAND

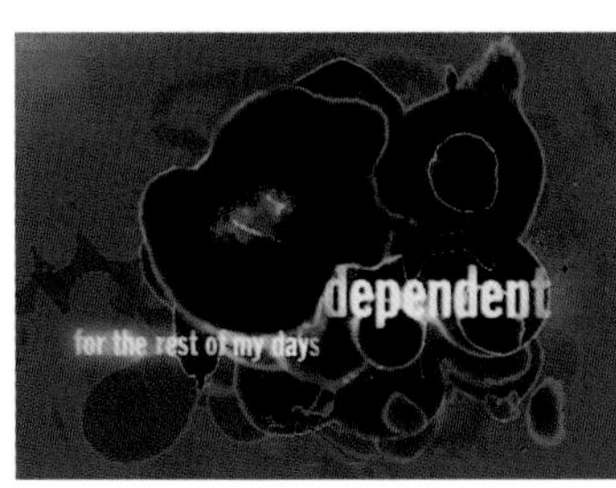

Directors
SIMON TAYLOR
GRAHAM WOOD

Producer
HELEN LANGRIDGE

Production Company
HELEN LANGRIDGE
ASSOCIATES

FOGGIE BUMMER

As we hear the gripping radio article we see the words appear on screen. The words help to dramatise the action.

MVO1:
An exercise I often do is write words like 'BOMBAIZE' and 'FORFOUGHEN' and words like that up on the board, you see. And they think things like, a foggie bummer, what's a foggie bummer? Then we'll ask one another, you see, and...

MVO 2:
What is a foggie bummer?

MVO 1:
Foggie bummer means a bumble bee! (laughs)

MVO 2:
I was away to say you could have got us struck off air then!

MVO 1:
Oh no no no! It's not that bad!

Mix up caption which reads, Re-discover the power of the spoken word.

Music ident.

Mix to end frame. We see the BBC Scotland logo and tuning device which demonstrates where to find the signal.

CAPTION:
UK National Station of the Year.

NAE HOPE

As we hear the gripping radio article, we see the words appear on screen. The words help to dramatise the action.

MVO:
*I'm 27 just now and I started using hard drugs when I was 22, it was that kinda day when everyone was using it so I had a wee shot and I liked it. And just recently there I had two overdoses. It was due to high purity heroin.
It was on streets about here. I think I'll be drug dependent for the rest of my days I think. Nae hope. Nae hope whatsoever.*

Mix up caption which reads, Re-discover the power of the spoken word.

Music ident.

*Mix to end frame.
We see the BBC Scotland logo and tuning device which demonstrates where to find the signal.*

CAPTION:
UK National Station of the Year.

GRAFFITI

As we hear the gripping radio article, we see the words appear on the screen. The words help to dramatise the action.
We hear a snippet from a BBC Scotland programme.

MVO:
If I can explain some of this graffiti that's on the ceiling of the car here. We got psycho and Demon. We got psycho from rolling 60's cripps. We got...er Junior from Ghetto boys...Um, as I'm looking, I'm starting to feel these real kind of er, emotions choking up in me because there's probably about 20 or 25 different gang members that are carved in here, Babyface here, and I'd say about a dozen of them, almost half of them are dead.

Mix up caption which reads: Re-discover the power of the spoken word.
Mix to end frame.
We see the BBC Scotland logo and tuning device which demonstrates where to find the signal.

CAPTION:
UK National Station of the Year.

COCKEREL

As we hear the gripping radio article, we see the words appear on the screen. The words help to dramatise the action.

We hear a snippet from a BBC Scotland programme.

MVO:
Line out. Outside the French 22. Back on the main...oop...now the referee has called a halt to the proceedings, it's now over to the Scottish 22 and heading upfield. It's a magnificant fellow with a black underbelly, a gold coloured back and a red cockscomb and the cockerel's over the Scot's 5 metre line, heading for touch and the stewards are looking just a little bit flushed/perplexed, a little bit perplexed and flushed, ...just selling them a wee dummy and a wee side step and away he goes. Yes, he's over the touch line, now he's on the running track, and he's almost away.

Mix up caption which reads: Re-discover the power of the spoken word.
Mix to end frame. We see the BBC Scotland logo and tuning device which demonstrates where to find the signal.

CAPTION:
UK National Station of the Year.

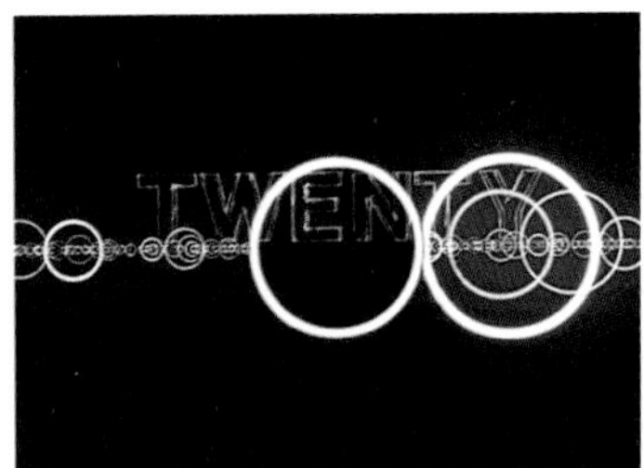

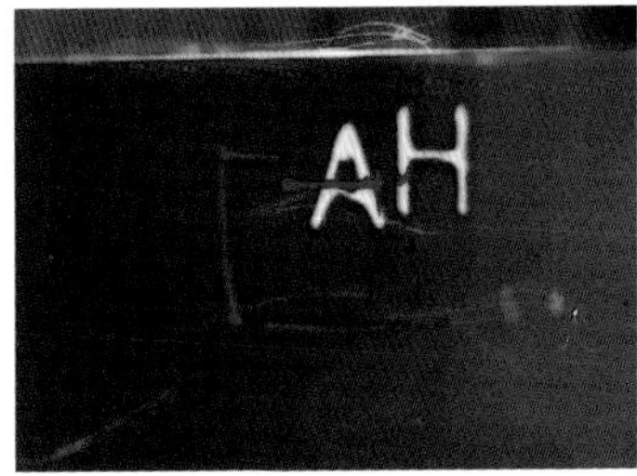

SILVER AWARD
for the Most
Outstanding
Photography Campaign

Photographer
TONY KAYE

Art Director
WALTER CAMPBELL

Copywriter
TOM CARTY

Typographer
ASHLEY PAYNE

Agency
ABBOTT MEAD
VICKERS.BBDO
LIMITED

Advertising Manager
TIM PATTEN

Client
BRITISH
TELECOMMUNICATIONS

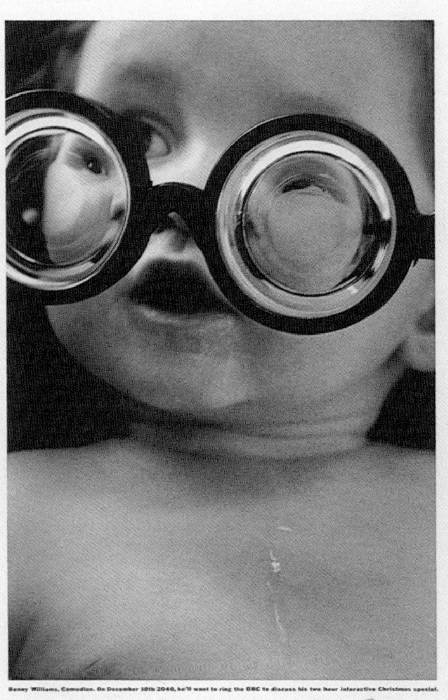

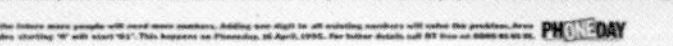

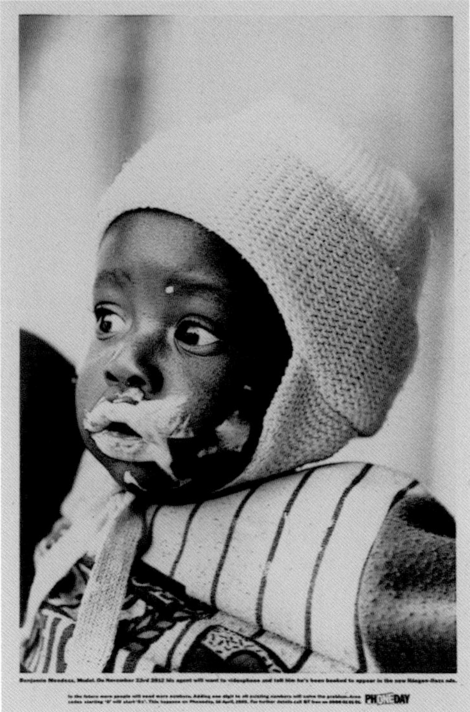

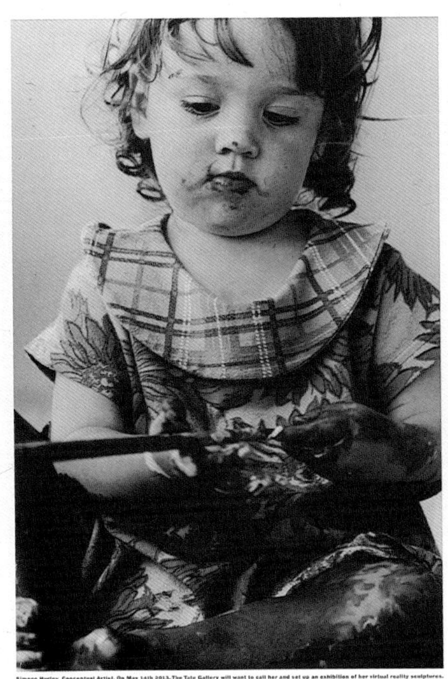
Simone Hurley, Conceptual Artist. On May 14th 2013, The Tate Gallery will want to call her and set up an exhibition of her virtual reality sculptures.
In the future more people will need more numbers. Adding one digit to all existing numbers will solve the problem. Area codes starting '0' will start '01'. This happens on Phoneday, 16 April, 1995. For further details call BT free on 0800 01 01 01.
PHONEDAY

Marlene Keaton, Session Musician. On October 15th 2012, Cliff Richard's manager will want to fax her the sheet music she'll be playing on Cliff's new single.
PHONEDAY

PHONEDAY

PHONEDAY

Mitzi Frecker, Fashion Designer. On 30th June 2029, she'll want to videophone Vogue to give them a sneak preview of her electronic haute couture.
PHONEDAY

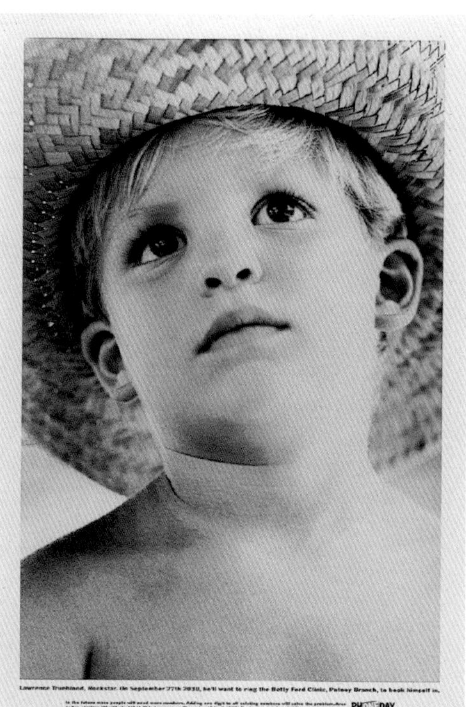
Lawrence Trumhand, Rockstar. On September 27th 2030, he'll want to ring the Betty Ford Clinic, Putney Branch, to book himself in.
PHONEDAY

Angela Jeffries, Agony Aunt. On March 18th 2024, a nervous women will want to call her radio chat show for advice on her husband's pregnancy.
PHONEDAY

SILVER AWARD NOMINATION
for the Most Outstanding Typography Individual

TRUE ROMANCE

As we hear the radio article, we see the words appear on the screen. The words help to dramatise the action.

SPEAKER:
These are the...these are the things that life is made of. I wanted to see what the Atlantic was like, you can only see it by going there. But much more importantly, I wanted to see what I was like on the Atlantic.

What's wrong with romance?

It brings light into life. Into your own life and into other peoples' lives.

God forbid that we were all practical pragmatists.

Silence.

Mix up caption which reads:

Re-discover the power of the spoken word.

Mix to end frame. We see the BBC Scotland logo and tuning device which demonstrates where to find the signal.

CAPTION:
UK National Station of the Year.

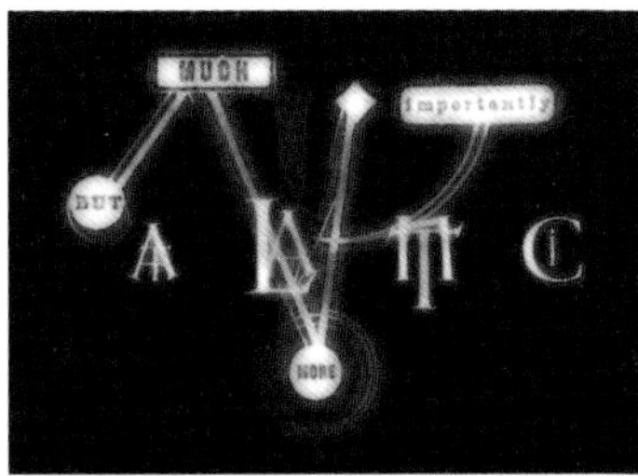

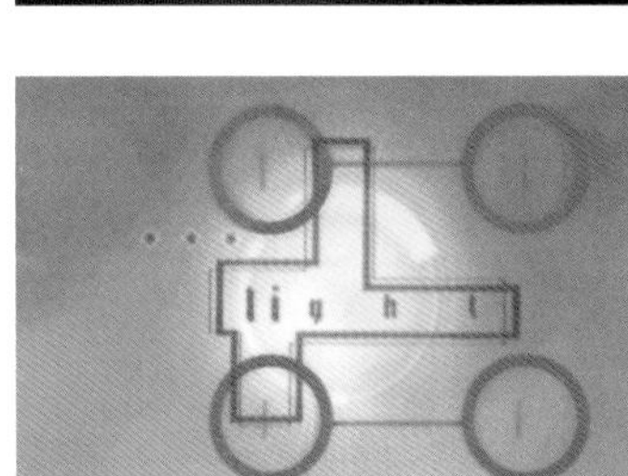

Director
JONATHAN BARNBROOK

Copywriter
ADRIAN JEFFERY

Art Director
LINDSEY REDDING

Creative Directors
SIMON SCOTT
ANDREW LINDSAY

Producer
YVONNE CHALK

Agency Producer
TIM MAGUIRE

Editor
JON HOLLIS

Music Composer/Arranger
LOGORHYTHM

Production Company
TONY KAYE FILMS

Agency
FAULDS ADVERTISING

Account Group Director
TOM GILL

Head of Presentation
PETER GOURD

Client
BBC RADIO SCOTLAND

SILVER AWARD NOMINATION
for the Most Outstanding Photography Individual

Photographer
TONY KAYE

Art Director
WALTER CAMPBELL

Copywriter
TOM CARTY

Typographer
ASHLEY PAYNE

Agency
ABBOTT MEAD VICKERS.BBDO LIMITED

Advertising Manager
TIM PATTEN

Client
BRITISH TELECOMMUNICATIONS

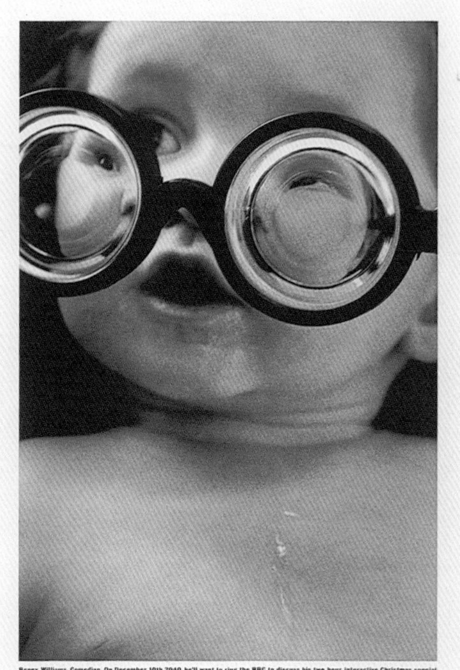

SILVER AWARD NOMINATION
for the Most Outstanding Photography Individual

Photographer
TONY KAYE

Art Director
WALTER CAMPBELL

Copywriter
TOM CARTY

Typographer
ASHLEY PAYNE

Agency
ABBOTT MEAD VICKERS.BBDO LIMITED

Advertising Manager
TIM PATTEN

Client
BRITISH TELECOMMUNICATIONS

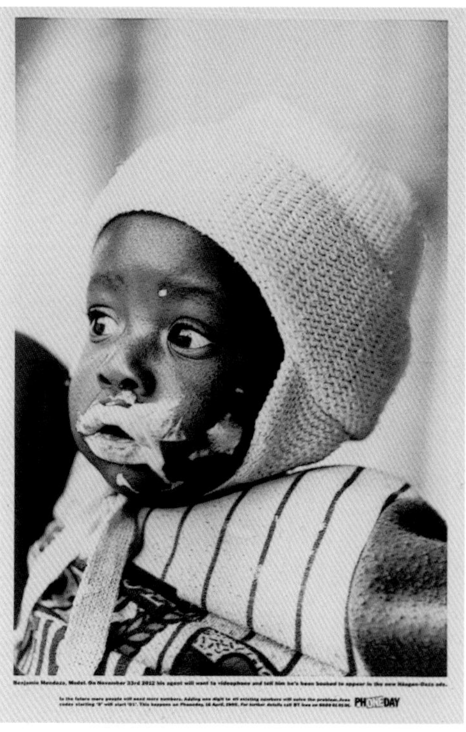

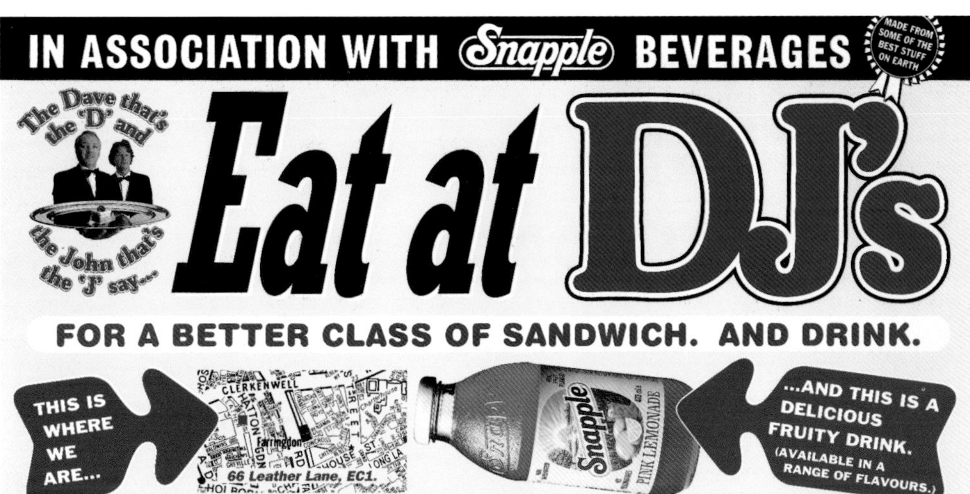

Typography Individual

Typographer
ANDY DYMOCK

Art Director
SIMON MORRIS

Copywriter
GEOFF SMITH

Photographer
STEVE CAVALIER

Agency
BANKS HOGGINS O'SHEA

International Marketing Director
JUNE BLOCKLIN

Client
SNAPPLE BEVERAGE CORPORATION

Typography Individual

Typographers
STEVEN WALLINGTON
PETER WOOD

Art Director
MARK REDDY

Copywriter
RICHARD GRISDALE

Photographer
DAVID STEWART

Agency
LEAGAS SHAFRON DAVIS AYER

Managing Director
COLIN PILGRIM

Client
HEAL'S

Typography Campaigns

Typographer
NIGEL WARD

Art Director
AJAB SAMRAI SINGH

Copywriter
GILES MONTGOMERY

Photographer
ALISTAIR THAIN

Agency
SAATCHI & SAATCHI

Marketing Executive
MARJORIE THOMPSON

Client
COMMISSION FOR RACIAL EQUALITY

THERE ARE LOTS OF PLACES IN BRITAIN WHERE RACISM DOESN'T EXIST.

In so many ways Britain is a racist country. In 1993 alone the police recorded over 9,000 incidents of racial harassment, abuse, assault, arson and murder. Thousands more incidents go unreported. As many as 120,000 a year, according to the Home Office. Worryingly, even this is still only half the problem.

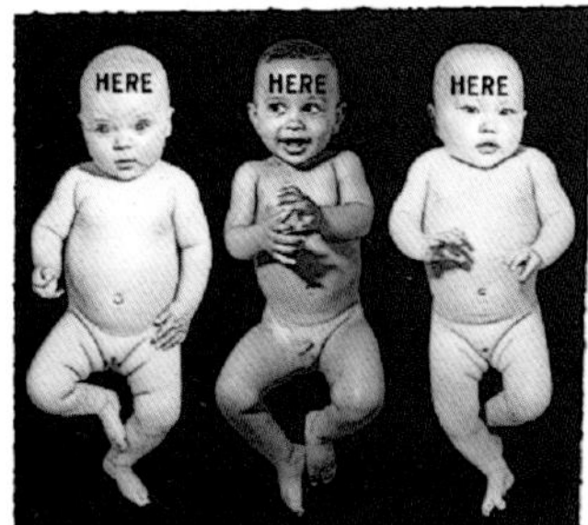

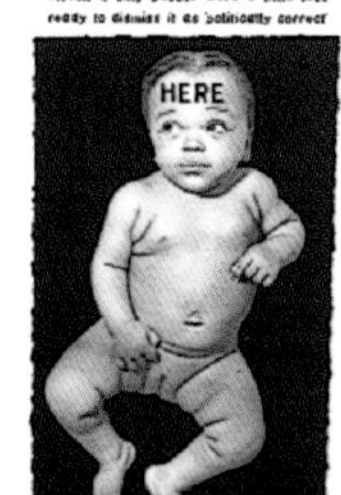

COMMISSION FOR RACIAL EQUALITY

Criminal

Typographer
TIM QUEST

Copywriter
AJAB SAMRAI SINGH

Photographers
TIM O'SULLIVAN
ALISTAIR THAIN

Openings

Typographer
NIGEL WARD

Copywriter
GILES MONTGOMERY

Photographer
JOHN TURNER

Worst Marks

Typographer
NIGEL WARD

Copywriters
AJAB SAMRAI SINGH
CHRIS KIRK

Photographer
BARRY LATEGAN

Junk Mail

Typographer
NIGEL WARD

Copywriter
GILES MONTGOMERY

Photographer
JOHN TURNER

CRIMINAL ISN'T IT?

A 1992 survey of Midlands crown courts revealed that some ethnic minorities are receiving longer prison sentences. On average, up to 9 months longer than white people for the same crimes. If this is typical, it leads to one simple and rather alarming conclusion.

Car theft 9 months.

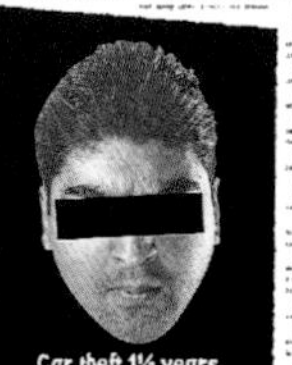

WHO SAYS ETHNIC MINORITIES CAN'T GET JOBS? THERE ARE OPENINGS EVERYWHERE.

Lavatory cleaner. Office cleaner. Somebody has to do all the low-paid, menial jobs, but why is it so often people from ethnic minorities? Prejudice, racial discrimination and harassment are denying people the chance of job they deserve. It's unjust and unfair. More than that, it's a terrible waste of British talent.

CHILDREN FROM ETHNIC MINORITIES OFTEN GET THE WORST MARKS AT SCHOOL.

Actually, studies show that some ethnic minorities get the best grades at school. But of course, you won't have heard about that. All you will have heard about are the kind of marks that grab the headlines. The vicious playground beatings, the horrific knife attacks and the senseless murders.

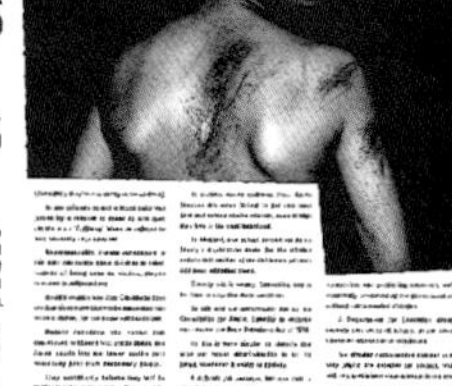

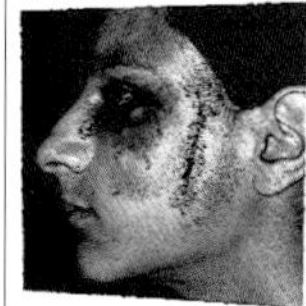

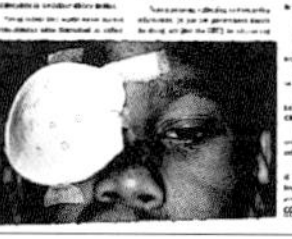

AND YOU GET ANNOYED ABOUT JUNK MAIL.

Imagine going to your door and finding, there, on the mat, not bills, or a paper, or junk mail, but pieces of dog excrement. As you stare, shocked, a heavy boot kicks the door. Hateful voices outside scream obscenities, telling you to get out, threatening your family. Why are they persecuting you? When will they stop?

Photography Individual

Photographers
THE DOUGLAS BROTHERS

Art Director
DAVE DYE

Copywriter
TIM DELANEY

Typographer
DAVE DYE

Agency
LEAGAS DELANEY

Senior Vice President, Marketing Communications
TOM HARRINGTON

Client
ADIDAS AG

Photography Individual

Photographers
THE DOUGLAS BROTHERS

Art Director
DAVE DYE

Copywriter
TIM DELANEY

Typographer
DAVE DYE

Agency
LEAGAS DELANEY

Senior Vice President, Marketing Communications
TOM HARRINGTON

Client
ADIDAS AG

Photography Individual

Photographer
TONY KAYE

Art Director
WALTER CAMPBELL

Copywriter
TOM CARTY

Typographer
ASHLEY PAYNE

Agency
ABBOTT MEAD
VICKERS.BBDO
LIMITED

Advertising Manager
TIM PATTEN

Client
BRITISH
TELECOMMUNICATIONS

Photography Individual

Photographer
DAVID STEWART

Art Director
MIKE KEANE

Copywriter
TONY VEAZEY

Typographer
MARCUS HASLAM

Agency
BROADBENT
CHEETHAM VEAZEY

Managing Director
PAUL MICHAEL

Marketing Director
PETER DELACY

Client
SLIMMER MAGAZINE

ON SALE NOW

Photography Individual

Photographer
TONY KAYE

Art Director
WALTER CAMPBELL

Copywriter
TOM CARTY

Typographer
ASHLEY PAYNE

Agency
ABBOTT MEAD
VICKERS.BBDO
LIMITED

Advertising Manager
TIM PATTEN

Client
BRITISH
TELECOMMUNICATIONS

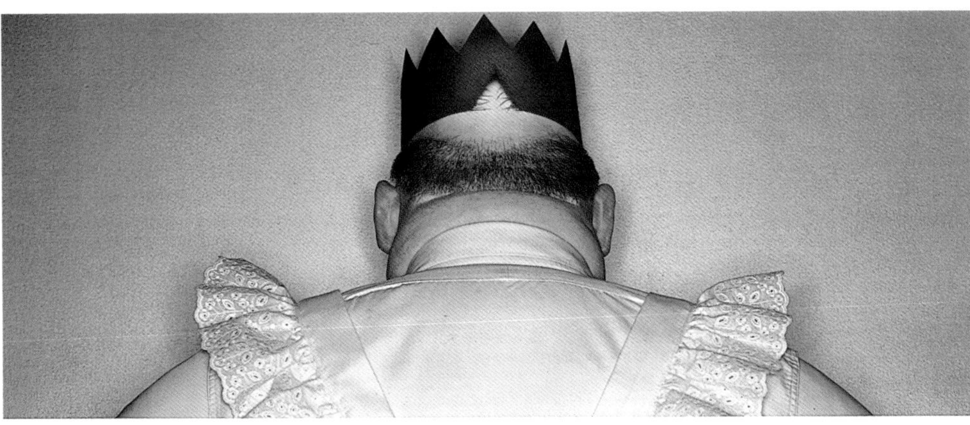

Photography Individual

Photographer
PAUL ARDEN

Art Director
ALEXANDRA TAYLOR

Copywriter
JIM SAUNDERS

Agency
SAATCHI & SAATCHI

Marketing Executive
MIKE HALL-TAYLOR

Client
GALLAHER TOBACCO
LIMITED

Photography Individual

Photographer
ALISTAIR MORRISON

Art Director
BILL GALLACHER

Copywriter
RICHARD MYERS

Typographer
ROGER KENNEDY

Agency
SAATCHI & SAATCHI

Marketing Controller
GARRY SMITH

Client
PORK FARMS
BOWYERS

A proud Parks is seen showing off his tasteful little number in prime pork, honey, spices and lemon juice. The whole ensemble set off perfectly, in the designer's own words, by 'some rather cunning herbs'. The creation was inspired by Tobago, or more accurately, the utter lack of a decent sausage when Parks set up home there. For a dedicated bangerphile, this was quite intolerable. But fortunately, while the digestive juices were starved,

the creative ones flowed. Fashion took a back seat to the frying pan as Parks perfected his recipe. The end result after three years work? The award-winning Famous Porkinson. Now available in three styles, Banger, Chipolata and Sausage Roll, at Harrods and well-known supermarkets. And also, ready-to-eat, at any number of appropriately fashionable restaurants, clubs and bars.

PORKINSON BANGER

The first sausage from an internationally renowned photographer.

After photographing the designs of Dior, Chanel & Shuji Tojo for forty five years, Norman Parkinson decided to model a creation of his own.

Photography
Campaigns

Photographer
NADAV KANDER

Art Director
ROB OLIVER

Copywriter
PETER RUSSELL

Agency
ABBOTT MEAD
VICKERS.BBDO
LIMITED

Marketing Director
NIALL BOWEN

Client
COW & GATE LIMITED

Photography
Campaigns

Photographer
DAVID STEWART

Art Director
MARK REDDY

Copywriter
RICHARD GRISDALE

Typographers
STEVE WALLINGTON
PETER WOOD

Agency
LEAGAS SHAFRON
DAVIS AYER

Managing Director
COLIN PILGRIM

Client
HEAL'S

Illustration Individual

Illustrator
JEFF FISHER

Art Director
TAN SHEN GUAN

Copywriter
TAN SHEN GUAN

Agency
J. WALTER THOMPSON, HONG KONG

Editor in Chief
DAVID ARMSTRONG

Client
SOUTH CHINA MORNING POST

Illustration Individual

Illustrator
JANET WOOLLEY

Art Director
GRAHAM WATSON

Copywriter
BRUCE CROUCH

Typographers
SID RUSSELL
GRAHAM WATSON

Agency
BARTLE BOGLE HEGARTY

Marketing Executive
MIKE DOWELL

Client
THE WHITBREAD BEER COMPANY

Illustration Individual

Illustrator
JEFF FISHER

Art Director
MICHAEL TAN

Copywriter
EUGENE CHEONG

Typographer
MICHAEL TAN

Agency
EURO RSCG BALL PARTNERSHIP, SINGAPORE

Marketing Executive
EDMUND KOH

Client
HONG KONG BANK

Illustration Campaigns

Illustrator
NEIL GOWER

Art Director
GUY MOORE

Copywriter
TONY MALCOLM

Typographer
JOHN TISDALL

Agency
SIMONS PALMER DENTON CLEMMOW & JOHNSON

Marketing Executive
ELAINE SNELL

Client
BRITISH HEART FOUNDATION

Illustration Campaigns

Illustrators
BRIAN GRIMWOOD
DAVID HOLMES
JEFF FISHER
SIMON SPILSBURY

Art Director
MICHAEL TAN

Copywriter
EUGENE CHEONG

Typographer
MICHAEL TAN

Agency
EURO RSCG BALL
PARTNERSHIP,
SINGAPORE

Marketing Executive
EDMUND KOH

Client
HONG KONG BANK

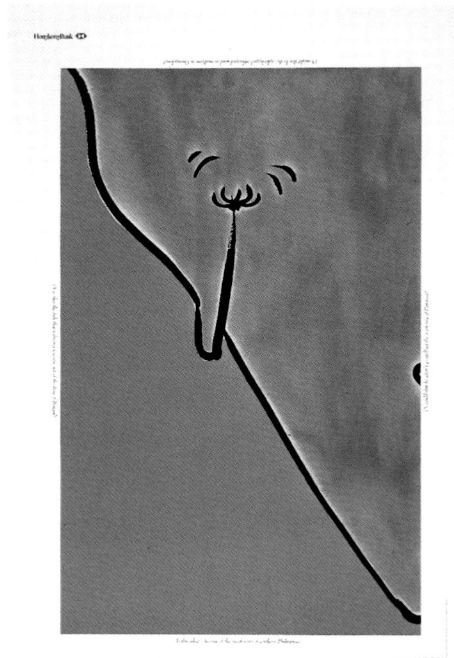

1995

PUBLIC SERVICE AND CHARITIES

Sponsored by GGT for Big Issue

SILVER AWARD
for the Most Outstanding Public Service TV or Cinema Advertisement

Director
MARTIJN VAN HEES

Copywriter
BARBARA TAMMES

Art Director
JACQUELINE DONKER

Creative Director
HARRY KRAMP

Producer
SJOERD HANNEMA

Agency Producer
ANNEMARIE SEMEIJN

Editor
MARTIJN VAN HEES

Lighting Cameraman
MAARTEN VAN KELLER

Music Composer/Arranger
DONNA SUMMER

Production Company
THE FILMSTONES

Agency
PPGH/JWT

Marketing Executive
HANS VERNHOUT

Client
MINISTRY OF SOCIAL AFFAIRS

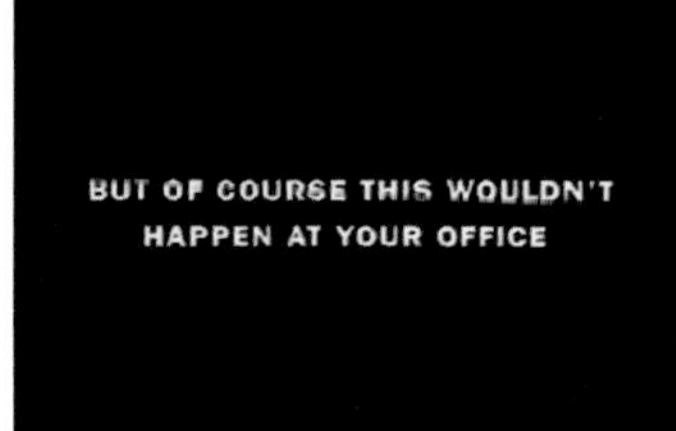

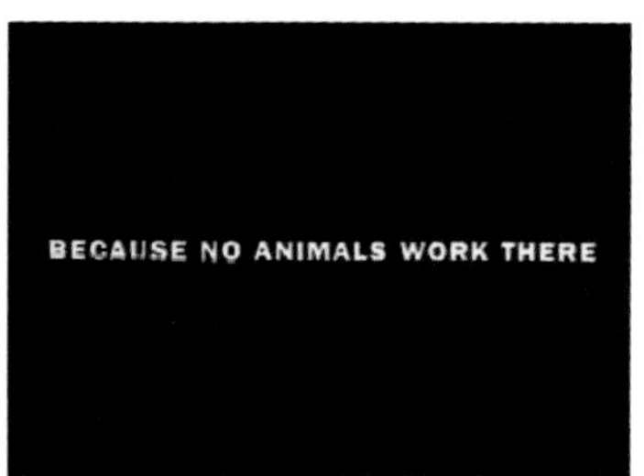

DOG

A man is standing at a photocopier. A dog trots up, licks his hand and mounts his leg. The man tries to push him away.

SUPER:
This is how women feel when sexually harrassed at work.

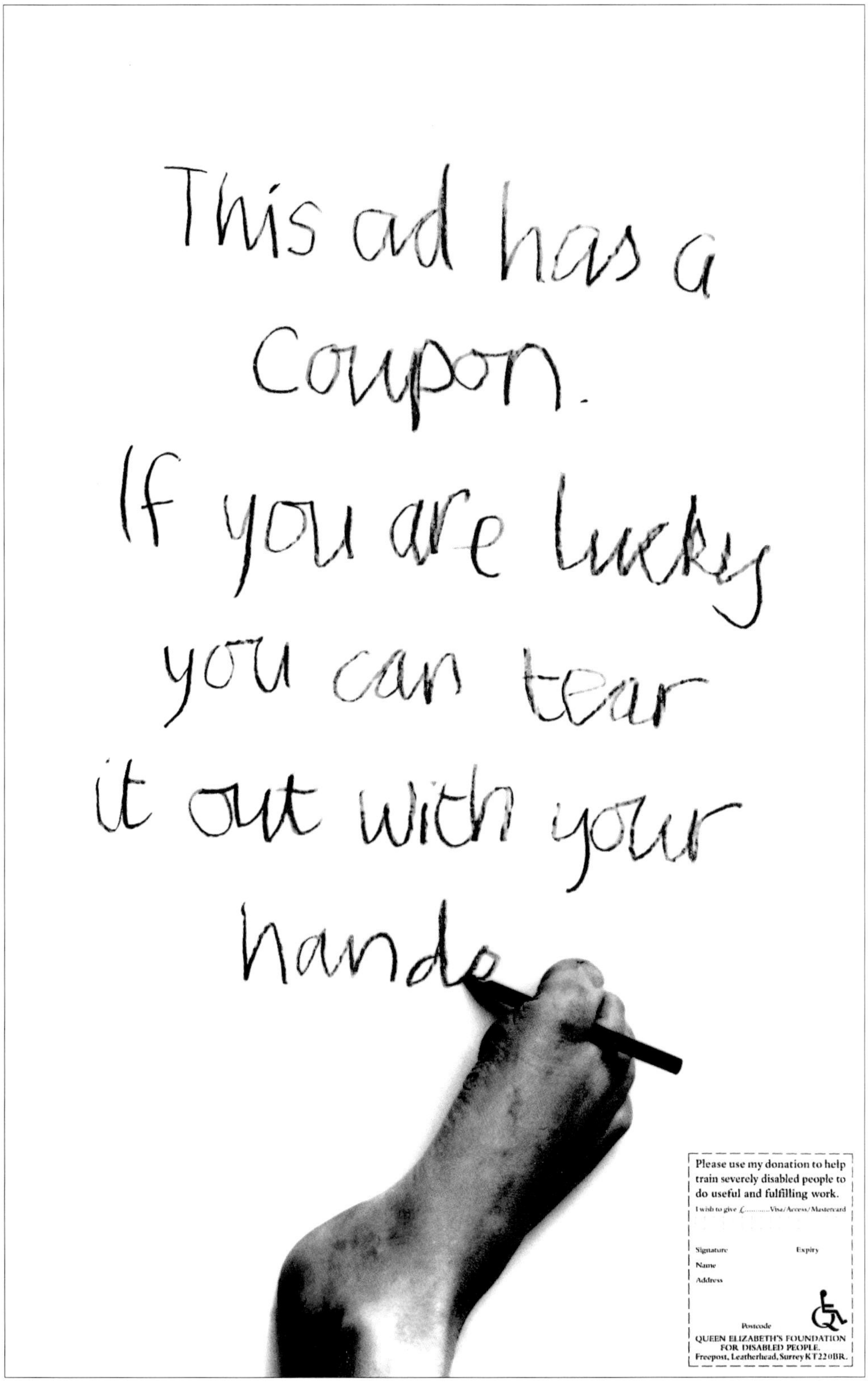

This ad has a
Coupon.
If you are lucky
you can tear
it out with your
hands

Please use my donation to help train severely disabled people to do useful and fulfilling work.

I wish to give £..........Visa/Access/Mastercard

Signature Expiry
Name
Address

Postcode

QUEEN ELIZABETH'S FOUNDATION FOR DISABLED PEOPLE.
Freepost, Leatherhead, Surrey KT22 0BR.

SILVER AWARD
for the Most Outstanding Charity Mixed Media Campaign

Art Director
PAUL BRAZIER

Copywriter
PETER SOUTER

Photographer
MIKE PARSONS

Typographer
JOE HOZA

Agency
ABBOTT MEAD VICKERS.BBDO LIMITED

Director of Fundraising
TONY RICHINS

Client
QUEEN ELIZABETH'S FOUNDATION FOR DISABLED PEOPLE

Director
DAVID GARFATH

Art Director
PAUL BRAZIER

Copywriter
PETER SOUTER

Creative Director
DAVID ABBOTT

Producer
MARY FRANCIS

Agency Producer
FRANCINE LINSEY

Editor
SIMON WILCOX

Lighting Cameraman
PETER HANNAN

Production Company
PAUL WEILAND FILM COMPANY

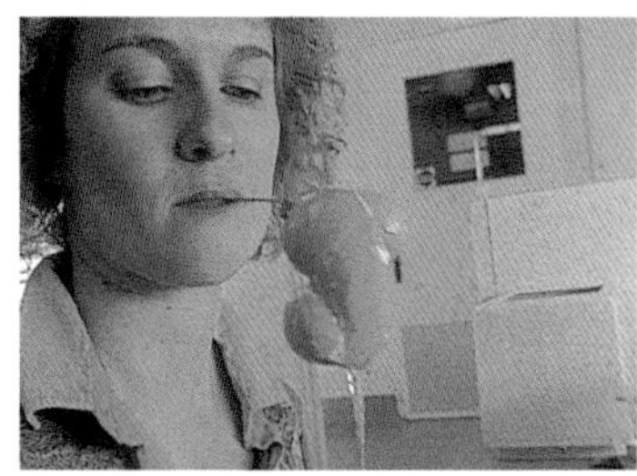

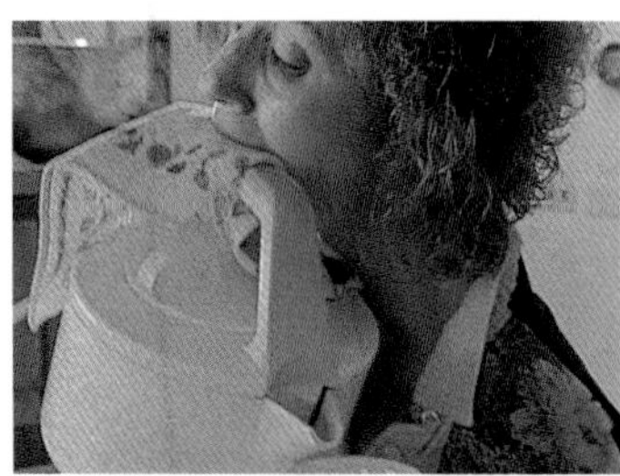

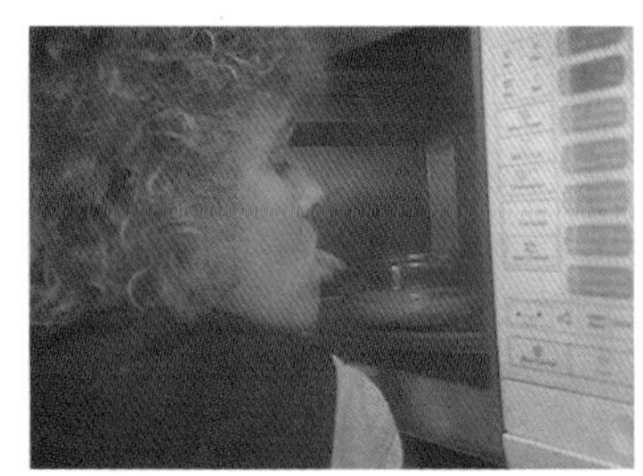

After what you've seen do you really find it so difficult to write a cheque?

EGGS

Open on a fridge. A young woman's head enters the frame and opens the fridge door with her mouth. The light from the fridge suddenly bathes her in brightness and for the first time we see she has no arms. The young woman sucks up an egg from the fridge, walks to a nearby table and sets it down. She returns to the fridge for another.

Cut to the young woman as she drops an egg into a mixing bowl. The egg breaks and the liquid and shell mix together. She lowers her head into the bowl and delicately lifts out the shell with her tongue. She repeats this process with the second egg.

Cut to the young woman as she beats the egg with a fork held between her teeth. We linger on the shot until her head movement makes us dizzy, then watch her pour the contents into a pan and place it in the microwave.

Cut to the young woman who is now wrapping a tea-towel around the handle of a hot kettle. She then lifts it up and, with difficulty, pours boiling water into some tea cups. These simple tasks require a Herculean effort.

V/O:
After what you've seen, do you really find it so difficult to write a cheque?

Cut back to the young woman presenting the finished breakfast.

TITLE:
Queen Elizabeth's Foundation For Disabled People.

Copywriters
PETER SOUTER
PAUL BRAZIER

Recording Engineer
NIGEL CROWLEY

Recording Studio
MAGMASTERS

ABBOTT MEAD VICKERS · BBDO LTD

191 Old Marylebone Road
London NW1 5DW
Telephone 071 402 4100
Telex 888876 MEDAVI
Fax 071 935 5883

Radio Script

Client QEFDP Date 11.11.94

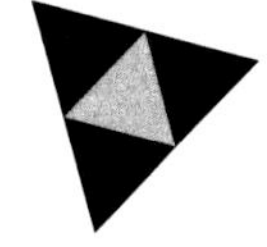

90 seconds

"Tapioca Pudding"

Andy: My name is Andy Dixon and I don't like Tapioca pudding. For the first 22 years of my life this was not a problem. I would just tell people.

Then I fell off a motorway bridge.

The fall left me virtually blind, spastic in all my limbs and speechless. In the hospital the nurses did everything they could for me and I was very grateful. Except at lunch-ime. That's when the gave me tapioca pudding. A lot of Tapioca pudding.

The only thing I could do to let them know I didn't like it was to spit it out. The doctors took my spitting as a sign of behavioural problems and classified me as a difficult patient.

Fortunately, after two years in various hospitals I was given one last chance. I was sent to a centre run by Queen Elisabeth's Foundation for Disabled People for assessment and rehabilitation.

They fixed me up with the specially adapted machine which is allowing me to talk to you now. I am tapping out letters using a pressure pad under my chin. It's a painfully slow process but it means I can do two things.

I can ask you to support QEFDP in any way you can. And I can say I don't like Tapioca pudding.

SILVER AWARD NOMINATION
for the Most Outstanding Public Service or Charity Press Advertisement

Art Director
SEAN THOMPSON

Copywriter
ROS SINCLAIR

Photographer
TERRY O'NEILL

Typographer
MARK OSBORNE

Agency
S P LINTAS

Marketing Executive
MARK SCOTHERN

Client
CRISIS

imaginative interiors

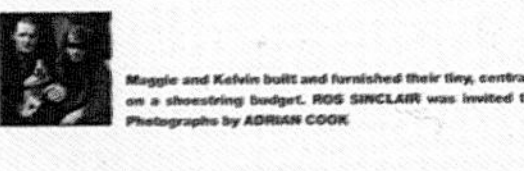

Maggie and Kelvin built and furnished their tiny, central London home on a shoestring budget. ROS SINCLAIR was invited to look around. Photographs by ADRIAN COOK

Compact & bijou

After their old home was burned down by unfriendly passers-by, Maggie 20 and Kelvin 26 had no option but to rebuild it. They didn't have enough money to rent a real apartment.

"This is the best place so far" says Maggie who has lived in a variety of shop doorways and cardboard shelters since she was 11.

"When I was 13, I lived in a cupboard in the boiler room of Marble Arch tube station. That's where I met Kelvin. There was a TV programme about us called 'The Subway Kids'. We stayed there three years, before they chucked us out."

Inside the shelter or 'bash' there is a strong smell of damp, rotting cardboard. "They only last about a month" says Maggie, prodding the collapsing cardboard roof with a small grubby finger. "I doubt this will keep the rain out much longer."

Through a little window Kelvin has carved in the cardboard and fitted with see-through plastic, we watch the rain pouring down.

The structure is built out of large packing boxes given to them by two cinemas in Leicester Square. Plastic sheeting covers a roof which is held up precariously by broken striplights.

The base is made out of plastic crates from McDonalds, carpet underlay and a foam mattress Kelvin found in a skip. Thin sleeping bags cover the lot.

Maggie has done her best to make the place more homely. Curtains made out of an old pillowcase hang on either side of the window, reminiscent of a Wendyhouse.

The walls are decorated with pictures ripped out of magazines and wrapping paper from a local florist. Two moth eaten bed-heads, given to them by a friendly landlord, form seating of sorts. A wicker tray serves as a bedside cabinet and small boxes form makeshift shelves which hang from the cardboard walls by string. Candles from the Bargain Pound Shop on Oxford Street sit on top of them.

Maggie's pride and joy has to be the cardboard table covered with a scarf, on which sits a pot plant, a toy clown and her collection of chipped miniature china houses. "I found them in rubbish bags. They're rejects from the tourist shops in Piccadilly."

She picks up a pretty cottage with roses around the door. "Maybe me and Kelvin will live in one like this someday." Maggie laughs at the idea ■

MAIN PICTURE: Maggie and Kelvin's home as it is now.
FUTURE PICTURE: Depends on you.
CALL: 071 377 0489 to find out how a donation of £10 can help the homeless.

CRISIS

SILVER AWARD NOMINATION
for the Most Outstanding Public Service or Charity Press Advertisement

Art Director
SEAN THOMPSON

Copywriter
ROS SINCLAIR

Photographer
ADRIAN COOK

Typographer
MARK OSBORNE

Agency
S P LINTAS

Marketing Executive
MARK SCOTHERN

Client
CRISIS

SILVER AWARD NOMINATION
for the Most Outstanding Charity TV or Cinema Advertisement

Director
DAVID GARFATH

Copywriter
PETER SOUTER

Art Director
PAUL BRAZIER

Creative Director
DAVID ABBOTT

Producer
MARY FRANCIS

Agency Producer
FRANCINE LINSEY

Editor
SIMON WILCOX

Lighting Cameraman
PETER HANNAN

Production Company
PAUL WEILAND FILM COMPANY

Agency
ABBOTT MEAD VICKERS.BBDO LIMITED

Director of Fundraising
TONY RICHINS

Client
QUEEN ELIZABETH'S FOUNDATION FOR DISABLED PEOPLE

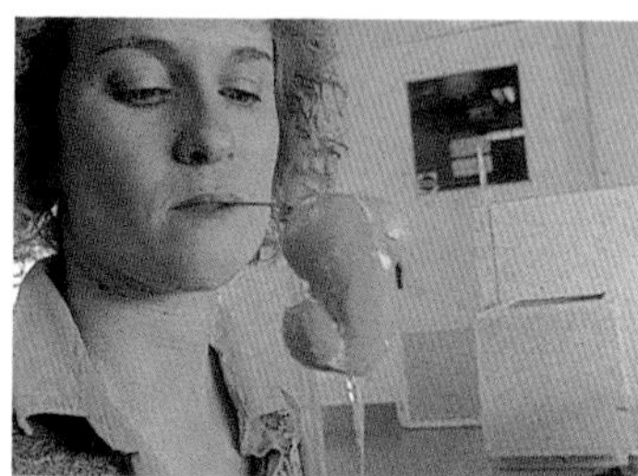

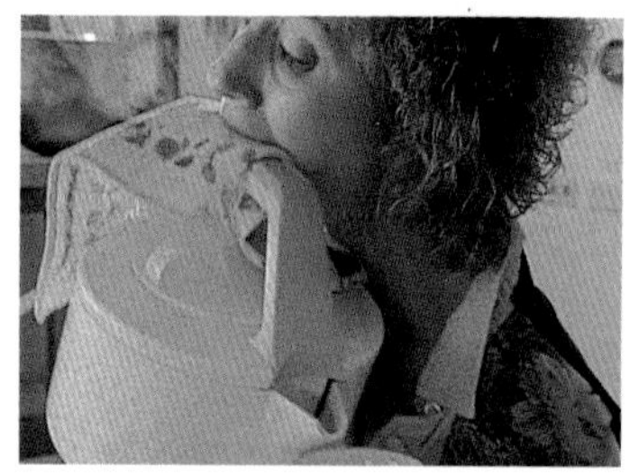

After what you've seen do you really find it so difficult to write a cheque?

EGGS

Open on a fridge. A young woman's head enters the frame and opens the fridge door with her mouth. The light from the fridge suddenly bathes her in brightness and for the first time we see she has no arms. The young woman sucks up an egg from the fridge, walks to a nearby table and sets it down. She returns to the fridge for another.

Cut to the young woman as she drops an egg into a mixing bowl. The egg breaks and the liquid and shell mix together. She lowers her head into the bowl and delicately lifts out the shell with her tongue. She repeats this process with the second egg.

Cut to the young woman as she beats the egg with a fork held between her teeth. We linger on the shot until her head movement makes us dizzy, then watch her pour the contents into a pan and place it in the microwave.

Cut to the young woman who is now wrapping a tea-towel around the handle of a hot kettle. She then lifts it up and, with difficulty, pours boiling water into some tea cups. These simple tasks require a Herculean effort.

V/O:
After what you've seen, do you really find it so difficult to write a cheque?

Cut back to the young woman presenting the finished breakfast.

TITLE:
Queen Elizabeth's Foundation For Disabled People.

SILVER AWARD NOMINATION
for the Most Outstanding Public Service or Charity Poster

Art Directors
ALEX BOGUSKY
PAT HARRIS
SHARON HARMS

Copywriter
PIETER BLIKSLAGER

Photographer
KARL STEINBRENNER

Agency
CRISPIN & PORTER ADVERTISING

Marketing Executive
JOE SHUTT

Client
FLORIDA COALITION TO STOP GUN VIOLENCE

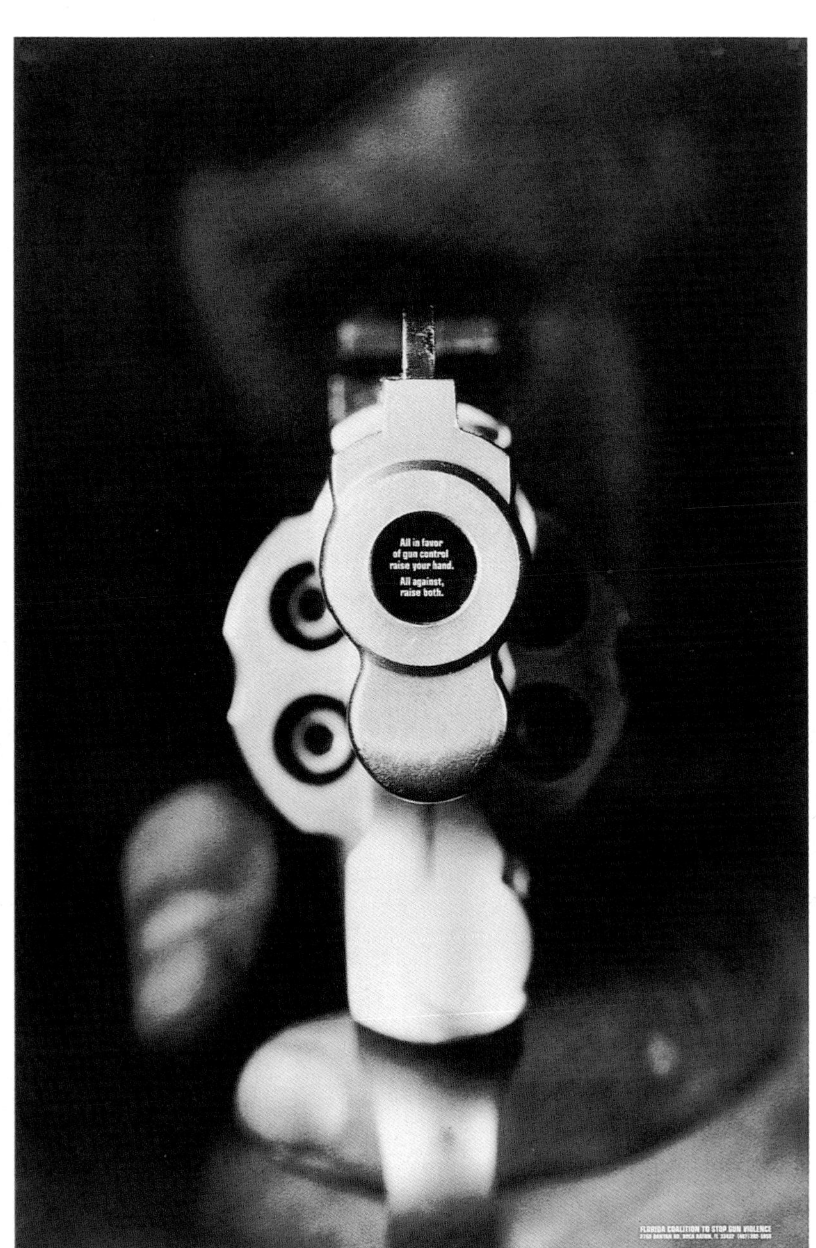

Press Advertising

Art Director
GUY MOORE

Copywriter
INDRA SINHA

Photographer
RAGHU RAI

Typographer
JEFF MERRELLS

Agencies
ANTENNAE COMMUNICATIONS
COLLETT DICKENSON PEARCE

Marketing Executive
SATINATH SARANGI

Client
SATINATH SARANGI

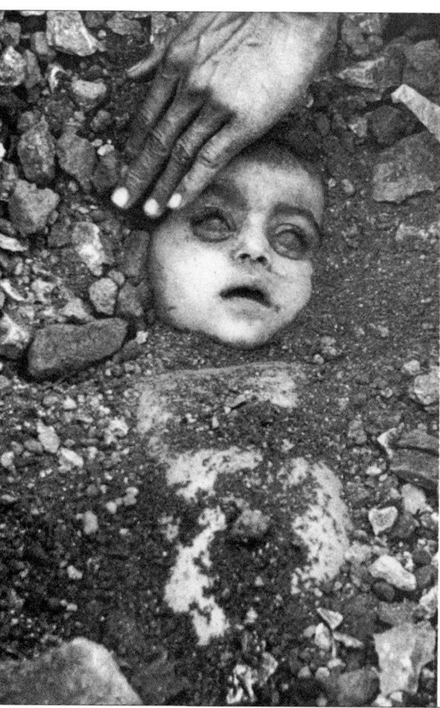

"THOUSANDS OF OUR CHILDREN WERE NOT SO LUCKY. THEY SURVIVED."

I WANT TO HELP THE BHOPAL GAS VICTIMS WHO HAVE SUFFERED FOR TEN YEARS WITHOUT RELIEF.

THE INTERNATIONAL MEDICAL APPEAL FOR BHOPAL

Press Advertising

Art Director
GREG MARTIN

Copywriter
NICK BELL

Typographer
JOE HOZA

Agency
ABBOTT MEAD VICKERS.BBDO LIMITED

Director of Campaigns and Public Relations
JERRY LLOYD

Client
RSPCA

Investigating this wasn't difficult. We had a lead.

We found Trudy tethered round the neck by a piece of rusting curtain wire.

Her three small puppies were just a few feet away.

Where Trudy had struggled to get to them, the sharp, rusty coil of the wire had cut deep into her throat.

From the depth of the wound and the amount of scar tissue formed, our vet estimated she had been tethered in this way for at least five weeks.

In his opinion, she would have suffered considerably.

All year round, our Inspectors are called to the aid of suffering animals like Trudy.

Last year alone, we responded to nearly 100,000 reports of animal

cruelty. Reports of horses that had been starved, dogs that had been beaten, kittens that had been kicked and maimed.

Our policy is never to refuse a call for help. But, of course, it's an expensive one.

The current cost of training, equipping and putting just one new Inspector on the road for a year is £32,407. Which is why we so desperately need your help.

The RSPCA doesn't receive any funding from the Government.

We rely entirely on the public's generosity.

Thanks to people like you, we were able to find a loving new home for Trudy and her puppies.

So please send as much money as you can. And help us save a few more necks.

TEL: 071 538 6001 — Telegraph APPOINTMENTS — FAX: 071 538 7816

COULD YOU MAKE YOUR PLATOON BLEND IN AS WELL AS THE ARMY OFFICER AD ON THE OTHER PAGE?

ARMY

Engineering Manager

When it comes to working overseas, some opportunities are *Taylor* made.

Export Regional Manager Scandinavian Markets

PRODUCT MANAGER

BRING YOUR NAME TO THE FRONT

TEL: 071 538 6001 — Telegraph APPOINTMENTS — FAX: 071 538 7816

SALES & TECHNICAL APPOINTMENTS

ESSOGAS LTD

TECHNICAL FACILITATOR

SALES FACILITATOR

The Telegraph plc

MANAGEMENT ACCOUNTANT

Press Advertising

Art Director
GREG MILBOURNE

Copywriter
GAVIN KELLETT

Typographer
NIGEL WARD

Agency
SAATCHI & SAATCHI

Marketing Executive
MAJOR TIM BRAND

Clients
DIRECTORATE OF ARMY RECRUITMENT
COI

I've got my mothers eyes.

This is Julie's story.

'Everyone in the village thinks my dad's really great. But I hate him.

They are always saying what a kind and helpful man he is. That's a load of rubbish. He's really horrible to me and my mum.

He's got his own business and is always coming home late. Sometimes he smells like he's been drinking. But if my mum ever complains he hits her.

The other night I could hear my mum screaming. I ran downstairs and saw him pulling her across the living room by her hair. When I tried to stop him, he hit me in the face.'

The next day, when a neighbour saw Julie's bruised eyes, she reported it. And now, thanks to her, Julie and her family are getting the help they need.

There are thousands of cases like Julie's every year. But they're only a small part of the problem.

When most people think of child abuse they think of cases like Julie's. But the fact is, children can actually be just as badly harmed by the kind of treatment that a lot of people might not even think of as abuse.

For instance, constantly ignoring or criticizing a child, or withdrawal of any signs of affection, can emotionally scar a child for the rest of his or her life.

They can lead to feelings of low self-worth, loneliness and an inability to form relationships with others.

Which is the reason why the NSPCC is launching a new campaign, 'A Cry For Children'. It's a cry to everyone to stop and think about how they behave towards children.

To recognise the impact that any form of cruelty can have on a child. And to realise the way children are treated can affect their whole lives.

Please answer the cry.

If you, or someone you know is suffering from abuse, please call the NSPCC Child Protection Helpline on 0800 800 500 any time, day or night.

Or if, after reading this, you would find more information helpful, please call us on 071 825 2775.

NSPCC
A cry for children.

Press Advertising

Art Directors
COLIN JONES
BILL GALLACHER

Copywriter
NEIL PAVITT

Photographer
GRAHAM CORNTHWAITE

Typographer
ROGER KENNEDY

Agency
SAATCHI & SAATCHI

Director of Public Policy
PHILIP NOYES

Client
NSPCC

Press Advertising

Art Director
DAVID WOODALL

Copywriter
CHARITY CHARITY

Typographer
DAVID WOODALL

Agency
J. WALTER THOMPSON

Exhibition/Tourism Manager
SANDRA MORETTO

Client
I.S.G.C. LIMITED

TO OVR MOST GRATIOVS AND MVNIFICENT PATRONS whether of this Scepter'd Isle or Nations Hesperian or yet Orient, wee the humble reed - binders, lime - plasterers and oake - sawyers of the famed NEW SHAKESPEARE GLOBE THEATRE

neering the end of our Travails and mindfull of your Great and Glorious *Largesse*, proceft our indebtedneffe to your singular Benevolence and pledge ourfelves to your efteemed Service in all Obedience, Honour & Duty

&c. &c. &c.

ANY CHANCE OF A BIT MORE DOSH?
071 928 7710

Press advertising

Art Director
STEVE CHETHAM

Copywriter
TREVOR BEATTIE

Photographer
LEON

Typographer
TIVY DAVIES

Agency
TBWA

Marketing Executives
JULIA FELTHOUSE
TONY SANDELL

Client
NATIONAL CANINE DEFENCE LEAGUE

TOYS AREN'T US.

AND YOU GET ANNOYED ABOUT JUNK MAIL.

Imagine going to your door and finding, there, on the mat, not bills, or a paper, or junk mail, but pieces of dog excrement. As you stare, shocked, a heavy boot kicks the door. Hateful voices outside scream obscenities, telling you to get out, threatening your family. Why are they persecuting you? When will they stop?

COMMISSION FOR RACIAL EQUALITY

Press Advertising

Art Director
AJAB SAMRAI SINGH

Copywriter
GILES MONTGOMERY

Photographer
JOHN TURNER

Typographer
NIGEL WARD

Agency
SAATCHI & SAATCHI

Marketing Executive
MARJORIE THOMPSON

Client
COMMISSION FOR RACIAL EQUALITY

WHO SAYS ETHNIC MINORITIES CAN'T GET JOBS? THERE ARE OPENINGS EVERYWHERE.

Lavatory attendant. Office cleaner. Somebody has to do all the low-paid, menial jobs, but why is it so often people from ethnic minorities? Prejudice, racial discrimination and harassment are denying people the choice of job they deserve. It's unjust and unfair. More than that, it's a terrible waste of British talent.

COMMISSION FOR RACIAL EQUALITY

Press Advertising

Art Director
AJAB SAMRAI SINGH

Copywriter
GILES MONTGOMERY

Photographer
JOHN TURNER

Typographer
NIGEL WARD

Agency
SAATCHI & SAATCHI

Marketing Executive
MARJORIE THOMPSON

Client
COMMISSION FOR RACIAL EQUALITY

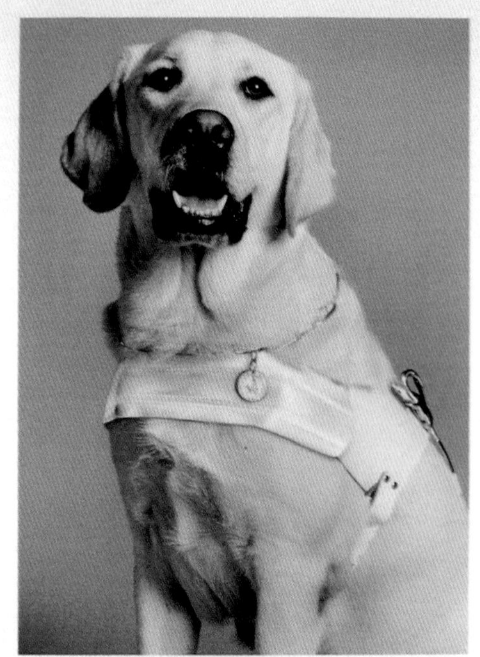

Press Advertising

Art Director
DERRICK HASS

Copywriter
JUSTIN ROGERS

Photographer
MALCOLM VENVILLE

Typographer
ROB WALLIS

Agency
McCANN-ERICKSON

Sales and Marketing Manager
ALISON RADEVSKY

Client
GUIDE DOGS FOR THE BLIND ASSOCIATION

Posters

Art Director
STEVE CHETHAM

Copywriter
TREVOR BEATTIE

Photographer
LEON

Typographer
TIVY DAVIES

Agency
TBWA

Marketing Executives
JULIA FELTHOUSE
TONY SANDELL

Client
NATIONAL CANINE DEFENCE LEAGUE

Posters

Art Director
STEVE CHETHAM

Copywriter
TREVOR BEATTIE

Photographer
LEON

Typographer
TIVY DAVIES

Agency
TBWA

Marketing Executives
JULIA FELTHOUSE
TONY SANDELL

Client
NATIONAL CANINE DEFENCE LEAGUE

VNPARALLEL'D
FANTASTICAL.
THE MOST ASTONISHING
SITE IN LONDON.

Posters

Art Director
DAVID WOODALL

Copywriter
CHARITY CHARITY

Typographer
DAVID WOODALL

Agency
J. WALTER THOMPSON

Exhibition/Tourism Manager
SANDRA MORETTO

Client
I.S.G.C. LIMITED

S	M	T	W	T	F	S
		1 Children	2 diagnosed	3 with	4 cancer	5 have
6 to	7 cherish	8 every	9 day.	10 Please	11 make	12 today
13 as	14 meaningful	15 to	16 you	17 as	18 it	19 is
20 to	21 them.	22 Send	23 a	24 donation	25 to	26 the
27 Children's	28 Cancer	29 Research	30 Fund.	31 (612) 929-5535		

Posters

Art Director
ELLEN STEINBERG

Copywriter
MIKE LESCARBEAU

Agency
FALLON McELLIGOTT

Executive Director
BRIAN NELSON

Client
CHILDREN'S CANCER RESEARCH FUND

Posters

Art Director
AJAB SAMRAI SINGH

Copywriter
GILES MONTGOMERY

Photographer
JOHN TURNER

Typographer
NIGEL WARD

Agency
SAATCHI & SAATCHI

Marketing Executive
MARJORIE THOMPSON

Client
COMMISSION FOR RACIAL EQUALITY

MOVIES

Super titles fading in and out.

Perfect Strangers

Fatal Attraction

The Apartment

Dangerous Liaisons

Dirty Harry

Exposed

The Naked Gun

Chitty Chitty Bang Bang

The Black Hole

Breathless

Tremors

The Verdict

Dying Young

The Fool

Sleeping With The Enemy

The End.

Action For Aids Singapore.

Wearing A Condom Can Protect You From Aids And Other Sexually Transmitted Diseases.

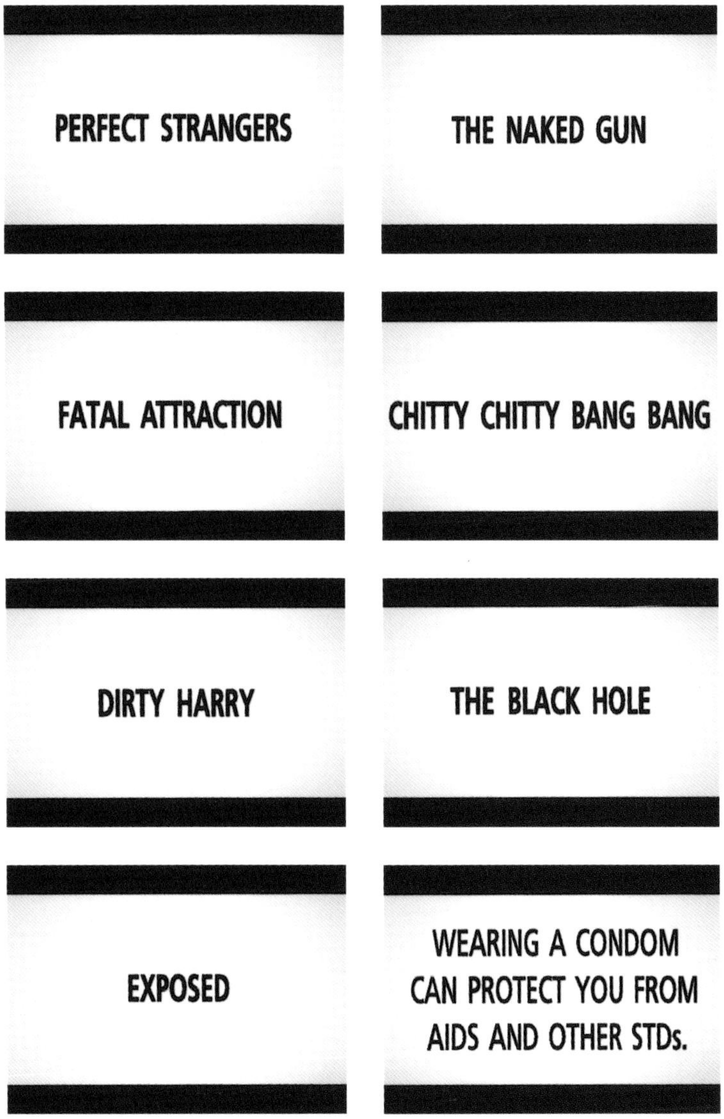

PERFECT STRANGERS

THE NAKED GUN

FATAL ATTRACTION

CHITTY CHITTY BANG BANG

DIRTY HARRY

THE BLACK HOLE

EXPOSED

WEARING A CONDOM
CAN PROTECT YOU FROM
AIDS AND OTHER STDs.

Television & Cinema

Director
EDDIE WONG

Copywriters
EDDIE WONG
WILTON BOEY

Art Directors
EDDIE WONG
WILTON BOEY

Producer
LARRY LAI

Editor
AARON EZEKIEL

Music Composer/Arranger
AARON EZEKIEL

Production Company
PETAL PRODUCTIONS

Client
ACTION FOR AIDS SINGAPORE

Television & Cinema

Director
MIKE STEPHENSON

Copywriter
ROB JANOWSKI

Art Director
STEVE GRIME

Creative Director
STEVE GRIME

Producer
PAUL ROTHWELL

Agency Producer
PETER GRAINGER

Editor
CYRIL METZGER

Lighting Cameraman
BARRY BROWN

Music Composer/Arrangers
JOE & CO

Production Company
PAUL WEILAND FILM COMPANY

Agency
LEAGAS SHAFRON DAVIS AYER

Head of Publicity, Home Office
CHARLES SKINNER

Client
COI

WALKMAN

The commercial is shot for real. Three young actors stage an incident in a shopping mall. The two older kids appear to rough up a smaller boy and try to steal his personal stereo.

YOUTH ACTORS:
What ya listening to mate? 'Ere gi's a listen!

TITLE:
These boys are the only actors in this scene. Through hidden cameras we record the natural reactions of the general public.

MVO:
It doesn't matter what walk of life you come from... If you can spare a few hours a week to help others... Most people don't want to know. Thankfully, one or two of the hundreds of shoppers step in to help the boy.

Cut to a Special Constable diverting traffic around an incident involving a burnt out car.

MVO:
...we'd like you to make enquiries. For more information about training for the Special Constabulary–the volunteer police service–ring 0345 272272.

MVO:
Would you care to help?

Cut back to shopping mall to show a different member of the public attempting to help.

Television & Cinema

Director
MIKE STEPHENSON

Copywriter
ROB JANOWSKI

Art Director
STEVE GRIME

Creative Director
STEVE GRIME

Producer
PAUL ROTHWELL

Agency Producer
PETER GRAINGER

Editor
CYRIL METZGER

Lighting Cameraman
BARRY BROWN

Music Composers/Arrangers
JOE & CO

Production Company
PAUL WEILAND FILM COMPANY

Agency
LEAGAS SHAFRON DAVIS AYER

Head of Publicity, Home Office
CHARLES SKINNER

Client
COI

BRIDGE

The commercial is shot for real. Open on a stuntman dressed as a businessman. He is hanging over the rail of a bridge showing obvious distress.

MVO:
It doesn't matter what walk of life you come from...

TITLE:
This man is the only actor in this scene. Through hidden cameras we record the natural reactions of the general public.

MVO:
If you can spare a few hours a week to help others... Most people don't want to know. Thankfully, one or two of the hundreds stop and try to coax the man back to safety. Cut to a Special Constable dealing with a disturbance at a late night fish and chip shop.

MVO:
...we'd like you to make enquiries. For more information about training for the Special Constabulary–the volunteer police service–ring 0345 272272.

MVO:
Would you care to help?

Cut back to bridge to show a different member of the public attempting to help.

BERYL'S LETTER

Open on a title which reads:

'An unedited letter from the files of The Guide Dogs for the Blind Association.'

Pauline Collins then reads the actual letter from a blind person's ex-girlfriend.

She explains that she left him because his newly acquired guide dog has made him a different person, giving him new-found independence.

As the letter is being read over, we see exciting, positive images which demonstrate the confidence a guide dog can inspire in a blind person.

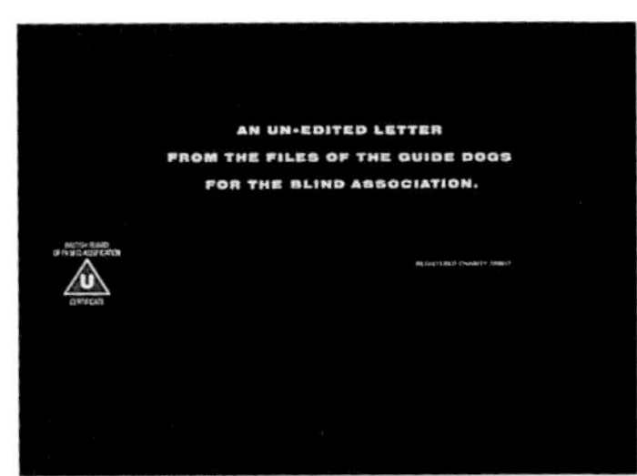

Television & Cinema

Director
THOMAS KRYGIER

Copywriter
DERRICK HASS

Art Director
DERRICK HASS

Creative Director
JENNY GREEN

Producer
DAVID KERR

Set Designer
RUSSELL DE ROZARIO

Agency Producers
SARAH MARTIN
KATE COURTNEY

Editor
SAM SNEADE

Lighting Cameraman
CINDERS FORSHAW

Music Composers/Arrangers
ANTHONY & GAYNOR SADLER

Production Company
ARDEN SUTHERLAND-DODD

Agency
McCANN-ERICKSON

Sales & Marketing Manager
ALISON RADEVSKY

Client
GUIDE DOGS FOR THE BLIND ASSOCIATION

Television & Cinema

Director
THOMAS KRYGIER

Copywriter
ADAM KEAN

Art Director
ALEXANDRA TAYLOR

Producer
DAVID KERR

Agency Producer
DAVID EDDON

Editor
MARTYN GOULD

Lighting Cameraman
GIUSEPPE MACCARI

Typographer
PAUL WINTER

Production Company
ARDEN SUTHERLAND-DODD

Agency
SAATCHI & SAATCHI

Director of Army Recruitment
BRIGADIER C.H.ELLIOTT

Client
THE ARMY

NIGHT DRIVING

SUPER:
Do You Want To Learn To Drive?

SFX:
(throughout)
Land Rover being driven.

Open on, from a driver's POV, a vehicle being driven down a country road at night. We hear a driving instructor giving instruction off camera, as we pass a road sign which says 'School' (showing children crossing).

INSTRUCTOR:
Get off the road.

Cut to instructor's face.

Cut to driver changing gear.

The driver responds by going off road so that we are driving along an uneven field, rolling side by side.

Then the driver issues another urgent instruction.

The vehicle's headlights are immediately switched off, so that now we can see nothing but blackness up ahead.

INSTRUCTOR:
Straight ahead. Straight ahead.

We continue driving in the dark for what seems an eternity, but is in fact only a few seconds. We hear the sounds of soldiers' voices as they are bumped around in the back.

SUPER:
Enjoying Your First Lesson?

INSTRUCTOR:
Right, Right, Right, Right...

Cut to British Flag Army Driver.

The word 'Driver' in super is then replaced by a series of quick cuts of other jobs you can do in the Army - Driver, Mechanic, Cook, Engineer, etc. and end with Army Soldier.

SFX:
Ticking.

SUPER:
Flag.

Army Soldier.

Be The Best.

0345 300 111.

SFX:
Stamping.

COT

We open this commercial on a close up of some silhouetted bars.

ALAN RICKMAN VO:
It's here where one in ten of all killings take place.

The camera begins to track along the bars.

ALAN RICKMAN VO:
There are one to two deaths every week.

The camera now begins to slowly pull out on the bars.

ALAN RICKMAN VO:
In a year there are over five thousand beatings. And over one thousand seven hundred sexual assaults including rape and buggery.

The camera has now pulled out and we see that the bars are in fact the bars of a child's cot.

Fade to black.

SUPER 1:
In Britain, 36,000 Children Live With The Threat Of Being Abused Everyday.

SUPER 2:
NSPCC. A Cry For Children.

Television & Cinema

Director
DAVID BAILEY

Copywriter
LINDA O'SULLIVAN

Art Director
NICK HINE

Producer
HOLLY HARTLEY

Agency Producer
FIONA WINBURN

Editor
CATHY O'SHEA

Lighting Cameraman
JOHN SWINNERTON

Production Company
RSA FILMS

Agency
SAATCHI & SAATCHI

Communications Manager
SIMON BERNSTEIN

Client
NSPCC

Television & Cinema

Director
RICHARD SLOGGETT

Copywriter
JAMES SINCLAIR

Art Director
ED MORRIS

Creative Director
DAVE TROTT

Producer
BROCK VAN DEN BOGAERDE

Set Designer
GAIL SMITH

Editor
RICHARD LEAROYD

Lighting Cameraman
SHAUN O'DELL

Music Composer/Arrangers
ANTHONY & GAYNOR SADLER

Production Company
SLOGGETT FILMS

Head of Development
RICHARD TYNEN

Client
WORLD DEVELOPMENT MOVEMENT

DEBT COLLECTORS

SFX:
Doorbell

MOTHER:
Who can it be James? It's too early for Daddy. Hello.

HEAVY 1:
Evening Madam. I have here an authorisation from your bank enabling us to seize all personal properties including any small children.

MOTHER:
What – you must be joking.

HEAVY 1:
It's not joking Madam. If you just take a look at this document you will find that this is all above board.

MOTHER:
Where are you going?

HEAVY 2:
To get the kid.

MOTHER:
What!

HEAVY 1:
I'm sorry Madam, but if you ring your branch in the morning I'm sure they'll be happy to explain it all to you.

MOTHER:
I didn't say you can come in...you can't just walk into my house...Get Out.

HEAVY 1:
Calm Down.

HEAVY 2:
Let's go Son.

MOTHER:
How dare you. Let go of me. James, James, James.

SON:
Mum.

HEAVY 1:
I've explained the situation.

MOTHER:
Let me go.

SON:
Mummy, Mummy.

MOTHER:
James. Help me. Help me.

MVO:
If there were high street banks that made interest rates so high you eventually paid for them with the lives of your children, would you use those banks? You probably are using those banks. They're just not doing it to you.

Every year the Third World pays for its debt with the lives of half a million children. If your bank is involved so are you.

MVO AND SUPER:
Find out who the big four debt collectors are and move your account or your credit card.

Contact the World Development Movement on 0171 737 6215.

TRUTH - VICTOR CRAWFORD

VICTOR CRAWFORD: *Maybe they'll get to your little brother or sister. Or maybe the kid down the block. But one thing is perfectly clear to me, tobacco companies are after children. Why? Because tobacco companies know that 90% of smokers start as children before they know any better. Of course, marketing to kids is unethical, so they just deny it.*

I'm Victor Crawford. I was a tobacco lobbyist for five years so I know how tobacco companies work. I lied. And I'm sorry.

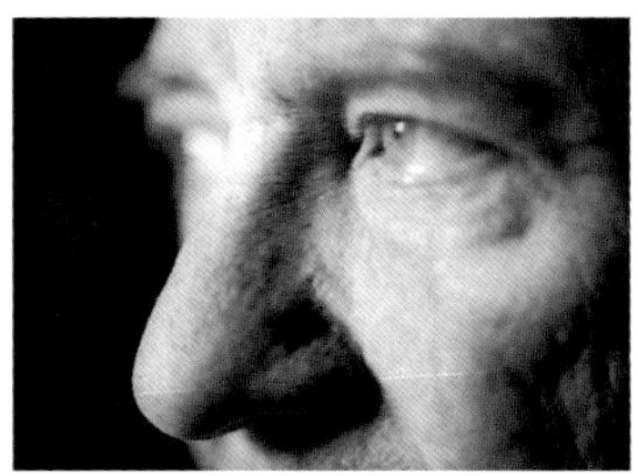

Television & Cinema

Director
NEIL ABRAMSON

Copywriters
KEN LEWIS
STU COOPERIDER

Art Director
DAVE GARDINER

Creative Directors
RICH HERSTEK
PETER FAVAT

Producer
JOHN BICK

Agency Producer
HARRY McCOY

Editor
SUZANNE HINES

Lighting Cameraman
NEIL ABRAMSON

Production Company
PALOMAR PICTURES

Agency
HOUSTON EFFLER HERSTEK FAVAT

Director, Tobacco Control Program
GREG CONNOLLY

Client
MASSACHUSSETTS DEPARTMENT OF PUBLIC HEALTH

Television & Cinema

Directors
DAVE RODETT
LUIS COOK

Copywriter
TONY MALCOLM

Art Director
GUY MOORE

Creative Directors
ANDY McKAY
PAUL HODGKINSON

Producer
JO ALLEN

Agency Producer
JO SAYER

Editor
DES

Music Composer/Arrangers
COLIN SMITH
SIMON ELMS

Production Company
AARDMAN ANIMATION

Agency
SIMONS PALMER DENTON CLEMMOW & JOHNSON

Fundraising Manager
LYNDALL STEIN

Client
TERRENCE HIGGINS TRUST

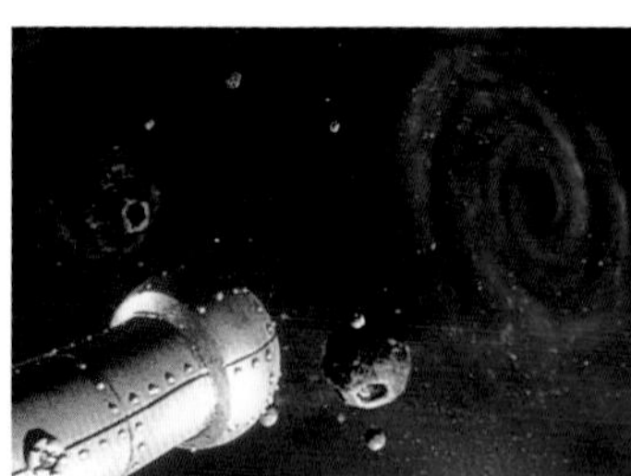

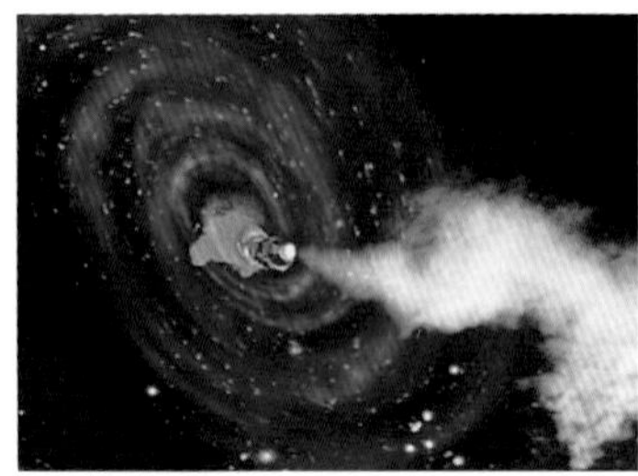

NOBS IN SPACE

A penis spaceship hurtles through space, to the sound of kitsch b-movie organ track, closely watched by a curious one-eyed planet.

He sees a black hole and rears up with excitement, his retro rockets cutting in. He shoots towards the black hole, who none too happy by his presence, closes on itself, reappearing in another part of space.

Undeterred, the eager spacehip banks round and heads towards it again. Once again, the uninterested black hole does its disappearing act.

Dejected, the penis-shaped ship limply splutters off into space.

He stops by a constellation of Sagittarius, who fires his arrow.

The arrow knocks aside a planet which is eclipsing a bright object.

A glow lights up the end of the spaceship as a shining condom is revealed.

The spaceship whizzes off and we hear the sound of stretching rubber.

Now wearing the condom, the spaceship hurtles back towards the hole, which now welcomes him by rotating even faster, literally sucking him in.

Flashes of blinding light hail his arrival and the words, "The Big Bang Theory" spin out, followed by the answer, "Wear A Condom".

TRUTH - JANET SACKMAN

JANET SACKMAN:
You may get cancer but I doubt you'll get the truth from tobacco companies. They keep saying you can't get hooked on cigarettes. Even though many smokers who lose their vocal cords can't quit.

I'm Janet Sackman.

I was a model on cigarette ads and convinced many young people to smoke. I hope I can convince you not to.

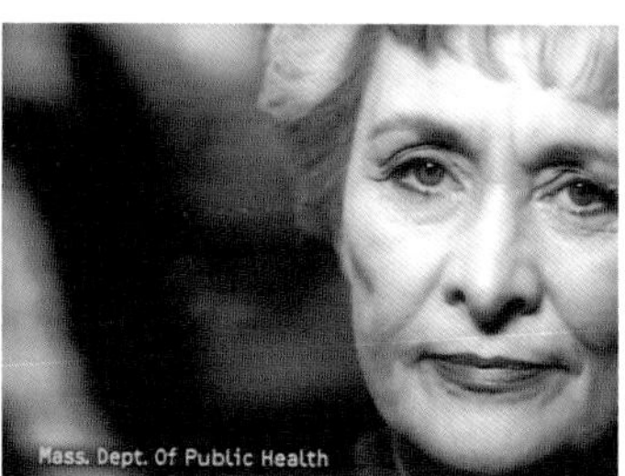

Television & Cinema

Director
NEIL ABRAMSON

Copywriters
KEN LEWIS
STU COOPERIDER

Art Director
DAVE GARDINER

Creative Directors
RICH HERSTEK
PETER FAVAT

Producer
JOHN BICK

Agency Producer
HARRY McCOY

Editor
SUZANNE HINES

Lighting Cameraman
NEIL ABRAMSON

Production Company
PALOMAR PICTURES

Agency
HOUSTON EFFLER
HERSTEK FAVAT

Director, Tobacco Control Program
GREG CONNOLLY

Client
MASSACHUSSETTS
DEPARTMENT OF
PUBLIC HEALTH

Television & Cinema

Copywriter
DAVID GEORGE

Art Director
MATTHEW SCHWARTZ

Creative Director
STANLEY R. BECKER

Agency Producer
JERRY BOYLE

Editor
ALAN EISENBERG

Agency
SAATCHI & SAATCHI, NY

Marketing Executive
DORIA STEEDMAN

Client
PARTNERSHIP FOR A DRUG-FREE AMERICA

CELEBRITIES

Slides of musicians/celebrities who have overdosed on drugs are projected onto a screen.

SFX:
Sound of a projector followed by click of next slide.

VO:
In advertising,

SFX:
Click

VO:
they say one of the surest ways

SFX:
Click

VO:
to get your message across

SFX:
Click

VO:
is to put celebrities in your commercial.

(Dramatic pause)

SFX:
Click

VO:
We hope they're right.

SFX:
Click

SLIDE WITH SUPER:
Partnership For A Drug-Free America.

SFX:
Click

Screen goes to black.

DECISION

Open on a hospital ward and corridor.

Camera pans around a corridor showing sick children. Soldier enters in background.

SOLDIER 1:
They say they can't operate on the kid - all the electric's gone.

Cut to soldier entering room joining three other soldiers standing over a sick child in bed. All the soldiers look directly and questioningly at the camera at once. They hold this anxious gaze for six or seven seconds, until one of them reminds "us" that they are waiting for an answer.

LANCE CORPORAL:
This one won't make it unless we get him out in the next 15 minutes.

SOLDIER 2:
But the truck's out of action.

SOLDIER 3:
No spares for 15 miles. With the checkpoints, it could take 4 hours.

LANCE CORPORAL:
What do we do Sir?

SOLDIER 3:
Sir?

SUPER:
If You Think You Know The Answer Call Army Officer On 0345 300 111.

SUPER:
Not Interested? Enjoy The Rest Of Your Evening.

Cut to Union Jack.

Army Officer.

SFX:
Stamping.

Be The Best

0345 300 111

SFX:
Stamping.

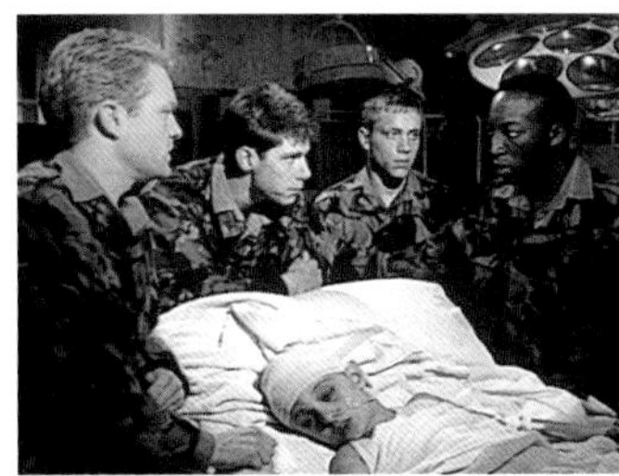

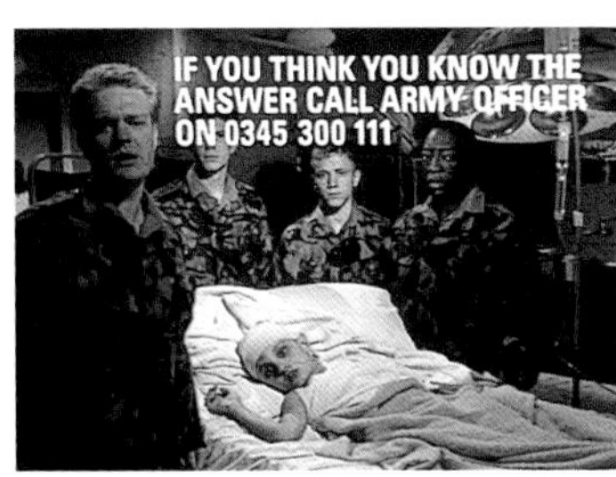

Television & Cinema

Director
THOMAS KRYGIER

Copywriter
ADAM KEAN

Art Director
ALEXANDRA TAYLOR

Producer
DAVID KERR

Agency Producer
DAVID EDDON

Editor
MARTIN GOULD

Lighting Cameraman
GIUSEPPE MACCARI

Typographer
PAUL WINTER

Production Company
ARDEN SUTHERLAND-DODD

Agency
SAATCHI & SAATCHI

Director of Army Recruitment
BRIGADIER C. H. ELLIOTT

Client
THE ARMY

Television & Cinema

Directors
SIMON TAYLOR
GRAHAM WOOD

Copywriter
ADRIAN JEFFERY

Art Director
LINDSEY REDDING

Creative Directors
SIMON SCOTT
ANDREW LINDSAY

Producer
HELEN LANGRIDGE

Agency Producer
TIM MAGUIRE

Editor
JON HOLLIS

Music Composers/Arrangers
LOGORHYTHM

Production Company
HELEN LANGRIDGE ASSOCIATES

Agency
FAULDS ADVERTISNG

Account Group Director
TOM GILL

Head of Presentation
PETER GOURD

Client
BBC RADIO SCOTLAND

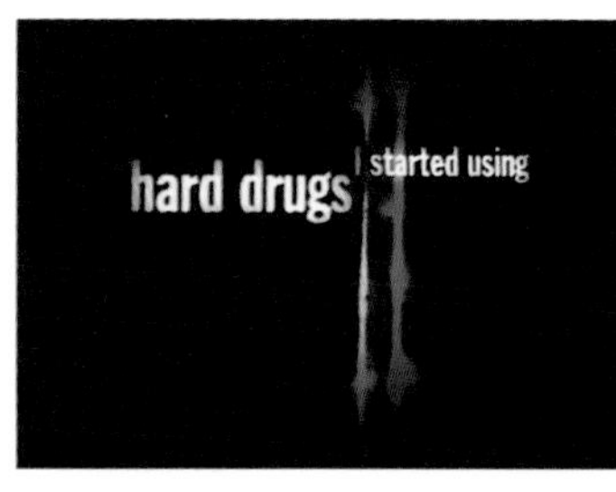

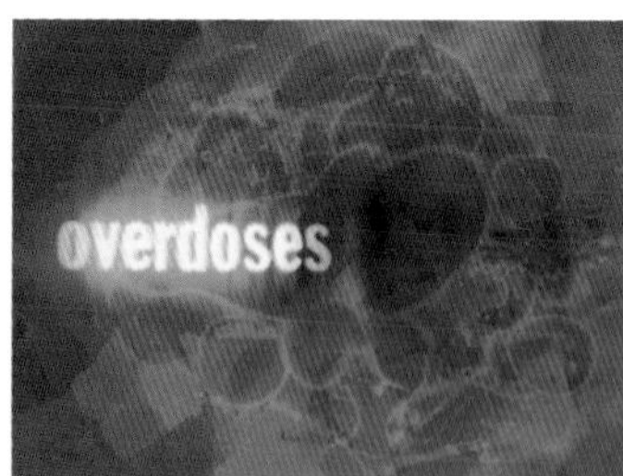

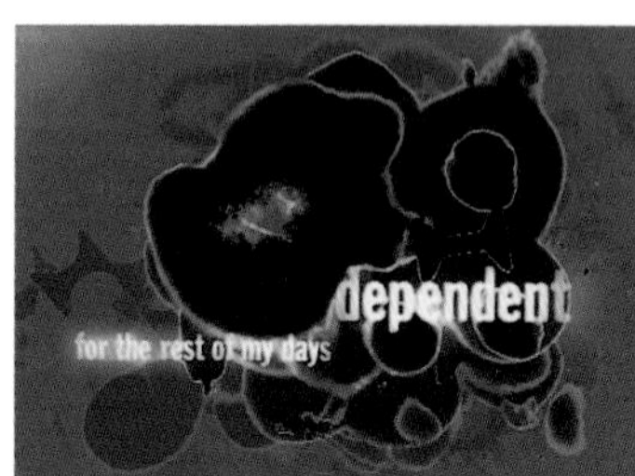

NAE HOPE

VIDEO:
As we hear the gripping radio article, we see the words appear on screen. The words help to dramatise the action.

MVO:
I'm 27 just now and I started using hard drugs when I was 22, it was that kinda day when everyone was using it so I had a wee shot and I liked it.

And just recently there I had two overdoses. It was due to high purity heroin.

It was on streets about here. I think I'll be drug dependent for the rest of my days I think. Nae hope. Nae hope whatsoever.

CAPTION:
Mix up caption which reads,

Re-discover the power of the spoken word.

Silence.

VIDEO
Mix to end frame.

SFX:
Music ident.

VIDEO:
We see the BBC Scotland logo and tuning device which demonstrates where to find the signal.

CAPTION:
UK National Station of the Year.

COCKEREL

As we hear the gripping radio article, we see the words appear on the screen. The words help to dramatise the action.

We hear a snippet from a BBC Scotland programme.

MVO:
Line out. Outside the French 22. Back on the main...oop...now the referee has called a halt to the proceedings, it's now over to the Scottish 22 and heading upfield. It's a magnificant fellow with a black underbelly, a gold coloured back and a red cockscomb and the cockerel's over the Scot's 5 metre line, heading for touch and the stewards are looking just a little bit flushed/perplexed, a little bit perplexed and flushed, ...just selling them a wee dummy and a wee side step and away he goes. Yes, he's over the touch line, now he's on the running track, and he's almost away.

Silence.

Mix up caption which reads:

Re-discover the power of the spoken word.

Mix to end frame. We see the BBC Scotland logo and tuning device which demonstrates where to find the signal.

SFX:
Music ident.

CAPTION:
UK National Station of the Year.

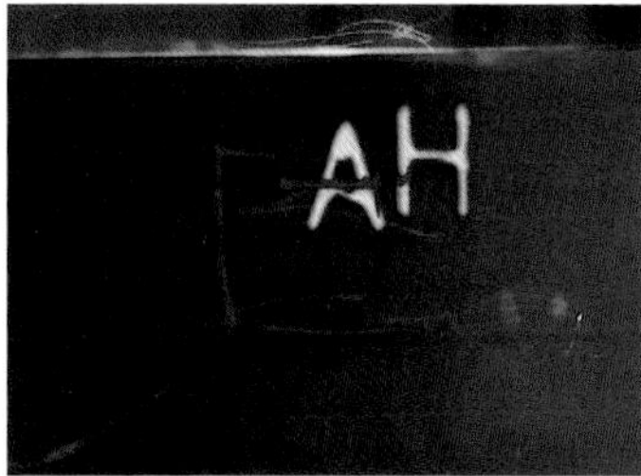

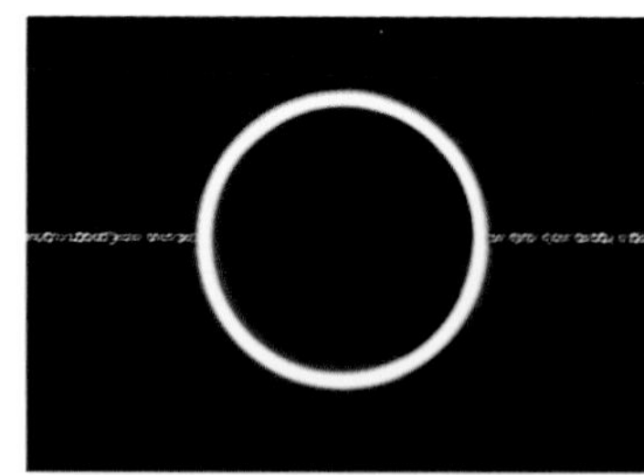

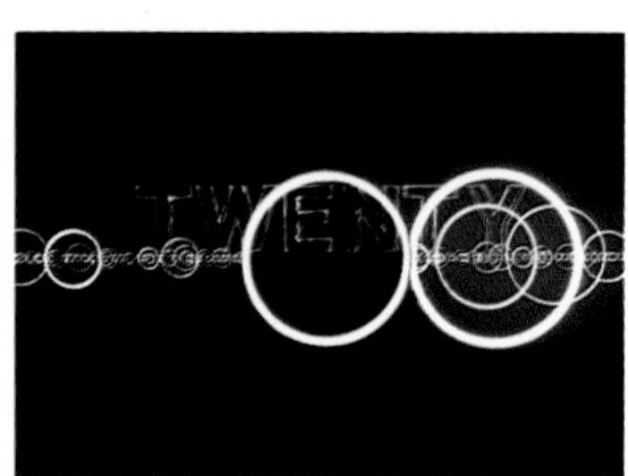

GRAFFITI

As we hear the gripping radio article, we see the words appear on the screen. The words help to dramatise the action.

We hear a snippet from a BBC Scotland programme.

MVO:
If I can explain some of this graffiti that's in the ceiling of the car here. We got psycho and Demon. We got psycho from rolling 60's cripps. We got...er Junior from Ghetto boys...Um, as I'm looking, I'm starting to feel these real kind of er, emotions choking up in me because there's probably about 20 or 25 different gang members that are carved in here, Babyface here, and I'd say about a dozen of them, almost half of them are dead.

Silence.

Mix up caption which reads:

Re-discover the power of the spoken word.

Mix to end frame.

SFX:
Music ident.

We see the BBC Scotland logo and tuning device which demonstrates where to find the signal.

CAPTION:
UK National Station of the Year.

TRUTH – JANET SACKMAN

JANET SACKMAN:
You may get cancer but I doubt you'll get the truth from tobacco companies. They keep saying you can't get hooked on cigarettes. Even though many smokers who lose their vocal cords can't quit.

I'm Janet Sackman.

I was a model on cigarette ads and convinced many young people to smoke. I hope I can convince you not to.

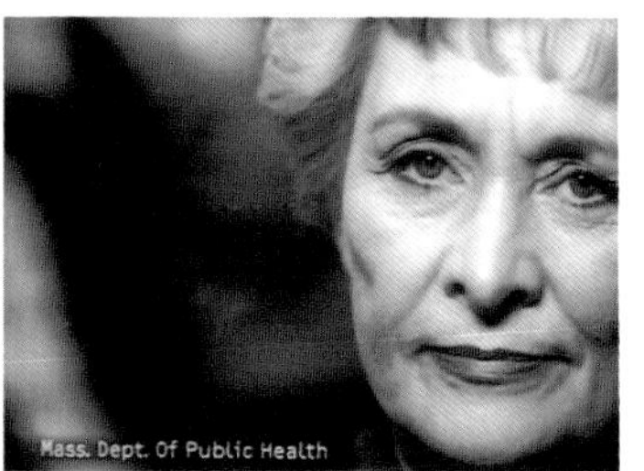

Television & Cinema Campaign

Director
NEIL ABRAMSON

Copywriters
KEN LEWIS
STU COOPERIDER

Art Director
DAVE GARDINER

Creative Directors
RICH HERSTEK
PETER FAVAT

Producer
JOHN BICK

Agency Producer
HARRY McCOY

Editor
SUZANNE HINES

Lighting Cameraman
NEIL ABRAMSON

Production Company
PALOMAR PICTURES

Agency
HOUSTON EFFLER
HERSTEK FAVAT

Director, Tobacco Control Program
GREG CONNOLLY

Client
MASSACHUSSETTS
DEPARTMENT OF
PUBLIC HEALTH

TRUTH – VICTOR CRAWFORD

VICTOR CRAWFORD: *Maybe they'll get to your little brother or sister. Or maybe the kid down the block. But one thing is perfectly clear to me, tobacco companies are after children. Why? Because tobacco companies know that 90% of smokers start as children before they know any better. Of course, marketing to kids is unethical, so they just deny it.*

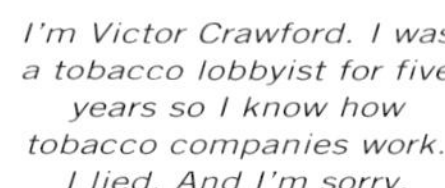

I'm Victor Crawford. I was a tobacco lobbyist for five years so I know how tobacco companies work. I lied. And I'm sorry.

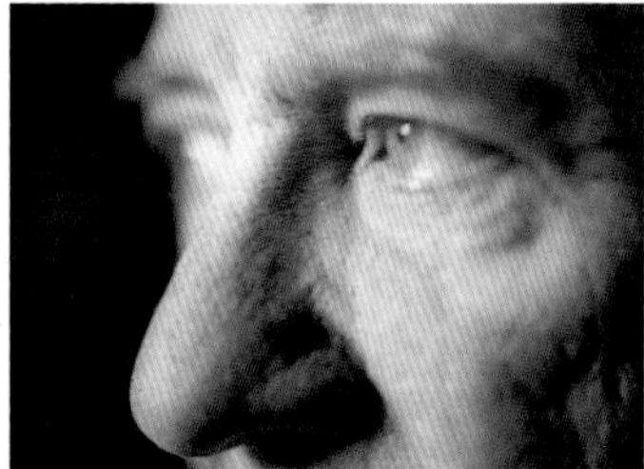

PATRICK REYNOLDS

PATRICK REYNOLDS: *Do you know what's in cigarettes? No. Because the last thing the tobacco companies want is for you to know how many poisonous chemicals there are in cigarettes. So they just don't tell you. Not on the pack, not in their ads.*

I'm Patrick Reynolds, the grandson of R.J. Reynolds. My family's name is printed on the side of 7 million packs a year. Why am I telling you this?

I want my family to be on the right side for a change.

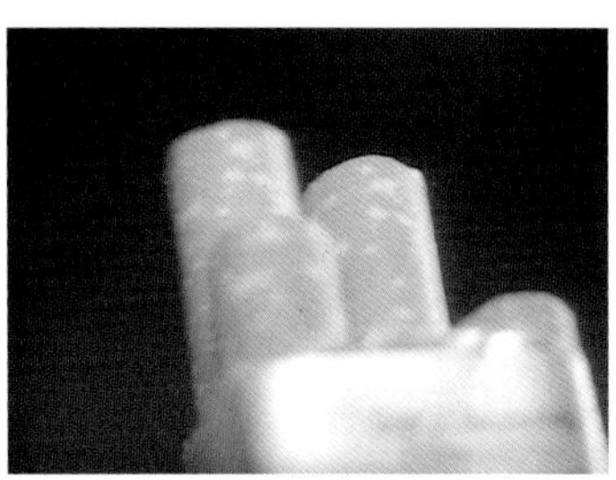

Television & Cinema

Director
MIKE STEPHENSON

Copywriter
ROB JANOWSKI

Art Director
STEVE GRIME

Creative Director
STEVE GRIME

Producer
PAUL ROTHWELL

Agency Producer
PETER GRAINGER

Editor
CYRIL METZGER

Lighting Cameraman
BARRY BROWN

Music Composers/Arrangers
JOE & CO

Production Company
PAUL WEILAND FILM COMPANY

Agency
LEAGAS SHAFRON DAVIS AYER

Head of Publicity
CHARLES SKINNER

Client
COI

BRIDGE

The commercial is shot for real.

SFX:
Music interlaced with extracts from an interview with a 'rescuer'.

Open on a stuntman dressed as a businessman. He is hanging over the rail of a bridge showing obvious distress.

MVO:
It doesn't matter what walk of life you come from...

TITLE:
This man is the only actor in this scene.

Through hidden cameras we record the natural reactions of the general public.

MVO:
If you can spare a few hours a week to help others...

Most people don't want to know.

Thankfully, one or two of the hundreds stop and try to coax the man back to safety.

Cut to a Special Constable dealing with a disturbance at a late night fish and chip shop.

MVO:
...we'd like you to make enquiries.

For more information about training for the Special Constabulary - the volunteer police service - ring 0345 272272.

TITLE:
0345 272272.

MVO:
Would you care to help?

Cut back to bridge to show a different member of the public attempting to help.

WALKMAN

The commercial is shot for real.

SFX:
Music with extracts from an interview with a 'rescuer'.

Three young actors stage an incident in a shopping mall. The two older kids appear to rough up a smaller boy and try to steal his personal stereo.

YOUTH ACTORS (AD LIB):
What ya listening to mate?

'Ere gi's a listen!

TITLE:
These boys are the only actors in this scene.

Through hidden cameras we record the natural reactions of the general public.

MVO:
It doesn't matter what walk of life you come from...

If you can spare a few hours a week to help others...

Most people don't want to know.

Thankfully, one or two of the hundreds of shoppers step in to help the boy.

Cut to a Special Constable diverting traffic around an incident involving a burnt out car.

MVO:
...we'd like you to make enquiries.

For more information about training for the Special Constabulary - the volunteer police service - ring 0345 272272.

TITLE:
0345 272272.

MVO:
Would you care to help?

Cut back to shopping mall to show a different member of the public attempting to help.

Radio

Concept Creators
CHRIS O'SHEA
KEN HOGGINS

Copywriters
CHRIS O'SHEA
KEN HOGGINS

Recording Engineer
IAN GRANT

Production Company
RORSCHACH

Agency
BANKS HOGGINS O'SHEA

Client
BRITISH RED CROSS

BANKS · HOGGINS · O'SHEA
PARTNERSHIP

RADIO

Client: Red Cross
Date: November 1994
Version: 1

Title: 999 Call
Product: First Aid Courses
Prepared by:

FVO: "If you've ever thought you were too busy to attend a first-aid course, we suggest you listen to the following recording of a 999 call. It's between a paramedic and a young mother, who's just discovered her 13 month old baby has stopped breathing and turned blue".

PARAMEDIC: Hello, have you got the baby with you?

MOTHER: She's on her back, in the cot, on her back.

PARAMEDIC: Lift her up. Are you left handed? Lift her up and put her in your left arm.

PARAMEDIC: Is her head flopping backwards, not a lot, just a little bit?

PARAMEDIC: Now put your mouth over her mouth and nose, and blow in gently.

MOTHER: Blow in her mouth?

PARAMEDIC: Blow in her mouth and nose gently. OK, so her chest rises a little bit.

(Pause.)

PARAMEDIC: Have you done that? Has she done anything?

MOTHER: No.

PARAMEDIC: Now do it again.
(Pause.)

PARAMEDIC: OK, is she breathing yet? No. OK, take two fingers, put them in the middle of her chest, right, and press gently about five times, quickly.

(Pause.)

PARAMEDIC: Is she doing anything now?

MOTHER: No. (distressed)

PARAMEDIC: OK, put your fingers in the middle of her chest again, fifteen times, quickly.

(Long pause)

PARAMEDIC: You've got to go quicker than that love.

MOTHER: Her arms are moving!!!

PARAMEDIC: Her arms are moving?

MOTHER: Her arms are moving, her chest isn't moving though.

PARAMEDIC: OK, her arms, take one of her arms and the muscle at the top, move it to one side and see if you can feel a pulse.

(Pause.)

MOTHER: She's moving her arms again!!!

PARAMEDIC: She's moving her arms, she must be breathing and her heart must be working. Is her arm still moving?

BABY: (Cry)

MOTHER: Yes.

PARAMEDIC: Is that her I can hear?

MOTHER: (Laughing) Yes.

BABY: (Crying)

PARAMEDIC: Sit down and relax now, sit down and relax. The ambulance is on its way and we're going to take her to hospital. Alright? (FVO: - crying. Yes.) Checked up at the hospital.

PARAMEDIC: You've done a wonderful job.

PARAMEDIC: Alright, the ambulance will be there shortly.

MOTHER: Thanks.

PARAMEDIC: OK, bye.

FVO: "Now call the Red Cross on 0245 490 090 and ask about short first-aid courses near you. "Unless that, is you're still too busy".

Radio

Concept Creator
SUZY DAVIDSON

Copywriter
SUZY DAVIDSON

Agency Producer
NOELEEN BURLEY

Recording Engineers
JOHN CULVERWELL
ALEC BOCCHINI

Production Company
SONOVISION STUDIOS

Agency
SONNENBERG MURPHY LEO BURNETT

Vice Chairman
CHRIS MILLER

Client
THE SALVATION ARMY

RADIO SCRIPT

No: SD
Client: SALVATION ARMY
Product: SHELTERS FOR BATTERED WOMEN
Prod. House: SONOVISION

Duration: 60"

TITLE: Battered woman/Sheila.

Sheila: (Very nasal, distorted, slurred, speaks with great difficulty.)
My name is Theila.
I am not talking thith thway becauthe I am drunk.
I am not deaf or mentally dithabled.
I am a dormal woman, mother (shuddery sob) ...and wife.
I am talking thith thway becauthe thith ith the thway my huthband wanth me to talk.
I know thith becauthe he bwroke my dose an' knocthed out my teeth lath night when I tried to talk to him like a dormal human being.

Anncr: Every year the Salvation Army provides shelter for thousands of women who can't take a little discipline.

Sheila: I'm juth glad that talking to you like thith...you can't thee me, becauthe I know I thound (starts to cry) muth better than I look.

Anncr: Help us to help them.

1995

COPY

SILVER AWARD
for the Most Outstanding Copy Campaign

Copywriter
ROS SINCLAIR

Art Director
SEAN THOMPSON

Photographer
TERRY O'NEILL

Typographer
MARK OSBORNE

Agency
S P LINTAS

Marketing Executive
MARK SCOTHERN

Client
CRISIS

Photographer
ADRIAN COOK

imaginative interiors

Maggie and Kelvin built and furnished their tiny, central Loudon home on a shoestring budget. ROS SINCLAIR was invited to look around. Photographs by ADRIAN COOK

Compact & bijou

MAIN PICTURE: Maggie and Kelvin's home as it is now. FUTURE PICTURE: Depends on you. CALL: 071 377 0489 to find out how a donation of £10 can help the homeless.

CRISIS

Photographer
KEVIN SUMMERS

Food & Drink

Dining Out

On those cold winter nights, what could be better than eating al fresco?
Ros Sinclair **discovers what's on the menu. Photographs by** Kevin Summers

**This page: Pot Luck.
Opposite page: Leftover Parcels.
To replace the food on these pages with hot soup, roast dinner and pudding, donate £10.
Call: 0800 374 717.
CRISIS**

Copy Individual

Copywriter
AJAB SAMRAI SINGH

Art Director
AJAB SAMRAI SINGH

Photographers
ALISTAIR THAIN
TIM O'SULLIVAN

Typographer
TIM QUEST

Agency
SAATCHI & SAATCHI

Marketing Executive
MARJORIE THOMPSON

Client
COMMISSION FOR RACIAL EQUALITY

CRIMINAL ISN'T IT?

A 1992 survey of Midlands crown courts revealed that some ethnic minorities are receiving longer prison sentences. On average, up to 9 months longer than white people for the same crimes. If this is typical, it leads to one simple and rather alarming conclusion.

The criminal justice system is heavily weighted against some ethnic minorities.

Sadly other similar investigations seem to bear this out.

Blacks and Asians are more likely to be charged than cautioned.

They are more likely to be refused bail.

Ethnic minorities are also more likely to be stopped by the police than whites.

(In one London borough Black people are four times more likely to be stopped by the police than whites.)

Mark a British born Afro-Caribbean is a case in point.

"I had never been involved or in trouble with the police before.

They said - 'I'm talking to you jungle bunnie.' I felt like it went on for hours and hours. I knew what he was trying to do, he was trying to coax me into causing trouble, start a fight, so he could have an excuse to arrest me."

Contrary to what some people might think, minorities are more often the victims of crime than the perpetrators.

Black and Asian people are more likely than whites to be the victims of violence against the person and property.

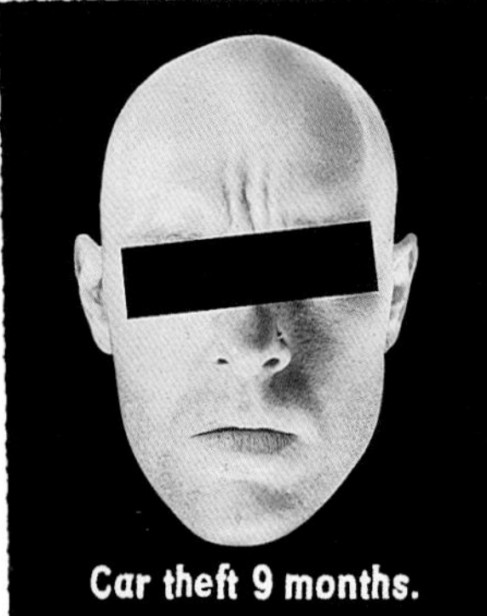

Car theft 9 months.

Car theft 1½ years.

And yet the stereotypical image of Black people is as aggressors.

It's a terrible slur on the vast majority of ethnic minorities in Britain who are law abiding contributors to society.

Moreover when Blacks and Asians are charged with a criminal offence, the courtroom ritual is quite daunting.

They are likely to be faced with a predominantly white institution.

From white judges and lawyers to white clerks of the courtroom.

(Out of 2,887 judges in England and Wales, only 32 are from ethnic minorities.)

The chances are they might not see a black face on the jury either.

They have to endure uncomfortable and humiliating displays of ignorance about their culture and lives.

It's a small wonder they find it difficult to co-operate with the system.

This then confirms the stereotypes of people who are alienated, hostile and aggressive to authority.

At the Commission for Racial Equality we believe there is hope.

We were set up in 1976 by the Race Relations Act to eliminate every kind of racial discrimination.

The CRE is an independent body funded by an annual Home Office grant.

The 1976 Race Relations Act quite simply states that people should not be discriminated against on the ground of colour, race or national origin.

It makes discrimination unlawful in jobs, training, housing and education.

The irony is it doesn't cover certain areas of the criminal justice process.

This basically means if you have been discriminated against in the justice process it is not possible to bring a complaint against a police officer or a judge under the Race Relations Act.

Clearly the Act should apply to these and many other similar institutions.

But the CRE are working to put an end to discrimination on how people are treated by the police force and other organisations and are working with the Association of Chief Police Officers to this end.

Secondly, we are influencing the judicial process to eliminate any kind of discrimination within their own system.

The judiciary is now undertaking training courses on racial equality issues and are planning to monitor sentencing trends to eradicate racial bias.

But what can you do?

If you feel you have been racially abused or harassed by a police officer, or if you feel you have been denied your rights and treated harshly because of your race or colour, complain.

Write to the superintendent at the station where the offending officer works.

Or, if you think you may have been unfairly discriminated against by the court system, complain.

Write to the Lord Chancellor's office.

You may be entitled to legal aid.

You could also apply to the CRE or contact your local Racial Equality Council for assistance and guidance.

We're not advocating special treatment for Britain's ethnic minorities.

(That would be positive discrimination, which is not allowed under our legislation.)

White or Black, if a person is found guilty of a criminal offence it's only right they should be justly punished.

Our criminal justice system is seen as being one of the best in the world.

It's something we can all be proud of.

But growing evidence suggests a more even handed approach is needed.

The sooner we can address these fundamental imbalances, the fairer the system will be for everyone.

If you're concerned about race issues, write to your MP and say so, or if you'd like a copy of the CRE report this advert was based on, write to the address below.

Prejudice and bigotry are passed from one generation to the next.

We have a simple choice, either take this opportunity to set an example, or ignore the problem altogether.

But that truly would be criminal.

COMMISSION FOR RACIAL EQUALITY

Copy Individual

Copywriter
PAUL BRINGLOE

Art Directors
DOMINIC CORP
BILL GALLACHER

Photographer
GRAHAM CORNTHWAITE

Typographer
ROGER KENNEDY

Agency
SAATCHI & SAATCHI

Director of Public Policy
PHILIP NOYES

Client
NSPCC

I know this is hard to read
My mother used to shake me like
a rag doll.

This is Karen's story.

'Writing isn't the only thing I find difficult. I can hardly talk. I have to rely on others to push my wheelchair, feed and dress me. I've got brain damage.

My mum caused it when I was a baby. I've been told that she used to shake me when she got angry with me.

Sometimes she did it so hard I would go unconscious.

It stopped me crying. But in the end it stopped me doing just about everything. If I think about it I get angry, like I am now. But I'm told I'm lucky to be alive at all.'

Karen's story will surprise a lot of people. Who would think that just shaking a child could be so dangerous? But even mild shaking can badly damage a child's brain.

That's not all. It can also cause blindness, deafness, paralysis and learning disabilities. It can kill.

Yet shaking is just one of several less obvious forms of cruelty that some people wouldn't even think of as abuse. For instance, imagine being constantly shouted at. Or ignored as if you didn't even exist. Or criticized, whatever you did.

While these may not cause brain damage, the emotional effects, such as low self-worth, humiliation and depression, can devastate a child.

Some children have even tried to take their own lives.

Because of all this, the NSPCC is launching a campaign called 'A Cry For Children.' It's a cry to everyone to stop and think about the way they behave towards children.

To recognise the impact that any form of cruelty can have on a child. And to realise that the way children are treated affects their whole lives.

Please answer the cry.

If you, or someone you know is suffering from abuse, please call the NSPCC Child Protection Helpline on 0800 800 500 any time, day or night.

Or if, after reading this, you would find further information helpful, please call us on 071 825 2775.

NSPCC
A cry for children

CHILDREN FROM ETHNIC MINORITIES OFTEN GET THE WORST MARKS AT SCHOOL.

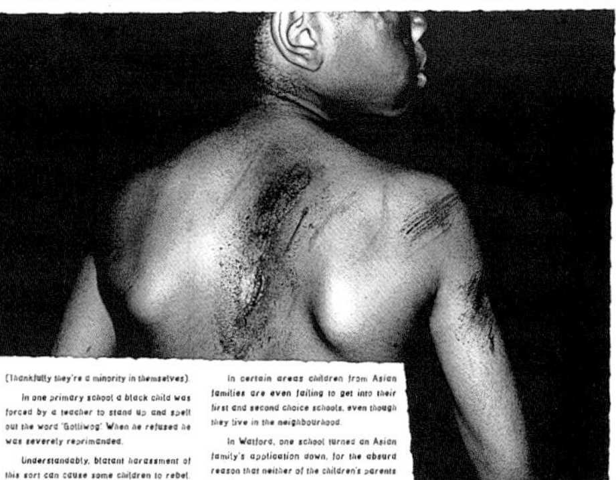

Actually, studies show that some ethnic minorities get the best grades at school. But of course, you won't have heard about that. All you will have heard about are the kind of marks that grab the headlines. The vicious playground beatings, the horrific knife attacks and the senseless murders.

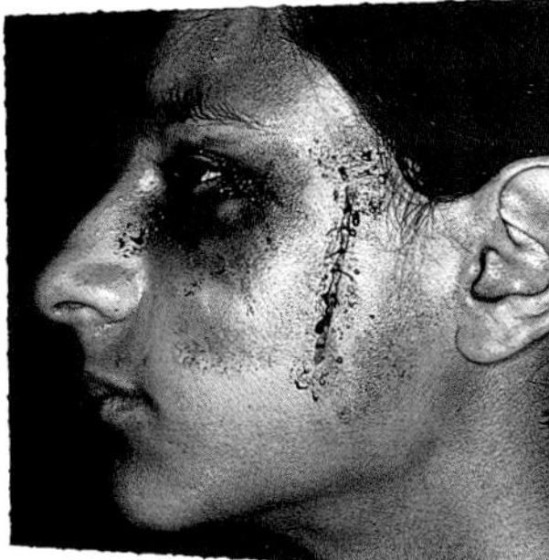

A disturbing Home Office report on 'racial attacks' in Britain, published a few years ago, estimated that Asians were 50 times more likely than whites to be the victims of racially motivated attacks.

In one extreme case in a Manchester school, a young Asian boy was senselessly stabbed to death by a 13 year old white pupil, simply for protecting other younger Asian boys from being bullied.

The scars verbal attacks leave behind may not be as visible as the physical ones, but they can be just as damaging.

'Coon', 'Paki', 'Nigger'.

Faced with racial taunts like this, a once smiling, untroubled child can quickly become shy and withdrawn.

A 7 year old Asian girl from the North West is a case in point. She became so traumatised by the persistent name calling, she tried to bleach her skin so she could be like everyone else and fit in.

What's more shocking, is that it's not just children who are the offenders.

In fact, some teachers can be racist too.

(Thankfully they're a minority in themselves).

In one primary school a black child was forced by a teacher to stand up and spell out the word 'Golliwog'. When he refused he was severely reprimanded.

Understandably, blatant harassment of this sort can cause some children to rebel. Instead of being seen as victims, they're branded troublemakers.

It might explain why Afro Caribbean boys are four times more likely to be suspended than white children, for the same misbehaviour.

Recent research has shown that sometimes teachers will place black and Asian pupils into the lower ability sets when they first start secondary school.

They mistakenly believe they will be unable to learn successfully with their white counterparts in the higher ability groups.

Young talent that would under normal circumstances have flourished, is stifled.

In certain areas children from Asian families are even failing to get into their first and second choice schools, even though they live in the neighbourhood.

In Watford, one school turned an Asian family's application down, for the absurd reason that neither of the children's parents had been educated there.

Clearly this is wrong. Something has to be done to stop this discrimination.

To this end the government set up the Commission for Racial Equality to enforce and review the Race Relations Act of 1976.

Its aim is very simple. To identify and wipe out racial discrimination in all its forms, wherever it exists in society.

A difficult job perhaps, but one that is obviously very necessary.

From monitoring, collecting, and recording information, (a job the government should be doing, not just the CRE), to supporting complaints and publishing research, we're constantly pressurising the government into making much needed changes.

A Department for Education circular recently sent out to all schools, on our advice, contained information on admissions.

The circular recommended changes in the way pupils are selected for schools, which will help to eliminate discrimination in this area.

(It would seem, that sometimes we have to educate the educators).

It's not just up to the government to help.

You can too.

If you suspect that your child has been unfairly treated at school, complain.

Write to the governors of the school, or write to your Local Education Authority.

Alternatively, contact your local Racial Equality Council for advice, or write to the CRE at the address below.

The onus is on all of us to make sure our children grow up respecting the different cultures that make up Britain today.

It would be a tragedy for the country if the only things our children learned at school were hatred, prejudice and racial intolerance.

COMMISSION FOR RACIAL EQUALITY

Copy Individual

Copywriters
AJAB SAMRAI SINGH
CHRIS KIRK

Art Director
AJAB SAMRAI SINGH

Photographer
BARRY LATEGAN

Typographer
NIGEL WARD

Agency
SAATCHI & SAATCHI

Marketing Executive
MARJORIE THOMPSON

Client
COMMISSION FOR RACIAL EQUALITY

WHO SAYS ETHNIC MINORITIES CAN'T GET JOBS? THERE ARE OPENINGS EVERYWHERE.

Lavatory attendant. Office cleaner. Somebody has to do all the low-paid, menial jobs, but why is it so often people from ethnic minorities? Prejudice, racial discrimination and harassment are denying people the choice of job they deserve. It's unjust and unfair. More than that, it's a terrible waste of British talent.

Getting into a skilled profession is hard enough for anyone these days.

But it's even harder for ethnic minorities.

For a start, qualifications count, but most ethnic minorities are still more likely to be unemployed than white people.

They have to apply for more jobs before they get one. In a recent investigation, one in three companies who were tested refused interviews to black and Asian applicants.

But they did offer interviews to white applicants with the same qualifications.

If they do find a job, ethnic minorities often find promotion harder to achieve than their white colleagues.

There's a disproportionately low number of ethnic minorities at managerial level.

For example, in one large transportation company 30% of the workforce are from ethnic minorities, but they account for only 3% of the management.

On top of all this ethnic minorities face racial harassment in the workplace.

If they complain about it they are often told to accept harassment as part of the job.

Sadly, most people do accept it.

Those who don't may have to take their employer to an industrial tribunal where hard evidence must be provided to support their complaint.

Whether or not they win their case they may well have to start the trying process of searching for a job all over again.

No wonder ethnic minorities have found it so difficult to make progress in Britain.

However, bad as the situation seems, some aspects have changed for the better.

A West Indian who came here in the fifties to work for British Rail remembers.

"It was hell. For the first ten years nobody would sit next to me in the lunch break. They gave you the worst job, paid you less, gave you no training.

They insulted you. There were 'No nigger' notices everywhere. It was very different then. There was no law against it."

Thankfully, the law has changed.

In 1976 the Race Relations Act was passed, making it unlawful for employers to discriminate on the grounds of colour, race, ethnic or national origin.

Those who do discriminate face hefty bills for compensation and legal costs, as well as having their guilt aired in public.

The Act certainly put an end to blatant discrimination like the 'No nigger' notices.

But it didn't put an end to the more subtle discrimination that still exists today.

Such as when an employer says "Sorry, there's someone else more qualified for the job." when there isn't.

Or when a manager 'forgets' to mention an opportunity for promotion to someone.

This is discrimination.

It's subtle, perhaps even unintentional, but it can still be very demoralising.

Imagine being told over and over again that you are not qualified enough for a job when you know very well that you are.

What could you do about it?

If your case is strong enough you could talk to the Commission for Racial Equality.

We are the independent body funded by the Home Office whose job it is to eliminate every kind of racial discrimination.

To this end we give support to victims of discrimination in industrial tribunals.

(It's not always ethnic minorities. We've dealt with cases of white workers being treated unfairly by black or Asian bosses.)

We're also working with trade unions to help them fight racial discrimination and harassment, within their own organisations as much as in the workplace.

Many trade unions now have specially designated officers who can give practical support and advice to people who have been discriminated against.

You'll find similarly qualified officers at your local Racial Equality Council and Citizens Advice Bureau.

What's more, with our help companies are adopting equal opportunity policies. These prevent discrimination before it can happen, giving everyone a fair chance.

If you'd like to talk to someone about implementing such a policy in your company, please write to us at the address below.

This is how we'll defeat racism.

Not by violence, but by accepting each other as equals. By opening our minds.

For the sake of ourselves and of the generation who are growing up now, this would be the most promising opening possible.

COMMISSION FOR RACIAL EQUALITY

Copy Individual

Copywriter
GILES MONTGOMERY

Art Director
AJAB SAMRAI SINGH

Photographer
JOHN TURNER

Typographer
NIGEL WARD

Agency
SAATCHI & SAATCHI

Marketing Executive
MARJORIE THOMPSON

Client
COMMISSION FOR RACIAL EQUALITY

Copy Individual

Copywriter
INDRA SINHA

Art Director
GUY MOORE

Photographer
RAGHU RAI

Typographer
JEFF MERRELLS

Agencies
ANTENNAE COMMUNICATIONS
COLLETT DICKENSON PEARCE

Marketing Executive
SATINATH SARANGI

Client
SATINATH SARANGI

"THOUSANDS OF OUR CHILDREN WERE NOT SO LUCKY. THEY SURVIVED."

I WANT TO HELP THE BHOPAL GAS VICTIMS WHO HAVE SUFFERED FOR TEN YEARS WITHOUT RELIEF.

THE INTERNATIONAL MEDICAL APPEAL FOR BHOPAL

Copy Individual

Copywriter
NICK BELL

Art Director
GREG MARTIN

Typographer
JOE HOZA

Agency
ABBOTT MEAD VICKERS.BBDO LIMITED

Director of Campaigns and Public Relations
JERRY LLOYD

Client
RSPCA

Investigating this wasn't difficult. We had a lead.

We found Trudy tethered round the neck by a piece of rusting curtain wire.

Her three small puppies were just a few feet away.

Where Trudy had struggled to get to them, the sharp, rusty coil of the wire had cut deep into her throat.

From the depth of the wound and the amount of scar tissue formed, our vet estimated she had been tethered in this way for at least five weeks.

In his opinion, she would have suffered considerably.

All year round, our Inspectors are called to the aid of suffering animals like Trudy.

Last year alone, we responded to nearly 100,000 reports of animal cruelty. Reports of horses that had been starved, dogs that had been beaten, kittens that had been kicked and maimed.

Our policy is never to refuse a call for help. But, of course, it's an expensive one.

The current cost of training, equipping and putting just one new Inspector on the road for a year is £32,407. Which is why we so desperately need your help.

The RSPCA doesn't receive any funding from the Government.

We rely entirely on the public's generosity.

Thanks to people like you, we were able to find a loving new home for Trudy and her puppies.

So please send as much money as you can. And help us save a few more necks.

RSPCA

DO YOU KNOW THIS MAN?

NEITHER DID HIS TORTURERS 50 YEARS AGO.

IT TOOK JUST SEVENTY DAYS FOR ONE EMPIRE TO EMERGE FROM THE DEBRIS OF ANOTHER.

DECEMBER 8, 1941. At exactly 4.15 am, the first Japanese bombs were sprinkled over Singapore.

Perched atop sturdy wooden poles, the sirens broke into a mournful song. A tortuous wailing that would linger in the heavy pre-dawn air long after the raid was over.

Hair tousled and sleepy-eyed, the inhabitants stumbled out of their homes for yet another air raid practice. Only this time, it was war.

For a while, it seemed as though dawn was breaking early. The sky glowed an infernal orange as Chinatown and its surrounds blazed vehemently.

The waking sun, peeking coyly from behind its sooty veil, revealed the fiery reality.

Cars were blasted to a molten mass; buildings reduced to mere rubble; and trees that once stood majestically, were now contorted into spastic silhouettes.

The lazy breeze carried the sickeningly sweet smell of burning flesh, as mangled bodies or their dismembered limbs freckled the streets with any last hope of peace.

February 15, 1942. The British conceded the tiny island of Singapore to her invaders.

Consequently, she became known as Syonan-to.

* * *

THERE WAS ALMOST A FEMININITY ABOUT THE MAN WHO WAS ONE OF THE MOST WANTED UNDERGROUND ACTIVISTS SOUGHT BY THE INFAMOUS JAPANESE MILITARY POLICE, THE *KEMPEITAI*.

LIM BO SENG's congenital shyness and unpretentious demeanour proved a perfect screen for his subversive activities.

(His charm impressed even the Japanese, and it was said, after his arrest, several of his Japanese friends went to the *kempeitai* to vouch for him and were severely beaten as a result.)

A tall, willowy figure with a spry step which at once betrayed his indefatigable vigour, his unassuming manner concealed a steel-wrought will that set country above everything else. Not least of all, himself.

Even before the Japanese campaign advanced southward to Malaya, Lim Bo Seng was already immersed in the anti-Japanese movement.

Once, 5,000 coolies working at a Japanese-owned iron mine went on strike at his instigation.

When they were subsequently replaced by Indian workers, he again engineered a walk-out, this time with the help of an Indian collaborator.

His position as an influential leader in the rich Amoy community ensured that funds were regularly expedited to the resistance forces in China.

Meanwhile, Japanese armoured columns sped inexorably towards Singapore.

And the unseeing artillery shells, whistling their tunes of wanton destruction, landed closer and closer.

It was inevitable that the man who had persistently plunged the spanner into the rampaging Japanese war machine should flee.

At least, for the time being.

Four days before the imminent surrender of Singapore, Lim Bo Seng stood in his Telok Ayer Street office, clutching his wife and seven children to his bosom. Then, tears scalding the concrete steps, the frail, mild-mannered man hatched into the night, knowing that this could be the last time he would ever see them.

For three exasperating years, his family never heard a word of him.

Finally, in 1945, some time after the war had ended, news broke.

A stunned Mrs Lim Bo Seng, escorted by her eldest son, travelled to Batu Gajah, Perak, to retrieve the remains of a man called Tan Choon Lim: her husband.

* * *

FEBRUARY 12, 1942. LIM BO SENG ESCAPED IN A *SAMPAN* TO A TINY DUTCH-HELD ISLAND NOT FAR FROM SINGAPORE.

HE WAS PICKED UP by a 30-ton steamer which inched its way to Sumatra, Indonesia. It was then across land to Padang on the west coast.

March 5, 1942. Lim Bo Seng stepped ashore in Colombo. The vessel he was in gratefully belched out its burden of refugees picked up along the way at sea.

He made his way to Calcutta where he was inducted into Force 136, the underground resistance section of the Supreme Allied Command, South-east Asia, and drilled in espionage and intelligence tactics in Khadakvasla, near Bombay.

April, 1943. Lim Bo Seng was despatched to Chungking, in China, to enlist resistance fighters for infiltration into Malaya.

He returned with about a hundred men, many of them Malayan Chinese who had fled at the start of the Japanese Occupation.

* * *

NOVEMBER 2, 1943. UNDER COVER OF THE MURKY SWELL, A METALLIC SHADOW SLIPPED INTO MALAYAN WATERS.

THE WAVES RUSHED eerily against each other, as the British submarine broke from under its watery veil.

Dim shadows emerged from the hatch; creeping into folding canvas boats, they stealthily manoeuvred the silent craft towards the coastline: Lim Bo Seng had landed at Bagan Datoh, Perak.

The sweltering Malayan rainforest itself was an impenetrable fortress, with pencil shafts of light piercing through the canopy of leaves.

It was also the home of the Malayan People's Anti-Japanese Army.

At its headquarters, Lim Bo Seng conferred with the guerrilla leaders.

They agreed that he should infiltrate Malayan towns to gather news of enemy movements. One of the many identities he assumed was Tan Choon Lim.

The Japanese patrols intensified. Doctors, medical supplies, food, weapons, money, were being smuggled to the guerrillas from Ipoh, Perak.

March 27, 1944. Information was betrayed to the Japanese about the resistance activities. Every road leading out of Ipoh was systematically blocked.

All the intelligence agents were alerted and instructed to withdraw at once. Still, the four agents in Tan Choon Lim's group failed to retreat.

Time was running out. He knew he had to escape immediately, but he insisted on waiting for them.

At the crossroad leading to Batu Gajah and Kuala Lumpur, Tan Choon Lim was arrested.

He was incarcerated in the Batu Gajah gaol.

* * *

FEW SURVIVED TORTURE BY THE *KEMPEITAI*. THEIR METHODS DEFIED EVEN THE MOST CRUEL IMAGINATION.

THE 'WATER TREATMENT' saw the victim strapped to a short bamboo ladder and continually doused headlong into a well of water. His head was usually threaded between two rungs, one rung at his throat, the other at the back of his head, to restrict all attempts to gasp for air.

In another version, the victim was pinned to the ground with a water hose shoved down his gullet (this prevented water rushing down the windpipe and drowning him).

As the water pumped incessantly into his gut, his tormentors bounced on an improvised see-saw balanced over his bulbously bloated belly. Water bled in torrents from every orifice of the body.

In the 'fire treatment', the victim was stripped and tied to a wooden cross. Under interrogation, every unsatisfactory answer was rewarded with the incandescent tip of a cigarette being lightly pressed onto some delicate part of the body, like a nipple, or the glans of the penis.

One of the most excruciating tortures employed by the *kempeitai* was the extraction of a victim's fingernails with a pair of pliers, one per day.

* * *

JUNE 29, 1944. AFTER ENDURING NEARLY THREE MONTHS OF TORTURE, LIM BO SENG DIED, AT THE AGE OF 35.

HE HAD NOT REVEALED a shred of information, not even his true identity, to his tormentors. He was buried in Batu Gajah as Tan Choon Lim.

There isn't anyone who can relate fully the last moments of his life. Because for those who survived, his screams, often heard echoing through the narrow, dingy corridors of the Batu Gajah gaol, are now but a painful testimony that is, perhaps, best forgotten.

Lim Bo Seng's body was exhumed and brought back to Singapore by his wife and eldest son.

January 13, 1946. He was laid to rest at MacRitchie Reservoir with full military honours.

Ironically, 50 years after his death, Singapore's first national hero, Lim Bo Seng, is just as unknown to a new generation of Singaporeans as he was to the *kempeitai*.

A humble memorial still stands at the Esplanade, a relic of our history.

LIM BO SENG IS PART OF SINGAPORE'S HERITAGE WHICH THE LITTLE ISLAND ENTERPRISE IS DEDICATED TO PRESERVE.

Copy Individual

Copywriter
DANIEL LIM

Art Directors
DANIEL LIM
GROVER THAM

Creative Director
JIM AITCHISON

Photographer
LYE KOK HONG

Typographer
GROVER THAM

Agency
BATEY ADS
SINGAPORE

Managing Director
VICTOR YEO

Client
THE LITTLE ISLAND
ENTERPRISE

Small.
Economical.
Reliable.

Edible.

Copy Individual

Copywriters
SIGGI HALLING
TREVOR DE SILVA

Art Director
DAVID MACKERSEY

Typographer
JOANNE CHEVLIN

Agency
J. WALTER
THOMPSON

Managing Director
DAVID HARRIS

Client
ROWNTREE PLC

Copy Individual

Copywriter
GEOFF SMITH

Art Director
SIMON MORRIS

Photographer
STEVE CAVALIER

Typographer
ANDY DYMOCK

Agency
BANKS HOGGINS O'SHEA

Managing Director
B. J. CUNNINGHAM

Client
THE ENLIGHTENED TOBACCO COMPANY

Enlightened Tobacco Company Plc:

13.5 MILLION SMOKERS WILL ADMIT IT'S BAD FOR THEM. ONLY ONE TOBACCO COMPANY WILL.

Ask any of the country's 13.5 million smokers and they'll probably admit, however grudgingly, that smoking is a health risk.

But ask any tobacco company, and their answer is likely to be very different.

In fact, tobacco companies usually have just two words to say on the subject of health: 'No' and 'Comment'.

They have never admitted that there is a proven link between smoking and lung cancer, or indeed any other smoking-related disease. Their only defence, therefore, is to say nothing.

Clearly, it is time for a tobacco company to break the silence. Enter the Enlightened Tobacco Company: the only cigarette manufacturer willing to tell it like it is.

There are currently 264 different brands of cigarette available in Great Britain. Yet, despite the stringent rules that apply to cigarette advertising, manufacturers are still able to lend their products an air of sophistication.

Often this is achieved simply by using esoteric photographs that have nothing at all to do with cigarettes.

Ironically, it is usually only the health warning at the bottom that gives any clue as to the nature of the product being advertised.

And neither is any clue given in the names of the cigarettes themselves. Many of them are still able to conjure up an image of something expensive, stylish, sophisticated or exotic.

Then there is Death.

The name alone leaves you in no doubt as to the risks you're taking. And neither does the pack.

Although all cigarettes must legally carry a health warning, our pack is, quite simply, the strongest warning it's possible to have short of speaking to your doctor.

Now it could be suggested that a cigarette company which appears to go out of its way to warn you not to smoke is a paradox every bit as insoluble as Joseph Heller's Catch 22. It isn't really. It's just being honest.

We are not anti-smoking. That would be ridiculous.

If you're a smoker we want you to buy our cigarettes. That's why both Death and Death Lights are made from the finest blends of luxury Virginia tobacco. But if we sell cigarettes, we should also be sufficiently honest to remind you of the dangers.

We don't believe, however,

that simply being truthful is enough. We openly admit to the link between smoking and lung cancer, so shouldn't we be prepared to do something about it? We're helping to create the problem after all.

That's precisely why the Enlightened Tobacco Company has decided to give 10% of all its pre-tax profits to non-vivisection cancer charities.

Obviously our donations won't lead to a miracle cure. Death smokers shouldn't look on this as some kind of life insurance policy. The best way to avoid dying of lung cancer remains the same. Stop smoking.

This advice is also offered to those wishing to avoid such unpleasant illnesses as heart disease, emphysema and bronchitis.

But if you do choose to continue, shouldn't you at least be honest with yourself?

Because, if you are, you'll have to admit that you already smoke death cigarettes.

They just happen to be called something else.

DEATH	DEATH LIGHTS
13mg TAR 1.0mg NICOTINE	7mg TAR 0.7mg NICOTINE

SMOKING KILLS

Health Departments' Chief Medical Officers

Copy Individual

Copywriter
DAVID NOBAY

Art Director
ANDRE COHEN

Creative Director
DAVID NOBAY

Typographer
ANDRE COHEN

Agency
COHN & WELLS, SAN FRANCISCO

Marketing Executive
BERT JENSSENS

Client
NEO GRAPHICS

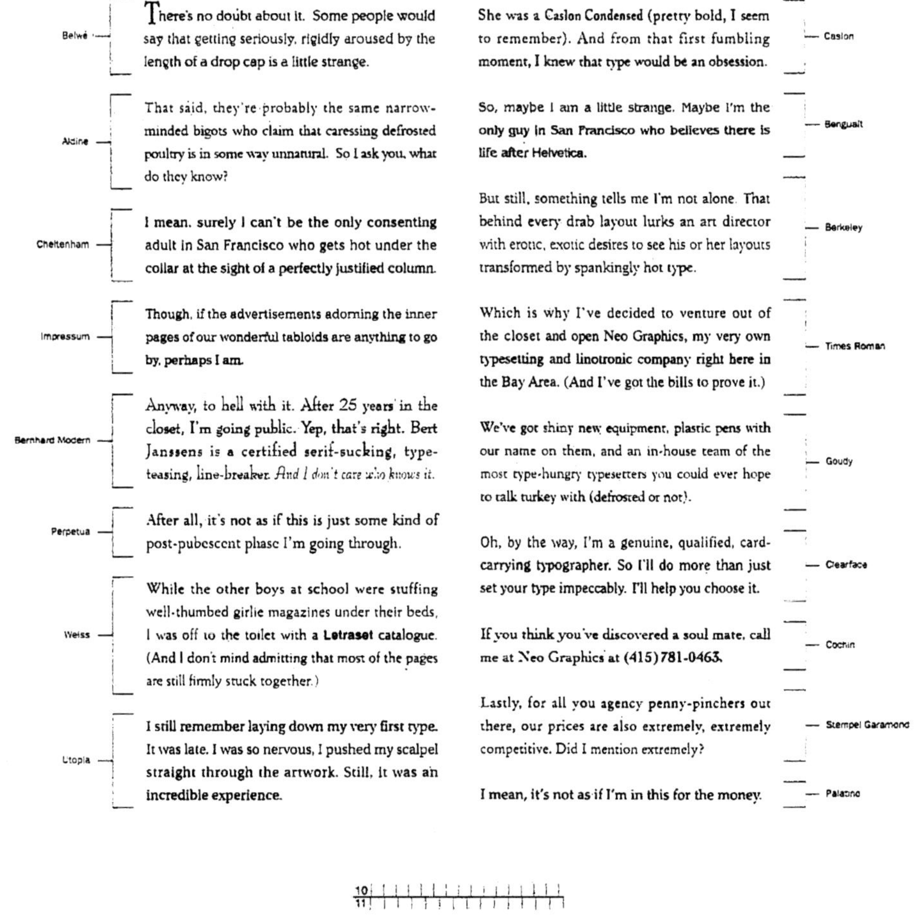

Copy Individual

Copywriter
NIGEL ROBERTS

Art Director
PAUL BELFORD

Agency
DMB&B

Marketing Director
RICHARD BREWSTER

Client
SCOPE

Spot the odd one out. If you didn't, maybe you'll appreciate why The Spastics Society has changed its name. People with cerebral palsy have enough to deal with as it is. And having the word spastic used as a term of abuse doesn't help. There are a lot more things we, as Scope, intend to change.

SCOPE
Formerly The Spastics Society

Copy Individual

Copywriter
NICK BELL

Art Director
GREG MARTIN

Typographer
JOE HOZA

Agency
ABBOTT MEAD VICKERS.BBDO LIMITED

Director of Campaigns and Public Relations
JERRY LLOYD

Client
RSPCA

Sorry if this is hard hitting but so was the man who did it.

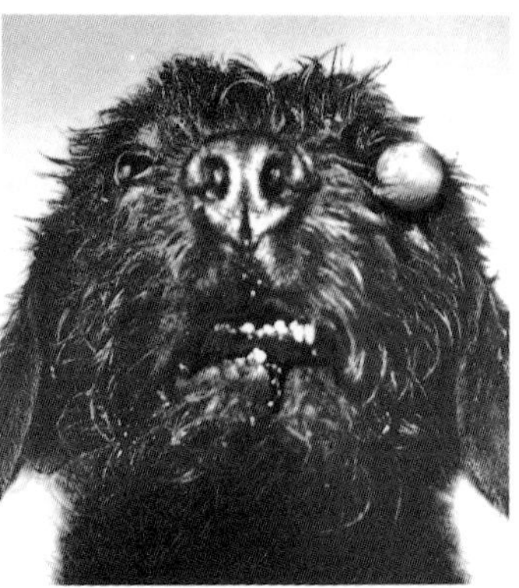

Max was beaten over the head with a garden spade.

According to witnesses, he was beaten repeatedly and viciously.

His teeth were shattered, his jaw was broken, his left eye was knocked out of its socket.

Our Inspector said they were the most horrific injuries he'd encountered in ten years with the RSPCA.

All year round, we're called to the aid of suffering animals like Max.

Last year, our Inspectors responded to nearly 100,000 reports of animal cruelty.

Reports of horses that had been starved, dogs that had been beaten, kittens that had been kicked and maimed.

Our policy is never to refuse a call for help. But, of course, it's an expensive one.

The current cost of training, equipping and putting just one new Inspector on the road for a year is £32,407.

Which is why we need your help so desperately.

The RSPCA receives no funding from the Government.

We rely entirely on the generosity of the public.

Indeed, it's thanks to people like you that we were able to save Max.

So please send as much money as you can.

Because it's cruelty like this that needs beating.

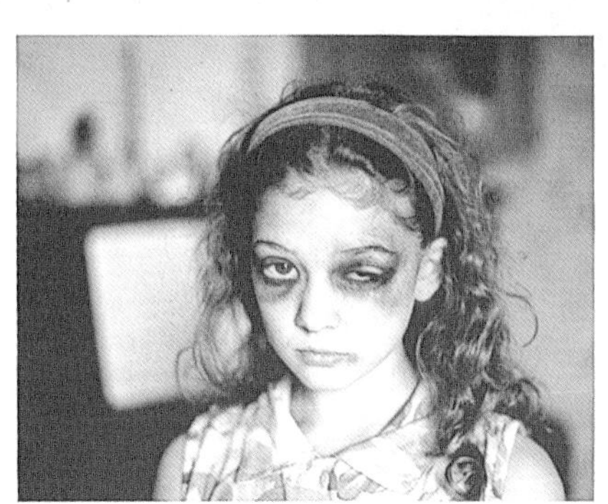

Ive got my mothers eyes.

This is Julie's story.

'Everyone in the village thinks my dad's really great. But I hate him.

They are always saying what a kind and helpful man he is. That's a load of rubbish. He's really horrible to me and my mum.

He's got his own business and is always coming home late. Sometimes he smells like he's been drinking. But if my mum ever complains he hits her.

The other night I could hear my mum screaming. I ran downstairs and saw him pulling her across the living room by her hair. When I tried to stop him, he hit me in the face.'

The next day, when a neighbour saw Julie's bruised eyes, she reported it. And now, thanks to her, Julie and her family are getting the help they need.

There are thousands of cases like Julie's every year. But they're only a small part of the problem.

When most people think of child abuse they think of cases like Julie's. But the fact is, children can actually be just as badly harmed by the kind of treatment that a lot of people might not even think of as abuse.

For instance, constantly ignoring or criticizing a child, or withdrawal of any signs of affection, can emotionally scar a child for the rest of his or her life.

They can lead to feelings of low self-worth, loneliness and an inability to form relationships with others.

Which is the reason why the NSPCC is launching a new campaign, 'A Cry For Children'. It's a cry to everyone to stop and think about how they behave towards children.

To recognise the impact that any form of cruelty can have on a child. And to realise the way children are treated can affect their whole lives.

Please answer the cry.

If you, or someone you know is suffering from abuse, please call the NSPCC Child Protection Helpline on 0800 800 500 any time, day or night.

Or if, after reading this, you would find more information helpful, please call us on 071 825 2775.

NSPCC
A cry for children.

Copy Individual

Copywriter
NEIL PAVITT

Art Directors
COLIN JONES
BILL GALLACHER

Photographer
GRAHAM CORNTHWAITE

Typographer
ROGER KENNEDY

Agency
SAATCHI & SAATCHI

Director of Public Policy
PHILIP NOYES

Client
NSPCC

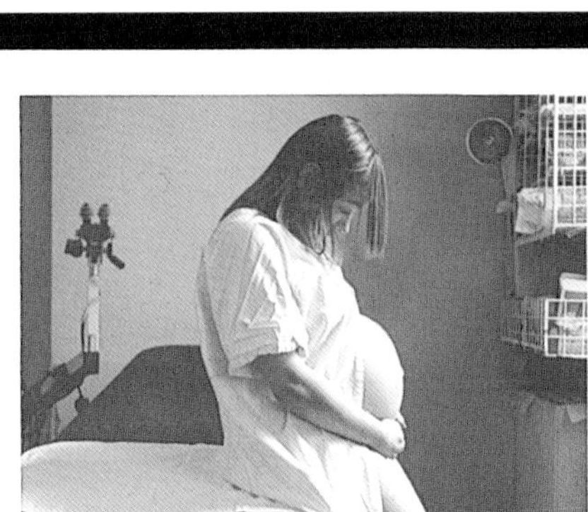

WE both have tHe same Father.

This is Sally's story.

'My mum died when I was twelve. One night when I had a bad dream my dad said I could sleep in his bed.

To start with he just cuddled me, but then he started doing other things. I wanted him to stop but he wouldn't. I hated it, it really hurt. He said it meant he loved me.

The next day when I was leaving for school he said I mustn't tell anyone about what happened. After that he wanted me to sleep with him every night. He called it our little secret.

Later, when my periods stopped my dad kept me off school. He told them that I was ill.

Sometimes I can feel the baby moving inside me, it feels horrible.'

Luckily Sally's school reported her absence and now she's getting all the support she needs.

Of course, there's more to her abuse than becoming pregnant.

She'll need long term counselling to tackle the emotional damage, such as feelings of guilt and an inability to form relationships.

In fact, all forms of abuse can cause emotional harm. Not just the more obvious forms involving sexual assault and physical brutality.

For example, withdrawal of any signs of affection, ignoring children, constantly criticizing or shouting at them can lead to emotional scars which last a lifetime. Sometimes, children can even be driven to commit suicide.

Because of all this, the NSPCC is launching 'A Cry for Children'. It's a cry to everyone to stop and think about their behaviour towards children.

To recognise the impact that any form of cruelty can have on a child. And to realise that the way children are treated affects their whole lives.

Please answer the cry.

If you, or someone you know is suffering abuse, call the NSPCC Child Protection Helpline on 0800 800 500.

Or if, after reading this, you would find more information helpful, please call us on 071 825 2775.

NSPCC
A cry for children.

Copy Individual

Copywriter
NEIL PAVITT

Art Directors
COLIN JONES
BILL GALLACHER

Photographer
GRAHAM CORNTHWAITE

Typographer
ROGER KENNEDY

Agency
SAATCHI & SAATCHI

Director of Public Policy
PHILIP NOYES

Client
NSPCC

Copy Campaigns

Copywriter
NICK BELL

Art Director
GREG MARTIN

Typographer
JOE HOZA

Agency
ABBOTT MEAD VICKERS.BBDO LIMITED

Director of Campaigns and Public Relations
JERRY LLOYD

Client
RSPCA

Investigating this wasn't difficult. We had a lead.

We found Trudy tethered round the neck by a piece of rusting curtain wire.

Her three small puppies were just a few feet away.

Where Trudy had struggled to get to them, the sharp, rusty coil of the wire had cut deep into her throat.

From the depth of the wound and the amount of scar tissue formed, our vet estimated she had been tethered in this way for at least five weeks.

In his opinion, she would have suffered considerably.

All year round, our Inspectors are called to the aid of suffering animals like Trudy.

Last year alone, we responded to nearly 100,000 reports of animal cruelty. Reports of horses that had been starved, dogs that had been beaten, kittens that had been kicked and maimed.

Our policy is never to refuse a call for help. But, of course, it's an expensive one.

The current cost of training, equipping and putting just one new Inspector on the road for a year is £32,407. Which is why we so desperately need your help.

The RSPCA doesn't receive any funding from the Government.

We rely entirely on the public's generosity.

Thanks to people like you, we were able to find a loving new home for Trudy and her puppies.

So please send as much money as you can. And help us save a few more necks.

Sorry if this is hard hitting but so was the man who did it.

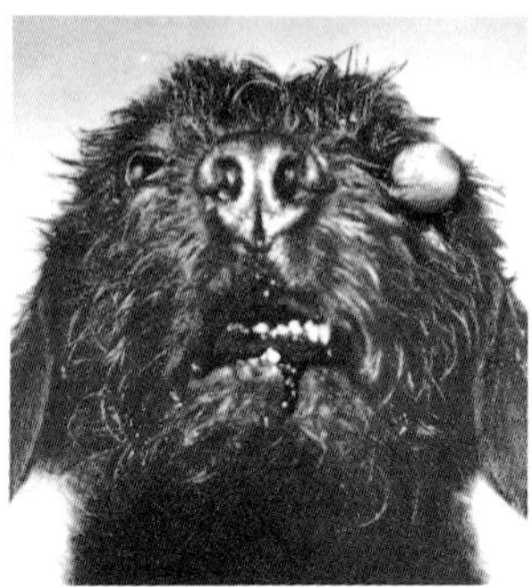

Max was beaten over the head with a garden spade.

According to witnesses, he was beaten repeatedly and viciously.

His teeth were shattered, his jaw was broken, his left eye was knocked out of its socket.

Our Inspector said they were the most horrific injuries he'd encountered in ten years with the RSPCA.

All year round, we're called to the aid of suffering animals like Max.

Last year, our Inspectors responded to nearly 100,000 reports of animal cruelty.

Reports of horses that had been starved, dogs that had been beaten, kittens that had been kicked and maimed.

Our policy is never to refuse a call for help. But, of course, it's an expensive one.

The current cost of training, equipping and putting just one new Inspector on the road for a year is £32,407.

Which is why we need your help so desperately.

The RSPCA receives no funding from the Government.

We rely entirely on the generosity of the public.

Indeed, it's thanks to people like you that we were able to save Max.

So please send as much money as you can.

Because it's cruelty like this that needs beating.

"How I put on 35 lbs in just 8 weeks."

Spot of Ipswich.

Me before the RSPCA diet.

Me after.

"Eighteen months ago, I had a weight problem.

My eyes were sunken, my ribs were showing; I looked awful.

Then I discovered the RSPCA. Or rather, they discovered me.

In no time, they had me eating sensibly again.

Plenty of the right things every day - even the occasional treat.

After just eight weeks, I'd reached my target weight."

When we discovered Spot, she was terribly underweight.

She had severe muscle wastage, she was weak with hunger and hadn't been fed properly for weeks.

But Spot is one of our many success stories. Because our Inspector reached her in time, we were able to save her and find her a loving new home.

Many animals aren't as fortunate.

All year round, our Inspectors are called to the aid of suffering animals like Spot.

Last year alone, we responded to nearly 100,000 reports of animal cruelty.

Reports of horses that had been starved, dogs that had been beaten, kittens that had been kicked and maimed.

Our policy is never to refuse a call for help. But, of course, it's an expensive one.

The current cost of training, equipping and putting just one new Inspector on the road for a year is £32,407.

Which is why we desperately need your help.

The RSPCA receives no funding from the Government.

We rely entirely on the generosity of people like you.

Please send as much money as you can.

We know plenty more animals that could do with a few pounds.

Some of our Inspectors can't tell one end of a dog from the other.

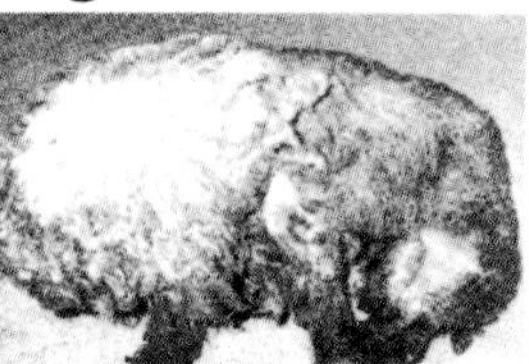

This poodle (yes, poodle) was found starving and miserable in the pouring rain.

His coat was so filthy and overgrown, our Inspector couldn't immediately tell which end his head was.

(If you're wondering, it's to the left.)

Every year, we deal with thousands of sad cases like this.

But we receive no funding from the Government, so we need your help to continue our good work.

Please give generously. Your donation will save us having to cut our coat.

Please tick the box if you are already a supporter. 1
Please tick the box if you would like information on becoming an RSPCA member. 2
Please use my donation to fight animal cruelty.
£60 £30 £12 £8 I prefer to give £
I wish to give via Visa/Access/RSPCA Mastercard no:
Signature Expiry
Name
Address
Postcode
To: RSPCA, Dept. TG1D, Freepost, Bristol BS3 3YY.
RSPCA

Copy Campaigns

Copywriter
SIGGI HALLING

Art Director
DAVID MACKERSEY

Typographer
JOANNE CHEVLIN

Agency
J. WALTER THOMPSON

Managing Director
DAVID HARRIS

Client
ROWNTREE PLC

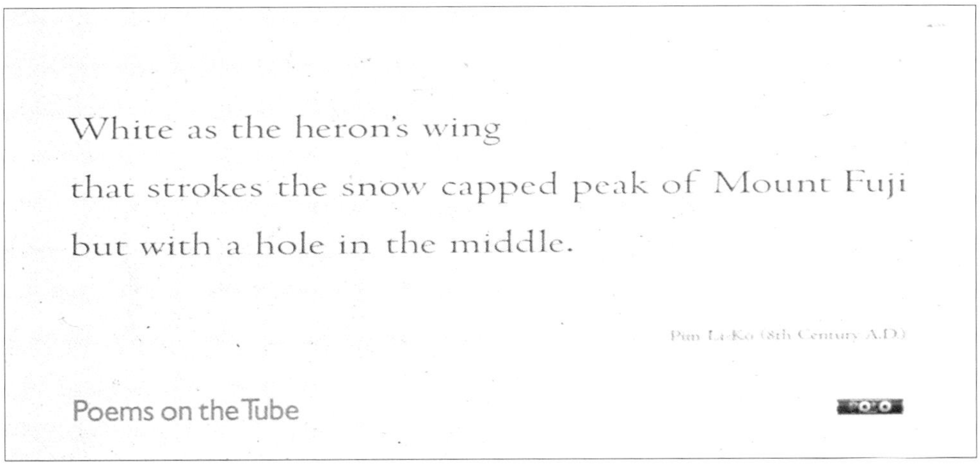

White as the heron's wing
that strokes the snow capped peak of Mount Fuji
but with a hole in the middle.

Pun Li-Ko (8th Century A.D.)

Poems on the Tube

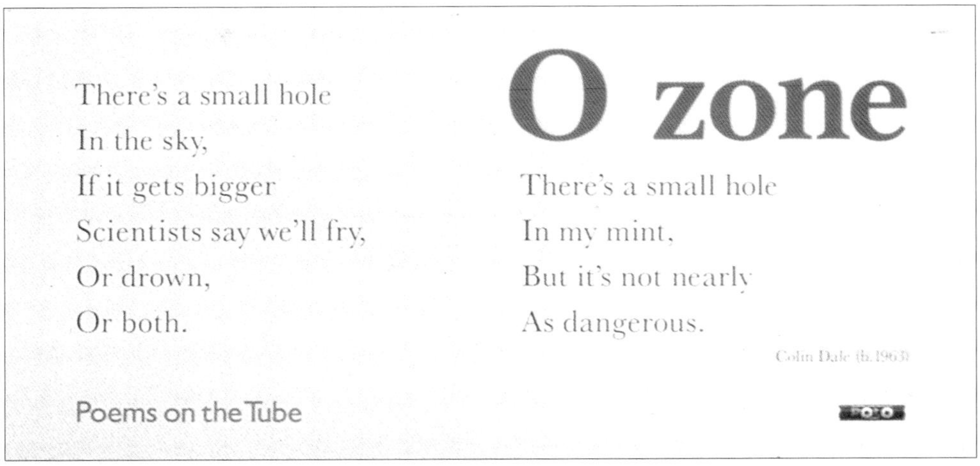

POLO

There's a small hole
In the sky,
If it gets bigger
Scientists say we'll fry,
Or drown,
Or both.

O zone

There's a small hole
In my mint,
But it's not nearly
As dangerous.

Colin Dale (b.1963)

Poems on the Tube

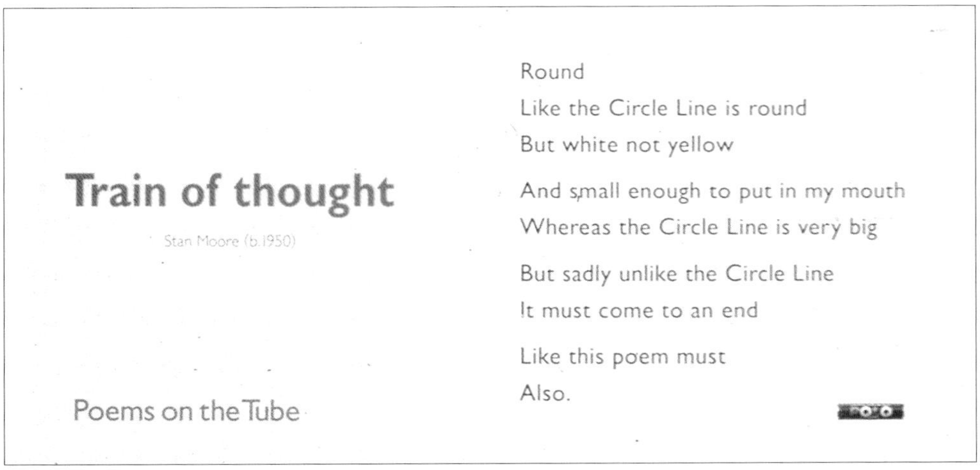

POLO

Train of thought

Stan Moore (b.1950)

Round
Like the Circle Line is round
But white not yellow
And small enough to put in my mouth
Whereas the Circle Line is very big
But sadly unlike the Circle Line
It must come to an end
Like this poem must
Also.

Poems on the Tube

POLO

Copy Campaigns

Copywriters
AJAB SAMRAI SINGH
CHRIS KIRK

Art Director
AJAB SAMRAI SINGH

Photographer
BARRY LATEGAN

Typographer
NIGEL WARD

Agency
SAATCHI & SAATCHI

Marketing Executive
MARJORIE
THOMPSON

Client
COMMISSION FOR
RACIAL EQUALITY

CHILDREN FROM ETHNIC MINORITIES OFTEN GET THE WORST MARKS AT SCHOOL.

Actually, studies show that some ethnic minorities get the best grades at school. But of course, you won't have heard about that. All you will have heard about are the kind of marks that grab the headlines. The vicious playground beatings, the horrific knife attacks and the senseless murders.

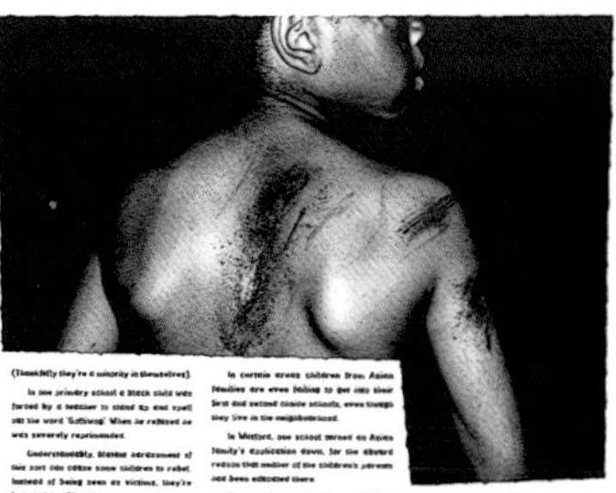

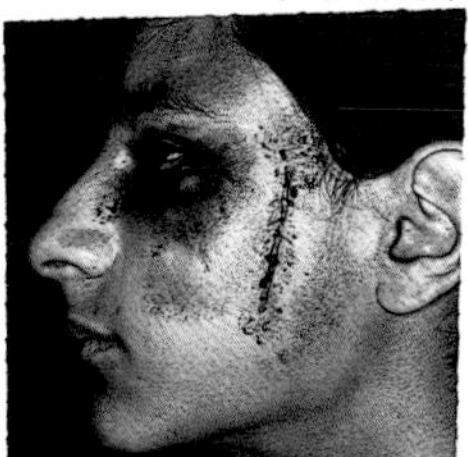

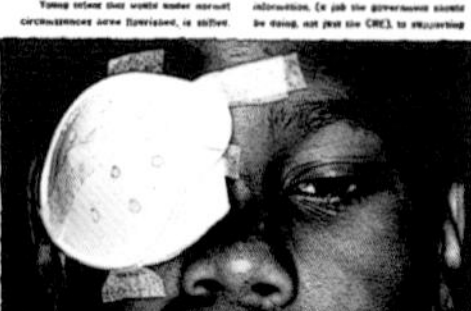

COMMISSION FOR RACIAL EQUALITY

Copywriter
AJAB SAMRAI SINGH

Photographers
ALISTAIR THAIN
TIM O'SULLIVAN

Typographer
TIM QUEST

CRIMINAL ISN'T IT?

A 1992 survey of Midlands crown courts revealed that some ethnic minorities are receiving longer prison sentences. On average, up to 9 months longer than white people for the same crimes. If this is typical, it leads to one simple and rather alarming conclusion.

Car theft 9 months.

Car theft 1½ years.

COMMISSION FOR RACIAL EQUALITY

Copywriter
GILES MONTGOMERY

Photographer
JOHN TURNER

Typographer
NIGEL WARD

WHO SAYS ETHNIC MINORITIES CAN'T GET JOBS? THERE ARE OPENINGS EVERYWHERE.

Lavatory attendant. Office cleaner. Somebody has to do all the low-paid, menial jobs, but why is it so often people from ethnic minorities? Prejudice, racial discrimination and harassment are denying people the choice of job they deserve. It's unjust and unfair. More than that, it's a terrible waste of British talent.

COMMISSION FOR RACIAL EQUALITY

THERE ARE LOTS OF PLACES IN BRITAIN WHERE RACISM DOESN'T EXIST.

In so many ways Britain is a racist country. In 1993 alone the police recorded over 9,000 incidents of racial harassment, abuse, assault, arson and murder. Thousands more incidents go unreported. As many as 120,000 a year, according to the Home Office. Worryingly, even this is still only half the problem.

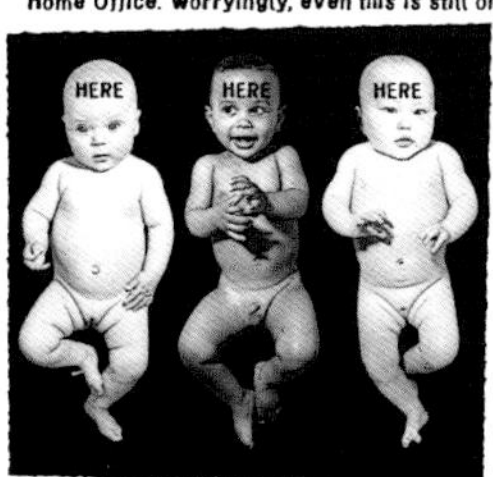

HERE

HERE

COMMISSION FOR RACIAL EQUALITY

Copywriter
GILES MONTGOMERY

Photographer
ALISTAIR THAIN

Typographer
NIGEL WARD

AND YOU GET ANNOYED ABOUT JUNK MAIL.

Imagine going to your door and finding, there, on the mat, not bills, or a paper, or junk mail, but pieces of dog excrement. As you stare, shocked, a heavy boot kicks the door. Hateful voices outside scream obscenities, telling you to get out, threatening your family. Why are they persecuting you? When will they stop?

COMMISSION FOR RACIAL EQUALITY

Copywriter
GILES MONTGOMERY

Photographer
JOHN TURNER

Typographer
NIGEL WARD

1995
POSTERS

Sponsored by More O'Ferrall

SILVER AWARD
for the Most
Outstanding 48 and
96 Sheet Poster

Art Director
ANDY McKAY

Copywriter
GILES MONTGOMERY

Photographers
NORBET SCHANER
SEAMUS RYAN

Typographer
JOHN TISDALL

Agency
SIMONS PALMER
DENTON CLEMMOW
& JOHNSON

Advertising Manager
TONY HILL

Client
NIKE UK LIMITED

SILVER AWARD NOMINATION
for the Most Outstanding 48 and 96 Sheet Poster

Art Director
TIGER SAVAGE

Copywriter
PAUL SILBURN

Photographer
SEAMUS RYAN

Typographer
JOHN TISDALL

Agency
SIMONS PALMER DENTON CLEMMOW & JOHNSON

Advertising Manager
TONY HILL

Client
NIKE UK LIMITED

SILVER AWARD NOMINATION
for the Most Outstanding 4 Sheet Poster

Art Director
JULIE HILL

Copywriter
MARK WALDRON

Typographer
ALEX MANOLATOS

Proprietor
PETER JOHNSON

Client
STATION GARAGE

SILVER AWARD NOMINATION
for the Most Outstanding 48 and 96 Sheet Poster

Art Director
TONY DAVIDSON

Copywriter
TONY DAVIDSON

Typographer
DAVID WAKEFIELD

Agency
BMP DDB NEEDHAM

Client
POWERBREAKER

SILVER AWARD NOMINATION
for the Most Outstanding Poster Campaign

Art Director
TIGER SAVAGE

Copywriter
PAUL SILBURN

Photographer
SEAMUS RYAN

Typographer
JOHN TISDALL

Agency
SIMONS PALMER DENTON CLEMMOW & JOHNSON

Advertising Manager
TONY HILL

Client
NIKE UK LIMITED

Art Director
ANDY McKAY

Copywriter
GILES MONTGOMERY

Photographers
NORBET SCHANER
SEAMUS RYAN

Art Director
TIGER SAVAGE

Copywriter
PAUL SILBURN

Photographer
PETER ANDERSON

SILVER AWARD NOMINATION
for the Most Outstanding Poster Campaign

Art Directors
NIGEL ROSE
STEVE CHETHAM

Copywriter
TREVOR BEATTIE

Creative Directors
NIGEL ROSE
TREVOR BEATTIE

Photographer
ELLEN VON UNWERTH

Typographer
TIVY DAVIES

Agency
TBWA

Marketing Executive
JOHN DIXEY

Account Director
SUSANNA HAILSTONE

Client
PLAYTEX UK LIMITED

PULL
YOURSELF
TOGETHER.

THE ORIGINAL PUSH-UP PLUNGE BRA. NOW AVAILABLE IN COOL COTTON

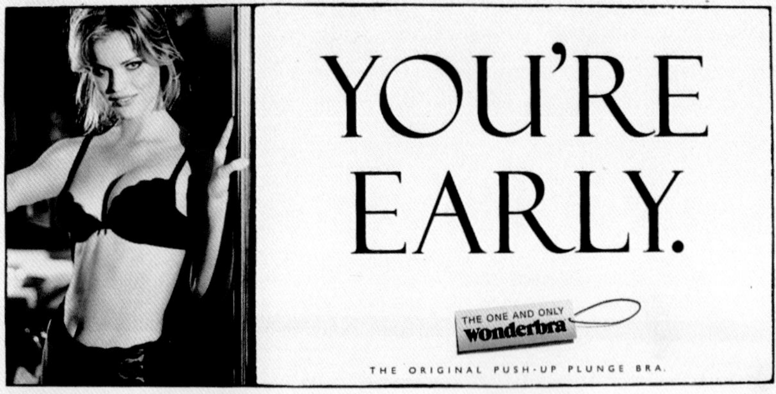

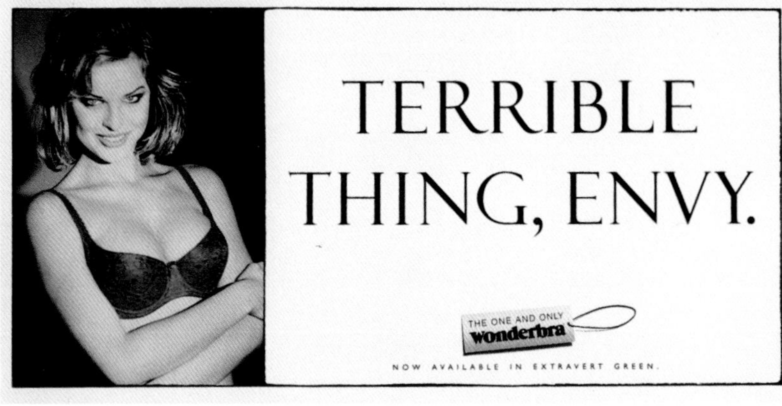

Art Director
NIGEL ROSE

Copywriter
NIGEL ROSE

Creative Director
NIGEL ROSE

Art Director
NIGEL ROSE

Copywriter
TREVOR BEATTIE

Creative Director
NIGEL ROSE

SILVER AWARD NOMINATION
for the Most Outstanding Poster Campaign

Art Director
JULIE HILL

Copywriter
MARK WALDRON

Typographer
ALEX MANOLATOS

Proprietor
PETER JOHNSON

Client
STATION GARAGE

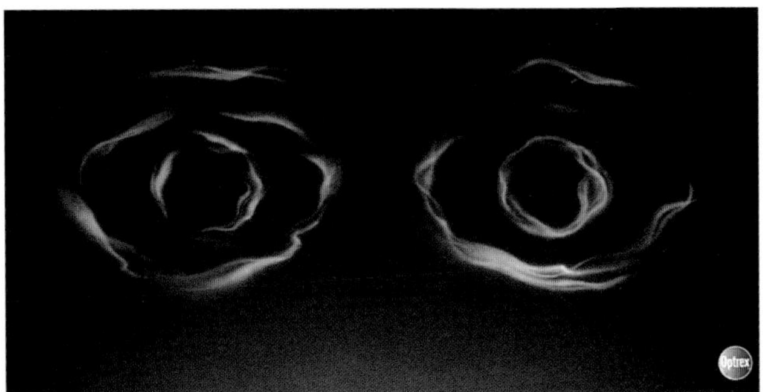

SILVER AWARD NOMINATION
for the Most Outstanding Poster Campaign

Art Director
JEREMY CARR

Copywriter
JEREMY CRAIGEN

Photographer
MIKE PARSONS

Agency
BMP DDB NEEDHAM

Client
CROOKES HEALTHCARE

Photographer
RUSSELL PORCAS

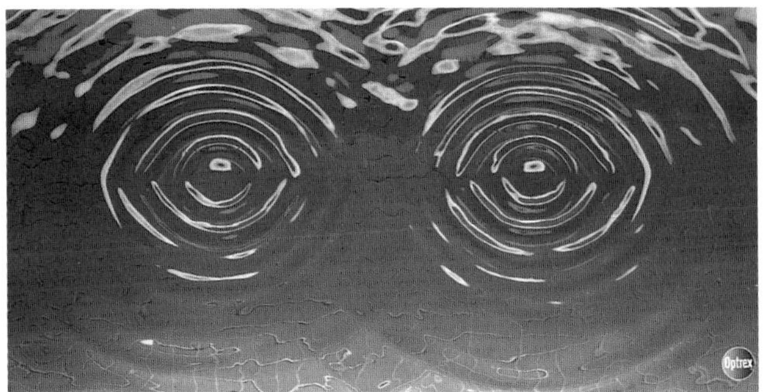

Photographer
DEREK SEAGRAM

SILVER AWARD NOMINATION
for the Most Outstanding Poster Any Other

Art Director
PAUL BELFORD

Copywriter
NIGEL ROBERTS

Agency
DMB&B

Advertising and Public Relations Manager
JANE RITCHIE

Client
QANTAS AIRWAYS LIMITED

SILVER AWARD NOMINATION
for the Most Outstanding Poster Any Other

Art Director
TONY DAVIDSON

Copywriter
TONY DAVIDSON

Typographer
DAVID WAKEFIELD

Agency
BMP DDB NEEDHAM

Client
POWERBREAKER

SILVER AWARD NOMINATION
for the Most Outstanding Poster Any Other

Art Director
TONY DAVIDSON

Copywriter
KIM PAPWORTH

Photographer
NICK RIGG

Typographer
KEVIN CLARKE

Agency
BMP DDB NEEDHAM

Client
CROOKES HEALTHCARE

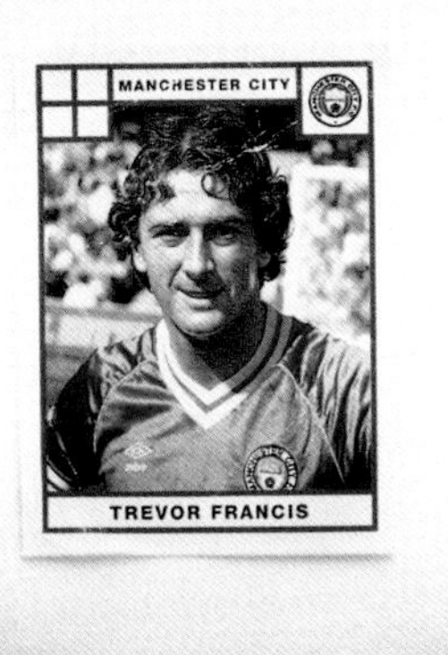

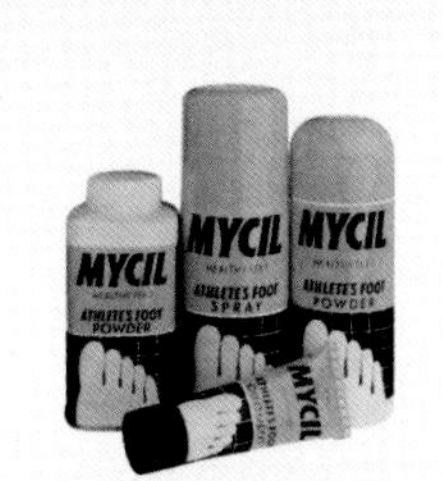

Fast relief from itchy feet.

48 and 96 Sheet

Art Directors
NIGEL ROSE
STEVE CHETHAM

Copywriter
TREVOR BEATTIE

Creative Directors
NIGEL ROSE
TREVOR BEATTIE

Photographer
ELLEN VON UNWERTH

Typographer
TIVY DAVIES

Agency
TBWA

Marketing Executive
JOHN DIXEY

Account Director
SUSANNA HAILSTONE

Client
PLAYTEX UK LIMITED

48 and 96 Sheet

Art Director
DEXTER GINN

Copywriter
DOMINIC GETTINS

Photographer
DAN TIERNEY

Typographer
ANDY PALMER

Agency
EURO RSCG WNEK
GOSPER

Marketing Director
ROBERT MacNEVIN

Client
GUINNESS BREWING
GB

48 and 96 Sheet

Art Director
JEREMY CARR

Copywriter
JEREMY CRAIGEN

Photographer
MIKE PARSONS

Agency
BMP DDB NEEDHAM

Client
CROOKES
HEALTHCARE

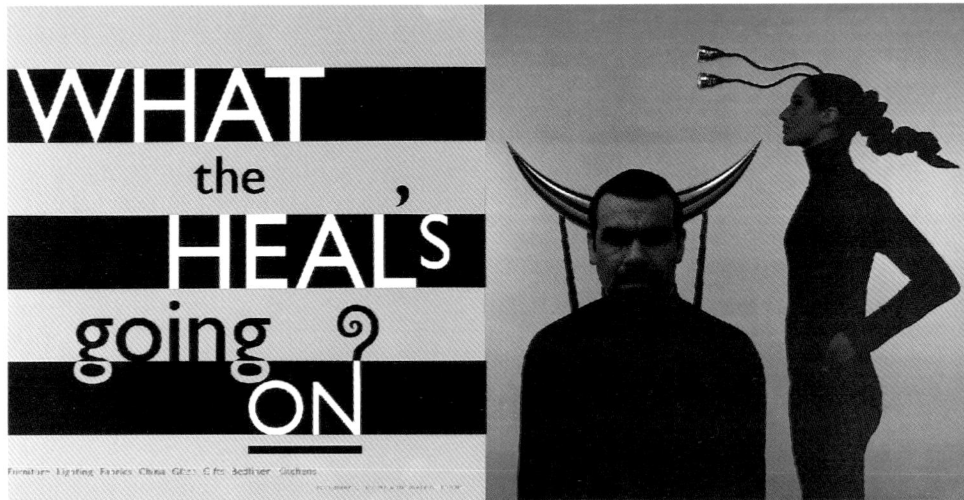

48 and 96 Sheet

Art Director
MARK REDDY

Copywriter
RICHARD GRISDALE

Photographer
DAVID STEWART

Typographers
PETER WOOD
STEVEN
WALLINGTON

Agency
LEAGAS SHAFRON
DAVIS AYER

Managing Director
COLIN PILGRIM

Client
HEAL'S

48 and 96 Sheet

Art Director
PAUL BRIGINSHAW

Copywriter
MALCOLM DUFFY

Typographer
JOE HOZA

Agency
ABBOTT MEAD
VICKERS.BBDO
LIMITED

Magazine Marketing Manager
CHANTAL HUGHES

Client
THE ECONOMIST

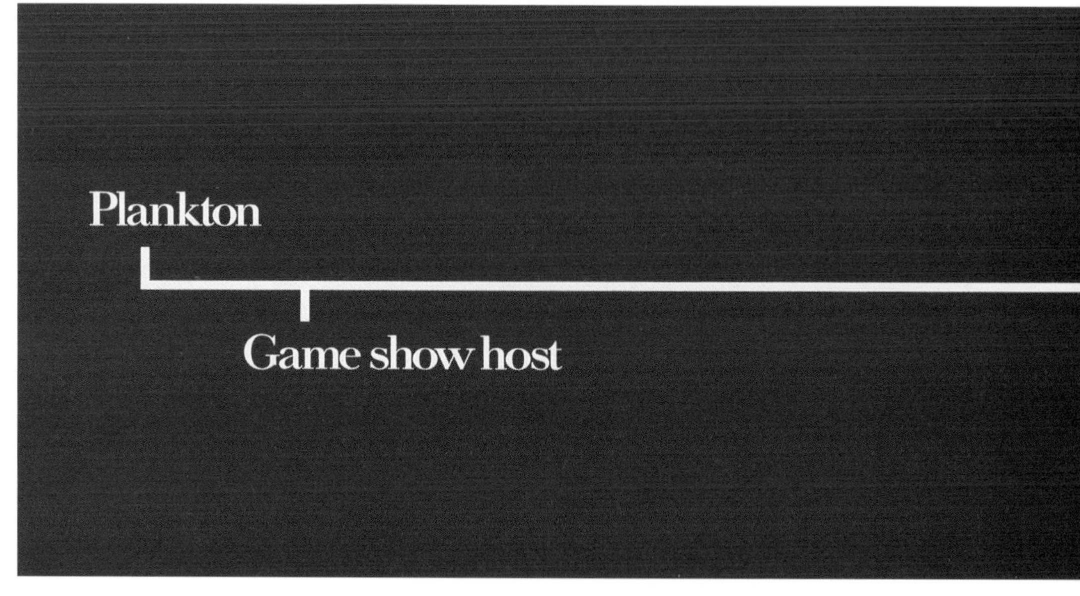

48 and 96 Sheet

Art Director
PAUL BRIGINSHAW

Copywriter
MALCOLM DUFFY

Photographer
NIGEL HAYNES

Typographer
JOE HOZA

Agency
ABBOTT MEAD
VICKERS.BBDO
LIMITED

Magazine Marketing Manager
CHANTAL HUGHES

Client
THE ECONOMIST

48 and 96 Sheet

Art Director
TIGER SAVAGE

Copywriter
PAUL SILBURN

Illustrator
MICK BROWNFIELD

Typographer
MATTHEW KEMSLEY

Agency
BARTLE BOGLE
HEGARTY

Vice President,
Director of Advertising
DAVID WHELDON

Client
THE COCA-COLA
COMPANY

48 and 96 Sheet

Art Director
MATT MURRAY

Copywriter
GILES HARGREAVES

Photographer
PAUL BEVITT

Typographer
STEVEN WALLINGTON

Agency
LEAGAS SHAFRON
DAVIS AYER

Standard Lagers Controller
MIKE DAVIES

Client
CARLSBERG-TETLEY

48 and 96 Sheet

Art Director
NIGEL ROSE

Copywriter
TREVOR BEATTIE

Creative Director
NIGEL ROSE

Photographer
ELLEN VON UNWERTH

Typographer
TIVY DAVIES

Agency
TBWA

Marketing Executive
JOHN DIXEY

Account Director
SUSANNA HAILSTONE

Client
PLAYTEX UK LIMITED

48 and 96 Sheet

Art Director
TIGER SAVAGE

Copywriter
PAUL SILBURN

Photographer
PETER ANDERSON

Typographer
JOHN TISDALL

Agency
SIMONS PALMER
DENTON CLEMMOW &
JOHNSON

Advertising Manager
TONY HILL

Client
NIKE UK LIMITED

48 and 96 Sheet

Art Director
TIM ASHTON

Copywriter
JOHN McCABE

Typographer
MATTHEW KEMSLEY

Agency
BARTLE BOGLE
HEGARTY

Marketing Executives
PHILIP LEY
SIMON MORRIS

Client
BSKYB

48 and 96 Sheet

Art Director
JEREMY CARR

Copywriter
JEREMY CRAIGEN

Photographer
MALCOLM VENVILLE

Typographer
KEVIN CLARKE

Agency
BMP DDB NEEDHAM

Client
VAG UK LIMITED

48 and 96 Sheet

Art Director
JAMES GILLHAM

Copywriter
ANDY LOCKLEY

Photographer
PAUL MYATT

Typographers
JAMES GILLHAM
ANDY LOCKLEY

Agency
GGT

General Manager, Marketing
STEVE HOLT

Client
TAUNTON CIDER PLC

48 and 96 Sheet

Art Director
KEITH TERRY

Copywriter
DAVE FOWLE

Photographer
ALLAN McPHAIL

Typographer
LYNNE McINTOSH

Agency
SAATCHI & SAATCHI

Marketing Manager
TOM HINGS

Client
CARLSBERG-TETLEY

Campaigns

Art Director
JON GREENHALGH

Copywriter
KES GRAY

Photographer
NICK GEORGHIOU

Typographers
JON GREENHALGH
KES GRAY

Agency
BMP DDB NEEDHAM

Client
VAG UK LIMITED

Campaigns

Art Director
MARK REDDY

Copywriter
RICHARD GRISDALE

Photographer
DAVID STEWART

Typographers
PETER WOOD
STEVEN
WALLINGTON

Agency
LEAGAS SHAFRON
DAVIS AYER

Managing Director
COLIN PILGRIM

Client
HEAL'S

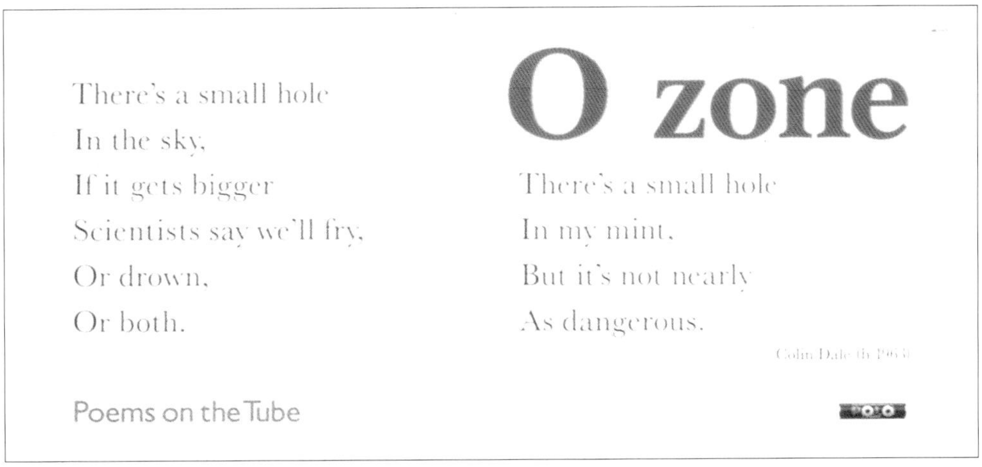

There's a small hole
In the sky,
If it gets bigger
Scientists say we'll fry,
Or drown,
Or both.

O zone

There's a small hole
In my mint,
But it's not nearly
As dangerous.

Poems on the Tube

Any Other

Art Director
DAVID MACKERSEY

Copywriter
SIGGI HALLING

Typographer
JOANNE CHEVLIN

Agency
J. WALTER
THOMPSON

Managing Director
DAVID HARRIS

Client
ROWNTREE PLC

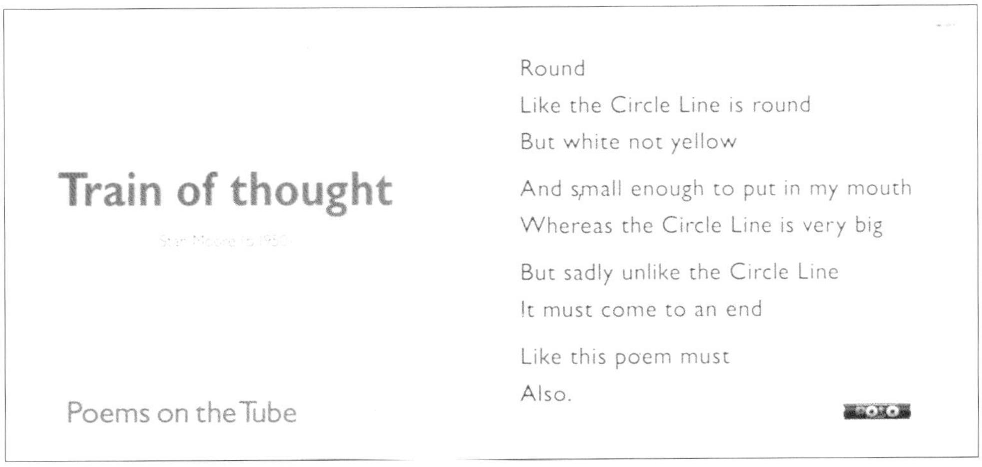

Train of thought

Round
Like the Circle Line is round
But white not yellow

And small enough to put in my mouth
Whereas the Circle Line is very big

But sadly unlike the Circle Line
It must come to an end

Like this poem must
Also.

Poems on the Tube

Any Other

Art Director
DAVID MACKERSEY

Copywriter
SIGGI HALLING

Typographer
JOANNE CHEVLIN

Agency
J. WALTER
THOMPSON

Managing Director
DAVID HARRIS

Client
ROWNTREE PLC

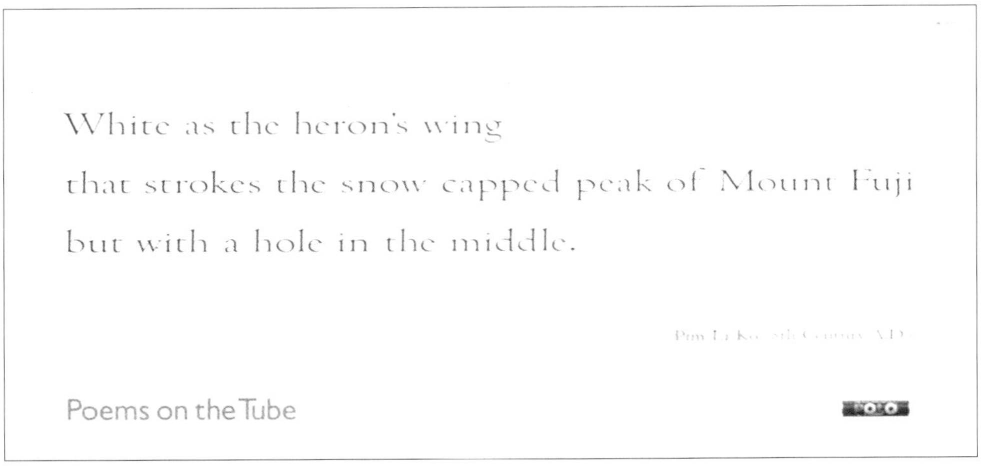

White as the heron's wing
that strokes the snow capped peak of Mount Fuji
but with a hole in the middle.

Poems on the Tube

Any Other

Art Director
DAVID MACKERSEY

Copywriter
SIGGI HALLING

Typographer
JOANNE CHEVLIN

Agency
J. WALTER
THOMPSON

Managing Director
DAVID HARRIS

Client
ROWNTREE PLC

Any Other

Art Director
TERRY TAYLOR

Copywriter
TOM DARBYSHIRE

Illustrator
STEVEN CHAVERS

Typographer
TOM DARBYSHIRE

Agency
EARLE PALMER BROWN

Client
DR GABRIEL A. BERREBI

Does it take you a long time to urinate? Or, once you start, do you find it difficult to stop? If you answered yes to either of these questions, you may be suffering from prostate disease. Prostate disease often causes swelling in the prostate gland, which is located at the upper part of the urethra. This swelling causes a disruption or slowing in the flow of urine from the bladder. Prostate disease afflicts four out of five men at some point in their lives. But since it isn't usually painful in the early stages, many men just don't take the symptoms seriously. This is often unfortunate, because when prostate disease is allowed to progress unchecked, it can lead to cancer, severe pain and, eventually, death. If you feel that you may have any of these symptoms, please see your physician immediately. In one office visit, your doctor can perform a simple and painless exam to check for prostate disease and recommend treatment. If you don't have a physician, please call Doctor Gabriel A. Berrebi: 301-869-9776. BECAUSE IF YOU'VE BEEN STANDING HERE LONG ENOUGH TO READ THIS MUCH INFORMATION ABOUT PROSTATE DISEASE, THEN YOU PROBABLY HAVE IT.

Any Other

Art Director
TARAS WAYNER

Copywriter
KEVIN RODDY

Photographer
ILAN RUBIN

Agency
EARLE PALMER BROWN

Client
GOLF CITY DRIVING RANGE

ABSOLUT X-RAY.

CLEARLY THERE IS NO PURER VODKA THAN ABSOLUT. DO IT JUSTICE DRINK IT NEAT AT 0°C.

Any Other

Art Directors
JOAN ELLIS
NIGEL ROSE

Copywriter
JOAN ELLIS

Typographer
TIVY DAVIES

Agency
TBWA

Marketing Executives
SIMON TURNBULL
SAM EYKEN

Client
ABSOLUT UK

1995

DIRECT MARKETING

SILVER AWARD NOMINATION
for the Most Outstanding Direct Response Press

Art Director
GREG MARTIN

Copywriter
NICK BELL

Typographer
JOE HOZA

Agency
ABBOTT MEAD VICKERS.BBDO LIMITED

Director of Campaigns and Public Relations
JERRY LLOYD

Client
RSPCA

Sorry if this is hard hitting but so was the man who did it.

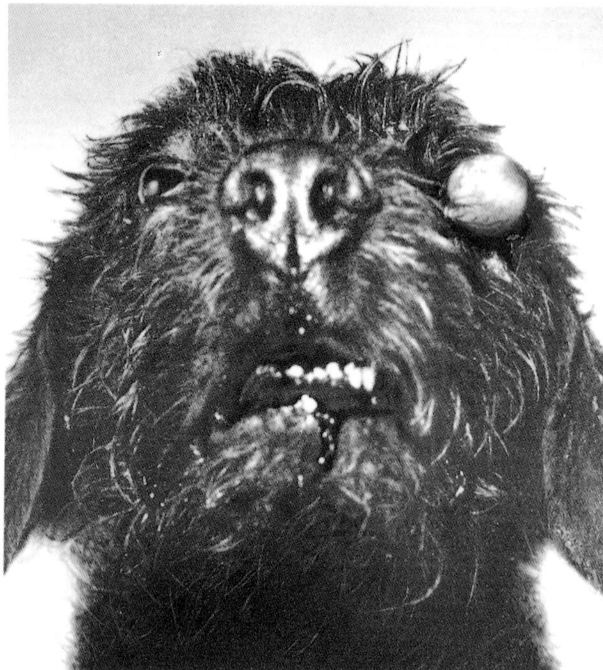

Max was beaten over the head with a garden spade.

According to witnesses, he was beaten repeatedly and viciously.

His teeth were shattered, his jaw was broken, his left eye was knocked out of its socket.

Our Inspector said they were the most horrific injuries he'd encountered in ten years with the RSPCA.

All year round, we're called to the aid of suffering animals like Max.

Last year, our Inspectors responded to nearly 100,000 reports of animal cruelty.

Reports of horses that had been starved, dogs that had been beaten, kittens that had been kicked and maimed.

Our policy is never to refuse a call for help. But, of course, it's an expensive one.

The current cost of training, equipping and putting just one new Inspector on the road for a year is £32,407.

Which is why we need your help so desperately.

The RSPCA receives no funding from the Government.

We rely entirely on the generosity of the public.

Indeed, it's thanks to people like you that we were able to save Max.

So please send as much money as you can.

Because it's cruelty like this that needs beating.

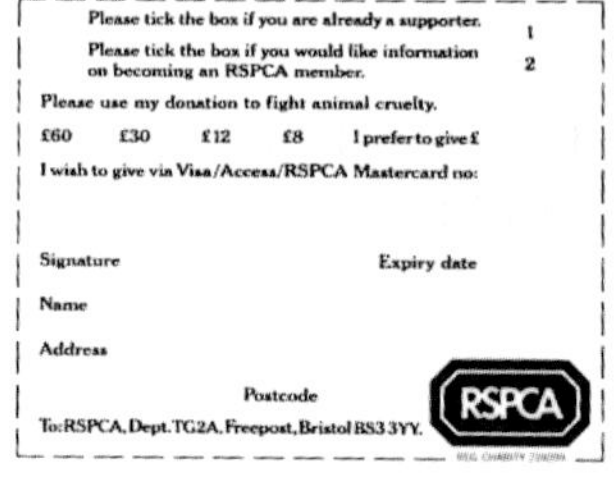
Please tick the box if you are already a supporter. 1
Please tick the box if you would like information on becoming an RSPCA member. 2
Please use my donation to fight animal cruelty.
£60 £30 £12 £8 I prefer to give £
I wish to give via Visa/Access/RSPCA Mastercard no:
Signature Expiry date
Name
Address
Postcode
To:RSPCA, Dept. TG2A, Freepost, Bristol BS3 3YY.

BRIDGE

The commercial is shot for real.

SFX:
Music interlaced with extracts from an interview with a 'rescuer'.

Open on a stuntman dressed as a businessman. He is hanging over the rail of a bridge showing obvious distress.

MVO:
It doesn't matter what walk of life you come from...

TITLE:
This man is the only actor in this scene.

Through hidden cameras we record the natural reactions of the general public.

MVO:
If you can spare a few hours a week to help others...

Most people don't want to know.

Thankfully, one or two of the hundreds stop and try to coax the man back to safety.

Cut to a Special Constable dealing with a disturbance at a late night fish and chip shop.

MVO:
...we'd like you to make enquiries.

For more information about training for the Special Constabulary - the volunteer police service - ring 0345 272272.

TITLE:
0345 272272.

MVO:
Would you care to help?

Cut back to bridge to show a different member of the public attempting to help.

Direct Response Television

Director
MIKE STEPHENSON

Copywriter
ROB JANOWSKI

Art Director
STEVE GRIME

Creative Director
STEVE GRIME

Producer
PAUL ROTHWELL

Agency Producer
PETER GRAINGER

Editor
CYRIL METZGER

Lighting Cameraman
BARRY BROWN

Music Composer/Arranger
JOE & CO

Production Company
PAUL WEILAND FILM COMPANY

Agency
LEAGAS SHAFRON DAVIS AYER

Head of Publicity
CHARLES SKINNER

Client
COI

Direct Response Television

Director
MIKE STEPHENSON

Copywriter
ROB JANOWSKI

Art Director
STEVE GRIME

Creative Director
STEVE GRIME

Producer
PAUL ROTHWELL

Agency Producer
PETER GRAINGER

Editor
CYRIL METZGER

Lighting Cameraman
BARRY BROWN

Music Composer/Arranger
JOE & CO

Production Company
PAUL WEILAND FILM COMPANY

Agency
LEAGAS SHAFRON DAVIS AYER

Head of Publicity
CHARLES SKINNER

Client
COI

WALKMAN

The commercial is shot for real.

SFX:
Music with extracts from an interview with a 'rescuer'.

Three young actors stage an incident in a shopping mall. The two older kids appear to rough up a smaller boy and try to steal his personal stereo.

YOUTH ACTORS (AD LIB):
What ya listening to mate?

'Ere gi's a listen!

TITLE:
These boys are the only actors in this scene.

Through hidden cameras we record the natural reactions of the general public.

MVO:
It doesn't matter what walk of life you come from...

If you can spare a few hours a week to help others...

Most people don't want to know.

Thankfully, one or two of the hundreds of shoppers step in to help the boy.

Cut to a Special Constable diverting traffic around an incident involving a burnt out car.

MVO:
...we'd like you to make enquiries.

For more information about training for the Special Constabulary - the volunteer police service - ring 0345 272272.

TITLE:
0345 272272.

MVO:
Would you care to help?

Cut back to shopping mall to show a different member of the public attempting to help.

2 MINUTE LAUNCH

Your first challenge is to get up at 6am to watch the commercials.

Then there are three further challenges. (One for soldiers, one for officers, one for T.A. members. All are addressed to you.)

1
A driving lesson at night. It starts innocently. Then the enemy is sighted. You (the driver) have to go off road and switch off your headlights. Could you handle it?

2
A dying boy in a war-torn hospital. The situation seems hopeless. The men turn to you, outline the facts and ask 'What do we do sir?' Call with the answer.

3
The TV screen becomes a cinema screen as we hear 'Saturday Night at the Movies' by the Drifters. Then the record gets stuck in a groove. Are you stuck in a groove or do you want to join the T.A. at the weekends? Some quick fire footage of the T.A. appears.

Your last challenge. Go back to bed or go to the phone.

ARMY. BE THE BEST.

DO YOU WANT TO LEARN TO DRIVE?

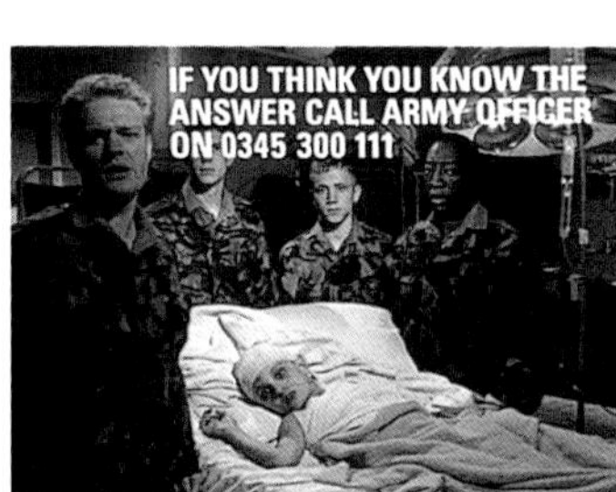

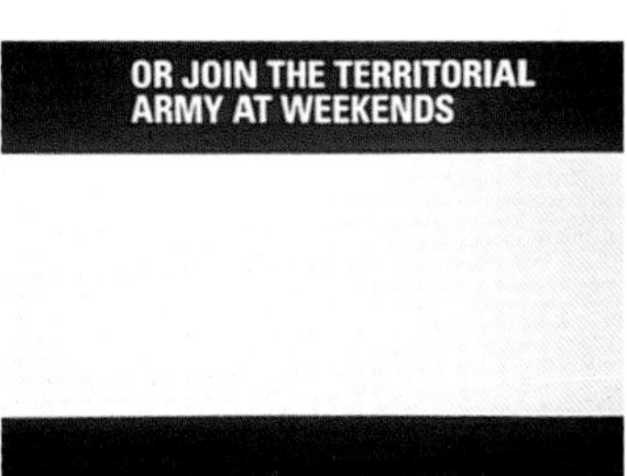

Direct Response Television

Art Director
ALEXANDRA TAYLOR

Copywriter
ADAM KEAN

Typographer
PAUL WINTER

Agency
SAATCHI & SAATCHI

Director of Army Recruitment
BRIGADIER C.H. ELLIOTT

Client
THE ARMY

1995

PACKAGING

Sponsored by Bowater

SILVER AWARD
for the Most Outstanding Individual Pack

Design Director
JOHN BLACKBURN

Designer
JOHN BLACKBURN

Copywriter
DEREK HODGETTS

Typographer
MATT THOMPSON

Illustrator
DOUGLAS SHELDRAKE

Design Group
BLACKBURN'S

Marketing Director
CHRIS ZANETTI

Client
HARVEYS OF BRISTOL

SILVER AWARD
for the Most Outstanding Range of Packaging

Design Director
TODD WATERBURY

Designer
TODD WATERBURY

Copywriter
PETER WEGNER

Typographer
TODD WATERBURY

Illustrators
DANIEL CLOWES
CHARLES BURNS
DAVID COWLES
CALEF BROWN

Agency
WIEDEN & KENNEDY, USA

Vice President, Marketing
BRIAN LANAHAN

Client
THE COCA-COLA COMPANY

SILVER AWARD
for the Most
Outstanding Range of
Packaging

Design Director
MARY LEWIS

Designer
BRYAN CLARK

Copywriter
MARY LEWIS

Typographers
KASIA RUST
MARY LEWIS
BRYAN CLARK

Photographer
STEPHEN HAYWARD

Design Group
LEWIS MOBERLY

Buying Controller
FIONA BAILEY

Client
THE BOOTS
COMPANY PLC

Boots
DUSTERS
100% COTTON
3

Boots
FLOOR CLOTH
TOUGH AND DURABLE
1

Boots
CLEANING CLOTHS
SOFT AND ABSORBENT
2

Boots
WINDOW CLOTH
NON SMEAR, FOR SPARKLING SURFACES
1

SILVER AWARD NOMINATION
for the Most Outstanding Range of Packaging

Design Director
ALAN COLVILLE

Designers
LINDSEY TURNHAM
ALAN COLVILLE

Typographers
LINDSEY TURNHAM
ALAN COLVILLE

Photographer
CLIVE WHITE

Design Group
THE IAN LOGAN DESIGN COMPANY

Group Product Manager
EILEEN NAIRN

Client
THE BOOTS COMPANY PLC

Individual Pack

Design Director
GARY COOKE

Designer
SARAH SHEPHERD

Typographer
SARAH SHEPHERD

Design Group
HORSEMAN COOKE

Client
MAKRO

Individual Pack

Design Director
MARY LEWIS

Designer
LUCILLA
SCRIMGEOUR

Typographer
LUCILLA
SCRIMGEOUR

Design Group
LEWIS MOBERLY

Retail Marketing Manager
SUE MYATT

Client
NEXT PLC

Individual Pack

Design Director
JOHN BLACKBURN

Designer
BELINDA DUGGAN

Copywriter
JOHN BLACKBURN

Typographer
BELINDA DUGGAN

Illustrator
SYD BRAK

Photographer
OWEN SMITH

Design Group
BLACKBURN'S

Marketing Director
CHRIS ZANETTI

Client
COCKBURN'S
SMITHES &
COMPANY LIMITED

Range of Packaging

Design Directors
HARRY PEARCE
DOMENIC LIPPA

Designer
HARRY PEARCE

Copywriter
GILES CALVER

Typographer
HARRY PEARCE

Photographer
RICHARD FOSTER

Design Group
LIPPA PEARCE
DESIGN

Two Wheel Buyer
WAYNE SHEPHERD

Client
HALFORDS LIMITED

Range of Packaging

Design Director
KATHY MILLER

Designer
KATHY MILLER

Typographer
KATHY MILLER

Design Group
MILLER SUTHERLAND

Chairman
LYN HARRIS

Client
HARRIS OILS

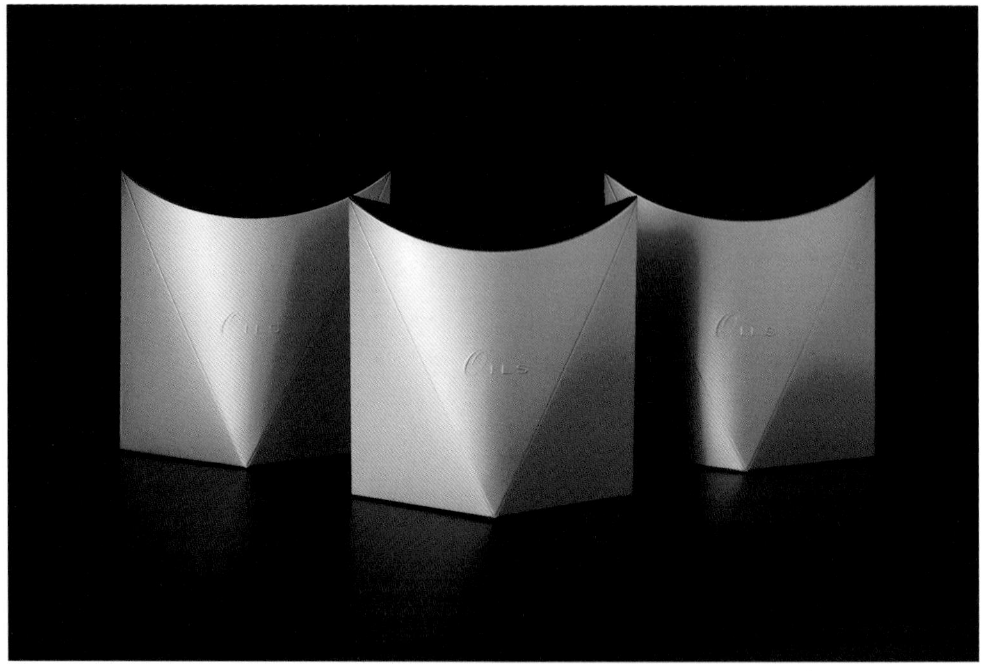

Range of Packaging

Design Directors
STEPHANIE NASH
ANTHONY MICHAEL

Designers
STEPHANIE NASH
ANTHONY MICHAEL

Design Group
MICHAEL NASH ASSOCIATES

Clients
MAUREEN DOHERTY
ASHA SARABHAI

Range of Packaging

Design Director
MARY LEWIS

Designer
BRYAN CLARK

Copywriters
MARY LEWIS
BRYAN CLARK

Typographer
BRYAN CLARK

Design Group
LEWIS MOBERLY

Group Product Manager
CAROLINE STEPHENS

Product Manager
WENDY EARP

Client
THE BOOTS COMPANY PLC

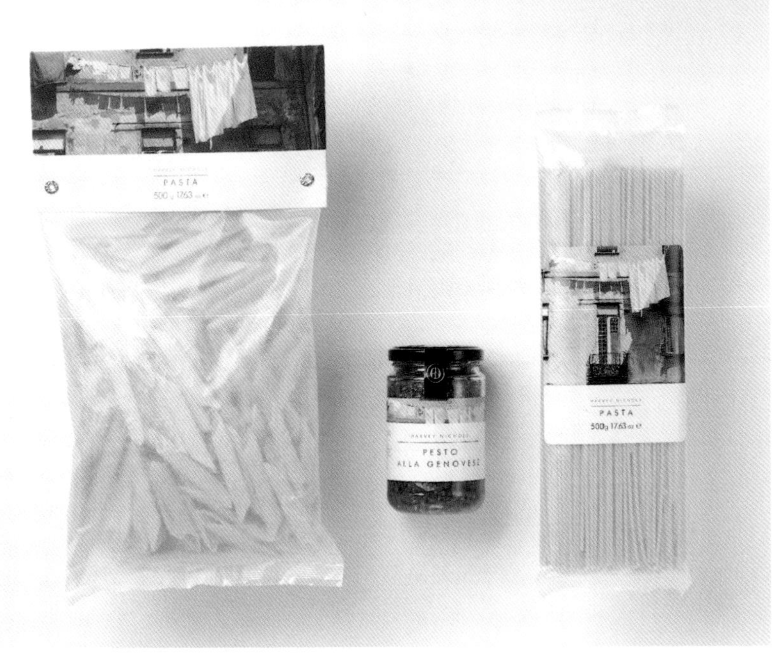

Range of Packaging

Design Directors
STEPHANIE NASH
ANTHONY MICHAEL

Designers
STEPHANIE NASH
ANTHONY MICHAEL
TERESA ROVIRAS

Photographer
TOBY GLANVILLE

Design Group
MICHAEL NASH ASSOCIATES

Director of Food and Beverage
DOMINIC FORD

Client
HARVEY NICHOLS

1995

GRAPHIC DESIGN

Sponsored by James McNaughton Paper Group

SILVER AWARD
for the Most Outstanding Annual Report

Design Director
DANA ARNETT

Designer
CURT SCHREIBER

Copywriters
MICHEAL OAKES
ANITA LISKEY

Photographer
FRANÇOIS ROBERT

Design Group
VSA PARTNERS, INC

Manager of Communication Services
MICHEAL OAKES

Client
CHICAGO BOARD OF TRADE

out cry

"Sell it at
4"
"Sell it at
4"
"Sell it at
4"

bid

offer

SILVER AWARD
for the Most Outstanding Direct Mail

Design Director
JOHN RUSHWORTH

Designers
JOHN RUSHWORTH
VINCE FROST
CHIEW YONG

Copywriter
PETER LESTER

Typographers
JOHN RUSHWORTH
VINCE FROST
CHIEW YONG

Design Group
PENTAGRAM DESIGN

Marketing Executive
CHARLIE YIANOULLOU

Client
POLAROID UK LIMITED

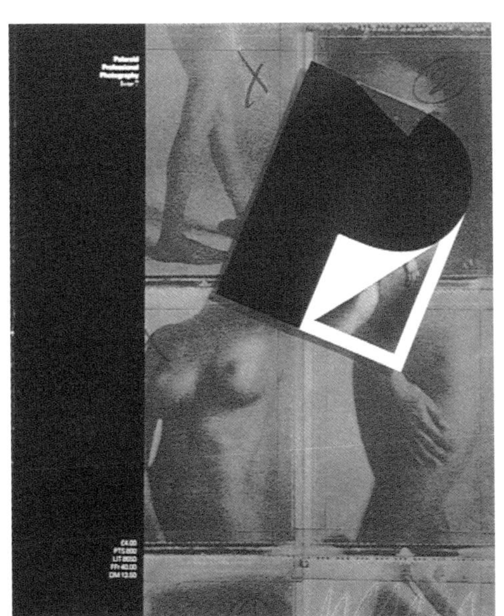

SILVER AWARD
for the Most Outstanding Direct Mail

Designers
LYNN TRICKETT
BRIAN WEBB
STEVE EDWARDS

Copywriter
NEIL MATTINGLEY

Design Group
TRICKETT & WEBB

Marketing Executive
CHARLES SWAN

Clients
THE SIMKINS PARTNERSHIP
ADVERTISING LAW INTERNATIONAL

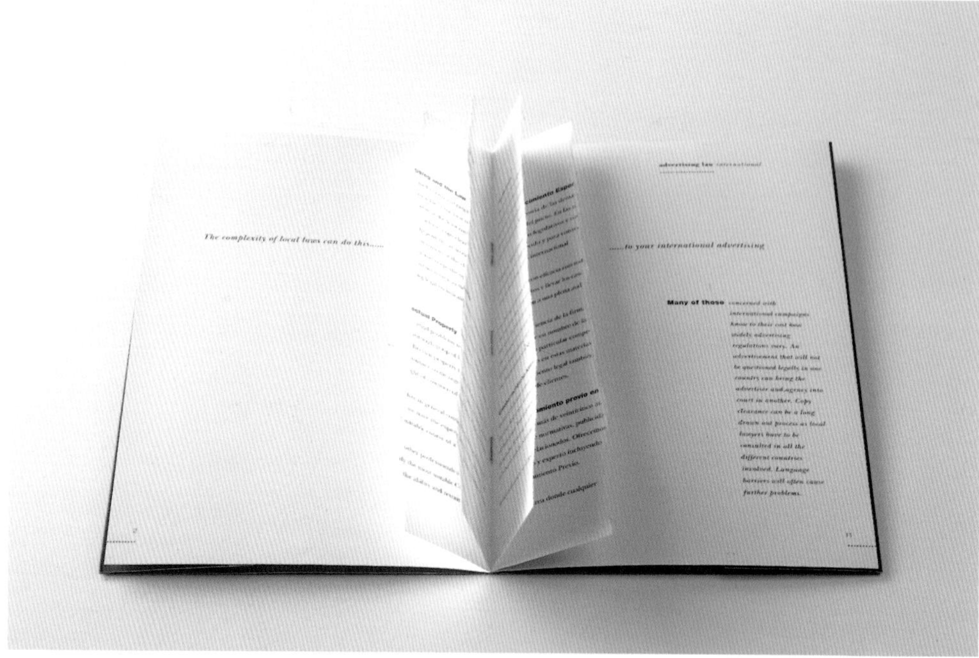

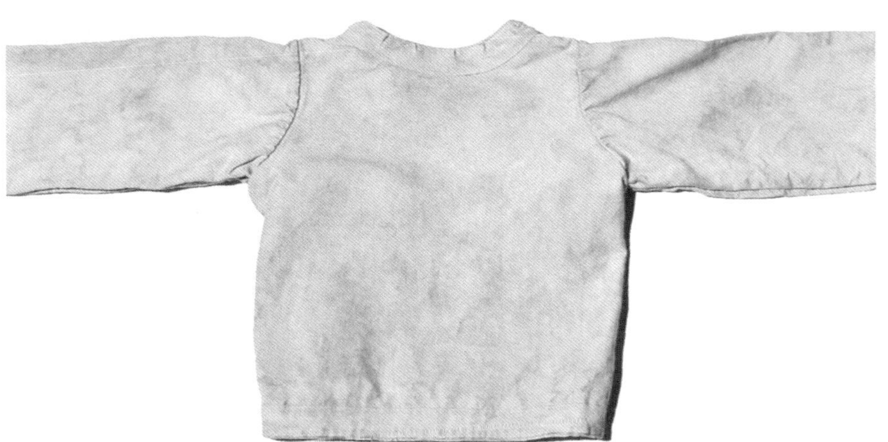

YESTERDAY, WHEN I WAS MAD.
PET SHOP BOYS

SILVER AWARD
for the Most Outstanding Individual Poster

Design Directors
MARK FARROW
NEIL TENNANT
CHRIS LOWE

Designers
PHIL SIMS
MARK FARROW
ROB PETRIE

Typographers
PHIL SIMS
MARK FARROW
ROB PETRIE

Photographer
RICHARD J. BURBRIDGE

Design Group
FARROW

Client
PSBP

SILVER AWARD
for the Most Outstanding Compact Disc and Record Sleeve

Design Directors
MARK FARROW
NEIL TENNANT
CHRIS LOWE

Designers
ROB PETRIE
MARK FARROW
PHIL SIMS

Typographers
PHIL SIMS
MARK FARROW
ROB PETRIE

Photographer
RICHARD J. BURBRIDGE

Design Group
FARROW

Client
PSBP

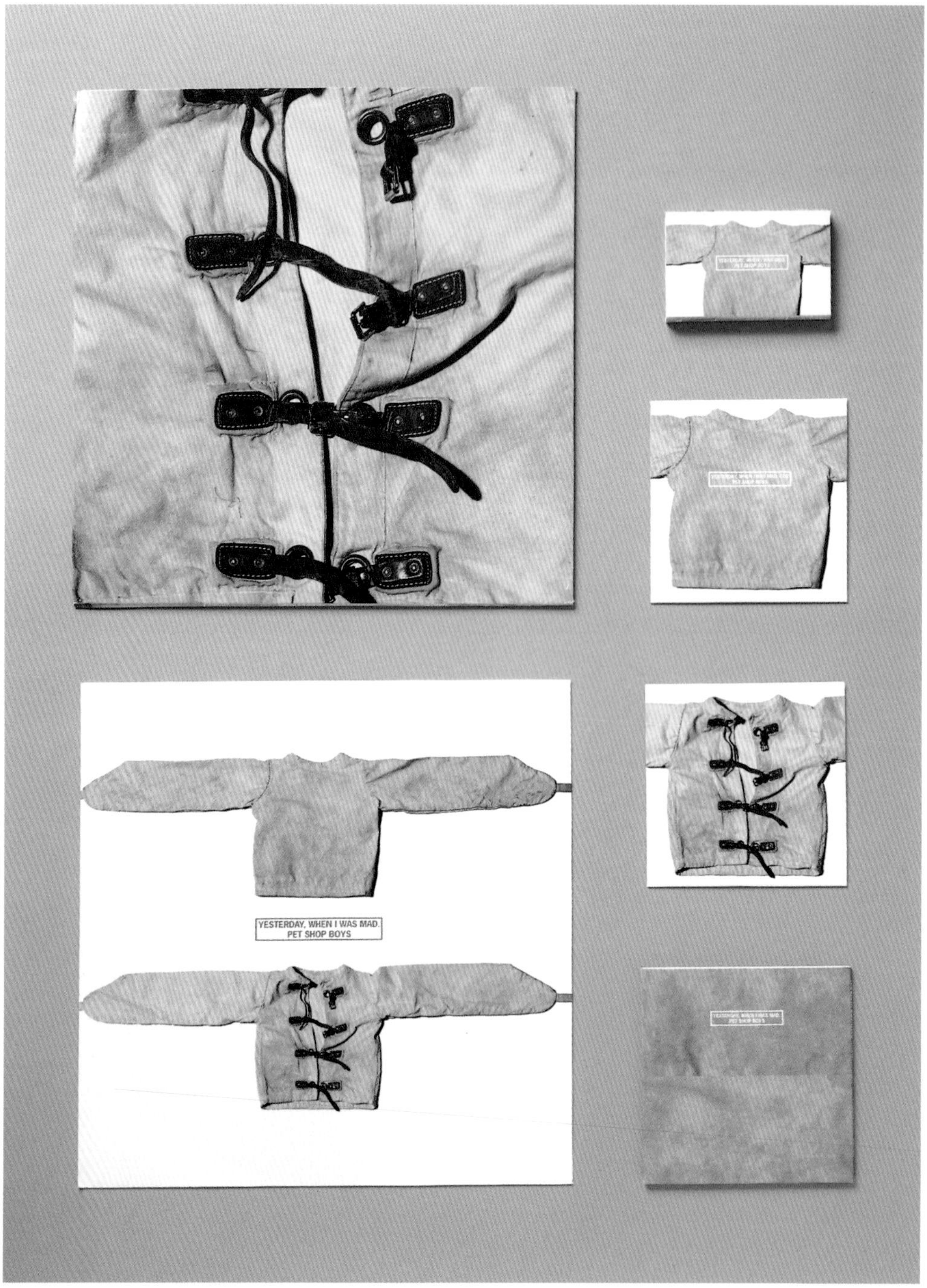

SILVER AWARD
for the Most Outstanding Compact Disc and Record Sleeve Campaign

Design Directors
STEPHANIE NASH
ANTHONY MICHAEL

Designers
STEPHANIE NASH
ANTHONY MICHAEL

Photographer
MATTHEW DONALDSON

Design Group
MICHAEL NASH ASSOCIATES

Head of Marketing
DANNY VAN EMDEN

Client
CIRCA RECORDS

SILVER AWARD
for the Most Outstanding Graphic Design Any Other

Design Directors
FRANCK SARFATI
OLIVIER STÉNUIT
JOEL VAN AUDENHAEGE

Designers
FRANCK SARFATI
OLIVIER STÉNUIT
JOEL VAN AUDENHAEGE

Typographers
FRANCK SARFATI
OLIVIER STÉNUIT
JOEL VAN AUDENHAEGE

Photographer
CHARLES VAN HOORIJK

Design Group
SIGN

Client
SIGN

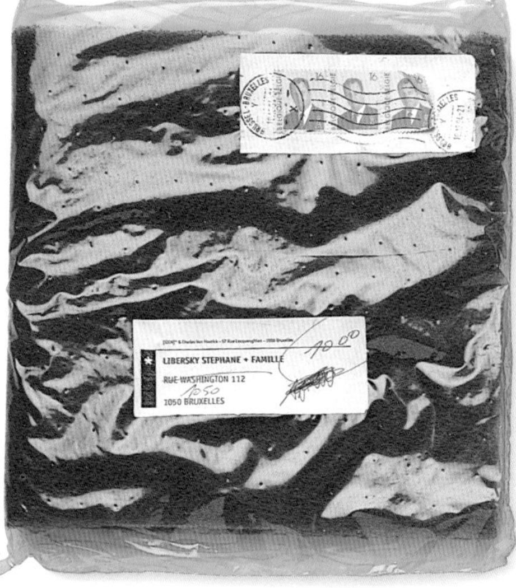

celebrate
DIVERSITY

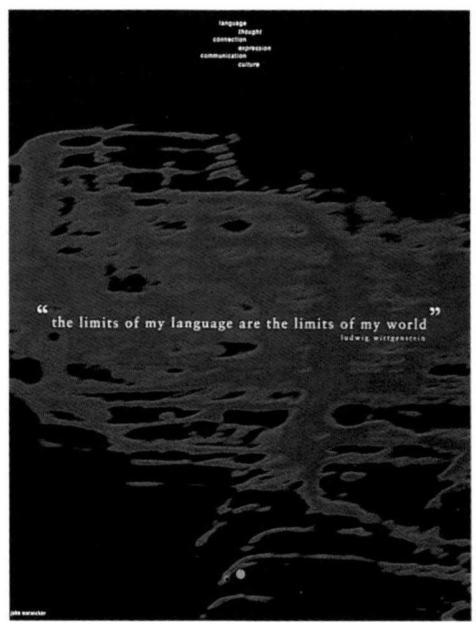

SILVER AWARD NOMINATION
for the Most Outstanding Brochure

Design Directors
JOHN WARWICKER
SIMON TAYLOR

Designers
CHRIS ASHWORTH
DAVID SMITH
JOHN WARWICKER
SIMON TAYLOR

Copywriters
JARON LANIER
MICHAEL HORSHAM
JOHN WARWICKER
CHRIS STEPHENSON
HIS HOLINESS THE DALAI LAMA

Typographers
CHRIS ASHWORTH
DAVID SMITH
JOHN WARWICKER
SIMON TAYLOR

Design Groups
TOMATO
INVISIBLE

Vice President, Marketing
CHRIS STEPHENSON

Client
MTV EUROPE

SILVER AWARD NOMINATION
for the Most Outstanding Brochure

Design Director
ALAN ABOUD

Designer
ALAN ABOUD

Typographers
TIM SPENCER
NICK FOLEY-OATES

Photographer
JULIAN BROAD

Design Group
ABOUD.SODANO

Client
PAUL SMITH LIMITED

THE CITY OF WESTMINSTER
ROAD SWEEPER'S JACKET.

THE GPO IS BASED ON
A SHIRT MANUFACTURED BY
R.NEWBOLD FOR THE
GENERAL POST OFFICE.

SILVER AWARD NOMINATION
for the Most Outstanding Brochure

Design Director
DANA ARNETT

Designer
CURT SCHREIBER

Copywriter
NANCY LERNER

Photographer
FRANÇOIS ROBERT

Design Group
VSA PARTNERS, INC

Marketing Executive
JIM LADWIG

Client
AGI, INC

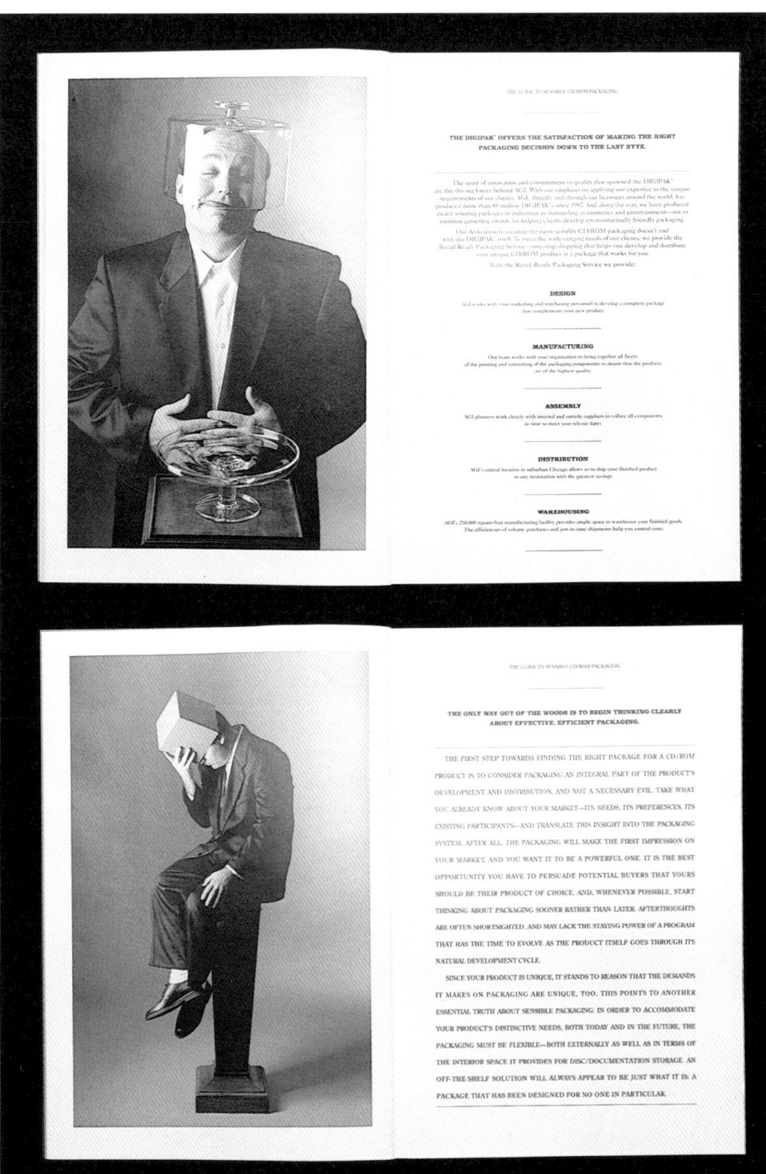

SILVER AWARD NOMINATION
for the Most Outstanding Brochure

Design Director
MARIA GRILLO

Designers
MARIA GRILLO
TIM BRUCE

Photographer
PETER FRAHM

Design Group
VSA PARTNERS, INC

Marketing Executives
LAURA SHORE
BETH BRIADDY

Client
MOHAWK PAPER MILLS, INC

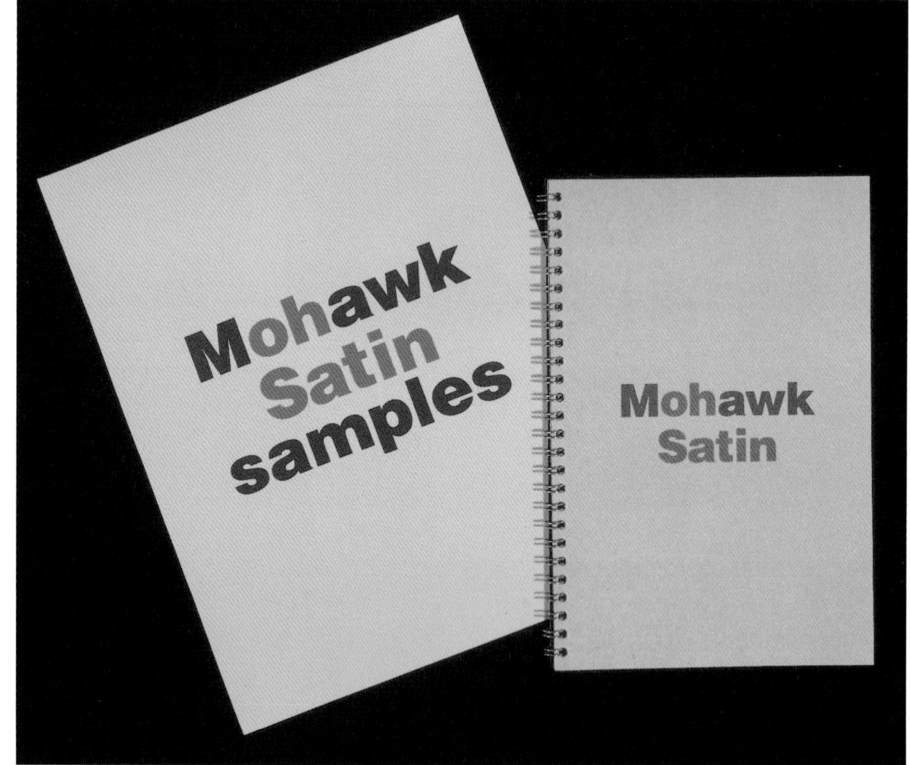

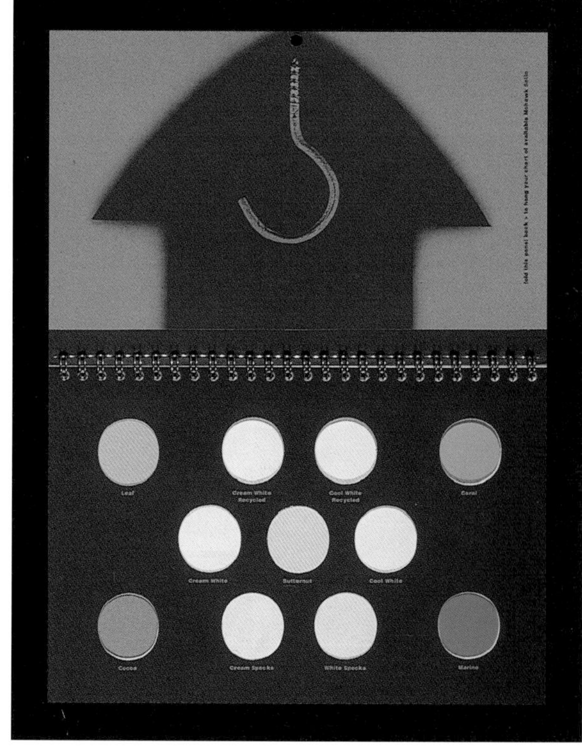

SILVER AWARD NOMINATION
for the Most Outstanding Catalogue

Design Directors
GIOVANNI BIANCO
SUSANNA CUCCO

Designers
GIOVANNI BIANCO
SUSANNA CUCCO

Copywriters
FRANCESCA PAGLIARINI
GIORGIO ANZANI

Illustrator
ANTONELLA PORTFIDO

Photographer
PAOLO LEONE

Design Group
BIANCO & CUCCO

Public Relations and Image Communication Manager
MARCO BRUSAMOLIN

Client
ITIERRE SPA FOR DOLCE & GABBANA

SILVER AWARD NOMINATION
for the most outstanding Catalogue

Design Directors
GIOVANNI BIANCO
SUSANNA CUCCO

Designers
GIOVANNI BIANCO
SUSANNA CUCCO

Copywriter
JOAO CARRASCOSA

Typographer
GIORGIO ANZANI

Photographer
ROBERTO CECATO

Design Group
BIANCO & CUCCO

Client
BRAZILIAN COUNCIL, MILAN

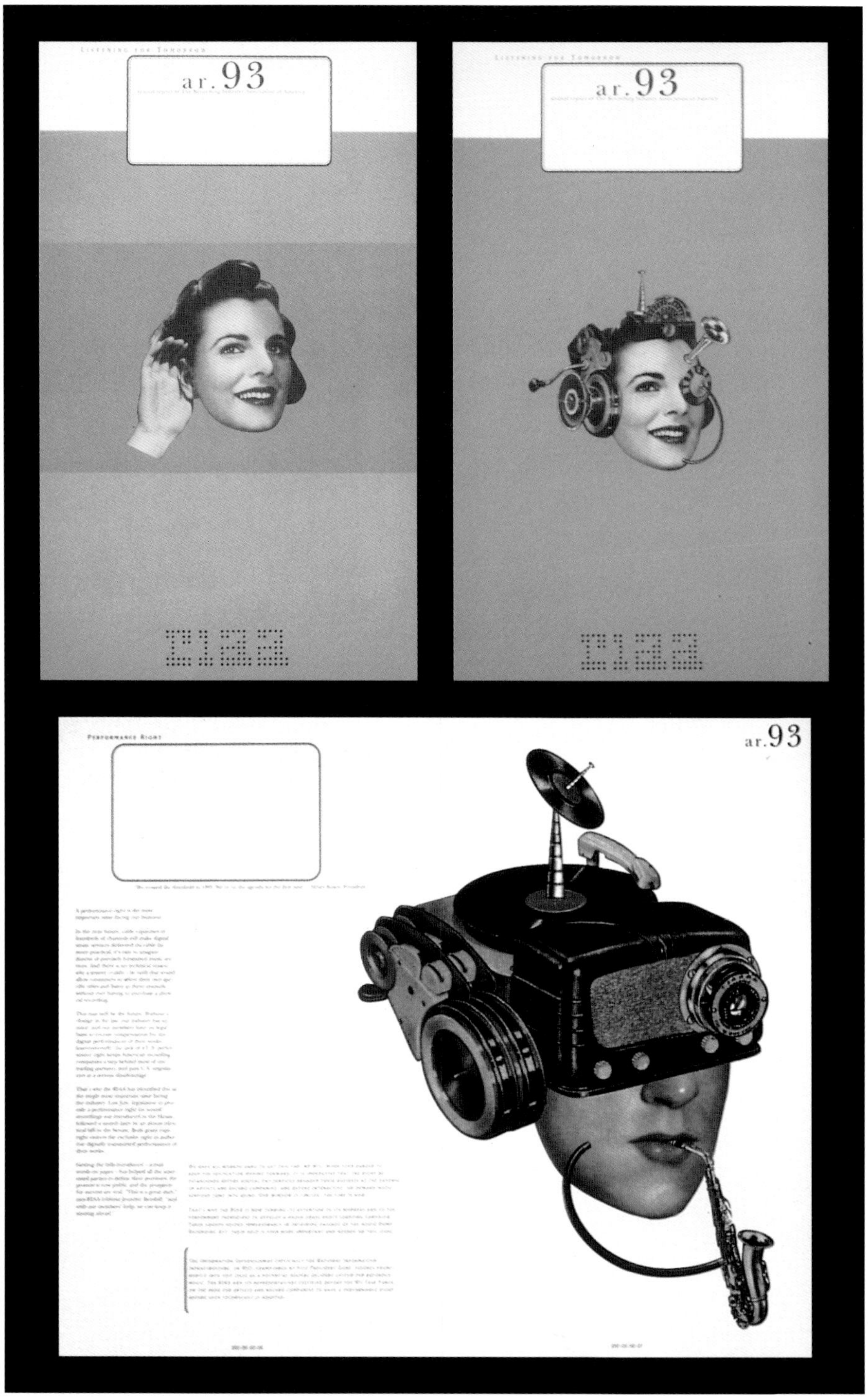

SILVER AWARD NOMINATION
for the Most Outstanding Annual Report

Design Director
NEAL ASHBY

Designer
NEAL ASHBY

Copywriter
FRED GUTHRIE

Typographer
NEAL ASHBY

Illustrator
DAVE PLUNKERT

Photographer
STEVE BIVER

Design Group
RECORDING INDUSTRY ASSOCIATION OF AMERICA

Client
RECORDING INDUSTRY ASSOCIATION OF AMERICA

SILVER AWARD NOMINATION
for the Most Outstanding Annual Report

Designer
ANDREA FUCHS

Editor
DR O.RIEWOLDT

Typographer
ANDREA FUCHS

Photographers
LEX VAN PIETERSON
GERRIT SCHREURS

Design Group
STUDIO DUMBAR

Client
ZUMTOBEL HOLDING AG

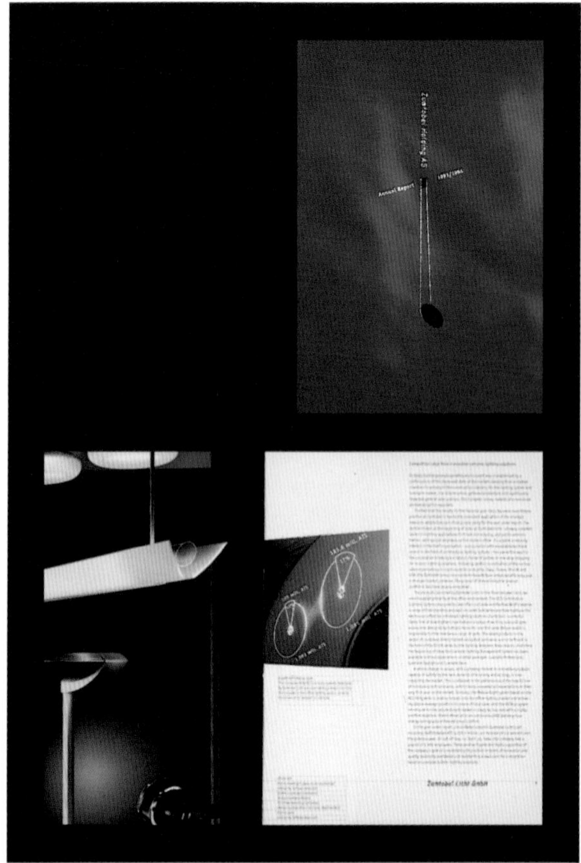

SILVER AWARD NOMINATION
for the Most Outstanding Direct Mail

Design Director
DAVID STUART

Designer
DAVID STUART

Copywriter
PETER COLLINGWOOD

Typographer
ROSA LOEFFEL

Design Group
THE PARTNERS

Client
THE DESIGN COUNCIL

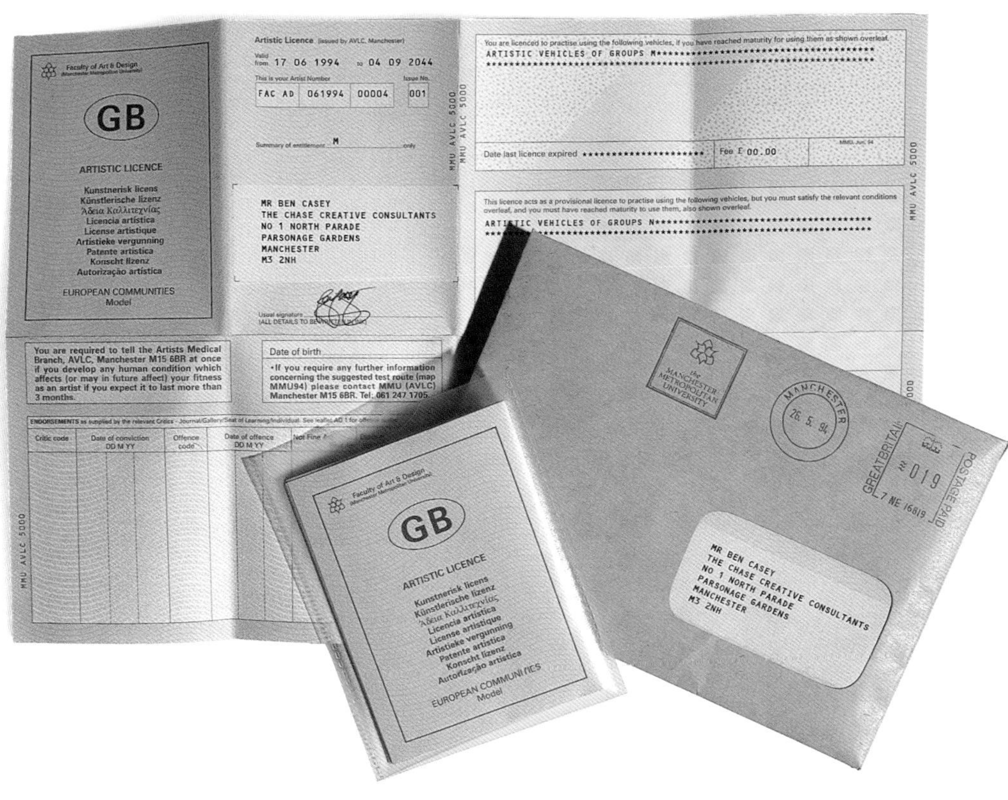

SILVER AWARD NOMINATION
for the Most Outstanding Direct Mail

Design Director
BEN CASEY

Designers
MARK HURST
CHARLIE HOLMES

Copywriters
MARK HURST
CHARLIE HOLMES

Design Group
THE CHASE CREATIVE CONSULTANTS

Pro Vice-Chancellor and Dean of Faculty
PROFESSOR ROGER WILSON

Client
MANCHESTER METROPOLITAN UNIVERSITY, FACULTY OF ART & DESIGN

SILVER AWARD NOMINATION
for the Most Outstanding Direct Mail

Design Director
SUE TURNER

Designer
SUE TURNER

Copywriter
IAN HENDERSON

Typographer
SUE TURNER

Illustrator
SALLY HYNARD

Design Group
BASTEN GREENHILL ANDREWS

Marketing Executive
FLOYD TIMMS

Client
HONDA UK

SILVER AWARD NOMINATION
for the Most Outstanding Calendar

Design Director
AZIZ CAMI

Designer
ANDREW HOWELL

Design Group
THE PARTNERS

Marketing Executive
PATRICK WILSON

Client
THRISLINGTON CUBICLES

SILVER AWARD NOMINATION
for the Most Outstanding Calendar

Design Director
BEN CASEY

Designer
MARK HURST

Design Group
THE CHASE CREATIVE CONSULTANTS

Director
THOMAS P. KEARNS

Client
SPECTRUM PRESS

SILVER AWARD NOMINATION
for the Most Outstanding Calendar

Design Director
PETER RAE

Designers
PAUL HOLDEN
DENNIS OU
MIKE CHAN

Typographers
PETER RAE
PAUL HOLDEN
MIKE CHAN
DENNIS OU

Photographer
ARTHUR SCHULTEN

Design Group
LEO BURNETT DESIGN GROUP, HONG KONG

Director of Marketing and Operations
BILL BETTENCOURT

Associate Account Director
JONATHAN BANNISTER

Client
REEBOK INTERNATIONAL

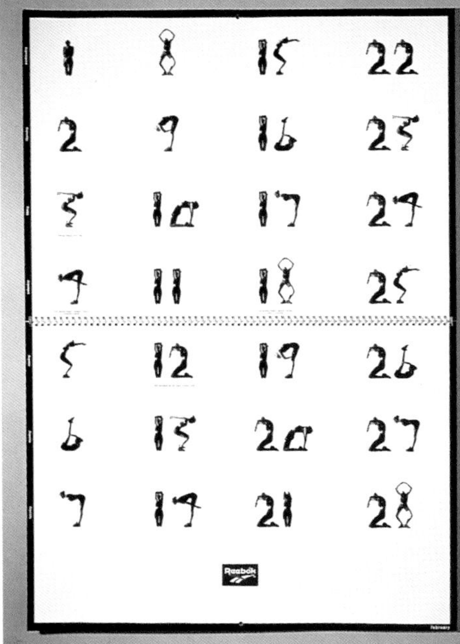

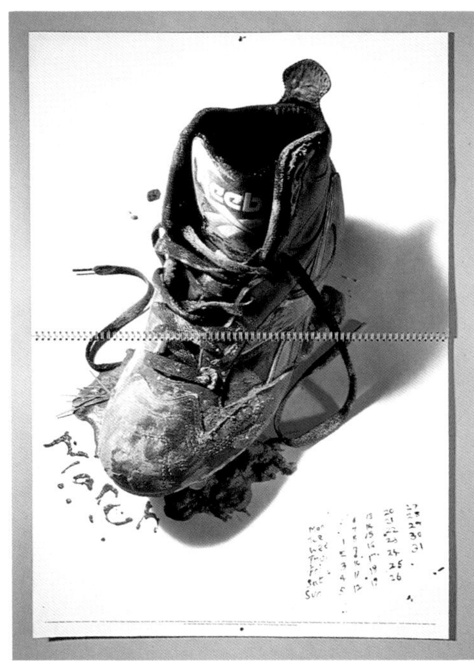

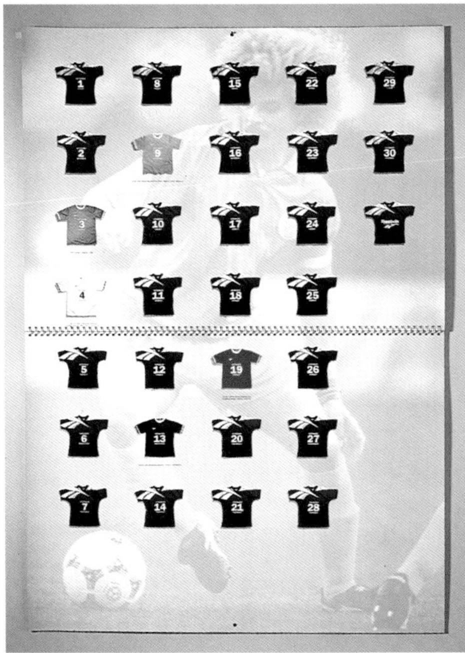

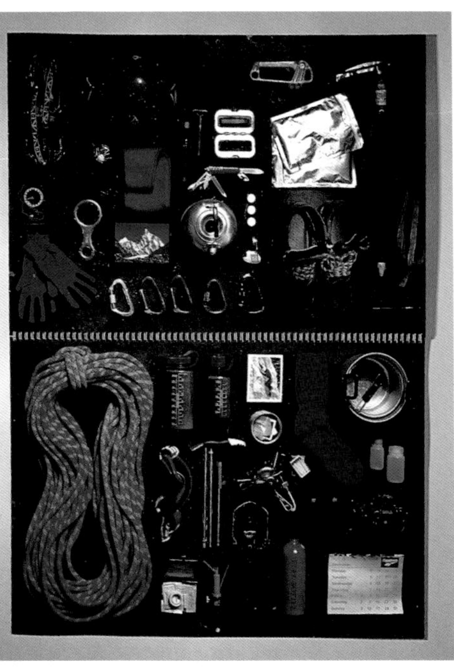

SILVER AWARD NOMINATION
for the Most Outstanding Individual Poster

Design Director
JOHN RUSHWORTH

Designers
JOHN RUSHWORTH
CHIEW YONG

Photographer
GILES REVELL

Design Group
PENTAGRAM DESIGN

Marketing Executive
DON DAVIDSON

Client
GANNETT OUTDOOR GROUP

SILVER AWARD NOMINATION
for the Most Outstanding Individual Poster

Design Directors
JACQUES KOEWEIDEN
PAUL POSTMA

Designers
JACQUES KOEWEIDEN
PAUL POSTMA

Typographers
JACQUES KOEWEIDEN
PAUL POSTMA

Photographers
GYULA KARDOS
ROBBERT FELS

Design Group
KOEWEIDEN POSTMA ASSOCIATES

Client
KOEWEIDEN POSTMA ASSOCIATES

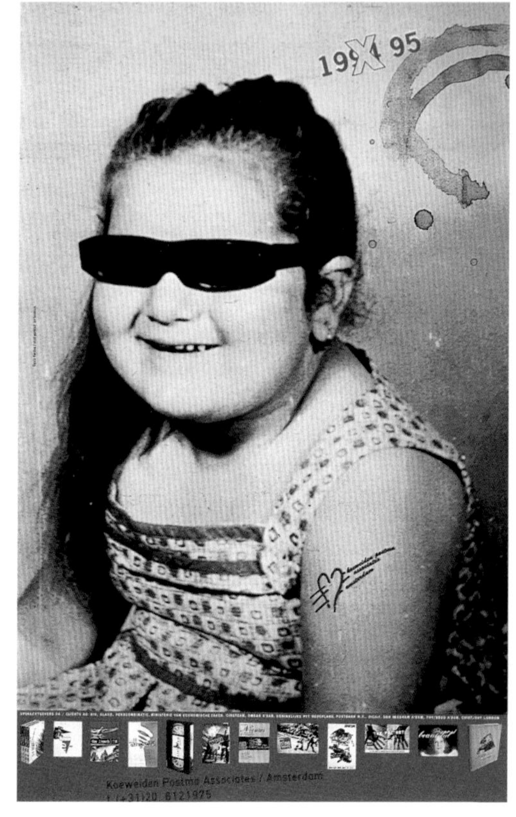

SILVER AWARD NOMINATION
for the Most Outstanding Poster Campaign

Art Director
JOHN C. JAY

Designers
CHRIS SHIPMAN
PETRA LANGHAMMER
JOHN C. JAY

Creative Director
DAN WIEDEN

Photographer
STANLEY BACH

Agency
WIEDEN & KENNEDY, USA

Client
NIKE N.Y.C.

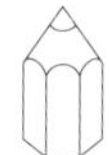

SILVER AWARD NOMINATION
for the Most Outstanding Poster Campaign

Design Director
MICHAEL JOHNSON

Designers
MICHAEL JOHNSON
NINA JENKINS
LUKE GIFFORD

Copywriter
MICHAEL JOHNSON

Typographers
MICHAEL JOHNSON
NINA JENKINS
LUKE GIFFORD

Photographer
MARTIN BARRAUD

Design Group
JOHNSON BANKS

Marketing Manager
WENDY MORRELL

Client
JAMES McNAUGHTON PAPER

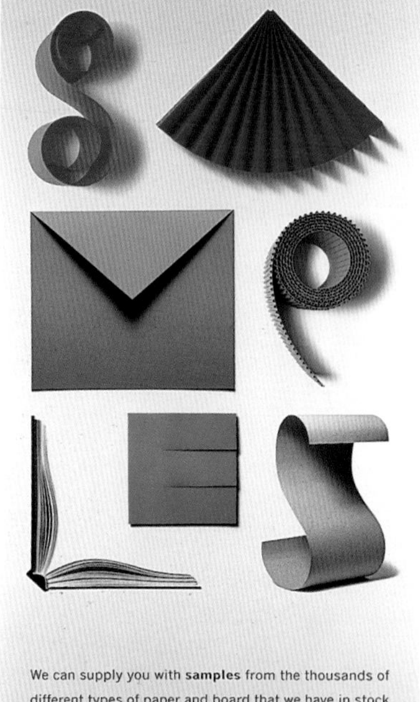

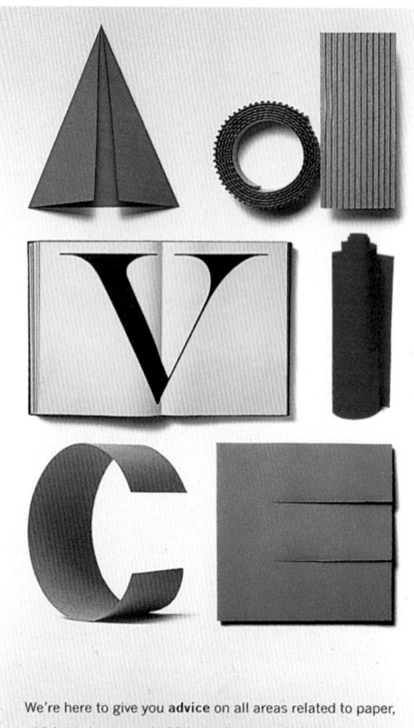

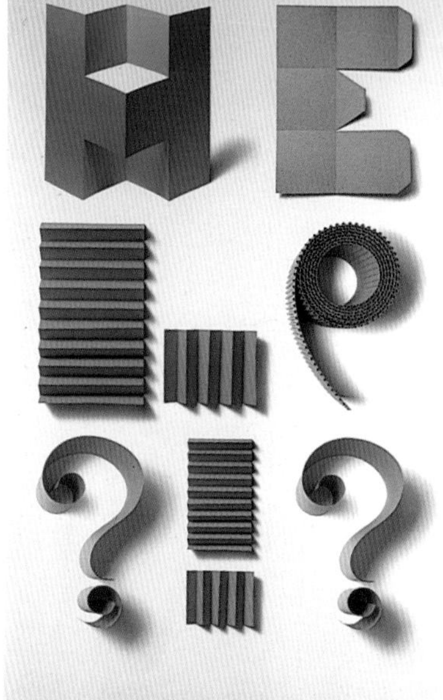

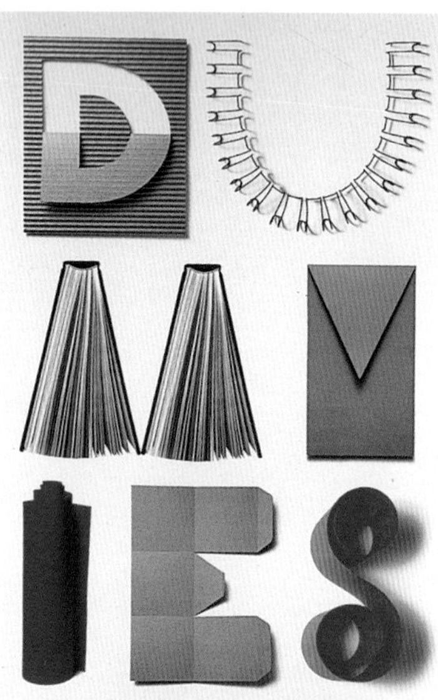

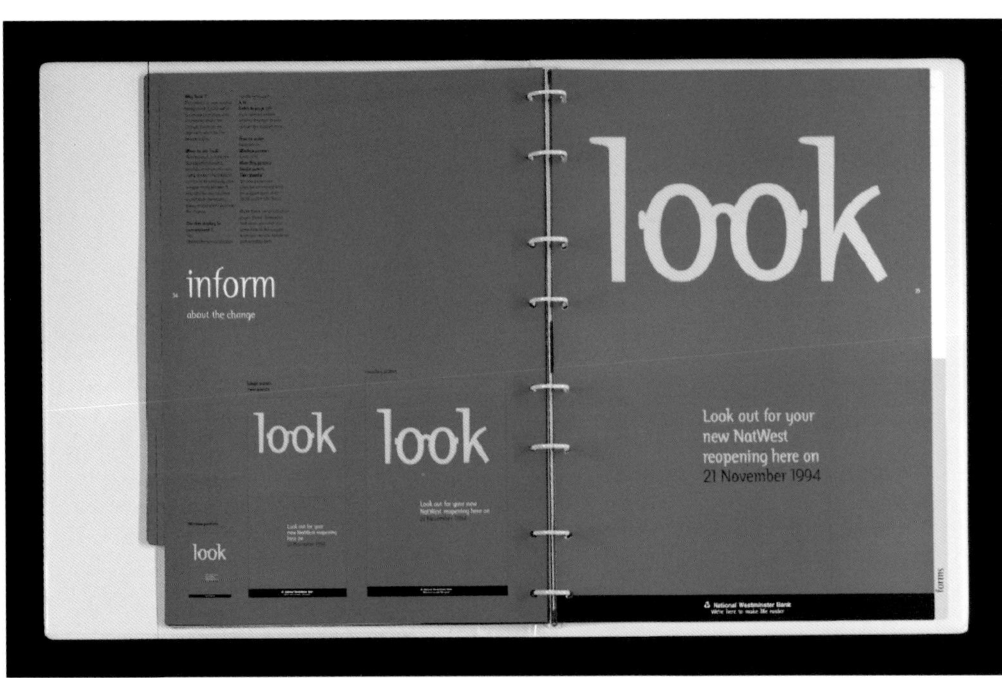

Technical Literature

Design Director
CHRIS BRADLEY

Designers
CHRIS BRADLEY
STUART RUSSELL

Copywriters
SUE NIPPARD
KIRSTY MORAN

Typographer
CHRIS BRADLEY

Illustrators
CHRIS BRADLEY
STUART RUSSELL
ANTHONY BILES

Design Group
SMITH & MILTON
ORIGINAL

Advertising Manager
EDWARD PERTWEE

Client
NATIONAL
WESTMINSTER BANK
PLC

Technical Literature

Design Director
NICHOLAS THIRKELL

Designer
NEIL WALKER

Editor
TOM LLOYD

Typographers
NEIL WALKER
KERRY HUMPHREYS

Design Group
CDT DESIGN

Marketing Executive
PETER BIELBY

Client
GEMINI CONSULTING

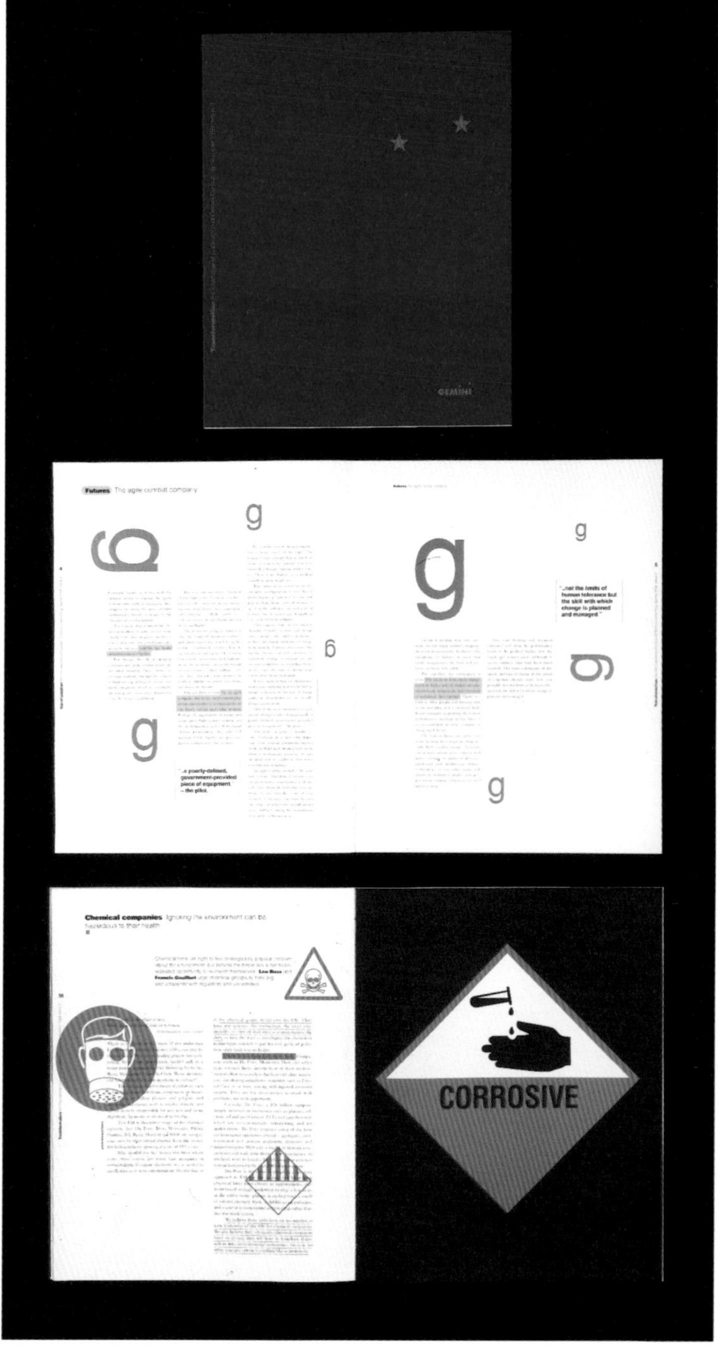

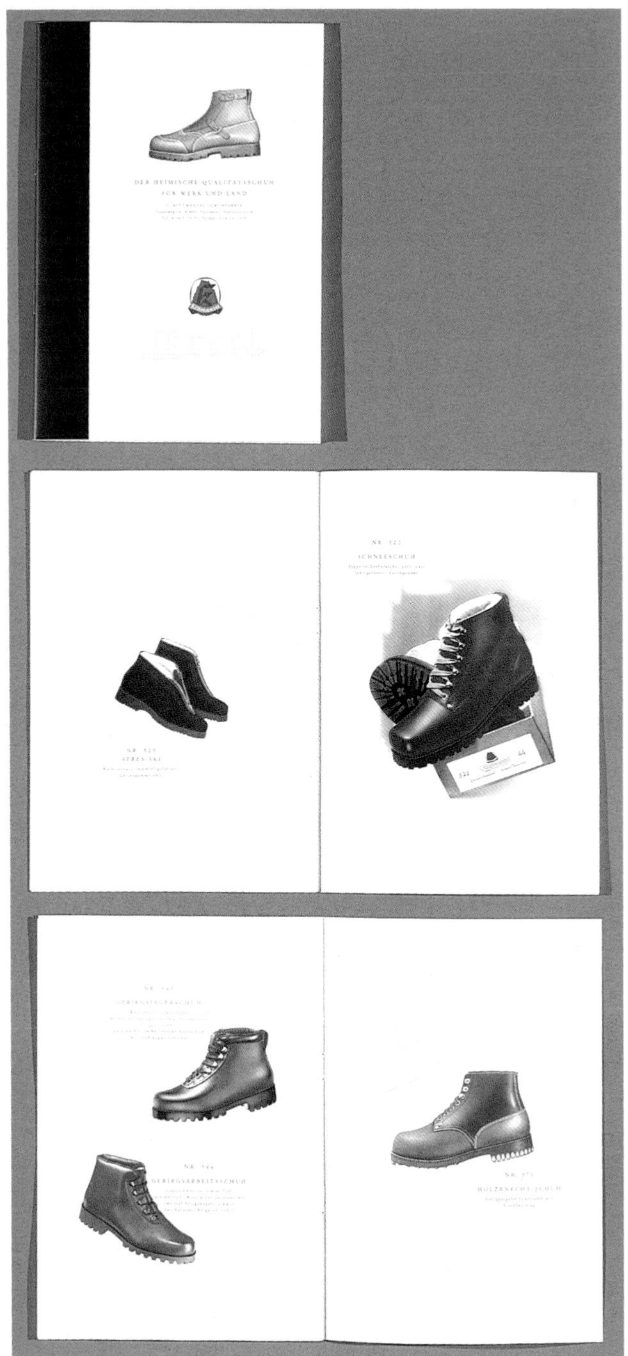

Brochures

Design Director
SIGI MAYER

Designer
SIGI MAYER

Copywriter
A. RICHTER

Typographer
SIGI MAYER

Photographer
HORST STASNY

Design Group
SIGI MAYER
PROJEKTAGENTUR

Marketing Executive
C. WEIXLBAUMER

Clients
A. RICHTER
KITZMANTEL
SCHUHMANIFAKTUR

Brochures

Design Director
PETER CHODEL

Designer
MIKE TURNER

Copywriter
JOE LANG

Typographer
MIKE TURNER

Photographer
FI McGHEE

Design Group
ADDISON DESIGN
COMPANY LIMITED

Client
AXIA ASSET
MANAGEMENT S.A.

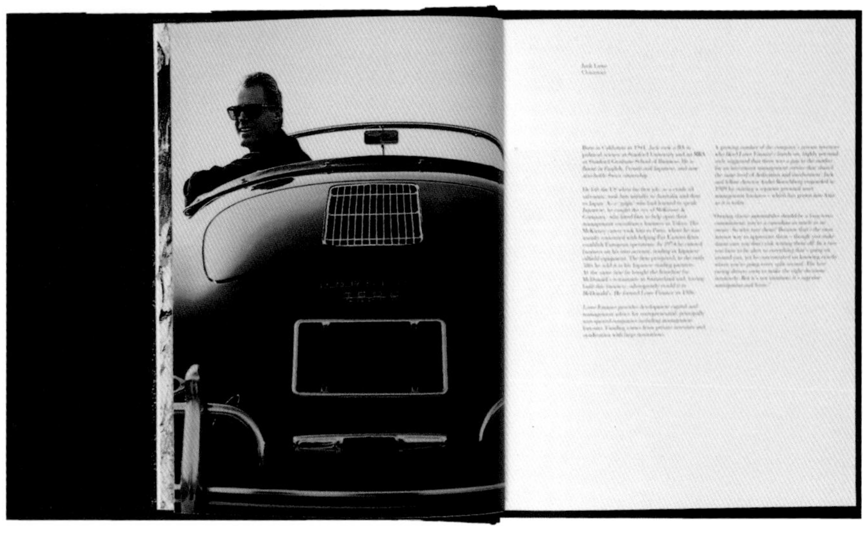

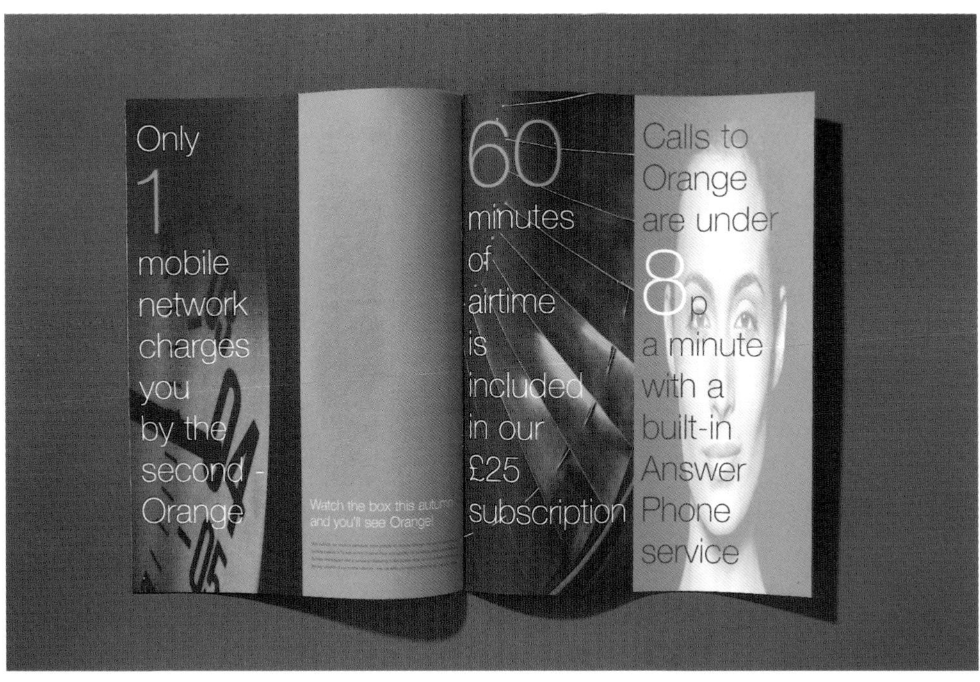

Brochures

Design Directors
DOMENIC LIPPA
HARRY PEARCE

Designer
RACHAEL DINNIS

Copywriter
GILES CALVER

Typographer
RACHAEL DINNIS

Design Group
LIPPA PEARCE
DESIGN LIMITED

Customer Communications Manager
KAREN MOTE

Client
ORANGE PERSONAL
COMMUNICATIONS
SERVICES LIMITED

Brochures

Design Director
SEAN PERKINS

Designers
KATE TREGONING
PAUL WINTER
ADRIAN CADDY
BRYAN EDMONDSON

Copywriter
ANDREA L. FINTER

Typographer
SEAN PERKINS

Photographers
RICHARD J.
BURBRIDGE
FI McGHEE

Design Group
IMAGINATION

Marketing Executives
TONY SHEERING
ANDREA L. FINTER

Client
INTERCRAFT

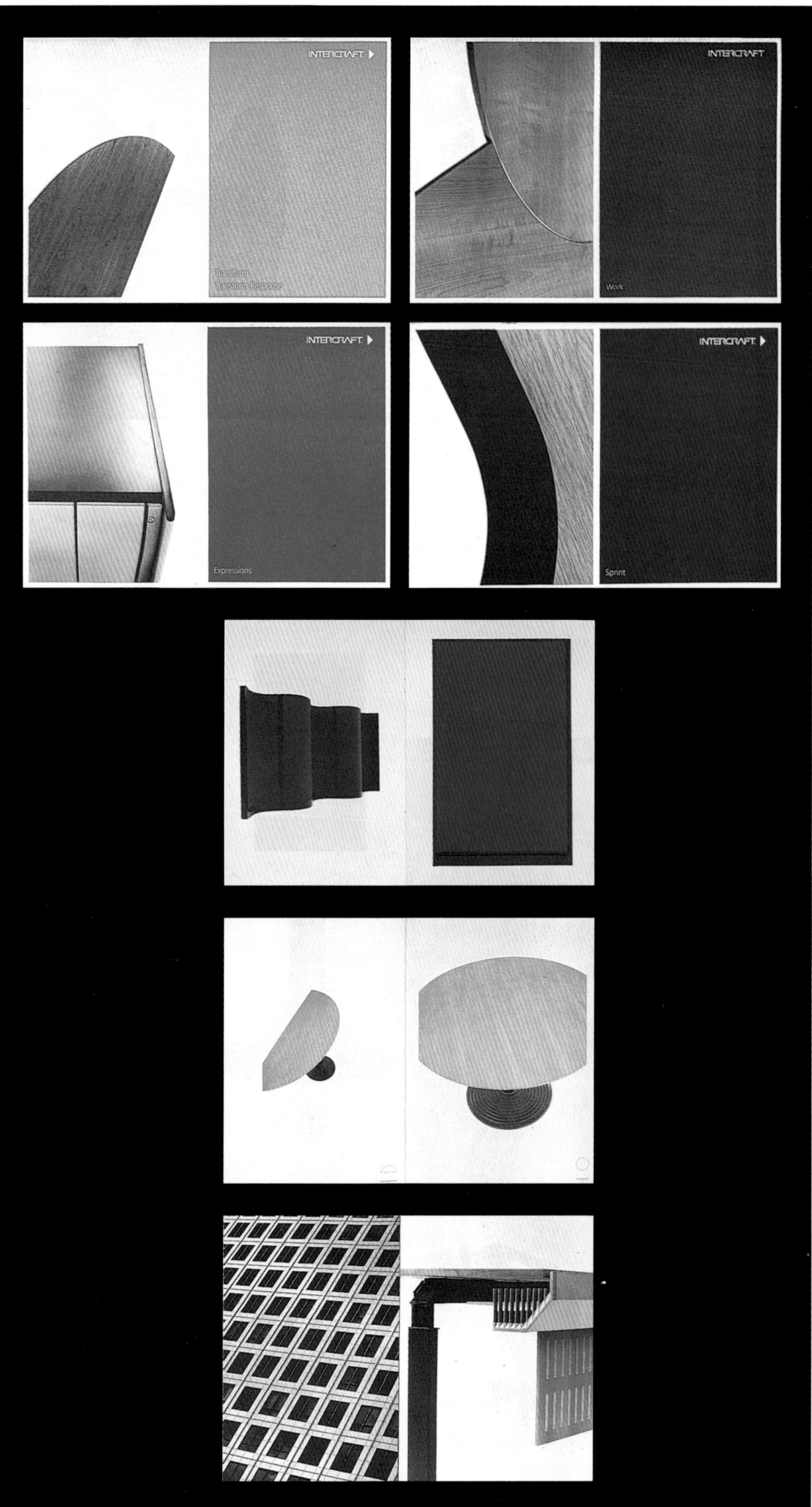

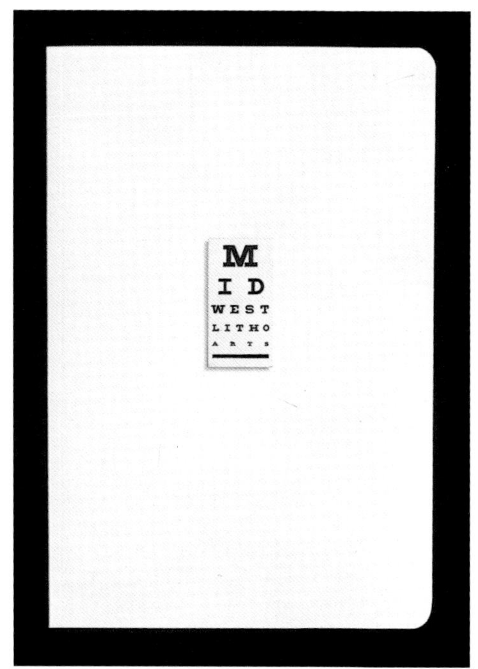

Brochures

Design Director
JAMES KOVAL

Designer
JAMES KOVAL

Copywriters
LINDA LAWRENCE
JOHN NITTI

Photographer
PAUL ELLEDGE

Design Group
VSA PARTNERS, INC

Vice President, Sales and Marketing
JOHN NITTI

Client
MIDWEST LITHO ARTS

Brochures

Design Director
CRAIG HUTTON

Designer
CRAIG HUTTON

Copywriter
CHIK LYNN

Typographer
CRAIG HUTTON

Photographer
HATTY GOTTSCHALK

Client
SIMEX

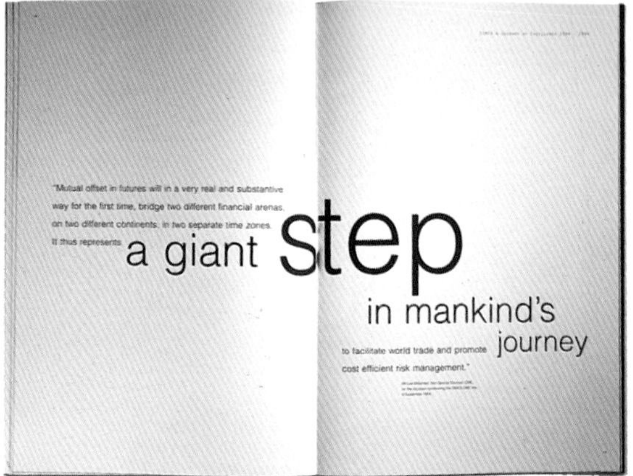

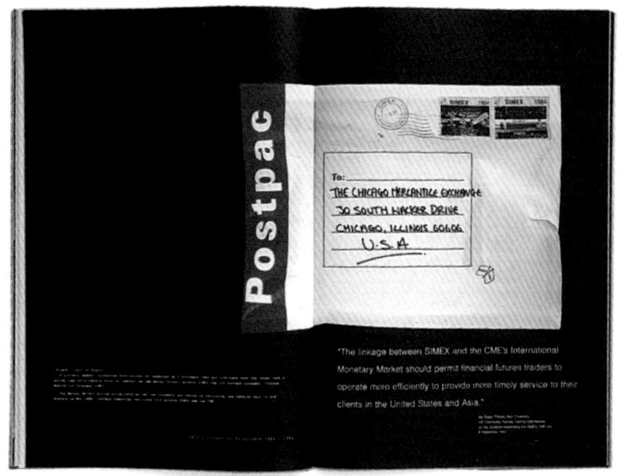

Catalogues

Design Director
ROBIN ROUT

Designer
ROBIN ROUT

Copywriter
ROBIN ROUT

Typographer
ROBIN ROUT

Photographer
JAMES MERRELL

Design Group
PHOTOGRAFT

Marketing Executive
IAIN RENWICK

Client
HABITAT UK

Catalogues

Design Director
TERESA ROVIRAS

Designer
TERESA ROVIRAS

Typographer
TERESA ROVIRAS

Photographers
BELA ADLER
RUIZ ARAGO

Design Group
TERESA ROVIRAS

Marketing Director
IGNACIO MALET

Clients
ANTONIO MIRO
ERMENEGILDO
ZEGNA

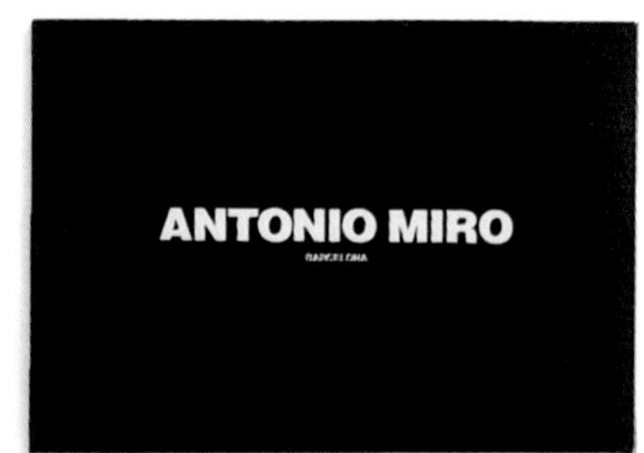

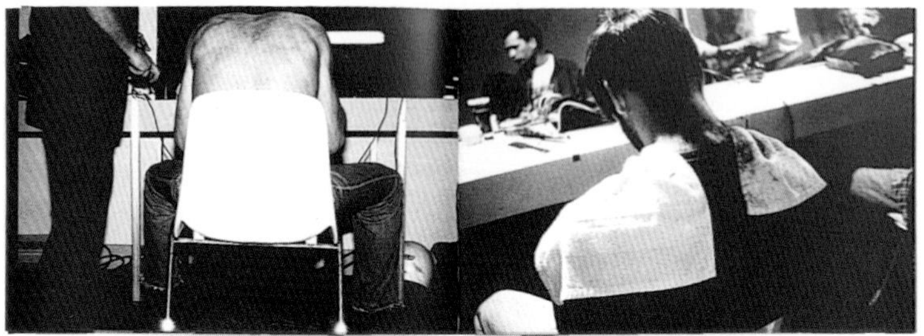

Annual Reports

Design Director
HANS BOCKTING

Designers
HANS BOCKTING
WILL DE L'ECLUSE

Copywriter
MEGHAN FERRILL

Typographer
WILL DE L'ECLUSE

Photographer
LEX VAN PIETERSON

Design Group
UNA

General Manager
A.W. JONKER

Client
F. VAN LANSCHOT
BANKIERS

Annual Reports

Designer
KATE STEPHENS

Sculptor
ANTONY GORMLEY

Director General
COLIN TWEEDY

Client
ABSA

Annual Reports

Design Director
JAMES KOVAL

Designer
JO-ANN BOUTIN

Copywriter
JOHN HARRIS

Illustrators
BILL GRAHAM
ILENE ROBINETTE

Photographer
HOWARD BJORNSON

Design Group
VSA PARTNERS, INC

Director of Communications
JOHN HARRIS

Client
THE MARMON GROUP

Direct Mail

Designers
IAN DAVID
DAVID WHITE

Copywriters
IAN DAVID
DAVID WHITE

Marketing Executive
MARK GORDON

Client
CALEDONIAN
PLUMBING

Direct Mail

Design Director
DAVID STUART

Designers
KATE EMAMOODEN
PETER CARROW

Copywriter
PETER
COLLINGWOOD

Typographer
KATE EMAMOODEN

Photographer
JOHN STONE

Design Group
THE PARTNERS

Marketing Executive
LISA BARWICK

Client
THE DESIGN
COUNCIL

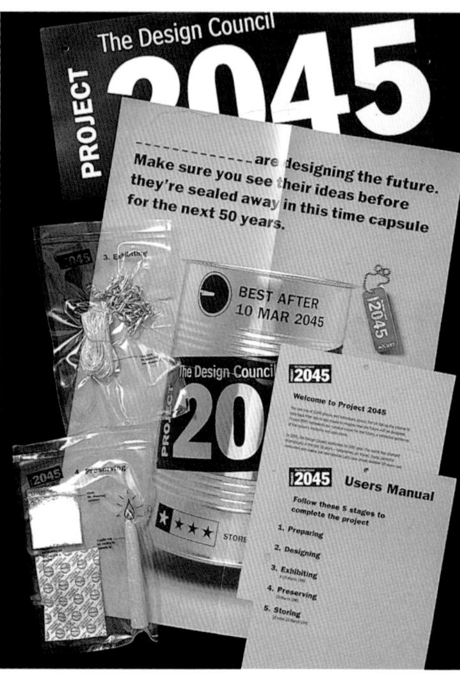

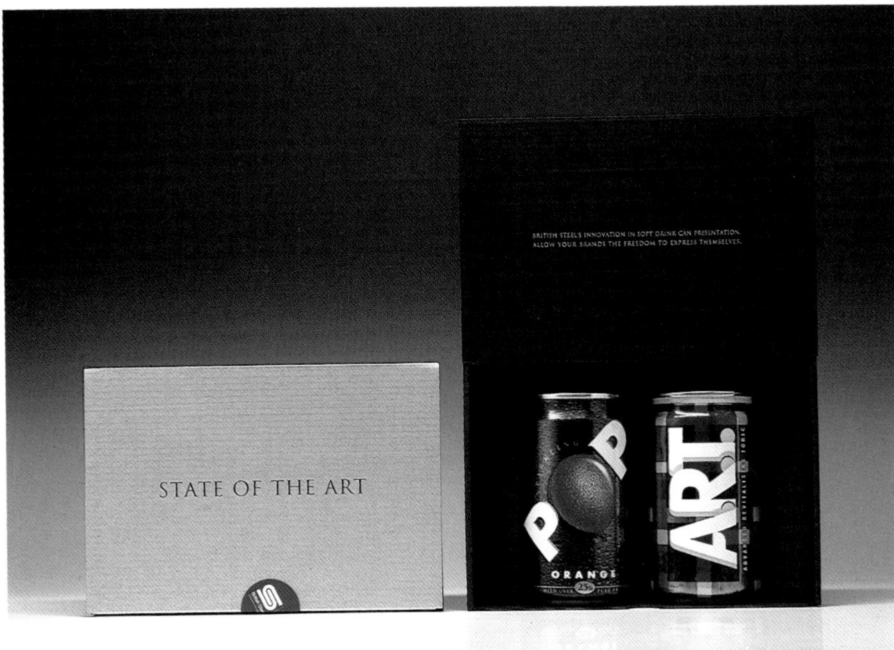

Direct Mail

Design Directors
BRUCE DUCKWORTH
DAVID TURNER

Designers
BRUCE DUCKWORTH
DAVID TURNER
JANICE L. DAVISON

Copywriter
BRUCE DUCKWORTH

Typographers
BRUCE DUCKWORTH
JANICE L. DAVISON

Illustrator
ANTON MORRIS

Photographer
LAURIE EVANS

Design Group
TURNER
DUCKWORTH

Public Relations Executive
HELEN WILLIAMS

Client
BRITISH STEEL
TINPLATE

Direct Mail

Art Director
GUY GUMM

Copywriter
GERRY FARRELL

Typographer
GUY GUMM

Photographer
VICTOR ALBROW

Agency
THE LEITH AGENCY

Brand Manager
JEREMY ELDER

Client
TULLIS RUSSELL &
CO LIMITED

Direct Mail

Design Director
MARCELLO MINALE

Designer
MARCELLO MINALE

Design Group
MINALE
TATTERSFIELD
& PARTNERS

Client
MINALE
TATTERSFIELD
& PARTNERS

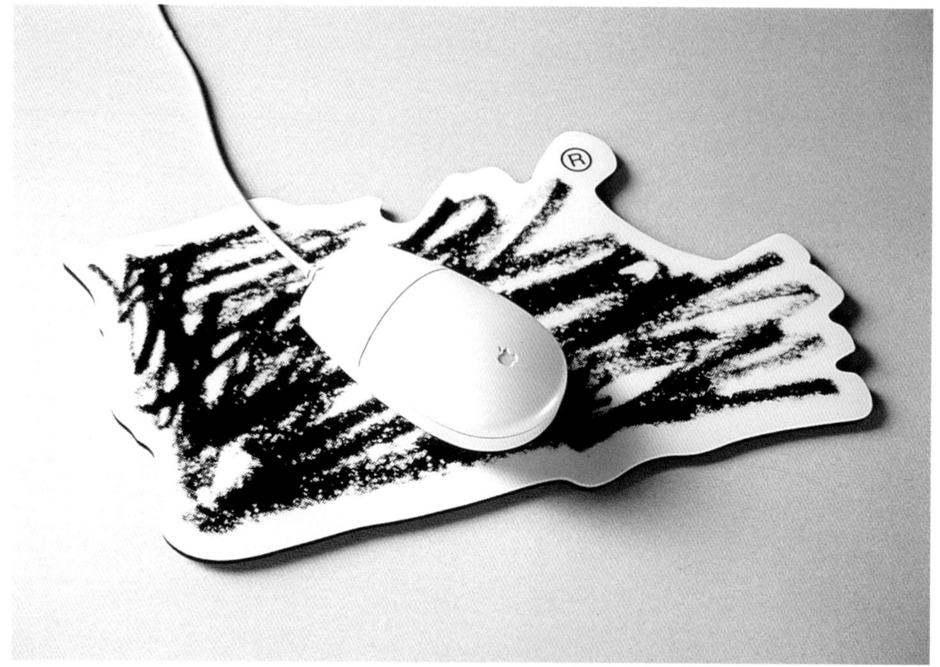

Direct Mail

Design Director
BEN CASEY

Designer
MARK HURST

Design Group
THE CHASE
CREATIVE
CONSULTANTS

Director
THOMAS P. KEARNS

Client
SPECTRUM PRESS

Calendars

Designers
LYNN TRICKETT
BRIAN WEBB
COLIN GIFFORD

Copywriter
NEIL MATTINGLEY

Illustrators
GEORGE HARDIE
ANDREW KULMAN
JEFF FISHER
MARION DEUCHARS
IAN BECK
PETER BLAKE
DAN FERN
LAWRENCE ZEEGAN
PHILLIPPE WEISBECKER
TOBY MORRISON
ANDRZEJ KLIMOWSKI
ROBERT SHADBOLT
BRIAN CRONIN

Design Group
TRICKETT & WEBB

Marketing Executive
LASCELLE BARROW

Clients
AUGUSTUS MARTIN
TRICKETT & WEBB

Calendars

Design Director
MICHAEL GORE

Designer
COLIN GOODHEW

Copywriter
RON NEWSHAM

Typographer
COLIN GOODHEW

Illustrator
COLIN GOODHEW

Design Group
NEWSHAM GORE

Client
NEWSHAM GORE

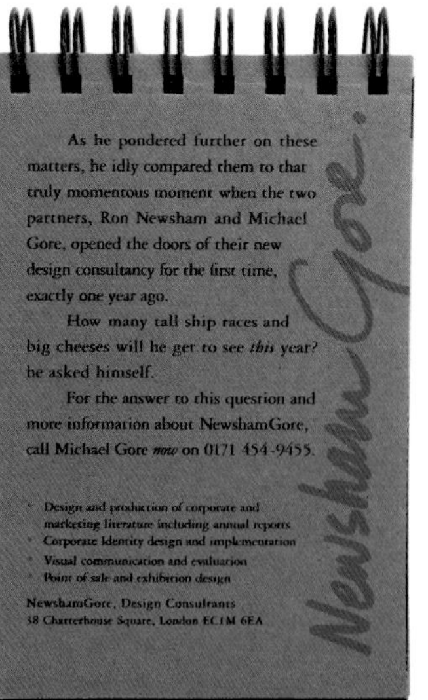

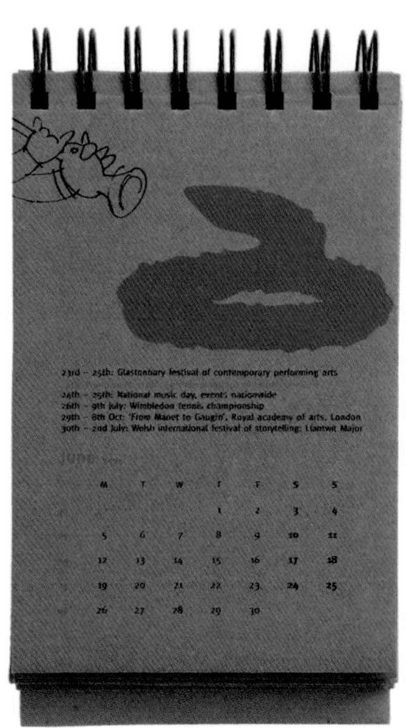

Self Promotional Items

Design Directors
ANTHONY BLURTON
ANDY BONE

Designer
MARTIN
McLOUGHLIN

Typographer
ANTHONY BLURTON

Design Group
FOUR IV

Client
DEBBIE GRAINGER

Self Promotional Items

Design Directors
ALAN HERRON
MARTYN HEY
MARK ROLLINSON
NEIL SMITH

Designers
SHARON CLAMPIN
ALAN FARRELLY
JULIET MacDONALD
NICK VEASEY
SUZANNE EVANS
VICTORIA HOPE
KARN RICHENS

Copywriter
MARTIN HEY

Design Group
GIANT

Client
GIANT

Self Promotional Items

Designer
GYLES LINGWOOD

Copywriter
GYLES LINGWOOD

Typographer
GYLES LINGWOOD

Photographer
GYLES LINGWOOD

Client
GYLES LINGWOOD

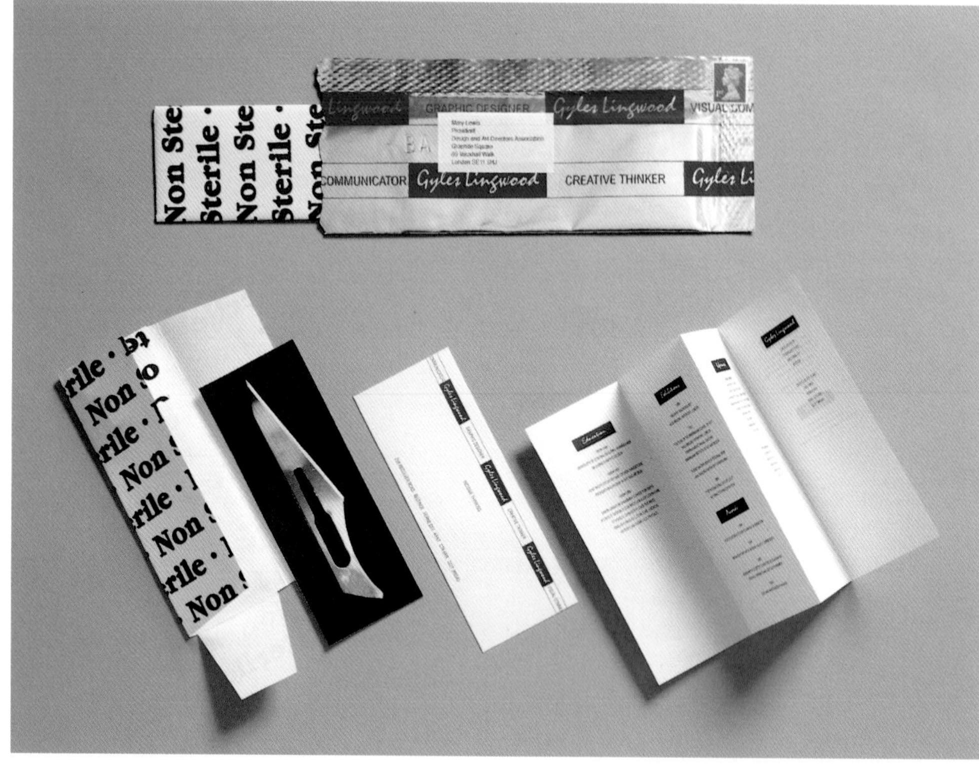

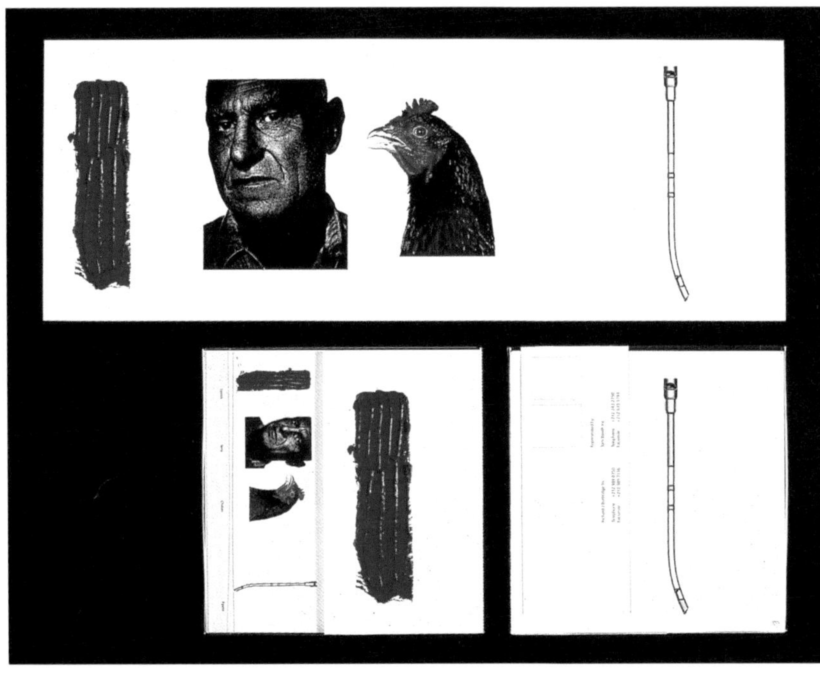

Self Promotional Items

Design Director
SEAN PERKINS

Designers
BRYAN EDMONDSON
ADRIAN CADDY
PAUL WINTER

Typographer
SEAN PERKINS

Photographer
RICHARD J. BURBRIDGE

Design Group
IMAGINATION

Client
RICHARD J. BURBRIDGE

Self Promotional Items

Design Director
SIMON BROADBENT

Designers
SIMON BROADBENT
LYNTON HEMSLEY

Copywriter
LINDA SPENCER

Typographer
CHRIS LLOYD

Photographer
ROBERT WALKER

Agency
BDH ADVERTISING

Marketing Executive
SIMON FARRELL

Client
SIMON FARRELL

Individual Posters

Design Director
PIERRE VERMEIR

Designer
JIM SUTHERLAND

Photographer
DUNCAN SMITH

Design Group
HALPIN GREY VERMEIR

Marketing Manager
JACQUI GELLMAN

Client
ALMEIDA THEATRE

Individual Posters

Design Director
MIKE DEMPSEY

Designer
NEIL WALKER

Typographer
NEIL WALKER

Design Group
CDT DESIGN

Client
ENGLISH NATIONAL OPERA

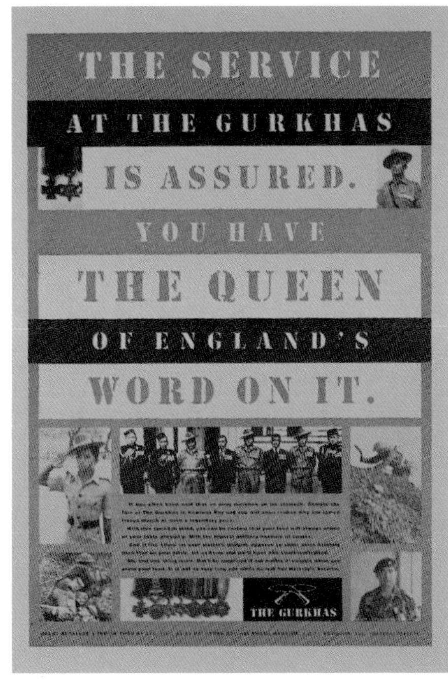

Poster Campaigns

Design Director
SHYAM MADIRAJU

Designers
SHYAM MADIRAJU
ALAN WONG

Copywriter
SHYAM MADIRAJU

Typographer
SHYAM MADIRAJU

Design Group
LEO BURNETT
DESIGN GROUP,
HONG KONG

President
PRAKASH PUN

Client
THE GURKHA'S CLUB

Compact Disc and
Record Sleeve
Individual

Design Directors
ROB O'CONNOR
CHRIS THOMSON

Designer
CHRIS THOMSON

Typographer
CHRIS THOMSON

Illustrator
CHRIS THOMSON

Design Group
STYLOROUGE

Marketing Executive
TERRY FELGATE

Client
PARLOPHONE/FOOD
RECORDS

Compact Disc and
Record Sleeve
Individual

Design Director
PAUL JENKINS

Designers
PAUL JENKINS
STEPHEN PARKER
PETER MAUDER
GRANT FULTON

Typographers
PAUL JENKINS
STEPHEN PARKER
PETER MAUDER

Photographers
SALLY HARDING
MARK HÄKANSSUN
CLAIRE GODFREY

Design Group
RANCH ASSOCIATES

Marketing Executive
ROB HOLDEN

Client
LONDON RECORDS

Compact Disc and
Record Sleeve
Individual

Design Director
MARK FARROW

Designers
ROB PETRIE
MARK FARROW
PHIL SIMS

Typographers
ROB PETRIE
MARK FARROW
PHIL SIMS

Photographer
PRUDENCE
CUMMING

Design Group
FARROW

Marketing Executive
PETE HADFIELD

Client
DECONSTRUCTION

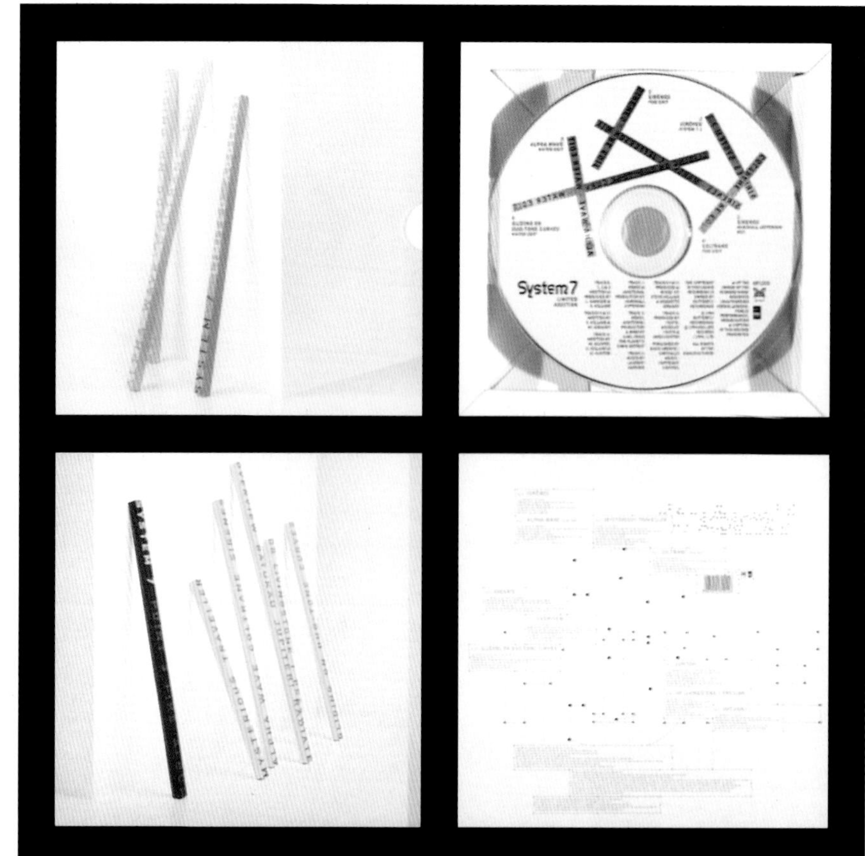

Compact Disc and Record Sleeve Individual

Design Director
DAVID JAMES

Designer
DAVID JAMES

Typographer
DAVID JAMES

Photographer
TREVOR KEY

Design Group
DAVID JAMES ASSOCIATES

Marketing Manager
SOPHY ASHMORE

Client
BIG LIFE RECORDS

Compact Disc and Record Sleeve Individual

Design Directors
MARK FARROW
NEIL TENNANT
CHRIS LOWE

Designers
ROB PETRIE
MARK FARROW
PHIL SIMS

Typographers
ROB PETRIE
MARK FARROW
PHIL SIMS

Illustrators
IAN BIRD
JOHN WAKE

Design Group
FARROW

Client
PSBP

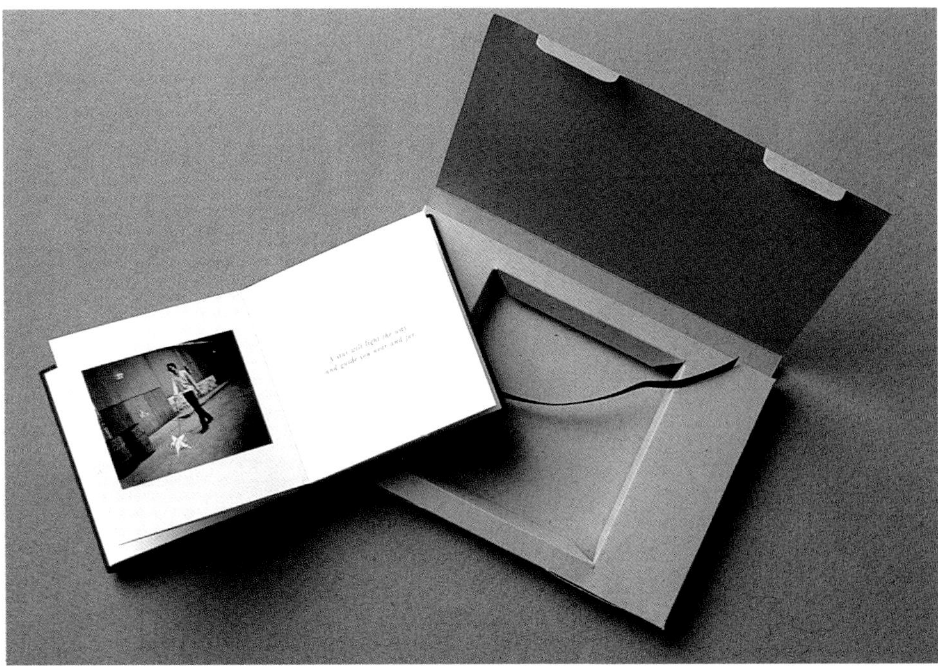

Any other

Design Director
BHANU INKAWAT

Designers
ALISSARA ONNOMPHUNT
PATTREE PORNNIMIT

Copywriters
BHANU INKAWAT
RICHARD IRVINE

Typographer
PATTREE PORNNIMIT

Producer
KOBKHAN THITACHAI

Photographer
JEREMY TAYLOR

Design Group
LEO BURNETT DESIGN GROUP, THAILAND

Client
LEO BURNETT, THAILAND

Any other

Design Director
NEVILLE BRODY

Designer
JOHN CRITCHLEY

Editor
JON WOZENCROFT

Typographers
ERIK VAN BLOKLAND
JUST VAN ROSSUM
LUCAS DE GROOT
IAN WRIGHT
PETER MILES
DAMON MURRAY
STEPHEN SORRELL

Design Group
RESEARCH STUDIOS

Marketing Manager
STEPHEN MILLER

Client
FONTWORKS UK

Any other

Design Directors
BRUCE DUCKWORTH
DAVID TURNER

Designer
JANICE L. DAVISON

Typographer
JANICE L. DAVISON

Design Group
TURNER
DUCKWORTH

Client
TIMOTHY & NICOLA
ASHTON

Any other

Art Director
GUY GUMM

Copywriter
GERRY FARRELL

Typographer
GUY GUMM

Agency
THE LEITH AGENCY

Marketing Executive
PAULINE KERR

Client
THE EDINBURGH
CLUB

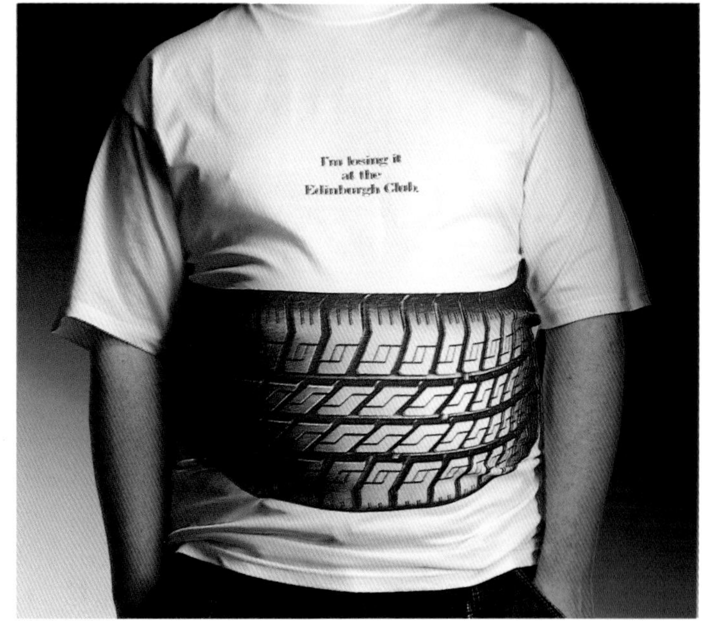

Any other

Design Director
BARRY KETTLEWELL

Designer
DOMINIC FRARY

Copywriter
BARRY KETTLEWELL

Typographer
DOMINIC FRARY

Design Group
...TALK DESIGN COMMUNICATIONS

Marketing Executive
KEVIN ELLIS

Client
...TALK DESIGN COMMUNICATIONS

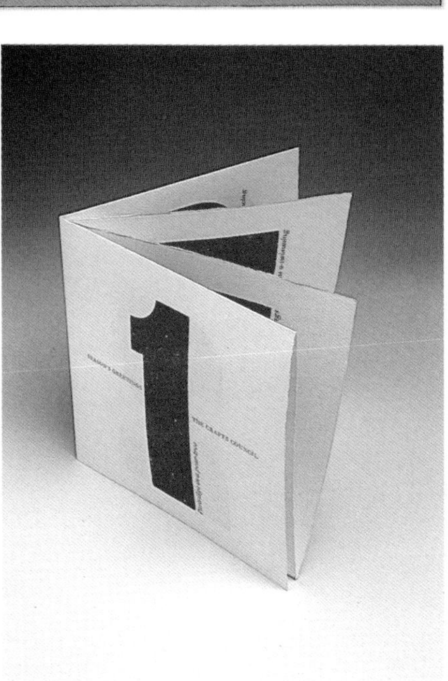

Any other

Design Director
ALAN KITCHING

Designer
ALAN KITCHING

Typographer
ALAN KITCHING

Design Group
THE TYPOGRAPHY WORKSHOP

Client
THE CRAFTS COUNCIL

1995

GRAPHIC DESIGN CRAFTS

Sponsored by CTD

SILVER AWARD
for the Most Outstanding Typography

Typographer
DAVID JAMES

Design Director
DAVID JAMES

Designer
DAVID JAMES

Photographer
TREVOR KEY

Design Group
DAVID JAMES ASSOCIATES

Marketing Manager
SOPHY ASHMORE

Client
BIG LIFE RECORDS

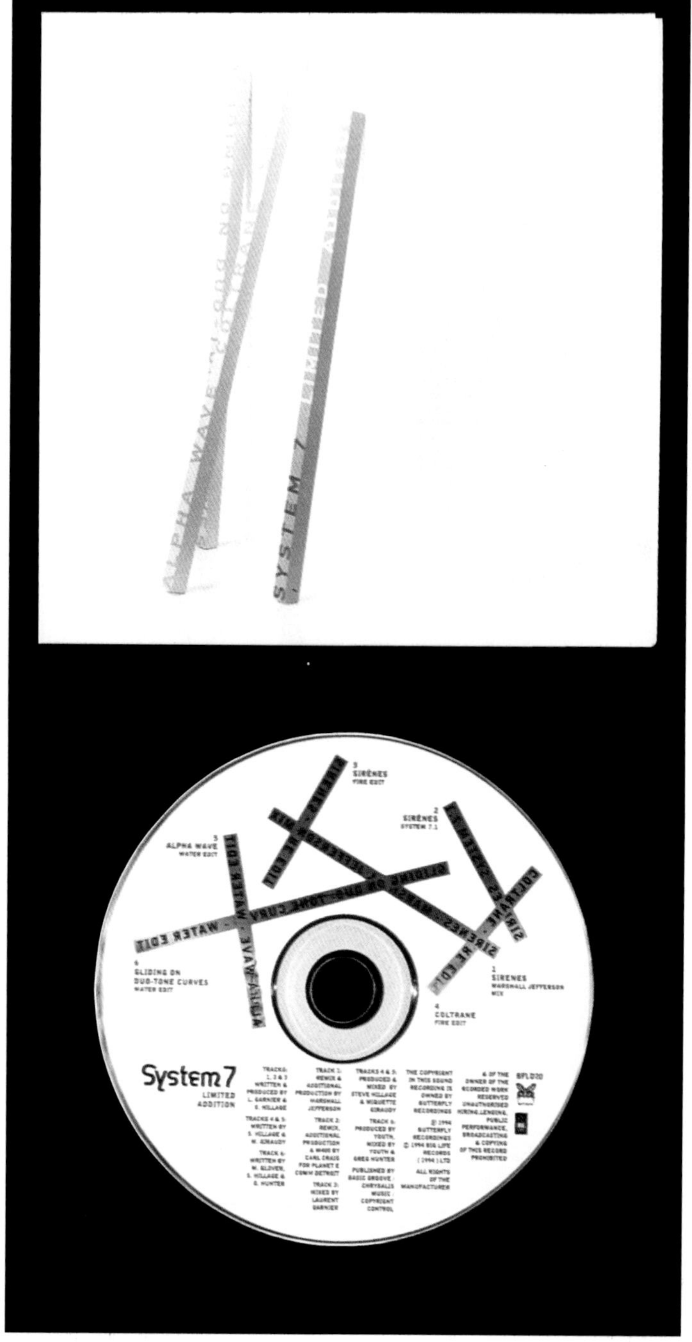

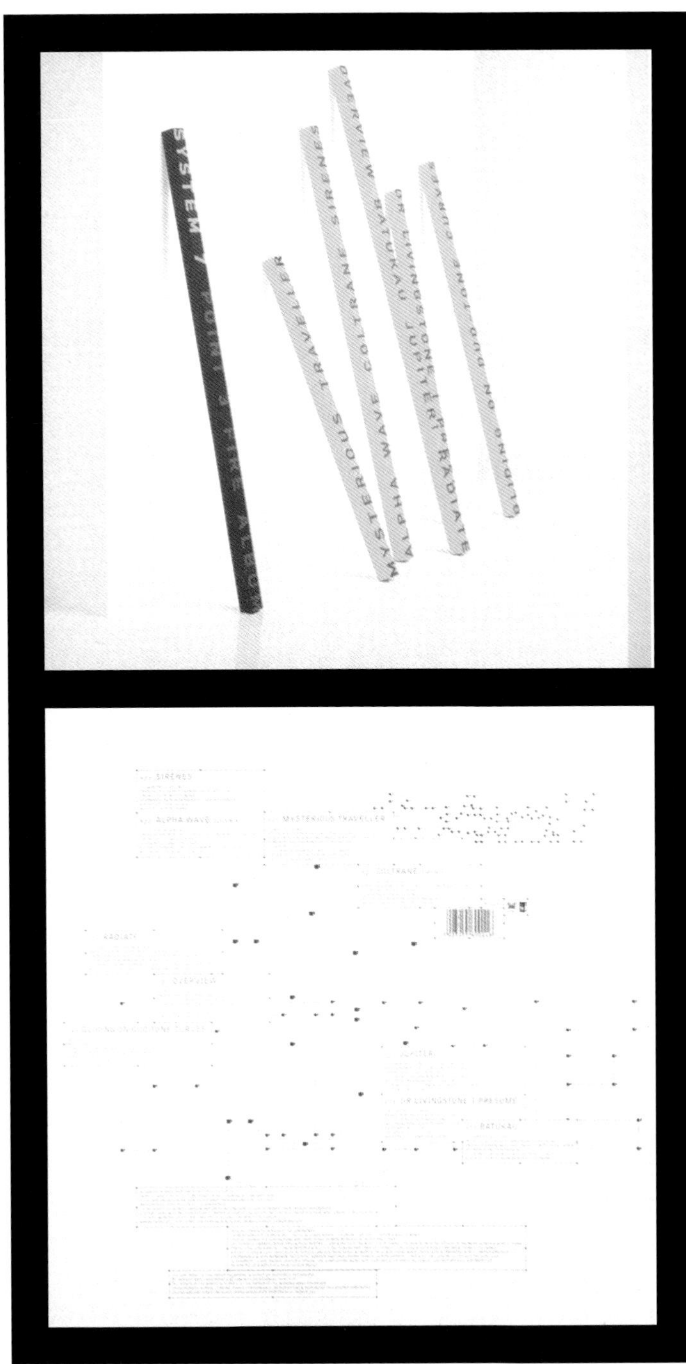
SYSTEM 7
MYSTERIOUS TRAVELLER
RADIATE

Typography

Typographers
CHRIS BRADLEY
DAVID HITNER

Design Director
NANCY WILLIAMS

Designers
CHRIS BRADLEY
DAVID HITNER
LEE FUNNELL

Copywriter
STEPHEN CALLOWAY

Photographer
TREVOR KEY
(cover and dividers)

Design Group
WILLIAMS & PHOA

Commissioning Editor
ROGER SEARS

Client
PHAIDON PRESS

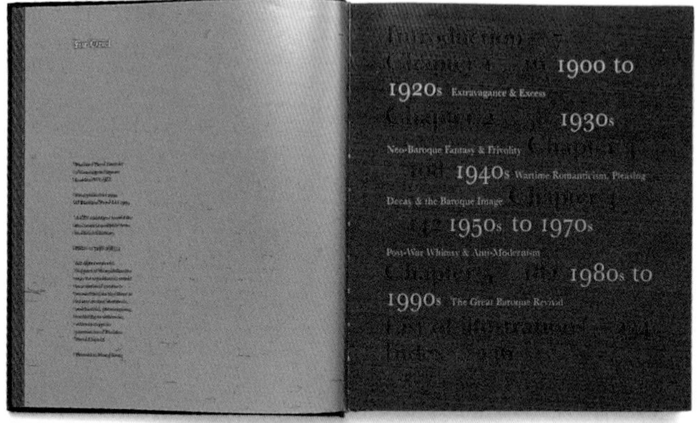

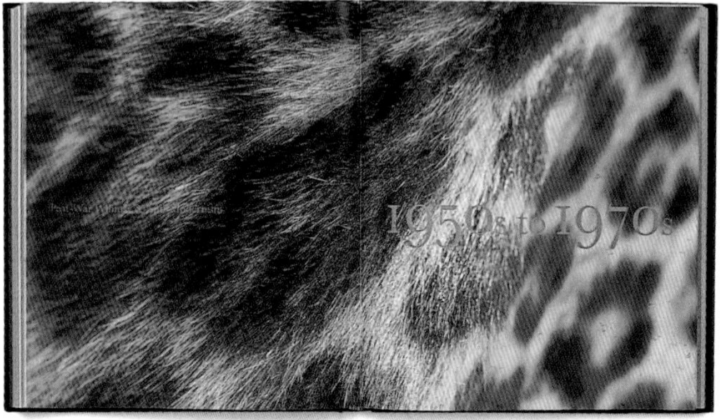

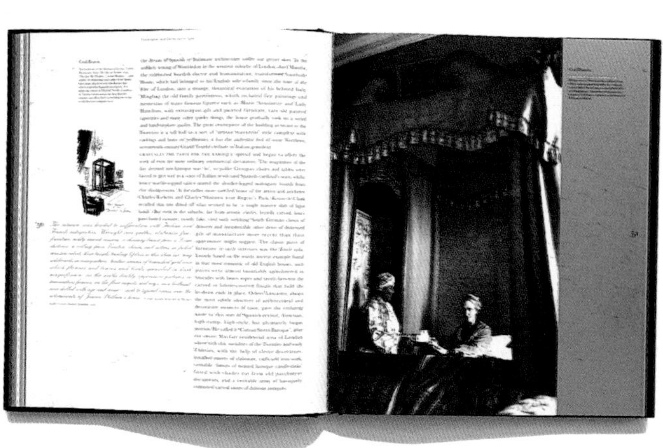

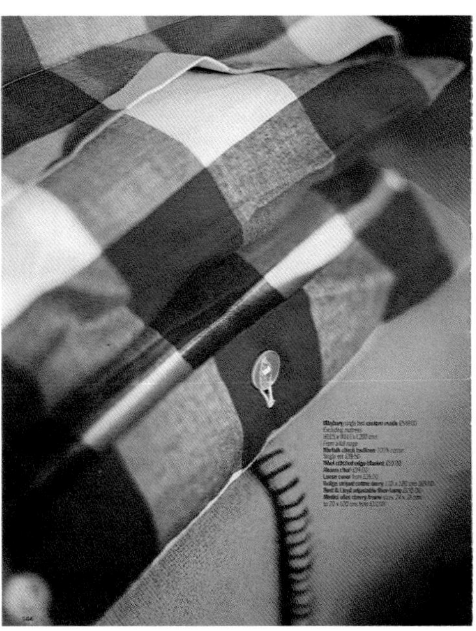

Photography

Photographer
JAMES MERRELL

Designer
ROBIN ROUT

Copywriter
ROBIN ROUT

Typographer
ROBIN ROUT

Stylists
SUE SKEEN
KARINA GARRICK

Design Group
PHOTOGRAFT

Marketing Director
IAIN RENWICK

Client
HABITAT UK

Photography

Photographer
ALVA BERNADINE

Designer
ALVA BERNADINE

Client
ALVA BERNADINE

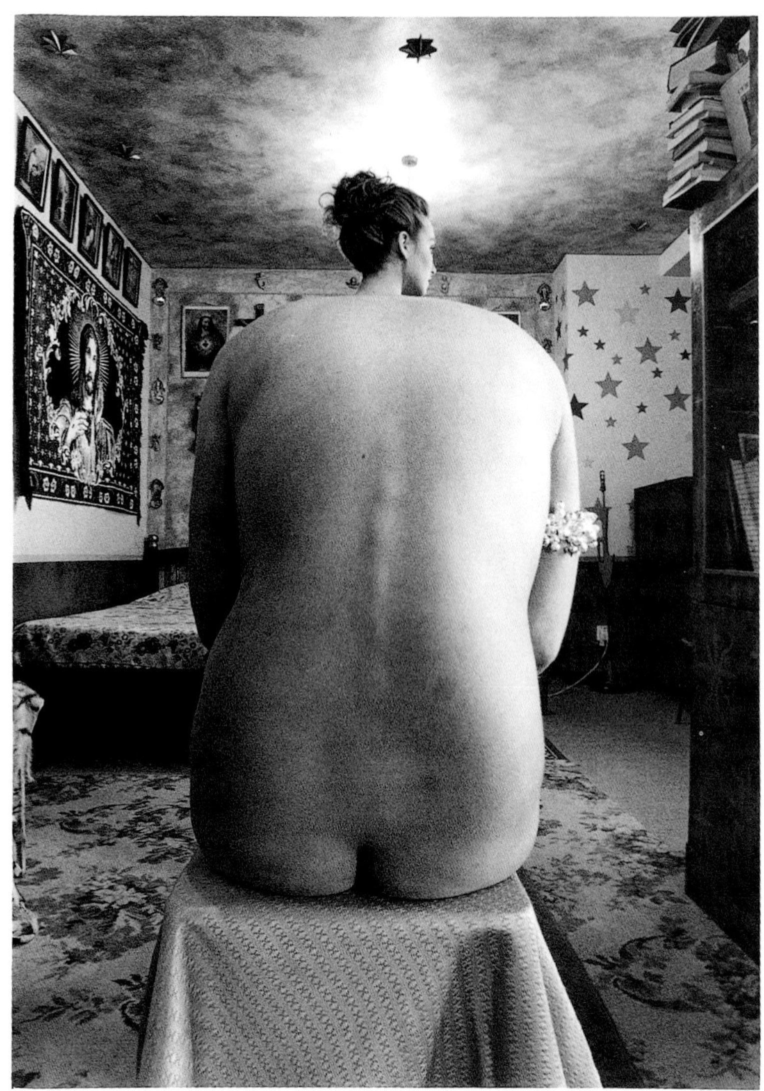

Perspective Nude

alva bernadine

23 EXBURY HOUSE FERNDALE ROAD LONDON SW9 8AZ TEL 071 326 4277

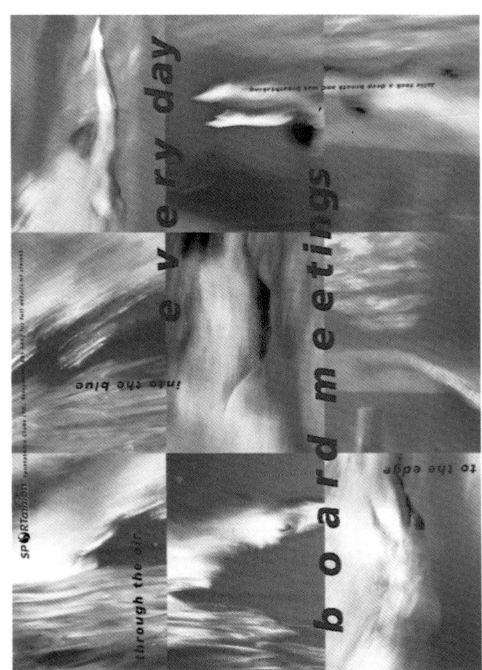

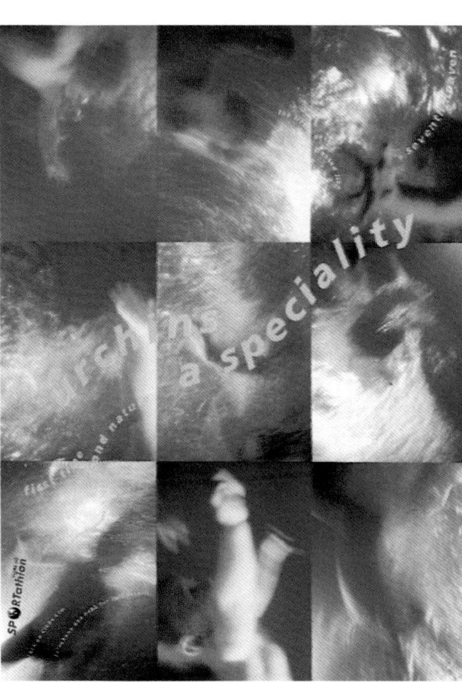

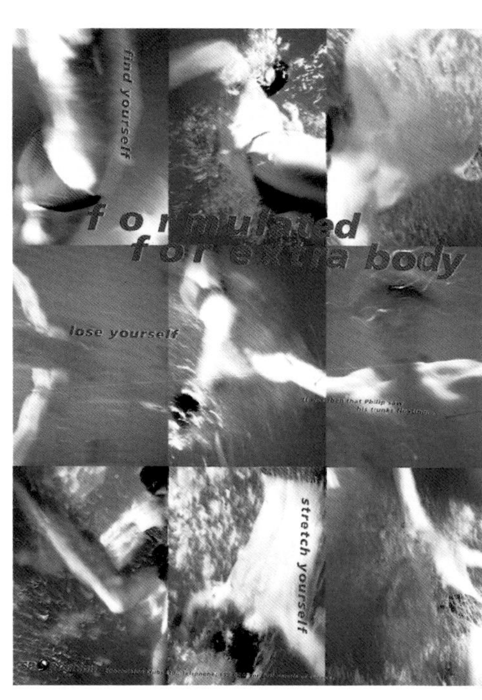

Photography

Photographer
CLAUDIA IMMIG

Designer
CLAUDIA IMMIG

Copywriter
GARY KNIGHT

Typographer
CLAUDIA IMMIG

Agency
BATES HONG KONG

Account Manager
LYNN CHOW

Client
SPORTATHALON

Illustration

Illustrator
MARION DEUCHARS

Design Directors
PHILIP CARTER
NICK DOWNES

Designer
PHILIP CARTER

Typographer
PHILIP CARTER

Design Group
CARTER WONG
& PARTNERS

Vice President, Commercial & Promotional Affairs
BERNIE
ECCLESTONE

Client
FEDERATION
INTERNATIONALE DE
L'AUTOMOBILE

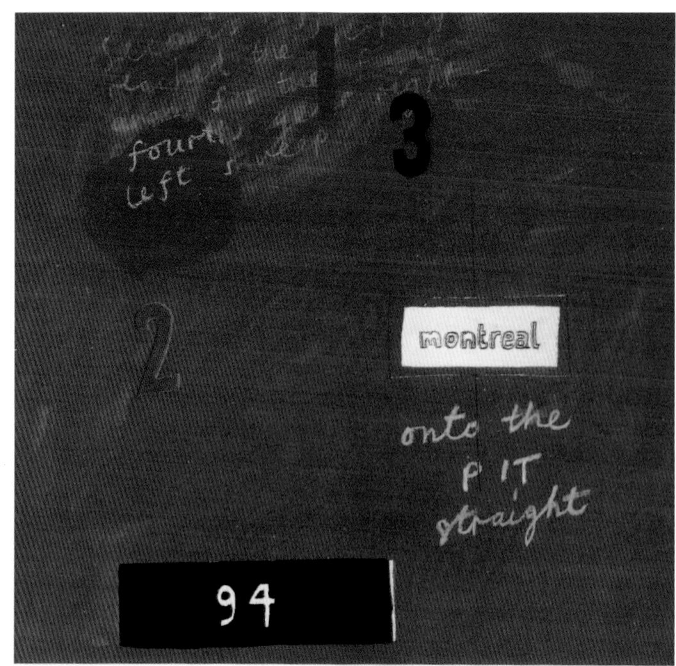

GRAND PRIX MOLSON DU CANADA
MEDIA INFORMATION
1994

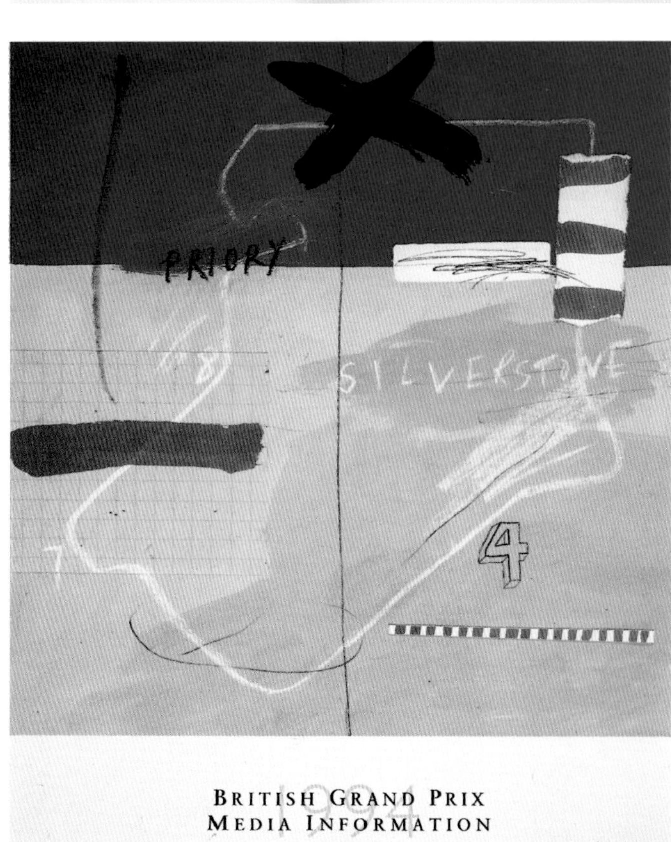

Illustration

Illustrator
RUSSELL BELL

Designer
RUSSELL BELL

Typographer
RUSSELL BELL

Design Group
LANDELS BELL

Client
LANDELS BELL

1995

IDENTITY

SILVER AWARD
for the Most
Outstanding Corporate
Identity Programme

Design Director
JOHN RUSHWORTH

Designers
JOHN RUSHWORTH
ERIKA RENNELL
BJÖRKMAN
CHIEW YONG

Copywriter
DAVID GIBBS

Typographers
JOHN RUSHWORTH
ERICA RENNELL
BJÖRKMAN
CHIEW YONG

Photographer
PETER WOOD

Design Group
PENTAGRAM DESIGN

Marketing Executives
RAMON PAJARES
CHARLOTTE
DOHERTY

Client
FOUR SEASONS
HOTEL GROUP

SILVER AWARD NOMINATION
for the Most Outstanding Corporate Identity Programme

Design Directors
DAVID STUART
SHAUN DEW
STEVE GIBBONS

Designers
PETER CARROW
ROSA LOEFFEL
MARK BONNER
DAVID KIMPTON
TRACY AVISON

Copywriter
LINDSAY CAMP

Illustrator
MICK BROWNFIELD

Photographer
JOHN STONE

Design Group
THE PARTNERS

Marketing Executive
CAMILLA HONEY

Client
J. WALTER THOMPSON

SILVER AWARD NOMINATION
for the Most Outstanding Corporate Identity Programme

Design Director
MARK FARROW

Designers
MARK FARROW
PHIL SIMS
ROB PETRIE

Typographers
MARK FARROW
PHIL SIMS
ROB PETRIE

Design Group
FARROW

Marketing Executive
VANESSA RAND

Client
CONCRETE

SILVER AWARD NOMINATION
for the Most Outstanding Stationery Range

Design Director
DAVID STUART

Designer
PETER CARROW

Copywriter
PETER COLLINGWOOD

Typographer
ROSA LOEFFEL

Design Group
THE PARTNERS

Client
THE DESIGN COUNCIL

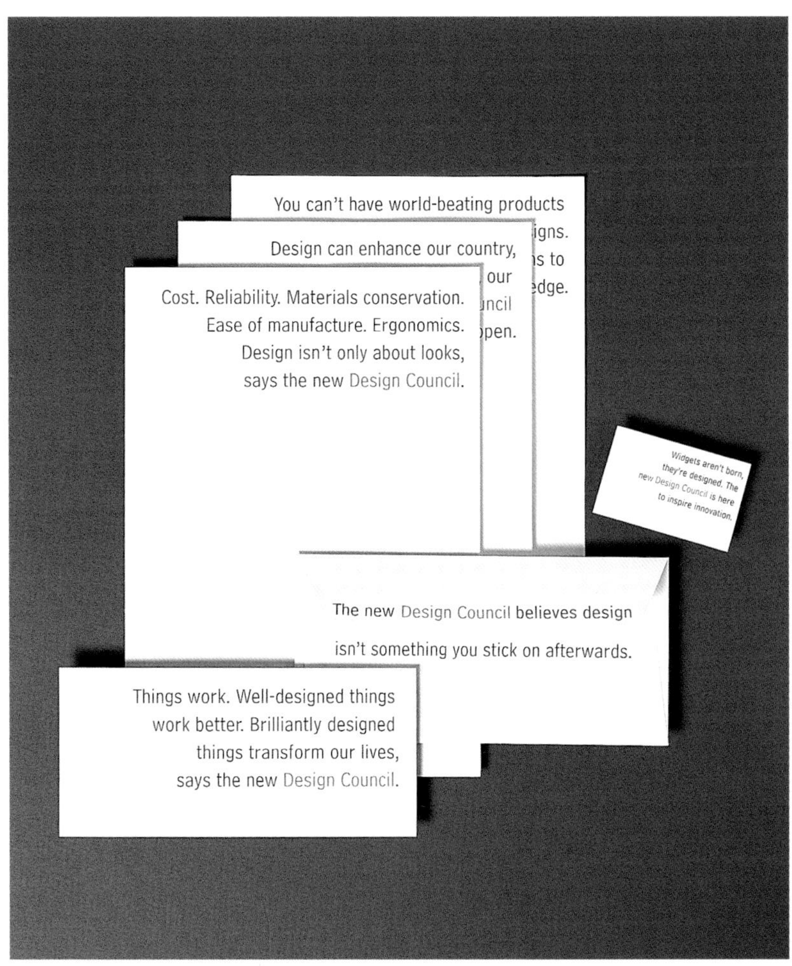

The new Design Council believes that words can speak as loud as logos.

SILVER AWARD NOMINATION
for the Most Outstanding Individual Letterhead

Design Director
SIGI MAYER

Designer
SIGI MAYER

Copywriters
GERHARD MERZEDER
SIGI MAYER

Typographer
SIGI MAYER

Photographer
GERHARD MERZEDER

Design Group
SIGI MAYER PROJEKTAGENTUR

Client
GERHARD MERZEDER FOTOSTUDI

gerhard /merzeder
fotograf

bismarckstr. 7
A-4020 linz/donau
austria
telefax 0732 / 78 41 44

gerhard /merzeder
fotograf

Corporate Identity Programmes

Design Directors
DAVID STUART
SHAUN DEW

Designers
PETER CARROW
ROSA LOEFFEL

Copywriter
PETER COLLINGWOOD

Typographer
ROSA LOEFFEL

Design Group
THE PARTNERS

Marketing Executive
LISA BARWICK

Client
THE DESIGN COUNCIL

Stationery Ranges

Design Director
AZIZ CAMI

Designer
MICHAEL WALLIS

Typographer
MICHAEL WALLIS

Design Group
THE PARTNERS

Chairman
STEPHANIE WILLIAMS

Client
CHILDREN'S EXPRESS

Stationery Ranges

Art Director
PHOA KIA BOON

Designers
SARAH JANE McKENZIE
TIM BEARD

Design Group
WILLIAMS & PHOA

Client
WILLIAMS & PHOA

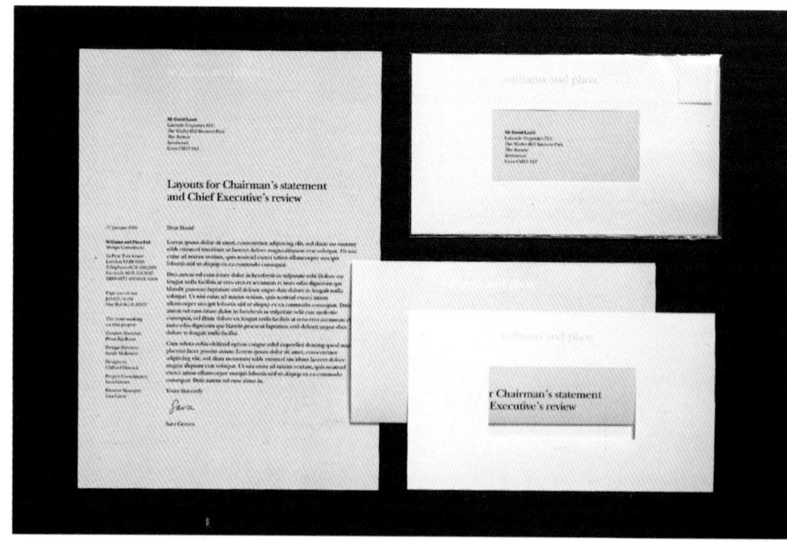

Stationery Ranges

Design Director
MARY LEWIS

Designer
BRYAN CLARK

Copywriter
MARY LEWIS

Typographer
BRYAN CLARK

Design Group
LEWIS MOBERLY

Joint Partners
KEITH CLARKE
GILL CLARKE

Client
STARLITE DANCE

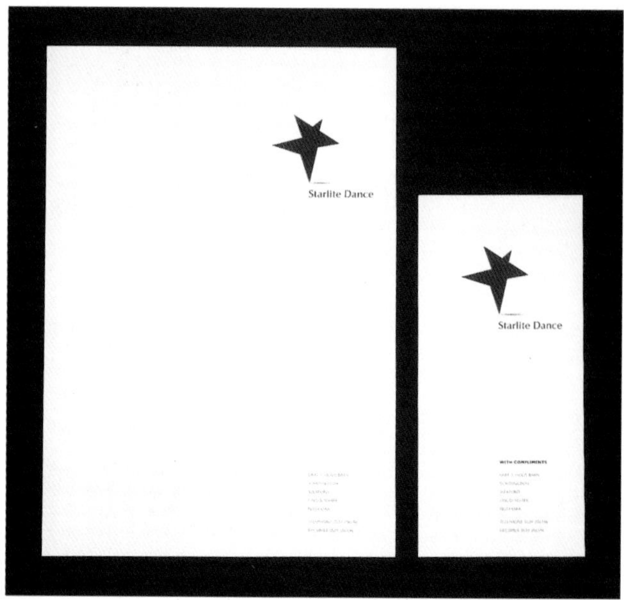

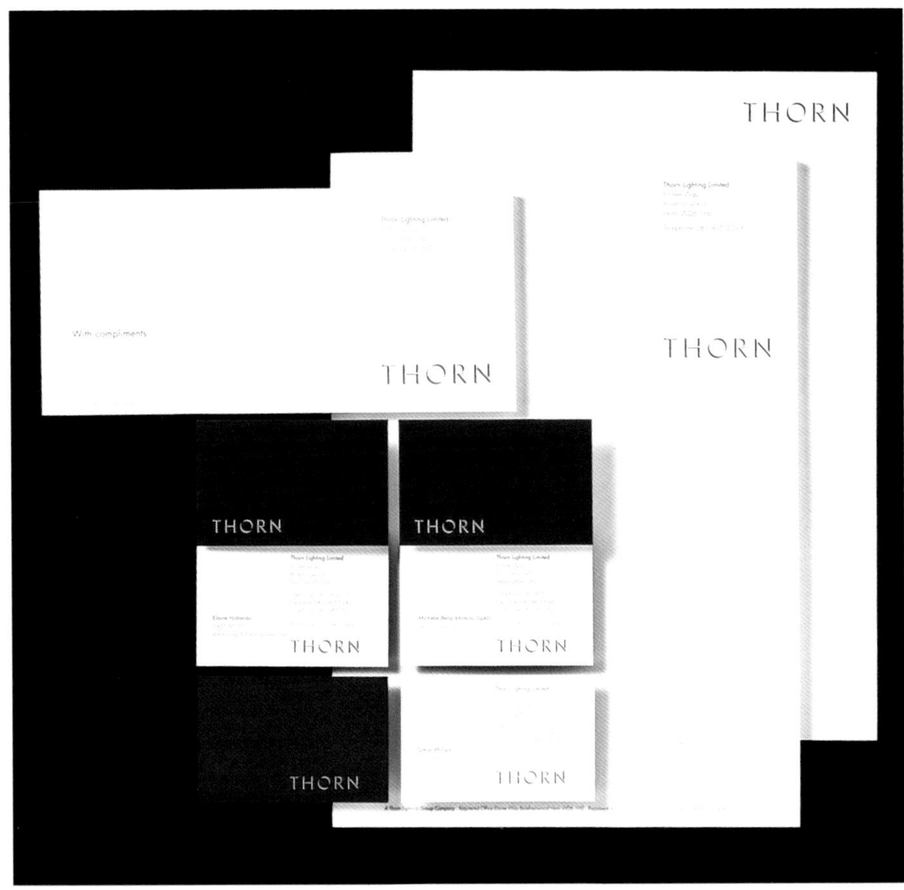

Stationery Ranges

Design Directors
FRANCES NEWELL
JOHN SORRELL
MARK-STEEN
ADAMSON

Designer
CHESTER

Typographer
CHESTER

Design Group
NEWELL AND
SORRELL

**Strategic Development
Manager**
HILARY REID

Client
THORN LIGHTING
LIMITED

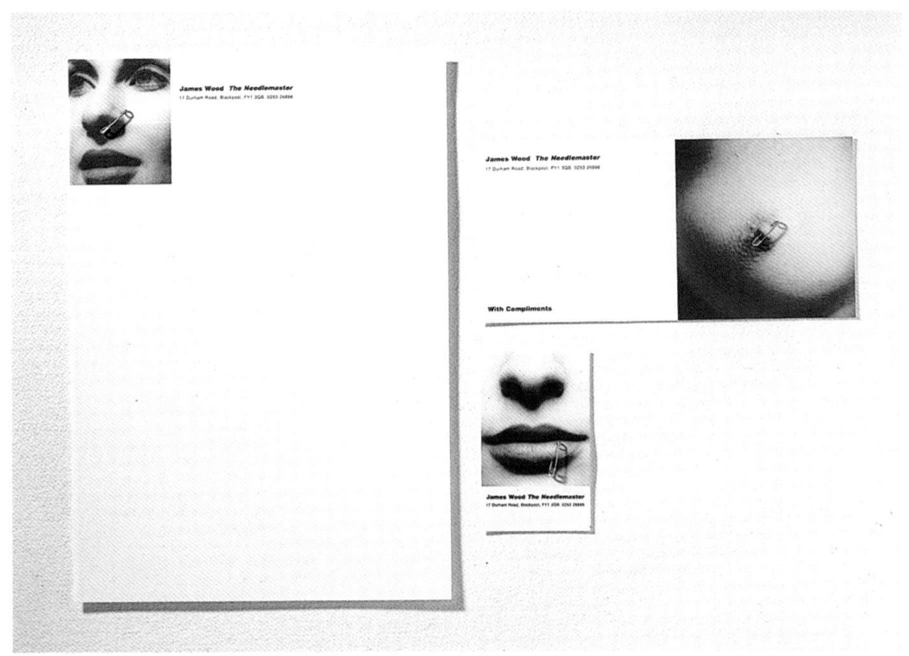

Stationery Ranges

Design Director
SIMON BROADBENT

Designers
SIMON BROADBENT
LYNTON HEMSLEY

Copywriter
LINDA SPENCER

Typographer
CHRIS LLOYD

Photographer
MOY WILLIAMS

Agency
BDH ADVERTISING

Marketing Executive
JAMES WOOD

Client
THE NEEDLEMASTER

Symbols and Logotypes

Designers
STEPHEN PAYNE
MAX CARRINGTON
DEREK JOHNSTON

Design Group
SAATCHI & SAATCHI DESIGN

Client
CAMELOT GROUP PLC

Symbols and Logotypes

Design Director
PIERRE VERMEIR

Typographer
GEOFF HALPIN

Design Group
HALPIN GREY VERMEIR

Managing Director
RONALD STERN

Client
STERNSTAT LIMITED

Symbols and Logotypes

Design Director
LINDON GRAY LEADER

Designers
JOHN LUTZ
LINDON GRAY LEADER

Creative Director
COURTNEY REESER

Design Group
LANDOR ASSOCIATES, SAN FRANCISCO

Marketing Director
GAYLE CHRISTIENSEN

Client
FEDERAL EXPRESS CORPORATION

Symbols and Logotypes

Design Director
STEVE GIBBONS

Designers
TRACY AVISON
LOUISE EDWARDS

Typographer
PETER HALE

Illustrator
TRACY AVISON

Design Group
THE PARTNERS

Marketing Executive
SIOBHAN LYNCH

Client
ASDA

Symbols and Logotypes

Design Director
MARY LEWIS

Designer
BRYAN CLARK

Copywriter
MARY LEWIS

Typographer
BRYAN CLARK

Design Group
LEWIS MOBERLY

Joint Partners
KEITH CLARKE
GILL CLARKE

Client
STARLITE DANCE

1995

ENVIRONMENTAL DESIGN

SILVER AWARD
for the Most Outstanding Retail Design

Designers
MARTYN BULLOCK
RICHARD GREENLEAF

Design Group
RED JACKET

Client
HMV UK LIMITED

Listen
Listen

Singles
Listen

Listen
First Floor
Classical, Video
Specialist Music

SILVER AWARD
for the Most Outstanding Exhibition Design

Design Director
PROFESSOR DANIEL WEIL

Designer
PROFESSOR DANIEL WEIL

Design Team
FIRST YEAR INDUSTRIAL DESIGN STUDENTS
JEAN PIERRE GÉNÉREUX

Client
ROYAL COLLEGE OF ART

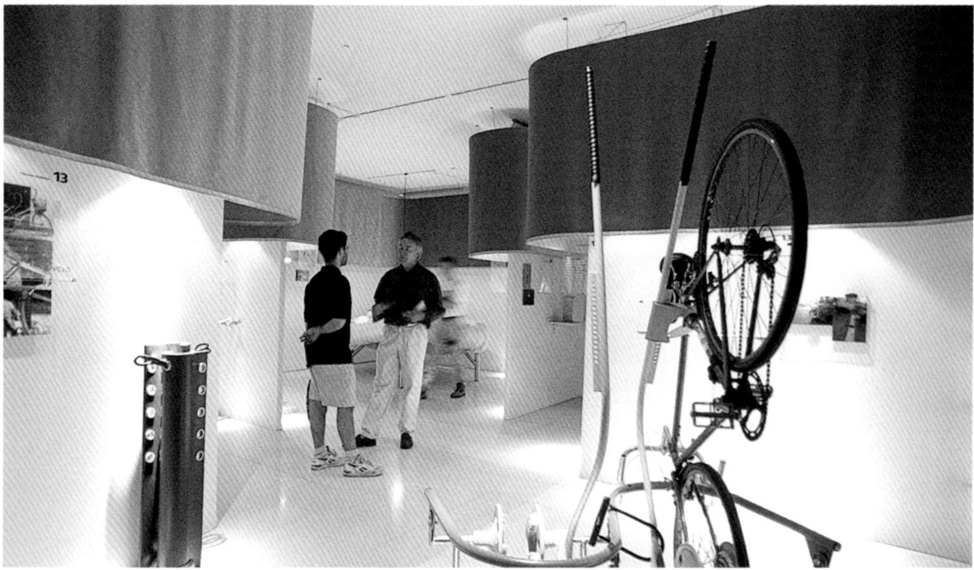

SILVER AWARD NOMINATION
for the Most Outstanding Exhibition Design

Design Director
STEPHEN DOYLE

Architect
MIGUEL OKS

Design Team
ROSEMARY TURK
GARY TOOTH

Design Group
DRENTTEL DOYLE PARTNERS

Marketing Executive
WILLIAM DRENTTEL

Client
THE WORLD FINANCIAL CENTER

SILVER AWARD NOMINATION
for the Most Outstanding Applied Graphic Design

Design Group
CLIFFORD SIEBERT DESIGN COLLABORATIVE

Project Director
MAURY BLITZ

Project Manager
SUZANNE DEMERS

Client
WORLD CUP 1994

Retail Design

Design Director
JOHN HARVEY

Designers
ANGELA DRINKALL
PHILIP DOLMAN
PAUL DEAN

Design Group
DIN ASSOCIATES

Client
NICOLE FARHI FOR FRENCH CONNECTION

Retail Design

Design Director
JEFF KINDLEYSIDES

Designers
JEFF KINDLEYSIDES
DAVID WRIGHT

Design Team
DAVID WRIGHT
MAGGIE WRIGHT
JO DALE
CARL MURCH
RICHARD WHITMORE
MATTHEW FAWELL

Design Group
CHECKLAND
KINDLEYSIDES

Marketing Executive
AMANDA LE ROUX

Client
LEVI STRAUSS UK
LIMITED

Non Retail Interior

Designers
DAVID HARPER
KEN RORRISON

Design Group
HARPER MACKAY

Client
FRAMESTORE

Exhibition Design

Design Director
MARIANNE VOS

Designers
MARIANNE VOS
EDWIN VERKOOYEN
PETER VAN DE PALM

Photographers
CHRIS VAN DEURSEN
PAUL ROMIJN
MAARTEN VAN DE VELDE

Design Team
YVETTE VALKENBURG
DICK DE JONG

Design Group
SAMENWERKENDE ONTWERPERS

Director De Hoep Centre
PIET DUIZER

Client
NV PWN

Exhibition Design

Design Director
CLAUS KOCH

Designers
PETER ENGELHARDT
CLAUS KOCH

Design Group
CLAUS KOCH
CORPORATE
COMMUNICATIONS

Client
MAUSER
WALDECK AG

1995

PRODUCT DESIGN

SILVER AWARD
for the Most
Outstanding Product
for Health and Leisure

Designers
DAVID J. HEARNE
PAUL K. RAND

Design Team
RICHARD WALKER
IAN CUDE
NICK COLE
PHIL FARR
ANDREW GRANT
PETER BRAND

Manufacturer
GLAXO OPERATIONS
UK LIMITED

Design Group
GLAXO RESEARCH
AND DEVELOPMENT,
DEVICE
DEVELOPMENT UNIT

Client
GLAXO RESEARCH
AND DEVELOPMENT
LIMITED

THE GLAXO MULTI DOSE POWDER INHALER

This new Inhaler, for the treatment of asthma, has been designed after extensive customer research, specifically patients and healthcare professionals, to give greatly enhanced levels of useability and performance. Particular emphasis has been placed on providing for the needs of children, teenagers, and those of low manual dexterity to ensure successful self-administration and improved compliance.

The compact shape, ergonomic design and minimal operating steps, provide a device which is easy and comfortable to use, discrete, convenient to carry and store, and is without separate parts which can be misplaced or lost.

Intensive development and testing has been carried out with the mechanism design to ensure high levels of reliability, robustness and resistance against the effects of misuse.

Efficient clinical performance has been obtained by careful design and optimisation of the airflow through the device.

The drug, in powder form, is contained as individual unit doses, within pockets on a foil strip, hermetically sealed with a peelable lid, giving excellent environmental protection and consistent dose delivery.

In use the patient simply slides open the outer case, pushes the lever, (which peels opens the strip and exposes a dose), inhales, and recloses the case. The closing operation automatically resets the mechanism ready for the next dose. When closed the integral outer case covers the mouthpiece preventing the entry of foreign bodies. A numerical display shows the exact number of doses that are left in the device.

Components have been designed to interact and work within a relatively large tolerance range, so ensuring a non-critical, robust production process utilising full automation and robotic assembly methods.

Throughout the project simultaneous development methods have been used, integrating the needs of the various in-house disciplines involved ensuring a user centred, quality and friendly product.

SILVER AWARD NOMINATION
for the Most Outstanding Product for Work

Industrial Design
MARTIN RIDDIFORD
JAMES DAWTON

Software Design
CHARLES DAVIES
BILL BATCHELOR
DAVID WOOD
NICK HEALEY

OS & Electronic Design
COLLY MYERS
MARK GRETTON
MARK KOVANDZICH

Product Design Engineering
KENNETH McALPINE

Marketing Executive
STEPHEN PANG

Client
PSION

SERIES 3A PALM TOP COMPUTER (PSION PLC)

The Series 3a palmtop computer measures 165mm x 22mm, runs for months on two AA size batteries and fits comfortably in a jacket pocket. Despite its modest dimensions it features built-in Database, Time Management, Word Processing and Spreadsheet facilities. The large LCD screen accommodates a full page width of text comfortably and the software applications are of the same scale and sophistication as those found on desk-bound computers. Yet the intuitive, Windows-like user interface makes it inviting to use for both novices and computer experts.

The Psion Series 3 range was launched in the United Kingdom in Autumn 1991, with initial production volumes of 4,000 units per month. Four years later over 500,000 units have been sold, and sales including software and peripherals have advanced to £39.8 million in 1994.

International markets accounted for 54% of the Group's computer sales. Psion's main markets are in continental Europe and North America. International sales increased 50% to £29.13 million, reflecting a particularly strong performance in the European markets. These figures make Psion the world leader in the palmtop market.

Products for the Home

Designer
JACK WOOLLEY

Technical Designer
BRIAN TAYLOR

Design Team
JACK WOOLLEY
RICHARD WHITEHALL
MING LEUNG

Design Group
ISIS UK LIMITED

Marketing Executive
MAHESH PATEL

Client
IMPULSE LOUDSPEAKERS

IMPULSE SPEAKERS

Impulse's exponential horn principle speaker construction produces an exceptionally high degree of realism. The casework has to reflect this acoustic sophistication, yet move the design away from black box electronic culture towards an aesthetic more appropriate to domestic interiors.

The curved front panel of solid maple emphasises quality. The grain is carefully matched on individual pairs. Spikes ensure stable coupling to the floor and damping material on the integral stand ensures consistent performance in a wide variety of environments.

Products for the Home

Design Group
SEYMOUR POWELL

Photographer
JEROME YEATS

Client
KEF AUDIO UK LIMITED

KEF HOME THEATRE SPEAKER SYSTEM

The 70S satellite/surround speakers and 40B powered sub-woofer have been designed to provide extremely high quality sound when coupled to a Dolby Pro-Logic Theatre System.

40B SUBWOOFER
This features 2x200m bass drivers in a dual coupled-cavity configuration fitted with KEF's unique force cancelling rod, to provide quite exceptional low frequency performance. The unit is powered by an integral 100w power amplifier.

70S SATELLITE SURROUND SPEAKERS
These compact but high quality speakers feature Kef's patented Uni-Q drivers. The renowned Uni-Q comprises a 19mm HF unit mounted at the acoustic centre of a 160mm mid-bass unit, making the composite driver both co-axial and co-planar. It provides a wide, even sound stage and a flat, smooth frequency response – especially off axis. The units can be wall hung, bookshelf mounted, or matched into a series of floor-standing or universally-jointed wall brackets via a purpose built mounting system.

Products for the Home

Designer
JAMES DYSON

Design Team
DYSON DESIGN TEAM

Design Group
DYSON APPLIANCES

Marketing Executive
JAMES DYSON

Client
DYSON APPLIANCES

DYSON DC02 DUAL CYLINDER VACUUM CLEANER

The Dyson DC02 Dual Cyclone Cylinder vacuum cleaner combines all of the advantages of the patented dual cyclone system with features designed to make vacuuming much less of a chore.

Dual Cyclone power means no bags, so no mess and no continual maintenance costs. It guarantees 100% power, 100% of the time, so all of the power necessary to remove stubborn dust and dirt from deep down is maintained constantly.

The Dual Cyclone uses the centrifugal forces of two sequential cyclones to spin the dirt and fine dust out, allowing the air to continue through the vacuum cleaner unimpeded without loss of power. By their very nature, a bag or other barrier filter must block continually in order to function, thus losing suction power from the minute the machine is turned on. The clear collection bin also makes it obvious when it's full and the dirt is simply tipped away.

The unique step-hugging profile makes the DC02 stable on the stairs, revolutionising the cleaning of the most awkward areas. Two high-area pleated electrostatic cartridge filters are fitted as standard to enhance the already excellent dual cyclonic filtration. As a result the exhaust air is near free from the minute particles now found to cause respiratory ailments. Additionally, the Dual Cyclone dirt separation process means that the exhaust air does not carry the odours of the dirt out of the Dyson into the room.

The Dyson DC02 also sports a 130w motor, concealed on-board tools, automatic cable rewind, foot operated controls, ergonomic handles and trigger suction control.

The total package combines to offer a truly fresh and innovative design solution to an already saturated and traditional market.

Products for Work

Designers
ANDY PIDGEON
ADRIAN LEES
MARTIN GAZE
STEPHEN GREEN
LIN ROWORTH-STOKES
DAVID HADLEY
PHIL FENTON

Manufacturer
DESKING SYSTEMS LIMITED

Design Group
BIB DESIGN CONSULTANTS

Client
DESKING SYSTEMS LIMITED

ARTEMIS

Designed by BIB Desking Systems, Artemis combines the elegance of classical shapes and lines to create an exceptional British product with broad European and International appeal.

Artemis' striking design is centred on 3 different structural elements for the workstations base, the 'T' leg, Panel and Skeletal. These complementary bases can be mixed and matched within the same office environment to provide a consistent design theme.

The bases are attached to an elegant wing shaped element that supports the desk-tops and provides continuity throughout the range.

A multi level rotalink can be used to link 2 or more work stations together at any angle providing a landscaped look to an office and additional working space.

Artemis is fully cable managed, the split level work surfaces allowing the desk-tops to slide open to reveal the cabling without the need to move any furniture or disturb the desk contents.

The range uses bold colours, materials and form to enliven the working environment. A wide variety of work stations, storage units and personal screening give Artemis users a huge choice of layouts.

Products for Work

Designers
IAN GRAVATT
ADRIAN
TYTHERLEIGH

Technical Designers
IAN GRAVATT
ADRIAN
TYTHERLEIGH

Manufacturer
JAMES BURN
INTERNATIONAL

Design Group
WORKS DESIGN

Client
JAMES BURN
INTERNATIONAL

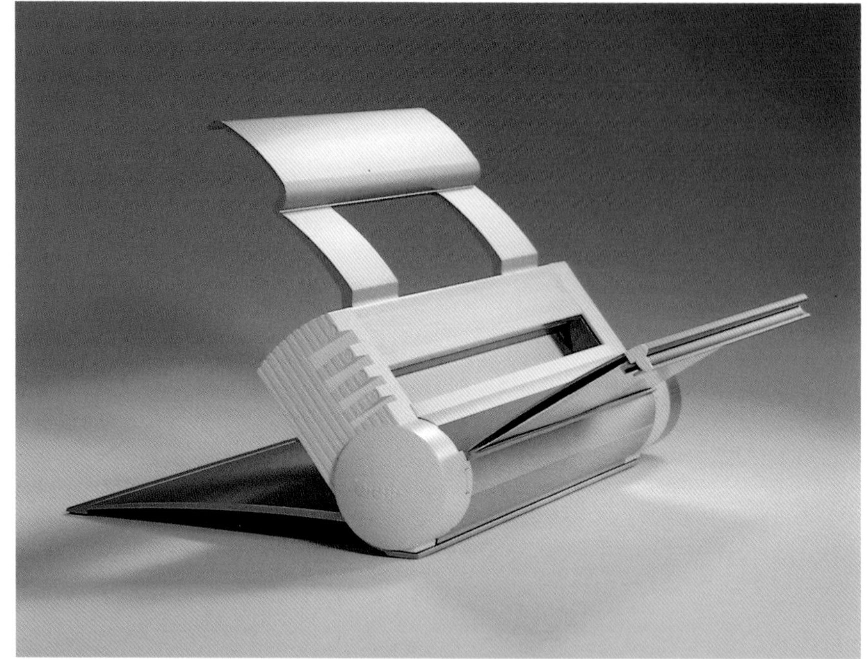

JAMES BURN INTERNATIONAL – WIRE-O DESKTOP

The Desktop is a new addition to the range of machines produced by James Burn International for use with their Wire-O binding system. It is an entry level machine for the office and small business environment and is dedicated to binding reports and other documents of up to 85 sheets of A4 paper.

Producing a bound report involves two main stages, firstly punching 34 holes through the sheets making up the report and them assembling the report by closing a binding wire thought the punched holes. The Desktop is manually operated by pressing a handle and has been designed to minimise the effort a user must apply.

The Desktop includes a number of new features to simplify the production of a bound report.

A stepped adjustment knob sets the machine to suit the number of pages.
A slide out instruction card reminds new or infrequent users of the operation procedure.

An extruded feature holds the binding wire steady while the punched sheets are inserted onto it.

The design is based around anodised aluminium extrusions; facilitating components which work as finished structural parts on the outside, giving the machine a strong visual identity, and as cost effective mechanical components on the inside.

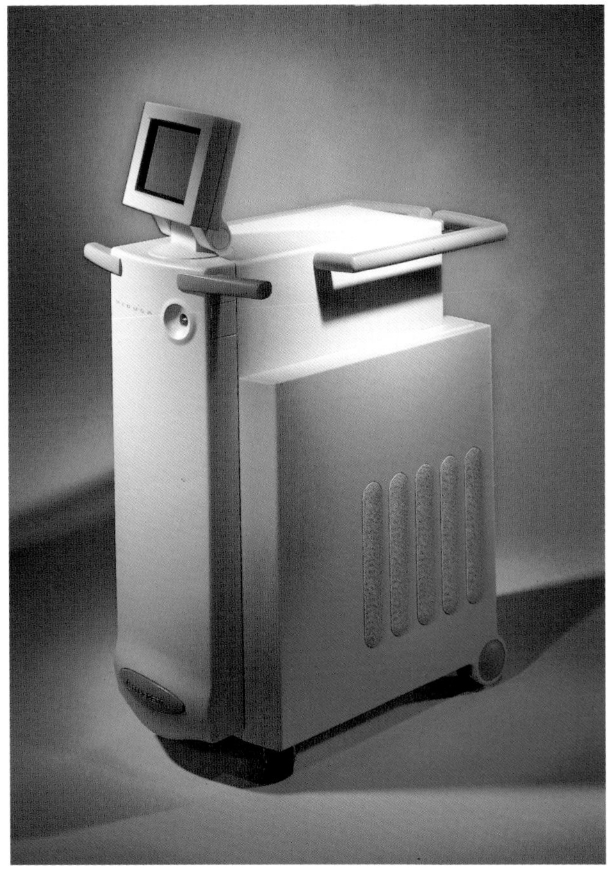

Products for Health and Leisure

Designers
MAX YOSHIMOTO
GIL WONG
BJARKI HALLGRIMMSON
GERARD FURBERSHAW

Design Team
KEVIN CONNORS
JOHN ONDO
DAVID TROST
ROBERT ESTRADA
ED REED

Manufacturer
COHERENT MEDICAL

Design Group
LUNAR DESIGN, INC

Client
COHERENT MEDICAL

COHERENT VERSAPULSE SELECT SURGICAL LASER

The designers were charged with developing a product that incorporated Coherent's state-of-the-art technology into a surgical laser product that would communicate value, quality and longevity, as well as meet ergonomic and other user demands. The designers also wanted to establish a complementary design language for this new surgical product that previously has been developed for the company's ophthalmic devices.

The most important design objectives for the VersaPulse Select were to ensure that; 1 the product took up as little floor space as possible, 2 that the controls and 'action panel' would be visible from anywhere in the operation room, and 3 that the product could be easily moved from surgical suite to surgical suite.

Designed as a tall, compact device, the Coherent VersaPulse Select surgical laser reduces the invasiveness of various operating procedures, including knee, spine and shoulder. By incorporating the innovative laser technology into a tall, slender enclosure, the designers saved on floor space and created a visually sophisticated product, as well as one whose control panel is at the appropriate height for optimum viewing. The VersaPulse Select's backlit, touchscreen panel (with built-in tilt/swivel mechanism) is used for the main display. This allows the company to easily change text for international language applications.

The display, mounted toward the front of the unit, allows the surgeon (in the sterile zone) to view the readout, yet the panel can be controlled by a nurse in the non-sterile area. An optional remote device (with display) is located at the rear of the unit to allow non-sterile users dedicated access to control the output of the laser. The remote can be 'bagged' and placed in the sterile zone to allow the surgeon control of the laser.

Handles in the front and rear of the unit allow it to be easily moved in either direction and from room to room without tipping due to optimal weight distribution. The rear wrap around handle extends beyond the side panels to provide protection and also provide a space to store a patient information clipboard and packaging for laser delivery devices. The rear of the handle is detailed to accommodate the remote control usage and storage. A heat dissipation area was needed on the main body of the surgical laser, so the designers incorporated side panels as an integral part of the overall design.

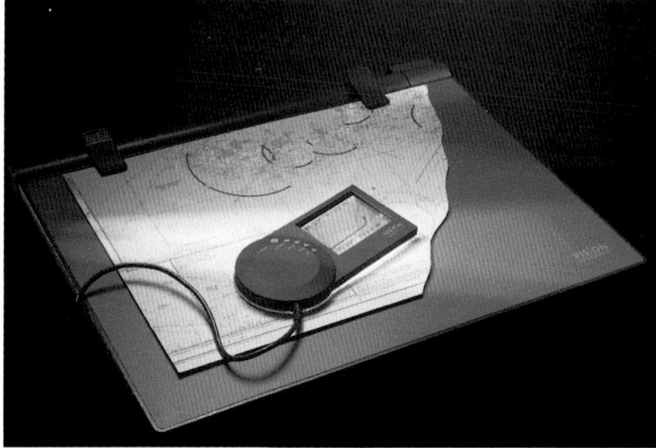

Products for Industry and Transport

Designers
DAVID GOODWIN
NICK HAMNETT
TOM TIVENDALE

Manufacturer
GEOGRAFIX
NAVIGATION
SYSTEMS UK

Design Group
GOODWIN EMCK

Client
GEOGRAFIX
NAVIGATION
SYSTEMS UK

GEOGRAFIX YACHT NAVIGATION AID

The Vision GPS displays navigation information in a new and 'user friendly' way. It displays the boat's position and track directly on a paper chart thus simplifying navigation and eliminating the need to plot. The navigator can see his progress in real time and adjust his course accordingly.

The display unit consists of a 'magic window' which is a transparent LCD. The chart can be viewed through the window and the navigational information is shown graphically on the LCD, relative to the chart. The display is illuminated to enable the chart to be viewed in all conditions.

The chart is positioned over the digitising surface to which both chart and display are referenced. To navigate, the user simply places the display over the chart and watches his track as it is drawn in the window.

The product is portable and contains a rechargeable battery pack and is also designed to float.

1995

EDITORIAL AND BOOKS

SILVER AWARD NOMINATION
for the Most Outstanding Book Cover

Design Directors
JACQUES KOEWEIDEN
PAUL POSTMA

Designers
JACQUES KOEWEIDEN
PAUL POSTMA

Typographers
JACQUES KOEWEIDEN
PAUL POSTMA

Photographer
MARC VAN PRAAG

Design Group
KOEWEIDEN POSTMA ASSOCIATES

Marketing Executive
WOUTER VOS

Client
BIS PUBLISHERS

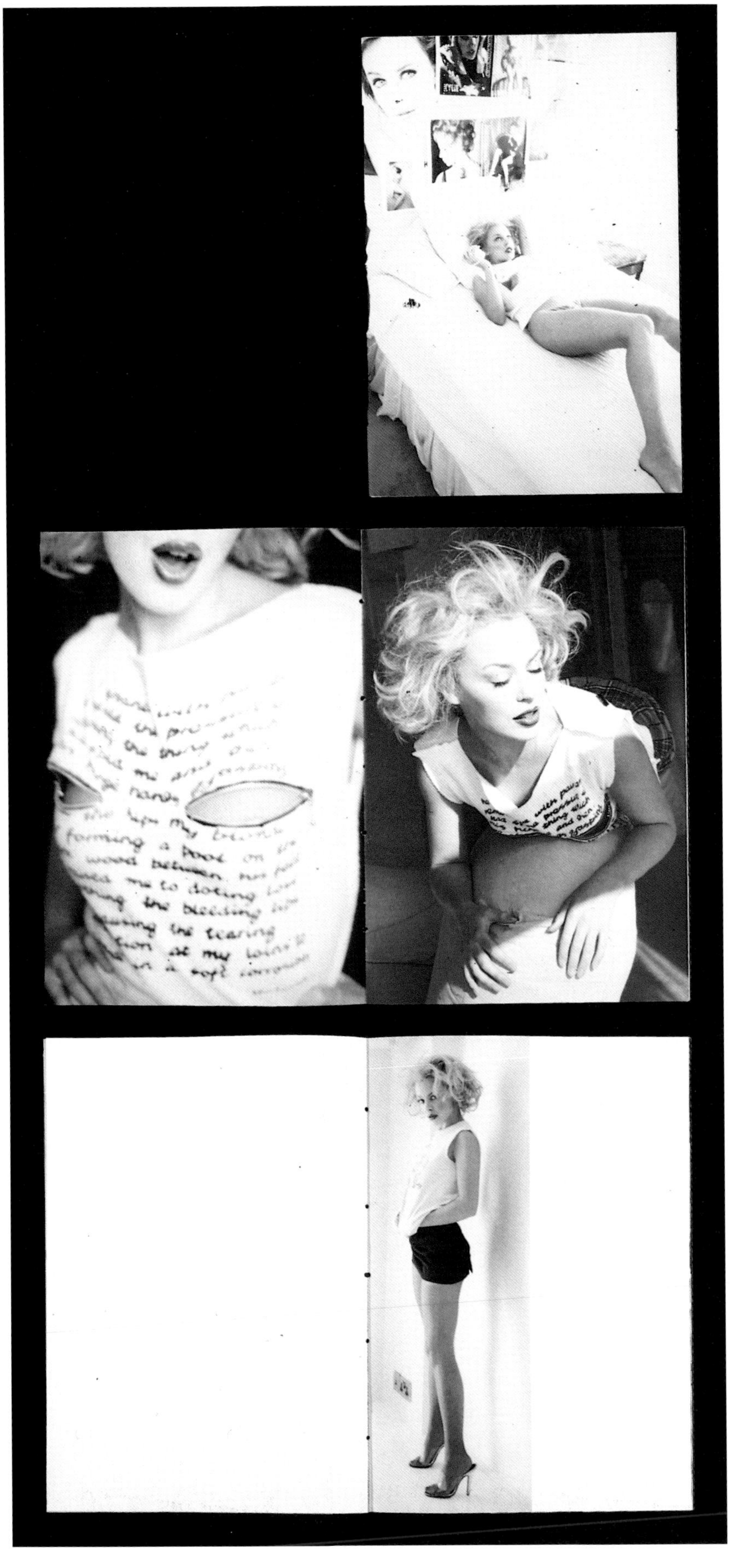

SILVER AWARD NOMINATION
for the Most Outstanding Complete Book

Design Director
MARK FARROW

Designers
ROB PETRIE
PHIL SIMS
MARK FARROW

Typographers
MARK FARROW
PHIL SIMS
ROB PETRIE

Photographers
ELLEN VON UNWERTH
KATERINA JEBB

Design Group
FARROW

Marketing Executive
PETE HADFIELD

Client
DECONSTRUCTION

Book Covers

Designer
JOOST ROOZEKRANS

Typographer
JOOST ROOZEKRANS

Design Group
STUDIO DUMBAR

Project Leader
DHR. L. VAN KAMPEN

Clients
MINISTERIE VAN BINNENLANDSE ZAKEN
MINISTERIE VAN JUSTITIE

Complete Books

Designers
ANGUS HYLAND
SILVIA GASPARDO
MORO

Copywriter
LIZ FARRELLY

Photographer
ARREN ELVIDGE

Publisher
EDWARD
BOOTH-CLIBBORN

Client
BOOTH-CLIBBORN
EDITIONS

Urgentimages: The graphic language of the fax.

MOM'S CUTE IN A LIVED IN SORT OF WAY WHEN SHE PUTS ON HER RED SCARF. THE CURL IN HER HAIR ISN'T QUITE WHAT IT USED TO BE.

Complete Books

Design Directors
JACQUES KOEWEIDEN
PAUL POSTMA

Designers
JACQUES KOEWEIDEN
PAUL POSTMA

Typographers
JACQUES KOEWEIDEN
PAUL POSTMA

Photographer
MARC VAN PRAAG

Design Group
KOEWEIDEN POSTMA
ASSOCIATES

Marketing Executive
WOUTER VOS

Client
BIS PUBLISHERS

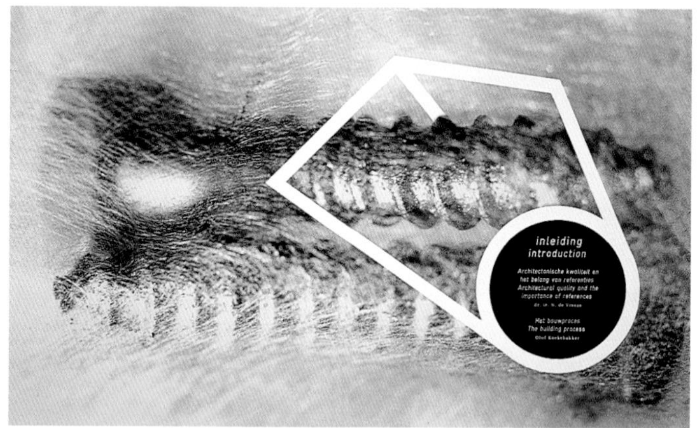

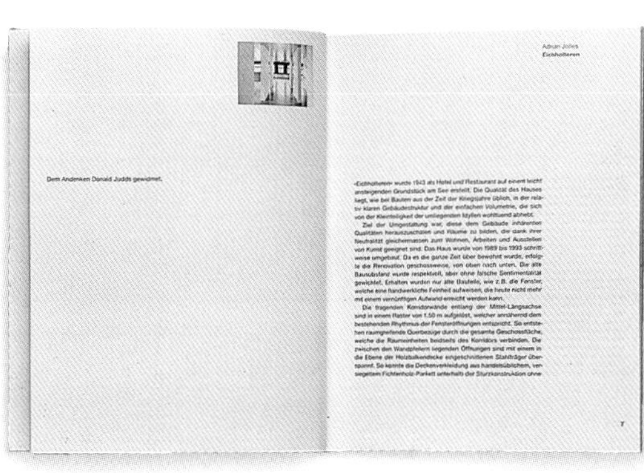

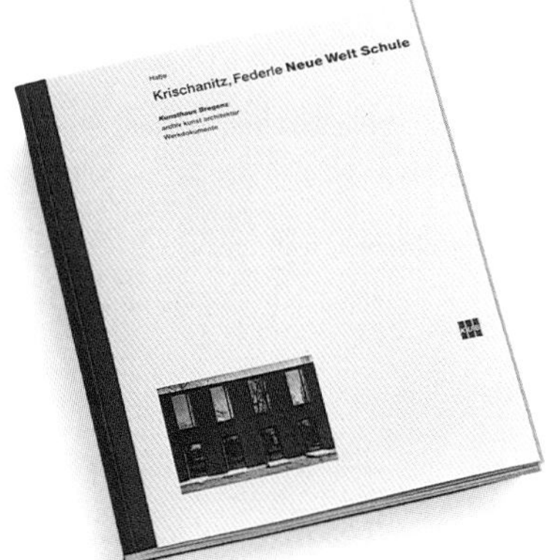

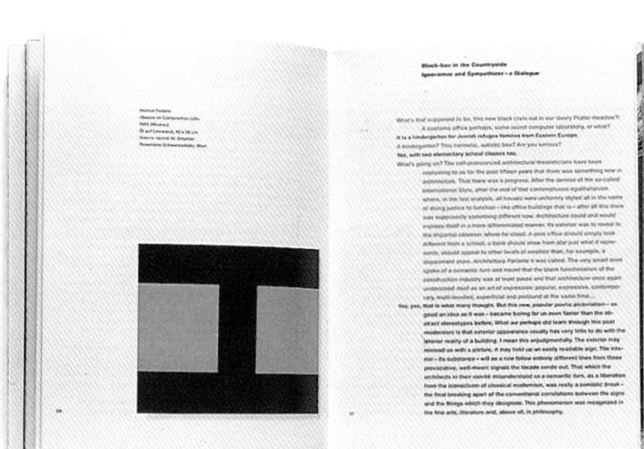

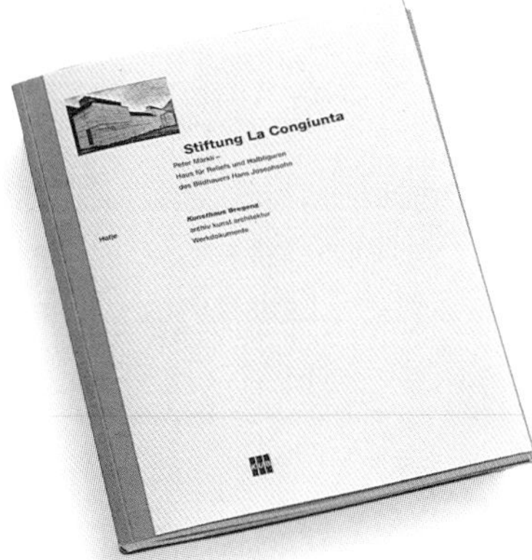

Complete Books

Art Director
CLEMENS SCHEDLER

Designer
CLEMENS SCHEDLER

Author
OTTO KAPFINGER

Typographer
CLEMENS SCHEDLER

Photographer
MARGHERITA SPILUTTINI

Design Group
BOHATSCH AND SCHEDLER GMBH

Marketing Executive
PROFESSOR EDELBERT KÖB

Client
KUNSTHAUSS BREGENZ

1995

RADIO

Sponsored by Capital Radio

SILVER AWARD
for the most outstanding Radio Commercial Campaign

Concept Creators
TREVOR ROBINSON
ALAN YOUNG

Copywriters
TREVOR ROBINSON
ALAN YOUNG

Agency Producer
KATHLEEN RAINEY

Recording Engineer
ANDY HUMPHRIES

Agency
HOWELL HENRY CHALDECOTT LURY & PARTNERS

Brand Manager
DAVID ATTER

Client
BRITVIC SOFT DRINKS LIMITED

HOWELL | HENRY | CHALDECOTT | LURY + PARTNERS

Although all the telephone conversations in the AppleTango radio campaign were planned out as a basic structure first, no actual scripts exist.

All the commercials were recorded live. All the people called were genuine, unsuspecting members of the public.

MISTER TUNNEY

The irate caller rings a lawyer, Mister Tunney for legal advice. He says he wants to sue Britvic, the makers of apple Tango.

He explains to the lawyer that a can of apple Tango talks to him, she makes him do things like eating dead dogs and wearing women's clothes. The caller is at pains to point out he didn't actually eat the dead dogs – '...I'm not stupid – right Mister Tunney!'

The Lawyer tells him he will need medical evidence to mount a case. The caller responds – '...I don't need medical evidence, I've got a flat full of dead dogs.'

The caller becomes more and more angry with the lawyer eventually threatening to sue him. The lawyer says go ahead. The caller asks if he knows any good lawyers before he hangs up.

LOST PROPERTY

A Desperate caller gets in touch with a B.R. lost property office. He explains he's lost a can of apple Tango on a train from London to Glasgow. He explains that it was in a briefcase with a round window in the front. It was packed with ice, although the ice would have melted since he lost it several weeks ago.

He pleads with the man in the lost property office to go and find it.

Apparently totally unphased, the lost property man goes off to look for the soft drink . He comes back saying it's not there. Our caller becomes frantic – 'what if some skanky Scotsman's got her and he's drinking her out of a paper cup?' The lost property man hangs up.

The caller rings back and accuses the lost property man of kidnapping the can '...you've got her haven't you, you've drunk my can of apple Tango.' Not surprisingly the lost property man hangs up again.

BLACK & WHITE & COLOUR

The caller contacts the Black & White & Colour processing lab. He explains that he needs a roll of film developed discreetly. He is assured of complete discretion.

He then goes on to explain that the film contains pictures of him cavorting naked with a can of apple Tango in his flat. The man in the photo lab is happy to develop the pictures but obviously doesn't want to know the details. The caller insists on telling him everything, including dressing the can up in doll's clothes.

Finally the caller asks if it's okay to bring the can when he drops off the film. 'We're in love and I take her everywhere with me...' he explains.

Not surprisingly the 'victim' doesn't understand what he's talking about. The caller then hangs up just before he bursts out laughing.

Kent House, 14-17 Market Place, Great Titchfield Street, London W1N 7AJ. Telephone: 0171 436 3333. Facsimile: 0171 436 2677. E-mail: postbox @ hhcl. com
Howell Henry Chaldecott Lury Ltd. Registered Office as above. Registered No. 2158210. England.

Single

Concept Creators
ERIC SILVER
MIKE HENRY

Copywriter
ERIC SILVER

Agency Producer
MIKE HENRY

Recording Engineer
JOE SHEETS

Production Company
SEVEN PRODUCTIONS

Agency
EARLE PALMER BROWN

Marketing Executive
ADDISON MOSS

Client
THE TEXAS WISCONSIN BORDER CAFE

EARLE PALMER BROWN

1710 EAST FRANKLIN STREET
RICHMOND, VIRGINIA 23223
804 775-0700
FAX 804 775-0795

RESTAURANT NOISES AND ROMANTIC VIOLIN IN BACKGROUND

MAN: Jane I wanted to tell you... that... this is kind of hard to say... but... I love you... and I wanna... what I'm trying to say is I can't live without you... and... I really think together... we could make a go of this thing...

MAN IS INTERRUPTED BY A VERY IMPRESSIVE BURP

JANE: (giggles / embarrassed) Sorry. I had chalupas for lunch.

MAN: At The Border. See I love that restaurant. That's what I'm talking about. It's like we're just totally meant to be together. We're perfect. Now I know forever's a long time, but Jane would you be my...

MAN IS INTERRUPTED BY WICKED FLATULENCE

JANE: (embarrassed) Oh. Sor-ree. I also had Gretchen's green chili burrito.

MAN: Yeah.

AWKWARD SILENCE

JANE: So as you were saying?

MAN: (meek) I really like that restaurant?

JANE: No. No. Before that.

MAN: Nothin' really.

PIANO AND VIOLIN BEGIN PLAYING IN UNISON

ANNCR: The Texas-Wisconsin Border Cafe. It's sure to be a meal you'll never forget. Whether you want to or not.

ADVERTISING / DATABASE MARKETING / DIRECT MARKETING / GRAPHIC DESIGN / PUBLIC RELATIONS / SALES PROMOTION
BETHESDA • NEW YORK • NORFOLK • PHILADELPHIA • RICHMOND • TAMPA BAY

1995

TELEVISION AND CINEMA COMMERCIALS

CINEMA

Sponsored by Framestore

SILVER AWARD
for the Most Outstanding Commercial up to 10 seconds

Directors
TREVOR ROBINSON
ALAN YOUNG

Copywriter
ALAN YOUNG

Art Director
TREVOR ROBINSON

Creative Director
STEVE HENRY

Producer
JANE FULLER

Editor
RICK LAWLEY

Lighting Cameraman
ZUBIN MISTRY

Production Company
JANE FULLER ASSOCIATES

Agency
HOWELL HENRY CHALDECOTT LURY & PARTNERS

Marketing Manager
JEREMY WOODS

Client
GOLDEN WONDER

RANDY

We super behind Phil:

NEW POTS OF THE WORLD.

We open on Phil wearing a string vest and a studded collar. A dog sits quietly beside him on the desk, also wearing a string vest and a studded collar. The three new Pot flavours are in front of Phil.

PHIL:
New Pots of the World range including Spicy Szechuan flavour.

Experiment with something more exotic like Randy and I do.

SUPER:
Intense.

CHAIN

MUSIC:
'We Have All The Time In The World' sung by Louis Armstrong.

In this commercial, we embark on a timeless journey through a glass of swirling Draught Guinness. Everything is rendered in Guinness tones.

We push inside a bubble, cross a strange universe, then descend upon a mysterious planet.

We sweep down towards an enormous tower set against a turbulent sky. The camera favours an open window as we move into a room packed with unusual souvenirs.

We glance past a television set. The familiar face of the Man in Black appears on the screen. He smiles at us, before we make a beeline for the centre piece; a swirling pint of Guinness set on a table.

The camera lingers. We think the journey is over when the chain of events begins to repeat itself. It's as if the journey might go on for some time.

TITLE:
Pure Genius.

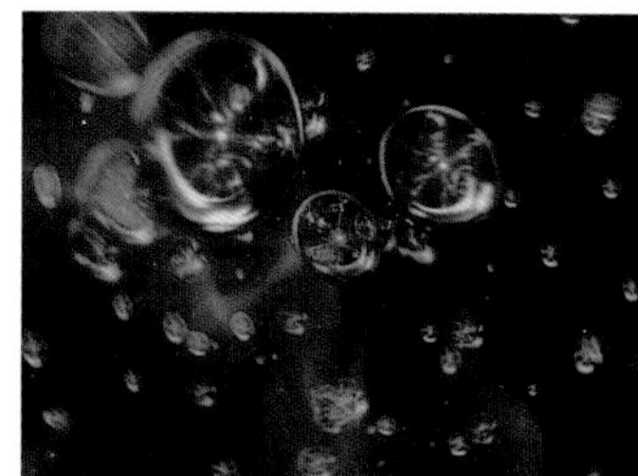

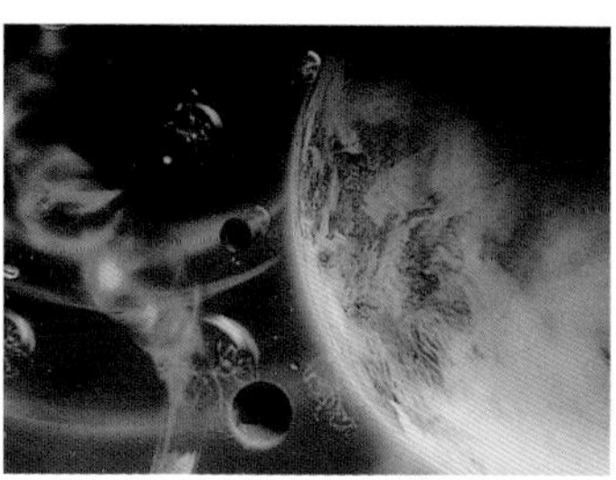

SILVER AWARD
for the Most Outstanding Television Commercial up to 60 seconds

Director
DOUG FOSTER

Copywriter
SIMON LEARMAN

Art Director
BRIAN FRASER

Creative Directors
SIMON LEARMAN
BRIAN FRASER

Producer
MICHELLE JAFFE

Animators
GRAHAME ANDREW
BEN HAYDEN
PAUL KAVANAGH
LAURENT HUGUENOIT

Production Company
BLINK PRODUCTIONS

Set Designer
ASSHETON GORTON

Agency Producer
JOHN MONTGOMERY

Editor
TIM BURKE

Lighting Cameramen
DOUG FOSTER
DAVID WYNN JONES

Music Composer/Arranger
JOHN BARRY

Agency
OGILVY & MATHER

Account Director
NEIL QUICK

Marketing Director
ROB McNEWIN

Client
GUINNESS BREWING GB

SILVER AWARD
for the Most Outstanding Television Commercial over 60 seconds

Director
MICHEL GONDRY

Copywriter
NICK WORTHINGTON

Art Director
JOHN GORSE

Creative Director
JOHN HEGARTY

Producers
TOBY COURLANDER
GEORGES BERMANN
PETE CHAMBERS

Set Designer
ROBBIE FREED

Agency Producer
PHILIPPA CRANE

Editor
RUSSELL ICKE

Lighting Cameraman
TIM MAURICE JONES

Music Composer/Arranger
GEIR JENSSEN

Production Company
PARTIZAN MIDI MINUIT

Agency
BARTLE BOGLE HEGARTY

Senior Marketing Manager
ROBERT HOLLOWAY

Client
LEVI STRAUSS & CO EUROPE SA

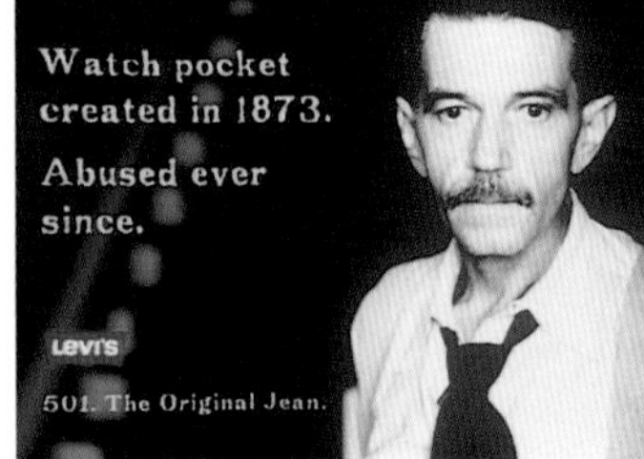

DRUGSTORE (MALE)

MUSIC:
Techno.

We see the view through the windscreen of an old truck heading into town. It's 1930, the American depression.

The truck comes to a stop outside a drugstore, as a train rumbles by.

We don't see the driver, just their view as they enter the store.

The shopkeeper, a woman and child and two girls, all turn to look.

At the counter, the driver asks for something.

The chemist hands over a tin of condoms, with a knowing smile. The driver tucks them into the watch pocket of his jeans and heads out of the door, leaving the woman in a state of shock and embarrassment.

We dissolve to the truck later that evening. It's waiting while a train thunders by. We then see it pulling up outside a white clapboard house.

A girl is waiting on the balcony.

The driver goes to the door. It opens, but it's not the girl. It's the chemist.

We see the driver for the first time, he's a young man in his teens. The chemist puts two and two together. Then, realising what's going on, trys to stop his daughter, but is powerless.

The chemist watches the young man climb into the vehicle and drive off with his daughter.

SUPER:
Watch Pocket Created in 1873.

Abused Ever Since.

Batwing logo.

SUPER:
501. The original Jean.

SILVER AWARD
for the Most Outstanding Television Campaign

Director
JEFF PRIESS

Copywriters
IZZY DEBELLIS
PAUL HIRSCH
JASON PETERSON

Art Directors
JASON PETERSON
PAUL HIRSCH
IZZY DEBELLIS

Creative Director
ANDY BERLIN

Producer
DEBORAH SULLIVAN

Music Composers/Arrangers
TOMANDANDY

Production Company
EPOCH FILMS

Agency
FALLON McELLIGOTT BERLIN

Vice President of Business Development
BILL DAUGHERTY

Client
NATIONAL BASKETBALL ASSOCIATION

PRESS CONFERENCE

AHMAD:
We are moments away from the much anticipated press conference. It's about to begin. Let's listen in.

MURRAY:
Thank you for coming out. I have an announcement to make that will come as a shock and surprise to some of you. I have decided to retire from the field of entertainment so that I may pursue a dream. I want to play in the NBA. I know that some of you will have questions.

REPORTER:
Why are you doing this?

MURRAY:
I have achieved everything possible in my own field. I am at the pinnacle of my industry and I have nothing else to prove.

REPORTER:
Have you ever won an Oscar?

MURRAY:
No. Not an Oscar.

REPORTER:
Were you ever nominated?

MURRAY:
No. I wasn't nominated either - no. But, I have an Emmy for writing.

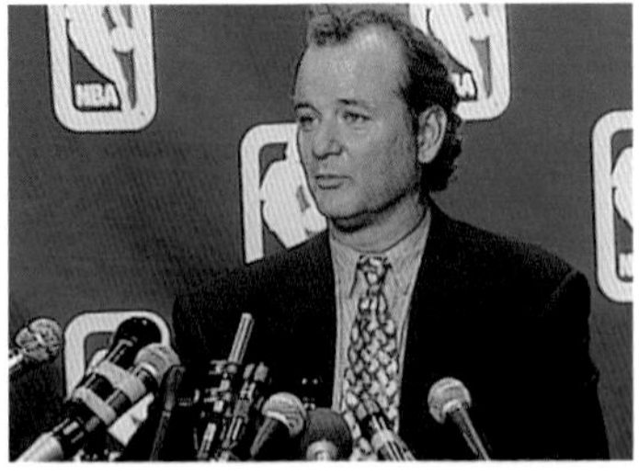

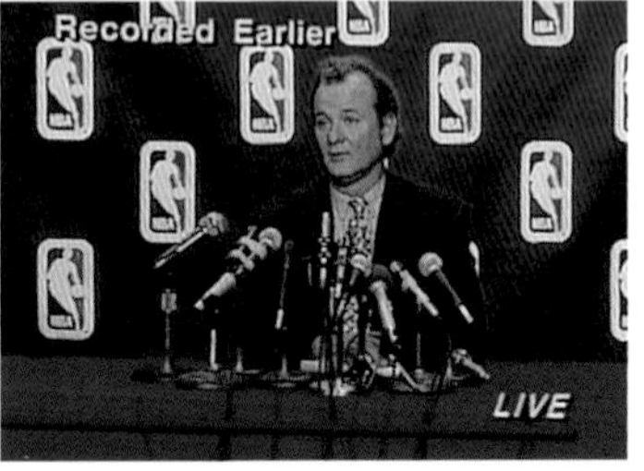

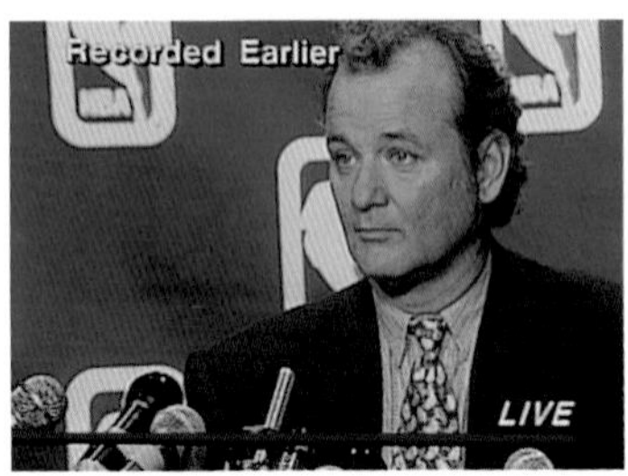

I HAD A DREAM

MURRAY:
I started thinking about basketball and I started dreaming about it and I had the same dream like three nights out of six and I thought to myself, "maybe this is real" and I went to someone who knows...you know...a lot about the future and they said that it was a real possibility.

REPORTER:
What was the dream exactly like?

MURRAY:
I scored the winning basket and then they hoisted me into the rafters and my whole body went up to the rafters of the stadium.

MOTHER

MURRAY:
I got a foul.

KID:
Foul?

MURRAY:
Right here.

KID:
It wouldn't have been a foul if you made the shot!

MURRAY:
It's the first one I've called, man. Come on, it's still game point. O.K., you ready? What, is this your mother coming to get you right here?

See that? In the NBA, some guy starts talking about your mama you don't listen up. You stay right here. My mother, my father, my dog, my brothers, my sisters. I'm all about the game. Baby -

KID:
I got it.

MURRAY:
You better get hungry or you're not going to be there with me.

STREET DRIBBLER

MURRAY:
It's like a religion with me. I believe in myself. I'm there for me. I believe in the ball and the ball is there for me. I believe in the court. But I just can't find the court. I have a ball and I'm here - I just can't find my court. I know it's out there somewhere.

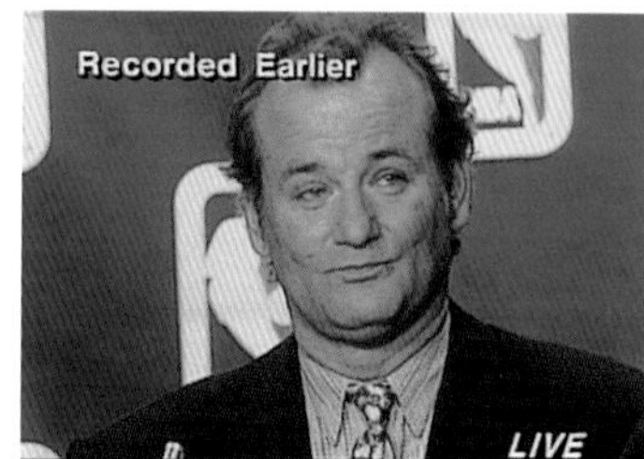

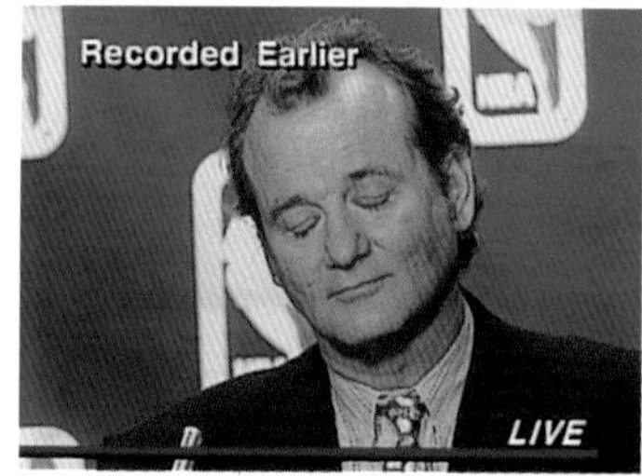

EATING

MURRAY:
What I got to worry about is the road, man. Hotel rooms, you know, room service, food. I'm gonna bring a vegetable juicer with me, you know just travel with it. When I get to a town I'm just going to find a farmer's market, go get fresh vegetables and juice. I got a really powerful will, but I just don't know where to direct it sometimes, you know. Like, I knew I was hungry and I knew I had to get food and I did. You know that's an example of my will power. You know, I just didn't have time to get the vegetables this morning.

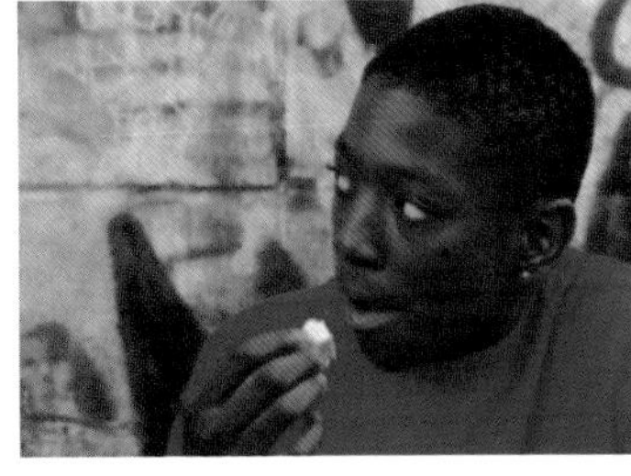

WHY SO TOUGH

MURRAY:
You know, I don't understand why you're being so tough on me, Mr Rashad. You weren't this tough on Michael Jordan or Scottie Pippen. I mean, just because I want to play? Maybe you and I should play sometime, you know?

REPORTER:
Mr Murray, I'm not trying to play in the National Basketball Association.

MURRAY:
You can call me Bill, I mean, not 'Mr Murray', you know, I know it's...think of this as the locker room.

REPORTER:
You were calling a press conference saying that you were going to play basketball and we found out here today you never played in college - you never played in high school.

MURRAY:
S...so?

BEACH LOVE AFFAIR

This commercial dips into a romantic day for a naturally beautiful woman and a 300 year old machiavellian duke called Drum. It was a few precious hours of wholesome innocence, of frolicking and fun that left her completely enchanted forever by Drum's extreme rudeness.

SILVER AWARD
for the Most Outstanding Cinema Commercial

Director
SEAN HINES

Copywriter
ALAN MOSELEY

Art Director
GRAHAM CAPPI

Creative Directors
ALAN MOSELEY
GRAHAM CAPPI

Producer
DAVID BURGESS

Agency Producer
SUZIE ROGERS

Lighting Cameraman
SEAN HINES

Music Composer/Arranger
FERN KINNEY

Production Company
HARRY FILMS

Agency
COWAN KEMSLEY TAYLOR

New Product Development Director
TIM ROPER

Client
TAUNTON CIDER PLC

SILVER AWARD NOMINATION
for the Most Outstanding Television Commercial up to 30 seconds

Director
JOHAN GULBRANSON

Copywriter
OISTEIN BORGE

Art Director
JOHAN GULBRANSON

Producer
KNUT E. JENSEN

Lighting Cameraman
KJELL VASSDAL

Music Composers/Arrangers
BOHREN & AASERUD

Production Company
LEO FILM

Agency
LEO BURNETT, OSLO

Marketing Executive
TERJE THORSRUD

Client
TIME FOTO

SNAPSHOT

Two young men walk by a couple of elderly ladies sunbathing. When they spot a camera by the side of the ladies, one of the men quickly has his friend take a close-up of his private parts. The camera is returned without the ladies noticing.

Develop and enlarge your favourite holiday picture at Time Foto.

CANTONA

VIDEO:
Cantona speaks on camera throughout. Dramatic black and white film capturing his intensity.

AUDIO:
I've been punished for striking a goalkeeper...

...for spitting at a supporter...

...for throwing my shirt at a referee...

...and for...

...calling my manager a bag of shit.

Then I called...

...the jury who punished me a bunch of idiots...

I thought I might have trouble finding a sponsor.

VIDEO:
Nike logo.

SILVER AWARD NOMINATION
for the Most Outstanding Television Commercial up to 30 seconds

Copywriter
BOB MOORE

Art Director
WARREN EAKINS

Creative Directors
BOB MOORE
MICHAEL PRIEVE

Producer
LILLY WEINGARTEN

Agency Producer
JANE DRIMBLECOMBE

Editor
DAVE BRIXTON

Production Company
PYTKA

Agency
WIEDEN & KENNEDY, AMSTERDAM

Client
NIKE INTERNATIONAL

SILVER AWARD NOMINATION
for the Most Outstanding Television Commercial up to 30 seconds

Director
JONATHAN BARNBROOK

Copywriter
ADRIAN JEFFERY

Art Director
LINDSEY REDDING

Creative Directors
SIMON SCOTT
ANDREW LINDSAY

Producer
YVONNE CHALK

Agency Producer
TIM MAGUIRE

Editor
JON HOLLIS

Music Composers/Arrangers
LOGORHYTHM

Animators
SARAH LEWIS
JONATHAN BARNBROOK

Production Company
TONY KAYE FILMS

Agency
FAULDS ADVERTISING

Client
BBC RADIO SCOTLAND

FOGGIE BUMMER

VIDEO:
As we hear the gripping radio article we see the words appear on screen. The words help to dramatise the action.

MVO1:
An exercise I often do is write words like 'BOMBAIZE' and 'FORFOUGHEN' and words like that up on the board, you see. And they think things like, a foggie bummer, what's a foggie bummer? Then we'll ask one another, you see, and...

MVO 2:
What is a foggie bummer?

MVO 1:
Foggie bummer means a bumble bee! (laughs)

MVO 2:
I was away to say you could have got us struck off air then!

MVO 1:
Oh no no no! It's not that bad!

CAPTION:
Mix up caption which reads,

Re-discover the power of the spoken word.

Silence.

SFX:
Music ident.

VIDEO:
Mix to end frame. We see the BBC Scotland logo and tuning device which demonstrates where to find the signal.

CAPTION:
UK National Station of the Year.

LINCOLN

ANNCR:
Abraham Lincoln did not have Cable. If he did have Cable, he could have taken advantage of our 'Buy one get one free deal.' Just get HBO or Showtime and we'll give you the other premium channel free. He'd have been home watching Indecent Proposal or The Firm or Last Action Hero. But he didn't. He went to Ford's Theatre and got shot. Think about it. Cable. If you don't get it, you'll just die.

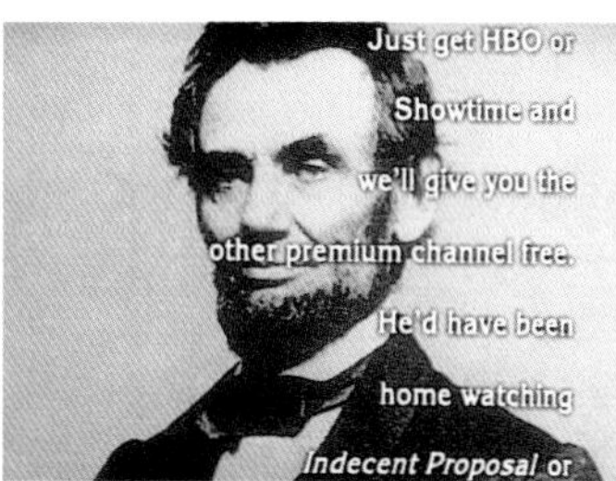

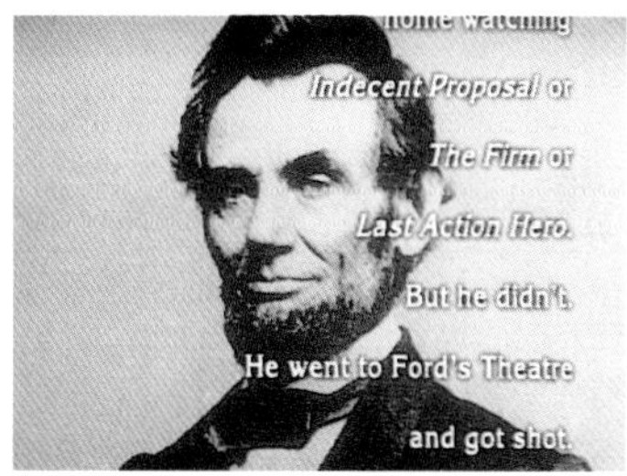

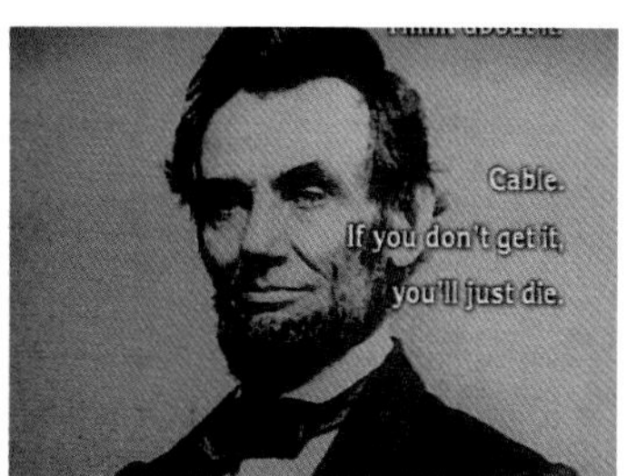

SILVER AWARD NOMINATION
for the Most Outstanding Television Commercial up to 30 seconds

Directors
PETER FAVAT
RICH HERSTEK

Copywriter
RICH HERSTEK

Art Director
PETER FAVAT

Creative Directors
PETER FAVAT
RICH HERSTEK

Producer
LARRY ANDERSON

Agency Producer
JENNIFER GLEBUS

Production Company
NATIONAL VIDEO

Agency
HOUSTON EFFLER HERSTEK FAVAT

Client
ADELPHIA CABLE

SILVER AWARD NOMINATION
for the Most Outstanding Television Commercial up to 40 seconds

Director
MICHEL GONDRY

Copywriter
NICK WORTHINGTON

Art Director
JOHN GORSE

Creative Director
JOHN HEGARTY

Producers
TOBY COURLANDER
GEORGES BERMANN
PETE CHAMBERS

Set Designer
ROBBIE FREED

Agency Producer
PHILIPPA CRANE

Editor
RUSSELL ICKE

Lighting Cameraman
TIM MAURICE JONES

Music Composer/Arranger
GEIR JENSSEN

Production Company
PARTIZAN MIDI MINUIT

Agency
BARTLE BOGLE HEGARTY

Senior Marketing Manager
ROBERT HOLLOWAY

Client
LEVI STRAUSS & CO EUROPE SA

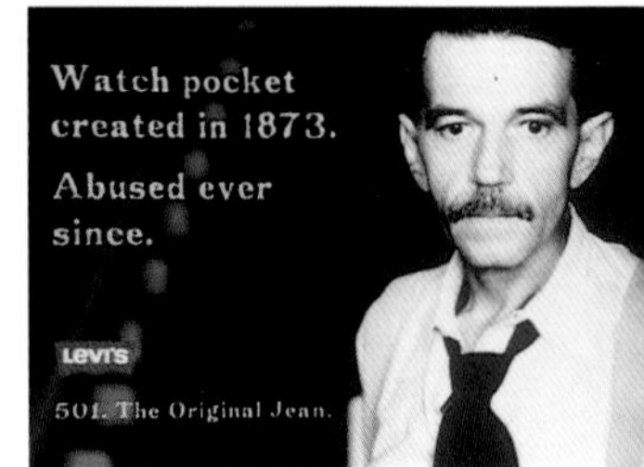

DRUGSTORE (MALE)

MUSIC:
Techno.

We see the view through the windscreen of an old truck heading into town. It's 1930, the American depression.

The truck comes to a stop outside a drugstore, as a train rumbles by.

We don't see the driver, just their view as they enter the store.

The shopkeeper, a woman and child and two girls, all turn to look.

At the counter, the driver asks for something.

The chemist hands over a tin of condoms, with a knowing smile. The driver tucks them into the watch pocket of his jeans and heads out of the door, leaving the woman in a state of shock and embarrassment.

We dissolve to the truck later that evening. It's waiting while a train thunders by. We then see it pulling up outside a white clapboard house.

A girl is waiting on the balcony.

The driver goes to the door. It opens, but it's not the girl. It's the chemist.

We see the driver for the first time, he's a young man in his teens. The chemist puts two and two together. Then, realising what's going on, trys to stop his daughter, but is powerless.

The chemist watches the young man climb into the vehicle and drive off with his daughter.

SUPER:
Watch Pocket Created in 1873.

Abused Ever Since.

Batwing logo.

SUPER:
501. The original Jean.

THE WORLD ACCORDING TO FRONTERA

Two African women are walking at what is apparently an impossible 45 degree angle. A Frontera drives past them, seemingly on the level.

Cut to a Frontera travelling through water which is at an odd 45 degree angle. The car passes Filipino fishermen on poles in the water.

Cut to the car in front of a waterfall. However, the water is running at a 45 degree angle.

Cut to Mongolian horsemen leading their horses past a Frontera apparently on the level. The horses are walking in a strange manner. The camera then reveals that they are not on the level but descending a steep slope.

Cut to a Frontera on a 45 degree icy slope. A sleigh full of Eskimo children slides past the car. Oddly, however, the sleigh is going uphill.

SUPER:
See a different world.

Cut to a rock climber abseiling across screen. He passes a Frontera parked on the level. In reality, though, the car is hanging on a cliff-face and he is dropping down vertically.

SUPER:
The Frontera 4x4 and Vauxhall logo.

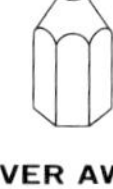

SILVER AWARD NOMINATION
for the Most Outstanding Television Commercial up to 40 seconds

Director
FRANK BUDGEN

Copywriter
PHIL DEARMAN

Art Director
CHARLES INGE

Creative Director
PAUL WEINBERGER

Producer
PAUL ROTHWELL

Set Designer
TONY NOBLE

Agency Producer
CHARLES CRISP

Editor
SAM SNEADE

Lighting Cameraman
HENRY BRAHAM

Production Company
PAUL WEILAND FILM COMPANY

Agency
LOWE HOWARD-SPINK

Marketing Executive
PHIL HARWOOD

Client
VAUXHALL MOTOR COMPANY

SILVER AWARD NOMINATION
for the Most Outstanding Television Commercial up to 40 seconds

Directors
TREVOR ROBINSON
ALAN YOUNG

Copywriter
ALAN YOUNG

Art Director
TREVOR ROBINSON

Creative Director
AXEL CHALDECOTT

Producer
JANE FULLER

Agency Producer
ZOE BELL

Editor
KEVIN CHICKEN

Lighting Cameraman
HOWARD ATHERTON

Production Company
JANE FULLER ASSOCIATES

Agency
HOWELL HENRY CHALDECOTT LURY & PARTNERS

Brand Manager
DAVID ATTER

Client
BRITVIC SOFT DRINKS LIMITED

BOSS'S OFFICE

A phone call interrupts a tense meeting. It's answered by the boss who hands the phone to a younger guy, 'the victim'.

He nervously explains the call – 'It's my mother.'

We cut away to see a can of apple Tango on the other end of the phone.

The can taunts him – 'You've been thinking about me haven't you? Picture condensation running down my sleek sides.'

The victim smiles, vainly pretending nothing is wrong. His boss eyes him suspiciously.

The can asks him to talk dirty to her. He mumbles into the mouthpiece, 'Big juicy apples.'

'Louder' the can commands.

'Big juicy apples' the victim says with a bit more volume.

The can demands he says it louder still. He throws caution to the wind – it's too late to worry about what his boss thinks.

The victim bellows at the top of his voice:

'Big juicy apples dagnammit.'

MADNESS

We see footage taken by police cameras, of people driving dangerously on the road. The track 'Madness' by Madness plays throughout.

Finally, we cut to title:

Volvo. Because you never know who's round the bend.

SILVER AWARD NOMINATION
for the Most Outstanding Television Commercial up to 40 seconds

Copywriter
NICK BELL

Art Director
GREG MARTIN

Creative Director
DAVID ABBOTT

Agency Producer
YVONNE CHALKLEY

Editor
NICK SPENCER

Music Composers/Arrangers
MADNESS
EMI MUSIC SERVICES

Agency
ABBOTT MEAD VICKERS.BBDO LIMITED

Communications Manager
CRAIG FABIAN

Client
VOLVO CARS UK LIMITED

SILVER AWARD NOMINATION
for the Most Outstanding Television Commercial up to 60 seconds

Copywriter
NICK BELL

Art Director
GREG MARTIN

Creative Director
DAVID ABBOTT

Agency Producer
YVONNE CHALKLEY

Editor
NICK SPENCER

Music Composers/Arrangers
MADNESS
EMI MUSIC SERVICES

Agency
ABBOTT MEAD VICKERS.BBDO LIMITED

Communications Manager
CRAIG FABIAN

Client
VOLVO CARS UK LIMITED

BECAUSE YOU NEVER KNOW
WHO'S ROUND THE BEND.

MADNESS

We see footage taken by police cameras, of people driving dangerously on the road. The track 'Madness' by Madness plays throughout.

Finally, we cut to title:

Volvo. Because you never know who's round the bend.

SILVER AWARD NOMINATION
for the Most Outstanding Television Commercial over 60 seconds

Director
TONY KAYE

Copywriter
TOM CARTY

Art Director
WALTER CAMPBELL

Creative Director
DAVID ABBOTT

Producer
MIRANDA DAVIS

Agency Producer
FRANK LIEBERMAN

Editor
PETER GODDARD

Lighting Cameraman
TONY KAYE

Sound Designers
ROHAN YOUNG
MALCOLM BRISTOW

Music Composers/Arrangers
JENKINS & RATLEDGE

Production Company
TONY KAYE FILMS

Agency
ABBOTT MEAD VICKERS.BBDO LIMITED

Communications Manager
CRAIG FABIAN

Client
VOLVO CARS UK LIMITED

PHOTOGRAPHER

A documentary studying the life of war photographer Jana Schneider.

She talks about her working life and the importance of equipment. Eyes, camera, car.

We see Schneider in a dangerous assignment. She drives her Volvo 850 out onto a deserted runway to photograph a suspicious plane. The plane starts to taxi toward take off.

However, Schneider has an amazing camera rig mounted on the side of her car, which is activated by a cable release on the steering wheel. This allows her to get the shots she needs whilst driving close alongside the hurtling plane.

The situation is made even more deadly as cargo bales are being thrown from the plane into her path.

Volvo. A car you can believe in.

PHOTOGRAPHER:
My photography is about life, even when I photograph death.

*When you're stabbed or hit by a bullet it doesn't hurt like you'd imagine.
It burns. It's almost like a fast racing burn.*

My job isn't to judge. My job is to get in and get out.

I do all this, because it's about believing my pictures are the truth.

*I'm basically isolating a milli second in time.
If you're documenting life, a moment only happens once.*

Being in the bush makes me deal with a different rhythm.

What makes me laugh is, you know, is getting through the tiniest keyhole and getting it all when they say it's impossible.

*Your photographs are only as good as the position you get in. I can't get a photograph if I'm not in position.
This car gets me into that position.*

In my business everything's a one shot deal, you get it or you don't.

Equipment is everything. Eyes, camera, car.

SILVER AWARD NOMINATION
for the Most Outstanding Television Campaign

Directors
PETER FAVAT
RICH HERSTEK

Copywriter
RICH HERSTEK

Art Director
PETER FAVAT

Creative Directors
PETER FAVAT
RICH HERSTEK

Producer
LARRY ANDERSON

Agency Producer
JENNIFER GLEBUS

Production Company
NATIONAL VIDEO

Agency
HOUSTON EFFLER
HERSTEK FAVAT

Client
ADELPHIA CABLE

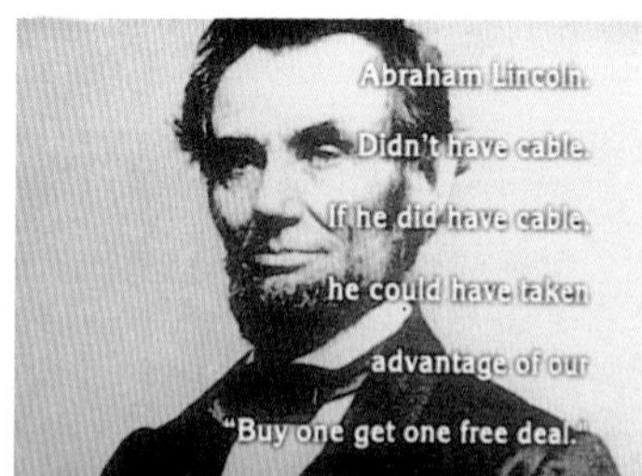

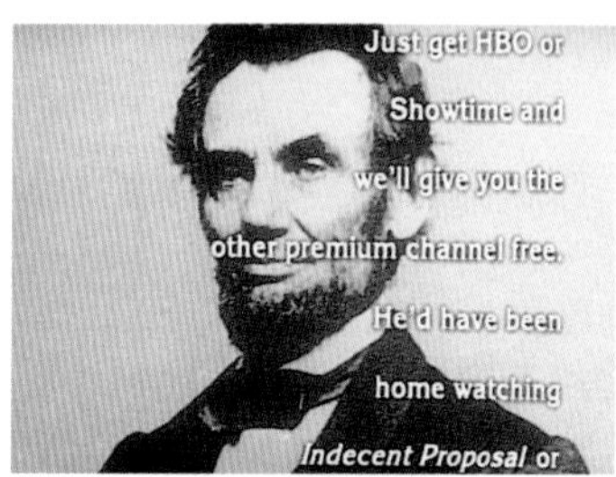

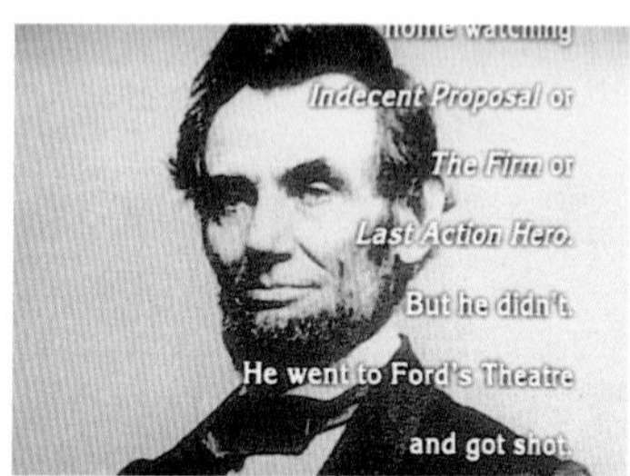

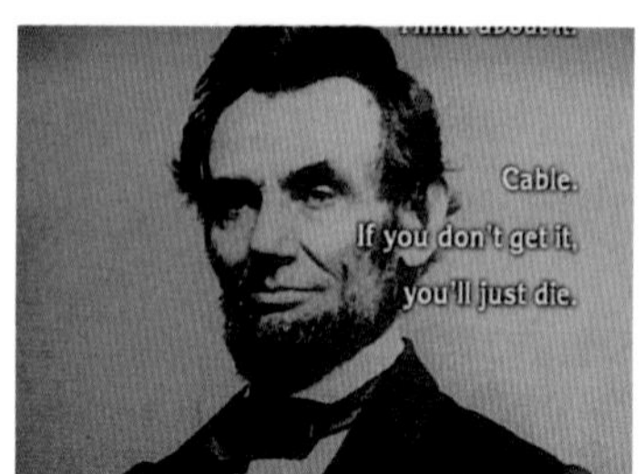

LINCOLN

ANNCR:
Abraham Lincoln did not have Cable. If he did have Cable, he could have taken advantage of our 'Buy one get one free deal.' Just get HBO or Showtime and we'll give you the other premium channel free. He'd have been home watching Indecent Proposal or The Firm or Last Action Hero. But he didn't. He went to Ford's Theatre and got shot. Think about it. Cable. If you don't get it, you'll just die.

HENDRIX

ANNCR:
Jimi Hendrix. Totally dope rocker. Awesome blacklight poster. Didn't have Cable. If he did have Cable, he could have watched the Discovery Channel. And he would have learned that, well, drugs are bad. He could have seen himself on MTV instead of on some astral plane. But he didn't. What can you learn from the Jimi Hendrix Experience? Get Cable. If you don't, you'll just die.

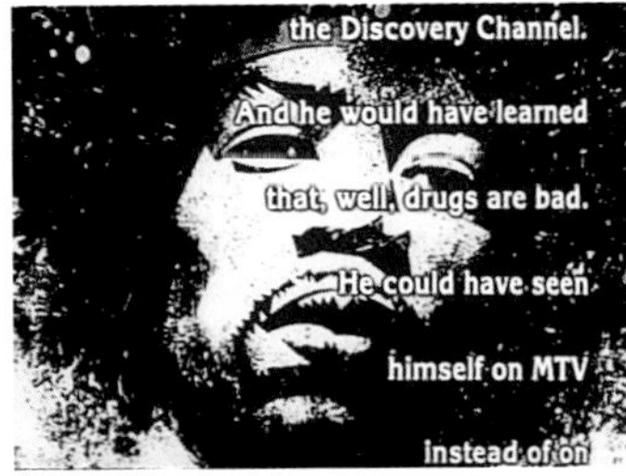

DINOSAURS

ANNCR:
The Dinosaurs. They didn't have Cable. If they did have Cable they could have watched the Weather Channel! They would have seen the ice-age coming. And they could have got inside. Or put on something warm. Were they too cheap to spend the $9.95 to get hooked up, plus get a free premium upgrade deal like the one we're offering now? All we know is, they didn't get Cable. And now they're gone. Cable. If you don't get it, you'll just die.

TRUE ROMANCE

As we hear the radio article, we see the words appear on the screen. The words help to dramatise the action.

SPEAKER:
These are the...these are the things that life is made of. I wanted to see what the Atlantic was like, you can only see it by going there. But much more importantly, I wanted to see what I was like on the Atlantic.

What's wrong with romance?

It brings light into life. Into your own life and into other peoples' lives.

God forbid that we were all practical pragmatists.

Silence.

Mix up caption which reads:

Re-discover the power of the spoken word.

Mix to end frame. We see the BBC Scotland logo and tuning device which demonstrates where to find the signal.

CAPTION:
UK National Station of the Year.

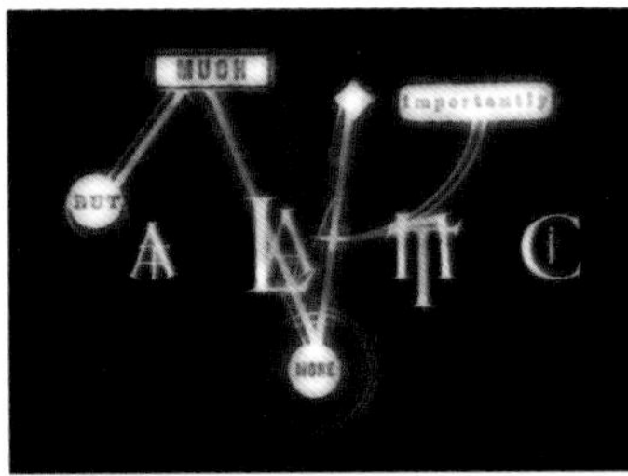

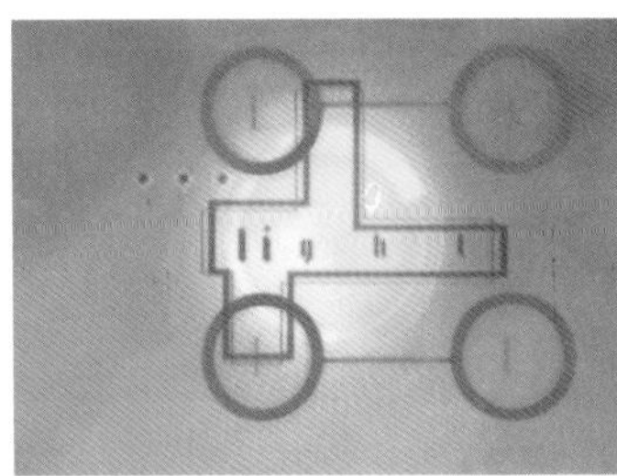

SILVER AWARD NOMINATION
for the Most Outstanding Television Campaign

Director
JONATHAN BARNBROOK

Copywriter
ADRIAN JEFFERY

Art Director
LINDSEY REDDING

Creative Directors
SIMON SCOTT
ANDREW LINDSAY

Producer
YVONNE CHALK

Agency Producer
TIM MAGUIRE

Editor
JON HOLLIS

Music Composers/Arrangers
LOGORHYTHM

Production Company
TONY KAYE FILMS

Agency
FAULDS ADVERTISING

Account Group Director
TOM GILL

Head of Presentation
PETER GOURD

Client
BBC RADIO SCOTLAND

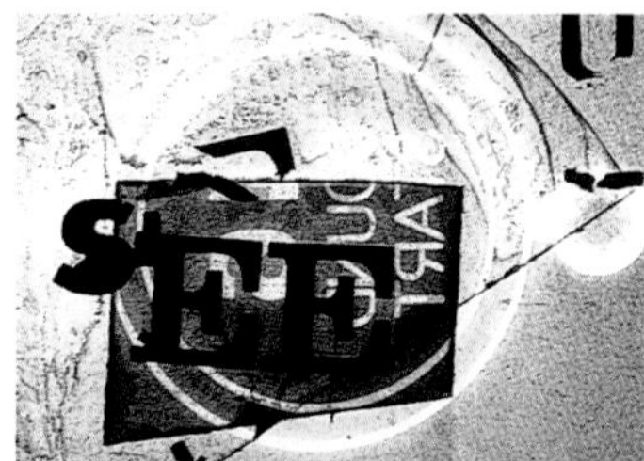

FOGGIE BUMMER

VIDEO:
As we hear the gripping radio article we see the words appear on screen. The words help to dramatise the action.

MVO1:
An exercise I often do is write words like 'BOMBAIZE' and 'FORFOUGHEN' and words like that up on the board, you see. And they think things like, a foggie bummer, what's a foggie bummer? Then we'll ask one another, you see, and...

MVO 2:
What is a foggie bummer?

MVO 1:
Foggie bummer means a bumble bee! (laughs)

MVO 2:
I was away to say you could have got us struck off air then!

MVO 1:
Oh no no no! It's not that bad!

CAPTION:
Mix up caption which reads,

Re-discover the power of the spoken word.

Silence.

SFX:
Music ident.

VIDEO:
Mix to end frame. We see the BBC Scotland logo and tuning device which demonstrates where to find the signal.

CAPTION:
UK National Station of the Year.

TARTAN TOYBOYS

As we hear the radio article, we see the words appear on the screen. The words help to dramatise the action.

MUM:
I'm looking forward to seeing the Tartan Toyboys.

DAUGHTER:
What do you think they're going to be like, though?

MUM:
Well, I hope they're going to have long legs and wee bums and broad shoulders, and I hope they're going to wear kilts. I'll be terribly disappointed if they don't have kilts on (laughs). I'll be equally disappointed if they don't have them off before the night's over.

Silence.

Mix up caption which reads:

Re-discover the power of the spoken word.

Mix to end frame. We see the BBC Scotland logo and tuning device which demonstrates where to find the signal.

CAPTION:
UK National Station of the Year.

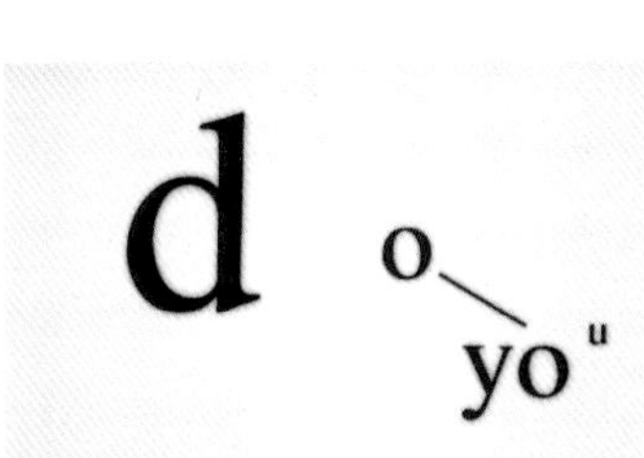

Directors
SIMON TAYLOR
GRAHAM WOOD

Copywriter
ADRIAN JEFFERY

Art Director
LINDSEY REDDING

Creative Directors
SIMON SCOTT
ANDREW LINDSAY

Producer
HELEN LANGRIDGE

Production Company
HELEN LANGRIDGE ASSOCIATES

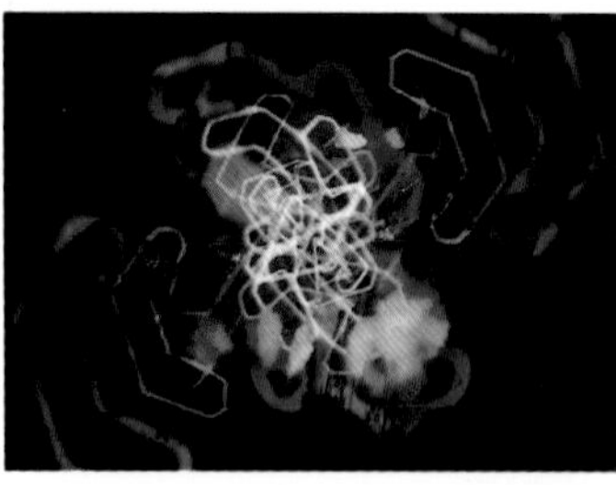

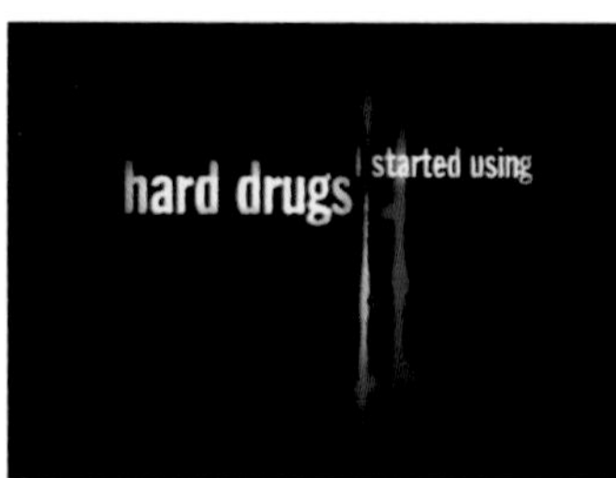

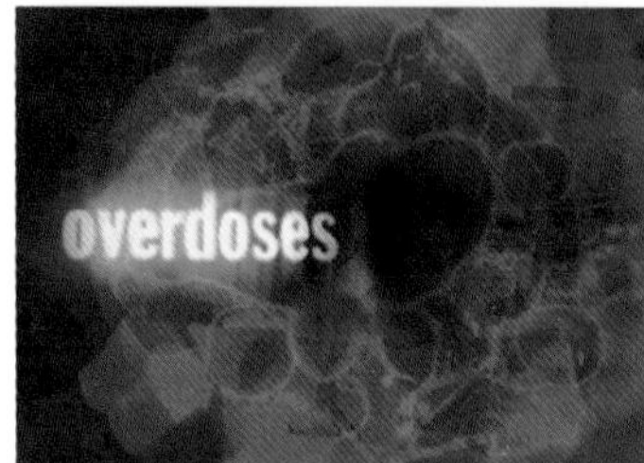

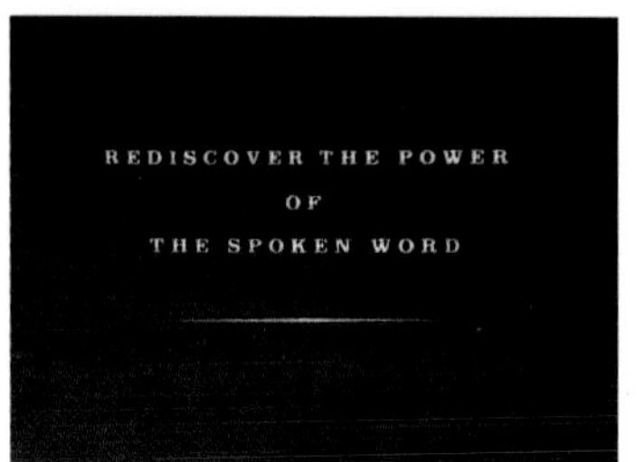

NAE HOPE

VIDEO:
As we hear the gripping radio article, we see the words appear on screen. The words help to dramatise the action.

MVO:
I'm 27 just now and I started using hard drugs when I was 22, it was that kinda day when everyone was using it so I had a wee shot and I liked it.

And just recently there I had two overdoses. It was due to high purity heroin.

It was on streets about here. I think I'll be drug dependent for the rest of my days I think. Nae hope. Nae hope whatsoever.

CAPTION:
Mix up caption which reads,

Re-discover the power of the spoken word.

Silence.

VIDEO
Mix to end frame.

SFX:
Music ident.

VIDEO:
We see the BBC Scotland logo and tuning device which demonstrates where to find the signal.

CAPTION:
UK National Station of the Year.

GRAFFITI

As we hear the gripping radio article, we see the words appear on the screen. The words help to dramatise the action.

We hear a snippet from a BBC Scotland programme.

MVO:
If I can explain some of this graffiti that's in the ceiling of the car here. We got psycho and Demon. We got psycho from rolling 60's cripps. We got...er Junior from Ghetto boys...Um, as I'm looking, I'm starting to feel these real kind of er, emotions choking up in me because there's probably about 20 or 25 different gang members that are carved in here, Babyface here, and I'd say about a dozen of them, almost half of them are dead.

Silence.

Mix up caption which reads:

Re-discover the power of the spoken word.

Mix to end frame.

SFX:
Music ident.

We see the BBC Scotland logo and tuning device which demonstrates where to find the signal.

CAPTION:
UK National Station of the Year.

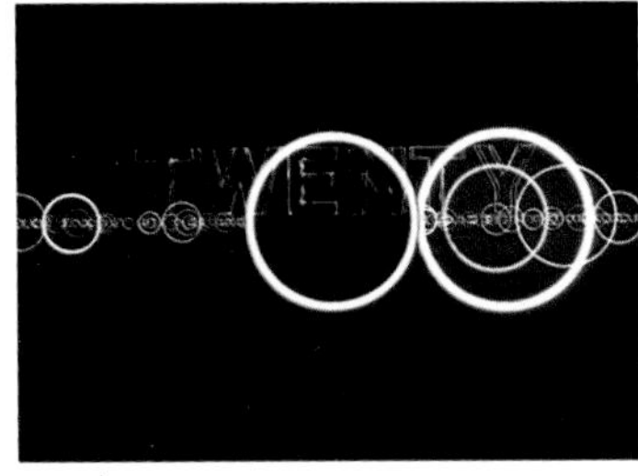

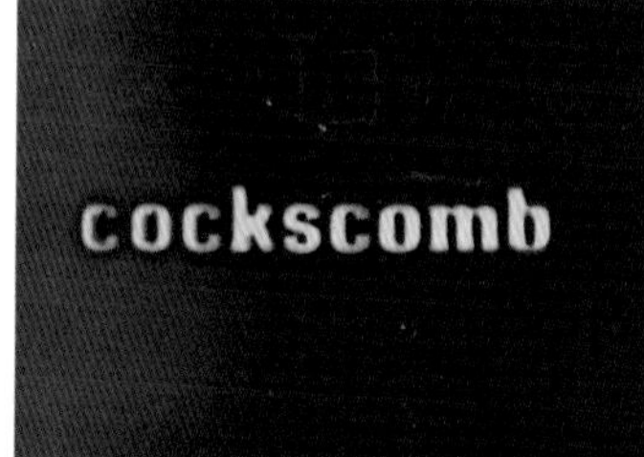

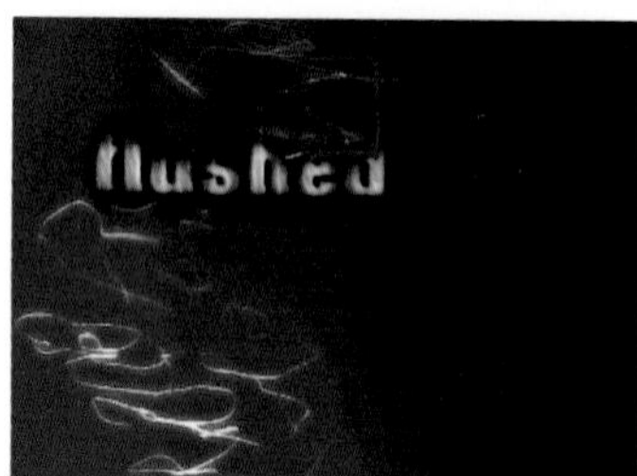

COCKEREL

As we hear the gripping radio article, we see the words appear on the screen. The words help to dramatise the action.

We hear a snippet from a BBC Scotland programme.

MVO:
Line out. Outside the French 22. Back on the main...oop...now the referee has called a halt to the proceedings, it's now over to the Scottish 22 and heading upfield. It's a magnificent fellow with a black underbelly, a gold coloured back and a red cockscomb and the cockerel's over the Scot's 5 metre line, heading for touch and the stewards are looking just a little bit flushed/perplexed, a little bit perplexed and flushed, ...just selling them a wee dummy and a wee side step and away he goes. Yes, he's over the touch line, now he's on the running track, and he's almost away.

Silence.

Mix up caption which reads:

Re-discover the power of the spoken word.

Mix to end frame. We see the BBC Scotland logo and tuning device which demonstrates where to find the signal.

SFX:
Music ident.

CAPTION:
UK National Station of the Year.

GEORGIES

We are looking at the exterior of the shop.

ROBERT:
Georgies, brought to you in association with the Snapple Beverage Corporation makers of delicious fruit juice drinks and iced teas.

We cut to interior of the shop.

CUSTOMER:
Excuse me.

GEORGIE:
Welcome to Georgies. The biggest little shop in London.

ROBERT:
Hey Georgie where do you keep the Snapple?

Georgie points.

Camera bumps fridge.

ROBERT:
Why don't you carry all the flavours?

GEORGIE:
No Room. Yes please?

Camera pans around, jostles with customers.

CUSTOMER:
(Geoffrey)
Excuse me.

ROBERT:
(Wildtrack only)
Pardon me. Oops...sorry.

CUSTOMER:
(Karen)
Excuse me.

We cut to exterior of shop.

Pan up to Snapple logo on awning.

GEORGIE:
So come to Georgies, 78b Log Acre, Covent Garden, because biggest isn't always best.

SUPER:
Made from some of the best stuff on earth.

SILVER AWARD NOMINATION
for the Most Outstanding Television Campaign

Director
MARK STORY

Copywriter
GEOFF SMITH

Art Director
SIMON MORRIS

Creative Directors
CHRIS O'SHEA
KEN HOGGINS

Producer
LUCINDA WALLOP

Executive Producers
LISA BRYER
CAROL HEYWOOD

Agency Producer
SUSIE STOCK

Editor
IAN WEIL

Lighting Cameraman
DAVID WALSH

Production Company
COWBOY FILMS

Agency
BANKS HOGGINS O'SHEA

International Marketing Director
JUNE BLOCKLIN

Client
SNAPPLE BEVERAGE CORPORATION

JOHN C. EWENS

We are looking at the exterior of the shop.

ROBERT:
John C. Ewens, brought to you in association with the Snapple Beverage Corporation, makers of delicious fruit juice drinks and iced teas.

We cut to interior of the shop.

CHRIS:
Remember those great sweets you had as a kid?

Well, we've still got them. Pear drops, Acid drops, Pineapple chunks...We also have...

ROBERT:
Hey Chris! What are those green things on the top shelf?

Chris looks round for Choc Limes.

CHRIS:
(turns his back - shows jacket logo)

...Those ones? They're Chocolate Limes.

ROBERT:
(Voice Over off screen)

So how's the Snapple moving?

CHRIS:
Yeah fine - we also have an extensive range of toys and games. Show them, Mum.

RAE:
This professional football trainer has been marked down yet again, to this unrepeatable low, low price.

Pan off to Snapple.

RAE:
(off screen)

Cut to exterior of shop.

Pan to Snapple bottle in window.

CHRIS:
So remember Jand C. Ewans, Golborne Road W10. Your first choice for papers, sweets and toys.

SUPER:
Made from some of the best stuff on earth.

MISTRY'S

We are looking at the exterior of the shop.

Mandy and K.D. in front of shop.

ROBERT:
Mistry's Health Foods, brought to you in association with the Snapple Beverage Corporation, makers of delicious fruit juice drinks and iced teas.

We cut to interior of the shop.

MANDY:
Health food's no mystery at Mistry's. We've got Icelandic kelp tablets.

Close-ups of Mandy and K.D.

K.D.
Naturally.

MANDY:
Blue Wheat Tortilla Chips.

K.D.
Naturally.

MANDY:
And Organic Honey from Africa.

K.D.
Naturally.

ROBERT:
And Snapple.

K.D.
Naturally.

MANDY:
We also have a full range of Mistry's Health products.

K.D.
Naturally.

MANDY:
Frankincense and Myrhh.

K.D.
Naturally.

MANDY:
Herbal eye patches.

K.D.
Naturally.

Cut to exterior of shop.

MANDY:
If you think about what you eat, think about us.

Pan off to Snapple in window during.

K.D.
Mistry's Health Food Store, 20 Station Parade, Willesden Green, NW2.

SUPER:
Made from some of the best stuff on earth.

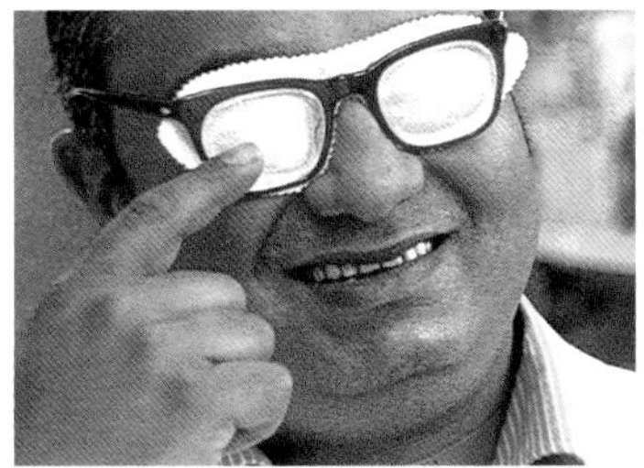

SILVER AWARD NOMINATION
for the Most Outstanding Cinema Commercial

Director
JOE PUBLIC

Copywriter
HUGH TODD

Art Director
ADAM SCHOLES

Creative Directors
JOHN DEAN
SIMON GREEN

Producer
CHRIS STEVENSON

Agency Producer
PATRICK MURPHY

Editor
MARK RICHARDS

Lighting Cameraman
SIMON RICHARDS

Music Composer/Arranger
SERGE GAINSBOURG

Production Company
STARK FILMS

Agency
BUTTERFIELD DAY DEVITO HOCKNEY

Managing Director
JOHN WARR

Client
WARR'S HARLEY DAVIDSON

GRANDAD

Open on an old man with the support of a zimmer frame, in a suburban front room.

He talks to camera (understandingly):

I suppose my son's right......I don't really need an electric wheelchair right now......it would've got me out of the house a bit more - and I could have had a pint with my mates......but like he says...I can wait.

MUSIC:
Brigitte Bardot, 'Harley Davidson'.

Cut to his son standing proudly next to a brand spanking new Harley Davidson motorbike outside Warr's Harley Davidson shop.

Super logo and line:

Harley Davidson - A Completely Irresponsible Thing To Do.

Reprise to old man sitting by gas fire. The fire goes out. He attempts to stand up.

SILVER AWARD NOMINATION
for the Most Outstanding Cinema Commercial

STUNTMAN

A documentary style commercial featuring the work and philosophies of a stuntman.

He talks about the importance of belief, not only in himself, but in his car; a Volvo 850.

The climax of the film shows the stuntman driving over a bridge. But this is no ordinary bridge, it has no centre, so the car must travel on the supports of the bridge which are only a tyre's width in thickness.

VOLVO. A car you can believe in.

STUNTMAN:
I used to be a stunt kid before I was a stuntman.

I learnt one thing early on, belief is everything.

My interest in cars started on my fourth birthday.

I've loved driving cars ever since.

That's why I like this car.

It's great to drive.

I do stunts people think can't be done.

They think my stunts are crazy.

I've never been afraid of heights, ever.

I guess I have a pretty healthy fear of death.

You can conquer fear through knowledge.

One centimetre this way or that, and it's four hundred miles down.

When I ask it to do something it responds.

Control.

I'm a control freak.

You know some people say I'll believe it when I see it.

I prefer to say you'll see it when you believe it.

They think my stunts are crazy.

Director
TONY KAYE

Copywriter
TOM CARTY

Art Director
WALTER CAMPBELL

Creative Director
DAVID ABBOTT

Producers
YVONNE CHALK
MIRANDA DAVIS

Agency Producer
LINDSAY HUGHES

Editor
PETER GODDARD

Lighting Cameraman
TONY KAYE

Sound Designers
WARREN HAMILTON
ROHAN YOUNG
MALCOLM BRISTOW

Music Composers/Arrangers
JENKINS & RATLEDGE

Production Company
TONY KAYE FILMS

Agency
ABBOTT MEAD VICKERS.BBDO LIMITED

Communications Manager
CRAIG FABIAN

Client
VOLVO CARS UK LIMITED

SILVER AWARD NOMINATION
for the Most Outstanding Cinema Commercial

Director
MICHEL GONDRY

Copywriter
NICK WORTHINGTON

Art Director
JOHN GORSE

Creative Director
JOHN HEGARTY

Producers
TOBY COURLANDER
GEORGES BERMANN
PETE CHAMBERS

Set Designer
ROBBIE FREED

Agency Producer
PHILIPPA CRANE

Editor
RUSSELL ICKE

Lighting Cameraman
TIM MAURICE JONES

Music Composer/Arranger
GEIR JENSSEN

Production Company
PARTIZAN MIDI MINUIT

Agency
BARTLE BOGLE HEGARTY

Senior Marketing Manager
ROBERT HOLLOWAY

Client
LEVI STRAUSS & CO EUROPE SA

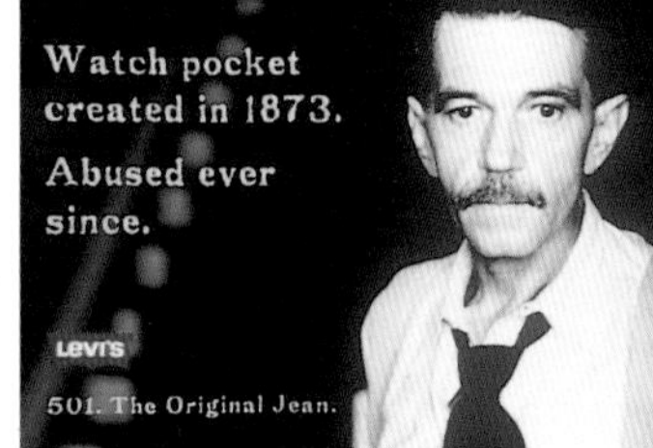

DRUGSTORE (MALE)

MUSIC:
Techno.

We see the view through the windscreen of an old truck heading into town. It's 1930, the American depression.

The truck comes to a stop outside a drugstore, as a train rumbles by.

We don't see the driver, just their view as they enter the store.

The shopkeeper, a woman and child and two girls, all turn to look.

At the counter, the driver asks for something.

The chemist hands over a tin of condoms, with a knowing smile. The driver tucks them into the watch pocket of his jeans and heads out of the door, leaving the woman in a state of shock and embarrassment.

We dissolve to the truck later that evening. It's waiting while a train thunders by. We then see it pulling up outside a white clapboard house.

A girl is waiting on the balcony.

The driver goes to the door. It opens, but it's not the girl. It's the chemist.

We see the driver for the first time, he's a young man in his teens. The chemist puts two and two together. Then, realising what's going on, trys to stop his daughter, but is powerless.

The chemist watches the young man climb into the vehicle and drive off with his daughter.

SUPER:
Watch Pocket Created in 1873.

Abused Ever Since.

Batwing logo.

SUPER:
501. The original Jean.

WIFE

Open on a woman standing on a street corner at night.

SFX:
Cars swishing by.

She talks to camera (positively):

What with things being so tight at the moment, my husband persuaded me to take a second job...I couldn't get the hang of it to begin with, but I'm improving...

...one good thing though, the hours are flexible and I do get to meet people. Some of them are a bit strange though....

...I do get a bit exhausted sometimes 'cos I have to concentrate so hard. But like he says...we need every penny we can get.

MUSIC:
Brigitte Bardot, 'Harley Davidson'.

Cut to her husband standing proudly next to a brand spanking new Harley Davidson motorbike outside Warr's Harley Davidson shop.

Super logo and line:

Harley Davidson - A Completely Irresponsible Thing To Do.

Reprise to his wife leaning into a car window

'Hundred pounds, alright?'. She smiles at the camera and gets into the car.

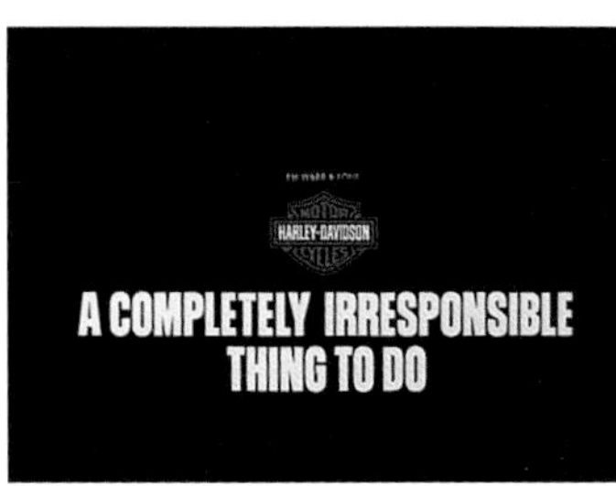

SILVER AWARD NOMINATION
for the Most Outstanding Cinema Commercial

Director
JOE PUBLIC

Copywriter
HUGH TODD

Art Director
ADAM SCHOLES

Creative Directors
JOHN DEAN
SIMON GREEN

Producer
CHRIS STEVENSON

Agency Producer
PATRICK MURPHY

Editor
MARK RICHARDS

Lighting Cameraman
SIMON RICHARDS

Music Composer/Arranger
SERGE GAINSBOURG

Production Company
STARK FILMS

Agency
BUTTERFIELD DAY DEVITO HOCKNEY

Managing Director
JOHN WARR

Client
WARR'S HARLEY DAVIDSON

Up to and including 10 seconds

Director
BRIAN MORRIS

Copywriter
BARBERA TAMMES

Art Director
JACQUELINE DONKER

Creative Director
HARRY KRAMP

Producer
DANIËLLE VAN BERKEL

Agency Producer
MAARTEN FENENGA

Lighting Cameraman
HARRO VAN SCHOONHOVEN

Music Composer/Arranger
MARCEL WALVISCH

Production Company
T&T FILM PRODUCTIONS

Agency
PPGH/JWT

Marketing Executive
MARION MEYS

Client
ELIDA ANDRÉLON

ANDRÉLON

A bottle of shampoo is shown in a snow storm scene in a glass bell. The bell is turned upside down and put back in place. Nothing happens, not a snowflake drifts down.

SUPER & VO:
The anti-dandruff shampoo. One of Andrélon's special shampoos.

CHIHUAHUA

SFX:
Phone ringing.

VIDEO:
Telephone on a little dainty pillow on the table.

Hand reaches in to grab phone receiver, instead picks up chihuahua.

GUY:
Hello.

AVO:
Time to have your eyes checked?

SFX:
Dog yelp!

ART CARD:
$50 Eye Exam Rebate.

AVO:
We'll pay for your eye exam, up to $50.

ART CARD:
Family Eye Care Month.

AVO:
Right now at EyeMasters.

LOGO:
EyeMasters.

Your Eyes. Our Focus.

$50 Eye Exam Rebate

Up to and including 10 seconds

Director
ROBERT HANNANT

Copywriters
DAVID COATS
KEVIN SUTTON

Art Director
KENT JOHNSON

Creative Directors
GLENN DADY
MIKE MALONE

Producer
CAROL LEFTWICH

Editor
MICHAEL VAN DE KAMER

Music Composer/Arranger
TOM FALKNER

Production Company
CROSSROADS FILMS

Agency
THE RICHARDS GROUP

Marketing Executive
GARY HOSS

Client
EYEMASTERS

Up to and including 10 seconds

Director
SERGIO SIMONETTI

Copywriter
SIMON BERE

Art Director
MARC BENNETT

Creative Director
TREVOR BEATTIE

Producer
MALCOLM BUBB

Animator
SERGIO SIMONETTI

Agency Producer
GILBERT KING

Editor
SERGIO SIMONETTI

Lighting Cameraman
SERGIO SIMONETTI

Rostrum Cameraman
SERGIO SIMONETTI

Production Companies
SIMONETTI FILMS
JAMES GARRETT & PARTNERS

Agency
TBWA

Account Director
NEIL CHRISTIE

Marketing Executive
DAVID HORNCASTLE

Client
NISSAN GB LIMITED

SPIDER

We see a spider repeatedly trying and failing to scale the wall of a ceramic bathtub.

Cut to shot of Terrano II coming over hill.

SUPER:
You can with a Nissan.

JOINED BY:
The 4 X 4 Terrano II.

SNO DANDRUFF

Open on a close up of a Father Christmas snow shaker.

A woman's hand reaches into shot, picks up the snow shaker and vigorously shakes it.

She gently places it back down on the table. No snow falls.

SUPER:
Merry Christmas from Head & Shoulders.

Up to and including 10 seconds

Director
TIFF HUNTER

Copywriter
CHRIS KIRK

Art Director
BRUCE WATT

Producer
HARRY RANKIN

Agency Producer
SAM TAYLOR

Editor
DAVE ROSE

Lighting Cameraman
TIFF HUNTER

Production Company
ECLIPSE FILMS

Agency
SAATCHI & SAATCHI

Marketing Executive
MATTHEW PRICE

Client
PROCTER & GAMBLE LIMITED

Up to and including 10 seconds

Director
FRANK BUDGEN

Copywriter
PHIL DEARMAN

Art Director
CHARLES INGE

Creative Director
PAUL WEINBERGER

Producer
PAUL ROTHWELL

Agency Producer
AMANDA DICKS

Editor
SIMON WILCOX

Lighting Cameraman
STEVE BLACKMAN

Music Composer/Arranger
DAVID MOTION

Production Company
PAUL WEILAND FILM COMPANY

Agency
LOWE HOWARD-SPINK

Marketing Executive
CAROLYN BRADLEY

Client
TESCO STORES LIMITED

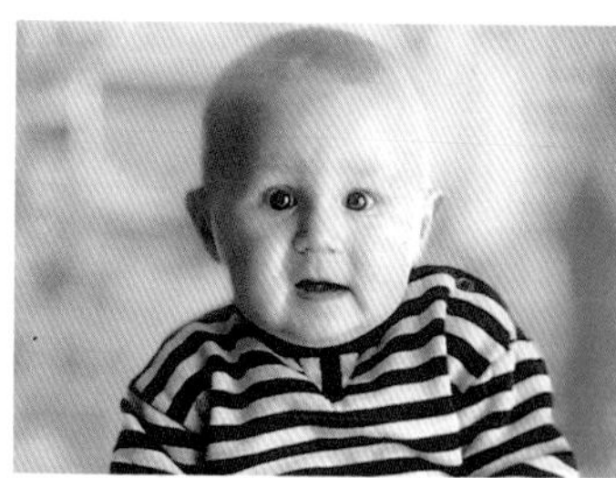

WOBBLING BABY

Open on a baby seated in a Tesco shopping trolley which is being pushed along.

His cheeks are wobbling wildly.

MVO:
Should you find yourself with a wobbly wheel...

...we'll transfer you and your groceries to a new trolley instantly.

Tesco. Every little helps.

SUPER:
Tesco. Every little helps.

TRAP DOOR

JACK:
John Smith's Extra Smooth Bitter slips down like a penguin through a trap door.

PENGUIN:
Gulp!

SFX:
Squeaking as penguin shuffles out of frame.

Clunk.

Up to and including 10 seconds

Director
MANDIE FLETCHER

Copywriters
JOHN WEBSTER
ANDREW FRASER
JACK DEE

Art Directors
JOHN WEBSTER
ALAN CINNAMOND

Creative Director
JOHN WEBSTER

Producers
MADELEINE SANDERSON
DAVID MORLEY

Set Designer
ROGER HALL

Agency Producer
LUCINDA KER

Editor
ALASTER JORDON

Lighting Cameraman
SUE GIBSON

Music Composers/Arrangers
PAUL HART
JOE CAMPBELL

Production Companies
FLETCHER SANDERSON FILMS
OPEN MIKE PRODUCTIONS

Agency
BMP DDB NEEDHAM

Group Marketing Controller
JOHN ROBERTS

Client
COURAGE LIMITED

Up to and including 20 seconds

Director
DAVID DENNEEN

Copywriter
PAUL FISHLOCK

Art Director
RON MATHER

Creative Director
RON MATHER

Producer
ANNA FAWCETT

Agency Producer
IVAN ROBINSON

Editor
SUE JONES

Lighting Cameraman
GRAHAM LIND

Music Composer/Arranger
STEPHEN RAE

Production Company
FILM GRAPHICS

Agency
THE CAMPAIGN PALACE

General Manager, Marketing
JIM WILLETT

Client
BBC HARDWARE PTY LIMITED

SMALL PRICES

VIDEO:
Limbo studio with height scale on the back wall. A very short couple walk on. The man speaks to camera.

MAN:
I'm Norman Price and this is my wife. I believe you're looking for us.

ANNCR:
Looking for small prices?

VIDEO:
Cut to a label gun rapidly applying prices.

ANNCR:
Hardwarehouse has hundreds.

SUPER:
Hardwarehouse logo.

LITTLE GIRL

Open on a precocious child.

She begins to dance and launches into an atrocious rendition of 'Daddy wouldn't buy me a bow wow.'

Suddenly, a giant foot wearing a British Knights shoe appears from off screen and crushes her.

SFX:
Splat!

MUSIC:
That's what you gotta do, you gotta keep on steppin' on.

SUPER:
British Knights.
The B-K's.

Up to and including 20 seconds

Director
JOE PUBLIC

Copywriter
GILES HARGREAVES

Art Director
MATT MURRAY

Creative Director
STEVE GRIME

Producer
ROBERT BRAY

Agency Producer
HELEN WHITELEY

Editor
CYRIL METZGER

Lighting Cameraman
GEOFF BOYLE

Production Company
STARK FILMS

Agency
LEAGAS SHAFRON DAVIS AYER

Marketing Executive
MALCOLM NATHAN

Client
BRITISH KNIGHTS

Up to and including 20 seconds

Director
JEFF STARK

Copywriter
ROBERT CAMPBELL

Art Director
MARK ROALFE

Creative Directors
ROBERT CAMPBELL
MARK ROALFE

Producer
CATHY GREEN

Set Designer
JIM STEWART

Agency Producer
ALISON CUMMINS

Editor
SAM SNEADE

Lighting Cameraman
JIM BAMBRICKS

Production Company
STARK FILMS

Agency
RAINEY KELLY CAMPBELL ROALFE

General Manager, Marketing
RUTH BLAKEMORE

Client
VIRGIN ATLANTIC AIRWAYS

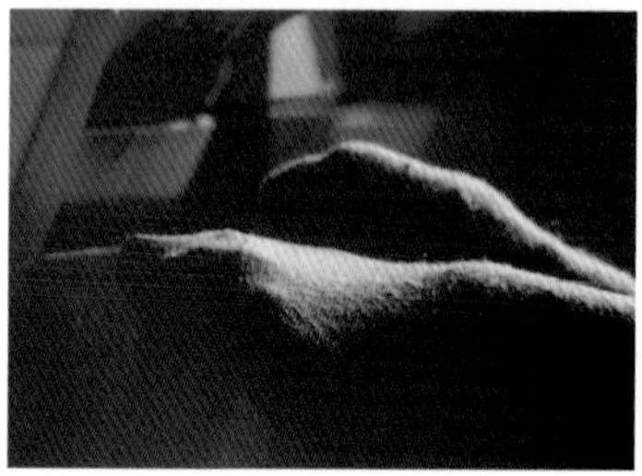

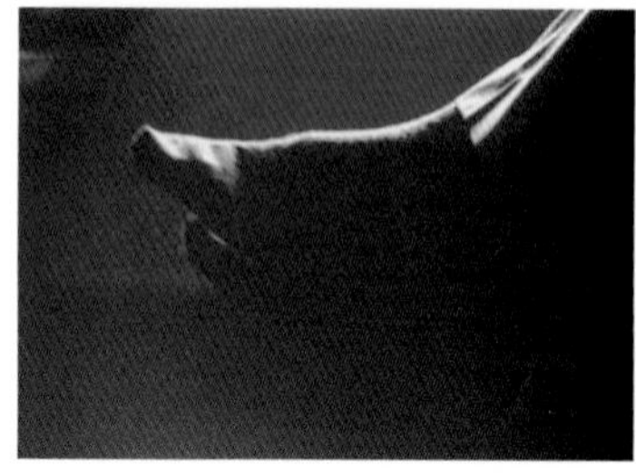

LEG ROOM

Open on Terence Stamp in Upper Class.

TERENCE:
If you're six foot, as I am, next time you're flying business class try this simple test...

VIDEO:
The camera pans down to Terence's legs. We go through a long sequence of him kicking off his shoes and stretching out his legs. However much he stretches, his toes do not touch the seat in front.

Cut back to Terence in close up.

TERENCE:
If your toes touch the seat in front, you're on the wrong plane.

CUT TO:
Upper Class. Virgin Atlantic.

CHAIN

MUSIC:
'We Have All The Time In The World' sung by Louis Armstrong.

In this commercial, we embark on a timeless journey through a glass of swirling Draught Guinness.

(Everything is rendered in Guinness tones)

We push inside a bubble, cross a strange universe, then descend upon a mysterious planet.

We sweep down towards an enormous tower set against a turbulent sky. The camera favours an open window as we move into a room packed with unusual souvenirs.

We glance past a television set. The familiar face of the Man in Black appears on screen. He smiles at us, before we make a beeline for the centre piece - a swirling pint of Guinness set on a table.

The camera lingers.

TITLE:
Pure Genius.

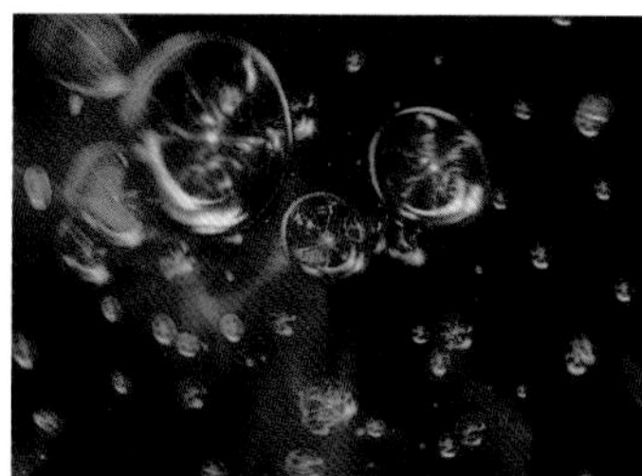

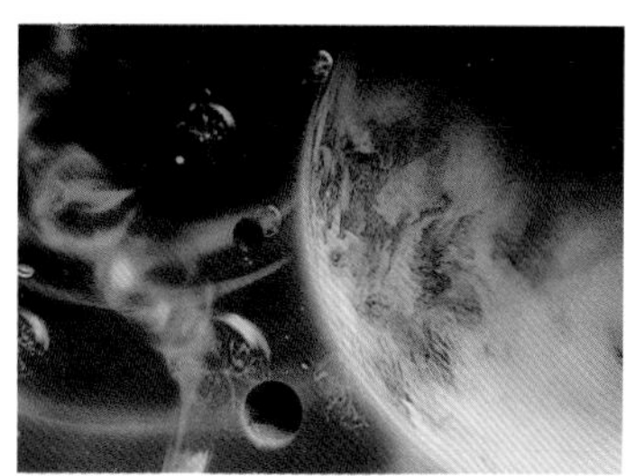

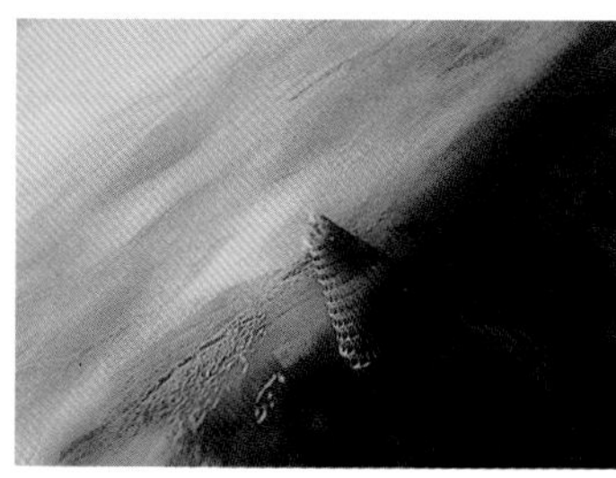

Up to and including 30 seconds

Director
DOUG FOSTER

Copywriter
SIMON LEARMAN

Art Director
BRIAN FRASER

Creative Directors
SIMON LEARMAN
BRIAN FRASER

Producer
MICHELLE JAFFE

Set Designer
ASSHETON GORTON

Animators
GRAHAME ANDREW
BEN HAYDEN
PAUL KAVANAGH
LAURENT HUGUENOIT

Agency Producer
JOHN MONTGOMERY

Editor
TIM BURKE

Lighting Cameramen
DOUG FOSTER
DAVID WYNN JONES

Music Composer/Arranger
JOHN BARRY

Production Company
BLINK PRODUCTIONS

Agency
OGILVY & MATHER

Marketing Director
ROB McNEWIN

Account Director
NEIL QUICK

Client
GUINNESS BREWING GB

Up to and including 30 seconds

Director
PAUL MIDDLEDITCH

Art Directors
PAUL RAUCH
MARIO SANASI

Creative Director
GUY WINSTON

Producer
PHILIP DAGG

Agency Producer
DENISE McKEON

Editor
ROSS SIMMONS

Lighting Cameraman
DAVID BURR

Agency
LINTAS SYDNEY

Assistant General Manager
KEN THOMPSON

Client
NEC HOME ELECTRONICS

PRESENTER

We open on two men facing camera. They are both characters and are wearing brightly coloured suits. The man behind is talking enthusiastically about the NEC Parabola and its features. The man in front is politely trying to interrupt to talk about the Parabola also.

MAN 1:
Bob and I are here to tell you about something that's got us very excited. NEC's Parabola range of Televisions. They've got a three year warranty which we think is fantastic. They're from the people who've sold over a million Australian made colour TV's. Superb sound comes from the slimline shell speakers. BUT, the best feature of the NEC Parabola is its...

After repeatedly trying to say his part the man in front picks up a remote control, points it towards the man behind and switches him off. The camera pulls back to reveal him standing in front of the NEC Parabola. The man behind was only a life-like image on the TV screen.

MAN 2:
...life like picture.

SUPER:
Parabola logo.

NEC logo.

VOODOO CHILE

TITLE:
Music That Means Something. Vic And Bob.

VIDEO:
Vic and Bob are standing in limbo talking about music that means something to them.

VIC:
Voodoo Chile's my favourite. I first heard Voodoo Chile when I was at Butlin's in Filey in 1970 when it was re-released...

...My Dad used to say, 'Anyone could play the guitar like that. I could play the guitar like that.' And I thought one day when I'd got enough money I'd get a guitar and stick it in my Dad's hands and say, 'Now do Voodoo Chile.'

MUSIC:
Riff from Voodoo Chile.

CUT TO TITLE:
If Music Means Something To You There's A New TV Channel.

We cut back to Vic and Bob.

VIC:
Voodoo's good enough isn't it?

BOB:
Voodoo is good, but it's a very powerful thing.

MUSIC:
Riff from Voodoo Chile.

CUT TO TITLE:
Music That Means Something.

Up to and including 30 seconds

Director
ROB SANDERS

Copywriter
ROBERT CAMPBELL

Art Director
MARK ROALFE

Creative Directors
ROBERT CAMPBELL
MARK ROALFE

Producer
HELEN LANGRIDGE

Set Designer
CLARE ANDRADE

Agency Producer
ALISON CUMMINS

Editor
MARK REYNOLDS

Lighting Cameraman
BOB PENDAR HUGHES

Production Company
HELEN LANGRIDGE ASSOCIATES

Agency
RAINEY KELLY CAMPBELL ROALFE

Vice President of Marketing
CHRIS STEPHENSON

Marketing Manager
GILES THOMAS

Client
VH1

Up to and including 30 seconds

Director
ERIC SAARINEN

Copywriters
GARY TOPOLEWSKI
PETE POHL

Art Director
ANDY OZARK

Creative Director
GARY TOPOLEWSKI

Agency Producer
JOHN VAN OSDOL

Music Composer/Arranger
ERIC PILHOFER

Production Company
PLUM PRODUCTIONS

Agency
BOZELL WORLDWIDE, INC

General Manager
ED BRUST

Client
CHRYSLER CORPORATION

SNOW COVERED

Open on a snow mountain vista.

SFX:
Desolate wind.

Suddenly a mole-like burrow (a la Bugs Bunny) comes through the foreground moving away from camera.

SFX:
Music up.

We follow the burrow zigzagging across the snowscape.

Cut to new shot of pristine snow and camera pans right.

Pan stops when the top of a 'Stop' sign appears poking out of snow.

Burrow pulls to stop by the sign. There's a red glow from where tail lights should be, 'Turn' signal flashes.

Burrow turns left.

SUPER:
There's only one jeep.

Tri-bar logo.

A division of Chrysler Corporation.

Jeep is a registered trademark of Chrysler Corporation

DINOSAURS

ANNCR:
The Dinosaurs. They didn't have Cable. If they did have Cable they could have watched the Weather Channel! They would have seen the ice-age coming. And they could have got inside. Or put on something warm. Were they too cheap to spend the $9.95 to get hooked up, plus get a free premium upgrade deal like the one we're offering now? All we know is, they didn't get Cable. And now they're gone. Cable. If you don't get it, you'll just die.

Up to and including 30 seconds

Directors
PETER FAVAT
RICH HERSTEK

Copywriter
RICH HERSTEK

Art Director
PETER FAVAT

Creative Directors
PETER FAVAT
RICH HERSTEK

Producer
LARRY ANDERSON

Agency Producer
JENNIFER GLEBUS

Production Company
NATIONAL VIDEO

Agency
HOUSTON EFFLER HERSTEK FAVAT

Client
ADELPHIA CABLE

Up to and including 30 seconds

Director
MURRAY SAVIDAN

Copywriter
MICHAEL BOSWELL

Art Director
STUART ROBINSON

Creative Director
MICHAEL BOSWELL

Producer
TIM CODDINGTON

Set Designer
KAI HAWKINS

Editor
MIKE HORTON

Lighting Cameraman
RICHARD MICHALAK

Production Company
ROLLING FILMS

Agency
THE CAMPAIGN PALACE

Manager, Pharmacy Products
SHARON CALLAGHAN

Client
MERCK SHARP & DOHME

ACID CASUALTY

Our commercial begins on the characterful face of a man in his late 30s. He looks a little unhappy.

We cut to a wide shot showing our man standing on a viewing platform looking at the wild volcanic hot springs of Rotorua. We see shots of mud pools, geysers going off and steam rising everywhere.

We cut back to a shot of our hero looking more dyspeptic; the state of his stomach is reflected in the scene we see before us.

Our hero takes a packet of Pepcid AC from his pocket and pops one of the small pink tablets into his mouth. Being so small it slips through his fingers and drops through the grating of the walkway into the boiling, bubbling mud.

Unperturbed our hero pops another Pepcid AC and puts it in his mouth.

We cut back to a shot of the volcanic landscape. Suddenly the mud stops bubbling, the steam disappears and the geysers die to nothing. Silence.

Our hero looks incredulously at the now quiet landscape, then glances down at the packet of Pepcid.

We see the look of realisation on his face and then his eyes dart shiftily around to see if anybody has seen what has happened. A group of tourists bedecked with cameras are rapidly approaching, so our hero furtively slips away.

VO:
Pepcid AC gives you control over excess stomach acid...

We cut to pack shot.

VO:
...for up to nine hours.

SUPER:
Now available. Only from your pharmacist.

We cut back to the group of tourists waiting patiently, cameras at the ready. It's the middle of the night.

DAN BROOKS

One day, Dan Brooks was walking down the street minding his own business.

What he didn't realise is that he was about to bump into a beautiful woman.

A woman who would have his three children.

The woman who would graduate from law school and go on to become a successful politician.

The woman who would change his life forever.

But rather than insisting on a Seiko, Dan settled for an ordinary watch.

And unfortunately, Dan was running one second late.

Up to and including 30 seconds

Director
PAUL WEILAND

Copywriter
KEN SHULDMAN

Art Director
KEN FERRIS

Creative Directors
ROB SCHLAUSSENBERG
DAVID ANGELO

Producer
ALICIA BERNARD

Set Designer
GEOFFREY KIRKLAND

Agency Producer
STEVE AMATO

Editor
MICHAEL SAIA

Lighting Cameraman
STEPHEN RAMSEY

Music Composers/Arrangers
THE WOJAHN BROTHERS

Production Company
PAUL WEILAND FILM COMPANY

Agency
DDB NEEDHAM WORLDWIDE

Marketing Executive
BOB SWANSON

Client
SEIKO

Up to and including
30 seconds

Copywriter
J. J. JORDAN

Art Director
FRANK COSTANTINI

Creative Directors
FRANK COSTANTINI
J. J. JORDAN

Agency Producer
MAYA BREWSTER

Editor
DON WAHLBERG

Agency
J. WALTER
THOMPSON, NY

Client
LES HALLES

FRENCH STYLE

The scene slowly unravels to support the premise of American beef served in a French style restaurant that has arrived in the nation's capital on Pennsylvania Avenue.

NEW YORK

SFX:
Busy New York street.

Open on a large cream carpet in the centre of a New York street.

Through the course of the day we see it takes all that the city can throw at it. A taxi-cab drives over it. Hundreds of various characters trample across. A fat woman dribbles mayonnaise, followed by a ranting barefoot vagrant who leaves a trail of dirty footprints, then a garishly dressed old lady dropping her powder puff. It explodes in close up like a pink powder bomb onto the carpet. Cut to a girl starting to clean the now filthy carpet with a VAX wet and dry machine.

MVO 1:
The VAX New Wave...

FVO:
1300 watt suction power!

A half empty cup of coke is carelessly discarded onto the carpet from a parked police car. Cut to close up of various features of the cleaner.

MVO 2:
Unique spill pick up!

FVO:
And a deep washing action!

The girl surveys the thoroughly cleaned carpet as New York bustles in the background.

MVO 1:
How else can you clean up the streets of New York single handed?

TITLE:
VAXIMUM CLEANING POWER.

Up to and including 30 seconds

Director
BARRY KINSMAN

Copywriter
TREVOR WEBB

Art Director
STEPHEN CAMPBELL

Creative Director
STEVE GRIME

Producer
DIANA HAYWOOD

Agency Producer
ANGELA KING

Editor
LYNN DAVIS

Lighting Cameraman
GABRIEL BERSTIAN

Production Company
KINSMAN & CO

Agency
LEAGAS SHAFRON DAVIS AYER

Director, Sales & Marketing
KIM RAWSON

Client
VAX LIMITED

Up to and including 30 seconds

Director
FRANK BUDGEN

Copywriter
ROBERT SAVILLE

Art Director
JAY POND-JONES

Creative Director
TIM MELLORS

Producer
PAUL ROTHWELL

Set Designer
JULIA SHERBORNE

Agency Producer
DIANE CROLL

Editor
SAM SNEADE

Lighting Cameraman
ADRIAN BIDDLE

Music Composers
MR BARRY
MR KIM

Arranged By
RICHARD MYHILL

Production Company
PAUL WEILAND FILM COMPANY

Agency
GGT

Marketing Director
PHIL PLOWMAN

Client
HOLSTEN DISTRIBUTORS LIMITED

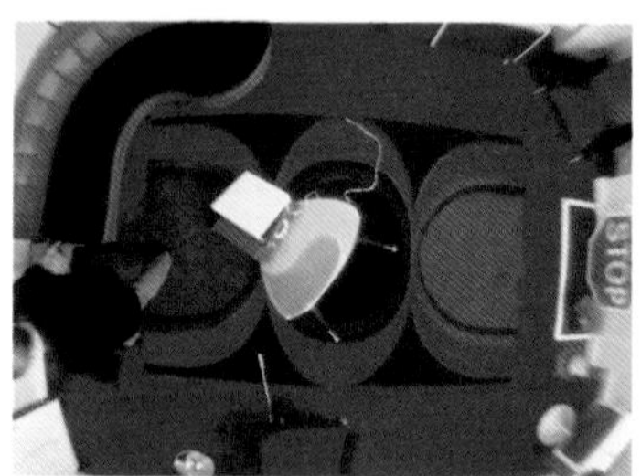

SUGAR SUGAR

Open on a Dansette record player in CU.

MUSIC:
Sugar Sugar by the Archies.

Enter Denis Leary on one of his rants in a retro room.

DL:
Back in the seventies, I must have heard this record at least 5,128 times. To the point where if I have to listen to it one more time, I think my head's gonna blow up. I hate it. I hate the seventies. I hate nostalgia. I hate clogs. I hate lava lamps. I hate burnt sienna corduroy bell bottoms. But most of all I hate Sugar Sugar.

Denis picks up a bottle of Holsten Pils.

DL:
This I don't hate. Holsten Pils. Because it's brewed twice so that all of the sugar turns to alcohol. That's no sugar, no honey honey and totally candy girl free.

Denis walks over to the record player and accidentally knocks it over with his foot.

DL:
Whoops!

TITLE:
Sugar? Get Real!

NEWTON'S CRADLE

Throughout this commercial we watch a Newton's Cradle.

As the silver ball on the right hand side lifts, we see a businessman on the phone.

As the ball comes back to obscure him, we hear the French businessman that he's talking to.

This conversation happens in time to the motion of the Newton's Cradle.

Finally, we close on the end sequence as they continue to talk, boxes and logo.

MUSIC:
(fade up)

Dire Straits.

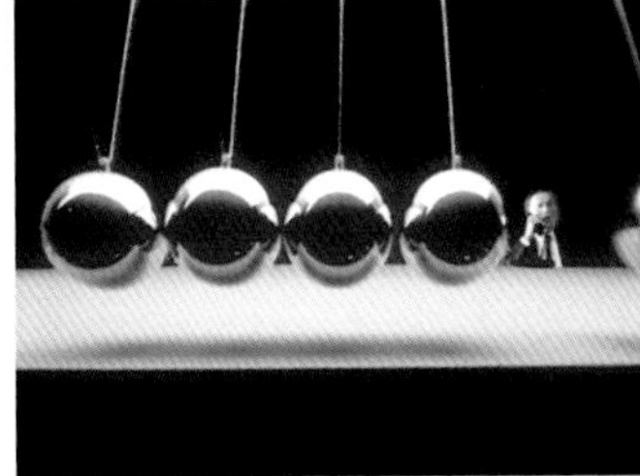
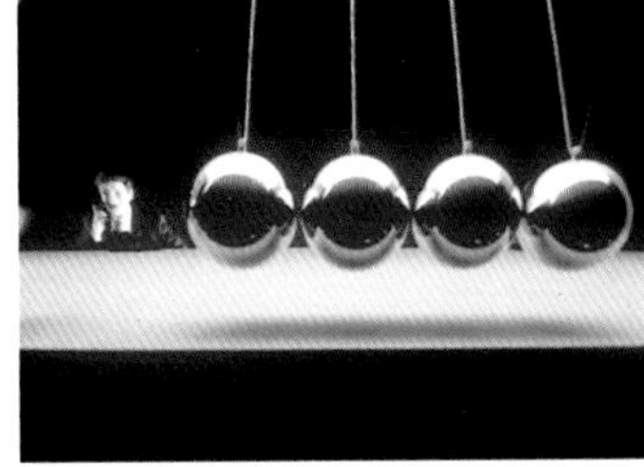

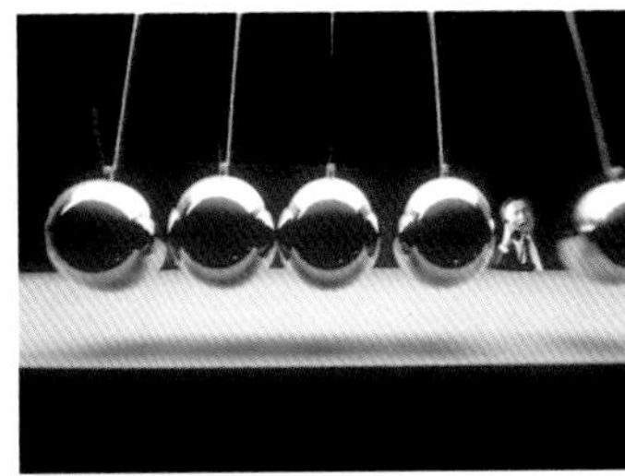

Up to and including 30 seconds

Director
PAUL ARDEN

Copywriter
JOHN DEAN

Art Director
SIMON GREEN

Producer
NICK SUTHERLAND-DODD

Set Designer
VOYTEK

Agency Producer
MARNIE CORAZZA

Editor
BRIAN DYKE

Lighting Cameraman
ALEX THOMSON

Production Company
ARDEN SUTHERLAND-DODD

Agency
BUTTERFIELD DAY DEVITO HOCKNEY

Account Director
PAUL VENN

Client
BRITISH TELECOMMUNICATIONS

Up to and including 30 seconds

Director
DOUG WERBE

Copywriter
TOM WITT

Art Director
MICHAEL RYLANDER

Creative Directors
MICHAEL RYLANDER
TOM WITT

Animator
JOEL HLADECHEK

Editor
DOUG WERBE

Production Company
RED SKY FILMS

Agency
WITT/RYLANDER

Artistic Director
TANDY BEALE

Consultant
BARBARA KIBBE

Client
THE NEW PICKLE CIRCUS

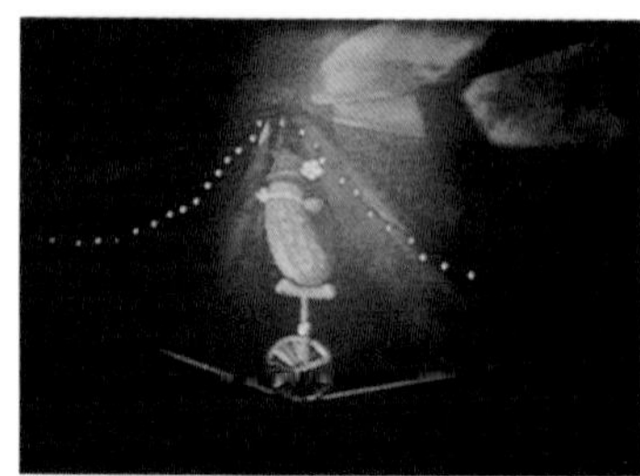

POOP

Open with the sound of a shrieking chimpanzee against an aged and distressed black/white title card.

TITLE CARD:
No monkey poop.

SFX:
Film chattering through gate, simulating a silent movie.

TITLE CARD:
No tiger poop.

SFX:
Tiger Roar.

TITLE CARD:
No elephant poop.

SFX:
Elephant bugle.

TITLE CARD:
But diapers for your toddlers are recommended.

SFX:
Baby gurgling and giggling punctuated by a short fart.

Cut to a circus tent set with a tightrope strung left to right.

SFX:
Crowd cheers.

Entering from left, we see a pickle, wearing a hobo hat and red clown nose, peddling a unicycle.

The pickle momentarily falters to the hushed gasp of the audience, then regains balance and continues out of frame to the delight of all.

TITLE CARD:
The New Pickle Circus.

SFX:
Forced, canned laughter.

TITLE CARD:
Ford Mason Center. December 8 to January 1.

SFX:
Laughter becomes louder and more obnoxious.

TITLE CARD:
To procure seats, kindly ring (415) 392 4400.

GERMAN

A German beer lover is testing the difference between Lysholmer Light Beer and a German light beer. When giving his verdict he suddenly resembles Adolf Hitler!

Up to and including 30 seconds

Director
JOHAN GULBRANSON

Copywriter
OISTEIN BORGE

Art Director
JOHAN GULBRANSON

Producers
KNUT E.JENSEN
ANNA SOMLMAN

Set Designer
KALLE BOMAN

Lighting Cameraman
THOMAS BOMAN

Music Composers/Arrangers
BOHREN & AASERUD

Production Company
LEO FILM

Agency
LEO BURNETT, NORWAY

Project Manager
STIG NYHEIM

Client
RINGNES

Up to and including 30 seconds

Director
MICHAEL GRASSO

Copywriter
RICK DENNIS

Art Director
MICHAEL CORBEILLE

Creative Director
GARY TOPOLEWSKI

Agency Producer
JIM BROWN

Music Composer/Arranger
MICHAEL MONTEZ

Production Company
GARDNER/GRASSO

Agency
BOZELL WORLDWIDE, INC

General Manager
ED BRUST

Client
CHRYSLER CORPORATION

GATES

MUSIC:
Classical theme, up full.

VIDEO:
Open on Beverly Hills street. The camera dollies past huge homes protected by hedges, walls and iron gates. We see a few luxury cars driving through the gates. The camera settles on home surrounded by a pile of boulders several feet high. A Jeep Grand Cherokee pulls up and drives over the rocks and boulders.

A newspaper boy peddles by and throws paper over rock wall.

SFX:
Bicycle sound and thud of newspaper landing.

SUPER:
There's only one Jeep...

Tri Bar logo.

Jeep is a registered trademark of Chrysler Corporation.

KLINGONESE

MUSIC:
Star Trek music.

VIDEO:
We open on the USS Enterprise warping impressively through space.

Cut to Klingon spaceship.

Cut to inside Klingon spaceship.

The Klingons are watching the speedy approach of the USS Enterprise on their screen.

They are understandably worried.

KLINGON LEADFR:
Quob Klow?

KLINGONS:
Klow doha RITKE PLIC.

VIDEO:
They do the twirl.

Cut to Klingon spaceship exploding.

MUSIC:
Klingon version of 'Hey Hey'.

VIDEO:
Cut to Next Generation cups.

MVO:
Sklid triksha von flunk, ecche tek Bratek Slucks, rach sok sok sok.

VIDEO:
Cut to Pizza Hut in a hail of laser rays. Two of the Klingons are firing their guns at camera. They stop when a waitress gives them a withering look.

Cut to the same two Klingons happily slurping their Next Generation drinks.

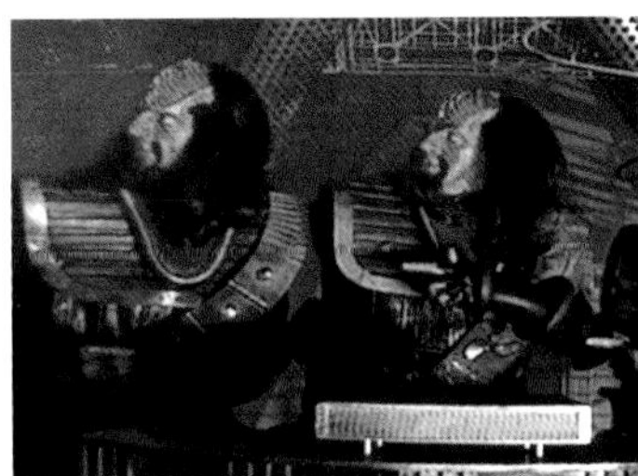

Up to and including 30 seconds

Director
RICHARD PHILLIPS

Copywriter
ANDY McLEOD

Art Director
RICHARD FLINTHAM

Creative Directors
PAUL GRUBB
DAVE WATERS

Producer
CHRISSIE PHILLIPS

Set Designer
STEVE SMITHWICK

Agency Producer
KATE O'MULLOY

Editor
RICHARD LEAROYD

Lighting Cameraman
KARL WATKINS

Music Composer/Arranger
ROY HEAD

Production Company
R. J. PHILLIPS & CO

Agency
DUCKWORTH FINN GRUBB WATERS

Marketing Director
STEVE DUNN

Client
PIZZA HUT UK LIMITED

Up to and including 30 seconds

Director
MARY COOKE

Copywriter
LIONEL HUNT

Art Director
RON MATHER

Creative Director
RON MATHER

Producer
ROGER WILSON

Agency Producer
IVAN ROBINSON

Editor
SETH LOCKWOOD

Lighting Cameraman
ELLERY RYAN

Music Composer/Arranger
ANDREW THOMAS WILSON

Production Company
THIRTY SECOND STREET

Agency
THE CAMPAIGN PALACE

Group Divisional Manager, Consumer Products
PAUL FRANCIS

Client
HANIMEX PTY LIMITED

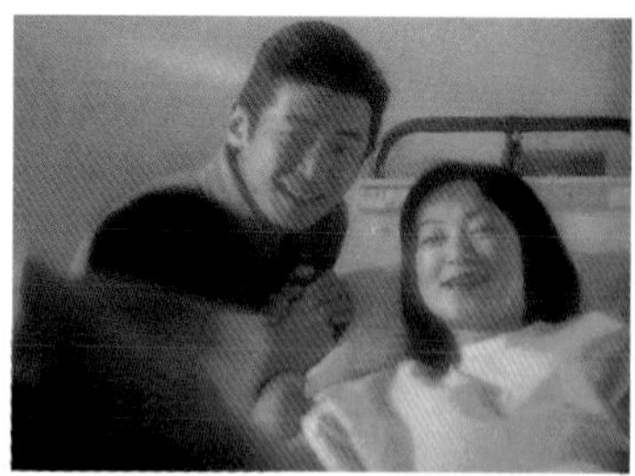

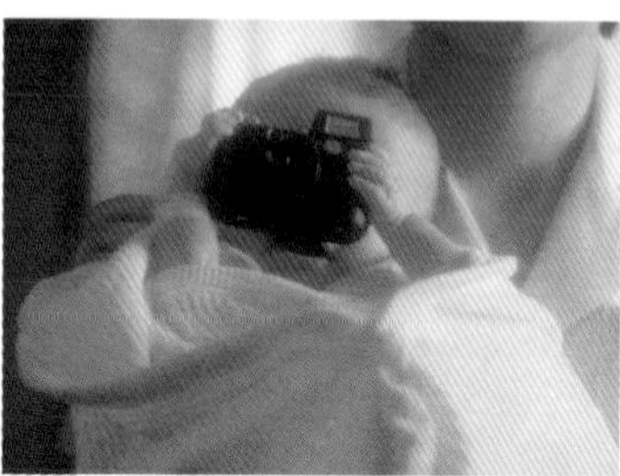

BORN PHOTOGRAPHER

We are at the bedside of a Japanese woman about to give birth. Husband at her side, Japanese doctor and nurses at the end of the bed.

Baby boy is born, nurses quickly clean up the baby and hold him up to show his parents.

Baby holds up a little camera and takes flash photo of his astonished parents.

VO & SUPER:
Fuji Better Colour Film.

As used by the worlds top photographers.

70'S DANCE SOW

Open on the set of a TV dance show, circa 1976. A woman in an orange dress with matching orange hair is on stage doing a spoken word reading of Wild Cherry's 'Play that Funky Music.'

People in assorted seventies garb are awkwardly dancing on the surrounding stages even though there is no music. Shots of the woman performing are intercut with shots of the dancers.

SFX:
Natural sounds like feet clomping.

FEMALE PERFORMER:
Yeah, they were dancing and singing and moving to the grooving and just then it hit me...

Woman dancer with large afro plays air guitar. Blonde woman does a drugged-out frug.

FEMALE PERFORMER:
...and somebody turned around and shouted...

Black couple dances for the camera. Blonde guy does a kung-fu kick.

FEMALE PERFORMER:
...play that funky music white boy...

SUPER:
If you're not listening to Kenwood,

FEMALE PERFORMER:
...play that funky music right, play that funky music white boy...

Blonde guy does Travolta-esque arm gyrations.

SUPER:
there might as well be no music at all.

FEMALE PERFORMER:
...lay down the boogie and play that funky music 'til you die, oh 'til you die.

SFX:
Microphone feedback.

TITLE:
Kenwood. Do the music justice.

Up to and including 30 seconds

Director
JOE PYTKA

Copywriter
BRYAN BEHAR

Art Director
BOB PULLUM

Creative Directors
KIRK CITRON
MATT HALIGMAN

Producer
NAIA HALL

Agency Producer
ROB SONDIK

Editor
ADAM LIEBOWITZ

Production Company
PYTKA

Agency
CITRON HALIGMAN BEDECARRE

Client
KENWOOD USA CORPORATION

Up to and including 30 seconds

Director
JOE PYTKA

Copywriters
JIM LEMAITRE
DEREK BARNES

Art Directors
ANDREW CHRISTON
ERIK KING

Creative Directors
DAN WIEDEN
SUSAN HOFFMAN

Producer
PHILIP BROOKS

Agency Producer
DONNA PORTARO

Editor
ADAM LIEBOWITZ

Production Company
PYTKA

Agency
WIEDEN & KENNEDY, USA

Client
NIKE INTERNATIONAL

ORGAN

TITLE CARD:
Day 10.

AUDIO:
Organ playing the usual baseball warm-up song.

VIDEO:
Cut to various shots of empty baseball stadium.

Cut to fan in the organ booth. We see it was him playing the organ.

The fan looks round to see if anyone is looking. When he doesn't see anybody, he starts playing again.

AUDIO:
Hear 'chopsticks' being played.

TITLE CARD:

Play ball.

Please.

Nike w/swoosh logo.

MAGAZINE WARS

Open on a storeman reading newspaper in a quiet magazine store.

Jim Courier comes to life on the cover of a tennis magazine and smashes a backhand.

Agassi stretches for a forehand from the cover of Tennis Match magazine.

John MacEnroe ducks as the ball clips the magazine where he is featured on the cover. A card falls out of the magazine.

The storeman looks up from his newspaper. MacEnroe climbs up his magazine cover trying to get a better view.

Pioline returns the ball with a back hand. He grunts as he hits the ball.

Krajicek smashes the ball.

Ball flies past bride magazine and surprises bride on cover.

Pioline turns to follow the path of the ball.

SFX:
Glass breaking

Gabby catches ball with one hand.

The store owner gets out of his chair.

Gabby throws ball out of magazine.

A ball boy appears from behind a stand and retrieves the ball.

Storeman enters room with a dustpan and brush.

The pages of a tennis magazine flick over as the tennis players in the photograph play out a point.

The ball flies through an art magazine and smashes the plate on the cover.

Courier and Krajicek face camera.

Nike Air logo.

Storeman cleans up the broken glass.

Up to and including 30 seconds

Director
DAVID FINCHER

Copywriter
EVELYN MONROE GUDE

Art Director
SUSAN HOFFMAN

Creative Director
DAN WIEDEN

Producer
CEAN CHAFFIN

Agency Producer
JANE BRIMBLECOMBE

Lighting Cameraman
HARRY SAVIDES

Sound Designer
REN KLYCE

Production Company
PROPAGANDA FILMS

Agency
WIEDEN & KENNEDY, AMSTERDAM

Marketing Executive
SCOTT GARRET

Client
NIKE EUROPE

Up to and including 30 seconds

Director
CHARLES WITTENMEIER

Copywriter
ARTHUR BIJUR

Art Director
DONNA WEINHEIM

Creative Directors
ARTHUR BIJUR
DONNA WEINHEIM

Agency Producer
ANNE KURTZMAN

Editor
IAN MACKENZIE

Music Composer/Arranger
MICHAEL CARROLL

Production Company
HARMONY PICTURES

Agency
CLIFF FREEMAN & PARTNERS

Client
LITTLE CAESARS ENTERPRISES

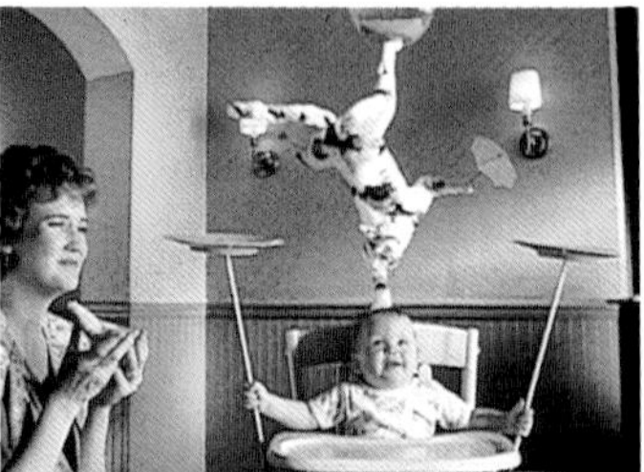

SINGING BABY

Open on a Father and Grandmother at dining table admiring two Little Caesars Pizzas.

GRANNY:
Have you ever seen anything more amazing than Little Caesars Italian sausage pizza?

Father looks up. Cut to reveal a baby sitting in a high chair spinning plates on sticks. On baby's head is a cat doing a hand stand while balancing a full goldfish bowl on its foot. Baby sings "Give My Regards To Broadway."

Cut back to Father.

FATHER:
...No.

Cut to food section.

ANNCR:
Italian sausage pizza! Loaded with sausage, peppers and onions. The newest from a whole menu of Little Caesar Pleasers.

Any two for $9.98!

LITTLE CAESAR:
Pizza! Pizza!

ANNCR:
Or get one for $5.99!

LITTLE CAESAR:
Pizza!

COUNTRY ROAD

Open on Mr Illitch, the owner of Little Caesars, driving a convertible along a country road.

SUPER:
Mike Illitch. Founder and owner of Little Caesars.

ANNCR:
How does the owner of Little Caesars think up his next great pizza idea?

What are his influences... His inspirations?

The car keeps driving. Suddenly, an old truck loaded with wooden crates filled with live chickens comes roaring up behind the convertible, honking loudly.

CHICKENS:
Buck! Buck! Buck! Buck!

The chicken truck speeds past the convertible, sending one chicken flying out of the truck and onto Mr Illitch's windshield.

CHICKEN:
(flattened against windshield)
Buck! Buck! BUCK!

The windscreen wipers knock the chicken into the back seat of the convertible. Mr Illitch has no idea it is there.

MR I:
That's it! Pizza for a buck!!! Where do I come up with this stuff?

CHICKEN:
(woozily)
Buuuck!

Cut to Little Caesar character snapping a dollar bill, followed by beauty shots of Little Caesars Pizzas.

ANNCR:
Get pizza for a buck - your Pizza Pizza Bonus - when you buy two pizzas with two toppings for $8.98!

LITTLE CAESAR:
Pizza! Pizza!

ANNCR:
Plus a third...

LITTLE CAESAR:
Pizza for a Buck!

Up to and including 30 seconds

Director
MARK STORY

Copywriters
CLIFF FREEMAN
HAROLD EINSTEIN
MICHELLE ROUFA

Art Director
BRUCE HURWIT

Creative Directors
CLIFF FREEMAN
DONNA WEINHEIM

Agency Producers
ANNE KURTZMAN
MELANIE KLEIN

Production Company
CROSSROADS FILMS

Agency
CLIFF FREEMAN & PARTNERS

Client
LITTLE CAESARS ENTERPRISES

Up to and including 30 seconds

Director
GREG WINTER

Copywriter
BILL JOHNSON

Art Director
RANDY HUGHES

Creative Director
JAC COVERDALE

Producer
PHIL SIMS

Agency Producer
JENEE SCHMIDT

Editor
JEFF STICKLES

Lighting Cameraman
GREG WINTER

Music Composer/Arranger
ERIC PHILHOFER

Production Company
WILSON GRIAK

Agency
CLARITY COVERDALE FURY

Promotions Manager
CHRIS OSHIKATA

Client
PIONEER PRESS

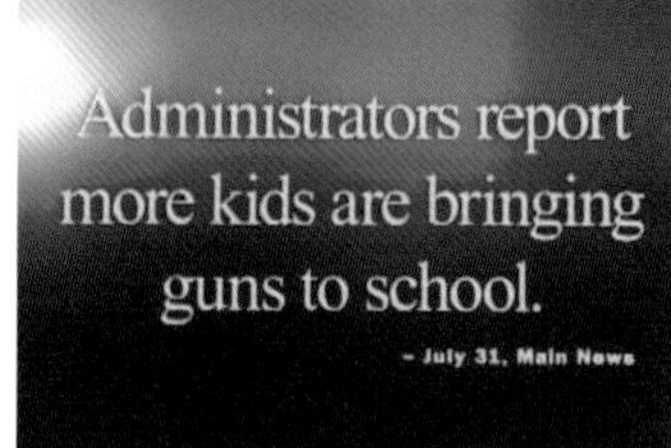

LOCKER

SFX:
School bell rings, classroom doors open, kids pour into hallway.

A locker slams shut loudly, like a gunshot.

Kids hit the floor, everything goes silent.

GIRL:
Sorry.

SUPER:
Administrators report more kids are bringing guns to school.

July 31, Main News.

SUPER:
Hey, you learn something new every day.

JAPANESE GARDEN

Classical Japanese music throughout.

MVO:
I tell the tale of Trapitaka...

...whose life was made misery...

...by the demons under the rim.

Until arrived her hero - Hu Clean-loo...

SFX:
Quack quack.

MVO:
...who vanquished them effortlessly...

...leaving the fresh fragrance of a Japanese Garden.

Old proverb: When demons lurk beneath the rim - duck!

SFX:
Quack quack.

MVO:
New Japanese Garden Toilet Duck.

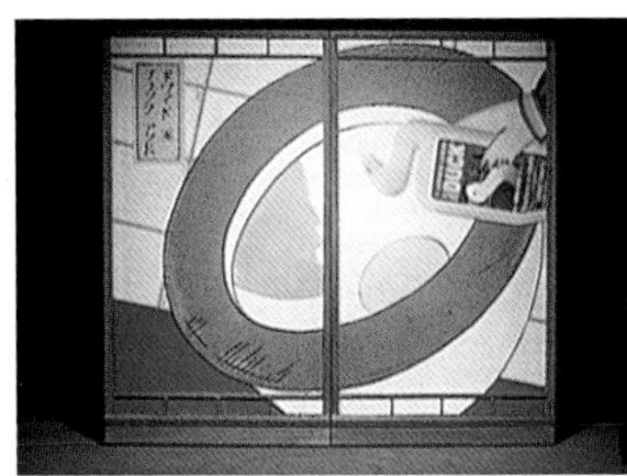

Up to and including 30 seconds

Director
BARRY PURVES

Copywriter
ALASDAIR GRAHAM

Art Director
FRAZER JELLEYMAN

Creative Director
TONY COX

Producer
GLENN HOLBERTON

Set Designer
BARRY PURVES

Animators
IAN MacKINNON
PETE SAUNDERS

Agency Producer
MICHAEL PARKER

Editor
TIM FULFORD

Lighting Cameraman
MARK STEWART

Music Composer/Arranger
ROB BOWKETT

Production Company
BARE BOARDS PRODUCTIONS

Agency
BMP DDB NEEDHAM

Commercials Director
IWAN WILLIAMS

Client
SC JOHNSON

Up to and including 30 seconds

Director
MICHAEL BAY

Copywriter
HARRY COCCIOLO

Art Director
SEAN EHRINGER

Creative Directors
RICH SILVERSTEIN
JEFFREY GOODBY

Producer
CINDY EPPS

Editor
TOM MULDOON

Lighting Cameraman
MARK PLUMMER

Music Composer/Arranger
KEN DOLLINGER

Production Company
PROPAGANDA FILMS

Agency
GOODBY, SILVERSTEIN & PARTNERS

Executive Director
JEFF MANNING

Client
CALIFORNIA FLUID MILK PROCESSOR ADVISORY BOARD

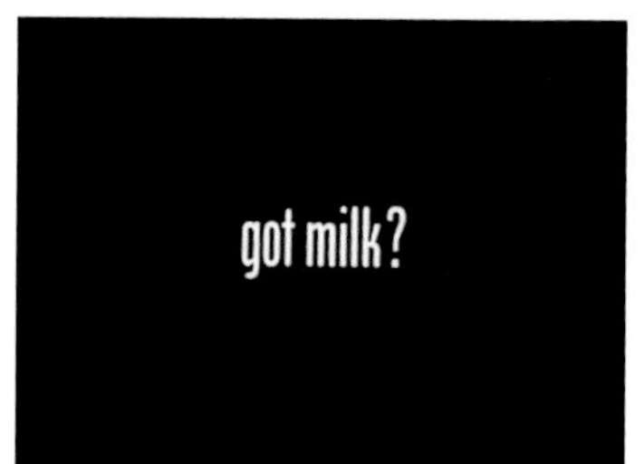

DINER

MUSIC:
(throughout)
'Groove Me.'

Open on young man sitting down at counter of boisterous American Diner. He is eating a large stack of pancakes.

Cook slams glass of ice water down on counter in front of young man.

YOUNG MAN:
(with mouth full)
Could I get some milk, please?

We see woman next to young man, sitting at counter, with glass of milk in front of her.

Young man looks over as she gets up and leaves the counter.

WOMAN:
(to cook)
Excuse me. I'll be right back, OK?

Young man places fork down in frustration, still with mouth full, staring at his ice water.

COOK V/O:
I need two specials!

Young man stares at woman's full glass of milk. He checks to see if woman is still gone, grabs glass and slides it down the counter towards him. He drinks half the milk and then realising what he has done, he leans forward and moans.

Young man picks up glass of ice water, holding back ice with knife, whilst refilling milk glass with water.

As he is doing this, a big man sits down where woman was sitting. He stares at young man pouring ice water.

Young man slides glass of milk in front of big man without noticing him.

We see c/u of big man, mystified.

Just then woman returns and hugs big man.

WOMAN:
Hi, sweet.

Realising he has been caught, young man looks away in fear.

SFX:
Plates breaking.

YOUNG MAN V/O:
Check please.

SUPER:
Got Milk?

ROCKING CHAIR

Open on an old man in his living room rocking gently back and forth in creaking rocking chair.

He stands up and walks to an adjacent window; the creaking continues.

It becomes apparent that it is, in fact, the old man's legs that creak, not the rocking chair.

TITLES:
Aching Joints?

Alchemilla Complex by Vogel.

Vogel Helps.

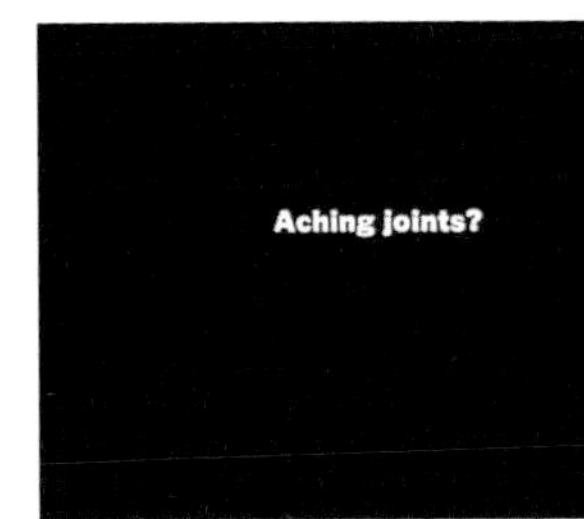
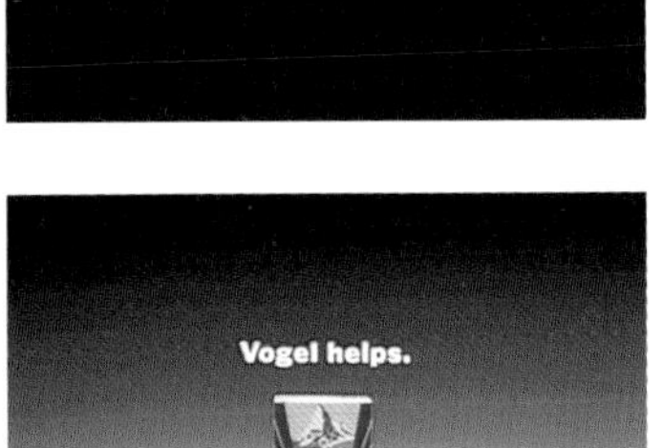

Up to and including 30 seconds

Director
BOB BROOKS

Copywriter
LYSBETH BIJLSTRA

Art Director
BELA STAMENKOVITS

Creative Director
BELA STAMENKOVITS

Producer
CASPAR DELANEY

Set Designer
STEWART ROSE

Agency Producer
MIRIAM BUISE

Editor
TIM FULFORD

Lighting Cameraman
HOWARD ATHERTON

Production Company
BFCS

Agency
TBWA/CAMPAIGN COMPANY

Marketing Director
BEN BOUTER

Client
BIOHORMA BEHEER B.V. (A.VOGEL)

Up to and including 30 seconds

Director
JOE PYTKA

Copywriters
JIM LEMAITRE
DEREK BARNES

Art Directors
ANDREW CHRISTON
ERIK KING

Creative Directors
DAN WIEDEN
SUSAN HOFFMAN

Producer
PHILIP BROOKS

Agency Producer
DONNA PORTARO

Editor
ADAM LIEBOWITZ

Production Company
PYTKA

Agency
WIEDEN & KENNEDY, USA

Client
NIKE INTERNATIONAL

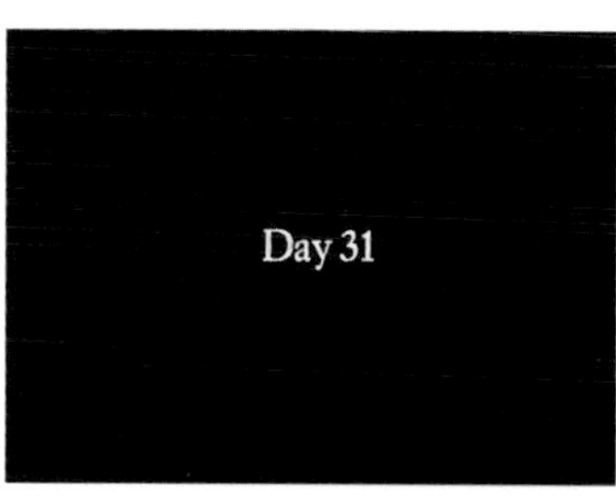

WAVE

TITLE CARD:
Day 6

Open on pan of empty basketball stadium seats.

Camera 'finds' lone fan who rises to do the wave and sits back down.

Camera continues to pan beyond fan to more empty seats.

TITLE CARD:
Play ball.

Please.

Nike w/swoosh logo.

GORILLA

SFX:
Rock Music.

SUPER:
(shaky)
The Good Guys! (How Good Are They?)

Cut to man standing in front of Good Guys! store knowingly pointing at his baseball cap. Arrow points to cap.

SUPER:
Hidden camera.

The man turns towards the store. In store a Good Guys! employee is listening to man.

MAN:
Over at the zoo we can't get the gorillas to mate, so we need a TV to show them some videos of other gorillas, uh, to inspire them. And we need it delivered.

EMPLOYEE:
Gotcha.

SUPER:
Set-up and Delivery Available.

SFX:
Drum Music.

Employee is seen, hand under chin, questioning the man. Customer walks past in background.

MAN:
Yeah, into the cage.

EMPLOYEE:
Am I gonna' be in any danger?

SUPER:
Not If You Wear The Suit.

SFX:
Drum Music.

EMPLOYEE:
Oh, I wear a gorilla suit.

MAN:
Yeah, Sparky.

EMPLOYEE:
No way to remove the gorilla from the area?

SUPER:
That Would Be Too Easy.

SFX:
Drum Music.

MAN:
Can you do it today?

EMPLOYEE:
I can do it today.

SFX:
Rock Music.

Cut to exterior of a Good Guys! store entrance. A hand raises in front of the store, underneath the store name.

SIGN:
They Really Are.

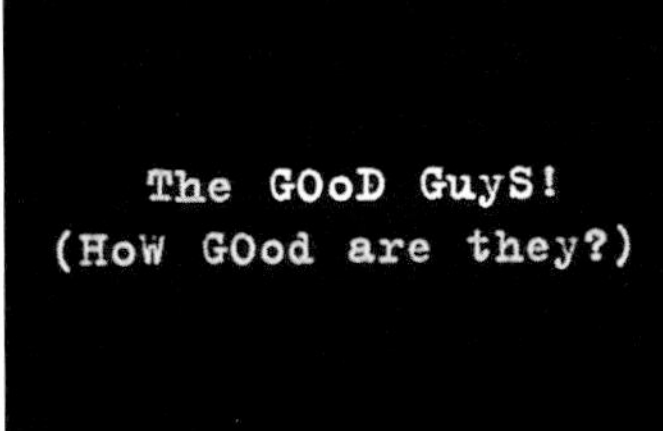

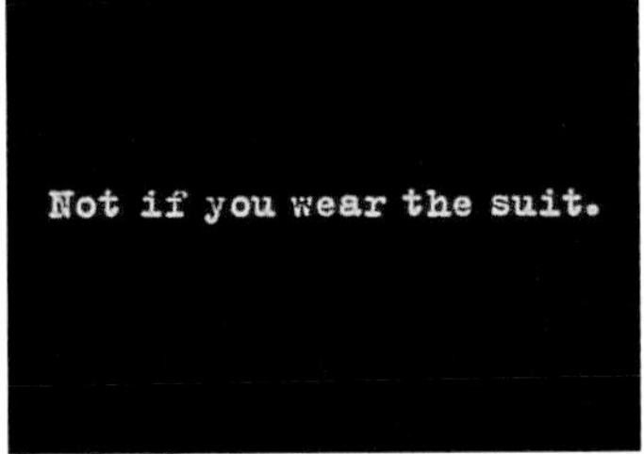

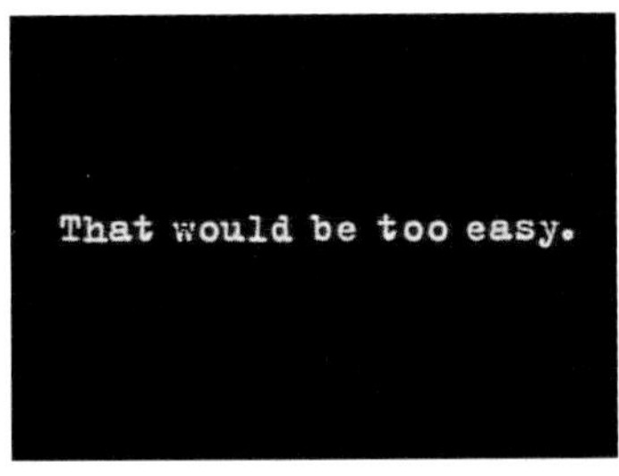

Up to and including 30 seconds

Copywriters
SCOTT AAL
GEOFF BOLT

Art Director
DAVE AYRISS

Creative Directors
RICH SILVERSTEIN
JEFFREY GOODBY

Producer
STACY McCLAIN

Editor
BOB SPECTOR

Lighting Cameraman
SHELDON ROUTH

Music Composer/Arranger
PETE SCATURRO

Production Company
GOODBY, SILVERSTEIN & PARTNERS

Agency
GOODBY, SILVERSTEIN & PARTNERS

Client
THE GOOD GUYS!

Up to and including 30 seconds

Director
RICHARD PHILLIPS

Copywriter
PAUL GRUBB

Art Director
DAVE WATERS

Creative Directors
PAUL GRUBB
DAVE WATERS

Producer
CHRISSIE PHILLIPS

Set Designer
STEVE SMITHWICK

Agency Producer
KATE O'MULLOY

Editor
RICHARD LEAROYD

Lighting Cameraman
KARL WATKINS

Music Composers/Arrangers
ROY HEAD
ANTHONY & GAYNOR SADLER

Production Company
R. J. PHILLIPS & CO

Agency
DUCKWORTH FINN GRUBB WATERS

Marketing Director
STEVE DUNN

Client
PIZZA HUT UK LIMITED

TWO

Open on huge Gill Bold number 2 on limbo backdrop.

A huge glob of paint splashes into it from the side...

SFX:
Splooooosh!!

The paint drips off the 2 for a few moments.

A man, face covered in paint splats, pops his head up in screen and speaks to camera, doing the Pizza Hut point and flicking more paint at the lens.

MAN:
...two erm...pizzas for the price of one...when you...erm...Hit The Hut!

Cut to painter with his wife and child in a Pizza Hut, as the waitress pops their pizzas on the table in front of them.

MVO:
Buy any medium or large pizza from Pizza Hut any weekday after 4, and get another one absolutely free.

As they begin to tuck in, a huge metal sharp-edged two thunks into the table, point first, just in front of them. They reel back in surprise.

SFX:
Thrrrannnggg!!!

The painter looks up above him...

MAN:
Whooa...could've had somebody's eye out...

Cut to Pizza Hut logo falling onto a flour background with an almighty thud.

MVO:
Two pizzas for the price of one when you Hit The Hut.

BLIMP

SFX:
Rock Music.

SUPER:
The Good Guys! (How Good Are They?)

Cut to man standing in front of Good Guys! store knowingly pointing to his baseball cap. Arrow points to cap.

SUPER:
Hidden Camera.

The man turns towards the store. In the store, a Good Guys! employee is listening to man.

MAN:
I know you guys have a low price guarantee and I saw...

Cut to tight shot of Good Guys! newspaper ad in man's hands. He is pointing to a stereo unit that is on sale.

MAN:
...this unit selling for less somewhere else.

SUPER:
They'll Beat Any Advertised Price.

MAN:
I saw it on this blimp at the ball park...

Cut to employee examining a photograph with a magnifying glass.

MAN:
...you know, in that thing that lights up, that gizmo?

Cut to photo showing a blimp in a blue sky with clouds as seen through the magnifying glass.

MAN:
Can you see it?

EMPLOYEE:
A gizmo?

Employee explains situation to his manager.

SUPER:
Ads Must Be Visible To The Naked Eye.

Employee still intently studies the photo with magnifying glass.

MAN:
Maybe this magnifying glass is dirty.

Cut to series of quick shots with the Good Guys! logo on them. Cut to photo as seen through the magnifying glass.

MAN:
See the pilot waving?

Cut to blurry TV screens. Camera cuts to single screen.

SUPER:
They Really Are.

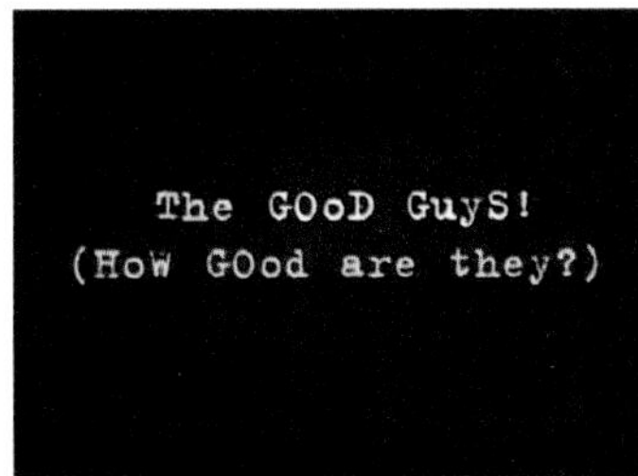

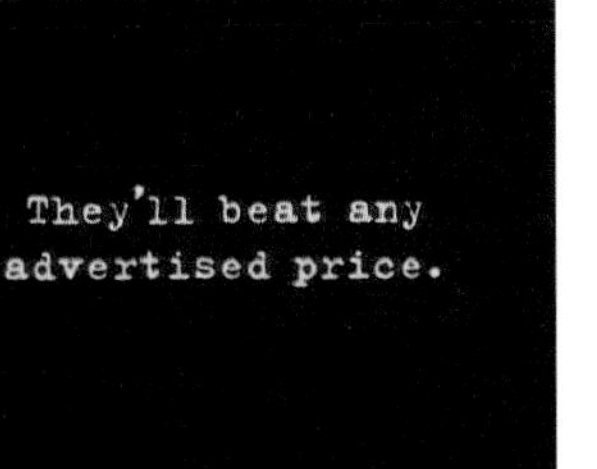

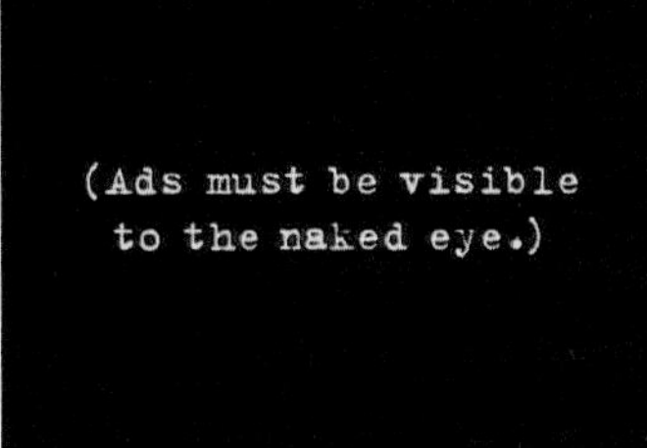

Up to and including 30 seconds

Copywriters
SCOTT AAL
GEOFF BOLT

Art Director
DAVE AYRISS

Creative Directors
RICH SILVERSTEIN
JEFFREY GOODBY

Producer
STACY MCCLAIN

Editor
BOB SPECTOR

Lighting Cameraman
SHELDON ROUTH

Music Composer/Arranger
PETE SCATURRO

Production Company
GOODBY, SILVERSTEIN & PARTNERS

Agency
GOODBY, SILVERSTEIN & PARTNERS

Client
THE GOOD GUYS!

Up to and including 30 seconds

Director
BRUCE HURWIT

Copywriter
ARTHUR BIJUR

Art Director
BRUCE HURWIT

Creative Director
ARTHUR BIJUR

Agency Producer
MARY ELLEN DUGGAN

Production Company
CROSSROADS FILMS

Agency
CLIFF FREEMAN & PARTNERS

Client
LITTLE CAESARS ENTERPRISES

ORANGUTAN

Open on a orangutan in testing lab. In front of him on counter is one button with a sign that reads '1' and another big button that reads '2'. A mechanical hand enters and shows the orangutan a single banana.

VOICE:
(through speaker) One banana...

(another hand presents two bananas)

...Or two bananas?

Orangutan ponders, scratches head and then pushes button marked '2'. Button lights up.

SFX:
Buzzz.

Cut to an orangutan wearing a nighty in a come hither pose.

ANNCR:
One female orangutan?...

(pan to reveal two orangutans blowing kisses)

...Or two female orangutans?

Immediately cut back to male hitting '2' buzzer almost before sentence is completed.

SFX:
Buzzzzzzz!

Cut to pizza graphic on an easel of one pizza and two pizzas.

ANNCR:
One pizza for $9.98?...Or two for $9.98?

Cut back to orangutan, now flanked by the two females who are kissing him, stroking his hair etc. He smiles a huge smile.

VOICE:
He seems to prefer two.

Cut to food.

ANNCR:
Two is better than one, so why settle for one supreme pizza when you can get two at Little Caesars for just $9.98!

LITTLE CAESAR:
Pizza Pizza.

LITTLE ANT & ELEPHANT

We see a sexy little ant lying in bed whilst she's smoking.

The camera pulls back and we see that her partner is an elephant, lying beside her with a glass of whisky in his hand.

Cut to pack and title:

Tulipan lubricant gel. Very lubricant.

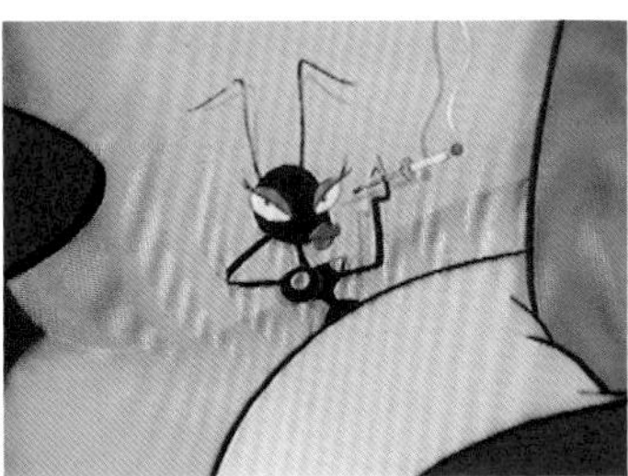

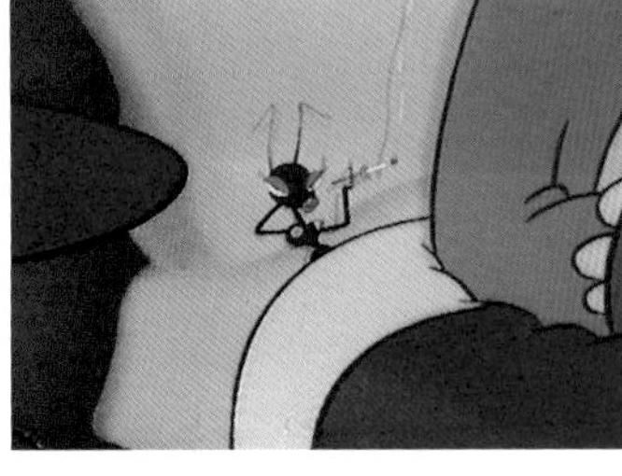

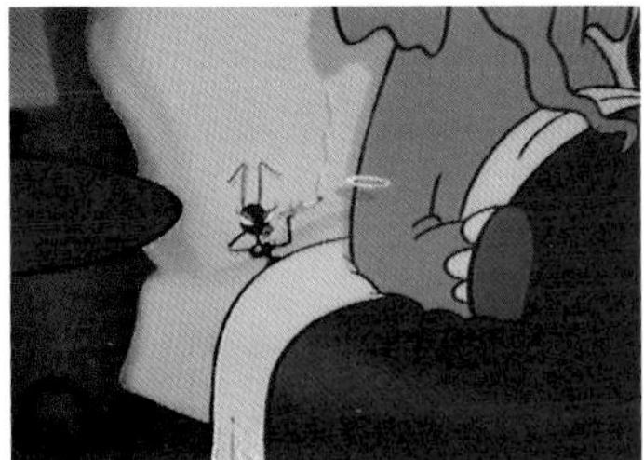

Up to and including 30 seconds

Copywriter
ALBERTO PONTE

Art Director
MARCELO BURGOS

Creative Directors
HERNAN PONCE
CARLOS BAYALA

Producer
JAIME DIAZ

Animator
JAIME DIAZ

Agency Producers
LUIS POMPEO
HORACIO CIANCIA

Production Company
METROVISION

Agency
YOUNG & RUBICAM, BUENOS AIRES

President
DR ALBERTO KOPELOWICZ

Commercial Director
DR JORGE AGOFF

Client
KOPELCO

Up to and including 30 seconds

Directors
IAIN ALLAN
ROSS THOMSON

Copywriter
ROSS THOMSON

Art Director
IAIN ALLAN

Creative Directors
SIMON SCOTT
ANDREW LINDSAY

Producers
IAIN ALLEN
ROSS THOMSON

Agency Producer
TIM MAGUIRE

Editor
CRAWFORD REILLY

Production Company
IN-VIDEO

Agency
FAULDS ADVERTISING

Marketing Executive
FIONA LITTLEJOHN

Client
SCOTTISH OPERA

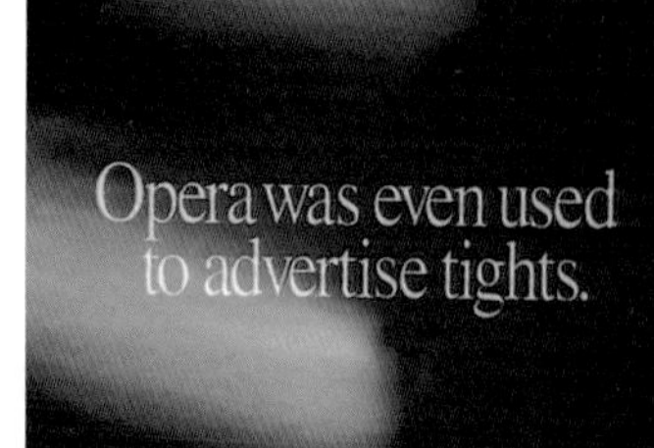

FROGS

'Bud.'
'Bud.'
'Weis.'
'Bud.'
'Bud.'
'Weis.'
'Bud.'
'Er.'
'Bud.'
'Weis.'
'Bud.'
'Er.'
'Weis.'
'Bud.'
'Bud.'
'Weis.'
'Er.'
'Bud.'
'Weis.'
'Er.'
'Bud.'
'Weis.'
'Er.'
'Bud.'
'Weis.'
'Er.'

Up to and including 40 seconds

Director
GORE VERBINSKI

Copywriter
DAVID SWAINE

Art Director
MICHAEL SMITH

Creative Director
RIC ANELLO

Producer
KATHY RHODES

Set Designer
LAURYN LECLERE

Animator
STAN WINSTON

Agency Producer
CHAN HATCHER

Editor
CRAIG WOOD

Lighting Cameraman
STEPHEN RAMSEY

Sound Design
HUMMING BIRD

Production Company
PALOMAR PICTURES

Agency
DMB&B, USA

Director, Budweiser Marketing
MICHAEL BROOKS

Client
ANHEUSER-BUSCH, INC

Up to and including 40 seconds

Director
MIKE STEPHENSON

Copywriter
JOHN BEDFORD

Art Director
PAUL SIMBLETT

Creative Directors
JOHN BEDFORD
PAUL SIMBLETT

Producer
ALICIA BERNARD

Agency Producer
JO BOURNE

Editor
CYRIL METZGER

Lighting Cameraman
ALEXANDER WITT

Production Company
PAUL WEILAND FILM COMPANY

Agency
BURKITT EDWARDS MARTIN

Marketing Manager
KEN HEHIR

Client
COORS UK LIMITED

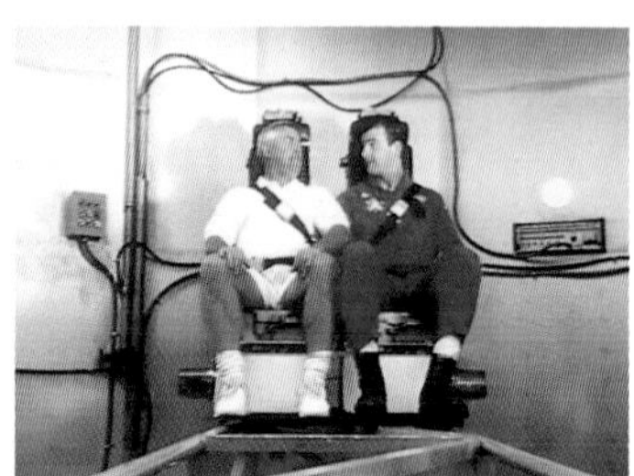

SPACE

SFX:
Stirring music.

JOHN:
The conquest of space. The American Dream. But what about the men behind that dream - Coors drinking men.

(John struggles with a large suitcase, duty free bag, golf clubs etc.)

ASTRONAUT:
Carryin' a little excess baggage there John?

(John drops his golf clubs etc.)

JOHN:
Not anymore!

(John tries to grab a proffered glass of Coors but has to walk off with the astronauts.)

JOHN:
Roger, Roger. So, space cadet, I bet after sitting around all day, you could really go for a Coors - Whoaaa...

(The centrifuge starts up)

ASTRONAUT:
Bye John.

JOHN:
See you later!

(Dizzy, John walks past the proffered glass of Coors)

JOHN:
Talking of gravity, the original gravity of Coors is...

(John reaches for a glass of Coors but his helmet begins to mist over)

JOHN:
Hey, I'm steaming up...don't they fit these things with wipers?

(Losing his balance, John falls into the anti-gravity unit. He floats into the bar.)

WORKERS:
Coors here etc.

(One turns to John)

Don't worry, John, it'll wear off soon...

(John suddenly drops to the floor)

SFX:
Loud crash.

WORKERS:
(Chuckling)

Told you!

ALL NIGHT STORE

Our victim is woken in the night by a phone call. A can of apple Tango demands to see him.

'Meet me at the all night store and wear the special outfit.'

We cut to later. He rushes into the store wearing ridiculous clothes.

We hear the can calling out to him: 'You want my big juicy apples. Go on peel my top off.'

He waits for his moment, under the watchful gaze of a security guard. He snatches the can from the shelf then runs out of the store yelling what he plans to do to the can.

'I'm going to have you, you'll see! Oh yes!'

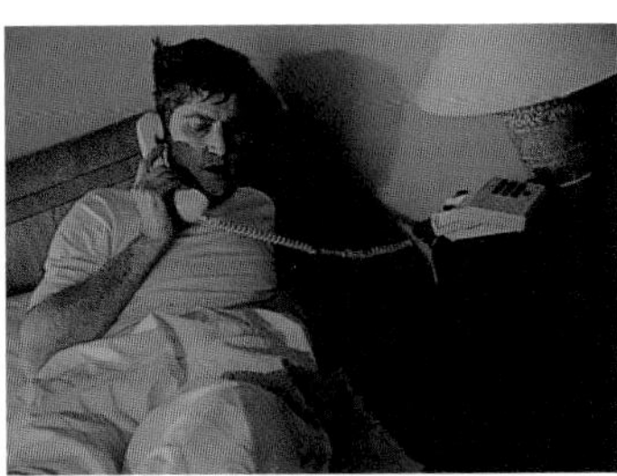

Up to and including 40 seconds

Directors
TREVOR ROBINSON
ALAN YOUNG

Copywriter
ALAN YOUNG

Art Director
TREVOR ROBINSON

Creative Director
AXEL CHALDECOTT

Producer
JANE FULLER

Editor
KEVIN CHICKEN

Lighting Cameraman
HOWARD ATHERTON

Production Company
JANE FULLER ASSOCIATES

Agency
HOWELL HENRY CHALDECOTT LURY & PARTNERS

Brand Manager
DAVID ATTER

Client
BRITVIC SOFT DRINKS LIMITED

Up to and including 40 seconds

Director
JEFF STARK

Copywriter
NICK WORTHINGTON

Art Director
JOHN GORSE

Creative Director
JOHN HEGARTY

Producer
CHRIS STEVENSON

Agency Producer
GEOFF STICKLER

Editor
JOHN SMITH

Lighting Cameraman
ADRIAN BIDDLE

Music Composers/Arrangers
SIMON ELMS
COLIN SMITH

Production Company
STARK FILMS

Agency
BARTLE BOGLE HEGARTY

Brand Manager
TIM DRAKE

Client
THE WHITBREAD BEER COMPANY

SUNCREAM

This commercial is a parody of a glamorous suncream commercial shot on an idyllic beach, set to the song 'Stay just a little bit longer.'

We see a series of beautiful people lounging on the beach in the midday sun.

MVO:
Now there's a cream that helps you stay in the sun just a little bit longer.

We pan up the body of a beautiful woman. She has a blob of cream on her nose. As we watch, she lifts a pint of beer to her lips and takes a noisy slurp.

WOMAN:
By 'eck, I could stay here as long as you like, chuck.

From her point of view, we see a bronzed man with an ice bucket, silhouetted against a pure blue sky.

MAN:
'Ere Vera, fancy a top up?'

The pure blue is not sky, it's the side of a chip van, which pulls away to reveal they are in fact in Blackpool.

WOMAN:
Not 'alf and give us another rub down with that chip fat.

Cut to Blackpool Tower, as a small plane towing a yellow banner, flies into frame with the words: Boddingtons. The Cream of Manchester printed on it.

V/O:
Boddingtons. The Cream of Manchester.

KEVIN'S STORY

MVO:
(Documentary style)

Kevin is a home-made beefburger. He is single and shares the third floor of a fridge with a limp lettuce called Tarquin.

Tonight is his big night. He has a date with a beautiful girl called Mary.

But, disaster.

Kevin has barely uttered a word and Mary seems more interested in Matthew, a tall, dark gateaux from The Black Forest.

MOTHER'S V/O:
Do you want some Heinz Salad Cream darling?

MVO:
(Documentary style)
Extraordinary, Kevin has instantly become more attractive...

...and Mary... well let's just say Kevin didn't get home last night.

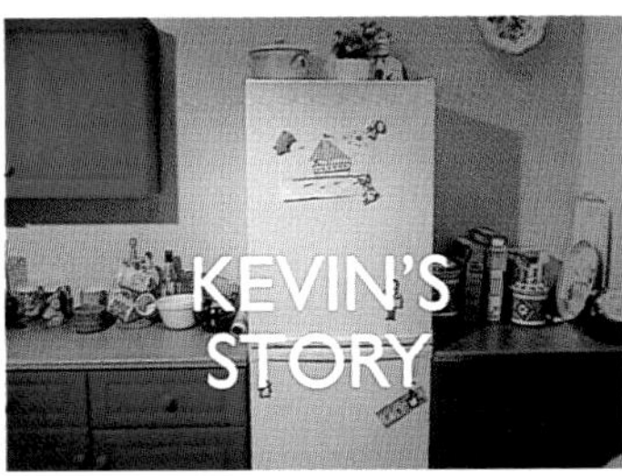

Up to and including 40 seconds

Director
JULIAN LEEFE GRIFFITHS

Copywriter
NICK GILL

Art Director
TONY DAVIDSON

Creative Director
TONY COX

Producer
JEREMY GOOLD

Agency Producer
FRANCIS CASTELLI

Editor
PAUL WATTS

Lighting Cameraman
JOHN TAYLOR

Production Company
TAYLOR McMILLAN

Agency
BMP DDB NEEDHAM

Client
HJ HEINZ COMPANY LIMITED

Up to and including 40 seconds

Director
FRANK BUDGEN

Copywriters
VICTORIA FALLON
STEVE HUDSON

Art Directors
STEVE HUDSON
VICTORIA FALLON

Creative Director
TONY COX

Agency Producer
SARAH POLLIT

Editor
PHIL METZER

Lighting Cameraman
HENRY BRAHAM

Production Company
PAUL WEILAND FILM COMPANY

Agency
BMP DDB NEEDHAM

Marketing Manager
MICHELLE REARDON

Marketing Director
KEN LEE

Client
POWERBREAKER

AN EVENING IN

We see the outside of a house at dusk.

A light is on in a downstairs room.

V/O:
Tonight, Mr and Mrs Hudson have decided to stay in. At the moment they're enjoying a chicken kiev in the dining room.

Another light comes on.

V/O:
Now they're having coffee and after dinner mints in the comfort of the lounge.

A light upstairs comes on:

V/O:
Ah, Mrs Hudson has gone upstairs to unwind in a nice hot bath.

Another light comes on.

V/O:
Finally, they both retire for the evening to snuggle up in bed. Mr and Mrs Hudson are staying at The Royal Hotel, Paris, and what you've been watching are their KingShield Security Time Switches in action. If they fooled you they could fool a burglar.

Cut to packshot and title:

KingShield. We Do Everything To Make You Feel Secure.

SOUND DOWN

We open on a Mazda Xedos 6, shot in a studio - overall the look is very minimal, but beautiful, and the feel seductive.

V/O:
With a car this special we don't need to shout. If you'd like to know more, please turn up your volume now.

There follows a sequence of about 35 simple and evocative close-up images of detail after detail of the Xedos 6.

The sound level for this section is made incredibly low - so people can choose to turn the volume up if they wish to hear the sound more clearly. If they do turn the sound up, they can listen to information about the effort or thought that has gone into the design of each particular detail that is shown.

The montage of sound is summarised at the end with a voice which says:

'The Mazda Xedos 6. Every detail matters.'

We end on the Mazda logo and the telephone number 0345 48 48 48 then a final super, reading '(special)'.

Finally, if you have the volume up you hear the voice-over say:

'Please return your volume to its normal level.'

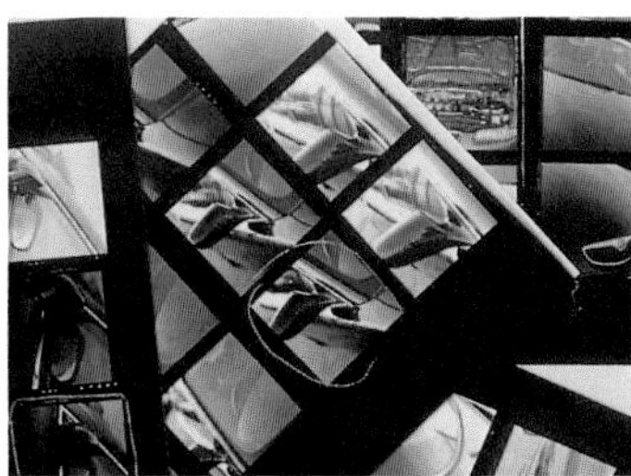

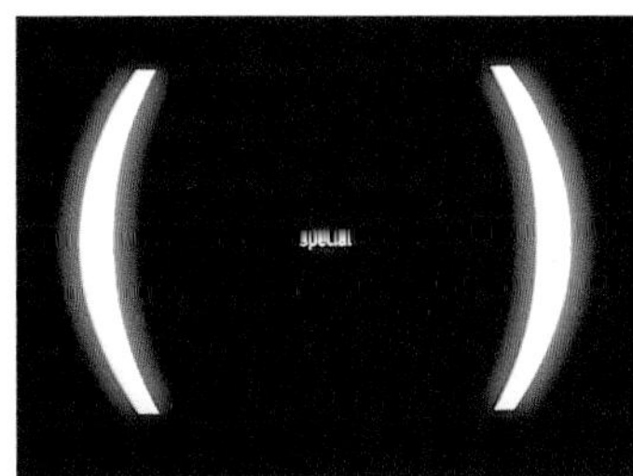

Up to and including 40 seconds

Director
TONY KAYE

Copywriter
JONATHAN KNEEBONE

Art Director
DAVE JOHNSON

Typographer
JONATHAN BARNBROOK

Creative Director
STEVE HENRY

Producer
MIRANDA DAVIS

Set Designer
JENNY SELDON

Sculptor
TOM DIXON

Agency Producer
JENNY SELBY

Editor
PETER GODDARD

Lighting Cameraman
TONY KAYE

Music Composer/Arranger
ROD SYERS

Production Company
TONY KAYE FILMS

Agency
HOWELL HENRY CHALDECOTT LURY & PARTNERS

Marketing Director
JAN SMITH

Client
MAZDA CARS UK LIMITED

Up to and including 40 seconds

Director
JONATHAN BARNBROOK

Copywriter
ADRIAN JEFFERY

Art Director
LINDSEY REDDING

Creative Directors
SIMON SCOTT
ANDREW LINDSAY

Producer
YVONNE CHALK

Agency Producer
TIM MAGUIRE

Editor
JON HOLLIS

Music Composers/Arranger
LOGORHYTHM

Animators
SARAH LEWIS
JONATHAN BARNBROOK

Production Company
TONY KAYE FILMS

Agency
FAULDS ADVERTISING

Account Group Director
TOM GILL

Head of Presentation
PETER GOURD

Client
BBC RADIO SCOTLAND

FOGGIE BUMMER

VIDEO:
As we hear the gripping radio article we see the words appear on screen. The words help to dramatise the action.

MVO1:
An exercise I often do is write words like 'BOMBAIZE' and 'FORFOUGHEN' and words like that up on the board, you see. And they think things like, a foggie bummer, what's a foggie bummer? Then we'll ask one another, you see, and...

MVO 2:
What is a foggie bummer?

MVO 1:
Foggie bummer means a bumble bee! (laughs)

MVO 2:
I was away to say you could have got us struck off air then!

MVO 1:
Oh no no no! It's not that bad!

CAPTION:
Mix up caption which reads,

Re-discover the power of the spoken word.

Silence.

SFX:
Music ident.

VIDEO:
Mix to end frame. We see the BBC Scotland logo and tuning device which demonstrates where to find the signal.

CAPTION:
UK National Station of the Year.

NAE HOPE

VIDEO:
As we hear the gripping radio article, we see the words appear on screen. The words help to dramatise the action.

MVO:
I'm 27 just now and I started using hard drugs when I was 22, it was that kinda day when everyone was using it so I had a wee shot and I liked it.

And just recently there I had two overdoses. It was due to high purity heroin.

It was on streets about here. I think I'll be drug dependent for the rest of my days I think. Nae hope. Nae hope whatsoever.

CAPTION:
Mix up caption which reads,

Re-discover the power of the spoken word.

Silence.

VIDEO
Mix to end frame.

SFX:
Music ident.

VIDEO:
We see the BBC Scotland logo and tuning device which demonstrates where to find the signal.

CAPTION:
UK National Station of the Year.

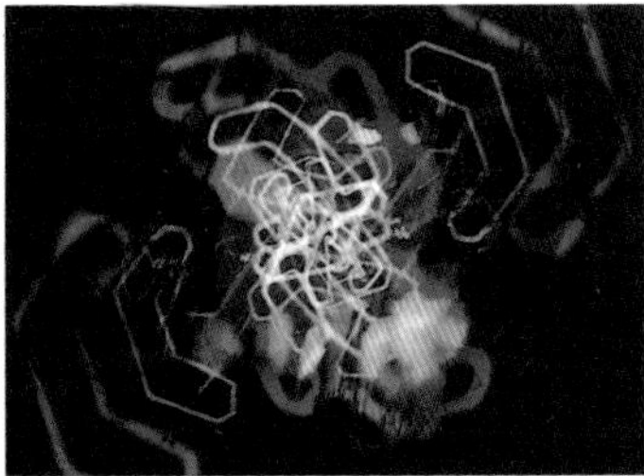

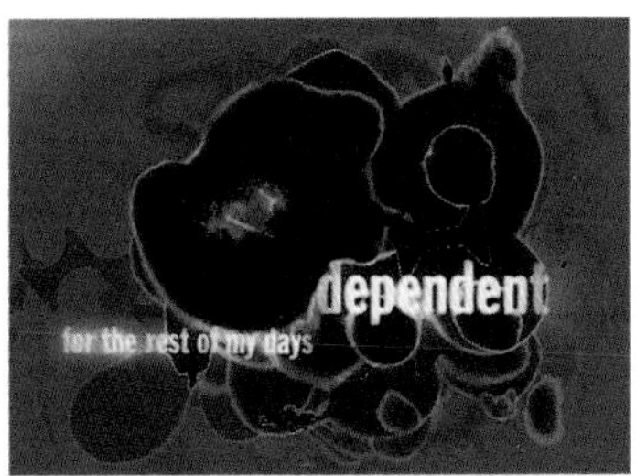

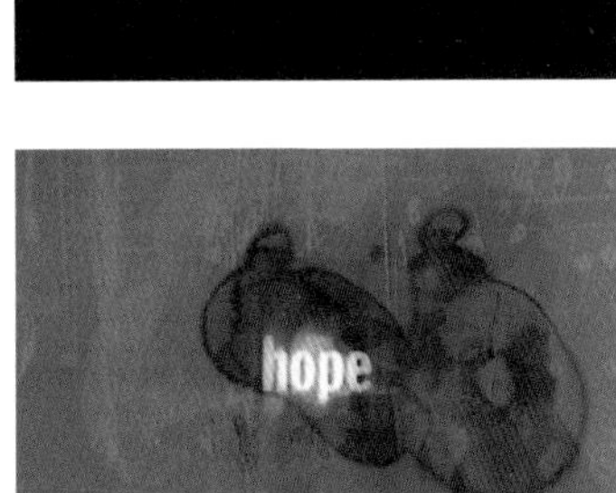

Up to and including 40 seconds

Directors
SIMON TAYLOR
GRAHAM WOOD

Copywriter
ADRIAN JEFFERY

Art Director
LINDSEY REDDING

Creative Directors
SIMON SCOTT
ANDREW LINDSAY

Producer
HELEN LANGRIDGE

Agency Producer
TIM MAGUIRE

Editor
JON HOLLIS

Music Composers/Arrangers
LOGORHYTHM

Production Company
HELEN LANGRIDGE ASSOCIATES

Agency
FAULDS ADVERTISING

Account Group Director
TOM GILL

Head of Presentation
PETER GOURD

Client
BBC RADIO SCOTLAND

Up to and including 40 seconds

Director
FRANK BUDGEN

Copywriter
ROBERT SAVILLE

Art Director
JAY POND-JONES

Creative Director
TIM MELLORS

Producer
PAUL ROTHWELL

Set Designer
JULIA SHERBORNE

Agency Producer
DIANE CROLL

Editor
SAM SNEADE

Lighting Cameraman
ADRIAN BIDDLE

Music Composer/Arranger
RICHARD MYHILL

Production Company
PAUL WEILAND FILM COMPANY

Agency
GGT

Marketing Director
PHIL PLOWMAN

Client
HOLSTEN DISTRIBUTORS LIMITED

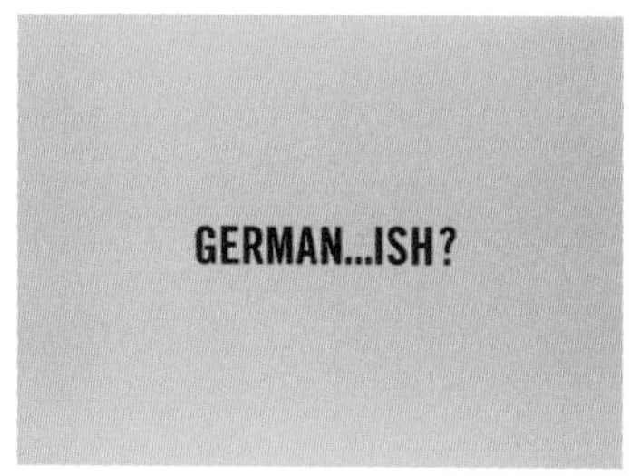

ELVISH

Denis Leary enters shot and paces back and forth as he does. He holds up a really OTT bottle to camera. We notice that something is not quite right about his performance.

DENIS LEARY:
It's delicious, it's hops, it's barley, it's yeast, it's water, it's got some additives, it's got a few other bits and pieces I can't pronounce and it's German...ish.

As the camera follows him left to right he walks straight into another Denis Leary (the real one). He grabs the dodgy bottle and reads it.

DENIS LEARY 2:
(to camera)
Fakenhoff Bier?

The real Denis Leary pulls the other Leary's mask off (a la Mission Impossible) and the guy underneath looks nothing like Leary.

FAKE LEARY:
You were busy...

DENIS LEARY:
Get out of here. You can stein and frau and gluck and schtuck as much as you like but if you don't say 'brewed in Germany' its as authentic as a Chinese Elvis.

He walks off and Denis continues with a real bottle of Holsten Pils.

DENIS LEARY:
Holsten Pils. It's hops, it's barley, it's yeast, it's water, it's made in Germany and it's authentic.

He paces back and forth until coming across a Chinese Elvis.

DENIS LEARY:
Don't even think about it.

TITLE:
Germanish? Get Real!

THE ROACH

Open on a hand dropping a live cockroach into a toilet. The roach frantically swims around in the calm water. The toilet is flushed, the music starts and the roach fatally makes its exit.

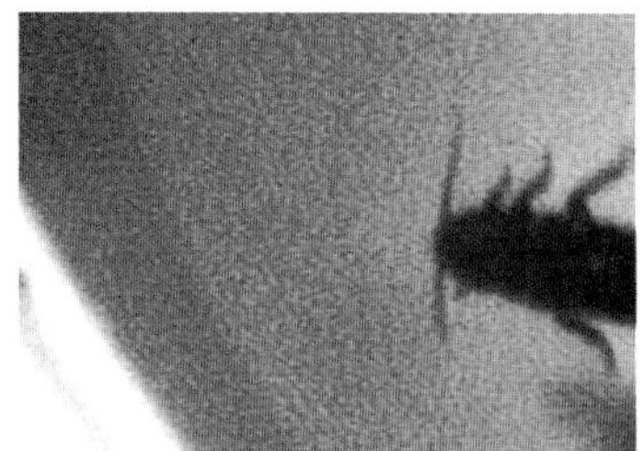

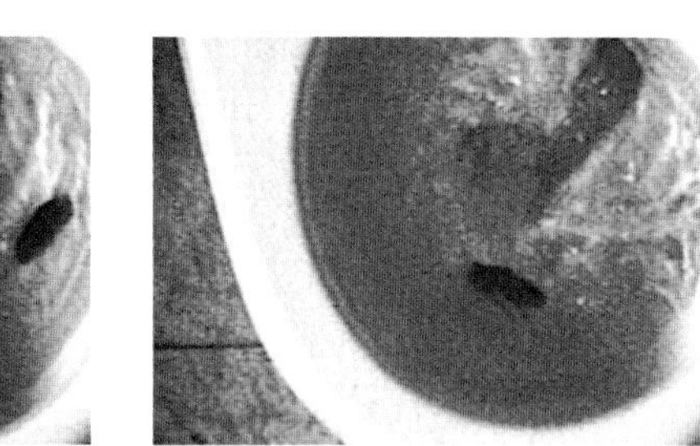

Up to and including 40 seconds

Director
SCOTT DUCHON

Copywriter
TOM KUNTZ

Art Director
RICHARD YELLAND

Agency Producer
STEVEN CHEIFITZ

Music Composer/Arranger
VITO DESARIO

Production Company
DUCHON KUNTZ YELLAND

Client
LUCY'S SURF BAR

Up to and including 40 seconds

Director
JOE PYTKA

Copywriter
BOB MOORE

Art Director
WARREN EAKINS

Creative Directors
DAN WIEDEN
SUSAN HOFFMAN

Producer
LILLY WEINGARTEN

Agency Producer
JANE BRIMBLECOMBE

Lighting Cameraman
JOE PYTKA

Production Company
PYTKA

Agency
WIEDEN & KENNEDY, AMSTERDAM

Marketing Executive
SCOTT GARRETT

Client
NIKE EUROPE

THE WALL

Open on a shot of stormy Paris. Thunder crashing in background.

A wall featuring Eric Cantona is seen.

We see a ball flying past the Eiffel Tower.

Close up of the Cantona wall. The ball flies into the picture. He beats an opponent and kicks the ball, destroying a part of the wall with his shoe.

We hear the noise of the ball flying with rocket like speed, the crowd cheering, the noise of the power kick and bricks smashing.

The ball flies past the Brandenberg gate to a wall in Berlin featuring Michael Schulz.

Schulz takes the ball on his chest, dribbles for a couple of steps and passes the ball, destroying part of the wall.

The ball flies to a city in Italy, upsetting some pigeons, where Maldini comes to life on his wall and heads the ball back to London. Bricks fly from the wall.

Ian Wright kicks the ball from his wall, past Tower Bridge, removing some bricks with his kick.

The ball flies across the ocean to Brazil and into Rio de Janeiro where Romario and Bebeto are seen on two side by side walls. Romario heads the ball to Bebeto, who kicks it to Mexico where Campos dives across three buildings to catch it.

Smashing bricks, kicking sound and moving ball noise continue.

Campos dislodges a Nike logo with his arms on the third building. The sign swings loose from one corner.

Sound of broken glass as he hits logo.

Sound of sign swinging.

BALL

These commercials all take place in a television studio in Sydney, Australia. They are anchored by two presenters. One is male, the other is female. The show is sponsored by Tooheys Export, and consequently called Channel Tooheys.

SFX:
Music intro.

Open on Joy and Jonno sitting in the studio.

Beside them is the singing Cocky. As Jonno and Joy chat with a bloke called Peter Jackson, the Cocky bobs excitedly up and down.

JONNO:
Welcome back to Channel Tooheys. I think we're just about ready now to go live to one of the organisers of tonight's Batchelor and Spinster Ball, are you there Peter Jackson?

PETER JACKSON:
G'day Jonno, G'day Joy. Well, we've got a huge night happening here at the Sydney cricket ground. We've got 100,000 people rocking up. Get this, we've got a million sausages and 200,000 cans of beer.

JOY:
More sausages than beer?

Jonno and Joy look at Peter. Peter looks a bit worried.

PETER JACKSON:
Yeah.

JONNO:
Anyway, we're getting the nod from the prod, the signal's breaking up slightly...

SUPER & END DEVICE:
Brewed In Sydney Since 1869.

SFX:
Music fades up.

Sponsors of the Batchelor and Spinster Ball, Battersea Park, July 16th.

Up to and including 40 seconds

Director
JOHN MARLES

Copywriter
JOHN McCABE

Art Director
TIM ASHTON

Creative Director
JOHN HEGARTY

Producer
ADRIAN HARRISON

Agency Producer
REBECCA AITKINSON

Editor
PETER WHITMORE

Lighting Cameraman
BRIAN BANSGROVE

Music Composer/Arranger
JOE GLASSMAN

Production Company
RSA FILMS

Agency
BARTLE BOGLE HEGARTY

Marketing Executive
ADAM OAKES

Client
THE WHITBREAD BEER COMPANY

Up to and including 40 seconds

Director
RICHARD GOLESZOWSKI

Copywriter
GORDON GRAHAM

Art Director
NEIL SULLIVAN

Creative Director
PAUL WEINBERGER

Producer
JULIE LOCKHART

Animator
RICHARD GOLESZOWSKI

Agency Producer
SUE BRALEY

Editors
TAMSIN PARRY
ROD HOWICK

Lighting Cameraman
FRANK PASSINGHAM

Music Composers
FISHER, LASKY, STERN

Arranged By
JOE & CO

Production Company
AARDMAN ANIMATIONS

Agency
LOWE HOWARD-SPINK

Senior Brand Manager
PAUL TROY

Client
WEETABIX LIMITED

PIRATES

MUSIC:
'My Brudda Sylveste'.

Open on one pirate ship sailing on the sea. Cut to crew on board the Marie Celeste looking menacing.

SUNG:
There was a ship all the other pirates feared
Even Black, Blue, Red and Yellow Beard.

We see a cage suspended with black, blue, red and yellow beard in it. They look frightened. The Captain swipes his sword and the cage drops through a trap door in the deck.

SUNG:
Now the Captain was as rotten as they come
And never once thought to write to his mum
On...the...Marie Celeste.

Cut to the rest of the Marie Celeste crew looking menacing as they move across the deck to join the Captain, who is sitting beside a cannon. He fires it and the cannon ball shoots through the legs of a lookout on the rigging of the ship.

PARROT:
What's it got?

SUNG:
It's got the meanest, cruellest pirates ever pressed.
Until the bosun cried from the crow's nest. There's a ship to the west.

Cut to the crow's nest where the bosun spies the Weetabix ship in the distance.

SUNG:
Shiver me timbers, walk the plank. SOS, swim for shore, pieces of eight... Abandon ship.

Cut to the Captain wearing a rubber ring as he dives overboard.

Mix through to the Weetabix ship where we see the crew sitting around a table eating their Weetabix.

SUNG:
It wasn't magic or ghostly tricks,

PARROT:
What was it?

SUNG:
It was down to a bowl of Weetabix.

Cut to the deserted deck of the Marie Celeste in ghostly mist.

SUNG:
That's why they found no pirates aboard the Marie Celeste.

PACKSHOT & SUPER:
Have You Had Your Weetabix?

SILENT RUNNING

An Aborigine stands in the outback.

His heightened awareness of the natural world allows him to hear the smallest sounds.

His hearing is so good that he reacts to a gecko licking its eye, a snake moving across the sand and a bird taking flight.

He sees movement on the horizon, but he is confused because he can't hear what it is. The dot reveals itself to be a car travelling at speed across the desert floor.

Still he can't hear. He puts his ear to the ground.

The silent car passes him. He turns to watch it go and a pebble is thrown up by the wheel. This bounces noisily to his feet.

Confused by the silence of the car, the Aborigine gazes after the fast disappearing Calibra.

MVO:
The Calibra from Vauxhall. The most aerodynamic production coupe on earth.

SUPER:
The Calibra from Vauxhall.

Up to and including 40 seconds

Director
TARSEM

Copywriter
PHIL DEARMAN

Art Director
CHARLES INGE

Creative Director
PAUL WEINBERGER

Producers
SIMON TURTLE
PHIL CONTOMICHALOS

Set Designer
FATIMA ANDRADE

Agency Producer
SARAH HORRY

Editor
ROBERT DUFFY

Lighting Cameraman
PAUL LAUFER

Production Company
SPOTS FILM SERVICES

Agency
LOWE HOWARD-SPINK

Marketing Executive
MARTIN BROWN

Client
VAUXHALL MOTOR COMPANY

Up to and including 40 seconds

Director
DANIEL BARBER

Copywriters
LARRY BARKER
LEON JAUME

Art Director
ROONEY CARRUTHERS

Creative Directors
LARRY BARKER
ROONEY CARRUTHERS

Producer
KAREN CUNNINGHAM

Set Designer
JOHNA BUTLER

Agency Producer
SIMON WELLS

Editor
BRIAN DYKE

Lighting Cameraman
STEVE CHIVERS

Music Composer/Arranger
PHILIP GLASS

Production Company
ROSE HACKNEY BARBER PRODUCTIONS

Agency
WCRS

Head of Marketing Services
SEAN GARDENER

Client
HUTCHISON TELECOM

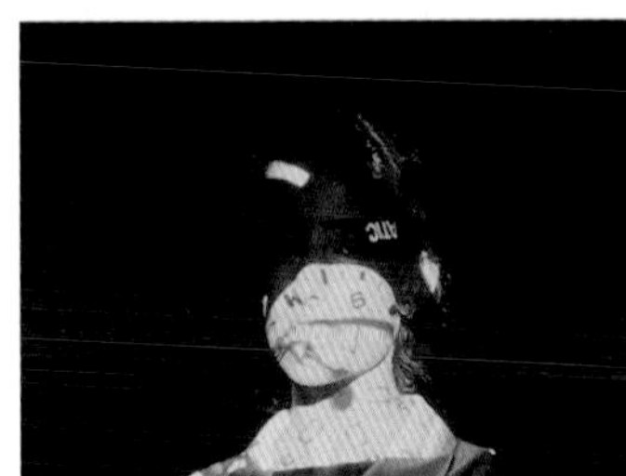

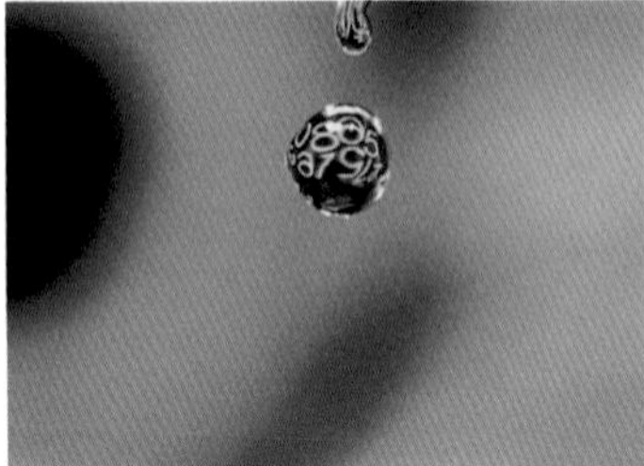

PER SECOND

SFX:
Orange theme.

The commercial begins with extremely tight close-ups of a stopwatch. Various shots of people are superimposed over the watch face. Their lips are moving in time to the counting of numbers in the music.

MVO:
Orange think it unfair that you should pay for time you haven't used.

We see more images superimposed over the watch face. We now see a single droplet of water with numbers reflected on its surface.

MVO:
And in the future maybe everyone will think that way.

We watch as the droplet falls and splashes into a pool of water.

MVO:
Until then, Orange is the only mobile network to charge you one second at a time...

SUPER:
1.

SFX:
Music stops - silence except for fast ticking.

Dissolve to extreme close-up of the stopwatch. The hand on the stopwatch ticks on alone.

Cut to an extreme close-up of a woman's eye. It blinks and dissolves through to the face of a clock.

MVO:
...Instead of rounding up to the next minute or half minute.

SFX:
Music re-starts.

We see a close-up of a child's face. She smiles. We cut to endframe and logo.

MVO:
The Future's Bright. The Future's Orange.

HELP YOURSELF

MUSIC:
Help Yourself.

PENGUINS:
(sing)

Just help yourself to John Smiths
to its charms
Just say the word and it is yours
Just help yourself to the flavour in its heart
Your lips can open up the door

(continues under)

JACK:
There's something completely new in the pub, John Smiths Extra Smooth Bitter, pure silk in a glass.

Mmmm...

So you still don't need gimmicks.

PENGUINS:
(sing)

...and your lips...(stop)

(mutter mutter)

SFX:
Clunk.

Up to and including 40 seconds

Director
MANDIE FLETCHER

Copywriters
JOHN WEBSTER
JACK DEE

Art Director
JOHN WEBSTER

Creative Director
JOHN WEBSTER

Producers
MADELEINE SANDERSON
DAVID MORLEY

Set Designer
ROGER HALL

Agency Producer
LUCINDA KER

Editor
ALASTER JORDON

Lighting Cameraman
SUE GIBSON

Music Composers/Arrangers
PAUL HART
JOE CAMPBELL

Production Companies
FLETCHER SANDERSON FILMS
OPEN MIKE PRODUCTIONS

Agency
BMP DDB NEEDHAM

Group Marketing Controller
JOHN ROBERTS

Client
[illegible]

Up to and including 60 seconds

Director
DAVID TAYLOR

Copywriter
KES GRAY

Art Director
JON GREENHALGH

Producer
BEN SWAFFER

Agency Producer
ARNOLD PEARCE

Editor
PAUL WATTS

Lighting Cameraman
MARTIN TESTER

Music Composer/Arranger
PAUL HART

Production Company
THE SHOP

Agency
SAATCHI & SAATCHI

Marketing Executive
JANE PACKER

Client
JANE PACKER

PRIVET ON PARADE

Open on a 'hard man' soldier, talking in a subdued fashion to camera.

MVO:
It was a year ago to this day...

We were on manoeuvres at a secret location, when suddenly I just cracked.

I went to pieces.

I tried to fight it, but I knew deep down what was wrong.

I was tired of privet and hawthorn.

I couldn't take any more.

A humorous sequence of cameos follow as various flowers are presented in isolation as part of a camouflage manoeuvre.

MVO:
With a little more thought, there's so much more you can do with a camouflage outfit.

Dried yarrow for instance, (yarrow on the helmet)

bright yellow florets that look simply sublime nestled alongside the, rubbery rouche of an ornamental cabbage. (cabbage on his shoulders)

For sheer fiery impact, consider the explosive reds of virginia creeper. (virginia creeper on his gun)

If it's prickles you want try thistles emboldened with hydrangea blues. (thistles, hydrangea down his arm)

Go wild with sunflowers or Gerbera, each arrangement can be so exciting so personal. (sunflowers, gerbera up both legs)

We cut finally to see the soldier on a wide, careering across the Sussex Downs dressed like a pot pourri, and struggling to keep up with the three soldiers in front of him.

FVO:
For every floral occasion.

Jane Packer Flowers.

SUPER:
Jane Packer Flowers (logo)

London. Tokyo.

DRUGSTORE (FEMALE)

We see the view through the windscreen of an old truck heading into town. It's 1930, the American depression.

The truck comes to a stop outside a drugstore, as a train rumbles by.

We don't see the driver, just their view as they enter the store.

The shopkeeper, a woman and child and two girls, all turn to look.

At the counter, the driver asks for something.

The chemist hands over a tin of condoms, with a knowing smile. The driver tucks them into the watch pocket of the jeans and heads out of the door, leaving the woman in a state of shock and embarrassment.

We dissolve to the truck later that evening. It's waiting while a train thunders by. We then see it pulling up outside a white clapboard house.

The driver bangs on the door. It opens. It's the chemist. The chemist is a little confused.

From the chemist's point of view, we see the driver for the first time. It's a teenage girl. She smiles at the chemist, as a young boy slips past his dad. The chemist, realising what's going on, trys to stop his son, but is powerless. He watches, as his son climbs into the truck and drives off with the girl.

SUPER:
Watch Pocket Created in 1873.

Abused Ever Since.

Batwing logo.

SUPER:
501. The Original Jean.

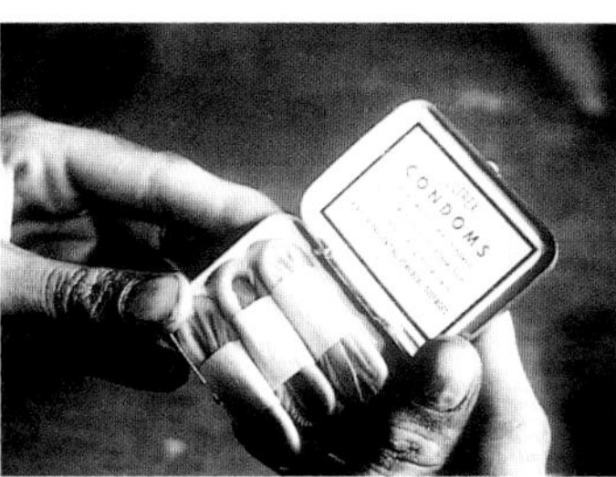

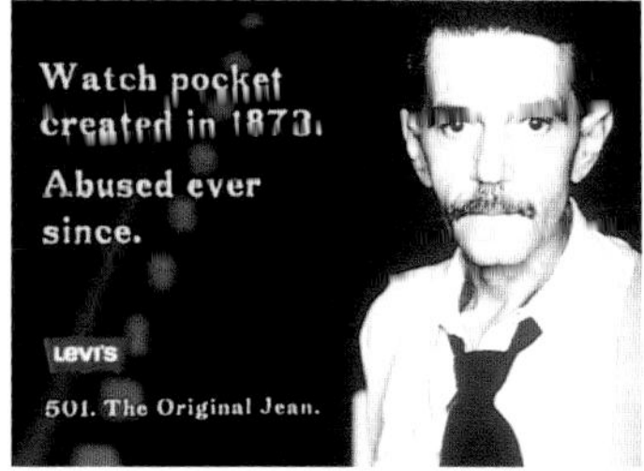

Up to and including 60 seconds

Director
MICHEL GONDRY

Copywriter
NICK WORTHINGTON

Art Director
JOHN GORSE

Creative Director
JOHN HEGARTY

Producers
TOBY COURLANDER
GEORGES BERMANN
PETE CHAMBERS

Set Designer
ROBBIE FREED

Agency Producer
PHILIPPA CRANE

Editor
RUSSELL ICKE

Lighting Cameraman
TIM MAURICE JONES

Music Composer/Arranger
GEIR JENSSEN

Production Company
PARTIZAN MIDI MINUIT

Agency
BARTLE BOGLE HEGARTY

Senior Marketing Manager
ROBERT HOLLOWAY

Client
LEVI STRAUSS & CO EUROPE SA

Up to and including 60 seconds

Director
ALEX PROYAS

Copywriter
ALISTAIR WOOD

Art Director
TOM NOTMAN

Creative Director
PAUL WEINBERGER

Producer
MARGOT FITZPATRICK

Set Designer
MIKE BUCHANAN

Agency Producer
SARAH HORRY

Editor
IAN WEIL

Lighting Cameraman
DAREK WOLSKI

Music Composers/Arrangers
DE WOLFE/JOE & CO

Production Company
PROPAGANDA FILMS

Agency
LOWE HOWARD-SPINK

Marketing Executive
SUSAN PURCELL

Client
THE WHITBREAD BEER COMPANY

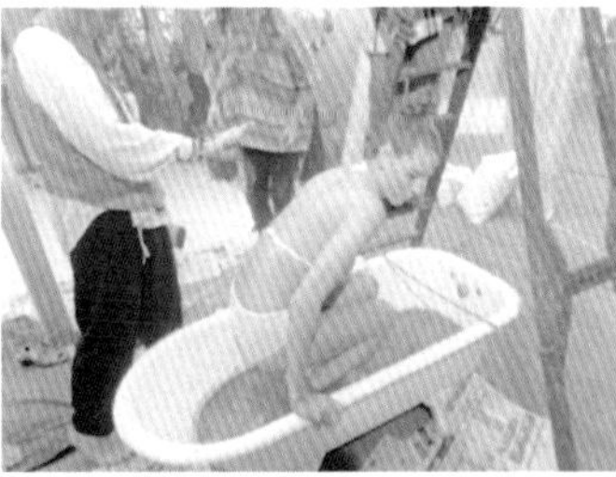

BOTTLE

This documentary charts an artist's life-long search for 'Strong Yet Light' art, from his early feather paintings through to illuminated hammers, polystyrene rooms, balloon animals and early film work, culminating in his classic short 'Bottle', a simple depiction of a bottle of 'Strong Yet Light' Stella Dry.

LAUNCH

SFX:
Orange theme.

Out of black fades up a baby floating in water. A series of numbers, written and numerical, appear on screen in time with the music. We dissolve through to a close-up of a baby. The word 'Cry' appears.

We see more numbers appearing and disappearing on screen superimposed over the baby's mouth. The word 'Laugh' appears.

We fade up a close-up of a child's ear, again superimposed numbers appear and disappear. The word 'Listen' appears.

CHILD V/O:
In the future you won't change what you say...just how you say it.

We see a close-up of a child's mouth, again in the midst of superimposed numbers. The word 'Talk' appears.

We see two boys running over fields. We dissolve to see them standing talking on a tin can walkie-talkie.

CHILD V/O:
In the future we'll think it strange that voices ever travelled down wires.

We see various shots of telephone posts and telegraph wires being cut.

CHILD V/O:
In the future no-one will be tied down.

Cut to a child sitting on a rock looking out over a valley. We pull back to reveal the scale of the vista.

CHILD V/O:
And in the future the skies will be clearer because the world of communications will be wire-free.

We cut to see the sun setting over office buildings, fields and office windows. The windows are bright orange. This changes into the orange logo.

CHILD V/O:
The future's Bright. The future's Orange.

Up to and including 60 seconds

Director
FRANK BUDGEN

Copywriter
LARRY BARKER

Art Director
ROONEY CARRUTHERS

Creative Directors
LARRY BARKER
ROONEY CARRUTHERS

Producer
PAUL ROTHWELL

Set Designer
LAUREN LECLERE

Agency Producer
BRENDA DYKES

Editor
SAM SNEADE

Lighting Cameraman
ALEXANDER WITT

Music Composer/Arranger
PHILIP GLASS

Production Company
PAUL WEILAND FILM COMPANY

Agency
WCRS

Marketing Director
LISA GERNON

Client
HUTCHISON TELECOM

Up to and including 60 seconds

Director
DAVID WILD

Copywriter
TOM CAMPION

Art Director
DOUG LYON

Creative Directors
GUY BOMMARITO
SCOTT MACKEY
DAVID CRAWFORD

Editor
HANK POLONSKY

Production Company
WILD SCIENTIFIC

Agency
GSD&M ADVERTISING

Vice-President of Marketing Services
RICK STEFFEN

Client
ROYAL CROWN COLA COMPANY

FISH-O-RAMA

Open on a dock in a harbour. A huge banner indicates the Coke and Pepsi Fishing Competition. Magnificent state-of-the-art boats with gleaming white hulls flying Coke and Pepsi banners from their masts.

Our boats motor away from the dock and head out to sea, where seagulls are dipping into the water. It's a beautiful day. The boats race to be the first to the fishing hole.

Cut to shot of a Coke crew member. He reaches into a cooler for a can of Coke, which he pops open and puts on the end of his line and casts it.

Cut to Pepsi boat where the same scenario is taking place.

On both boats each fisherman is reacting to a hit. Both start reeling in. The fight is on. We see our quarry jump out of the water. It is a man.

Cut to Pepsi guy who is trying to land another fish. Cut to Coke boat as they net a person. Cut back to Pepsi guy who is trying to land a housewife. The Pepsi boat pulls a guy onto the boat, throws him to the deck where he flops around with the rest of the 'fish'.

Cut to a 20-year-old guy buying an RC from a machine at the foot of the dock. As he's pulling out the RC, he looks back and notices something on the horizon. He walks down the dock.

Cut to shot over his shoulder. We see that just beyond his RC can the boats are coming in.

ANNCR:
Hey, you don't have to swallow that.

Cut to boats docking and fish being unloaded and weighed. Our RC guy walks over to one of the fish hanging upside down. He looks at him as if to say, 'What's going on?'

ANNCR:
Drink RC and you'll look at colas in a whole new way.

Cut to pov of the fish upside down and swinging slightly, looking at a kid who is also looking at the fish with an RC in his hand.

ANNCR & LOGO:
RC Cola. Shake things up.

ALPINE VILLAGE

We open on a glass of milk, which is suspended in mid air against a beautiful blue sky. The pint of milk revolves to reveal the Diesel logo. We reveal the Diesel man in close up. Close up of the cow's head. They walk gracefully towards the camera.

Hero's point of view of Alpine village. We see a young Adolf Hitler outside a bar. He appears to be very drunk. He receives a drink. This puts him off balance and he falls backwards out of frame.

From the hero's pov, he sees a strange shop and has to give a double take.

Close up of Jesus. He looks straight into the camera with a pitiful expression on his face. As the camera pulls back an empty hand drops into frame. Money is placed into his palm as the other hand produces fish and chips wrapped for the customer.

The hero now knows he is in the twilight zone. He sees a group of people wearing lycra and leder-hosens. They are all deep into formation aerobics which progresses into slapping each other around the face.

The hero spots a drunk Santa. He is sitting on his sledge, trying to motivate a pack of sheep wearing fake antlers and red and white underwear. Santa eventually [illegible] the sledge and out of frame, to our hero's amazement.

Hero and cow stroll around the corner to see Hitler staggering towards a beautiful buxom barmaid. Hitler tries to grab her breasts. She slaps him round the face and he falls over and out of frame.

Hero's pov. He turns into the next street to see a dwarf in close up. To the left of the street there is a field with a group of golfers dressed as pimps. Their aim is to hit the dwarfs as they are thrown down the road.

Hitler skips into frame wearing a wedding dress. He looks up to see our hero and partner. As this happens a piano drops from the heavens onto Hitler. Hero looks on in amazement. As the camera pivots 180 degrees, we see for the first time that the hero wears Diesel and the cow has a Diesel stamp burnt on its butt.

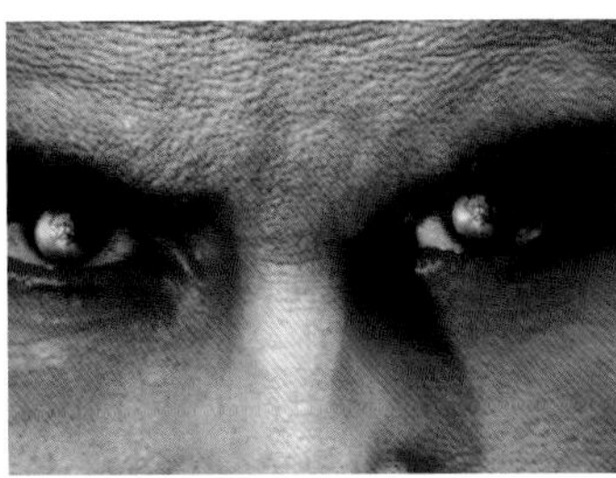

Up to and including 60 seconds

Directors
TERENCE O'CONNOR
MAREK LOSEY

Copywriter
LINUS KARLSON

Art Director
JOAKIM JONASSON

Producer
PHILIPPA TEDDER

Editor
TONY KEARNS

Lighting Cameraman
SHAUN O'DELL

Production Company
TRADEMARK PRODUCTIONS

Client
PLANET DIESEL

Up to and including 60 seconds

Director
PETER MAGUIRE

Copywriter
GEOFF DENMAN

Art Director
LYNDA THOMPSON

Creative Director
DAVID BLACKLEY

Producer
JULIE RUTHERFORD

Agency Producer
PIP HEMING

Editor
KARL SODERSTEN

Lighting Cameraman
MIKE MOLLOY

Music Composer/Arranger
TERRY GARLAND

Production Company
NEWBLOOD & OLDMONEY

Agency
CLEMENGER MELBOURNE PTY

Manager, Marketing Communications
WILLIAM BURLACE

Client
YELLOW PAGES

ZIPPER

Open on a shot of a man standing outside an office building. The building has dark glass windows, the kind that many people forget that they can still be seen from inside.

The man is standing, apparently waiting to meet someone, when he realises from the odd stares he is getting, that his fly is undone.

In embarrassment he quickly turns to the building and tries to fix the broken fly. Unknown to him, however, is the fact that he has just turned to full view of a woman inside the building. In fact the fly is right at her eye level. She is suitably shocked.

Finally the man only succeeds in pulling the zipper from his pants altogether.

The man moves across the glass wall, still with his back to the street.

Unknown to him, his actions are now being watched by several people inside the building.

Cut to shot of man in phono box looking through Yellow Pages. His fingers stop on listing 'Tailor'.

Cut to shot of man happily walking out of tailor's shop.

He stops, bends over to pick up an orange dropped by a pregnant woman. In doing so he splits the bottom out of his pants. He then walks off happily unaware of what's just happened.

Cut to Yellow Pages logo.

A STAR IS BORN (LAUNCH)

We open on a view of outer space. It's a magical sight.

Constellations begin to swirl around and become sucked together to form an amorphous mass of multi-coloured, twinkling particles.

We cut to POV from space as we descend down through cloud layers towards the earth and the shape of Great Britain.

We dissolve through further cloud layers to aerial view approaching rugged coastline.

We cut to lighthouse keeper and trawlermen (unaware), ancient stone circle; (breeze created as it passes) and aquaduct.

We cut to 'presence' forming into the shape of a hand.

Cut to hand making silhouette of rabbit's head from POV of child's window against moon.

Track along streets of detached homes.

Cut to hand passing over stadium.

Cut to hand passing train window.

Cut to hand approaching window, we see a man watching TV, surrounded by his family. It taps on window.

Cut to close up of delighted man illuminated by a magical glow as he turns to see hand. In the background, his family looks thrilled.

The whole room begins to sparkle magically.

Cut to his POV through window of hand pointing at camera.

The hand dematerialises in a burst of (silent) firework-like effects.

Logo and titles.

It Could Be You.

The National Lottery.

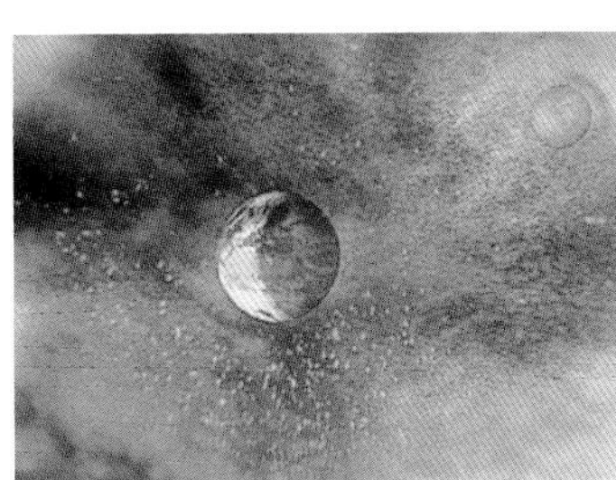

Up to and including 60 seconds

Director
KEVIN MOLONY

Copywriter
JOHN PALLANT

Art Director
MATT RYAN

Producer
SOPHIE HUMPHREYS

Agency Producer
MARK HANRAHAN

Editor
RICHARD LEAROYD

Lighting Cameraman
CURTIS CLARK

Music Composers/Arrangers
ANTHONY & GAYNOR SADLER

Production Company
T.T.O

Agency
SAATCHI & SAATCHI

Marketing Director
JON KINSEY

Client
CAMELOT GROUP PLC

Up to and including 60 seconds

Director
SPROTE

Copywriter
PAUL SILBURN

Art Director
TIGER SAVAGE

Creative Director
JOHN HEGARTY

Producer
BASY ROBERTSON

Set Designer
STEVE SMITHWICK

Agency Producer
FRANCES ROYALE

Editor
MIKE GILDING

Lighting Cameraman
DENIS CROSSAN

Music Composers/Arrangers
ANTHONY & GAYNOR SADLER

Production Company
REDWING FILM COMPANY

Agency
BARTLE BOGLE HEGARTY

Brand Manager
JENS HENNING KOCK

Client
HUGO BOSS AG

THE BOSS

MUSIC:
Zadoq the Priest by Handel.

We are at a big football match. We see our Boss suited hero, the manager of one of the teams, enduring the pressure of a vital game.

Things are going badly, so the boss decides to make a management decision. To the surprise of his staff and the TV commentators, he makes a substitution.

In the dying seconds, the substitute breaks through and is brought down in the penalty area.

He gets up and takes the penalty, scoring the winning goal.

The crowd goes wild, as the final whistle blows.

The players celebrate and the boss finds himself being embraced by his goalkeeper, who leaves mud down the front of his immaculate suit. For a moment, we think the boss will explode, but he simply smiles and turns to congratulate the goalscorer.

As he turns, we see he hasn't noticed the mud on his back.

SUPER:
Men At Work.

Hugo Boss.

BRITISH AIRWAYS WORLD OFFERS

This commercial is shot from camera point of view.

Open on a man waking up in the morning.

SFX:
Beep, beep, beep, of a digital alarm clock.

His hand reaches out and switches off the alarm. He throws an arm across the bed to reach for his wife. She's not there.

He walks down the stairs and calls out.

MAN:
Carol!

He looks in the kitchen but she's not there.

MAN:
Carol?

He passes the goldfish tank and notices the fish isn't there.

The man leaves the house, climbs into his car and drives off.

He drives through deserted streets, not a car or person in sight. He looks at his watch, it's 8.15am, rush hour.

He runs into a railway station. It's completely deserted.

He looks in a cafe. There's no one there.

He runs through more deserted streets desperately trying to find any sign of life. He runs up a flight of stairs and emerges into a large open plan office. Again, there's nobody there at all, only his reflection in a mirror.

In desperation he runs into the middle of a deserted street and screams.

MAN:
Where Is Everybody?!

SFX:
Festive music.

TITLES:
Rio from £299 return.

LA from £199 return.

Rome from £99 return.

Paris from £59 return.

New York from £168 return.

British Airways World Offers.

Up to and including 60 seconds

Director
PAUL MEIJER

Copywriter
KEITH BICKEL

Art Director
CARLOS ANUNCIBAY

Producer
ROBERT CAMPBELL

Agency Producer
TIM BERRIMAN

Editor
MARTYN GOULD

Lighting Cameraman
IVAN BIRD

Production Company
SPOTS FILM SERVICES

Agency
SAATCHI & SAATCHI

Marketing Executive
DEREK DEAR

Client
BRITISH AIRWAYS

Up to and including 60 seconds

Director
TONY KAYE

Art Director
KIM BOWEN

Creative Director
JEFF WEISS

Producer
EILEEN TERRY

Agency Producer
NATHALIE ROSS

Editor
BOB JENKINS

Lighting Cameraman
TONY KAYE

Production Company
TONY KAYE FILMS

Agency
MERGEOTES
FERTITTA & WEISS

Client
START, INC

BIRDS

OLD MAN:
I have a lovely marriage probably because I have a wife who's obsessed with birds.

OLD WOMAN:
I can't stand these things that cost a thousand dollars.

OLD MAN:
What is money?

OLD WOMAN:
Why does he think I love them so much when I hate them?

OLD WOMAN:
Especially this eagle.

Now how can that be an eagle when it looks like a vulture and it's a turkey?

OLD MAN:
And if she likes the eagle, I like the eagle.

OLD WOMAN:
You have to dust them, clean them, wash them.

All that money we could have saved.

All that money wasted.

Birds! Birds!

Flying!

Bang!

I mean, really, where does the money go? It just flies away.

OLD MAN:
I love to see them strut.

OLD WOMAN:
He thinks he's doing me a great big favour.

OLD MAN:
I would have to say that the birds have saved my marriage - I'm no dummy.

TRUE ROMANCE

As we hear the radio article, we see the words appear on the screen. The words help to dramatise the action.

SPEAKER:
These are the...these are the things that life is made of. I wanted to see what the Atlantic was like, you can only see it by going there. But much more importantly, I wanted to see what I was like on the Atlantic.

What's wrong with romance?

It brings light into life. Into your own life and into other peoples' lives.

God forbid that we were all practical pragmatists.

Silence.

Mix up caption which reads:

Re-discover the power of the spoken word.

Mix to end frame. We see the BBC Scotland logo and tuning device which demonstrates where to find the signal.

CAPTION:
UK National Station of the Year.

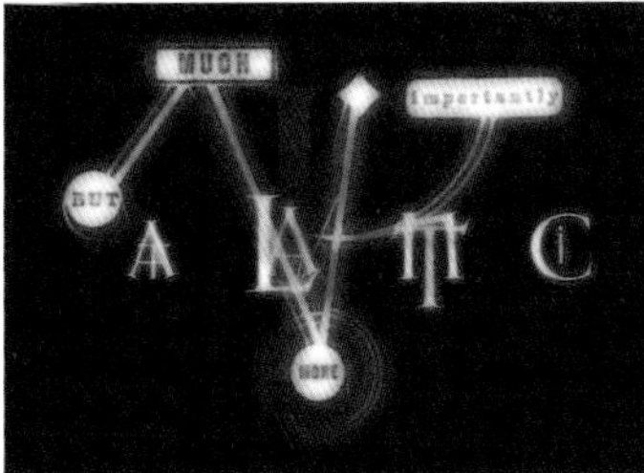

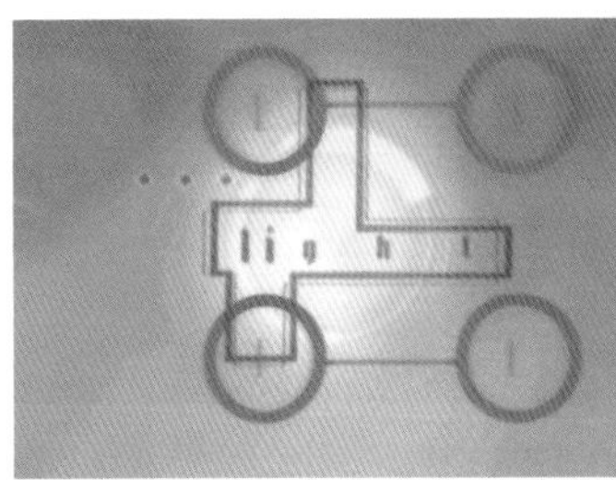

Up to and including 60 seconds

Director
JONATHAN BARNBROOK

Copywriter
ADRIAN JEFFERY

Art Director
LINDSEY REDDING

Creative Directors
SIMON SCOTT
ANDREW LINDSAY

Producer
YVONNE CHALK

Agency Producer
TIM MAGUIRE

Editor
JON HOLLIS

Music Composers/Arrangers
LOGORHYTHM

Production Company
TONY KAYE FILMS

Agency
FAULDS ADVERTISING

Account Group Director
TOM GILL

Head of Presentation
PETER GOURD

Client
BBC RADIO SCOTLAND

Up to and including 60 seconds

Directors
SIMON TAYLOR
GRAHAM WOOD

Copywriter
ADRIAN JEFFERY

Art Director
LINDSEY REDDING

Creative Directors
SIMON SCOTT
ANDREW LINDSAY

Producer
HELEN LANGRIDGE

Agency Producer
TIM MAGUIRE

Editor
JON HOLLIS

Music Composers/Arrangers
LOGORHYTHM

Production Company
HELEN LANGRIDGE ASSOCIATES

Agency
FAULDS ADVERTISING

Account Group Director
TOM GILL

Head of Presentation
PETER GOURD

Client
BBC RADIO SCOTLAND

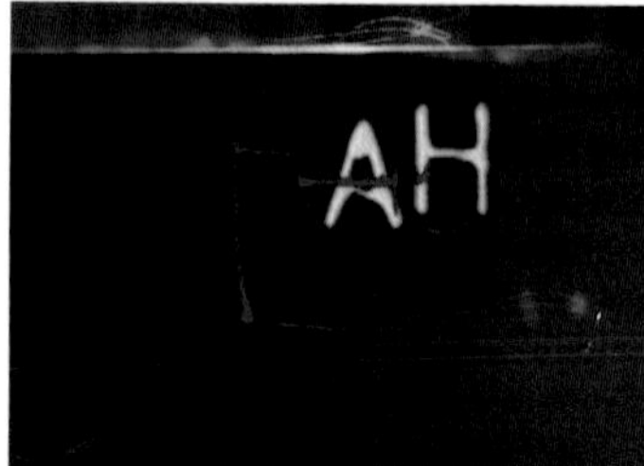

COCKEREL

As we hear the gripping radio article, we see the words appear on the screen. The words help to dramatise the action.

We hear a snippet from a BBC Scotland programme.

MVO:
Line out. Outside the French 22. Back on the main...oop...now the referee has called a halt to the proceedings, it's now over to the Scottish 22 and heading upfield. It's a magnificent fellow with a black underbelly, a gold coloured back and a red cockscomb and the cockerel's over the Scot's 5 metre line, heading for touch and the stewards are looking just a little bit flushed/perplexed, a little bit perplexed and flushed, ...just selling them a wee dummy and a wee side step and away he goes. Yes, he's over the touch line, now he's on the running track, and he's almost away.

Silence.

Mix up caption which reads:

Re-discover the power of the spoken word.

Mix to end frame. We see the BBC Scotland logo and tuning device which demonstrates where to find the signal.

SFX:
Music ident.

CAPTION:
UK National Station of the Year.

MIND GAMES

Creatively, the TAG Heuer commercial captures an attitude that is inspirational and fits within a sporting context. As a result, a platform of mental strength is developed, based on the recognition that the difference between success and failure is yourself. Winners create their own imaginary pressure in order to win. TAG Heuer associates itself with such an attitude, presenting it in a prestigious way.

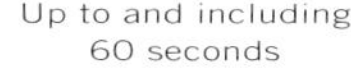

Up to and including 60 seconds

Director
TONY KAYE

Copywriter
REMY NOEL

Art Director
ERIC HOLDEN

Producer
SOPHIE JACOBS

Set Designer
JULIA JASON

Agency Producer
FRANCOISE KORB

Editor
PETER GODDARD

Lighting Cameraman
TONY KAYE

Production Company
1/33 PRODUCTIONS

Agency
BDDP PARIS

Client
TAG HEUER

Up to and including 60 seconds

Director
MARK CHAPMAN

Copywriter
PAUL BURKE

Art Director
PETER GATLEY

Creative Director
TONY COX

Producer
GLYNIS SANDERS

Set Designer
TONY NOBLE

Agency Producer
MICHAEL PARKER

Editor
IAN WEIL

Lighting Cameraman
JOHN IGNATIUS

Rostrum Cameraman
MARTIN KENZIE

Music Composer/Arranger
HOWARD GOODALL

Production Company
TIGER ASPECT PRODUCTIONS

Agency
BMP DDB NEEDHAM

Manager of Marketing and Advertising
JOHN LAIDLOW

Client
BARCLAYCARD

WHITEHALL

LATHAM:
...So there is no better way of serving your Queen and country...than to choose a career in MI7. Are there any questions?

CANDIDATE 1:
What's the financial package?401

LATHAM:
Financial package??

BOUGH:
You do get issued with a Barclaycard, Sir.

LATHAM:
Bough...

CANDIDATE 2:
Oh yeah, with Barclaycard can't you get medical help abroad?

CANDIDATE 3:
...and legal advice?

CANDIDATE 4:
...and some sort of purchase insurance?

BOUGH:
Ah yes, both at home and abroad.

LATHAM:
Bough!! These people will have to survive in locations rather more dangerous than a record shop.

CANDIDATE 5:
Ah, can I ask about Eastern Europe?

LATHAM:
Ah, yes...

CANDIDATE 5:
Do they take Barclaycard?

BOUGH:
Ah, well most countries actually take...

LATHAM:
I remember when all an agent had was his charm, his cunning, and if he was lucky...

CANDIDATE 6:
A biro?

LATHAM:
No ordinary biro...two clicks of the cap will render any assailant immobile...very dangerous in the wrong hands. Take over for a Bough, would you moment?

BOUGH:
Well, Barclaycard is widely accepted, in fact you can use it in over 200 countries around the world...

(fade out)

TARTAN TOYBOYS

As we hear the radio article, we see the words appear on the screen. The words help to dramatise the action.

MUM:
I'm looking forward to seeing the Tartan Toyboys.

DAUGHTER:
What do you think they're going to be like, though?

MUM:
Well, I hope they're going to have long legs and wee bums and broad shoulders, and I hope they're going to wear kilts. I'll be terribly disappointed if they don't have kilts on (laughs). I'll be equally disappointed if they don't have them off before the night's over.

Silence.

Mix up caption which reads:

Re-discover the power of the spoken word.

Mix to end frame. We see the BBC Scotland logo and tuning device which demonstrates where to find the signal.

CAPTION:
UK National Station of the Year.

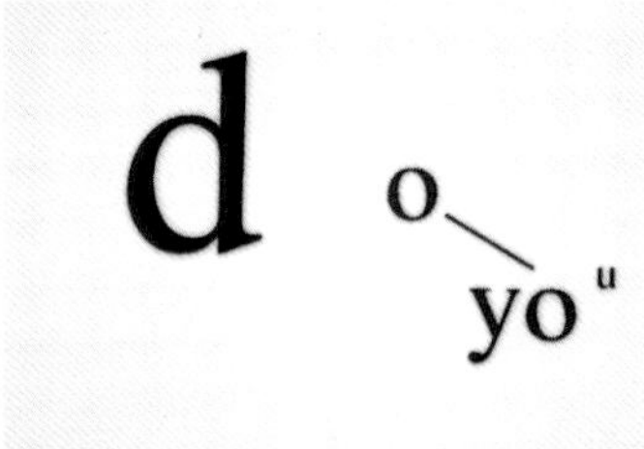

Up to and including 60 seconds

Director
JONATHAN BARNBROOK

Copywriter
ADRIAN JEFFERY

Art Director
LINDSEY REDDING

Creative Directors
SIMON SCOTT
ANDREW LINDSAY

Producer
YVONNE CHALK

Agency Producer
TIM MAGUIRE

Editor
JON HOLLIS

Music Composers/Arrangers
LOGORHYTHM

Production Company
TONY KAYE FILMS

Agency
FAULDS ADVERTISING

Account Group Director
TOM GILL

Head of Presentation
PETER GOURD

Client
BBC RADIO SCOTLAND

Up to and including 60 seconds

Director
JOE PYTKA

Copywriter
BOB MOORE

Art Director
WARREN EAKINS

Creative Directors
BOB MOORE
WARREN EAKINS

Producer
LILLY WEINGARTEN

Agency Producers
DEREK RUDDY
JANE BRIMBLECOMBE

Editor
ROB WATZKE

Production Company
PYTKA

Agency
WIEDEN & KENNEDY, AMSTERDAM

Client
NIKE INTERNATIONAL

THE WALL

Open on a shot of stormy Paris. Thunder crashing in background.

A wall featuring Eric Cantona is seen.

We see a ball flying past the Eiffel Tower.

Close up of the Cantona wall. The ball flies into the picture. He beats an opponent and kicks the ball, destroying a part of the wall with his shoe.

We hear the noise of the ball flying with rocket like speed, the crowd cheering, the noise of the power kick and bricks smashing.

The ball flies past the Brandenberg gate to a wall in Berlin featuring Michael Schulz.

Schulz takes the ball on his chest, dribbles for a couple of steps and passes the ball, destroying part of the wall.

The ball flies to a city in Italy, upsetting some pigeons, where Maldini comes to life on his wall and heads the ball back to London. Bricks fly from the wall.

Ian Wright kicks the ball from his wall, past Tower Bridge, removing some bricks with his kick.

The ball flies across the ocean to Brazil and into Rio de Janeiro where Romario and Bebeto are seen on two side by side walls. Romario heads the ball to Bebeto, who kicks it to Mexico where Campos dives across three buildings to catch it.

Smashing bricks, kicking sound and moving ball noise continue.

Campos dislodges a Nike logo with his arms on the third building. The sign swings loose from one corner.

Sound of broken glass as he hits logo.

Sound of sign swinging.

THE BEAUTIFUL GAME

Outside a stadium in Rio de Janeiro, we hear the sound of a football match and commentary in Portuguese. We see a Madonna swinging next to a football.

A businessman in a car passes the stadium. He is engrossed in the game.

We move to a backyard. A family are watching the game on a portable television. A young boy is holding the aerial trying to get a good picture.

Next we see a young couple kissing and cuddling on a bed in an apartment. The boy seems more interested in the football match, he is peeking at the screen.

Cut to a cafe/bar. It is packed with customers watching the game. The tension rises as the commentary becomes increasingly loud.

We hear a piercing whistle. It's a penalty!

The businessman stops, he's outside a TV shop.

The family are frozen in front of their TV. The boy holding the aerial wobbles nervously.

The customers in the bar are frozen, staring up at the TV in silence.

The boy clutches his girlfriend.

Cut to shots of the deserted town. The penalty is taken. 'Goal'.

We see the different reactions of the various scenarios.

The Umbro logo and super appear on the screen of a television.

'The heart and soul of football'.

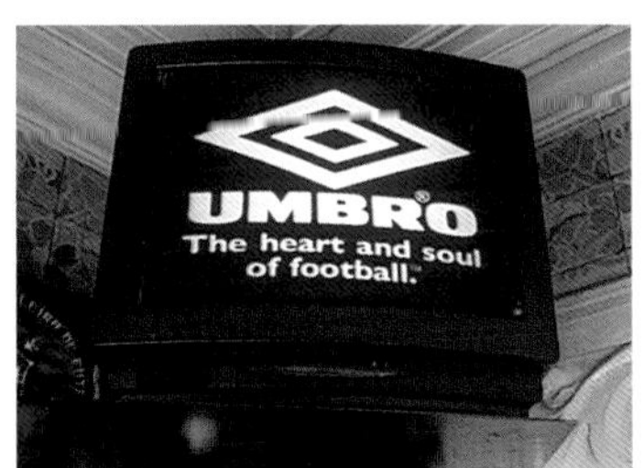

Up to and including 60 seconds

Director
TREVOR MELVIN

Copywriter
HOWARD FLETCHER

Art Director
JEREMY PEMBERTON

Creative Director
JEREMY PEMBERTON

Producer
JAMES STUDHOLME

Agency Producer
EMMA STRACHEN

Editor
RICH LAWLEY

Music Composer/Arranger
STEVE PARSONS

Production Company
BLINK PRODUCTIONS

Agency
DMB&B, LONDON

Marketing Director
PETER DRAPER

Client
UMBRO INTERNATIONAL

Over 60 seconds

Director
MARK COPPOS

Copywriter
JOHN BROCKENBROUGH

Art Director
LEE GARFINKEL

Creative Director
LEE GARFINKEL

Producer
MICHAEL APPEL

Set Designer
JACK WRIGHT

Agency Producer
BOB NELSON

Editor
CRAIG WARNICK

Lighting Cameraman
PETER BROWN

Production Company
COPPOS SATO THOMAS

Agency
LOWE & PARTNERS/SMS

Director of Marketing
MICKEY FOSTER

Client
HANSON INDUSTRIES

GRADUATION PARTY

Open on Ken's graduation party. Two women approach Ken to congratulate him. Man approaches Ken and puts his hand on his shoulder.

MAN 1:
I've got just one word for you. Plastics.

KEN:
Exactly what do you mean, sir?

MAN 1:
Plastics, Ken. Great opportunity. Remember it.

Ken goes back inside where another man approaches him. Mrs Parkinson is on sofa in background looking on.

MAN 2:
One word, Ken – aggregates.

KEN:
Sir?

MAN 2:
Sand, gravel, old as the planet, Ken.

Cut to third man at party offering Ken advice.

MAN 3:
Now remember one thing Ken...bricks. Will you remember that?

KEN:
Yes sir, I will.

Cut to fourth man offering Ken advice.

MAN 4:
One word, asphalt.

Cut to fifth man.

MAN 5:
Do you ever think about lumber, Ken?

Ken leaves party and dashes up steps where sixth man offers him advice.

MAN 6:
One word Ken - coal...it's power, Ken!

Ken runs into room and closes door where he encounters Mrs Parkinson.

MRS P:
One word, Ken. Hanson.

KEN:
Mrs Parkinson, are you trying to seduce me?

MRS P:
I'm trying to teach you about the basics, Ken.

Fade to flashing supers:

Plastics
Aggregates
Bricks
Asphalt
Lumber
Coal

Hanson – Just Your Basic 15 Billion Dollar Company.

ALIEN HATMAN

VIDEO:
Close up of man with alien hat.

MAN:
I first met the aliens when I was on a trip with my family...in a station wagon, right outside of Jacksonville, and he told me how to build this hat...see right then I was talking to them...I'm talking to them again...actually, an alien has met with every President since Washington...8am...time has stopped and an alien will come down and talk to the President, and he'll say, hey, how's it going...

SUPER:
Everybody Knows the Best Nuts Come From California.

Product drops down.

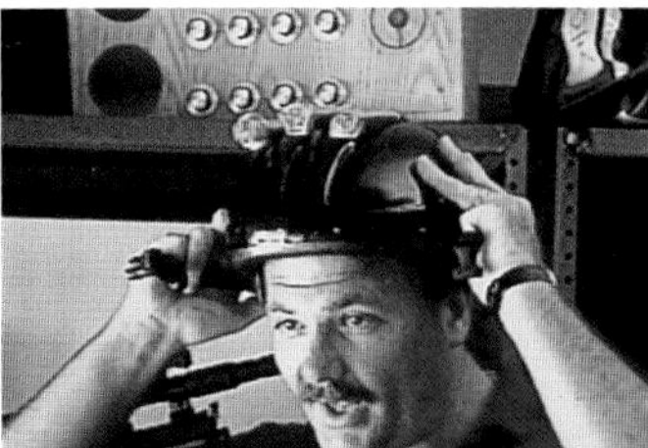

EVERYBODY KNOWS
THE BEST NUTS COME
FROM CALIFORNIA.

Television Campaigns

Director
JEFF GORMAN

Copywriter
JERRY GENTILE

Art Director
STEVE RABOSKY

Production Company
JOHNS & GORMAN FILMS

Agency
CHIAT DAY, INC

Client
SUNKIST/PISTACHIO GROWERS

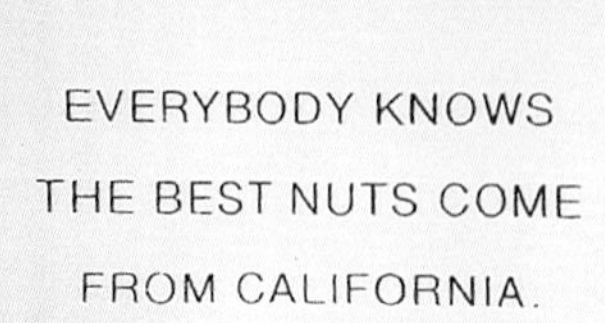

UFO COUPLE

VIDEO:
Couple walking along beach.

WOMAN:
I feel very certain that this is the biggest story of the 20th century...I had an extraterrestrial appear in my apartment...you see them a lot in Malibu...the extraterrestrials are taking a great risk when they manifest in front of us...

MAN:
I mean, she asked them, "Why don't you just land and step out and say hello and they said, "Cause we would be shot at." I mean, you know what it's like around here, some of these pretty rough neighbourhoods...

SUPER:
Everybody Knows the Best Nuts Come From California.

Product drops down.

CYBORG HELMET PEOPLE

VIDEO:
Interior. Couple in garage.

O.C. ANNCR:
What do we have here?

MAN:
Well, this is basically 25th Century technology that we feel is going to be the saviour of the planet in the coming years. What we have right here is an alien anti-abduction rifle that puts out this positive force field that negative entities such as aliens, spirits, etc. cannot stand. It works by sending actual energies from your head...

SUPER:
Everybody Knows the Best Nuts Come From California.

Product drops down.

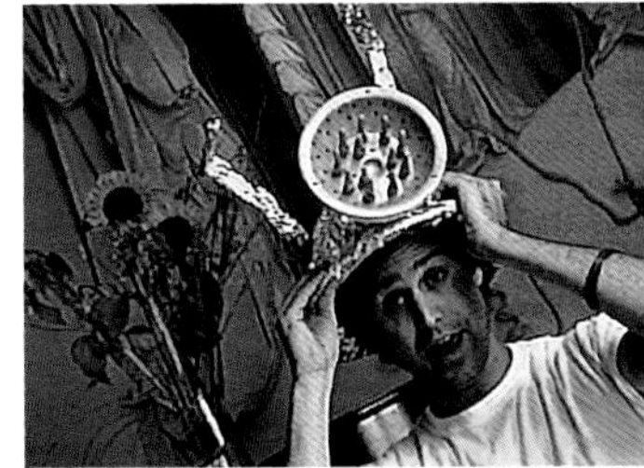

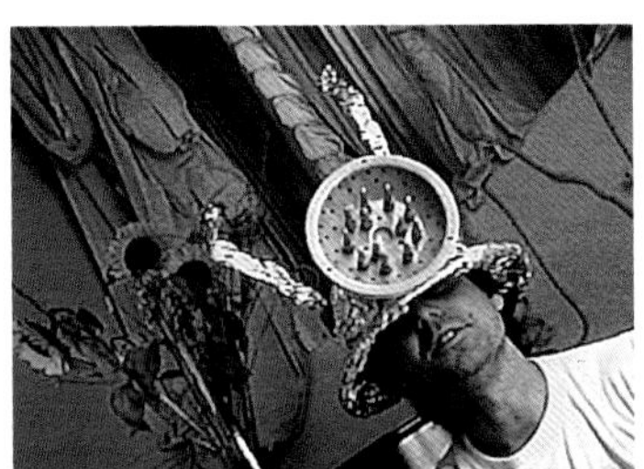

EVERYBODY KNOWS
THE BEST NUTS COME
FROM CALIFORNIA.

Television Campaigns

Director
JAN KOUNEN

Copywriter
WILL FARQUHAR

Art Director
IAN DUCKER

Creative Director
TIM DELANEY

Producer
ROSIE MUCH

Set Designer
KIM BUDDEE

Agency Producer
NICKY GREGOROWSKI

Lighting Cameraman
EDUARDO SERRA

Music Composer/Arranger
PETER LAWLOR

Production Company
HELEN LANGRIDGE ASSOCIATES

Agency
LEAGAS DELANEY

Head of Marketing and Communications
TOM HARRINGTON

Client
ADIDAS AG

BRAZILIAN

Open on a pale skinned young man.

MVO:
How to play soccer like a Brazilian.

Suddenly he is transported to a Brazilian beach and through a series of transformations, changes into a samba dancing, ball juggling Brazilian footballer.

MVO:
Squeeze into a yellow shirt and some sexy blue shorts. Gyrate suggestively. Learn some tricks.

Cut to his feet. A pair of Predator Boots magic on. He is then transported to a stadium where he outplays an entire team of bad guys.

MVO:
Invest in a pair of Predator Boots by Adidas. These revolutionary boots will soon have you making your friends look like complete burros.

SFX:
Eeyore, Eeyore.

MVO:
As well as adding more swerve to your banana shot and just a little more power. Gooaaalll!!

Cut to our hero as he lands from his spectacular volley. As camera tilts up, his hair grows into a terrible Brazilian style hair-do.

MVO:
And don't forget the haircut.

The now fully transformed Brazilian pleads in fluent Portuguese.

BRAZILIAN:
Ei! Posso Ficar so com as chuteiras?

SUBTITLE:
Hey! Can I just take the boots?

Cut to close up of the boot screaming towards camera.

TITLES:
More Swerve. More Power. Adidas. Earn Them.

FIFA

We open on a series of graphic shots, illustrating the fairness and evenness of the game of football.

MVO:
Soccer. A game played on a level pitch between two equal sides of eleven players, each in possession of one left foot and one right.

Each team defends their half. The game is divided into two 45 minute periods, the object to project the ball into your opponent's goal, as many times as you can.

Both teams wear FIFA approved boots, which now include an entirely new boot, the Predator by Adidas.

We see that one team is wearing Predator boots and, as we cut to a series of action shots, we see how this gives them an obvious advantage over their opponents.

TITLES:
More Control.

More Swerve.

More Power.

Cut to a despondent goalkeeper dropping to his knees, then dissolve to a shot of the FIFA headquarters.

MVO:
All complaints should be made to FIFA, PO Box 85, Zurich, Switzerland. Thank you.

Cut to close up of the boot screaming towards camera. It turns and comes to rest.

TITLES:
100% Legal. 0% Fair.

Adidas. Earn Them.

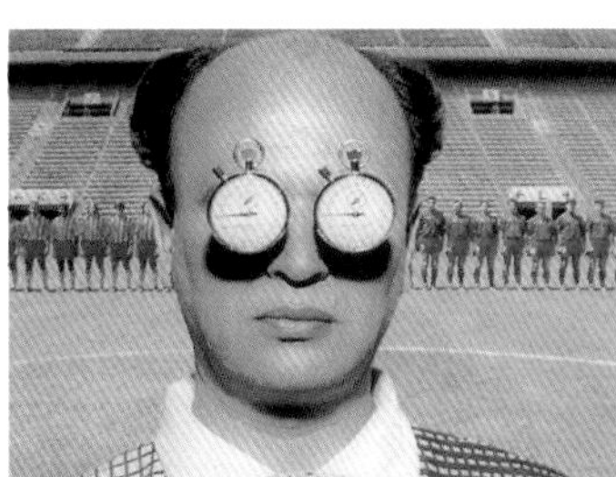

Director
MEHDI NOROWZIAN

Copywriter
WILL FARQUHAR

Art Director
IAN DUCKER

Creative Director
TIM DELANEY

Producer
DESLEY GREGORY

Agency Producer
JANE JOYCE

Lighting Cameraman
EDUARDO SERRA

Sound Design
ROSS GREGORY

Production Company
REDWING FILM COMPANY

Director
GERARD DE THAME

Copywriter
WILL FARQUHAR

Art Director
IAN DUCKER

Creative Director
TIM DELANEY

Producer
FABYAN DAW

Agency Producer
NICKY GREGOROWSKI

Editor
PETER GODDARD

Lighting Cameraman
PASCAL MARTI

Special Effects
THE MILL

Production Company
GERARD DE THAME FILMS

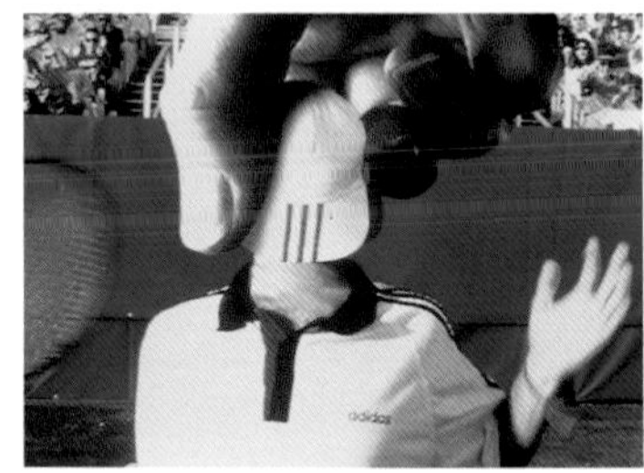

GOELLNER

Open on a tennis match in progress. We recognise one of the players as Marc Kevin Goellner. He is wearing his trademark cap back to front.

We hear the voices of stuffy, elderly officials.

MVO 1:
This Marc Goellner fellow, is he allowed to wear his cap backwards?

MVO 2:
Oh absolutely not.

Suddenly, a big hand drops into shot and straightens his cap, twisting his head around so it now faces backwards.

MVO 1:
That's better.

His head spins back round and he plays a series of winners.

MVO 2:
No, no that was a direct violation of club rules...

MVO 1:
Oh how tiresome.

MVO 2:
Well don't worry. This'll fix him...

The big hand drops in again and twists his head around twice.

MVO 1:
And again please. Thank you.

Goellner's head spins back and he plays a spectacular forehand down the line.

MVO 2:
Oh what a frightful cheek. We shall have to ban him.

MVO 1:
Can't we fine him as well?

MVO 2:
Good idea!

Goellner looks up at the officials, defiantly turning his cap sideways.

TITLES:
Adidas. Earn Them.

SHOE DEAL

MUSIC:
Hip Hop throughout.

Open on a rooftop Streetball game.

Cut to one of the Streetball players standing outside an enormous mansion with his manager.

MANAGER:
23.2 Million Dollars? We'll take it.

PLAYER:
I don't need this.

Cut back to see the Streetball player in action.

MANAGER:
(under)
You can be the man.

Cut to the Streetball player, as a young kid holds up replica doll of him.

KID:
Hey would you sign my doll, please?

PLAYER:
I don't need any of this.

Cut to our player involved in more Streetball action. Cut to player in a TV commercial.

PLAYER:
(over sincerely)
...With a specially reinforced outdoor toe!

I don't need all of this.

Cut back to more Streetball action. Cut to our player about to sign a sponsorship deal.

PLAYER:
And I don't need no shoe deal.

Cut quickly to the Streetball player's POV.

DAD:
What do you mean you don't want no shoe deal?!!!

MUM:
Boy, what is the matter with you?

BROTHER:
You're lonely.

TITLES:
Adidas.

Streetball.

Earn them.

Cut back to the player on the Streetball court having second thoughts.

MAN:
Well, maybe...

SFX:
Cash register.

Directors
VAUGHAN & ANTHEA

Copywriter
ROB BURLEIGH

Art Director
DAVID BEVERLEY

Creative Director
TIM DELANEY

Producer
ADAM SAWARD

Agency Producer
LINDA DOWNS

Lighting Cameraman
JOSEPH YACOE

Music Composers/Arrangers
THE WASCALS

Production Company
LEWIN & WATSON

Directors
ANDREW DOUGLAS
STUART DOUGLAS

Copywriter
TIM DELANEY

Creative Director
TIM DELANEY

Art Director
MARTIN GALTON

Producer
CLARE MITCHELL

Agency Producer
MATTHEW JONES

Editor
TIM THORNTON-ALLEN

Lighting Cameramen
ANDREW DOUGLAS
STUART DOUGLAS

Music Composer/Arranger
KEVIN SARGENT

Production Company
DELANEY & HART

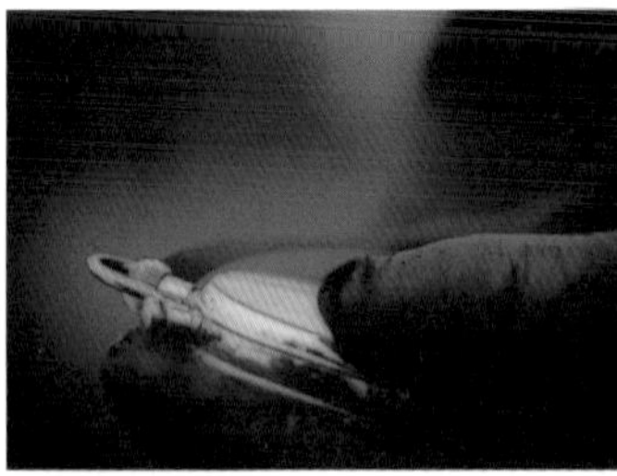

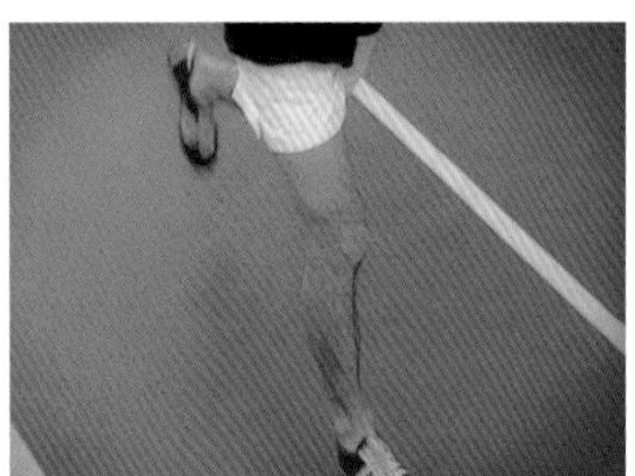

ZATOPEK

SFX:
Music.

A coach waits in an empty stadium with stop watch in hand. He is timing a young man who we see running through woodland in army boots, with a back pack on his back. The young man runs into the stadium exhausted.

MVO:
In the early 1950's, a young Czech army captain developed a training method that would change running forever. Stamina was everything.

Cut to a riot. We see the runner, now in full uniform, has worked his way to the front of a resisting crowd.

MVO:
But he wasn't just a committed athlete. When his country was invaded he made a personal stand.

The runner is recognised by the Tank Commander, who decides not to have him shot.

MVO:
This dedication to ideals and his training methods won him 3 Olympic gold medals in one week. A record which even today remains unbroken.

Dissolve to the empty stadium. The runner wears Adidas shoes and runs through the winning tape.

Dissolve to close up of an old man.

OLD MAN:
My name is Emil Zatopek.

Cut to Emil Zatopek's Training Boot 1950.

TITLE:
Emil Zatopek's Training Shoe 1950.

Dissolve to the new 'cardio-vascular' training shoe.

TITLE:
Adidas Training Shoe 1995.

LITTLE GIRL

Open on a precocious child.

She begins to dance and launches into an atrocious rendition of 'Daddy wouldn't buy me a bow wow.'

Suddenly a giant foot wearing a British Knights shoe appears from off screen and crushes her.

SFX:
Splat!

MUSIC:
That's what you gotta do, you gotta keep on steppin' on.

*A super and end device appears:
British Knights.
The B-K's.*

MATCHSTICK MAN

Open on an elderly man standing in a potting shed. Next to him there is a model replica of the Empire State Building made entirely of matches.

MAN:
(In a tedious, dull delivery) Five years, six days in the making, seventy six thousand, four hundred and seventy eight matches, each individually stained. Just common or garden matches... If I may demonstrate...

Whilst his back is turned, a giant foot wearing a British Knights shoe appears from off screen and crushes his beloved tower.

SFX:
Scrunch!

MUSIC:
That's what you gotta do, you gotta keep on steppin' on.

*A super and end device appears:
British Knights.
The B-K's.*

Television Campaigns

Director
JOE PUBLIC

Copywriter
GILES HARGREAVES

Art Director
MATT MURRAY

Creative Director
STEVE GRIME

Producer
ROBERT BRAY

Agency Producer
HELEN WHITELEY

Editor
CYRIL METZGER

Lighting Cameraman
GEOFF BOYLE

Production Company
STARK FILMS

Agency
LEAGAS SHAFRON DAVIS AYER

Marketing Executive
MALCOLM NATHAN

Client
BRITISH KNIGHTS

AMERICAN TOURISTS

Open on two fat American tourists. He is holding a video camera and his wife poses.

WOMAN:
No, don't...

The man films up and down her body, while she squeals and giggles for the camera.

MAN:
Ohhh that's good Edith... This one's for Jessie and Ellie back home, darlin...

He looks to the sky and screams in horror. A giant foot wearing a British Knights shoe appears from above and crushes them both.

SFX:
Splat!

MUSIC:
That's what you gotta do, you gotta keep on steppin' on.

A super and end device appears:
British Knights.
The B-K's.

FOLKIES

Open on a 60's folk group.

They launch into an awful rendition of 'All around my hat.'

GROUP:
All around my hat, I will wear a green willow. All around my ha...

Suddenly a giant foot wearing a British Knights shoe appears off screen and crushes them.

SFX:
Spat!

MUSIC:
That's what you gotta do, you gotta keep on steppin' on.

A super and end device appears:
British Knights.
The B-K's.

INTRO

We see a man asleep in front of TV with 'You are watching' projected above in reverse as if coming from the TV.

VO:
You are watching the Coors Light Channel... (Hero shot of Coors Light can.) ...where there is always something going on.

Up next, its The Sideways Show. Man walks on camera, camera turns sideways, man pours beer, beer flows sideways.

VO:
Then join Dave and Chris in Coors Light. Camera. Action.

CHRIS:
The acting is there, the cinematography is there, everything's beautiful. The Coors Light can makes the film.

VO:
We'll be back after these messages, so don't move.

We see mannequins on a beach. Volleyball on sand next to coffee cup. Cup is replaced with Coors Light can.

SUPER AND VO:
Coors Light. Cause coffee's nasty after volleyball.

Picture of cow eyeing Coors Light can.

SUPER:
What Cows Would Rather Give.

Chalkboard with scribblings and message 'You + Coors Light = 21'.

VO:
It's simple, you plus Coors Light must equal 21. Got a problem with that?

Woman in front of wall with a picture on either side.

TITLE CARD:
Coors Light party tip number 34.

WOMAN:
A warm beer is an angry beer. A cold beer is...

VO:
Say 'good'.

Camera pans across guests on talk show set. Stops on host.

FRED:
Men who drink Coors Light. And, the women who love them. Today, on Fred.

VO:
Coors Light Channel. Always on.

Channel Logo.

SUPER:
Always On.

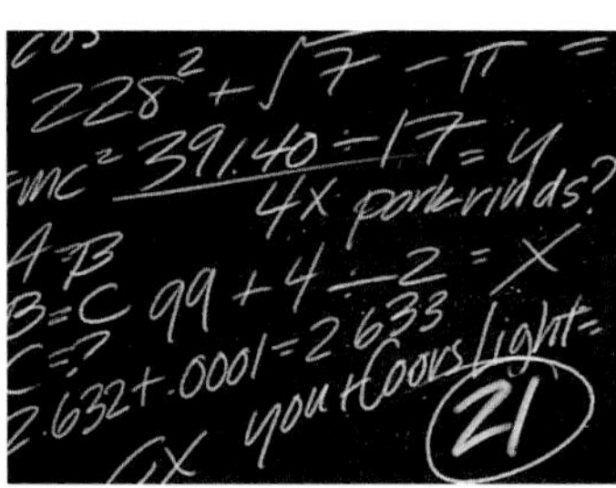

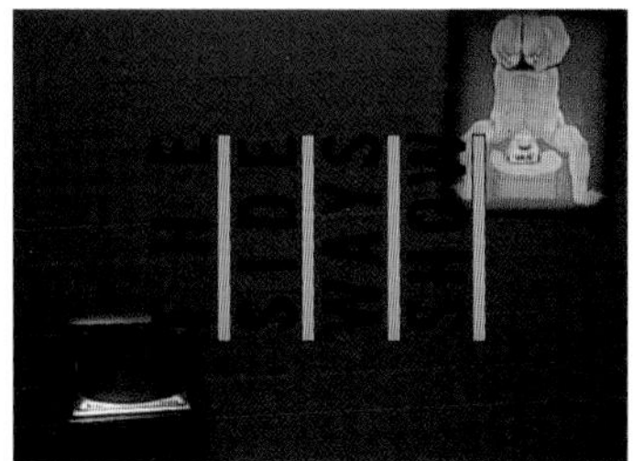

Television Campaigns

Director
MARK FENSKE

Copywriter
AMY KROUSE-ROSENTHAL

Art Director
DAVID T. JONES

Creative Director
GEOFF THOMPSON

Agency Producer
CHRIS BING

Agency
FCB, CHICAGO

Client
COORS BREWING COMPANY

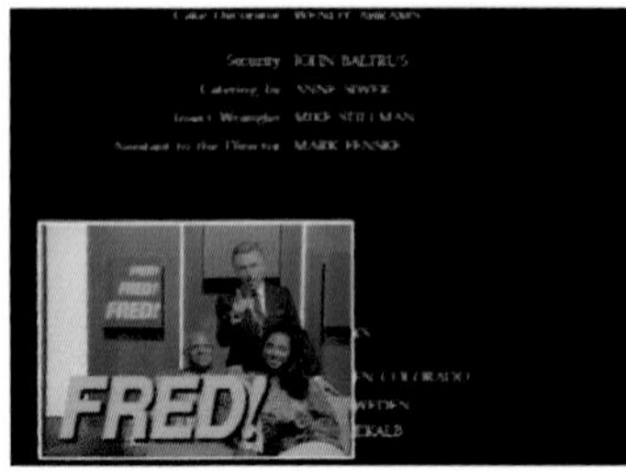

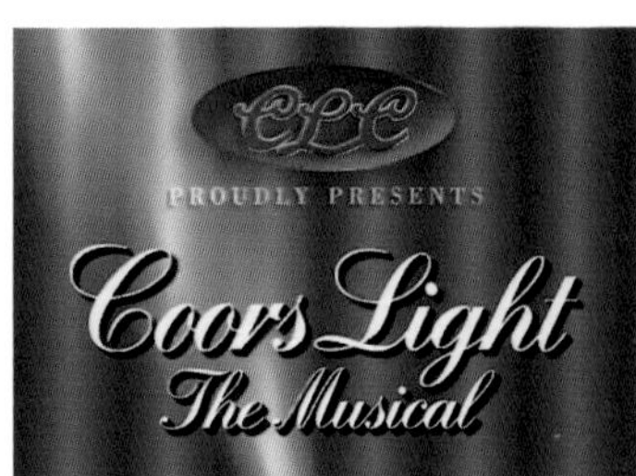

MUSICAL

We see a man in front of TV. TV projects image of name tag.

TITLE:
Hello My Name is CLC – The Coors Light Channel.

VO:
You're watching the Coors Light Channel where there's always something...

TITLE:
CLC Update.

ANNCR:
This just in...
(Thumb wipes frost off beer glass. Reveals Coors Light name)
Coors Light. It's good cold.
We now return to our programme already in progress.

TITLE:
CLC proudly presents Coors Light The Musical.
(Man and woman on fake mountain set)

LADY:
I can't breathe cause my dress is too tight. I'd rather leave here and go have a Coors Light.
(Movie credits roll.)

ANNCR:
Up next on CLC, it's Beerweek with Jordana Capra.

CAPRA:
Tonight's topic: Pretzels versus peanuts.

ANNCR:
Then, couples who met while touring the Coors Light Brewery.

VISUAL:
Fred Programme.

TITLE:
A Coors Light Production.

FRED:
Today, on Fred.

VO:
There's more after these messages.
(We see a man on street being interviewed.)

ANNCR:
What do you think of Coors Light?

MAN:
Should I say something nice?

TITLE:
Drink In Moderation.

Woman speaking into phone.

TITLE:
The Coors Light Fantasy Line.

LADY:
Everyone has a fantasy. Maybe you want to talk about the fermentation process. Call me.

TITLE:
Peace. Love. Beer.
CLC Always On.

VO:
The Coors Light Channel. Always on.

MANOR

Coors Light Channel logo treatment.

VO:
You're watching the Coors Light Channel.

ANNCR:
Previously on Coors Light Manor.

Man enters parlor and speaks to the woman.

MAN:
I'm leaving.

WOMAN:
Is it because of Tom?

MAN:
No, I didn't know about that...I'm just going to get some more Coors Light.

Coors Light can sweeps across the screen followed by Coors Light Manor title card, followed by can sweep.

ANNCR:
Stay tuned for Coors Light Manor.

But first, these messages.

(TV flashing on empty chair)

SUPER:
Paid Advertisement.

We see Coors Light in an elevator.

SUPER:
Smooth Going Down.

VO:
Coors Light. Smooth going down.

ANNCR:
Remember, to drink Coors Light you must be 21.

(Illustration of hand holding can tranforms into number '21')

Channel logo treatment.

VO:
The Coors Light Channel. Always on.

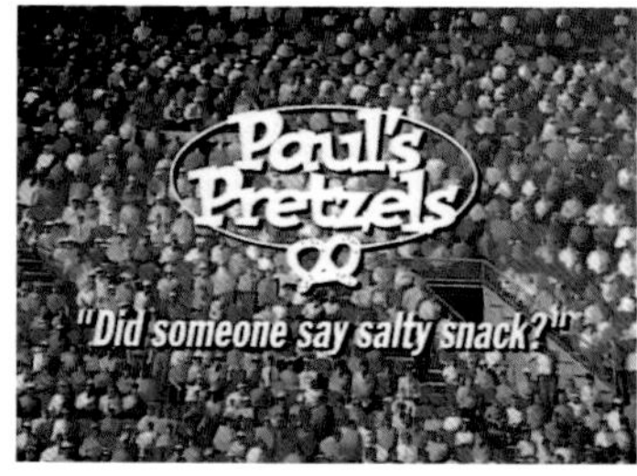

BOWL

We see Coors Light channel logo on psychedelic 60's-style background.

VO:
You're watching The Coors Light Channel.

ANNCR:
Welcome to the 39th Annual Coors Light Bowl.

Open on shot of cardboard Coors Light blimp.

TITLE:
Coors Light Bowl XX1V

We see Coors Light cans versus toy electric football players on electric football field.

Fictitious company, Paul's Pretzels is supered over a fake football crowd followed by super for Coors Light, "So Good It's scary."

ANNCR:
The Coors Light Bowl has been brought to you by Paul's Pretzels and by Coors Light, the beer that's so good it's scary.

We see a dog sniffing around in the grass. Coors Light logo appears on screen and the dog is scared away.

ANNCR:
Stay tuned for the Coors Light Bowl post-game wrap-up.

Coors Light Bowl graphics appear on screen with face of Johnny Seven.

Coors Light Channel logo.

VO:
The Coors Light Channel.

Always on.

GAME SHOW

VO:
You're watching The English Channel...
(Stock Footage of English Channel.)

Cut to CLC-Coors Light Channel logo.

TITLE:
The Beer Is Light.
(next to Coors Light can)

VO:
The Coors Light Channel.
And now back to Jay Dandy on the Beer Is Light.

JACK:
OK, Doris. You've won the million dollars. Now let's see what you would have won had you chosen door number two.

DORIS:
Coors Light! I don't believe it.

TITLE & VO:
And Now These Messages.

Note pad with messages:
'David - call Amy.'
'Chris - pick up a 6-pack of Coors Light - KT.'

We see bottom of Coors Light can with superimposed message:
'If you can read this, thank a teacher.'

Cut to Victor Jory sitting in a lounge chair with a Coors beer on the coffee table.

JORY:
Hello, we're about to bring you another story of Canhunt.

TITLE:
Canhunt.

SFX:
Music.

Cut to Coors Light can on target eluding arrows shot at the target.

JORY:
Hope you enjoyed tonight's Canhunt presented by Coors Light beer.

TV smashes on road.

SFX:
Laughter.

Girl jogging trips on sandy beach.

VO:
Oops. Watch out.

Party tip woman realizes she has forgotten to put her glasses on.

VO:
Uh, oh. Try again.
And now when you tune into the Coors Light Channel, you'll get CLC Bloopers absolutely free.
The Coors Light Channel.
Always on.

Coors Light Channel logo.

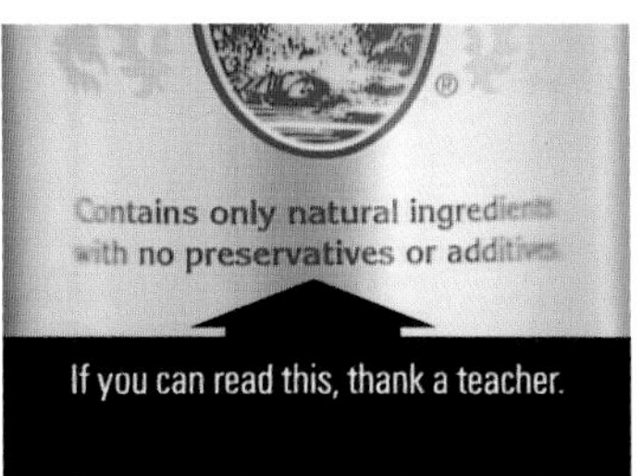

Television Campaigns

Director
TONY KAYE

Copywriter
JONATHAN KNEEBONE

Art Director
DAVE JOHNSON

Creative Director
STEVE HENRY

Typographer
JONATHAN BARNBROOK

Producer
MIRANDA DAVIS

Set Designer
JENNY SELDON

Sculptor
TOM DIXON

Agency Producer
JENNY SELBY

Editor
PETER GODDARD

Lighting Cameraman
TONY KAYE

Music Composers/Arrangers
ROD SYERS
EVELYN GLENNIE

Production Company
TONY KAYE FILMS

Agency
HOWELL HENRY CHALDECOTT LURY & PARTNERS

Marketing Director
JAN SMITH

Client
MAZDA CARS UK LIMITED

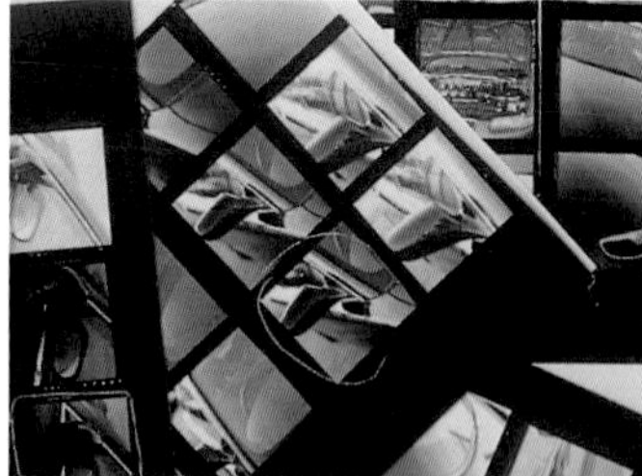

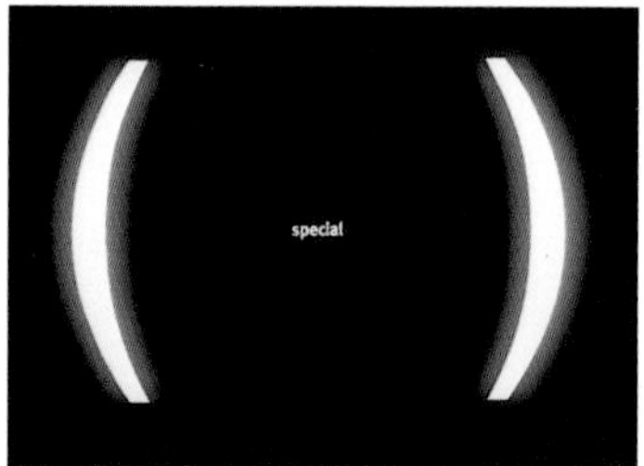

SOUND DOWN

We open on a Mazda Xedos 6, shot in a studio - overall the look is very minimal, but beautiful, and the feel seductive.

V/O:
With a car this special we don't need to shout. If you'd like to know more, please turn up your volume now.

There follows a sequence of about 35 simple and evocative close-up images of detail after detail of the Xedos 6.

The sound level for this section is made incredibly low - so people can choose to turn the volume up if they wish to hear the sound more clearly. If they do turn the sound up, they can listen to information about the effort or thought that has gone into the design of each particular detail that is shown.

The montage of sound is summarised at the end with a voice which says:

'The Mazda Xedos 6. Every detail matters.'

We end on the Mazda logo and the telephone number 0345 48 48 48 then a final super, reading '(special)'.

Finally, if you have the volume up you hear the voice-over say:

'Please return your volume to its normal level.'

WHITE

We open on a stationary white Mazda 323 shot against a white metal backdrop in a studio. The 323 is shot from fresh and seductive angles.

V/O & TITLE:
With a car as special as the new Mazda 323, we don't need to shout. If you'd like to know more, please video this commercial.

Halfway through the commercial, the car cuts out of frame and is replaced with three information panels. When seen at normal speed, this is easily noticeable to the eye but not readable. However, when viewed on video, the viewer can freeze the frame and read the information clearly.

After about eighteen frames, the panel is removed and the car returns to the precise position as before in frame.

Finally, the commercial ends with the Mazda logo, the telephone number 0345 48 48 48 and an endline reading: '(special)'.

An additional super now appears reading:

To win a car this special press rewind and search. This allows the viewer to access a message instructing them to search for the hidden Japanese password, Kansei.

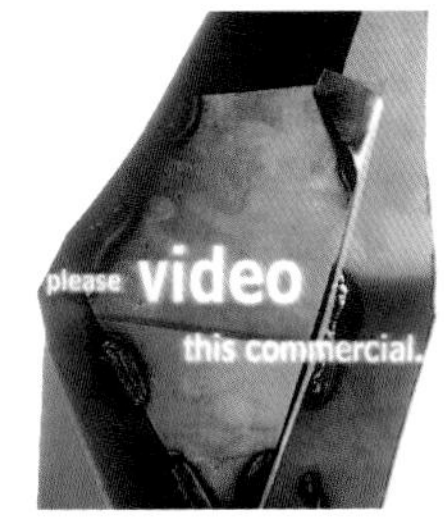

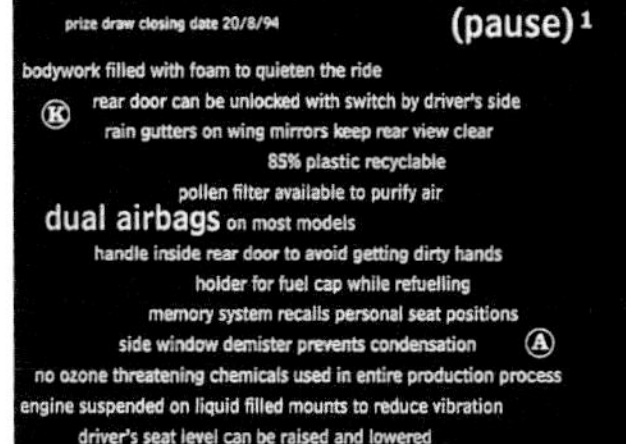

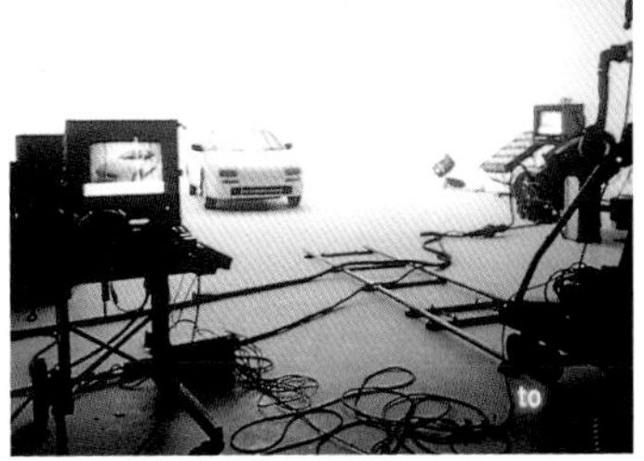

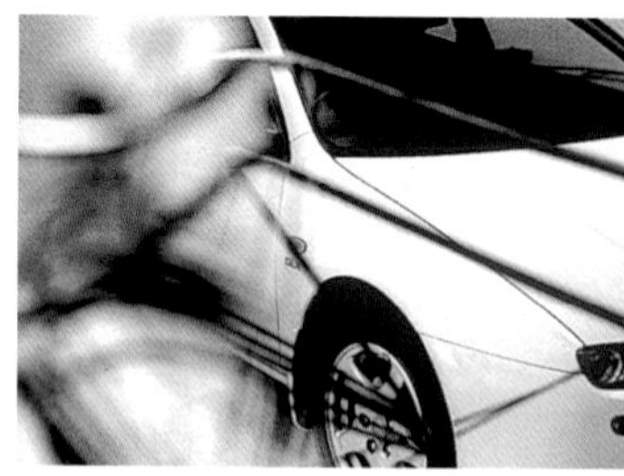

WHITE CHRISTMAS

We see a succession of black and white images of the Mazda 323.

V/O:
If you'd like to know what makes the Mazda 323 special, page teletext 888 during this commercial.

SUPER:
Page teletext 888 during this commercial.

If the viewer pages 888 they will see selected details of the car during the commercial.

These details concentrate on certain aspects of the car that make it special.

A title appears for all to see.

TITLE:
For further details, page 559 (C4) at any time.

V/O:
Mazda. Special.

1345 48 48 48

The commercial ends with the Mazda logo and the word "(special)".

Television Campaigns

Directors
JOHAN KRAMER
ERIK KESSELS

Copywriter
JOHAN KRAMER

Art Director
ERIK KESSELS

Producer
ROBERT CAMPBELL

Agency Producer
BART OVERES

Editor
STRUAN CLAY

Lighting Cameraman
PETER DE BONT

Music Composer/Arranger
MARCEL WALVISCH

Production Company
SPOTS FILM SERVICES

Agency
KRAMER/KESSELS

Client
HANS BRINKLER BUDGET HOTELS

WAKE-UP CALL

A drunk guest of this budget hotel returns after a late night out and, on his way back to his room, he hits almost every door with his head.

SUPER:
Our wake-up call.

BRIDAL SUITE

A just-married couple hurry to their room in this budget hotel. When they enter, there's only a bunkbed.

SUPER:
Our bridal suite.

NIGHT PORTER

It's evening.

A homeless person sits down on the pavement next to the entrance of this budget hotel and starts sleeping.

SUPER:
Our night porter.

VISITORS BOOK

We are in the public toilet of this budget hotel.

Lots of guests come in and write their names on the walls.

SUPER:
Our visitors book.

PRIVATE PARKING

We see three bicycles being parked in front of the hotel.

SUPER:
Our private parking.

Suddenly, the bikes are gone.

SUPER:
Our security system.

Television Campaigns

Directors
DAVID GARFATH
TARSEM

Copywriters
PHIL COCKRELL
PHIL DEARMAN

Art Directors
GRAHAM STOREY
CHARLES INGE

Creative Director
PAUL WEINBERGER

Producers
MARY FRANCIS
SIMON TURTLE
PHIL CONTOMICHALOS

Set Designers
TONY NOBLE
FATIMA ANDRADE

Agency Producer
SARAH HORRY

Editors
GREG WILLCOX
ROBERT DUFFY

Lighting Cameramen
MIKE GARFATH
PAUL LAUFER

Music Composers/Arrangers
JOE & CO

Production Companies
PAUL WEILAND FILM COMPANY
SPOTS FILM SERVICES
AFRICAN SKY PRODUCTION SERVICES

Agency
LOWE HOWARD-SPINK

Marketing Executive
MARTIN BROWN

Client
VAUXHALL MOTOR COMPANY

ONE OF THOSE DAYS

We see a Cavalier driver taking the same uneventful route to work, day after day after day. Suddenly the unpredictable happens, making him thankful that his car now has ABS as standard.

SILENT RUNNING

An Aborigine stands in the outback.

His heightened awareness of the natural world allows him to hear the smallest sounds.

His hearing is so good that he reacts to a gecko licking its eye, a snake moving across the sand and a bird taking flight.

He sees movement on the horizon, but he is confused because he can't hear what it is. The dot reveals itself to be a car travelling at speed across the desert floor.

Still he can't hear. He puts his ear to the ground.

The silent car passes him. He turns to watch it go and a pebble is thrown up by the wheel. This bounces noisily to his feet.

Confused by the silence of the car, the Aborigine gazes after the fast disappearing Calibra.

MVO:
The Calibra from Vauxhall. The most aerodynamic production coupe on earth.

SUPER:
The Calibra from Vauxhall

TIGRA

MUSIC:
The Pogues 'Fiesta'.

Man ironing jeans.

MVO:
People who iron creases in their jeans.
(Couple in restaurant.)
People who always work out their exact share of the bill.
(Man folding pyjamas.)
People who always fold their jim-jams.

(Iris reveal of tunnel.)
They're not going to like this at all.

Car driving down row of balls.
(music speeds up)
Car collides with pyramid of balls.

SFX:
Needle skidding off record.

End frame with title.

MVO:
The Tigra from Vauxhall.
Fun...if you like that sort of thing.

THE WORLD ACCORDING TO FRONTERA

Two African women are walking at what is apparently an impossible 45 degree angle. A Frontera drives past them, seemingly on the level.

Cut to a Frontera travelling through water which is at an odd 45 degree angle. The car passes Filipino fishermen on poles in the water.

Cut to the car in front of a waterfall. However, the water is running at a 45 degree angle.

Cut to Mongolian horsemen leading their horses past a Frontera apparently on the level. The horses are walking in a strange manner. The camera then reveals that they are not on the level but descending a steep slope.

Cut to a Frontera on a 45 degree icy slope. A sleigh full of Eskimo children slides past the car. Oddly, however, the sleigh is going uphill.

SUPER:
See a different world.

Cut to a rock climber abseiling across screen. He passes a Frontera parked on the level. In reality, though, the car is hanging on a cliff-face and he is dropping down vertically.

SUPER:
The Frontera 4x4 and Vauxhall logo.

Directors
MEHDI NOROWZIAN
FRANK BUDGEN

Copywriters
JOHN SILVER
PHIL DEARMAN

Art Directors
KEVIN THOMAS
CHARLES INGE

Creative Director
PAUL WEINBERGER

Producers
JOANNE HOLLAND
PAUL ROTHWELL

Set Designers
STEVEN SMITHWICK
TONY NOBLE

Agency Producers
ANDY McLEAN
CHARLES CRISP

Editors
MARK LANGLEY
SAM SNEADE

Lighting Cameramen
KEITH GODDARD
HENRY BRAHAM

Music Composers/Arrangers
CHRIS BLACKWELL
THE POGUES
DAVID MOTION

Production Company
PAUL WEILAND FILM COMPANY

Television Campaigns

Director
GRAHAM ROSE

Copywriter
MARTIN LORAINE

Art Director
STEVE JONES

Creative Directors
SLIM FOSTER
MIKE ELLIOTT

Producer
RON HOLBROOK

Set Designer
JIM CLAY

Agency Producer
AMANDA LOWIT

Editor
IAN WEIL

Lighting Cameraman
TONY PIERCE-ROBERTS

Music Composer
IRVING BERLIN

Arranged By
SIMON FRAGLIN

Production Company
ROSE HACKNEY BARBER PRODUCTIONS

Agency
GREY

Marketing Communications Manager
DAVID SIMS

Client
ALLIED DUNBAR

CUBICLE

This commercial takes place in a company toilet. With relish, two businessmen discuss the 'retirement' of Morrison, a colleague.

MAN 1:
I never thought he'd retire.

The other man smiles maliciously.

MAN 2:
Neither did he.

We then look inside to see the ashen face of Morrison. He's hearing the news for the first time.

To the embarrassment of the two men, Morrison leaves the cubicle. Then, in a style reminiscent of Dennis Potter, Morrison lip-syncs to a Nat King Cole soundtrack.

MORRISON:
There may be trouble ahead...

The men appear to find nothing unusual in Morrison's behaviour. They carry on as normal, drying hands and straightening ties. Their movements however, become synchronised to the beat. Hands are shaken to a brass rhythm, ties adjusted to a trumpet blast.

MORRISON:
...but while there's moonlight and music and love and romance...

Morrison confidently finishes the song.

MORRISON:
Let's face the music and dance.

MVO:
You needn't worry if your life changes. Allied Dunbar financial plans adapt, to help you cope with the unexpected.

As the music fades everything returns to normal.

We see the logo and endline.

MVO:
Allied Dunbar. For the life you don't yet know.

THEATRE

During a routine operation, surgeons discover that their patient's illness is more serious than they thought.

SURGEON 1:
I think we're going to be seeing rather a lot of this chap.

SURGEON 2:
Mmm. Hope he's got an understanding boss.

As the surgeons work away at an incision in the patient's abdomen, the patient looks to camera, appalled at the news. He pulls off his oxygen mask and in a style reminiscent of Dennis Potter, lip-syncs to a Nat King Cole soundtrack.

PATIENT:
There may be trouble ahead...

No one in the theatre reacts with any surprise to the patient's behaviour. The surgeons and nurses work on, but gradually their movements become synchronised to the beat. Forceps whirl to the rhythm, the anaesthetist moves in pirouettes.

PATIENT:
but while there's moonlight and music and love and romance...

The patient, now completely reassured, enjoys a lungful of gas.

PATIENT:
Let's face the music and dance.

MVO:
You needn't worry if your life changes. Allied Dunbar financial plans adapt, to help you cope with the unexpected.

As the music fades everything returns to normal.

We see the logo and endline.

MVO:
Allied Dunbar. For the life you don't yet know.

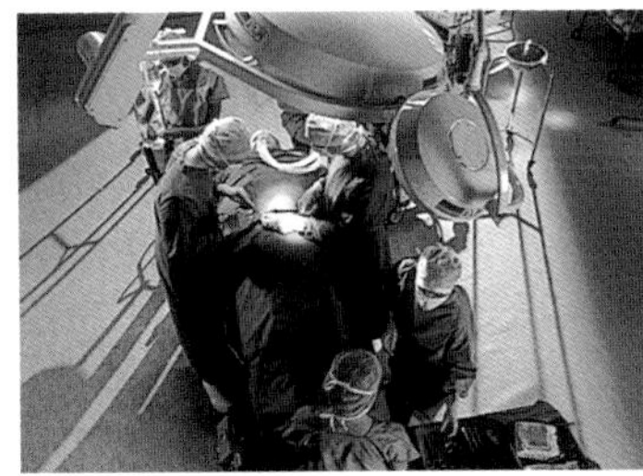

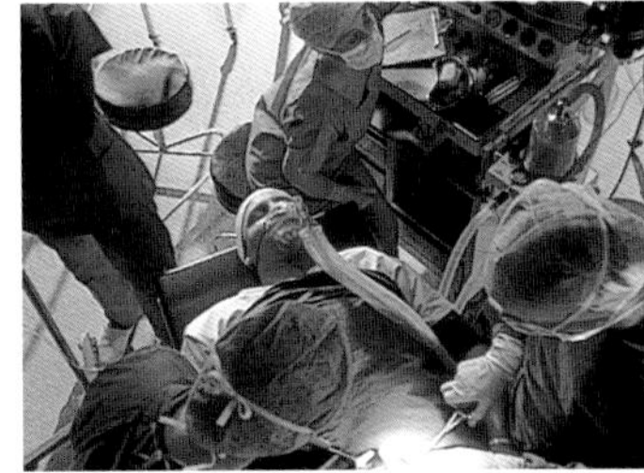

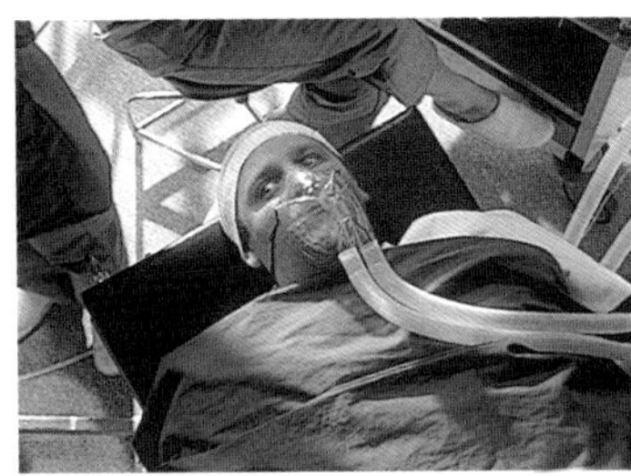

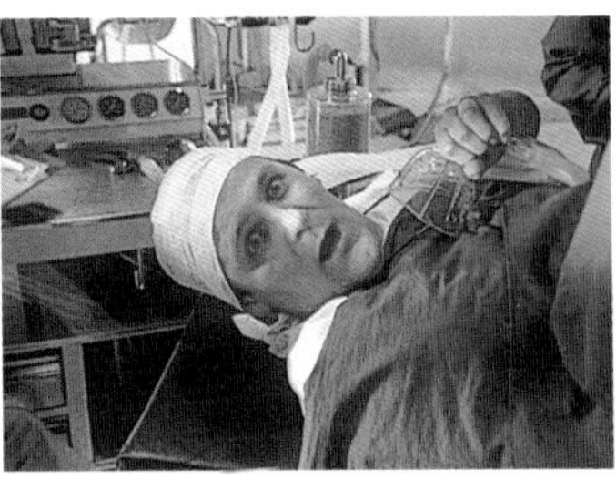

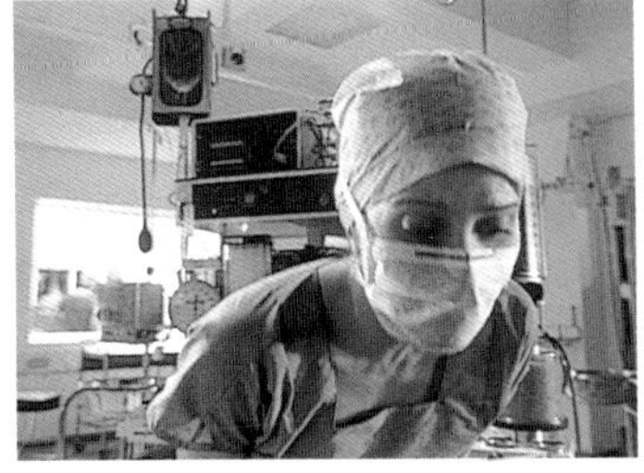

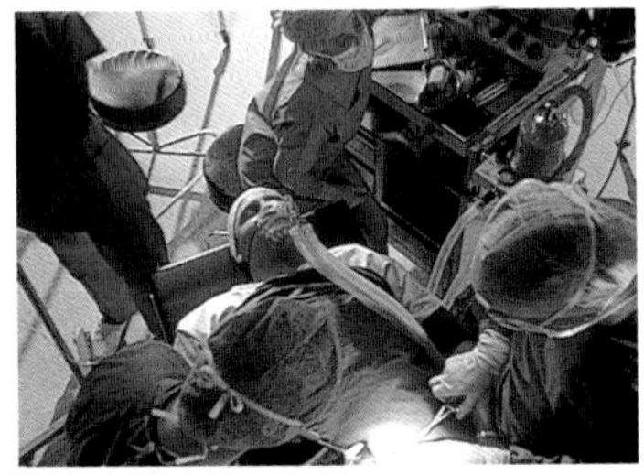

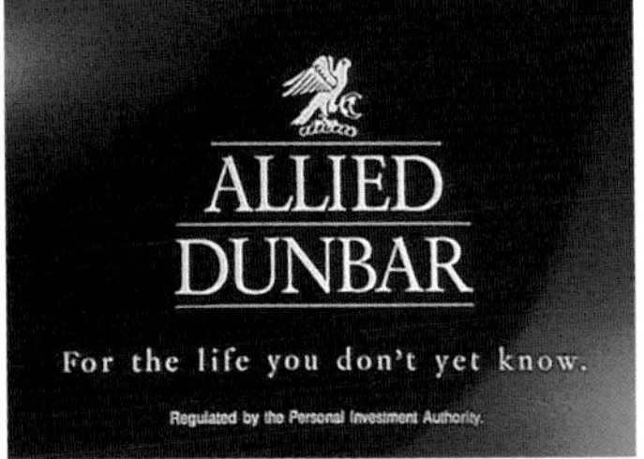

Director
FRANK BUDGEN

Copywriter
MARTIN LORAINE

Art Director
STEVE JONES

Creative Directors
MIKE EVERETT
PAUL SMITH

Producer
MARY FRANCIS

Set Designer
ROD McLEAN

Editor
SIMON WILCOX

Lighting Cameraman
PETER HANNAN

Production Company
PAUL WEILAND FILM COMPANY

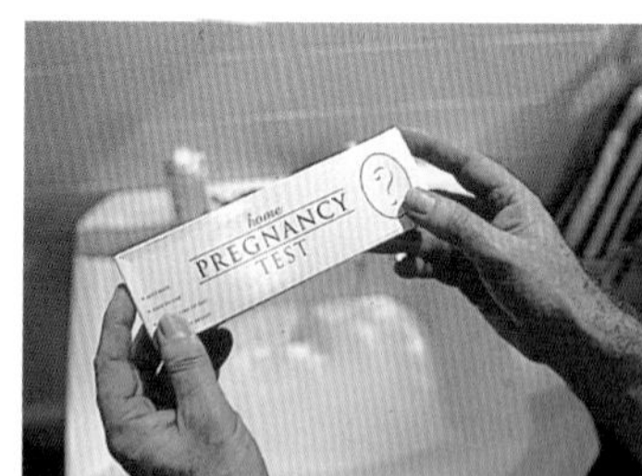

TEST

Whilst looking for his razor, a middle-aged man finds a pregnancy test. Brimming with righteous indignation, he storms into the kitchen to confront his teenage daughters.

When both girls deny knowledge of the test, his frustration grows.

DAD:
I thought we told you to be careful.

His wife interrupts.

MUM:
John. We're the ones who should have been careful.

Finally, realising that the pregnancy test belongs to his wife, the man is flabbergasted. Then in a style reminiscent of Dennis Potter, he lip-syncs to a Nat King Cole sound track.

DAD:
There may be trouble ahead...

His family don't seem to find his behaviour unusual. They continue to slice and butter toast absently. However, every move becomes synchronised to the song's rhythm.

DAD:
but while there's moonlight and music and love and romance...

As he mimes, he grows in confidence.

DAD:
Let's face the music and dance.

MVO:
If your family suddenly grows, so too will your responsibilities. That's why Allied Dunbar financial plans adapt, so you can face the unexpected.

As the music fades everything returns to normal. We see the logo and endline.

MVO:
Allied Dunbar. For the life you don't yet know.

WHITEHALL

LATHAM:
...So there is no better way of serving your Queen and country...than to choose a career in MI7. Are there any questions?

CANDIDATE 1:
What's the financial package?

LATHAM:
Financial package??

BOUGH:
You do get issued with a Barclaycard, Sir.

LATHAM:
Bough...

CANDIDATE 2:
Oh yeah, with Barclaycard can't you get medical help abroad?

CANDIDATE 3:
...and legal advice?

CANDIDATE 4:
...and some sort of purchase insurance?

BOUGH:
Ah yes, both at home and abroad.

LATHAM:
Bough!! These people will have to survive in locations rather more dangerous than a record shop.

CANDIDATE 5:
Ah, can I ask about Eastern Europe?

LATHAM:
Ah, yes...

CANDIDATE 5:
Do they take Barclaycard?

BOUGH:
Ah, well most countries actually take...

LATHAM:
I remember when all an agent had was his charm, his cunning, and if he was lucky...

CANDIDATE 6:
A biro?

LATHAM:
No ordinary biro...two clicks of the cap will render any assailant immobile...very dangerous in the wrong hands. Take over for a Bough, would you moment?

BOUGH:
Well, Barclaycard is widely accepted, in fact you can use it in over 200 countries around the world...

(fade out)

Television Campaigns

Director
MARK CHAPMAN

Copywriter
PAUL BURKE

Art Director
PETER GATLEY

Creative Director
TONY COX

Producer
GLYNIS SANDERS

Set Designer
TONY NOBLE

Agency Producer
MICHAEL PARKER

Editor
IAN WEIL

Lighting Cameraman
JOHN IGNATIUS

Rostrum Cameraman
MARTIN KENZIE

Music Composer/Arranger
HOWARD GOODALL

Production Company
TIGER ASPECT PRODUCTIONS

Agency
BMP DDB NEEDHAM

Manager of Marketing and Advertising
JOHN LAIDLOW

Client
BARCLAYCARD

MOVING

LATHAM:
Come on.

BOUGH:
Wow, who say's crime doesn't pay?

LATHAM:
The bigger they are the harder they fall.

BOUGH:
I'm thinking of buying a house Sir.

LATHAM:
On your salary Bough...and how do you intend to pay for it...with your Barclaycard?

BOUGH:
Well funnily enough Sir, you can get up to £15,000 back from [illegible] with a new Barclays mortgage

LATHAM:
£15,000 Eh? Well, Belgravia beckons, Bough.

BOUGH:
I think it's a good offer Sir.

LATHAM:
Just leave the thinking to me...Ah ha, well Bough I think we can safely say this place will be on the market soon.

BOUGH:
I wouldn't move if I were you Sir.

LATHAM:
I have no intention of moving Bough, you're the one who's been wittering on about mortgages. Right let's get out of here.

BOUGH:
Don't worry Sir, I've got the evidence I'd better get...(fade out).

KNEES

TITLE:
An Easy To Follow Advertisement For Your Easy To Use Delta Card.

V/O:
Some people are confused

(man looking confused)

about the difference between a cheque (a cheque)

and a Delta card (Delta card).

No need!

(man with his knees missing)

Like a cheque (check material),

Delta comes out

(flamboyant man leaps out of closet)

of your current (a current)

account (Count Dracula),

and you get a receipt (a receipt)

for your records (old 78 playing).

It's just far, (sign to Mongolia) far, (sign to Venezuela)

faster (sign to Sydney followed by cuppa being stirred)

to use (two ewes).

So (sewing)

Delta (Delta logo)

has all of the good bits (nice shiny drill bits)

of a cheque (checks)

but (a bottom)

none (a nun)

of the bad bits (nasty, grotty old drill bits).

Visa's (Visa logo) Delta (Delta logo)

Blow (hammer hits toe)

To cheques.

(two Czechoslovakian gentlemen).

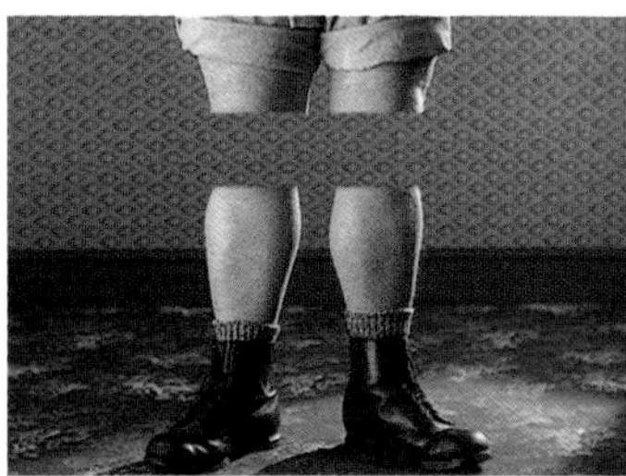

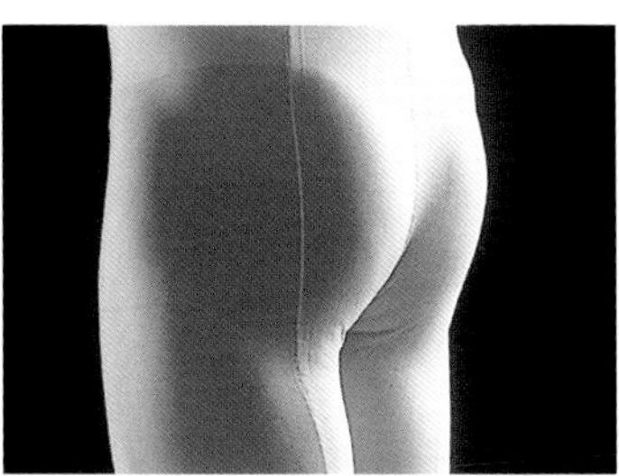

Television Campaigns

Director
MALCOLM VENVILLE

Copywriter
MARY WEAR

Art Director
DAMON COLLINS

Creative Directors
JAMES LOWTHER
SIMON DICKETTS

Producer
BASH ROBERTSON

Set Designer
MARC HOLMES

Agency Producer
EMMA SCOTT

Editor
ANNETTE WILLIAMS

Lighting Cameraman
MALCOLM VENVILLE

Production Company
THE REDWING FILM COMPANY

Agency
SAATCHI & SAATCHI

Marketing Executive
MARK GIFFIN

Client
VISA DELTA

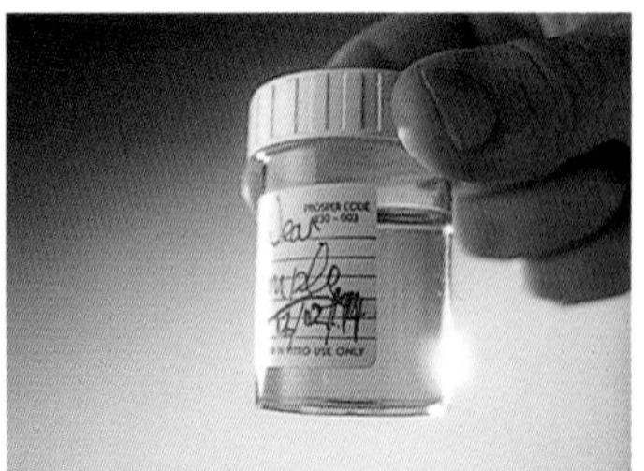

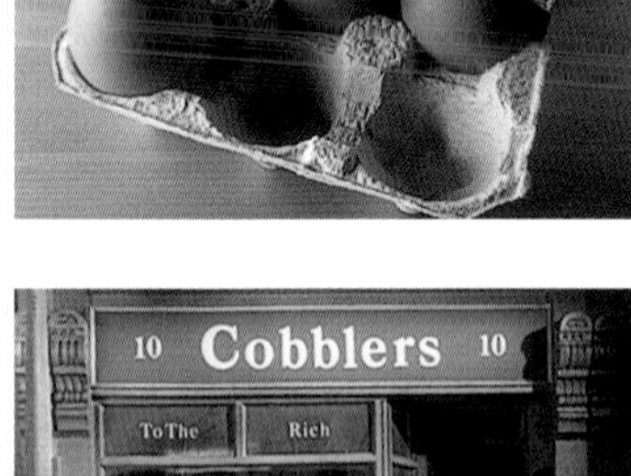

WELL

SUPER:
An Easy To Follow Advertisement For Your Easy To Use Delta Card.

V/O:
A lot of people (large crowd of people)

already use their Delta card (Delta card)

to pay for groceries (bag of groceries).

Well (a well) hey (a pile of hay)!

Great (a cheese grater) news (a newspaper)!

Delta (logo)

is welcome at (a door mat)

stacks (platform shoes)

more (Bobby Moore)

places (a selection of plaice).

For example (four eggs, a urine sample)

pharmacies (a farmer, sea),

stationers (a station, a nurse) and

hairdressers (a hare, two welsh dressers) and that's not (a knot)

just a load of old (cobblers shop)

...nonsense.

Visa's (logo) Delta (logo)

Blow (dynamite plunger)

To cheques

(two Czechoslovakians).

NUTTER

SUPER:
An Easy To Follow Advertisement For Your Easy To Use Delta Card.

V/O:
When you go shopping

(woman buying large cucumber)

are you still paying by cheque (hand writing cheque),

instead of your Delta card (Delta card)?

What an utter (a nutter)

waste (plump waist) of time (watch face)!

Delta (delta logo) is a lot (auction lot)

faster (map followed by saucepan being stirred)

than a cheque (chess piece in check)

which is (two witches)

an awfully (an oar followed by a flea)

tire (a tyre) some (a sum) way (scales)

to pay (man in dreadful toupee).

Yes, (thumbs up)

thanks to the Delta (Delta logo)

card (birthday card),

cheques (check material) are well and truly

(turkey being vigorously stuffed)

...scuppered.

Visa's (logo) Delta (logo)

Blow (man being punched)

To cheques

(two Czechoslovakians gentlemen).

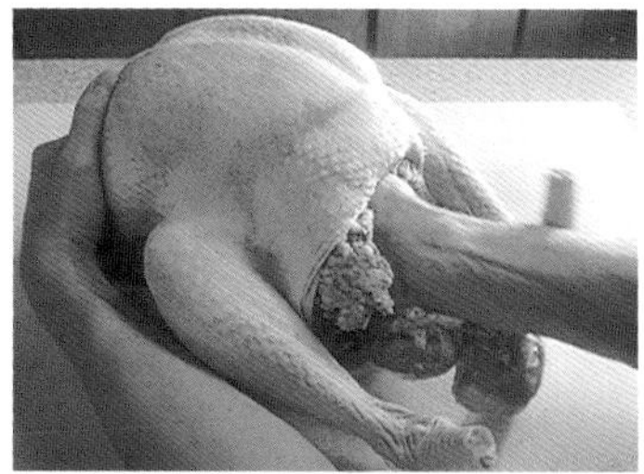

Television Campaigns

Director
RICHARD PHILLIPS

Copywriters
PAUL GRUBB
ANDY McLEOD
JAMES FRYER

Art Directors
DAVE WATERS
RICHARD FLINTHAM
MIKE LONDON

Creative Directors
PAUL GRUBB
DAVE WATERS

Producer
CHRISSIE PHILLIPS

Set Designer
STEVE SMITHWICK

Agency Producers
KATE O'MULLOY
ROS McLELLAN

Editor
RICHARD LEAROYD

Lighting Cameraman
KARL WATKINS

Music Composers/Arrangers
ROY HEAD
ANTHONY & GAYNOR SADLER

Production Company
R.J.PHILLIPS & CO

Agency
DUCKWORTH FINN GRUBB WATERS

Marketing Director
STEVE DUNN

Client
PIZZA HUT UK LIMITED

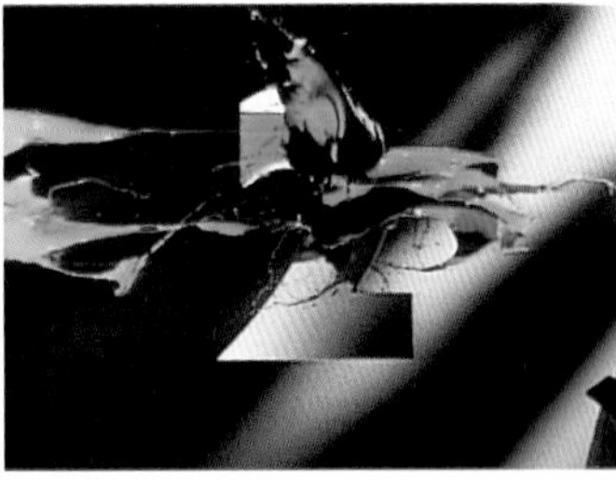

TWO

Open on huge Gill Bold number 2 on limbo backdrop. A huge glob of paint splashes into it from the side...The paint drips off the 2 for a few moments.

A man, face covered in paint splats, pops his head up in screen and speaks to camera, doing the Pizza Hut point and flicking more paint at the lens.

MAN:
...two erm...pizzas for the price of one...when you...erm...Hit The Hut!

Cut to painter with his wife and child in a Pizza Hut.

MVO:
Buy any medium or large pizza from Pizza Hut any weekday after 4, and get another one absolutely free.

As they begin to tuck in, a huge metal sharp-edged two thunks into the table, point first, just in front of them. They reel back in surprise.

MAN:
Whooa...could've had somebody's eye out...

Cut to Pizza Hut logo falling onto a flour background with an almighty thud.

MVO:
Two pizzas for the price of one when you Hit The Hut.

KLINGONESE

MUSIC:
Star Trek music.

VIDEO:
We open on the USS Enterprise warping impressively through space. Cut to inside Klingon spaceship who are watching the speedy approach of the USS Enterprise on their screen. They are understandably worried.

KLINGON LEADER:
Quob Klow?

KLINGONS:
Klow doha RITKE PLIC.

They do the twirl. Cut to Klingon spaceship exploding.

MUSIC:
Klingon version of 'Hey Hey'.

Cut to Next Generation cups.

MVO:
Sklid triksha von flunk, ecche tek Bratek Slucks, rach sok sok sok.

Cut to Pizza Hut in a hail of laser rays. Two of the Klingons are firing their guns at camera. They stop when a waitress gives them a withering look.

Cut to the same two Klingons happily slurping their Next Generation drinks.

KUNG FU

All the dialogue is dubbed out of sync, Kung Fu movie style.

Open on two men fighting off loads of baddies Kung Fu style.

SFX:
Kung Fu fighting noises.

They manage to beat them all in a comic book battle. The baddies are left lying around them.

SFX:
Groaning.

They dust their hands off.

MAN 1:
What now?

They both do a Kung Fu style point.

MAN 2:
Now we...Hit the Hut.

SFX:
Music, Hey, hey, hey.

MVO:
Get a Chinese Chicken Pizza only £5.99 at Pizza Hut.

Cut to food shots of the ingredients, the two beers and the pizza.

Cut to the Pizza Hut.

The waitress bursts in from the kitchen with pizzas balanced on either hand.

She serves the pizzas with a flourish of Kung Fu style movements.

SFX:
Kung Fu noises.

She serves our two men their beers, again Kung Fu style.

MAN 1:
Is that really necessary?

MVO:
For a Chinese pizza...Hit the Hut!

SUPER:

Pizza Hut offer and logo.

Television Campaigns

Director
MANDIE FLETCHER

Copywriters
JOHN WEBSTER
JACK DEE

Art Directors
JOHN WEBSTER

Creative Director
JOHN WEBSTER

Producers
MADELEINE SANDERSON
DAVID MORLEY

Set Designer
ROGER HALL

Agency Producer
LUCINDA KER

Editor
ALASTER JORDON

Lighting Cameraman
SUE GIBSON

Music Composers/Arrangers
PAUL HART
JOE CAMPBELL

Production Companies
FLETCHER SANDERSON FILMS
OPEN MIKE PRODUCTIONS

Agency
BMP DDB NEEDHAM

Group Marketing Controller
JOHN ROBERTS

Client
COURAGE LIMITED

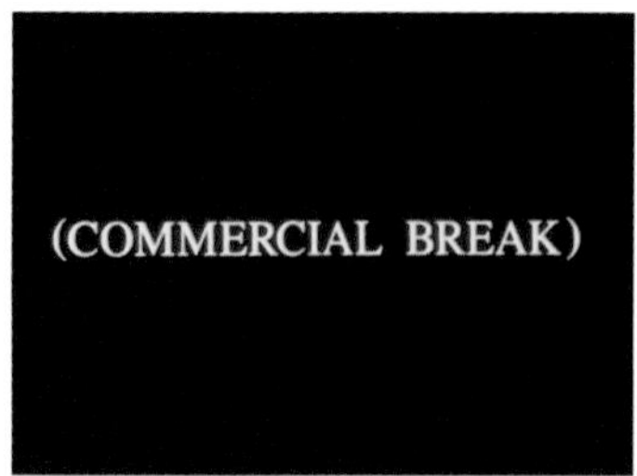

NOT READY

JACK:
New John Smiths Extra Smooth Bitter, look at that - pure silk in a glass.

BARMAN:
When it clears Sir.

JACK:
Now?

BARMAN:
Not quite yet Sir.

JACK:
(whinging)
Oh go on.

BARMAN:
Weather's warm for the time of the year Sir...I saw a snowdrop yesterday...

JACK:
Please let me have it now. I waited...please...

(Commercial break)

BARMAN:
Okay.

JACK:
Thanks.

SFX:
Clunk.

HELP YOURSELF

MUSIC:
Help Yourself.

PENGUINS:
(sing)
Just help yourself to John Smiths

to its charms

Just say the word and it is yours

Just help yourself to the flavour in its heart

Your lips can open up the door

(continues under)

JACK:
There's something completely new in the pub, John Smiths Extra Smooth Bitter, pure silk in a glass.

Mmmm

So you still don't need gimmicks.

PENGUINS:
(sing)
...and your lips...(stop)

(mutter mutter)

SFX:
Clunk.

TRAILER

JACK:
Something new is about to enter the pub from John Smiths.

What could it be?

SFX:
Psycho music.

Copywriters
JOHN WEBSTER
JACK DEE
ANDREW FRASER

Art Directors
JOHN WEBSTER
ALAN CINNAMOND

TRAP DOOR

JACK:
John Smith's Extra Smooth Bitter slips down like a penguin through a trap door.

PENGUIN:
Gulp!

SFX:
Squeaking as penguin shuffles out of frame.

Clunk.

WASTE

This ad finds Denis Leary behind a bar. He picks up A. N. OTHER bottle and starts to read from the label as he passes about. He dumps the bottle in a huge bin. He picks up a second bottle, reads then dumps it. Another and another as the cutting gathers more pace. Denis trashes bottle after bottle.

DENIS LEARY:
Deep in the American south for over 200 years they've started each and every day with a traditional breakfast. Eggs over easy. A rasher of crispy fried bacon and a bowl of hot hominy grits. Grits. Do you know what grits are? Well they're a tough, chewy mass of stuff that tastes of boiled over cat litter and it's just like rocks in my mouth. I hate grits and guess what, they're in this beer. Why? I don't know why. Maybe for the same reason that there's caramel in this beer. Caramel. If I want candy I buy a candy bar. Guess what? Seaweed. SEA WEED. That's weed that comes from the sea which is where fish go to the toilet. It's a free country, but personally I don't want fish urine in my beer. And of course, rice? RICE? Next time you go to a wedding try throwing one of these at the bride. Or one of these, or one of these, or...Ascorbic acid or citric acid, sorghum, sugar, fructose, glucose, sucrose, sulphur dioxide, potassium metabisulphate, propylene glyco agnate and bat faeces. I made up the last one but you never know.

Denis picks up a bottle of Holsten Pils and reads from the label. The bar is now clear of the other bottles except for one which rolls along the shelf behind and then falls off into the big bin.

DENIS LEARY:
Holsten Pils. Hops, barley, yeast, water and no shit.

TITLE:

Full Of Shit? Get Real!

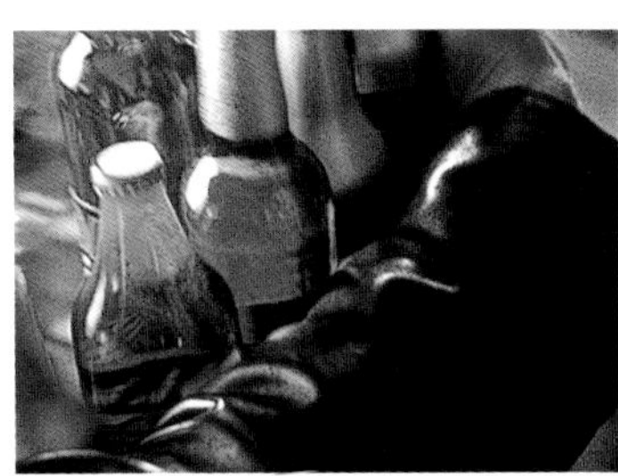

Cinema Commercials Single and Campaigns

Director
FRANK BUDGEN

Copywriter
ROBERT SAVILLE

Art Director
JAY POND-JONES

Creative Director
TIM MELLORS

Producer
PAUL ROTHWELL

Set Designer
JULIA SHERBORNE

Agency Producer
DIANE CROLL

Editor
SAM SNEADE

Lighting Cameraman
ADRIAN BIDDLE

Music Composer/Arranger
RICHARD MYHILL

Production Company
PAUL WEILAND FILM COMPANY

Agency
GGT

Marketing Director
PHIL PLOWMAN

Client
HOLSTEN DISTRIBUTORS LIMITED

Cinema Commercials
Single and Campaigns

Director
DOUG FOSTER

Copywriter
SIMON LEARMAN

Art Director
BRIAN FRASER

Creative Directors
SIMON LEARMAN
BRIAN FRASER

Producer
MICHELLE JAFFE

Set Designer
ASSHETON GORTON

Production Company
BLINK PRODUCTIONS

Animators
GRAHAME ANDREW
BEN HAYDEN
PAUL KAVANAGH
LAURENT HUGUENOIT

Agency Producer
JOHN MONTGOMERY

Editor
TIM BURKE

Lighting Cameramen
DOUG FOSTER
DAVID WYNN JONES

Music Composer/Arranger
JOHN BARRY

Agency
OGILVY & MATHER

Marketing Director
ROB McNEWIN

Account Director
NEIL QUICK

Client
GUINNESS BREWING GB

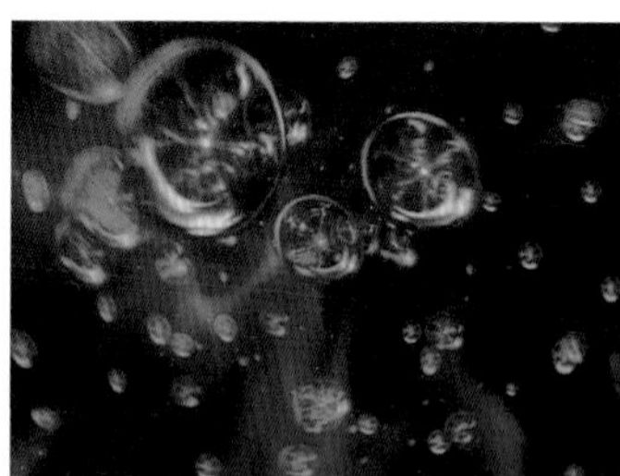
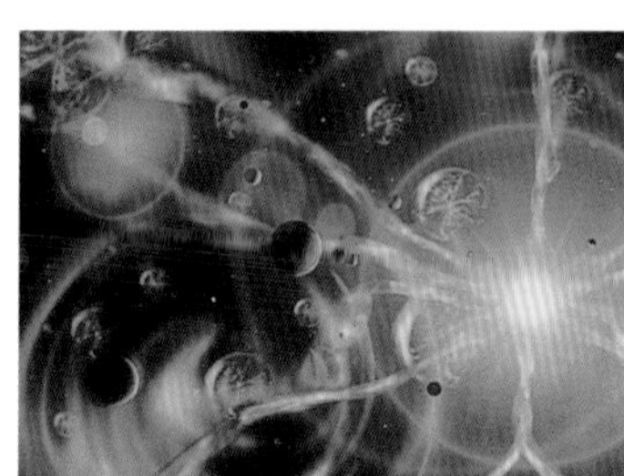
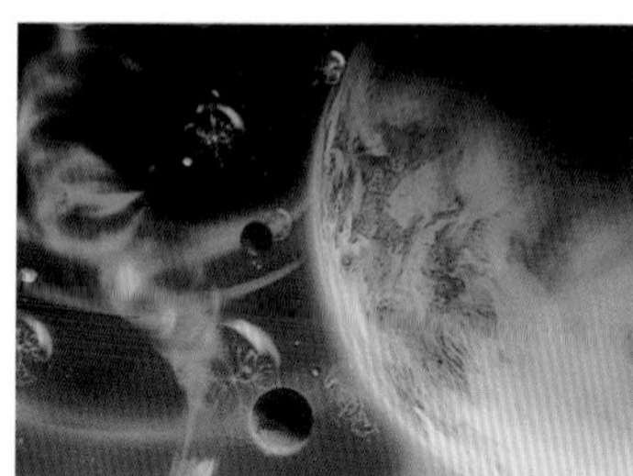

CHAIN

MUSIC:
'We Have All The Time In The World' sung by Louis Armstrong.

In this commercial, we embark on a timeless journey through a glass of swirling Draught Guinness. Everything is rendered in Guinness tones.

We push inside a bubble, cross a strange universe, then descend upon a mysterious planet.

We sweep down towards an enormous tower set against a turbulent sky. The camera favours an open window as we move into a room packed with unusual souvenirs.

We glance past a television set. The familiar face of the Man in Black appears on the screen. He smiles at us, before we make a beeline for the centre piece; a swirling pint of Guinness set on a table.

The camera lingers. We think the journey is over when the chain of events begins to repeat itself. It's as if the journey might go on for some time.

Title:

Pure Genius.

THE BOSS

MUSIC:
Zadoq the Priest by Handel.

We are at a big football match. We see our Boss suited hero, the manager of one of the teams, enduring the pressure of a vital game.

Things are going badly, so the boss decides to make a management decision. To the surprise of his staff and the TV commentators, he makes a substitution.

In the dying seconds, the substitute breaks through and is brought down in the penalty area.

He gets up and takes the penalty, scoring the winning goal.

The crowd goes wild, as the final whistle blows.

The players celebrate and the boss finds himself being embraced by his goalkeeper, who leaves mud down the front of his immaculate suit. For a moment, we think the boss will explode, but he simply smiles and turns to congratulate the goalscorer.

As he turns, we see he hasn't noticed the mud on his back.

SUPER:
Men At Work.

Hugo Boss.

Cinema Commercials
Single and Campaigns

Director
SPROTE

Copywriter
PAUL SILBURN

Art Director
TIGER SAVAGE

Creative Director
JOHN HEGARTY

Producer
BASY ROBERTSON

Set Designer
STEVE SMITHWICK

Agency Producer
FRANCES ROYALE

Editor
MIKE GILDING

Lighting Cameraman
DENIS CROSSAN

Music Composers/Arrangers
ANTHONY & GAYNOR SADLER

Production Company
REDWING FILM COMPANY

Agency
BARTLE BOGLE HEGARTY

Brand Manager
JENS HENNING KOCK

Client
HUGO BOSS AG

Cinema Commercials
Single and Campaigns

Directors
TERENCE O'CONNOR
MAREK LOSEY

Copywriter
ALAN MOSELEY

Art Director
GRAHAM CAPPI

Producer
ALAN TAYLOR

Agency Producer
ALISON TINKER

Editor
KAREN STEINIGER

Production Company
TRADEMARK PRODUCTIONS

Agency
COWAN KEMSLEY TAYLOR

Client
TAUNTON CIDER PLC

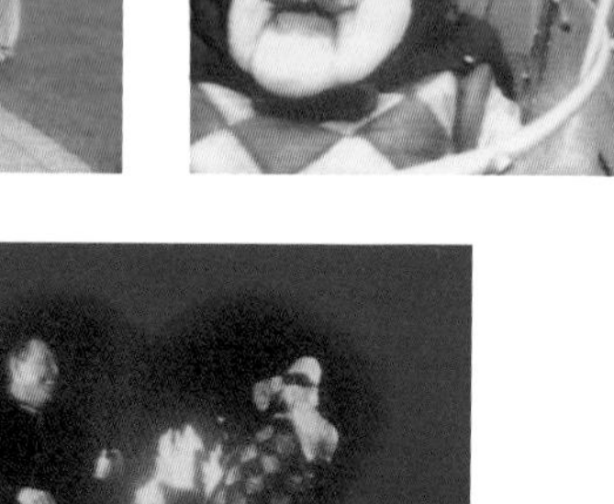

SUBURBAN BLISS

Love is an unpredictable beast, sometimes it strikes out in the most unlikely places.

This is the story of one man, mesmerised by Drum's inner beauty. As the lyrics of the song suggest, he would really give up his life, his heart and his Barratt home on the outskirts of Clacton-On-Sea, for a few moments of happiness that have alluded him all of his life.

WHITEHALL

LATHAM:
...So there is no better way of serving your Queen and country...than to choose a career in MI7. Are there any questions?

CANDIDATE 1:
What's the financial package?

LATHAM:
Financial package??

BOUGH:
You do get issued with a Barclaycard, Sir.

LATHAM:
Bough...

CANDIDATE 2:
Oh yeah, with Barclaycard can't you get medical help abroad?

CANDIDATE 3:
...and legal advice?

CANDIDATE4:
...and some sort of purchase insurance?

BOUGH:
Ah yes, both at home and abroad.

LATHAM:
Bough!! These people will have to survive in locations rather more dangerous than a record shop.

CANDIDATE 5:
Ah, can I ask about Eastern Europe?

LATHAM:
Ah, yes...

CANDIDATE 5:
Do they take Barclaycard?

BOUGH:
Ah, well most countries actually take...

LATHAM:
I remember when all an agent had was his charm, his cunning, and if he was lucky...

CANDIDATE 6:
A biro?

LATHAM:
No ordinary biro...two clicks of the cap will render any assailant immobile...very dangerous in the wrong hands. Take over for a Bough, would you moment?

BOUGH:
Well, Barclaycard is widely accepted, in fact you can use it in over 200 countries around the world...

(fade out)

Cinema Commercials
Single and Campaigns

Director
MARK CHAPMAN

Copywriter
PAUL BURKE

Art Director
PETER GATLEY

Creative Director
TONY COX

Producer
GLYNIS SANDERS

Set Designer
TONY NOBLE

Agency Producer
MICHAEL PARKER

Editor
IAN WEIL

Lighting Cameraman
JOHN IGNATIUS

Rostrum Cameraman
MARTIN KENZIE

Music Composer/Arranger
HOWARD GOODALL

Production Company
TIGER ASPECT PRODUCTIONS

Agency
BMP DDB NEEDHAM

Manager of Marketing and Advertising
JOHN LAIDLOW

Client
BARCLAYCARD

Cinema Commercials
Single and Campaigns

Director
TONY KAYE

Copywriter
TOM CARTY

Art Director
WALTER CAMPBELL

Creative Director
DAVID ABBOTT

Producer
MIRANDA DAVIS

Agency Producer
FRANK LIEBERMAN

Editor
PETER GODDARD

Lighting Cameraman
TONY KAYE

Music Composers/Arrangers
JENKINS & RATLEDGE

Sound Designers
ROHAN YOUNG
MALCOLM BRISTOW

Production Company
TONY KAYE FILMS

Agency
ABBOTT MEAD VICKERS.BBDO LIMITED

Communications Manager
CRAIG FABIAN

Client
VOLVO CARS UK LIMITED

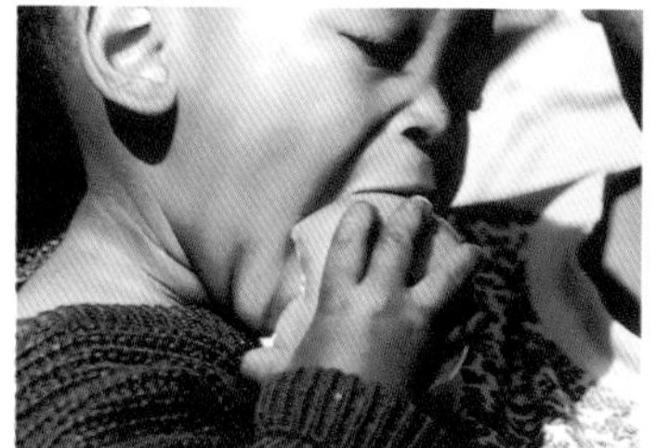

PHOTOGRAPHER

A documentary studying the life of war photographer Jana Schneider.

She talks about her working life and the importance of equipment. Eyes, camera, car.

We see Schneider in a dangerous assignment. She drives her Volvo 850 out onto a deserted runway to photograph a suspicious plane. The plane starts to taxi toward take off.

However, Schneider has an amazing camera rig mounted on the side of her car, which is activated by a cable release on the steering wheel. This allows her to get the shots she needs whilst driving close alongside the hurtling plane.

The situation is made even more deadly as cargo bales are being thrown from the plane into her path.

Volvo. A car you can believe in.

PHOTOGRAPHER:
My photography is about life, even when I photograph death.

*When you're stabbed or hit by a bullet it doesn't hurt like you'd imagine.
It burns. It's almost like a fast racing burn.*

My job isn't to judge. My job is to get in and get out.

I do all this, because it's about believing my pictures are the truth.

*I'm basically isolating a milli second in time.
If you're documenting life, a moment only happens once.*

Being in the bush makes me deal with a different rhythm.

What makes me laugh is, you know, is getting through the tiniest keyhole and getting it all when they say it's impossible.

*Your photographs are only as good as the position you get in. I can't get a photograph if I'm not in position.
This car gets me into that position.*

In my business everything's a one shot deal, you get it or you don't.

Equipment is everything. Eyes, camera, car.

Cinema Commercials
Single and Campaigns

TOUCH

A beautiful woman is reclining in a dream-like state.

She caresses her body and looks longingly into camera.

WOMAN:
Feel me...touch me...eat me.

We see her pick up a perfume box.

V/O:
Parfum de Mari Pepe.

C'est un petit bout d'animal.

She opens the box.

The smell is neat meat.

She reels away fast.

WOMAN:
...Stone me...!

A title comes on:

Mari Pepe.

C'est un petit bout d'animal.

SFX:
Evil Peperami cackle.

The letters change to:

Peperami.

It's a bit of an animal.

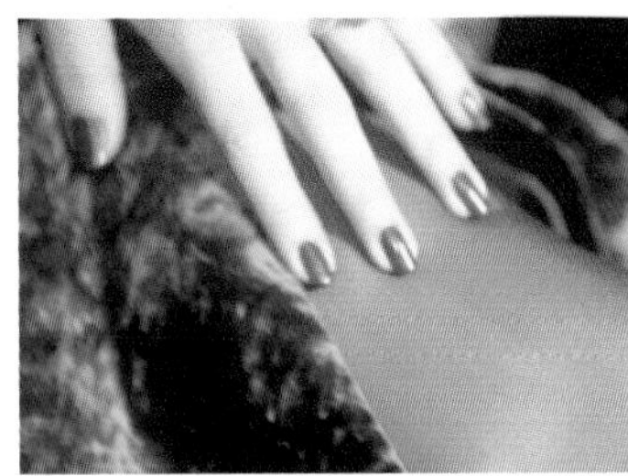

Director
KIM KNOTT

Copywriter
STEVE MEREDITH

Art Director
RAY BRENNAN

Creative Director
ALLAN CREW

Producer
HARRY RANKIN

Agency Producer
NICK PEERS

Editor
STEVE GANDOLFI

Lighting Cameraman
MIKE BREWSTER

Music Composer/Arranger
NICK PEERS

Production Company
ECLIPSE PRODUCTIONS

Agency
S P LINTAS

Marketing Director
SIMON TURNER

Client
VAN DEN BERGH LIMITED

Cinema Commercial Campaigns

Director
MICHEL GONDRY

Copywriter
NICK WORTHINGTON

Art Director
JOHN GORSE

Creative Director
JOHN HEGARTY

Producers
TOBY COURLANDER
GEORGES BERMANN
PETE CHAMBERS

Set Designer
ROBBIE FREED

Agency Producer
PHILIPPA CRANE

Editor
RUSSELL ICKE

Lighting Cameraman
TIM MAURICE JONES

Music Composer/Arranger
GEIR JENSSEN

Production Company
PARTIZAN MIDI MINUIT

Agency
BARTLE BOGLE HEGARTY

Senior Marketing Manager
ROBERT HOLLOWAY

Client
LEVI STRAUSS & CO EUROPE SA

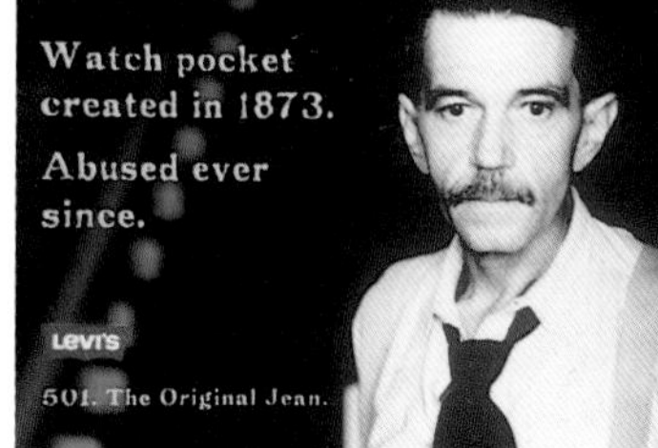

DRUGSTORE (MALE)

MUSIC:
Techno.

We see the view through the windscreen of an old truck heading into town. It's 1930, the American depression.

The truck comes to a stop outside a drugstore, as a train rumbles by.

We don't see the driver, just their view as they enter the store.

The shopkeeper, a woman and child and two girls, all turn to look.

At the counter, the driver asks for something.

The chemist hands over a tin of condoms, with a knowing smile. The driver tucks them into the watch pocket of his jeans and heads out of the door, leaving the woman in a state of shock and embarrassment.

We dissolve to the truck later that evening. It's waiting while a train thunders by. We then see it pulling up outside a white clapboard house.

A girl is waiting on the balcony.

The driver goes to the door. It opens, but it's not the girl. It's the chemist.

We see the driver for the first time, he's a young man in his teens. The chemist puts two and two together. Then, realising what's going on, trys to stop his daughter, but is powerless.

The chemist watches the young man climb into the vehicle and drive off with his daughter.

SUPER:
Watch Pocket Created in 1873.

Abused Ever Since.

Batwing logo.

SUPER:
501. The original Jean.

TAXI

MUSIC:
Retro 70's funk.

SFX:
Ambient city noises.

Open on a New York taxi cab rolling through a plume of steam in slow motion.

We're in 70's Manhattan on a hot summer's night where the streets glow bright with neon.

Our taxi cruises past a waiting couple and screeches to a halt beside a stunning young woman in 501 jeans and platform shoes. Cut to inside the cab. We watch a beauty shot of the woman as she looks toward the lecherous taxi driver. He nods approvingly.

The taxi sets off on its journey through the colourful city, allowing our cabbie to furtively leer at the woman's reflection as she teasingly touches up her make-up.

SFX:
Electric razor.

However, his passion is soon dampened when, to his horror, the woman whips out an electric razor and starts to shave some stubble from her chin.

Cut to reflection shot of the surprised taxi driver. A hint of anger flashes across his face as he realises that 'she' is in fact a 'he'.

The cab pulls over somewhere down-town and our 'hero' coolly gets out and vanishes into a cloud of steam.

SUPER:
Cut For Men Since 1850.

LOGO/ENDLINE:

501. The Original Jean.

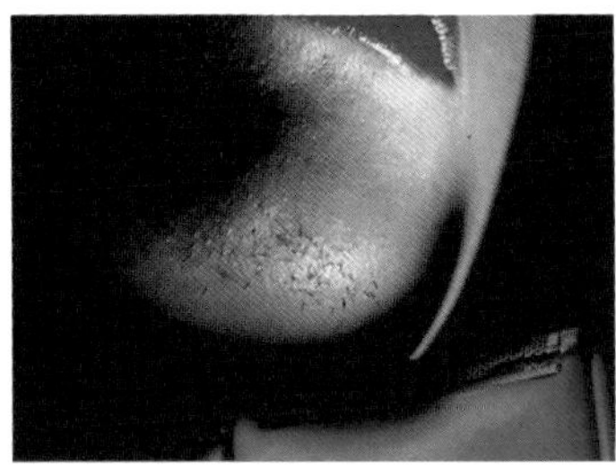

Director
BAILLIE WALSH

Copywriter
ROGER BECKETT

Art Director
ANDY SMART

Creative Director
JOHN HEGARTY

Producer
DICKIE JEFFARES

Set Designer
ALAN McDONALD

Agency Producer
PHILIPPA CRANE

Editor
ANDREA MACARTHUR

Lighting Cameraman
JOHN MATHIESON

Music Composer/Arranger
NORMAN COOK

Production Company
LIMELIGHT

Cinema Commercials
Single and Campaigns

Director
FRANK BUDGEN

Copywriter
ROBERT SAVILLE

Art Director
JAY POND-JONES

Creative Director
TIM MELLORS

Producer
PAUL ROTHWELL

Set Designer
JULIA SHERBORNE

Agency Producer
DIANE CROLL

Editor
SAM SNEADE

Lighting Cameraman
ADRIAN BIDDLE

Music Composer/Arranger
RICHARD MYHILL

Production Company
PAUL WEILAND FILM COMPANY

Agency
GGT

Marketing Director
PHIL PLOWMAN

Client
HOLSTEN DISTRIBUTORS LIMITED

WASTE

This ad finds Denis Leary behind a bar. He picks up A. N. OTHER bottle and starts to read from the label as he passes about. He dumps the bottle in a huge bin. He picks up a second bottle, reads then dumps it. Another and another as the cutting gathers more pace. Denis trashes bottle after bottle.

DENIS LEARY:
Deep in the American south for over 200 years they've started each and every day with a traditional breakfast. Eggs over easy. A rasher of crispy fried bacon and a bowl of hot hominy grits. Grits. Do you know what grits are? Well they're a tough, chewy mass of stuff that tastes of boiled over cat litter and it's just like rocks in my mouth. I hate grits and guess what, they're in this beer. Why? I don't know why. Maybe for the same reason that there's caramel in this beer. Caramel. If I want candy I buy a candy bar. Guess what? Seaweed. SEA WEED. That's weed that comes from the sea which is where fish go to the toilet. It's a free country, but personally I don't want fish urine in my beer. And of course, rice? RICE? Next time you go to a wedding try throwing one of these at the bride. Or one of these, or one of these, or...Ascorbic acid or citric acid, sorghum, sugar, fructose, glucose, sucrose, sulphur dioxide, potassium metabisulphate, propylene glyco agnate and bat faeces. I made up the last one but you never know.

Denis picks up a bottle of Holsten Pils and reads from the label. The bar is now clear of the other bottles except for one which rolls along the shelf behind and then falls off into the big bin.

DENIS LEARY:
Holsten Pils. Hops, barley, yeast, water and no shit.

TITLE:
Full Of Shit? Get Real!

ADDITIVES

We see Denis Leary standing in front of an over the top painted background of spectacular beauty. (Think 'Sound of Music'). Blue sky, snow capped mountains and a crystal clear lake.

To one side behind him is a really naff mixed race acapella group who are singing the most awful stomach churning song about 'living life in the glory of nature'.

Denis has sacks full of barley and hops around him. He picks handfuls of them. He enjoys the fragrances of the hops and lets the barley run through his fingers.

DENIS LEARY:
Hops. Barley. Yeast. Water. That's it! Hops, barley, yeast, water. That's it. Just those. Just lager. Delicious, full flavoured, authentic Holsten Pils. As nature inten...

(After a while the goody goody wonderment music of the singing gets to be too much and Denis snaps)

...Will you shut up! I'm talking down here.

Denis switches into his no bullshit attitude. He paces up and down.

DENIS LEARY:
Let me put it this way. I don't drink lager with a splash of additives. I don't drink lager with a preservative top. I don't drink lager and stabiliser shandy. Why not? Because I treat my body like a temple. That's why. I leave my boots on the outside.

Just as Denis is about to swig from a Holsten bottle, he hears a tambourine being dropped by one of the singers.

DENIS LEARY:
What are you looking at?

TITLE:
Additives? Get Real!

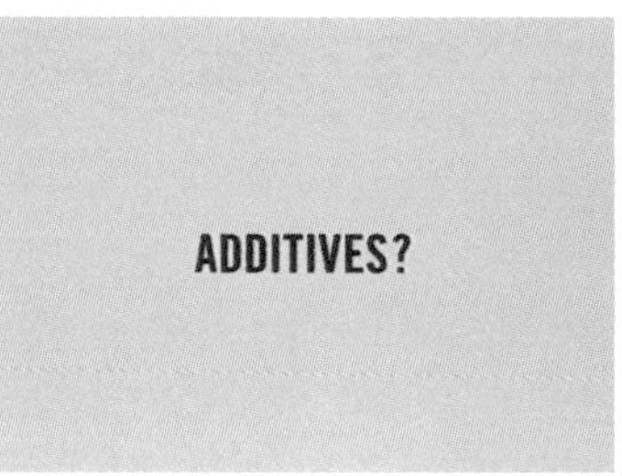

Cinema Commercials
Single and Campaigns

Directors
MARK STORY
BRUCE HURWIT
CHARLES WITTENMEIER

Copywriters
ARTHUR BIJUR
GREG BELL
JOHN LEU
CLIFF FREEMAN
MICHELLE ROUFA

Art Directors
JOHN LEU
GREG BELL
DONNA WEINHEIM

Creative Directors
CLIFF FREEMAN
ARTHUR BIJUR
DONNA WEINHEIM

Agency Producers
ANNE KURTZMAN
MARY ELLEN DUGGAN

Editors
CREW CUTS
IAN MACKENZIE

Music Composer/Arranger
MICHAEL CARROLL

Production Companies
CROSSROADS FILMS
HARMONY PICTURES

Agency
CLIFF FREEMAN & PARTNERS

Client
LITTLE CAESARS ENTERPRISES

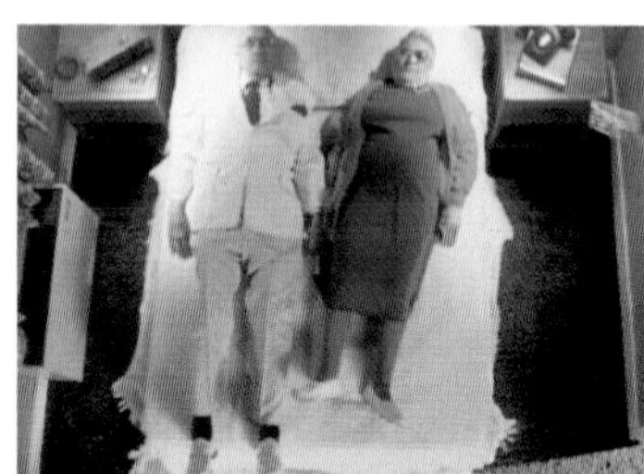

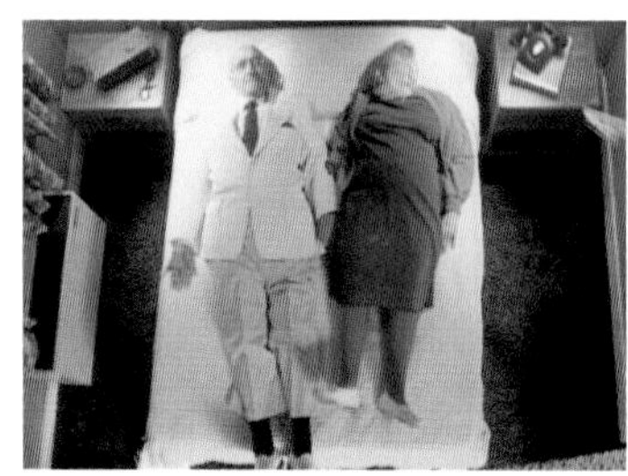

MAGIC FINGERS

Open on the 'Snugglers' Cove Motel".

SFX:
Romantic music on the radio.

Cut to the inside of a motel room. An older couple sit on the opposite sides of the bed. They smile at each other, as he takes her hand.

Cut to 'Magic Fingers' vibrating bed machine. The man puts $1.00 into the slot. The machine immediately sucks up the dollar bill, and the bed starts to vibrate noisily.

Cut to an overhead shot of the couple lying on the vibrating bed. They stare straight ahead, experiencing the moment. After a few seconds, the bed shudders to a stop. The woman turns to the man.

WOMAN:
We should've gotten the Pizza.

Cut to beauty shots of Little Caesars Pizzas.

SUPER:
$1

ANNCR:
Pizza for a buck! Now when you buy two pizzas with two toppings for $8.98, you get a third pizza for a buck!

Little Caesar appears, with the Little Caesars logo.

LITTLE CAESAR:

Pizza! Pizza!

SINGING BABY

Open on a Father and Grandmother at dining table admiring two Little Caesars Pizzas.

GRANNY:
Have you ever seen anything more amazing than Little Caesars Italian sausage pizza?

Father looks up. Cut to reveal a baby sitting in a high chair spinning plates on sticks. On baby's head is a cat doing a hand stand while balancing a full goldfish bowl on its foot. Baby sings 'Give My Regards To Broadway.' Cut back to Father.

FATHER:
...No.

Cut to food section.

ANNCR:
Italian sausage pizza! Loaded with sausage, peppers and onions. The newest from a whole menu of Little Caesar Pleasers.

Any two for $9.98!

LITTLE CAESAR:
Pizza! Pizza!

ANNCR:
Or get one for $5.99!

LITTLE CAESAR:

Pizza!

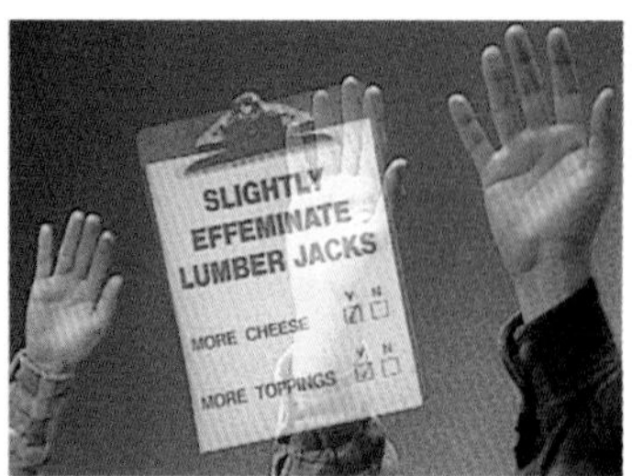

FOCUS GROUP

Open outside door of research facility. A researcher is sliding a placard reading 'pizzas' into slot on door.

SFX:
Heroic music starts low and builds throughout.

Move through door revealing focus group in session. Pan down table past group to moderator asking them questions. A group of researchers in suits observe the questioning.

MODERATOR:
O.K...how many of you would like more cheese on your pizza?

Cut to entire group slowly raising hands.

MODERATOR:
How many of you would like more toppings on your pizza?

Focus group again raises hands. MODERATOR: *O.K....more cheese?*

(Cut to group of kids raising their hands positively)

O.K....more toppings?

(Cut to group of war veterans raising hands)

O.K...more cheese?...More toppings...More?...More?... More?...More toppings?

Cut to group of people with big noses raising their hands. Cut to hands raising as different clipboards fly towards us and researchers celebrate. The clipboards read - Hairy Figure Skaters, Slightly Effeminate Lumberjacks, Over-the-hill Rock Stars, StarTrekkies, Clowns and a Brazilian Rainforest Tribe are all raising their hands.

Cut to researchers grouped around map of America totally covered in pushpins. One researcher fills in a final empty space.

RESEARCHER:
Well, that's every man, woman and child.

Cut to orangutans all raising hands. Moderator smiles.

ANNCR:
By popular demand, it's the new Little Caesars Pleasers Menu. More meat, more cheese, more pepperoni...more toppings. Any two for one low price. Satisfaction guaranteed or your money back.

LITTLE CAESAR:
Pizza! Pizza!

1995

TELEVISION AND CINEMA ADVERTISING CRAFTS

USE OF MUSIC

Sponsored by The Tape Gallery

SPECIAL EFFECTS

Sponsored by Rushes

SILVER AWARD
for the Most
Outstanding Direction

Director
MICHEL GONDRY

Copywriter
NICK WORTHINGTON

Art Director
JOHN GORSE

Creative Director
JOHN HEGARTY

Producers
TOBY COURLANDER
GEORGES BERMANN
PETE CHAMBERS

Set Designer
ROBBIE FREED

Agency Producer
PHILIPPA CRANE

Editor
RUSSELL ICKE

Lighting Cameraman
TIM MAURICE JONES

Music Composer/Arranger
GEIR JENSSEN

Production Company
PARTIZAN MIDI MINUIT

Agency
BARTLE BOGLE HEGARTY

Senior Marketing Manager
ROBERT HOLLOWAY

Client
LEVI STRAUSS & CO EUROPE SA

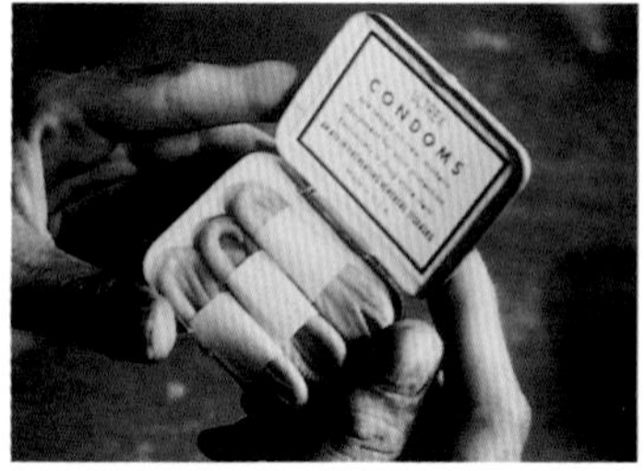

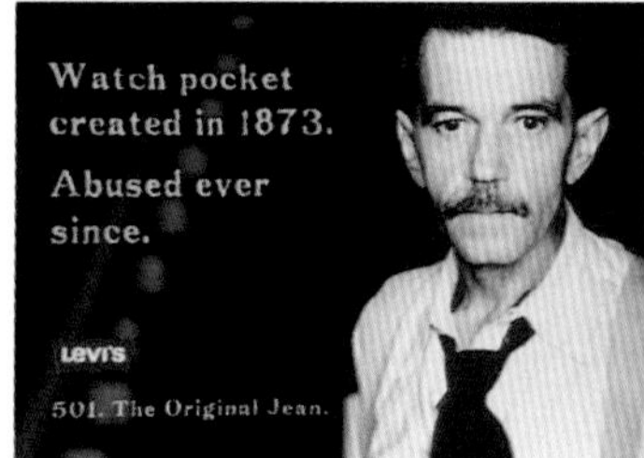

DRUGSTORE (MALE)

MUSIC:
Techno.

We see the view through the windscreen of an old truck heading into town. It's 1930, the American depression.

The truck comes to a stop outside a drugstore, as a train rumbles by.

We don't see the driver, just their view as they enter the store.

The shopkeeper, a woman and child and two girls, all turn to look.

At the counter, the driver asks for something.

The chemist hands over a tin of condoms, with a knowing smile. The driver tucks them into the watch pocket of his jeans and heads out of the door, leaving the woman in a state of shock and embarrassment.

We dissolve to the truck later that evening. It's waiting while a train thunders by. We then see it pulling up outside a white clapboard house.

A girl is waiting on the balcony.

The driver goes to the door. It opens, but it's not the girl. It's the chemist.

We see the driver for the first time, he's a young man in his teens. The chemist puts two and two together. Then, realising what's going on, trys to stop his daughter, but is powerless.

The chemist watches the young man climb into the vehicle and drive off with his daughter.

SUPER:
Watch Pocket Created in 1873.

Abused Ever Since.

Batwing logo.

SUPER:
501. The original Jean.

SILVER AWARD
for the Most Outstanding Use of Music

Director
MICHEL GONDRY

Copywriter
NICK WORTHINGTON

Art Director
JOHN GORSE

Creative Director
JOHN HEGARTY

Producers
TOBY COURLANDER
GEORGES BERMANN
PETE CHAMBERS

Set Designer
ROBBIE FREED

Agency Producer
PHILIPPA CRANE

Editor
RUSSELL ICKF

Lighting Cameraman
TIM MAURICE JONES

Music Composer/Arranger
GEIR JENSSEN

Production Company
PARTIZAN MIDI MINUIT

Agency
BARTLE BOGLE HEGARTY

Senior Marketing Manager
ROBERT HOLLOWAY

Client
LEVI STRAUSS & CO EUROPE SA

DRUGSTORE (MALE)

MUSIC:
Techno.

We see the view through the windscreen of an old truck heading into town. It's 1930, the American depression.

The truck comes to a stop outside a drugstore, as a train rumbles by.

We don't see the driver, just their view as they enter the store.

The shopkeeper, a woman and child and two girls, all turn to look.

At the counter, the driver asks for something.

The chemist hands over a tin of condoms, with a knowing smile. The driver tucks them into the watch pocket of his jeans and heads out of the door, leaving the woman in a state of shock and embarrassment.

We dissolve to the truck later that evening. It's waiting while a train thunders by. We then see it pulling up outside a white clapboard house.

A girl is waiting on the balcony.

The driver goes to the door. It opens, but it's not the girl. It's the chemist.

We see the driver for the first time, he's a young man in his teens. The chemist puts two and two together. Then, realising what's going on, trys to stop his daughter, but is powerless.

The chemist watches the young man climb into the vehicle and drive off with his daughter.

SUPER:
Watch Pocket Created in 1873.

Abused Ever Since.

Batwing logo.

SUPER:
501. The original Jean.

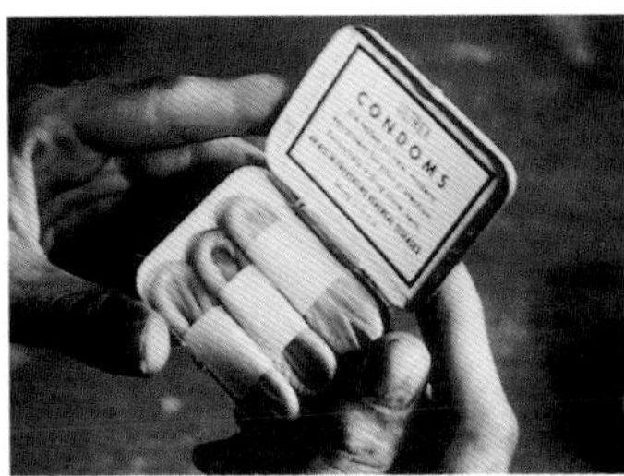

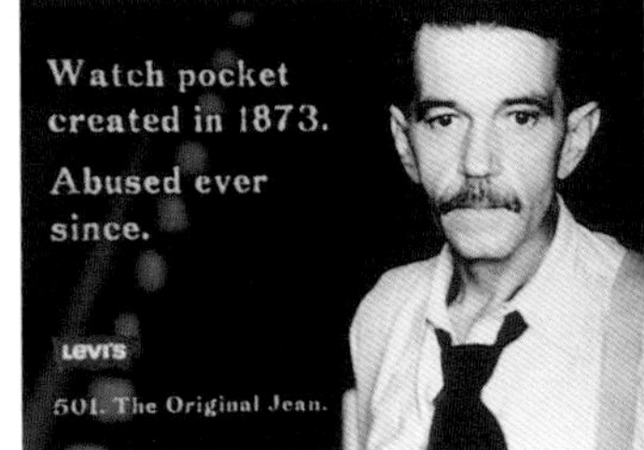

SILVER AWARD
for the Most Outstanding Editing

Director
TONY KAYE

Copywriter
TOM CARTY

Art Director
WALTER CAMPBELL

Producers
YVONNE CHALK
MIRANDA DAVIS

Agency Producer
LINDSAY HUGHES

Editor
PETER GODDARD

Lighting Cameraman
TONY KAYE

Music Composer/Arrangers
JENKINS & RATLEDGE

Sound Designers
WARREN HAMILTON
ROHAN YOUNG
MALCOLM BRISTOW

Production Company
TONY KAYE FILMS

Agency
ABBOTT MEAD VICKERS.BBDO LIMITED

Communications Manager
CRAIG FABIAN

Client
VOLVO CARS UK LIMITED

STUNTMAN

A documentary style commercial featuring the work and philosophies of a stuntman.

He talks about the importance of belief, not only in himself, but in his car; a Volvo 850.

The climax of the film shows the stuntman driving over a bridge. But this is no ordinary bridge, it has no centre, so the car must travel on the supports of the bridge which are only a tyre's width in thickness.

VOLVO. A car you can believe in.

STUNTMAN:
I used to be a stunt kid before I was a stuntman.

I learnt one thing early on, belief is everything.

My interest in cars started on my fourth birthday.

I've loved driving cars ever since.

That's why I like this car.

It's great to drive.

I do stunts people think can't be done.

They think my stunts are crazy.

I've never been afraid of heights, ever.

I guess I have a pretty healthy fear of death.

You can conquer fear through knowledge.

One centimetre this way or that, and it's four hundred miles down.

When I ask it to do something it responds.

Control.

I'm a control freak.

You know some people say I'll believe it when I see it.

I prefer to say you'll see it when you believe it.

They think my stunts are crazy.

PHOTOGRAPHER

A documentary studying the life of war photographer Jana Schneider.

She talks about her working life and the importance of equipment. Eyes, camera, car.

We see Schneider in a dangerous assignment. She drives her Volvo 850 out onto a deserted runway to photograph a suspicious plane. The plane starts to taxi toward take off.

However, Schneider has an amazing camera rig mounted on the side of her car, which is activated by a cable release on the steering wheel. This allows her to get the shots she needs whilst driving close alongside the hurtling plane.

The situation is made even more deadly as cargo bales are being thrown from the plane into her path.

Volvo. A car you can believe in.

PHOTOGRAPHER:
My photography is about life, even when I photograph death.

*When you're stabbed or hit by a bullet it doesn't hurt like you'd imagine.
It burns. It's almost like a fast racing burn.*

My job isn't to judge. My job is to get in and get out.

I do all this, because it's about believing my pictures are the truth.

*I'm basically isolating a milli second in time.
If you're documenting life, a moment only happens once.*

Being in the bush makes me deal with a different rhythm.

What makes me laugh is, you know, is getting through the tiniest keyhole and getting it all when they say it's impossible.

*Your photographs are only as good as the position you get in. I can't get a photograph if I'm not in position.
This car gets me into that position.*

In my business everything's a one shot deal, you get it or you don't.

Equipment is everything. Eyes, camera, car.

SILVER AWARD
for the Most Outstanding Editing

Director
TONY KAYE

Copywriter
TOM CARTY

Art Director
WALTER CAMPBELL

Creative Director
DAVID ABBOTT

Producer
MIRANDA DAVIS

Agency Producer
FRANK LIEBERMAN

Editor
PETER GODDARD

Lighting Cameraman
TONY KAYE

Music Composers/Arrangers
JENKINS & RATLEDGE

Sound Designers
ROHAN YOUNG
MALCOLM BRISTOW

Production Company
TONY KAYE FILMS

Agency
ABBOTT MEAD VICKERS.BBDO LIMITED

Communications Manager
CRAIG FABIAN

Client
VOLVO CARS UK LIMITED

SILVER AWARD
for the Most Outstanding Special Effects

Director
DOUG FOSTER

Copywriter
SIMON LEARMAN

Art Director
BRIAN FRASER

Creative Directors
SIMON LEARMAN
BRIAN FRASER

Producer
MICHELLE JAFFE

Set Designer
ASSHETON GORTON

Animators
GRAHAME ANDREW
BEN HAYDEN
PAUL KAVANAGH
LAURENT HUGUENOIT

Agency Producer
JOHN MONTGOMERY

Editor
TIM BURKE

Lighting Cameramen
DOUG FOSTER
DAVID WYNN JONES

Music Composer/Arranger
JOHN BARRY

Production Company
BLINK PRODUCTIONS

Agency
OGILVY & MATHER

Marketing Director
ROB McNEWIN

Account Director
NEIL QUICK

Client
GUINNESS BREWING GB

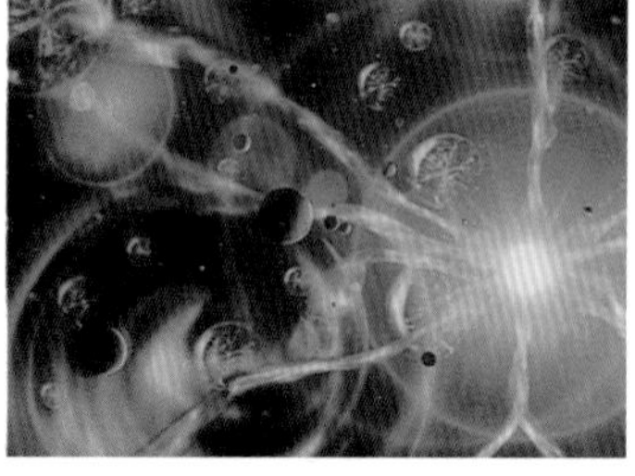

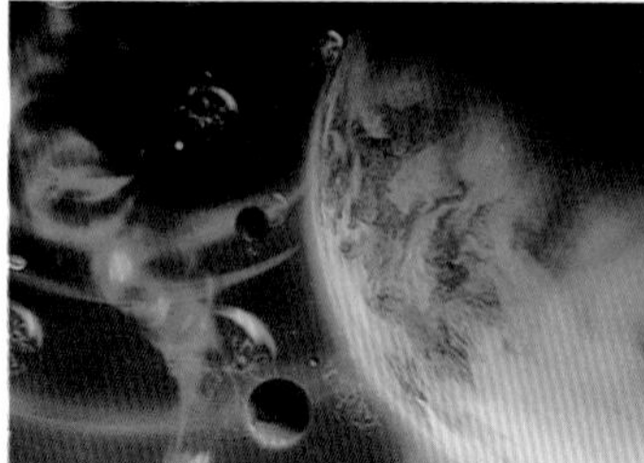

CHAIN

MUSIC:
'We Have All The Time In The World' sung by Louis Armstrong.

In this commercial, we embark on a timeless journey through a glass of swirling Draught Guinness. Everything is rendered in Guinness tones.

We push inside a bubble, cross a strange universe, then descend upon a mysterious planet.

We sweep down towards an enormous tower set against a turbulent sky. The camera favours an open window as we move into a room packed with unusual souvenirs.

We glance past a television set. The familiar face of the Man in Black appears on the screen. He smiles at us, before we make a beeline for the centre piece; a swirling pint of Guinness set on a table.

The camera lingers. We think the journey is over when the chain of events begins to repeat itself. It's as if the journey might go on for some time.

TITLE:
Pure Genius.

SILVER AWARD NOMINATION
for the Most Outstanding Direction

PHOTOGRAPHER

A documentary studying the life of war photographer Jana Schneider.

She talks about her working life and the importance of equipment. Eyes, camera, car.

We see Schneider in a dangerous assignment. She drives her Volvo 850 out onto a deserted runway to photograph a suspicious plane. The plane starts to taxi toward take off.

However, Schneider has an amazing camera rig mounted on the side of her car, which is activated by a cable release on the steering wheel. This allows her to get the shots she needs whilst driving close alongside the hurtling plane.

The situation is made even more deadly as cargo bales are being thrown from the plane into her path.

Volvo. A car you can believe in.

PHOTOGRAPHER:
My photography is about life, even when I photograph death.

*When you're stabbed or hit by a bullet it doesn't hurt like you'd imagine.
It burns. It's almost like a fast racing burn.*

My job isn't to judge. My job is to get in and get out.

I do all this, because it's about believing my pictures are the truth.

*I'm basically isolating a milli second in time.
If you're documenting life, a moment only happens once.*

Being in the bush makes me deal with a different rhythm.

What makes me laugh is, you know, is getting through the tiniest keyhole and getting it all when they say it's impossible.

*Your photographs are only as good as the position you get in. I can't get a photograph if I'm not in position.
This car gets me into that position.*

In my business everything's a one shot deal, you get it or you don't.

Equipment is everything. Eyes, camera, car.

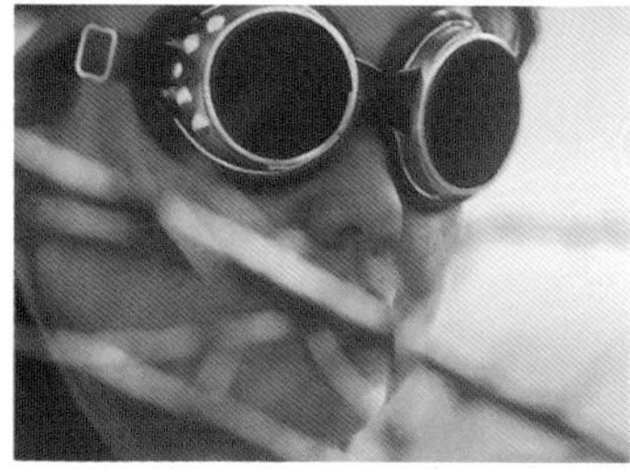

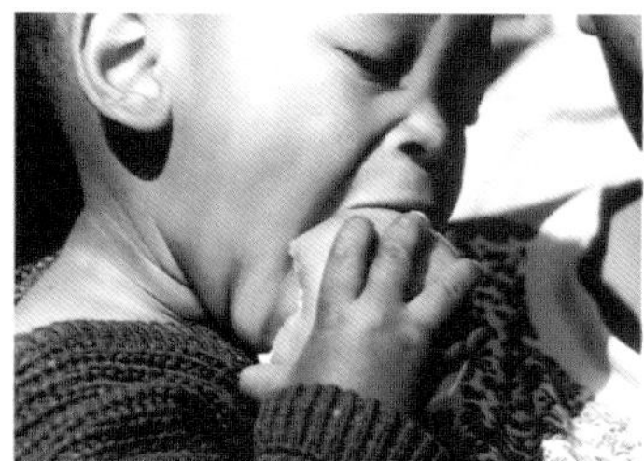

Director
TONY KAYE

Copywriter
TOM CARTY

Art Director
WALTER CAMPBELL

Creative Director
DAVID ABBOTT

Producer
MIRANDA DAVIS

Agency Producer
FRANK LIEBERMAN

Editor
PETER GODDARD

Lighting Cameraman
TONY KAYE

Music Composers/Arrangers
JENKINS & RATLEDGE

Sound Designers
ROHAN YOUNG
MALCOLM BRISTOW

Production Company
TONY KAYE FILMS

Agency
ABBOTT MEAD VICKERS.BBDO LIMITED

Communications Manager
CRAIG FABIAN

Client
VOLVO CARS UK LIMITED

SILVER AWARD NOMINATION
for the Most Outstanding Direction

Director
FRANK BUDGEN

Copywriter
PHIL DEARMAN

Art Director
CHARLES INGE

Creative Director
PAUL WEINBERGER

Producer
PAUL ROTHWELL

Set Designer
TONY NOBLE

Agency Producer
CHARLES CRISP

Editor
SAM SNEADE

Lighting Cameraman
HENRY BRAHAM

Music Composer/Arranger
DAVID MOTION

Production Company
PAUL WEILAND FILM COMPANY

Agency
LOWE HOWARD-SPINK

Marketing Executive
PHIL HARWOOD

Client
VAUXHALL MOTOR COMPANY

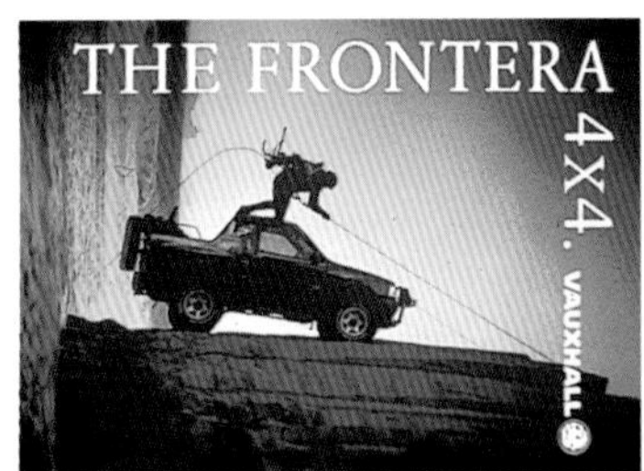

THE WORLD ACCORDING TO FRONTERA

Two African women are walking at what is apparently an impossible 45 degree angle. A Frontera drives past them, seemingly on the level.

Cut to a Frontera travelling through water which is at an odd 45 degree angle. The car passes Filipino fishermen on poles in the water.

Cut to the car in front of a waterfall. However, the water is running at a 45 degree angle.

Cut to Mongolian horsemen leading their horses past a Frontera apparently on the level. The horses are walking in a strange manner. The camera then reveals that they are not on the level but descending a steep slope.

Cut to a Frontera on a 45 degree icy slope. A sleigh full of Eskimo children slides past the car. Oddly, however, the sleigh is going uphill.

SUPER:
See a different world.

Cut to a rock climber abseiling across screen. He passes a Frontera parked on the level. In reality, though, the car is hanging on a cliff-face and he is dropping down vertically.

SUPER:
The Frontera 4x4 and Vauxhall logo.

SILVER AWARD NOMINATION
for the Most Outstanding Direction

STUNTMAN

A documentary style commercial featuring the work and philosophies of a stuntman.

He talks about the importance of belief, not only in himself, but in his car; a Volvo 850.

The climax of the film shows the stuntman driving over a bridge. But this is no ordinary bridge, it has no centre, so the car must travel on the supports of the bridge which are only a tyre's width in thickness.

VOLVO. A car you can believe in.

STUNTMAN:
I used to be a stunt kid before I was a stuntman.

I learnt one thing early on, belief is everything.

My interest in cars started on my fourth birthday.

I've loved driving cars ever since.

That's why I like this car.

It's great to drive.

I do stunts people think can't be done.

They think my stunts are crazy.

I've never been afraid of heights, ever.

I guess I have a pretty healthy fear of death.

You can conquer fear through knowledge.

One centimetre this way or that, and it's four hundred miles down.

When I ask it to do something it responds.

Control.

I'm a control freak.

You know some people say I'll believe it when I see it.

I prefer to say you'll see it when you believe it.

They think my stunts are crazy.

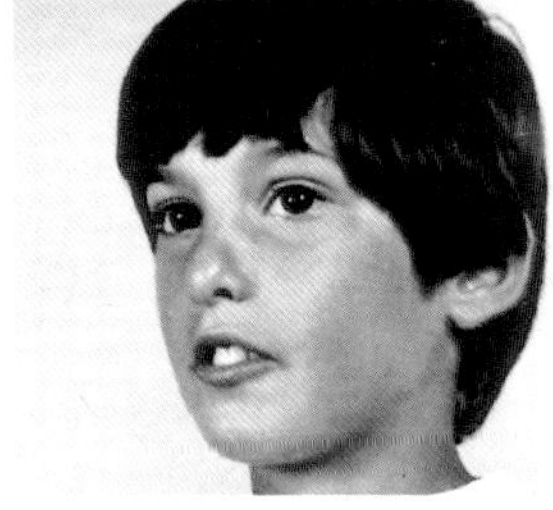

Director
TONY KAYE

Copywriter
TOM CARTY

Art Director
WALTER CAMPBELL

Creative Director
DAVID ABBOTT

Producers
YVONNE CHALK
MIRANDA DAVIS

Agency Producer
LINDSAY HUGHES

Editor
PETER GODDARD

Lighting Cameraman
TONY KAYE

Music Composer/Arrangers
JENKINS & RATLEDGE

Sound Designers
WARREN HAMILTON
ROHAN YOUNG
MALCOLM BRISTOW

Production Company
TONY KAYE FILMS

Agency
ABBOTT MEAD VICKERS.BBDO LIMITED

Communications Manager
CRAIG FABIAN

Client
VOLVO CARS UK LIMITED

SILVER AWARD NOMINATION
for the Most Outstanding Photography

Director
TONY KAYE

Copywriter
REMY NOEL

Art Director
ERIC HOLDEN

Producer
SOPHIE JACOBS

Set Designer
JULIA JASON

Agency Producer
FRANCOISE KORB

Editor
PETER GODDARD

Lighting Cameraman
TONY KAYE

Production Company
1/33 PRODUCTIONS

Agency
BDDP PARIS

Client
TAG HEUER

MIND GAMES

Creatively, the TAG Heuer commercial captures an attitude that is inspirational and fits within a sporting context. As a result, a platform of mental strength is developed, based on the recognition that the difference between success and failure is yourself. Winners create their own imaginary pressure in order to win. TAG Heuer associates itself with such an attitude, presenting it in a prestigous way.

DRUGSTORE (MALE)

MUSIC:
Techno.

We see the view through the windscreen of an old truck heading into town. It's 1930, the American depression.

The truck comes to a stop outside a drugstore, as a train rumbles by.

We don't see the driver, just their view as they enter the store.

The shopkeeper, a woman and child and two girls, all turn to look.

At the counter, the driver asks for something.

The chemist hands over a tin of condoms, with a knowing smile. The driver tucks them into the watch pocket of his jeans and heads out of the door, leaving the woman in a state of shock and embarrassment.

We dissolve to the truck later that evening. It's waiting while a train thunders by. We then see it pulling up outside a white clapboard house.

A girl is waiting on the balcony.

The driver goes to the door. It opens, but it's not the girl. It's the chemist.

We see the driver for the first time, he's a young man in his teens. The chemist puts two and two together. Then, realising what's going on, trys to stop his daughter, but is powerless.

The chemist watches the young man climb into the vehicle and drive off with his daughter.

SUPER:
Watch Pocket Created in 1873.

Abused Ever Since.

Batwing logo.

SUPER:
501. The original Jean.

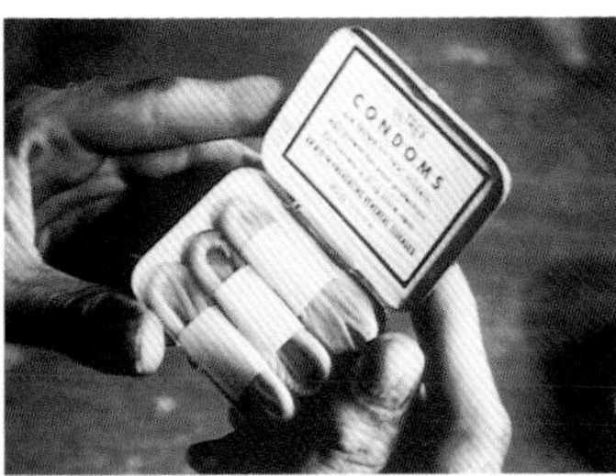

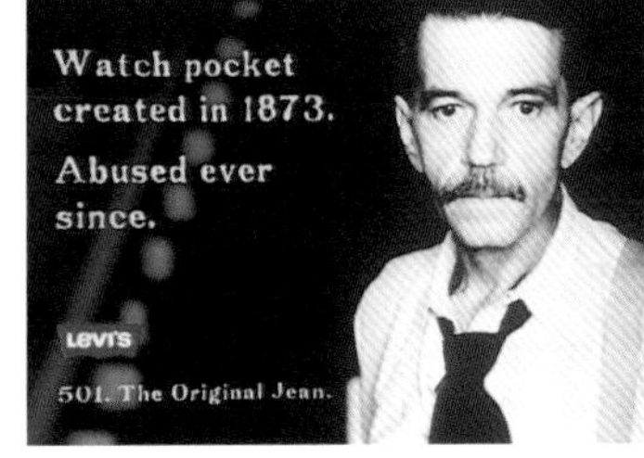

SILVER AWARD NOMINATION
for the Most Outstanding Photography

Director
MICHEL GONDRY

Copywriter
NICK WORTHINGTON

Art Director
JOHN GORSE

Creative Director
JOHN HEGARTY

Producers
TOBY COURLANDER
GEORGES BERMANN
PETE CHAMBERS

Set Designer
ROBBIE FREED

Agency Producer
PHILIPPA CRANE

Editor
RUSSELL ICKE

Lighting Cameraman
TIM MAURICE JONES

Music Composer/Arranger
GEIR JENSSEN

Production Company
PARTIZAN MIDI MINUIT

Agency
BARTLE BOGLE HEGARTY

Senior Marketing Manager
ROBERT HOLLOWAY

Client
LEVI STRAUSS & CO EUROPE SA

SILVER AWARD NOMINATION
for the Most Outstanding Photography

Director
TONY KAYE

Copywriter
TOM CARTY

Art Director
WALTER CAMPBELL

Creative Director
DAVID ABBOTT

Producers
YVONNE CHALK
MIRANDA DAVIS

Agency Producer
LINDSAY HUGHES

Editor
PETER GODDARD

Lighting Cameraman
TONY KAYE

Music Composers/Arrangers
JENKINS & RATLEDGE

Sound Designers
WARREN HAMILTON
ROHAN YOUNG
MALCOLM BRISTOW

Production Company
TONY KAYE FILMS

Agency
ABBOTT MEAD VICKERS.BBDO LIMITED

Communications Manager
CRAIG FABIAN

Client
VOLVO CARS UK LIMITED

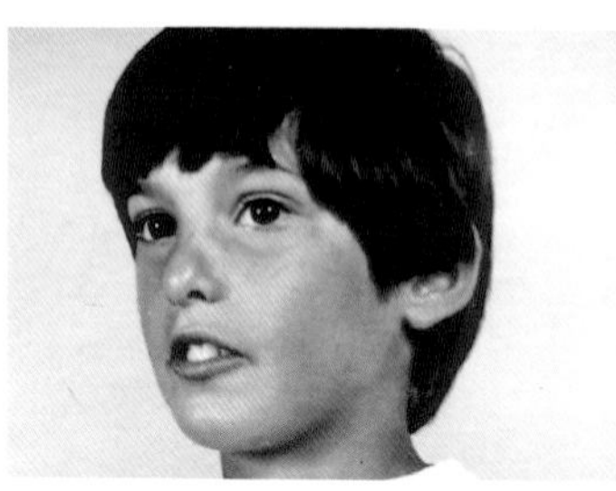

STUNTMAN

A documentary style commercial featuring the work and philosophies of a stuntman.

He talks about the importance of belief, not only in himself, but in his car; a Volvo 850.

The climax of the film shows the stuntman driving over a bridge. But this is no ordinary bridge, it has no centre, so the car must travel on the supports of the bridge which are only a tyre's width in thickness.

VOLVO. A car you can believe in.

STUNTMAN:
I used to be a stunt kid before I was a stuntman.

I learnt one thing early on, belief is everything.

My interest in cars started on my fourth birthday.

I've loved driving cars ever since.

That's why I like this car.

It's great to drive.

I do stunts people think can't be done.

They think my stunts are crazy.

I've never been afraid of heights, ever.

I guess I have a pretty healthy fear of death.

You can conquer fear through knowledge.

One centimetre this way or that, and it's four hundred miles down.

When I ask it to do something it responds.

Control.

I'm a control freak.

You know some people say I'll believe it when I see it.

I prefer to say you'll see it when you believe it.

They think my stunts are crazy.

THE WORLD ACCORDING TO FRONTERA

Two African women are walking at what is apparently an impossible 45 degree angle. A Frontera drives past them, seemingly on the level.

Cut to a Frontera travelling through water which is at an odd 45 degree angle. The car passes Filipino fishermen on poles in the water.

Cut to the car in front of a waterfall. However, the water is running at a 45 degree angle.

Cut to Mongolian horsemen leading their horses past a Frontera apparently on the level. The horses are walking in a strange manner. The camera then reveals that they are not on the level but descending a steep slope.

Cut to a Frontera on a 45 degree icy slope. A sleigh full of Eskimo children slides past the car. Oddly, however, the sleigh is going uphill.

SUPER:
See a different world.

Cut to a rock climber abseiling across screen. He passes a Frontera parked on the level. In reality, though, the car is hanging on a cliff-face and he is dropping down vertically.

SUPER:
The Frontera 4x4 and Vauxhall logo.

SILVER AWARD NOMINATION
for the Most Outstanding Photography

Director
FRANK BUDGEN

Copywriter
PHIL DEARMAN

Art Director
CHARLES INGE

Creative Director
PAUL WEINBERGER

Producer
PAUL ROTHWELL

Set Designer
TONY NOBLE

Agency Producer
CHARLES CRISP

Editor
SAM SNEADE

Lighting Cameraman
HENRY BRAHAM

Music Composer/Arranger
DAVID MOTION

Production Company
PAUL WEILAND FILM COMPANY

Agency
LOWE HOWARD-SPINK

Marketing Executive
PHIL HARWOOD

Client
VAUXHALL MOTOR COMPANY

SILVER AWARD NOMINATION
for the Most Outstanding Photography

Director
TONY KAYE

Copywriter
TOM CARTY

Art Director
WALTER CAMPBELL

Creative Director
DAVID ABBOTT

Producer
MIRANDA DAVIS

Agency Producer
FRANK LIEBERMAN

Editor
PETER GODDARD

Lighting Cameraman
TONY KAYE

Music Composers/Arrangers
JENKINS & RATLEDGE

Sound Designers
ROHAN YOUNG
MALCOLM BRISTOW

Production Company
TONY KAYE FILMS

Agency
ABBOTT MEAD VICKERS.BBDO LIMITED

Communications Manager
CRAIG FABIAN

Client
VOLVO CARS UK LIMITED

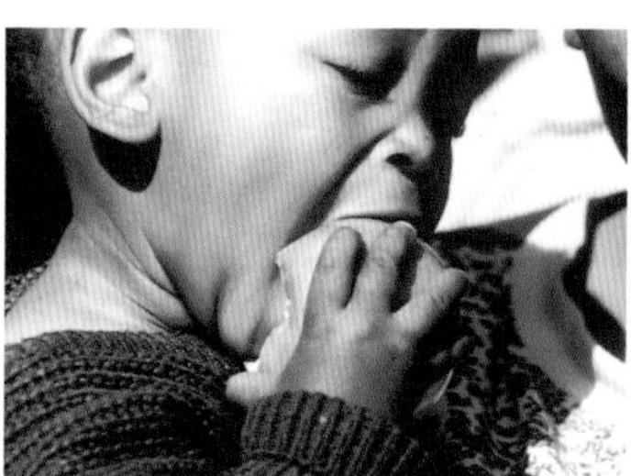

PHOTOGRAPHER

A documentary studying the life of war photographer Jana Schneider.

She talks about her working life and the importance of equipment. Eyes, camera, car.

We see Schneider in a dangerous assignment. She drives her Volvo 850 out onto a deserted runway to photograph a suspicious plane. The plane starts to taxi toward take off.

However, Schneider has an amazing camera rig mounted on the side of her car, which is activated by a cable release on the steering wheel. This allows her to get the shots she needs whilst driving close alongside the hurtling plane.

The situation is made even more deadly as cargo bales are being thrown from the plane into her path.

Volvo. A car you can believe in.

PHOTOGRAPHER:
My photography is about life, even when I photograph death.

*When you're stabbed or hit by a bullet it doesn't hurt like you'd imagine.
It burns. It's almost like a fast racing burn.*

My job isn't to judge. My job is to get in and get out.

I do all this, because it's about believing my pictures are the truth.

*I'm basically isolating a milli second in time.
If you're documenting life, a moment only happens once.*

Being in the bush makes me deal with a different rhythm.

What makes me laugh is, you know, is getting through the tiniest keyhole and getting it all when they say it's impossible.

*Your photographs are only as good as the position you get in. I can't get a photograph if I'm not in position.
This car gets me into that position.*

In my business everything's a one shot deal, you get it or you don't.

Equipment is everything. Eyes, camera, car.

CHAIN

MUSIC:
'We Have All The Time In The World' sung by Louis Armstrong.

In this commercial, we embark on a timeless journey through a glass of swirling Draught Guinness. Everything is rendered in Guinness tones.

We push inside a bubble, cross a strange universe, then descend upon a mysterious planet.

We sweep down towards an enormous tower set against a turbulent sky. The camera favours an open window as we move into a room packed with unusual souvenirs.

We glance past a television set. The familiar face of the Man in Black appears on the screen. He smiles at us, before we make a beeline for the centre piece; a swirling pint of Guinness set on a table.

The camera lingers. We think the journey is over when the chain of events begins to repeat itself. It's as if the journey might go on for some time.

TITLE:
Pure Genius.

SILVER AWARD NOMINATION
for the Most Outstanding Use of Music

Director
DOUG FOSTER

Copywriter
SIMON LEARMAN

Art Director
BRIAN FRASER

Creative Directors
SIMON LEARMAN
BRIAN FRASER

Producer
MICHELLE JAFFE

Set Designer
ASSHETON GORTON

Animators
BEN HAYDEN
PAUL KAVANAGH
LAURENT HUGUENOIT
GRAHAME ANDREW

Agency Producer
JOHN MONTGOMERY

Editor
TIM BURKE

Lighting Cameramen
DOUG FOSTER
DAVID WYNN JONES

Music Composer/Arranger
JOHN BARRY

Production Company
BLINK PRODUCTIONS

Agency
OGILVY & MATHER

Marketing Director
ROB McNEWIN

Account Director
NEIL QUICK

Client
GUINNESS BREWING GB

SILVER AWARD NOMINATION
for the Most Outstanding Use of Music

Copywriter
NICK BELL

Art Director
GREG MARTIN

Creative Director
DAVID ABBOTT

Agency Producer
YVONNE CHALKLEY

Editor
NICK SPENCER

Music Composers/Arrangers
MADNESS

Agency
ABBOTT MEAD VICKERS.BBDO LIMITED

Communications Manager
CRAIG FABIAN

Client
VOLVO CARS UK LIMITED

BECAUSE YOU NEVER KNOW WHO'S ROUND THE BEND.

MADNESS

We see footage taken by police cameras, of people driving dangerously on the road. The track 'Madness' by Madness plays throughout.

Finally, we cut to title:

Volvo. Because you never know who's round the bend.

CHAIN

MUSIC:
'We Have All The Time In The World' sung by Louis Armstrong.

In this commercial, we embark on a timeless journey through a glass of swirling Draught Guinness. Everything is rendered in Guinness tones.

We push inside a bubble, cross a strange universe, then descend upon a mysterious planet.

We sweep down towards an enormous tower set against a turbulent sky. The camera favours an open window as we move into a room packed with unusual souvenirs.

We glance past a television set. The familiar face of the Man in Black appears on the screen. He smiles at us, before we make a beeline for the centre piece; a swirling pint of Guinness set on a table.

The camera lingers. We think the journey is over when the chain of events begins to repeat itself. It's as if the journey might go on for some time.

TITLE:
Pure Genius.

SILVER AWARD NOMINATION
for the Most Outstanding Use of Animation

Director
DOUG FOSTER

Copywriter
SIMON LEARMAN

Art Director
BRIAN FRASER

Creative Directors
SIMON LEARMAN
BRIAN FRASER

Producer
MICHELLE JAFFE

Set Designer
ASSHETON GORTON

Animator
BEN HAYDEN
PAUL KAVANAGH
LAURENT HUGUENOIT
GRAHAME ANDREW

Agency Producer
JOHN MONTGOMERY

Editor
TIM BURKE

Lighting Cameramen
DOUG FOSTER
DAVID WYNN JONES

Music Composer/Arranger
JOHN BARRY

Production Company
BLINK PRODUCTIONS

Agency
OGILVY & MATHER

Marketing Director
ROB McNEWIN

Account Director
NEIL QUICK

Client
GUINNESS BREWING GB

SILVER AWARD NOMINATION
for the Most Outstanding Use of Animation

Director
RICHARD GOLESZOWSKI

Copywriter
GORDON GRAHAM

Art Director
NEIL SULLIVAN

Creative Director
PAUL WEINBERGER

Producer
JULIE LOCKHART

Animator
RICHARD GOLESZOWSKI

Agency Producer
SUE BRALEY

Editors
TAMSIN PARRY
ROD HOWICK

Lighting Cameraman
FRANK PASSINGHAM

Music Composers
FISHER, LASKY, STERN

Arranged By
JOE & CO

Production Company
AARDMAN ANIMATIONS

Agency
LOWE HOWARD-SPINK

Senior Brand Manager
PAUL TROY

Client
WEETABIX LIMITED

PIRATES

MUSIC:
'My Brudda Sylveste'.

Open on one pirate ship sailing on the sea. Cut to crew on board the Marie Celeste looking menacing.

SUNG:
There was a ship all the other pirates feared
Even Black, Blue, Red and Yellow Beard.

We see a cage suspended with black, blue, red and yellow beard in it. They look frightened. The Captain swipes his sword and the cage drops through a trap door in the deck.

SUNG:
Now the Captain was as rotten as they come
And never once thought to write to his mum
On...the...Marie Celeste.

Cut to the rest of the Marie Celeste crew looking menacing as they move across the deck to join the Captain, who is sitting beside a cannon. He fires it and the cannon ball shoots through the legs of a lookout on the rigging of the ship.

PARROT:
What's it got?

SUNG:
It's got the meanest, cruellest pirates ever pressed.
Until the bosun cried from the crow's nest. There's a ship to the west.

Cut to the crow's nest where the bosun spies the Weetabix ship in the distance.

SUNG:
Shiver me timbers, walk the plank. SOS, swim for shore, pieces of eight...
Abandon ship.

Cut to the Captain wearing a rubber ring as he dives overboard.

Mix through to the Weetabix ship where we see the crew sitting around a table eating their Weetabix.

SUNG:
It wasn't magic or ghostly tricks,

PARROT:
What was it?

SUNG:
It was down to a bowl of Weetabix.

Cut to the deserted deck of the Marie Celeste in ghostly mist.

SUNG:
That's why they found no pirates aboard the Marie Celeste.

PACKSHOT & SUPER:
Have You Had Your Weetabix?

FOGGIE BUMMER

VIDEO:
As we hear the gripping radio article we see the words appear on screen. The words help to dramatise the action.

MVO1:
An exercise I often do is write words like 'BOMBAIZE' and 'FORFOUGHEN' and words like that up on the board, you see. And they think things like, a foggie bummer, what's a foggie bummer? Then we'll ask one another, you see, and...

MVO 2:
What is a foggie bummer?

MVO 1:
Foggie bummer means a bumble bee! (laughs)

MVO 2:
I was away to say you could have got us struck off air then!

MVO 1:
Oh no no no! It's not that bad!

CAPTION:
Mix up caption which reads,

Re-discover the power of the spoken word.

Silence.

SFX:
Music ident.

VIDEO:
Mix to end frame. We see the BBC Scotland logo and tuning device which demonstrates where to find the signal.

CAPTION:
UK National Station of the Year.

SILVER AWARD NOMINATION
for the Most Outstanding Use of Animation

Director
JONATHAN BARNBROOK

Copywriter
ADRIAN JEFFERY

Art Director
LINDSEY REDDING

Creative Directors
SIMON SCOTT
ANDREW LINDSAY

Producer
YVONNE CHALK

Agency Producer
TIM MAGUIRE

Editor
JON HOLLIS

Music Composers/Arrangers
LOGORHYTHM

Animators
SARAH LEWIS
JONATHAN BARNBROOK

Production Company
TONY KAYE FILMS

Agency
FAULDS ADVERTISING

Account Group Director
TOM GILL

Head of Presentation
PETER GOURD

Client
BBC RADIO SCOTLAND

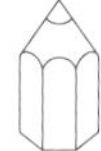

SILVER AWARD NOMINATION
for the Most Outstanding Use of Animation

Directors
SIMON TAYLOR
GRAHAM WOOD

Copywriter
ADRIAN JEFFERY

Art Director
LINDSEY REDDING

Creative Directors
SIMON SCOTT
ANDREW LINDSAY

Producer
HELEN LANGRIDGE

Agency Producer
TIM MAGUIRE

Editor
JON HOLLIS

Music Composers/Arrangers
LOGORHYTHM

Production Company
HELEN LANGRIDGE ASSOCIATES

Agency
FAULDS ADVERTISING

Account Group Director
TOM GILL

Head of Presentation
PETER GOURD

Client
BBC RADIO SCOTLAND

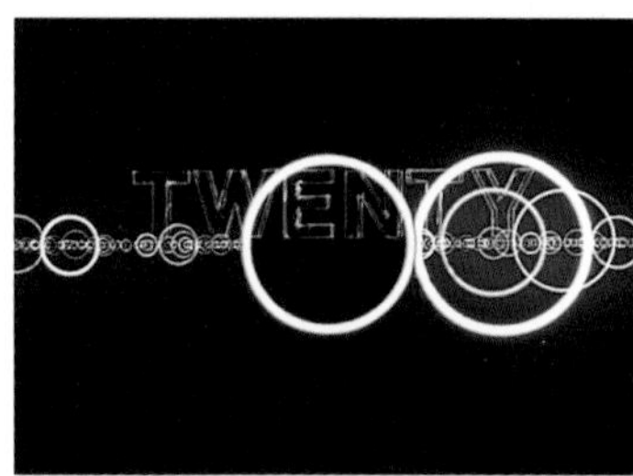

GRAFFITI

As we hear the gripping radio article, we see the words appear on the screen. The words help to dramatise the action.

We hear a snippet from a BBC Scotland programme.

MVO:
If I can explain some of this graffiti that's in the ceiling of the car here. We got psycho and Demon. We got psycho from rolling 60's cripps. We got...er Junior from Ghetto boys...Um, as I'm looking, I'm starting to feel these real kind of er, emotions choking up in me because there's probably about 20 or 25 different gang members that are carved in here, Babyface here, and I'd say about a dozen of them, almost half of them are dead.

Silence.

Mix up caption which reads:

Re-discover the power of the spoken word.

Mix to end frame.

SFX:
Music ident.

We see the BBC Scotland logo and tuning device which demonstrates where to find the signal.

CAPTION:
UK National Station of the Year.

THE WALL

Open on a shot of stormy Paris. Thunder crashing in background.

A wall featuring Eric Cantona is seen.

We see a ball flying past the Eiffel Tower.

Close up of the Cantona wall. The ball flies into the picture. He beats an opponent and kicks the ball, destroying a part of the wall with his shoe.

We hear the noise of the ball flying with rocket like speed, the crowd cheering, the noise of the power kick and bricks smashing.

The ball flies past the Brandenberg gate to a wall in Berlin featuring Michael Schulz.

Schulz takes the ball on his chest, dribbles for a couple of steps and passes the ball, destroying part of the wall.

The ball flies to a city in Italy, upsetting some pigeons, where Maldini comes to life on his wall and heads the ball back to London. Bricks fly from the wall.

Ian Wright kicks the ball from his wall, past Tower Bridge, removing some bricks with his kick.

The ball flies across the ocean to Brazil and into Rio de Janeiro where Romario and Bebeto are seen on two side by side walls. Romario heads the ball to Bebeto, who kicks it to Mexico where Campos dives across three buildings to catch it.

Smashing bricks, kicking sound and moving ball noise continue.

Campos dislodges a Nike logo with his arms on the third building. The sign swings loose from one corner.

Sound of broken glass as he hits logo.

Sound of sign swinging.

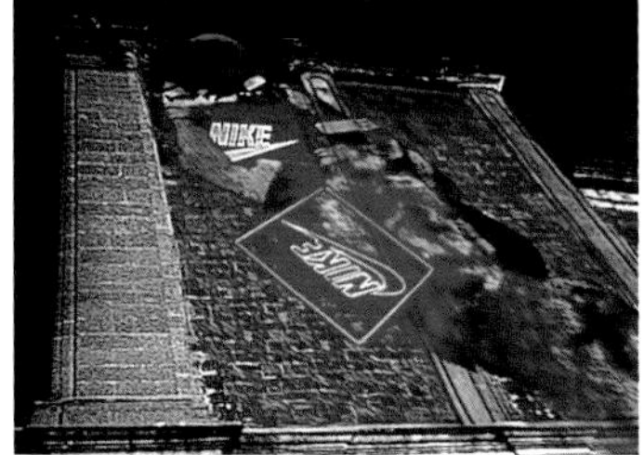

SILVER AWARD NOMINATION
for the Most Outstanding Special Effects

Director
JOE PYTKA

Copywriter
BOB MOORE

Art Director
WARREN EAKINS

Creative Directors
BOB MOORE
WARREN EAKINS

Producer
LILLY WEINGARTEN

Agency Producers
DEREK RUDDY
JANE BRIMBLECOMBE

Editor
ROB WATZKE

Production Company
PYTKA

Agency
WIEDEN & KENNEDY, AMSTERDAM

Client
NIKE INTERNATIONAL

Direction

Director
JOE PYTKA

Copywriter
BOB MOORE

Art Director
WARREN EAKINS

Creative Directors
BOB MOORE
WARREN EAKINS

Producer
LILLY WEINGARTEN

Agency Producers
DEREK RUDDY
JANE BRIMBLECOMBE

Editor
ROB WATZKE

Production Company
PYTKA

Agency
WIEDEN & KENNEDY, AMSTERDAM

Client
NIKE INTERNATIONAL

THE WALL

Open on a shot of stormy Paris. Thunder crashing in background.

A wall featuring Eric Cantona is seen.

We see a ball flying past the Eiffel Tower.

Close up of the Cantona wall. The ball flies into the picture. He beats an opponent and kicks the ball, destroying a part of the wall with his shoe.

We hear the noise of the ball flying with rocket like speed, the crowd cheering, the noise of the power kick and bricks smashing.

The ball flies past the Brandenberg gate to a wall in Berlin featuring Michael Schulz.

Schulz takes the ball on his chest, dribbles for a couple of steps and passes the ball, destroying part of the wall.

The ball flies to a city in Italy, upsetting some pigeons, where Maldini comes to life on his wall and heads the ball back to London. Bricks fly from the wall.

Ian Wright kicks the ball from his wall, past Tower Bridge, removing some bricks with his kick.

The ball flies across the ocean to Brazil and into Rio de Janeiro where Romario and Bebeto are seen on two side by side walls. Romario heads the ball to Bebeto, who kicks it to Mexico where Campos dives across three buildings to catch it.

Smashing bricks, kicking sound and moving ball noise continue.

Campos dislodges a Nike logo with his arms on the third building. The sign swings loose from one corner.

Sound of broken glass as he hits logo.

Sound of sign swinging.

DROP

At Volkswagen, we have learned to construct cars, of which qualities have become legendary.

Nowadays, you need a much smaller car. So we have conceived this car in the same frame of mind.

ABS and airbag for safety, 5 doors and a large interior space for comfort, exceptional construction and finish for reliability.

It is a new Volkswagen, a truc Volkswagen, but smaller.

New Polo the concentrate of Volkswagen.

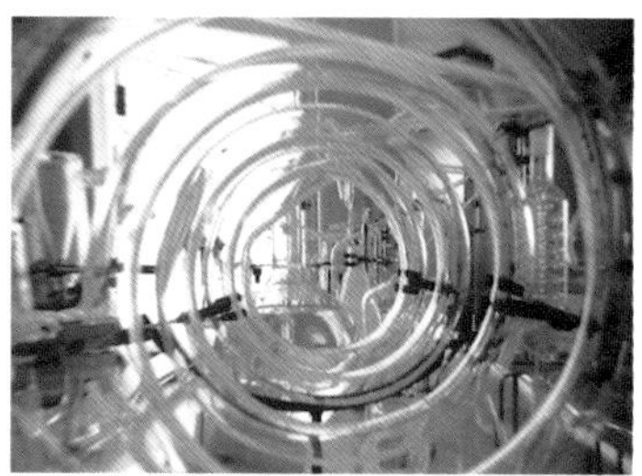

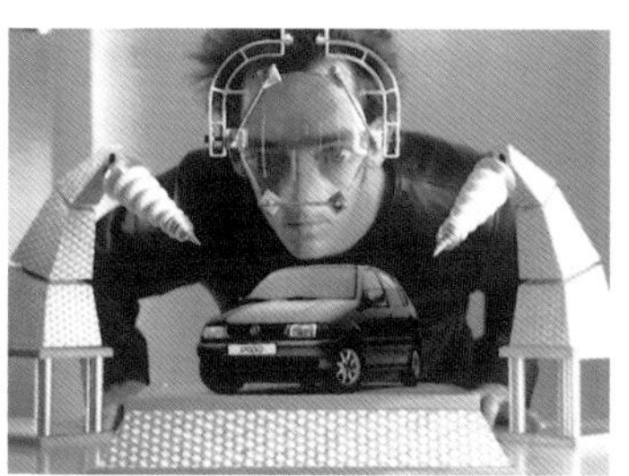

Direction

Director
TARSEM

Copywriter
BERNARD NAVILLE

Art Director
SOPHIE DUPONCHEL

Producer
SIMON TURTLE

Set Designer
LEO CLARKE

Agency Producer
PHILLIPPE GARNIER

Editor
GEOFF PAYNE

Lighting Cameraman
PAUL LAUFER

Production Companies
SPOTO FILM
SERVICES
PLANETE SPOTS
PARIS

Agency
DDB PARIS

Client
VW, FRANCE

Direction

Directors
VAUGHAN & ANTHEA

Copywriter
DEREK APPS

Art Director
VINCE SQUIBB

Creative Director
PAUL WEINBERGER

Producer
ADAM SAWARD

Set Designer
ROBIN BROWN

Agency Producer
CHARLES CRISP

Editor
RICK RUSSELL

Lighting Cameraman
STEVE CHIVERS

Special Effects Supervisor
MARK NELMES

Music Composer/Arranger
RONIN

Production Company
THE LEWIN & WATSON COMPANY

Agency
LOWE HOWARD-SPINK

Marketing Executive
PAUL DAVEY

Client
PIERRE SMIRNOFF COMPANY

REFLECTION

A photographer sees a darker side to a Russian wedding when he looks through a Smirnoff bottle.

He sees the demure bride turn into a snarling vampire.

Again the photographer looks at a woman in a beaded dress. The fat beads turn into crawling beetles.

He turns to see a meek waitress being bullied by a guest. But through the bottle she has her revenge as she plunges his head into the soup.

A sailor ogles a passing girl and turns into a leering vulture.

The bride shows off her sparkling wedding ring to a guest. But through the bottle instead of admiring it, the guest is lustfully sucking her finger.

Our hero sees a moustached man clapping along to the music. The bottle turns him into a giant walrus clapping its flippers.

A line of dancers pass by. Behind the bottle we see them in their underwear. The last little man in line is in fact wearing women's.

The bride throws her bouquet to three demure bridesmaids who, when seen behind the bottle, are having a snarling tussle for the prize.

Our man finally sees his reflection in a waiter's silver tray. Overcome by curiosity, he takes a look at himself through the bottle, only to see a frightening satyr staring back.

GOOD SAMARITAN

A passer-by comes to the aid of various characters, some waggoners beside a broken-down cart, a farmer with a heavily pregnant cow, an old man stranded by a fast-flowing river.

Their paths cross a second time in the local bar, where they offer him a beer. But when he orders a pint of 'reassuringly expensive' Stella Artois, they pretend not to know him.

Direction

Directors
VAUGHAN & ANTHEA

Copywriter
ALISTAIR WOOD

Art Director
TOM NOTMAN

Creative Director
PAUL WEINBERGER

Producer
ADAM SAWARD

Set Designer
ROBIN BROWN

Agency Producer
SUE BRALEY

Editor
RICK RUSSELL

Lighting Cameraman
PASCAL RABAUD

Music Composer/Arranger
JEAN-CLAUDE PETIT

Production Company
THE LEWIN AND WATSON COMPANY

Agency
LOWE HOWARD-SPINK

Marketing Executive
SUSAN PURCELL

Client
THE WHITBREAD BEER COMPANY

Direction

Director
PAUL MEIJER

Copywriter
KEITH BICKEL

Art Director
CARLOS ANUNCIBAY

Producer
ROBERT CAMPBELL

Agency Producer
TIM BERRIMAN

Editor
MARTYN GOULD

Lighting Cameraman
IVAN BIRD

Production Company
SPOTS FILM SERVICES

Agency
SAATCHI & SAATCHI

Marketing Executive
DEREK DEAR

Client
BRITISH AIRWAYS

BRITISH AIRWAYS WORLD OFFERS

This commercial is shot from camera point of view.

Open on a man waking up in the morning.

SFX:
Beep, beep, beep, of a digital alarm clock.

His hand reaches out and switches off the alarm. He throws an arm across the bed to reach for his wife. She's not there.

He walks down the stairs and calls out.

MAN:
Carol!

He looks in the kitchen but she's not there.

MAN:
Carol?

He passes the goldfish tank and notices the fish isn't there.

The man leaves the house, climbs into his car and drives off.

He drives through deserted streets, not a car or person in sight. He looks at his watch, it's 8.15am, rush hour.

He runs into a railway station. It's completely deserted.

He looks in a cafe. There's no one there.

He runs through more deserted streets desperately trying to find any sign of life. He runs up a flight of stairs and emerges into a large open plan office. Again, there's nobody there at all, only his reflection in a mirror.

In desperation he runs into the middle of a deserted street and screams.

MAN:
Where Is Everbody?!

SFX:
Festive music.

TITLES:
Rio from £299 return.

LA from £199 return.

Rome from £99 return.

Paris from £59 return.

New York from £168 return.

British Airways World Offers.

BOTTLE

This documentary charts an artist's life-long search for 'Strong Yet Light' art, from his early feather paintings through to illuminated hammers, polystyrene rooms, balloon animals and early film work, culminating in his classic short 'Bottle', a simple depiction of a bottle of 'Strong Yet Light' Stella Dry.

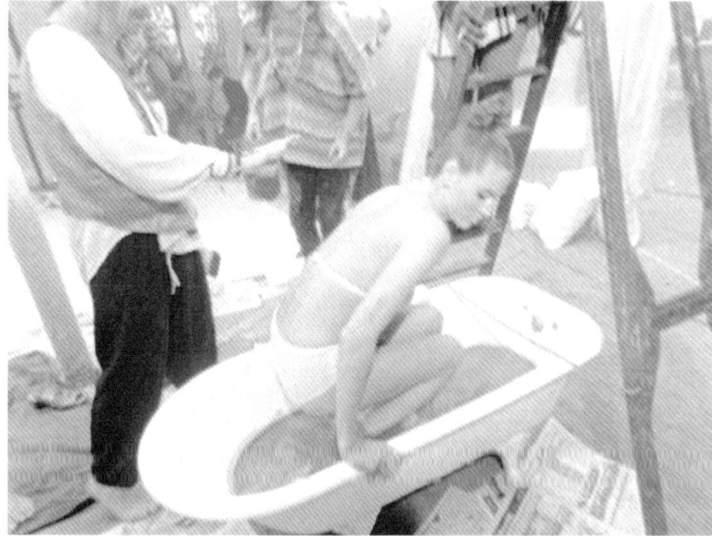

Direction

Director
ALEX PROYAS

Copywriter
ALISTAIR WOOD

Art Director
TOM NOTMAN

Creative Director
PAUL WEINBERGER

Producer
MARGOT FITZPATRICK

Set Designer
MIKE BUCHANAN

Agency Producer
SARAH HORRY

Editor
IAN WEIL

Lighting Cameraman
DAREK WOLSKI

Music Composers/Arrangers
DE WOLFE/JOE & CO

Production Company
PROPAGANDA FILMS

Agency
LOWE HOWARD-SPINK

Marketing Executive
SUSAN PURCELL

Client
THE WHITBREAD BEER COMPANY

Direction

Director
TONY KAYE

Copywriter
JONATHAN KNEEBONE

Art Director
DAVE JOHNSON

Creative Director
STEVE HENRY

Producer
MATTHEW BROWN

Set Designer
JULIA JASON

Agency Producer
JENNY SELBY

Editor
PETER GODDARD

Lighting Cameraman
TONY KAYE

Music Composer/Arranger
ROD SYERS

Production Company
TONY KAYE FILMS

Agency
HOWELL HENRY CHALDECOTT LURY & PARTNERS

Marketing Director
JAN SMITH

Client
MAZDA CARS UK LIMITED

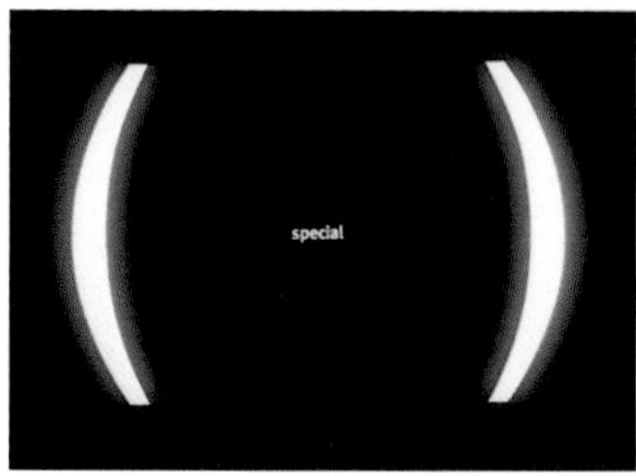

SOUND DOWN

We open on a Mazda Xedos 6, shot in a studio - overall the look is very minimal, but beautiful, and the feel seductive.

V/O:
With a car this special we don't need to shout. If you'd like to know more, please turn up your volume now.

There follows a sequence of about 35 simple and evocative close-up images of detail after detail of the Xedos 6.

The sound level for this section is made incredibly low - so people can choose to turn the volume up if they wish to hear the sound more clearly. If they do turn the sound up, they can listen to information about the effort or thought that has gone into the design of each particular detail that is shown.

The montage of sound is summarised at the end with a voice which says:

'The Mazda Xedos 6. Every detail matters.'

We end on the Mazda logo and the telephone number 0345 48 48 48 then a final super, reading '(special)'.

Finally, if you have the volume up you hear the voice-over say:

'Please return your volume to its normal level.'

WHITE

We open on a stationary white Mazda 323 shot against a white metal backdrop in a studio. The 323 is shot from fresh and seductive angles.

V/O & TITLE:
With a car as special as the new Mazda 323, we don't need to shout. If you'd like to know more, please video this commercial.

Halfway through the commercial, the car cuts out of frame and is replaced with three information panels. When seen at normal speed, this is easily noticeable to the eye but not readable. However, when viewed on video, the viewer can freeze the frame and read the information clearly.

After about eighteen frames, the panel is [illegible] and the car returns to the precise position as before in frame.

Finally, the commercial ends with the Mazda logo, the telephone number 0345 48 48 48 and an endline reading: '(special)'.

An additional super now appears reading:

To win a car this special press rewind and search. This allows the viewer to access a message instructing them to search for the hidden Japanese password, Kansei.

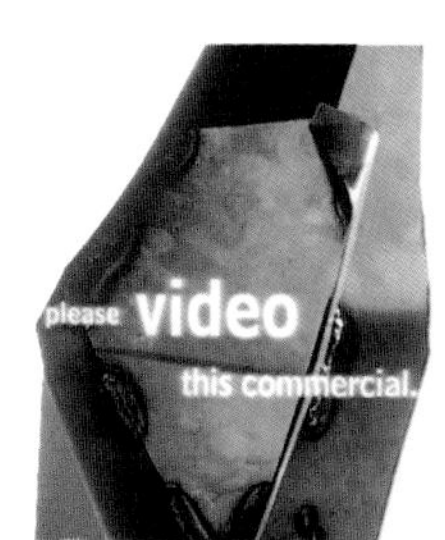

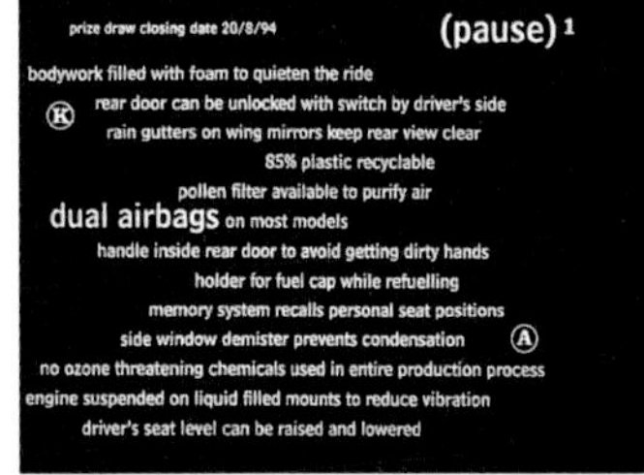

Direction

Director
TONY KAYE

Copywriter
JONATHAN KNEEBONE

Art Director
DAVE JOHNSON

Creative Director
STEVE HENRY

Producer
MATTHEW BROWN

Set Designer
JULIA JASON

Agency Producer
JENNY SELBY

Editor
PETER GODDARD

Lighting Cameraman
TONY KAYE

Music Composer/Arranger
EVELYN GLENNIE

Production Company
TONY KAYE FILMS

Agency
HOWELL HENRY CHALDECOTT LURY & PARTNERS

Marketing Director
JAN SMITH

Client
MAZDA CARS UK LIMITED

Direction

Director
FRANK BUDGEN

Copywriter
LARRY BARKER

Art Director
ROONEY
CARRUTHERS

Creative Directors
LARRY BARKER
ROONEY
CARRUTHERS

Producer
PAUL ROTHWELL

Set Designer
LAURFN LECLERE

Agency Producer
BRENDA DYKES

Editor
SAM SNEADE

Lighting Cameraman
ALEXANDER WITT

Music Composer/Arranger
PHILIP GLASS

Production Company
PAUL WEILAND FILM COMPANY

Agency
WCRS

Marketing Director
LISA GERNON

Client
HUTCHISON TELECOM

LAUNCH

SFX:
Orange theme.

Out of black fades up a baby floating in water. A series of numbers, written and numerical, appear on screen in time with the music. We dissolve through to a close-up of a baby. The word 'Cry' appears.

We see more numbers appearing and disappearing on screen superimposed over the baby's mouth. The word 'Laugh' appears.

We fade up a close-up of a child's ear, again superimposed numbers appear and disappear. The word 'Listen' appears.

CHILD V/O:
In the future you won't change what you say...just how you say it.

We see a close-up of a child's mouth, again in the midst of superimposed numbers. The word 'Talk' appears.

We see two boys running over fields. We dissolve to see them standing talking on a tin can walkie-talkie.

CHILD V/O:
In the future we'll think it strange that voices ever travelled down wires.

We see various shots of telephone posts and telegraph wires being cut.

CHILD V/O:
In the future no-one will be tied down.

Cut to a child sitting on a rock looking out over a valley. We pull back to reveal the scale of the vista.

CHILD V/O:
And in the future the skies will be clearer because the world of communications will be wire-free.

We cut to see the sun setting over office buildings, fields and office windows. The windows are bright orange. This changes into the orange logo.

CHILD V/O:
The future's Bright. The future's Orange.

FIFA

We open on a series of graphic shots, illustrating the fairness and evenness of the game of football.

MVO:
Soccer. A game played on a level pitch between two equal sides of eleven players, each in possession of one left foot and one right.

Each team defends their half. The game is divided into two 45 minute periods, the object to project the ball into your opponent's goal, as many times as you can.

Both teams wear FIFA approved boots, which now include an entirely new boot, the Predator by Adidas.

We see that one team is wearing [illegible] boots and, as we cut to a series of action shots, we see how this gives them an obvious advantage over their opponents.

TITLES:
More Control.

More Swerve.

More Power.

Cut to a despondent goalkeeper dropping to his knees, then dissolve to a shot of the FIFA headquarters.

MVO:
All complaints should be made to FIFA, PO Box 85, Zurich, Switzerland. Thank you.

Cut to close up of the boot screaming towards camera. It turns and comes to rest.

TITLES:
100% Legal. 0% Fair.

Adidas. Earn Them.

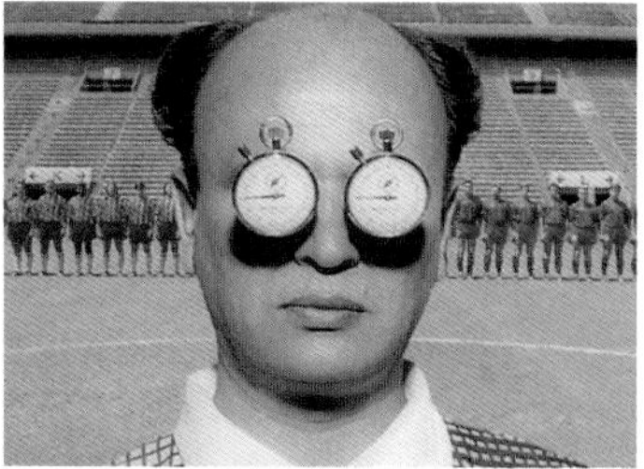

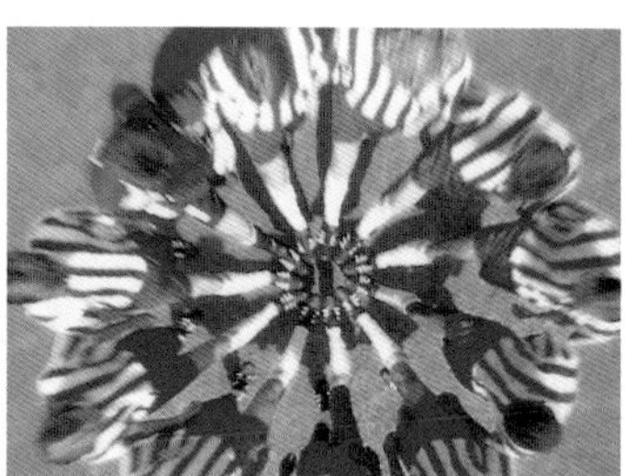

Direction

Director
MEHDI NOROWZIAN

Copywriter
WILL FARQUHAR

Art Director
IAN DUCKER

Creative Director
TIM DELANEY

Producer
DESLEY GREGORY

Agency Producer
JANE JOYCE

Lighting Cameraman
EDUARDO SERRA

Sound Designer
ROSS GREGORY

Production Company
REDWING FILM COMPANY

Agency
LEAGAS DELANEY

Head of Marketing and Communications
TOM HARRINGTON

Client
ADIDAS AG

Direction

Director
JEFF STARK

Copywriter
NICK WORTHINGTON

Art Director
JOHN GORSE

Creative Director
JOHN HEGARTY

Producer
CHRIS STEVENSON

Agency Producer
GEOFF STICKLER

Editor
JOHN SMITH

Lighting Cameraman
ADRIAN BIDDLE

Music Composer/Arrangers
SIMON ELMS
COLIN SMITH

Production Company
STARK FILMS

Agency
BARTLE BOGLE HEGARTY

Brand Manager
TIM DRAKE

Client
THE WHITBREAD BEER COMPANY

SUNCREAM

This commercial is a parody of a glamorous suncream commercial shot on an idyllic beach, set to the song 'Stay just a little bit longer.'

We see a series of beautiful people lounging on the beach in the midday sun.

MVO:
Now there's a cream that helps you stay in the sun just a little bit longer.

We pan up the body of a beautiful woman. She has a blob of cream on her nose. As we watch, she lifts a pint of beer to her lips and takes a noisy slurp.

WOMAN:
By 'eck, I could stay here as long as you like, chuck.

From her point of view, we see a bronzed man with an ice bucket, silhouetted against a pure blue sky.

MAN:
'Ere Vera, fancy a top up?'

The pure blue is not sky, it's the side of a chip van, which pulls away to reveal they are in fact in Blackpool.

WOMAN:
Not 'alf and give us another rub down with that chip fat.

Cut to Blackpool Tower, as a small plane towing a yellow banner, flies into frame with the words: Boddingtons. The Cream of Manchester printed on it.

V/O:
Boddingtons. The Cream of Manchester.

BIRDS

OLD MAN:
I have a lovely marriage probably because I have a wife who's obsessed with birds.

OLD WOMAN:
I can't stand these things that cost a thousand dollars.

OLD MAN:
What is money?

OLD WOMAN:
Why does he think I love them so much when I hate them?

OLD WOMAN:
Especially this eagle.

Now how can that be an eagle when it looks like a vulture and it's a turkey?

OLD MAN:
And if she likes the eagle, I like the eagle.

OLD WOMAN:
You have to dust them, clean them, wash them.

All that money we could have saved.

All that money wasted.

Birds! Birds!

Flying!

Bang!

I mean, really, where does the money go? It just flies away.

OLD MAN:
I love to see them strut.

OLD WOMAN:
He thinks he's doing me a great big favour.

OLD MAN:
I would have to say that the birds have saved my marriage - I'm no dummy.

Direction

Director
TONY KAYE

Art Director
KIM BOWEN

Creative Director
JEFF WEISS

Producer
EILEEN TERRY

Agency Producer
NATHALIE ROSS

Editor
BOB JENKINS

Lighting Cameraman
TONY KAYE

Production Company
TONY KAYE FILMS

Client
START, INC

Direction

Director
DANIEL BARBER

Copywriters
LARRY BARKER
LEON JAUME

Art Director
ROONEY
CARRUTHERS

Creative Directors
ROONEY
CARRUTHERS
LARRY BARKER

Producer
KAREN
CUNNINGHAM

Set Designer
JOHNA BUTLER

Agency Producer
SIMON WELLS

Editor
BRIAN DYKE

Lighting Cameraman
STEVE CHIVERS

Music Composer/Arranger
PHILIP GLASS

Production Company
ROSE HACKNEY
BARBER
PRODUCTIONS

Agency
WCRS

Head of Marketing Services
SEAN GARDENER

Client
HUTCHISON
TELECOM

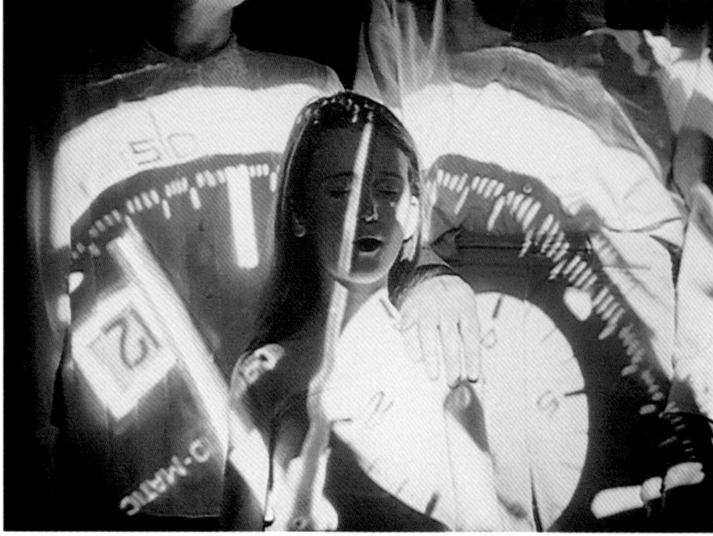

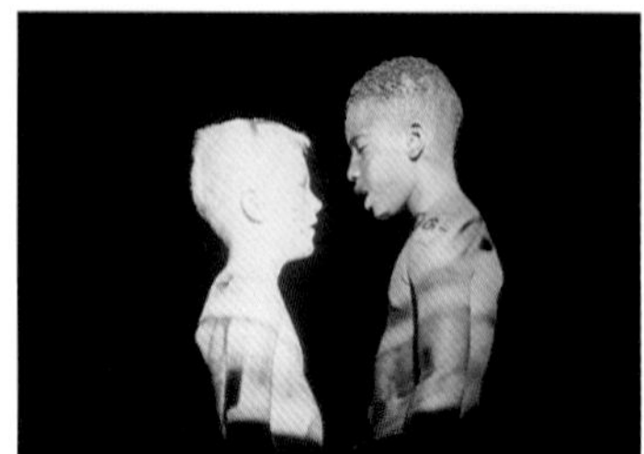

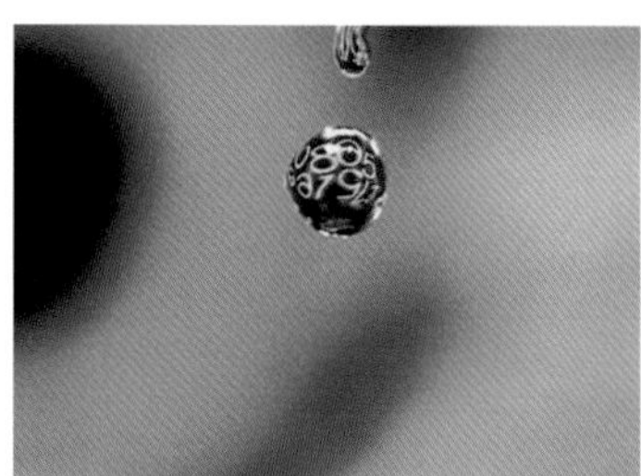

PER SECOND

SFX:
Orange theme.

The commercial begins with extremely tight close-ups of a stopwatch. Various shots of people are superimposed over the watch face. Their lips are moving in time to the counting of numbers in the music.

MVO:
Orange think it unfair that you should pay for time you haven't used.

We see more images superimposed over the watch face. We now see a single droplet of water with numbers reflected on its surface.

MVO:
And in the future maybe everyone will think that way.

We watch as the droplet falls and splashes into a pool of water.

MVO:
Until then, Orange is the only mobile network to charge you one second at a time...

SUPER:
1.

SFX:
Music stops - silence except for fast ticking.

Dissolve to extreme close-up of the stopwatch. The hand on the stopwatch ticks on alone.

Cut to an extreme close-up of a woman's eye. It blinks and dissolves through to the face of a clock.

MVO:
...Instead of rounding up to the next minute or half minute.

SFX:
Music re-starts.

We see a close-up of a child's face. She smiles. We cut to endframe and logo.

MVO:
The Future's Bright. The Future's Orange.

ROUNDEYE

SFX:
Music.

Over lyrical footage of a Korean family, we hear excerpts from a piece about prejudice that merge into each other.

BRODCASTER'S MVO:
It is the nature of prejudice that judgements are made about issues, people, indeed entire races without supporting evidence...

...Cultures that the West is somehow superior in matters to do with art, commerce, and [illegible]

...It is based on ignorance but that does not diminish its power to shape individual...

...Real experience of other cultures and the natural fear of the unknown, which makes preconceived ideas so comfortable for those who hold them...

...Confronting prejudice does not necessarily mean that it will recede. Although to leave it unchallenged simply allows opinions to harden...

...Sets in motion a complex series of barriers which prevent the real facts from emerging and being recognised...

...Entire races without supporting evidence does not diminish its power to shape individual or collective opinion...

...When the truth is established beyond doubt, it is possible that even a deeply held prejudice can be removed by knowledge and experience...

TITLE:
What is stopping you from buying a car from Korea?

TITLE:
Prejudice?

TITLE:
Hyundai.

Made in Korea.

Direction

Directors
ANDREW DOUGLAS
STUART DOUGLAS

Copywriter
TIM DELANEY

Art Director
MARTIN GALTON

Creative Director
TIM DELANEY

Producer
CLARE MITCHELL

Agency Producer
NICKY GREGOROWSKI

Editor
TIM THORNTON-ALLEN

Lighting Cameraman
ANDREW DOUGLAS
STUART DOUGLAS

Music Composer/Arranger
KEVIN SARGENT

Production Company
DELANEY & HART

Agency
LEAGAS DELANEY

Product Manager
GARY ELLIOTT

Client
HYUNDAI CAR UK LIMITED

Direction

Director
KEVIN MOLONY

Copywriter
ALEX GRIEVE

Art Director
ADRIAN ROSSI

Creative Director
RICHARD MYERS

Producers
RONNIE WEST
SOPHIE HUMPHRIES

Agency Producer
ARNOLD PEARCE

Editor
PIERS DOUGLAS

Lighting Cameraman
WIT DABAL

Music Composer/Arranger
BARRY KIRSCH

Production Company
TTO

Agency
SAATCHI & SAATCHI

Marketing Executive
OLIVER MANN

Marketing Director
GRAHAM SMITH

Client
TOYOTA UK

DON'T FORGET YOUR TROUSERS

The opening sequence outlines the basic theme of the commercial. It shows a series of nostalgic images from the 1950's. 'If you remember these events...' the voice-over says, 'then forget about buying a Toyota Rav 4, you're too old, you're the kind of person who wears driving gloves, buys his and hers matching coats and enjoys tearfully reminiscing about the wireless and Pearl Carr & Teddy Johnson. The Rav 4 is not for you.'

MUSIC:
Dvorak's New World Symphony.

MVO:
Remember that?
This?
And this?
Feel nostalgic? You do?
Oh dear, it's time to make the cocoa.

MUSIC:
Pulp fiction.

MVO:
I said it's time to make the cocoa. Because, we'll be honest, this will not interest you. We know what your cup of tea is.
It's a cup of tea.
And allotments.
Driving gloves.
His and hers matching coats.
And rambling.
Things confuse you.
Music. Fashion. Technology.
We'd like to explain. Honest.
But what we're selling today...is this. The Toyota Rav 4. A 4-wheel drive that handles like a GTI.Look at the press reviews. That's enough. You're never going to drive a Rav 4 and if you are, you shouldn't be.
Remember when you saw your parents dancing. Embarrassing.
The Rav 4 is a 2 litre, 0 to 60 in 9.9 seconds off-roader. What are you going to do off-road?
Go surfing. Forget it. That shouldn't be hard.
Making you angry?
Don't watch. Switch channels.
Our intention is not to antagonise, annoy, upset.
O.K. We lied. It is.
We just want you to accept the Rav 4 is not for you.
You may now return to tearful reminiscing. About the wireless. Peasoupers. The Boer war.

MUSIC:
In style of Carr/Johnson.

MVO:
And Pearl Carr and Teddy Johnson.
Thank you.
The Rav 4.
The car in front of you with the knitted steering wheel is a Toyota.

WASTE

This ad finds Denis Leary behind a bar. He picks up A.N. OTHER bottle and starts to read from the label as he passes about. He dumps the bottle in a huge bin. He picks up a second bottle, reads then dumps it. Another and another as the cutting gathers more pace. Denis trashes bottle after bottle.

DENIS LEARY:
Deep in the American south for over 200 years they've started each and every day with a traditional breakfast. Eggs over easy. A rasher of crispy fried bacon and a bowl of hot hominy grits. Grits. Do you know what grits are? Well they're a tough, chewy mass of stuff that tastes of boiled over cat litter and it's just like rocks in my mouth. I hate grits and guess what, they're in this beer. Why? I don't know why. Maybe for the same reason that there's caramel in this beer. Caramel. If I want candy I buy a candy bar. Guess what? Seaweed. SEA WEED. That's weed that comes from the sea which is where fish go to the toilet. It's a free country, but personally I don't want fish urine in my beer. And of course, rice? RICE? Next time you go to a wedding try throwing one of these at the bride. Or one of these, or one of these, or...Ascorbic acid or citric acid, sorghum, sugar, fructose, glucose, sucrose, sulphur dioxide, potassium metabisulphate, propylene glyco agnate and bat faeces. I made up the last one but you never know.

Denis picks up a bottle of Holsten Pils and reads from the label. The bar is now clear of the other bottles except for one which rolls along the shelf behind and then falls off into the big bin.

DENIS LEARY:
Holsten Pils. Hops, barley, yeast, water and no shit.

TITLE:
Full Of Shit? Get Real!

Direction

Director
FRANK BUDGEN

Copywriter
ROBERT SAVILLE

Art Director
JAY POND-JONES

Creative Director
TIM MELLORS

Producer
PAUL ROTHWELL

Set Designer
JULIA SHERBORNE

Agency Producer
DIANE CROLL

Editor
SAM SNEADE

Lighting Cameraman
ADRIAN BIDDLE

Music Composer/Arranger
RICHARD MYHILL

Production Company
PAUL WEILAND FILM COMPANY

Agency
GGT

Marketing Director
PHIL PLOWMAN

Client
HOLSTEN DISTRIBUTORS LIMITED

Photography

Directors
ANDREW DOUGLAS
STUART DOUGLAS

Copywriter
SIMON SCOTT

Art Director
ANDREW LINDSAY

Creative Directors
SIMON SCOTT
ANDREW LINDSAY

Producer
CLARE MITCHELL

Agency Producer
TIM MAGUIRE

Editor
CHRIS SHEARS

Lighting Cameramen
ANDREW DOUGLAS
STUART DOUGLAS

Music Composers/Arrangers
THE SILENCERS

Production Company
DELANEY & HART

Agency
FAULDS
ADVERTISING

Account Group Director
TOM GILL

Marketing Executive
DEREK REID

Client
SCOTTISH TOURIST
BOARD

WILD MOUNTAIN THYME

The wildness, the freedom, the romance and the poetry of Scotland are captured in the journey of a young woman to meet her lover in the Highlands of Scotland.

LAUNCH

SFX:
Orange theme.

Out of black fades up a baby floating in water. A series of numbers, written and numerical, appear on screen in time with the music. We dissolve through to a close-up of a baby. The word 'Cry' appears.

We see more numbers appearing and disappearing on screen superimposed over the baby's mouth. The word 'Laugh' appears.

We fade up a close-up of a child's ear, again superimposed numbers appear and disappear. The word 'Listen' appears.

CHILD V/O:
In the future you won't change what you say...just how you say it.

We see a close-up of a child's mouth, again in the midst of superimposed numbers. The word 'Talk' appears.

We see two boys running over fields. We dissolve to see them standing talking on a tin can walkie-talkie.

CHILD V/O:
In the future we'll think it strange that voices ever travelled down wires.

We see various shots of telephone posts and telegraph wires being cut.

CHILD V/O:
In the future no-one will be tied down.

Cut to a child sitting on a rock looking out over a valley. We pull back to reveal the scale of the vista.

CHILD V/O:
And in the future the skies will be clearer because the world of communications will be wire-free.

We cut to see the sun setting over office buildings, fields and office windows. The windows are bright orange. This changes into the orange logo.

CHILD V/O:
The future's Bright. The future's Orange.

Photography

Director
FRANK BUDGEN

Copywriter
LARRY BARKER

Art Director
ROONEY CARRUTHERS

Creative Directors
LARRY BARKER
ROONEY CARRUTHERS

Producer
PAUL ROTHWELL

Set Designer
LAUREN LECLERE

Agency Producer
BRENDA DYKES

Editor
SAM SNEADE

Lighting Cameraman
ALEXANDER WITT

Music Composer/Arranger
PHILIP GLASS

Production Company
PAUL WEILAND FILM COMPANY

Agency
WCRS

Marketing Director
LISA GERNON

Client
HUTCHISON TELECOM

Photography

Director
DANIEL BARBER

Copywriter
MARK COOPER

Art Director
GARRY HORNER

Creative Directors
LARRY BARKER
ROONEY
CARRUTHERS

Producer
KAREN
CUNNINGHAM

Agency Producer
VANESSA PICKFORD

Editor
SAM SNEADE

Lighting Cameraman
IVAN BIRD

Music Composer/Arranger
CHRIS BLACKWELL

Production Company
ROSE HACKNEY
BARBER
PRODUCTIONS

Agency
WCRS

Marketing Manager
MARTIN RUNNACLES

Client
BMW UK LIMITED

ART

This commercial features a BMW 7 Series going through its paces on a test track.

But just as this is no ordinary car, this is no ordinary test track. Instead of the usual strategically placed road cones, the car has to avoid an array of fragile, priceless object d'Art, which are arranged in the form of an obstacle course.
Ming vases, Chinese Xian terracotta warriors, Venetian glass, sculptures, paintings and delicate pottery. All are deftly avoided by the precise road-holding of the car.

MVO:
At BMW creating supreme comfort, handling and dynamic safety is not just a science. It is an Art.

The new BMW 7 series. Our finest work to date.

WHITE

We open on a stationary white Mazda 323 shot against a white metal backdrop in a studio. The 323 is shot from fresh and seductive angles.

V/O & TITLE:
With a car as special as the new Mazda 323, we don't need to shout. If you'd like to know more, please video this commercial.

Halfway through the commercial, the car cuts out of frame and is replaced with three information panels. When seen at normal speed, this is easily noticeable to the eye but not readable. However, when viewed on video, the viewer can freeze the frame and read the information [illegible] about eighteen frames, the panel is removed and the car returns to the precise position as before in frame.

Finally, the commercial ends with the Mazda logo, the telephone number 0345 48 48 48 and an endline reading: '(special)'.

An additional super now appears reading:

To win a car this special press rewind and search. This allows the viewer to access a message instructing them to search for the hidden Japanese password, Kansei.

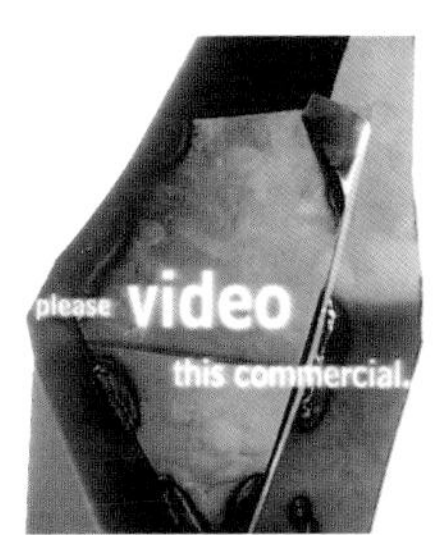

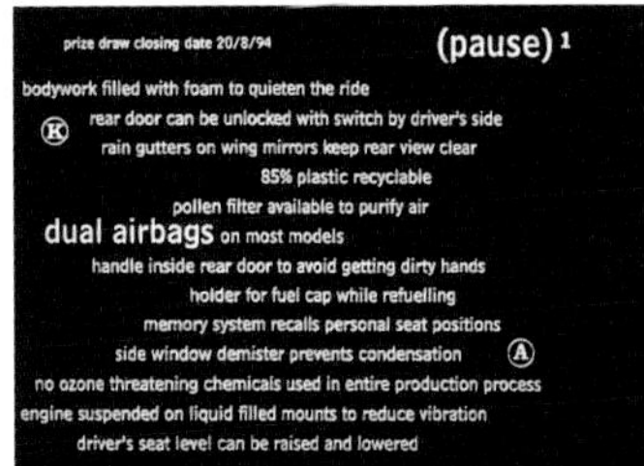

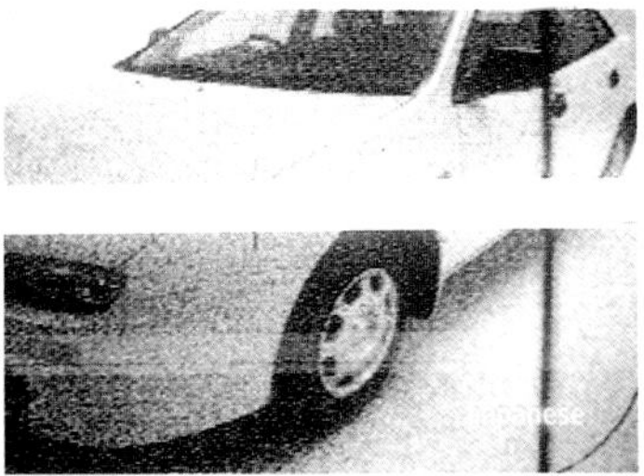

Photography

Director
TONY KAYE

Copywriter
JONATHAN KNEEBONE

Art Director
DAVE JOHNSON

Creative Director
STEVE HENRY

Producer
MATTHEW BROWN

Set Designer
JULIA JASON

Agency Producer
JENNY SELBY

Editor
PETER GODDARD

Lighting Cameraman
TONY KAYE

Music Composer/Arranger
EVELYN GLENNIE

Production Company
TONY KAYE FILMS

Agency
HOWELL HENRY CHALDECOTT LURY & PARTNERS

Marketing Director
JAN SMITH

Client
MAZDA CARS UK LIMITED

Photography

Director
ADRIAN MOAT

Copywriter
MALCOLM DUFFY

Art Director
PAUL BRIGINSHAW

Creative Director
DAVID ABBOTT

Producer
FRANCES SILOR

Agency Producer
LINDSAY HUGHES

Editor
RICK LAWLEY

Lighting Cameraman
PETER THWAITES

Music Composer/Arranger
SIMON EMMERSON

Production Company
RSA FILMS

Agency
ABBOTT MEAD VICKERS.BBDO LIMITED

Marketing Director
LAURA CANNON

Client
GOSSARD

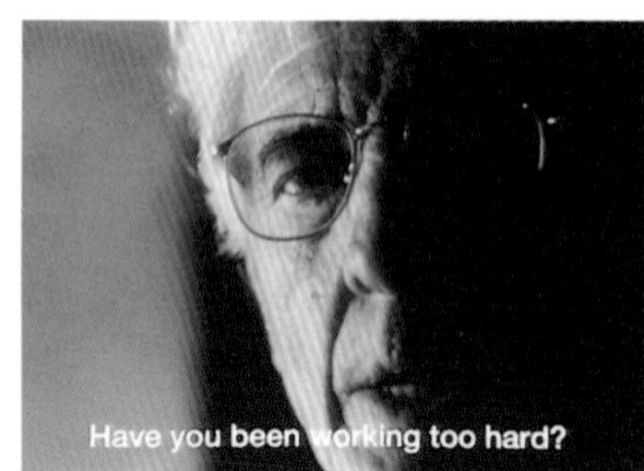

DOCTOR

Tense music.

Open on an old car travelling along a dusty road in Spain.

We see a solitary house. The car stops outside the house. The driver, an old doctor, goes into the house.

We see a muscular, dark-haired man, sitting on a wooden chair.

The doctor puts his bag down and takes the man's pulse. He speaks in Spanish.

SUBTITLE:
Have you been in the sun too long?

The young man shakes his head.

The doctor feels the young man's forehead. He speaks again.

SUBTITLE:
Have you been working too hard?

The young man shakes his head again.

The doctor shrugs and heads for the door. He speaks one more time.

SUBTITLE:
Call me if you feel faint again.

The doctor exits.

Then, at the bedroom door appears a beautiful, young woman. She is wearing the Gossard Gypsy bra and briefs.

Dramatic music punctuates the appearance of the girl.

She walks slowly towards the young man.

Cut to a close-up of the man's hand as he grips the arm of the chair.

With a mischievous smile the girl walks slowly past him.

SUPER:
Gypsy from Gossard.

A final title appears:

Not For The Faint-Hearted.

ZATOPEK

SFX:
Music.

A coach waits in an empty stadium with stop watch in hand. He is timing a young man who we see running through woodland in army boots, with a back pack on his back. The young man runs into the stadium exhausted.

MVO:
In the early 1950's, a young Czech army captain developed a training method that would change running forever. Stamina was everything.

Cut to a riot. We see the runner, now in full [illegible] way to the front of a resisting crowd.

MVO:
But he wasn't just a committed athlete. When his country was invaded he made a personal stand.

The runner is recognised by the Tank Commander, who decides not to have him shot.

MVO:
This dedication to ideals and his training methods won him 3 Olympic gold medals in one week. A record which even today remains unbroken.

Dissolve to the empty stadium. The runner wears Adidas shoes and runs through the winning tape.

Dissolve to close up of an old man.

OLD MAN:
My name is Emil Zatopek.

Cut to Emil Zatopek's Training Boot 1950.

TITLE:
Emil Zatopek's Training Shoe 1950.

Dissolve to the new 'cardio-vascular' training shoe.

TITLE:
Adidas Training Shoe 1995.

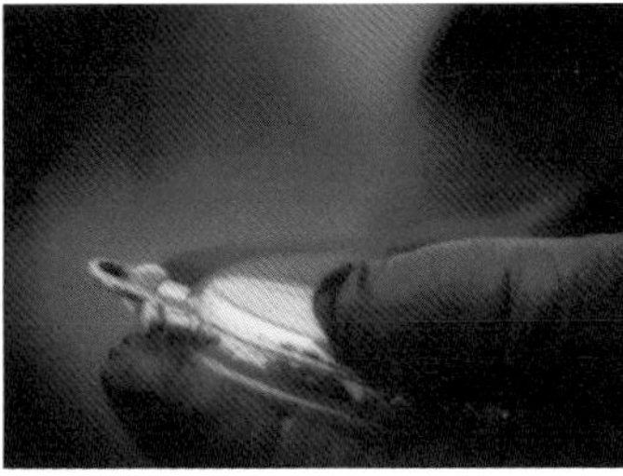

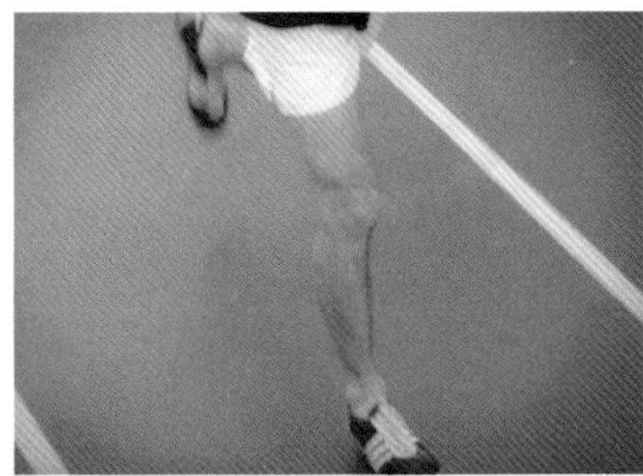

Photography

Directors
ANDREW DOUGLAS
STUART DOUGLAS

Copywriter
TIM DELANEY

Art Director
MARTIN GALTON

Creative Director
TIM DELANEY

Producer
CLARE MITCHELL

Agency Producer
MATTHEW JONES

Editor
TIM
THORNTON-ALLEN

Lighting Cameramen
[illegible]
STUART DOUGLAS

Music
Composer/Arranger
KEVIN SARGENT

Production Company
DELANEY & HART

Agency
LEAGAS DELANEY

Head of Marketing and Communications
TOM HARRINGTON

Client
ADIDAS AG

Photography

Director
DANIEL BARBER

Copywriters
LARRY BARKER
LEON JAUME

Art Director
ROONEY CARRUTHERS

Creative Directors
ROONEY CARRUTHERS
LARRY BARKER

Producer
KAREN CUNNINGHAM

Set Designer
JOHNA BUTLER

Agency Producer
SIMON WELLS

Editor
BRIAN DYKE

Lighting Cameraman
STEVE CHIVERS

Music Composer/Arranger
PHILIP GLASS

Production Company
ROSE HACKNEY BARBER PRODUCTIONS

Agency
WCRS

Head of Marketing Services
SEAN GARDENER

Client
HUTCHISON TELECOM

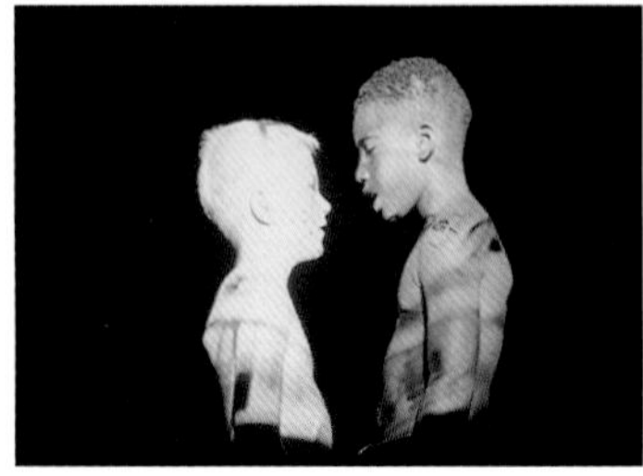

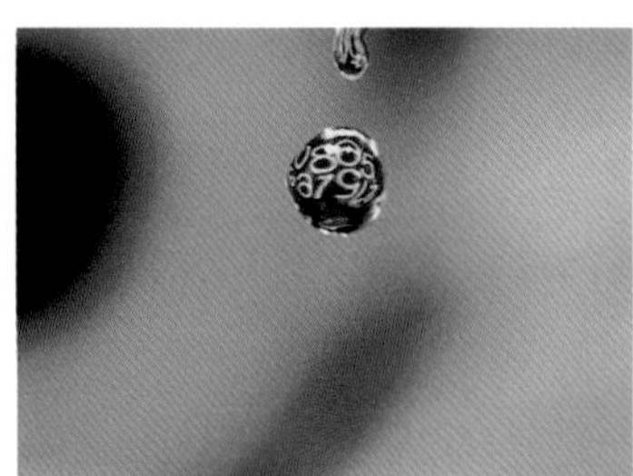

PER SECOND

SFX:
Orange theme.

The commercial begins with extremely tight close-ups of a stopwatch. Various shots of people are superimposed over the watch face. Their lips are moving in time to the counting of numbers in the music.

MVO:
Orange think it unfair that you should pay for time you haven't used.

We see more images superimposed over the watch face. We now see a single droplet of water with numbers reflected on its surface.

MVO:
And in the future maybe everyone will think that way.

We watch as the droplet falls and splashes into a pool of water.

MVO:
Until then, Orange is the only mobile network to charge you one second at a time...

SUPER:
1.

SFX:
Music stops - silence except for fast ticking.

Dissolve to extreme close-up of the stopwatch. The hand on the stopwatch ticks on alone.

Cut to an extreme close-up of a woman's eye. It blinks and dissolves through to the face of a clock.

MVO:
...Instead of rounding up to the next minute or half minute.

SFX:
Music re-starts.

We see a close-up of a child's face. She smiles. We cut to endframe and logo.

MVO:
The Future's Bright. The Future's Orange.

REFLECTIONS

SFX:
Music – sparse, electronic atmosphere.

We open on a dark front-view silhouette of the BMW Compact. The distorted angle gives the car the appearance of a strange, futuristic vehicle.

The sun breaks. The sky lights up. Clouds glide over, reflecting in the bonnet.

Cut to a group of men in silver suits and visors who stand before a mass of gleaming industrial pipes. We move in until one mirrored visor fills the screen.

We see the reflection of a BMW Compact move from left to right across it (The car appears as a space-age 'bubble car' shape because of the visor's distortion).

We see the car reflected as a stretched, pointed shape on a chrome oil-tanker.

Cut to a close-up of a roadside fish-eye mirror (as found on sharp bends where visibility is restricted). It appears as a distorted curved shape.

Cut to a huge green and blue glass building. The reflection of the car changes shape as it moves across.

Cut to a field of solar panels. We move to a close-up of one of the panels. The reflection of the car moves across it.

Cut to a close-circuit security camera. Cut to a close-up of the lens. The car appears as a ball-shape.

Cut a shot of the car appearing, as glimpses in mirrors, in the desert.

MVO:
The only way to predict the future is to shape it.

Cut to a shot of the car as it turns towards the camera and comes to a halt.

MVO:
The new BMW Compact.

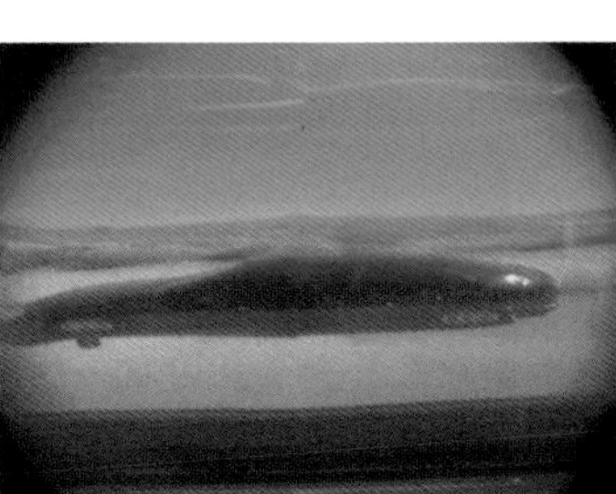

Photography

Director
FRANK BUDGEN

Copywriter
GARY KNIGHT

Art Director
ANDY DIBB

Creative Directors
LARRY BARKER
ROONEY
CARRUTHERS

Producer
ALICIA BARNARD

Set Designer
TOM FODEN

Agency Producer
VANESSA PICKFORD

Editor
SAM SNEADE

Lighting Cameraman
MICHAEL BARNARD

Music Composer/Arranger
DAVID MOTION

Production Company
PAUL WEILAND FILM COMPANY

Agency
WCRS

Marketing Manager
SIMON OLDFIELD

Client
BMW UK LIMITED

Photography

Director
TARSEM

Copywriter
PHIL DEARMAN

Art Director
CHARLES INGE

Creative Director
PAUL WEINBERGER

Producers
SIMON TURTLE
PHIL CONTOMICHALOS

Set Designer
FATIMA ANDRADE

Agency Producer
SARAH HORRY

Editor
ROBERT DUFFY

Lighting Cameraman
PAUL LAUFER

Production Company
SPOTS FILM SERVICES

Agency
LOWE HOWARD-SPINK

Marketing Executive
MARTIN BROWN

Client
VAUXHALL MOTOR COMPANY

SILENT RUNNING

An Aborigine stands in the outback.

His heightened awareness of the natural world allows him to hear the smallest sounds.

His hearing is so good that he reacts to a gecko licking its eye, a snake moving across the sand and a bird taking flight.

He sees movement on the horizon, but he is confused because he can't hear what it is. The dot reveals itself to be a car travelling at speed across the desert floor.

Still he can't hear. He puts his ear to the ground.

The silent car passes him. He turns to watch it go and a pebble is thrown up by the wheel. This bounces noisily to his feet.

Confused by the silence of the car, the Aborigine gazes after the fast disappearing Calibra.

MVO:
The Calibra from Vauxhall. The most aerodynamic production coupe on earth.

SUPER:
The Calibra from Vauxhall.

CUBICLE

This commercial takes place in a company toilet. With relish, two businessmen discuss the 'retirement' of Morrison, a colleague.

MAN 1:
I never thought he'd retire.

The other man smiles maliciously.

MAN 2:
Neither did he.

We then look inside to see the ashen face of Morrison. He's hearing the news for the first time.

To the embarrassment of the two men, Morrison leaves the cubicle. Then, in a style reminiscent of Dennis Potter, Morrison [illegible] a Nat King Cole soundtrack.

MORRISON:
There may be trouble ahead...

The men appear to find nothing unusual in Morrison's behaviour. They carry on as normal, drying hands and straightening ties. Their movements however, become synchronised to the beat. Hands are shaken to a brass rhythm, ties adjusted to a trumpet blast.

MORRISON:
...but while there's moonlight and music and love and romance...

Morrison confidently finishes the song.

MORRISON:
Let's face the music and dance.

MVO:
You needn't worry if your life changes. Allied Dunbar financial plans adapt, to help you cope with the unexpected.

As the music fades everything returns to normal.

We see the logo and endline.

MVO:
Allied Dunbar. For the life you don't yet know.

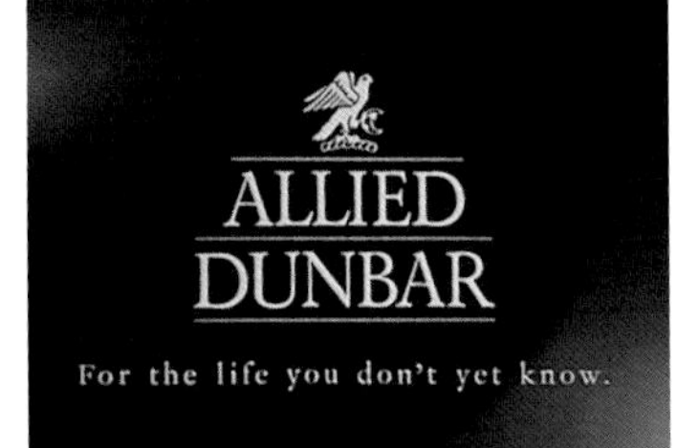

Use of Music

Director
GRAHAM ROSE

Copywriter
MARTIN LORAINE

Art Director
STEVE JONES

Creative Directors
SLIM FOSTER
MIKE ELLIOTT

Producer
RON HOLBROOK

Set Designer
JIM CLAY

Agency Producer
AMANDA LOWIT

Editor
IAN WEIL

Lighting Cameraman
TONY PIERCE-ROBERTS

Music Composers/Arrangers
IRVING BERLIN
SIMON FRAGLIN

Production Company
ROSE HACKNEY BARBER PRODUCTIONS

Agency
GREY

Marketing Communications Manager
DAVID SIMS

Client
ALLIED DUNBAR

Use of Music

Director
TONY KAYE

Copywriter
JONATHAN KNEEBONE

Art Director
DAVE JOHNSON

Creative Director
STEVE HENRY

Producer
MATTHEW BROWN

Set Designer
JULIA JASON

Agency Producer
JENNY SELBY

Editor
PETER GODDARD

Lighting Cameraman
TONY KAYE

Music Composer/Arranger
EVELYN GLENNIE

Production Company
TONY KAYE FILMS

Agency
HOWELL HENRY CHALDECOTT LURY & PARTNERS

Marketing Director
JAN SMITH

Client
MAZDA CARS UK LIMITED

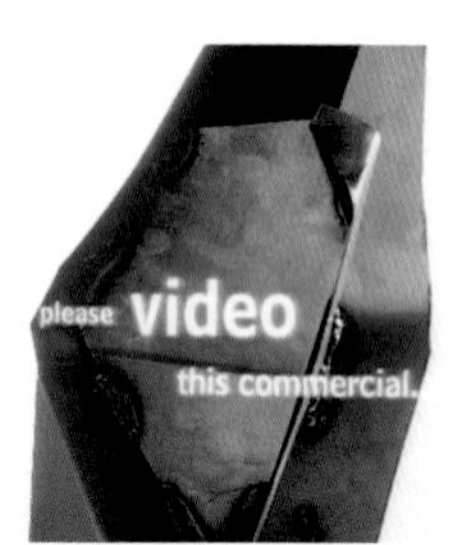

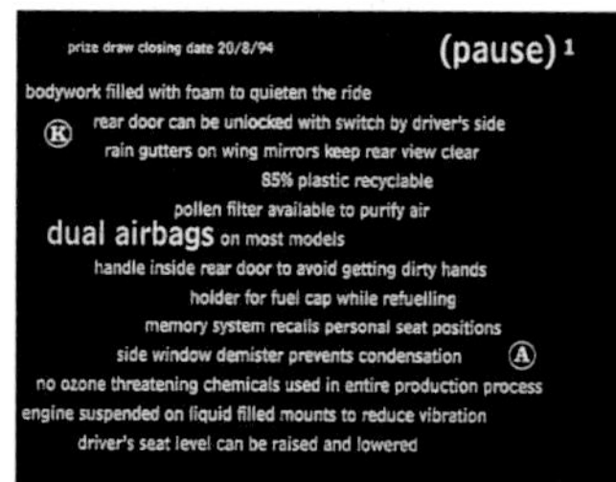

WHITE

We open on a stationary white Mazda 323 shot against a white metal backdrop in a studio. The 323 is shot from fresh and seductive angles.

V/O & TITLE:
With a car as special as the new Mazda 323, we don't need to shout. If you'd like to know more, please video this commercial.

Halfway through the commercial, the car cuts out of frame and is replaced with three information panels. When seen at normal speed, this is easily noticeable to the eye but not readable. However, when viewed on video, the viewer can freeze the frame and read the information clearly.

After about eighteen frames, the panel is removed and the car returns to the precise position as before in frame.

Finally, the commercial ends with the Mazda logo, the telephone number 0345 48 48 48 and an endline reading: '(special)'.

An additional super now appears reading:

To win a car this special press rewind and search. This allows the viewer to access a message instructing them to search for the hidden Japanese password, Kansei.

THE WORLD ACCORDING TO FRONTERA

Two African women are walking at what is apparently an impossible 45 degree angle. A Frontera drives past them, seemingly on the level.

Cut to a Frontera travelling through water which is at an odd 45 degree angle. The car passes Filipino fishermen on poles in the water.

Cut to the car in front of a waterfall. However, the water is running at a 45 degree angle.

Cut to Mongolian horsemen leading their horses past a Frontera apparently on the level. The horses are walking in a strange manner. The camera then reveals that they are not on the level but descending a steep slope.

Cut to a Frontera on a 45 degree icy slope. A sleigh full of Eskimo children slides past the car. Oddly, however, the sleigh is going uphill.

SUPER:
See a different world.

Cut to a rock climber abseiling across screen. He passes a Frontera parked on the level. In reality, though, the car is hanging on a cliff-face and he is dropping down vertically.

SUPER:
The Frontera 4x4 and Vauxhall logo.

Use of Music

Director
FRANK BUDGEN

Copywriter
PHIL DEARMAN

Art Director
CHARLES INGE

Creative Director
PAUL WEINBERGER

Producer
PAUL ROTHWELL

Set Designer
TONY NOBLE

Agency Producer
CHARLES CRISP

Editor
SAM SNEADE

Lighting Cameraman
HENRY BRAHAM

Music Composer/Arranger
DAVID MOTION

Production Company
PAUL WEILAND FILM COMPANY

Agency
LOWE HOWARD-SPINK

Marketing Executive
PHIL HARWOOD

Client
VAUXHALL MOTOR COMPANY

Use of Animation

Director
BARRY PURVES

Copywriter
ALASDAIR GRAHAM

Art Director
FRAZER JELLEYMAN

Creative Director
TONY COX

Producer
GLENN HOLBERTON

Set Designer
BARRY PURVES

Animators
IAN MacKINNON
PETE SAUNDERS

Agency Producer
MICHAEL PARKER

Editor
TIM FULFORD

Lighting Cameraman
MARK STEWART

Music Composer/Arranger
ROB BOWKETT

Production Company
BARE BOARDS PRODUCTIONS

Agency
BMP DDB NEEDHAM

Commercials Director
IWAN WILLIAMS

Client
SC JOHNSON

JAPANESE GARDEN

Classical Japanese music throughout.

MVO:
I tell the tale of Trapitaka...

...whose life was made misery...

...by the demons under the rim.

Until arrived her hero – Hu Clean-loo...

SFX:
Quack quack.

MVO:
...who vanquished them effortlessly...

...leaving the fresh fragrance of a Japanese Garden.

Old proverb: When demons lurk beneath the rim – duck!

SFX:
Quack quack.

MVO:
New Japanese Garden Toilet Duck.

A STAR IS BORN (LAUNCH)

We open on a view of outer space. It's a magical sight.

Constellations begin to swirl around and become sucked together to form an amorphous mass of multi-coloured, twinkling particles.

We cut to POV from space as we descend down through cloud layers towards the earth and the shape of Great Britain.

We dissolve through further cloud layers to aerial view approaching rugged coastline.

We cut to lighthouse keeper and trawlermen (unaware), ancient stone circle; (breeze created as it passes) and aquaduct.

We cut to 'presence' forming into the shape of a hand.

Cut to hand making silhouette of rabbit's head from POV of child's window against moon.

Track along streets of detached homes.

Cut to hand passing over stadium.

Cut to hand passing train window.

Cut to hand approaching window, we see a man watching TV, surrounded by his family. It taps on window.

Cut to close up of delighted man illuminated by a magical glow as he turns to see hand. In the background, his family looks thrilled.

The whole room begins to sparkle magically.

Cut to his POV through window of hand pointing at camera.

The hand dematerialises in a burst of (silent) firework-like effects.

Logo and titles.

It Could Be You.

The National Lottery.

Use of Animation

Director
KEVIN MOLONY

Copywriter
JOHN PALLANT

Art Director
MATT RYAN

Creative Director
JAMES LOWTHER

Producers
ALAN DEWHURST
RONNIE WEST

Animators
SHARON SMITH
LOST IN SPACE

3D Supervisor
CHRISTIAN HOGUE

Agency Producer
MARK HANRAHAN

Editors
IAN WEIL
ROD HOWICK

Visual Effects Director
CHRIS KNOTT

Production Company
PASSION PICTURES

Agency
SAATCHI & SAATCHI

Client
CAMELOT GROUP PLC

Use of Animation

Directors
SIMON TAYLOR
GRAHAM WOOD

Copywriter
ADRIAN JEFFERY

Art Director
LINDSEY REDDING

Creative Directors
SIMON SCOTT
ANDREW LINDSAY

Producer
HELEN LANGRIDGE

Agency Producer
TIM MAGUIRE

Editor
JON HOLLIS

Music Composers/Arrangers
LOGORHYTHM

Production Company
HELEN LANGRIDGE ASSOCIATES

Agency
FAULDS ADVERTISING

Account Group Director
TOM GILL

Head of Presentation
PETER GOURD

Client
BBC RADIO SCOTLAND

COCKEREL

As we hear the gripping radio article, we see the words appear on the screen. The words help to dramatise the action.

We hear a snippet from a BBC Scotland programme.

MVO:
Line out. Outside the French 22. Back on the main...oop...now the referee has called a halt to the proceedings, it's now over to the Scottish 22 and heading upfield. It's a magnificent fellow with a black underbelly, a gold coloured back and a red cockscomb and the cockerel's over the Scot's 5 metre line, heading for touch and the stewards are looking just a little bit flushed/perplexed, a little bit perplexed and flushed, ...just selling them a wee dummy and a wee side step and away he goes. Yes, he's over the touch line, now he's on the running track, and he's almost away.

Silence.

Mix up caption which reads:

Re-discover the power of the spoken word.

Mix to end frame. We see the BBC Scotland logo and tuning device which demonstrates where to find the signal.

SFX:
Music ident.

CAPTION:
UK National Station of the Year.

BRITISH AIRWAYS WORLD OFFERS

This commercial is shot from camera point of view.

Open on a man waking up in the morning.

SFX:
Beep, beep, beep, of a digital alarm clock.

His hand reaches out and switches off the alarm. He throws an arm across the bed to reach for his wife. She's not there.

He walks down the stairs and calls out.

MAN:
Carol!

He looks in the kitchen but she's not there.

MAN:
[illegible]

He passes the goldfish tank and notices the fish isn't there.

The man leaves the house, climbs into his car and drives off.

He drives through deserted streets, not a car or person in sight. He looks at his watch, it's 8.15am, rush hour.

He runs into a railway station. It's completely deserted.

He looks in a cafe. There's no one there.

He runs through more deserted streets desperately trying to find any sign of life. He runs up a flight of stairs and emerges into a large open plan office. Again, there's nobody there at all, only his reflection in a mirror.

In desperation he runs into the middle of a deserted street and screams.

MAN:
Where Is Everbody?!

SFX:
Festive music.

TITLES:
Rio from £299 return.

LA from £199 return.

Rome from £99 return.

Paris from £59 return.

New York from £168 return.

British Airways World Offers.

Editing

Director
PAUL MEIJER

Copywriter
KEITH BICKEL

Art Director
CARLOS ANUNCIBAY

Producer
ROBERT CAMPBELL

Agency Producer
TIM BERRIMAN

Editor
MARTYN GOULD

Lighting Cameraman
IVAN BIRD

Production Company
SPOTS FILM SERVICES

[illegible]
SAATCHI & SAATCHI

General Manager, Marketing Communications
DEREK DEAR

Client
BRITISH AIRWAYS

Editing

Director
MICHEL GONDRY

Copywriter
NICK WORTHINGTON

Art Director
JOHN GORSE

Creative Director
JOHN HEGARTY

Producers
TOBY COURLANDER
GEORGES BERMANN
PETE CHAMBERS

Set Designer
ROBBIE FREED

Agency Producer
PHILIPPA CRANE

Editor
RUSSELL ICKE

Lighting Cameraman
TIM MAURICE JONES

Music Composer/Arranger
GEIR JENSSEN

Production Company
PARTIZAN MIDI MINUIT

Agency
BARTLE BOGLE HEGARTY

Senior Marketing Manager
ROBERT HOLLOWAY

Client
LEVI STRAUSS & CO EUROPE SA

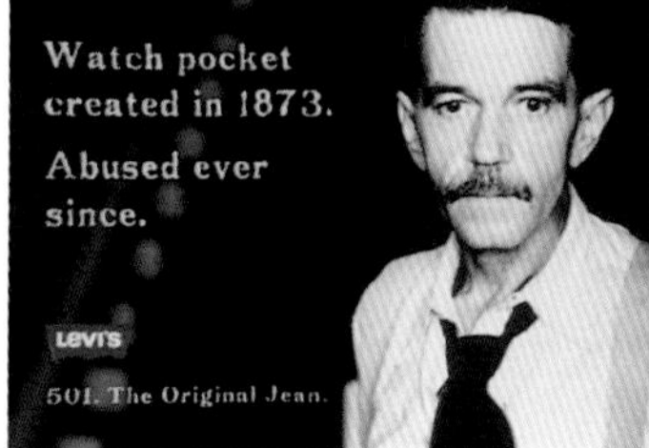

DRUGSTORE (MALE)

MUSIC:
Techno.

We see the view through the windscreen of an old truck heading into town. It's 1930, the American depression.

The truck comes to a stop outside a drugstore, as a train rumbles by.

We don't see the driver, just their view as they enter the store.

The shopkeeper, a woman and child and two girls, all turn to look.

At the counter, the driver asks for something.

The chemist hands over a tin of condoms, with a knowing smile. The driver tucks them into the watch pocket of his jeans and heads out of the door, leaving the woman in a state of shock and embarrassment.

We dissolve to the truck later that evening. It's waiting while a train thunders by. We then see it pulling up outside a white clapboard house.

A girl is waiting on the balcony.

The driver goes to the door. It opens, but it's not the girl. It's the chemist.

We see the driver for the first time, he's a young man in his teens. The chemist puts two and two together. Then, realising what's going on, trys to stop his daughter, but is powerless.

The chemist watches the young man climb into the vehicle and drive off with his daughter.

SUPER:
Watch Pocket Created in 1873.

Abused Ever Since.

Batwing logo.

SUPER:
501. The original Jean.

DON'T FORGET YOUR TROUSERS

The opening sequence outlines the basic theme of the commercial. It shows a series of nostalgic images from the 1950's. 'If you remember these events...' the voice-over says, 'then forget about buying a Toyota Rav 4, you're too old, you're the kind of person who wears driving gloves, buys his and hers matching coats and enjoys tearfully reminiscing about the wireless and Pearl Carr & Teddy Johnson. The Rav 4 is not for you.'

MUSIC:
Dvorak's New World Symphony.

MVO:
Remember that?
This?
And this?
Feel nostalgic? You do?
Oh dear, it's time to make the cocoa.

MUSIC:
Pulp fiction.

MVO:
I said it's time to make the cocoa. Because, we'll be honest, this will not interest you. We know what your cup of tea is.
It's a cup of tea.
And allotments.
Driving gloves.
His and hers matching coats.
And rambling.
Things confuse you.
Music. Fashion. Technology.
We'd like to explain. Honest.
But what we're selling today...is this. The Toyota Rav 4. A 4-wheel drive that handles like a GTI.Look at the press reviews. That's enough. You're never going to drive a Rav 4 and if you are, you shouldn't be. Remember when you saw your parents dancing. Embarrassing. The Rav 4 is a 2 litre, 0 to 60 in 9.9 seconds off-roader. What are you going to do off-road? Go surfing. Forget it. That shouldn't be hard.
Making you angry?
Don't watch. Switch channels.
Our intention is not to antagonise, annoy, upset.
O.K. We lied. It is.
We just want you to accept the Rav 4 is not for you.
You may now return to tearful reminiscing. About the wireless. Peasoupers. The Boer war.

MUSIC:
In style of Carr/Johnson.

MVO:
And Pearl Carr and Teddy Johnson.
Thank you.
The Rav 4.
The car in front of you with the knitted steering wheel is a Toyota.

Editing

Director
KEVIN MOLONY

Copywriter
ALEX GRIEVE

Art Director
ADRIAN ROSSI

Creative Director
RICHARD MYERS

Producers
RONNIE WEST
SOPHIE HUMPHRIES

Agency Producer
ARNOLD PEARCE

Editor
PIERS DOUGLAS

Lighting Cameraman
WIT DABAI

Composer/Arranger
BARRY KIRSCH

Production Company
TTO

Agency
SAATCHI & SAATCHI

Marketing Executive
OLIVER MANN

Marketing Director
GRAHAM SMITH

Client
TOYOTA UK

Editing

Director
FRANK BUDGEN

Copywriter
ROBERT SAVILLE

Art Director
JAY POND-JONES

Creative Director
TIM MELLORS

Producer
PAUL ROTHWELL

Set Designer
JULIA SHERBORNE

Agency Producer
DIANE CROLL

Editor
SAM SNEADE

Lighting Cameraman
ADRIAN BIDDLE

Music Composer/Arranger
RICHARD MYHILL

Production Company
PAUL WEILAND FILM COMPANY

Agency
GGT

Marketing Director
PHIL PLOWMAN

Client
HOLSTEN DISTRIBUTORS LIMITED

WASTE

This ad finds Denis Leary behind a bar. He picks up A.N. OTHER bottle and starts to read from the label as he passes about. He dumps the bottle in a huge bin. He picks up a second bottle, reads then dumps it. Another and another as the cutting gathers more pace. Denis trashes bottle after bottle.

DENIS LEARY:
Deep in the American south for over 200 years they've started each and every day with a traditional breakfast. Eggs over easy. A rasher of crispy fried bacon and a bowl of hot hominy grits. Grits. Do you know what grits are? Well they're a tough, chewy mass of stuff that tastes of boiled over cat litter and it's just like rocks in my mouth. I hate grits and guess what, they're in this beer. Why? I don't know why. Maybe for the same reason that there's caramel in this beer. Caramel. If I want candy I buy a candy bar. Guess what? Seaweed. SEA WEED. That's weed that comes from the sea which is where fish go to the toilet. It's a free country, but personally I don't want fish urine in my beer. And of course, rice? RICE? Next time you go to a wedding try throwing one of these at the bride. Or one of these, or one of these, or...Ascorbic acid or citric acid, sorghum, sugar, fructose, glucose, sucrose, sulphur dioxide, potassium metabisulphate, propylene glyco agnate and bat faeces. I made up the last one but you never know.

Denis picks up a bottle of Holsten Pils and reads from the label. The bar is now clear of the other bottles except for one which rolls along the shelf behind and then falls off into the big bin.

DENIS LEARY:
Holsten Pils. Hops, barley, yeast, water and no shit.

TITLE:
Full Of Shit? Get Real!

GIGGS

Imagine Manchester United's greatest-ever side.

Using old footage we put together a move involving United's greatest players, resulting in a magnificent goal from Ryan Giggs wearing Reebok boots.

Editing

Director
DAVID GARFATH

Copywriter
DEREK APPS

Art Director
VINCE SQUIBB

Creative Director
PAUL WEINBERGER

Producer
MARY FRANCIS

Agency Producer
TRACY JOHNSTON

Editor
SIMON WILCOX

Lighting Cameraman
ROGER PRATT

Music Composers/Arrangers
PAUL HART
JOE CAMPBELL

Production Company
PAUL WEILAND FILM COMPANY

Agency
LOWE HOWARD-SPINK

Marketing Executive
ROBERT FALLOW

Client
REEBOK UK LIMITED

Editing

Director
SPROTE

Copywriter
PAUL SILBURN

Art Director
TIGER SAVAGE

Creative Director
JOHN HEGARTY

Producer
BASY ROBERTSON

Set Designer
STEVE SMITHWICK

Agency Producer
FRANCES ROYALE

Editor
MIKE GILDING

Lighting Cameraman
DENIS CROSSAN

Music Composers/Arrangers
ANTHONY & GAYNOR SADLER

Production Company
REDWING FILM COMPANY

Agency
BARTLE BOGLE HEGARTY

Brand Manager
JENS HENNING KOCK

Client
HUGO BOSS AG

THE BOSS

MUSIC:
Zadoq the Priest by Handel.

We are at a big football match. We see our Boss suited hero, the manager of one of the teams, enduring the pressure of a vital game.

Things are going badly, so the boss decides to make a management decision. To the surprise of his staff and the TV commentators, he makes a substitution.

In the dying seconds, the substitute breaks through and is brought down in the penalty area.

He gets up and takes the penalty, scoring the winning goal.

The crowd goes wild, as the final whistle blows.

The players celebrate and the boss finds himself being embraced by his goalkeeper, who leaves mud down the front of his immaculate suit. For a moment, we think the boss will explode, but he simply smiles and turns to congratulate the goalscorer.

As he turns, we see he hasn't noticed the mud on his back.

SUPER:
Men At Work.

Hugo Boss.

MIND GAMES

Creatively, the TAG Heuer commercial captures an attitude that is inspirational and fits within a sporting context. As a result, a platform of mental strength is developed, based on the recognition that the difference between success and failure is yourself. Winners create their own imaginary pressure in order to win. TAG Heuer associates itself with such an attitude, presenting it in a prestigous way.

Editing

Director
TONY KAYE

Copywriter
REMY NOEL

Art Director
ERIC HOLDEN

Producer
SOPHIE JACOBS

Set Designer
JULIA JASON

Agency Producer
FRANCOISE KORB

Editor
PETER GODDARD

Lighting Cameraman
TONY KAYE

Production Company
1/33 PRODUCTIONS

Agency
BDDP PARIS

Client
TAG HEUER

Special Effects

Directors
VAUGHAN & ANTHEA

Copywriter
DEREK APPS

Art Director
VINCE SQUIBB

Creative Director
PAUL WEINBERGER

Producer
ADAM SAWARD

Set Designer
ROBIN BROWN

Agency Producer
CHARLES CRISP

Editor
RICK RUSSELL

Lighting Cameraman
STEVE CHIVERS

Special Effects Supervisor
MARK NELMES

Music Composer/Arranger
RONIN

Production Company
THE LEWIN & WATSON COMPANY

Agency
LOWE HOWARD-SPINK

Marketing Executive
PAUL DAVEY

Client
PIERRE SMIRNOFF COMPANY

REFLECTION

A photographer sees a darker side to a Russian wedding when he looks through a Smirnoff bottle.

He sees the demure bride turn into a snarling vampire.

Again the photographer looks at a woman in a beaded dress. The fat beads turn into crawling beetles.

He turns to see a meek waitress being bullied by a guest. But through the bottle she has her revenge as she plunges his head into the soup.

A sailor ogles a passing girl and turns into a leering vulture.

The bride shows off her sparkling wedding ring to a guest. But through the bottle instead of admiring it, the guest is lustfully sucking her finger.

Our hero sees a moustached man clapping along to the music. The bottle turns him into a giant walrus clapping its flippers.

A line of dancers pass by. Behind the bottle we see them in their underwear. The last little man in line is in fact wearing women's.

The bride throws her bouquet to three demure bridesmaids who, when seen behind the bottle, are having a snarling tussle for the prize.

Our man finally sees his reflection in a waiter's silver tray. Overcome by curiosity, he takes a look at himself through the bottle, only to see a frightening satyr staring back.

GIGGS

Imagine Manchester United's greatest-ever side.

Using old footage we put together a move involving United's greatest players, resulting in a magnificent goal from Ryan Giggs wearing Reebok boots.

Special Effects

Director
DAVID GARFATH

Copywriter
DEREK APPS

Art Director
VINCE SQUIBB

Creative Director
PAUL WEINBERGER

Producer
MARY FRANCIS

Agency Producer
TRACY JOHNSTON

Editor
SIMON WILCOX

Lighting Cameraman
ROGER PRATT

Special Effects Operator
HARRY JARMAN

Special Effects Producer
MARK BENSON

Music Composers/Arrangers
PAUL HART
JOE CAMPBELL

Production Company
PAUL WEILAND FILM COMPANY

Agency
LOWE HOWARD-SPINK

Marketing Executive
ROBERT FALLOW

Client
REEBOK UK LIMITED

Special Effects

Director
SIMON WEST

Director of Photography
STEVE RAMSEY

Copywriter
DONNA WEINHEIM

Art Director
DONNA WEINHEIM

Producer
OLIVER FUSELIER

Special Effects
NOVOCOM

Agency Producer
HYATT CHOATE

Editor
CHUCK WILLIS

Lighting Cameraman
STEVE RAMSEY

Production Company
SATELLITE FILMS

Agency
BBDO, NEW YORK

Client
PEPSI COLA, INC

INNERTUBE

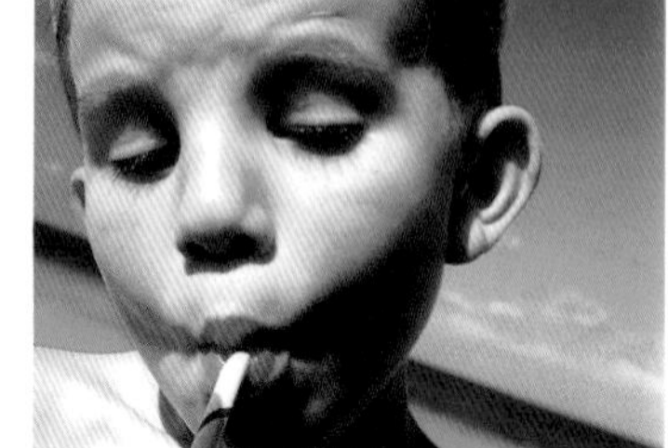

VENICE

A boy leaves his house with his elder brother after having eaten some Mulino Bianco cookies.

As they walk through Venice, they see that the city has been transformed; the canals are now full of wheat.

Nature has been brought to the city.

Special Effects

Director
TARSEM

Copywriter
GUIDO AVIGDOR

Art Director
ALBERTO BACCARI

Producer
SIMON TURTLE

Set Designer
LED CLARKE

Agency Producer
ALBERTO CARLONI

Editor
GEOFF PAYNE

Lighting Cameraman
PAUL LAUFER

Production Companies
[illegible]
SERVICES
BRW MILAN

Agency
ARMANDO TESTA

Client
BARILLA

Special Effects

Director
JEFF STARK

Copywriter
MARK COLLIS

Art Directors
MARK COLLIS
GRAHAM FINK

Creative Director
TIM MELLORS

Producer
CHRIS STEVENSON

Agency Producer
DIANE CROLL

Editor
JOHN SMITH

Lighting Cameraman
ROGER PRATT

Music Arranged By
RICHARD MYHILL

Production Company
STARK FILMS

Agency
GGT

Marketing Controller
GAUTAM DATAR

Client
NATIONWIDE
BUILDING SOCIETY

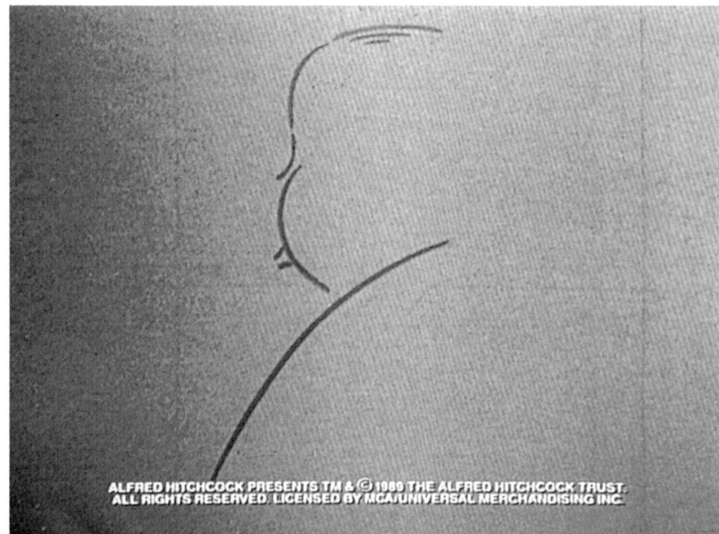

THE 'BUILDING' SOCIETY

HITCHCOCK

We open on the silhouette of Alfred Hitchcock, yes Alfred Hitchcock. Cut to him standing in his studio sitting in his grey suit.

In fact, it is an original piece of Hitchcock footage.

HITCHCOCK:
Good evening ladies and gentlemen and especially the homebuyers. All of you have at one time or another, worried about how much your monthly repayments might or might not be. Ah, but have you ever thought of finding out through Nationwide's Quick Quote?

Oh you haven't! Oh well, in that case you will be even more interested in the virtues of our sponsor's product.

V/O:
Home buying without a hitch.

Alfred Smiles.

MVO:
Building a future with Nationwide...The Building Society.

Cut to end device.

Nationwide. The Building Society.

1005

TELEVISION AND CINEMA GRAPHICS

SILVER AWARD
for the Most Outstanding Promotion

Director
WALTER STERN

Copywriters
JIM BOLTON
CHAS BAYFIELD

Producer
JOHN PAYNE

Lighting Cameraman
J. BENJAMIN

Editor
TOM MORRISH

Production Company
CURIOUS FILMS

Agency
HOWELL HENRY CHALDECOTT LURY & PARTNERS

Brand Manager
DAVID ATTER

Client
BRITVIC SOFT DRINKS LIMITED

THE WORD

A series of 102 different short sponsorship idents appear in and around Channel 4's programme, The Word. The idents fit into nine categories that have nothing in common with each other or The Word and which were chosen for no other reason than they made us laugh.

TV PRESENTER

Open on a pompous sounding fanfare and the familiar image of a TV studio. A seated newsreader is counted in by the floor manager. He proceeds to read the news in what appears to be a foreign language, but with the same confident tone of voice that is recognisable in any language.

Behind him is a huge video screen showing his face. The video image starts in synch with him but starts to glitch, prompting the reader to turn around. He continues to read, unperturbed.

The video image diverges [illegible] a series of nervous tics that continue to the end of the broadcast. By the time the lights go down on the newsreader, the video image is having its own version of a mental breakdown.

The caption appears, saying "MTV - We Speak Your Language".

SILVER AWARD
for the Most Outstanding Promotion

Director
MIKE BENNION

Copywriters
RALF RALF
MIKE BENNION

Producers
MARCO GIUSTI
GEORGINA POUSHKINE

Set Designer
CLIVE HOWARD

Music Composer
BEETHOVEN

Lighting Cameraman
DAVID WYNN JONES

Editors
[illegible]
ROB HARVEY

Production Company
TARANTULA COMMUNICATIONS

Senior Vice President
PETER DOUGHERTY

Client
MTV EUROPE

SILVER AWARD NOMINATION
for the Most Outstanding Brand Identity

Graphic Designer
DOUGLAS HAMILTON

Director
FRANK BUDGEN

Copywriter
LARRY BARKER

Producer
PAUL ROTHWELL

Set Designer
LAUREN LECLERE

Music Composer/Arranger
PHILIP GLASS

Lighting Cameraman
ALEXANDER WITT

Editor
SAM SNEADE

Production Company
PAUL WEILAND FILM COMPANY

Agency
WCRS

Marketing Director
LISA GERNON

Client
HUTCHISON TELECOM

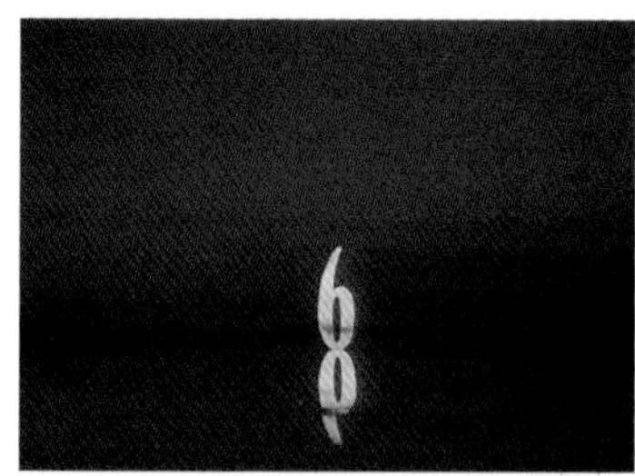

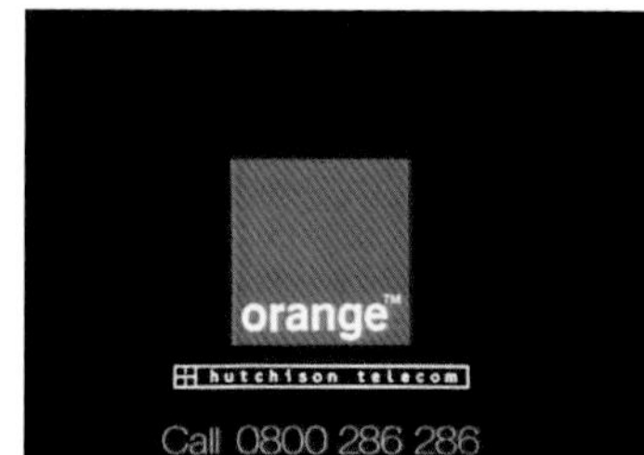

LAUNCH

SFX:
Orange theme.

Out of black fades up a baby floating in water. A series of numbers, written and numerical, appear on screen in time with the music. We dissolve through to a close-up of a baby. The word 'Cry' appears.

We see more numbers appearing and disappearing on screen superimposed over the baby's mouth. The word 'Laugh' appears.

We fade up a close-up of a child's ear, again superimposed numbers appear and disappear. The word 'Listen' appears.

CHILD V/O:
In the future you won't change what you say...just how you say it.

We see a close-up of a child's mouth, again in the midst of superimposed numbers. The word 'Talk' appears.

We see two boys running over fields. We dissolve to see them standing talking on a tin can walkie-talkie.

CHILD V/O:
In the future we'll think it strange that voices ever travelled down wires.

We see various shots of telephone posts and telegraph wires being cut.

CHILD V/O:
In the future no-one will be tied down.

Cut to a child sitting on a rock looking out over a valley. We pull back to reveal the scale of the vista.

CHILD V/O:
And in the future the skies will be clearer because the world of communications will be wire-free.

We cut to see the sun setting over office buildings, fields and office windows. The windows are bright orange. This changes into the orange logo.

CHILD V/O:
The future's Bright. The future's Orange.

TRUE ROMANCE

As we hear the radio article, we see the words appear on the screen. The words help to dramatise the action.

SPEAKER:
These are the...these are the things that life is made of. I wanted to see what the Atlantic was like, you can only see it by going there. But much more importantly, I wanted to see what I was like on the Atlantic.

What's wrong with romance?

It brings light into life. Into your own life and into other peoples' lives.

God forbid that we were all practical pragmatists.

Silence.

Mix up caption which reads:

Re-discover the power of the spoken word.

Mix to end frame. We see the BBC Scotland logo and tuning device which demonstrates where to find the signal.

CAPTION:
UK National Station of the Year.

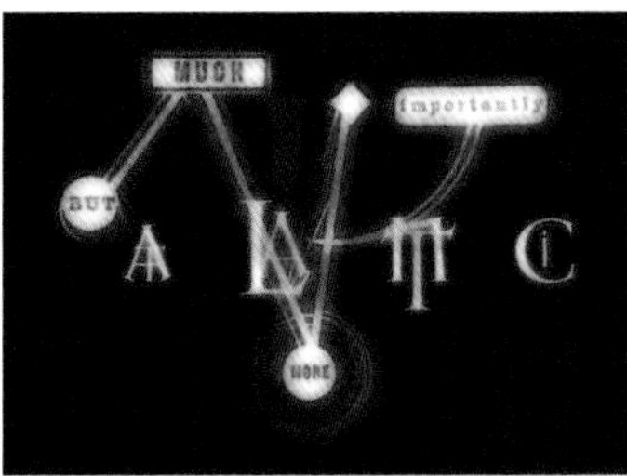

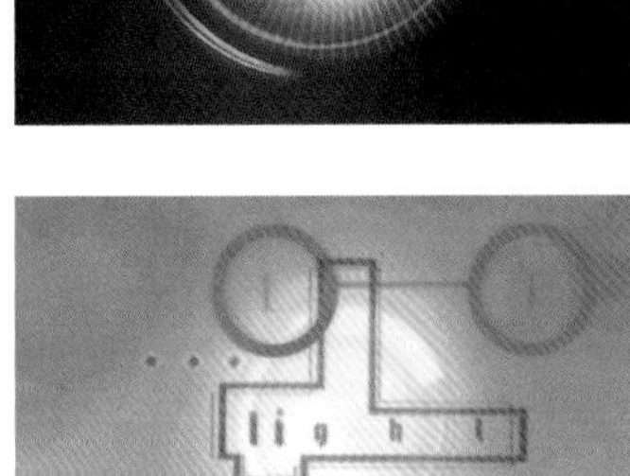

SILVER AWARD NOMINATION
for the Most Outstanding Promotion

Graphic Designer
JONATHAN BARNBROOK

Director
JONATHAN BARNBROOK

Copywriter
ADRIAN JEFFERY

Art Director
LINDSEY REDDING

Creative Directors
SIMON SCOTT
ANDREW LINDSAY

Producer
YVONNE CHALK

Agency Producer
TIM MAGUIRE

Music Composers/Arrangers
LOGORHYTHM

Editor
JON HOLLIS

Production Company
TONY KAYE FILMS

Agency
FAULDS ADVERTISNG

Account Group Director
TOM GILL

Head of Presentation
PETER GOURD

Client
BBC RADIO SCOTLAND

SILVER AWARD NOMINATION
for the Most Outstanding Promotion

Graphic Designer
JONATHAN BARNBROOK

Director
JONATHAN BARNBROOK

Copywriter
ADRIAN JEFFERY

Art Director
LINDSEY REDDING

Creative Directors
SIMON SCOTT
ANDREW LINDSAY

Producer
YVONNE CHALK

Animators
SARAH LEWIS
JONATHAN BARNBROOK

Agency Producer
TIM MAGUIRE

Editor
JON HOLLIS

Music Composers/Arranger
LOGORHYTHM

Production Company
TONY KAYE FILMS

Agency
FAULDS ADVERTISNG

Account Group Director
TOM GILL

Head of Presentation
PETER GOURD

Client
BBC RADIO SCOTLAND

FOGGIE BUMMER

VIDEO:
As we hear the gripping radio article we see the words appear on screen. The words help to dramatise the action.

MVO1:
An exercise I often do is write words like 'BOMBAIZE' and 'FORFOUGHEN' and words like that up on the board, you see. And they think things like, a foggie bummer, what's a foggie bummer? Then we'll ask one another, you see, and...

MVO 2:
What is a foggie bummer?

MVO 1:
Foggie bummer means a bumble bee! (laughs)

MVO 2:
I was away to say you could have got us struck off air then!

MVO 1:
Oh no no no! It's not that bad!

CAPTION:
Mix up caption which reads,

Re-discover the power of the spoken word.

Silence.

SFX:
Music ident.

VIDEO:
Mix to end frame. We see the BBC Scotland logo and tuning device which demonstrates where to find the signal.

CAPTION:
UK National Station of the Year.

TARTAN TOYBOYS

As we hear the radio article, we see the words appear on the screen. The words help to dramatise the action.

MUM:
I'm looking forward to seeing the Tartan Toyboys.

DAUGHTER:
What do you think they're going to be like, though?

MUM:
Well, I hope they're going to have long legs and wee bums and broad shoulders, and I hope they're going to wear kilts. I'll be terribly [illegible] have kilts on (laughs). I'll be equally disappointed if they don't have them off before the night's over.

Silence.

Mix up caption which reads:

Re-discover the power of the spoken word.

Mix to end frame. We see the BBC Scotland logo and tuning device which demonstrates where to find the signal.

CAPTION:
UK National Station of the Year.

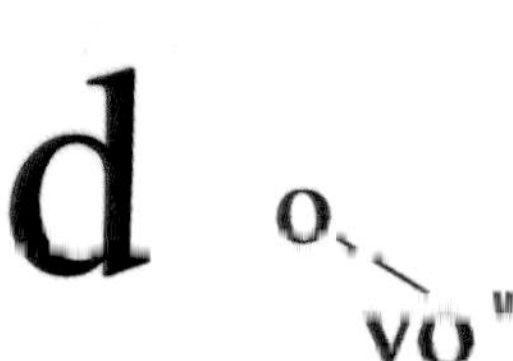

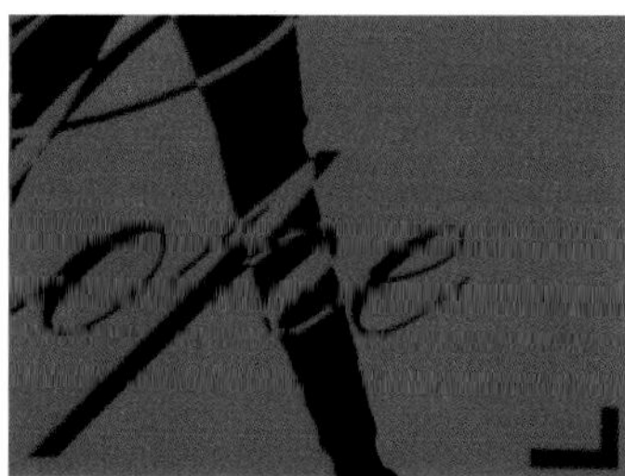

SILVER AWARD NOMINATION
for the Most Outstanding Promotion

Graphic Designer
JONATHAN BARNBROOK

Director
JONATHAN BARNBROOK

Copywriter
ADRIAN JEFFERY

Art Director
LINDSEY REDDING

Creative Directors
SIMON SCOTT
ANDREW LINDSAY

Producer
[illegible]

Agency [illegible]
TIM MAGUIRE

Editor
JON HOLLIS

Music Composers/Arrangers
LOGORHYTHM

Production Company
TONY KAYE FILMS

Agency
FAULDS ADVERTISNG

Account Group Director
TOM GILL

Head of Presentation
PETER GOURD

Client
BBC RADIO SCOTLAND

SILVER AWARD NOMINATION
for the Most Outstanding Promotion

Graphic Designers
PETER MILES
DAMON MURRAY
STEPHEN SORRELL

Directors
PETER MILES
DAMON MURRAY
STEPHEN SORRELL

Copywriters
PETER MILES
DAMON MURRAY
STEPHEN SORRELL

Producers
PETER MILES
DAMON MURRAY
STEPHEN SORRELL

Music Composer/Arrangers
FUEL
HAMOND ORGAN GREATS
ROY AYERS

Production Company
MTV EUROPE

Design Group
FUEL

Senior Vice President
PETER DOUGHERTY

Client
MTV EUROPE

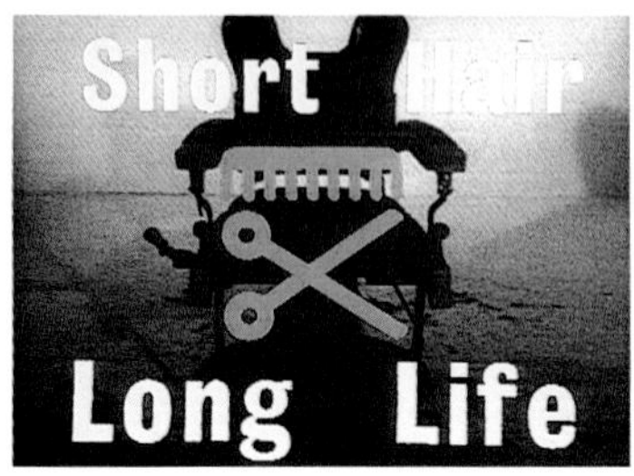

SAVE FUEL

Title appears as animated pegboard type.

Stills of coloured transport symbols appear one after another. Colours gradually darken as cuts become faster. Corresponding sounds of transport build up to a climax.

Cut to animated pump symbol and sound of birds singing.

'Save Fuel' appears.

Endframe:

MTV logo on pegboard.

HAIR

Title appears as animated pegboard type.

Live action Super 8 of hairdressers shop windows and signs.

Rapid stills sequence of head shots, faces spin around.

Cut to pixelated live action of a girl having her hair cut short.

'Short Hair, Long Life' appears.

Endframe:

MTV logo on pegboard.

FAST FOOD

Title appears as animated pegboard type.

Stills of fast food over which type alternates from EAT to FAT.

Cut to animated sequence of a large man spinning around.

Photographs of fast food on his stomach revolve in the opposite direction.

Cut to stills of fast food over which type alternates from FAT to FAST.

Endframe:

MTV logo on pegboard.

SILVER AWARD NOMINATION
for the Most Outstanding Television Graphics Any Other

Copywriters
MARK FAIRBANKS
MIKE BARKER

Agency
OGILVY & MATHER

Director of Sales
ROGER MURPHY

Client
DURACELL UK

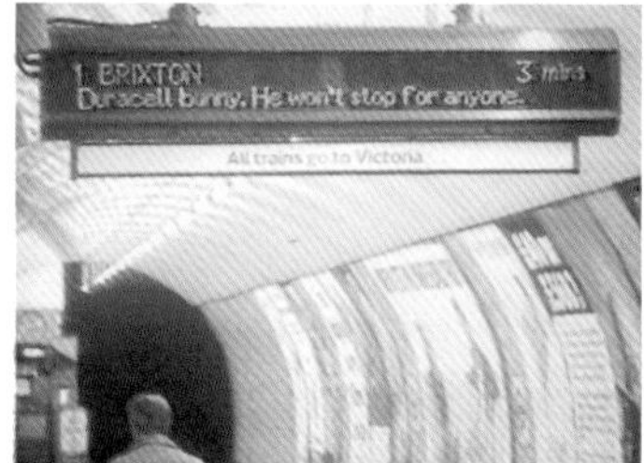

GOOD JOB YOUR NEXT TUBE

On the dot-matrix time indicator board at Warren Street tube station appears the following message.

'GOOD JOB YOUR NEXT TUBE ISN'T DRIVEN BY THE DURACELL BUNNY. HE WON'T STOP FOR ANYONE.'

IT'LL BE A HECK OF A LOT LONGER

On the dot-matrix time indicator board at Warren Street tube station appears the following message.

'IT'LL BE A HECK OF A LOT LONGER BEFORE THE DURACELL BUNNY STOPS.'

Brand Identity

Graphic Designers
IAIN GREENWAY
TIM PLATT
JANE FIELDER
BILL WILSON
MAYLIN LEE
PAULA WILLIAMS

Directors
IAIN GREENWAY
TIM PLATT
JANE FIELDER
BILL WILSON
MAYLIN LEE
PAULA WILLIAMS

Producers
ISABEL SLIEGHT
DAVE HOWE
JANIN MORGAN

Music Composers/Arrangers
MUSIC SCULPTORS

Animator
FRED REED

Lighting Cameraman
CARL WATKINS

Editor
TIM BURKE

Production Company
CELL ANIMATION

Design Group
BBC GRAPHIC DESIGN

Head of Presentation
PAM MASTERS

Client
BBC TELEVISION

Title Sequences

Graphic Designers
DAVID FLACK
NICOLAS CHARAVET

Director
DAVID FLACK

Music Composer/Arranger
DAN DONOVAN

Animators
DAVID FLACK
NICOLAS CHARAVET

Editor
DAVID FLACK

Production Company
MTV EUROPE

Client
MTV EUROPE

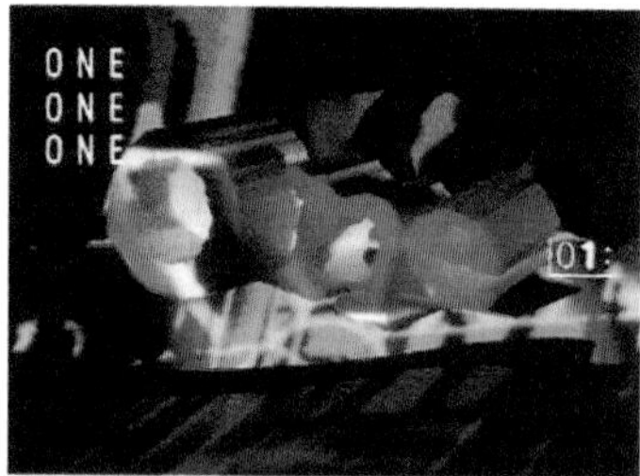

GRAFFITI

As we hear the gripping radio article, we see the words appear on the screen. The words help to dramatise the action.

We hear a snippet from a BBC Scotland programme.

MVO:
If I can explain some of this graffiti that's in the ceiling of the car here. We got psycho and Demon. We got psycho from rolling 60's cripps. We got...er Junior from Ghetto boys...Um, as I'm looking, I'm starting to feel these real kind of er, emotions choking up in me because there's probably about 20 or 25 different gang members that are carved in here, Babyface here, and I'd say about a dozen of them, almost half of them are dead

Silence.

Mix up caption which reads:

Re-discover the power of the spoken word.

Mix to end frame.

SFX:
Music ident.

We see the BBC Scotland logo and tuning device which demonstrates where to find the signal.

CAPTION:
UK National Station of the Year.

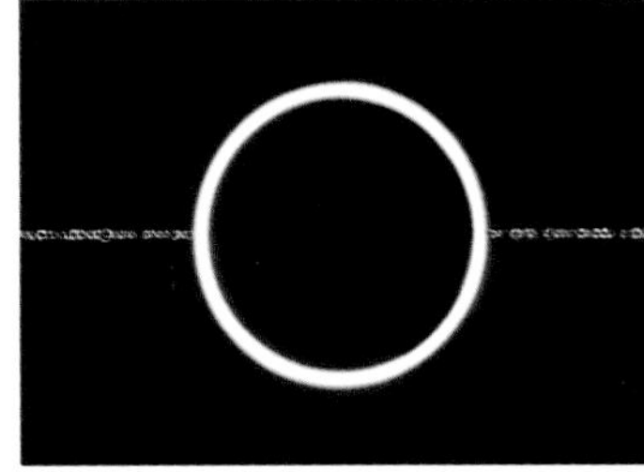

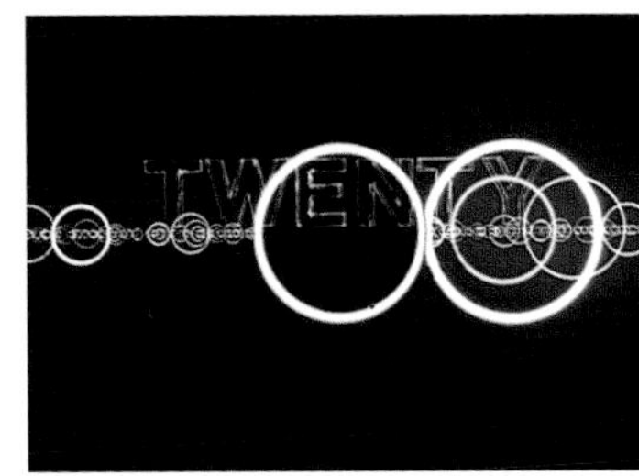

Promotion

Directors
SIMON TAYLOR
GRAHAM WOOD

Copywriter
ADRIAN JEFFERY

Art Director
LINDSEY REDDING

Creative Directors
SIMON SCOTT
ANDREW LINDSAY

Producer
HELEN LANGRIDGE

Agency Producer
TIM MAGUIRE

Editor
JON HOLLIS

Music Composers/Arrangers
LOGORHYTHM

Production Company
HELEN LANGRIDGE ASSOCIATES

Agency
FAULDS ADVERTISING

Account Group Director
TOM GILL

Head of Presentation
PETER GOURD

Client
BBC RADIO SCOTLAND

1995

POP PROMO VIDEOS

SILVER AWARD
for the Most
Outstanding Direction

Director
SPIKE JONZE

Director of Photography
SCOTT HERIKSON

Art Director
TERI WHITTAKER

Producer
VINCENT LANDAY

Editor
ERIC ZUMBRUNNEN

Production Company
SATELLITE FILMS

Client
THE DAVID GEFFEN COMPANY

SILVER AWARD
for the Most Outstanding Photography

Director
TONY KAYE

Art Director
JULIA JASON

Creative Director
JULIA JASON

Producer
MEREDYTH FRATLOLILLO

Set Designers
JULIA JASON
GILES CURTEIS

Editor
DUNCAN SHEPPARD

Lighting Cameraman
TONY KAYE

Record Company
EAST WEST RECORDS

Production Company
TONY KAYE FILMS

Marketing Executive
PAUL CHARLES

Client
EAST WEST RECORDS

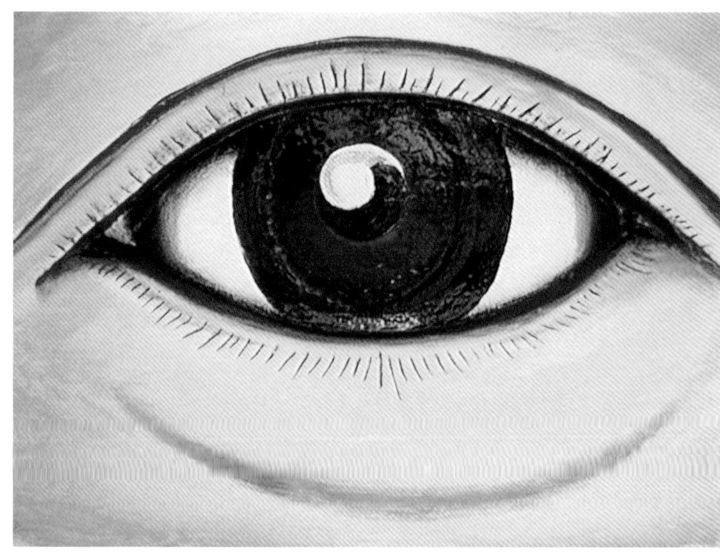

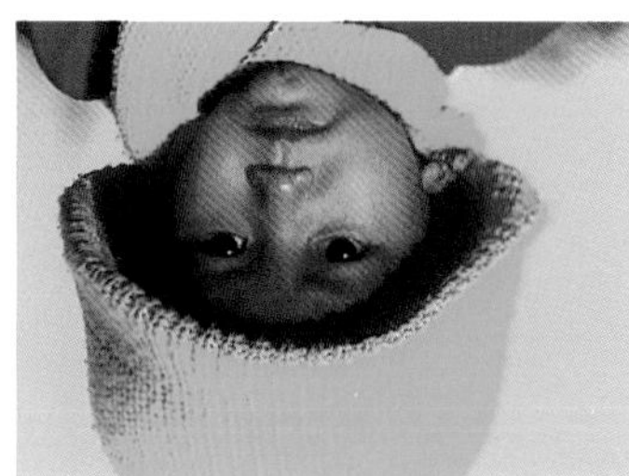

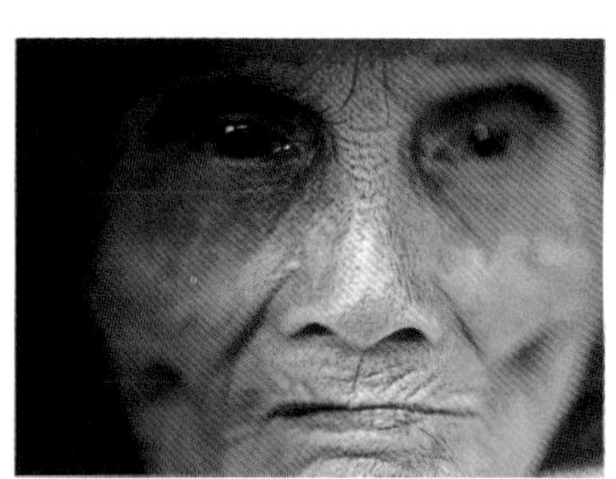

SILVER AWARD NOMINATION
for the Most Outstanding Pop Promo Video

Director
MARK ROMANEK

Director of Photography
HARRIS SAVIDES

Art Director
TOM FODEN

Producer
KRISTA MONTAGNA

Executive Producer
LARRY PEREL

Editor
ROBERT DUFFY

Production Company
SATELLITE FILMS

Client
NOTHING RECORDS

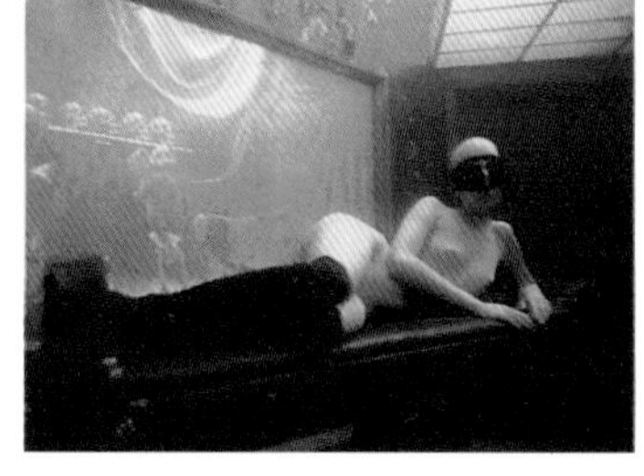

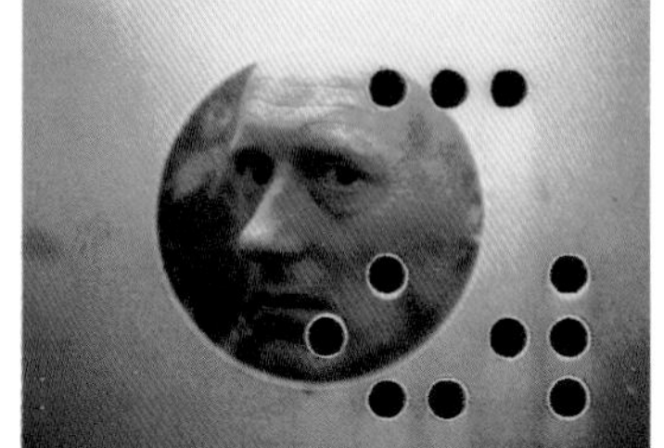

SILVER AWARD NOMINATION
for the Most Outstanding Pop Promo Video

Director
TONY KAYE

Art Director
JULIA JASON

Creative Director
JULIA JASON

Producer
MEREDYTH FRATLOLILLO

Set Designers
JULIA JASON
GILES CURTEIS

Editor
DUNCAN SHEPPARD

Lighting Cameraman
TONY KAYE

Recording Company
EAST WEST RECORDS

Production Company
TONY KAYE FILMS

Marketing Executive
PAUL CHARLES

Client
EAST WEST RECORDS

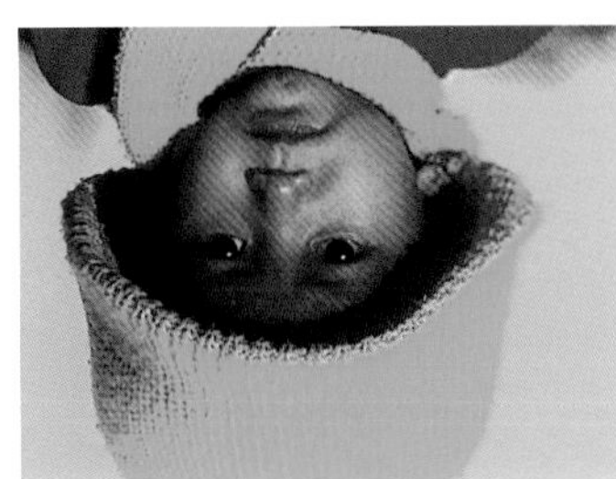

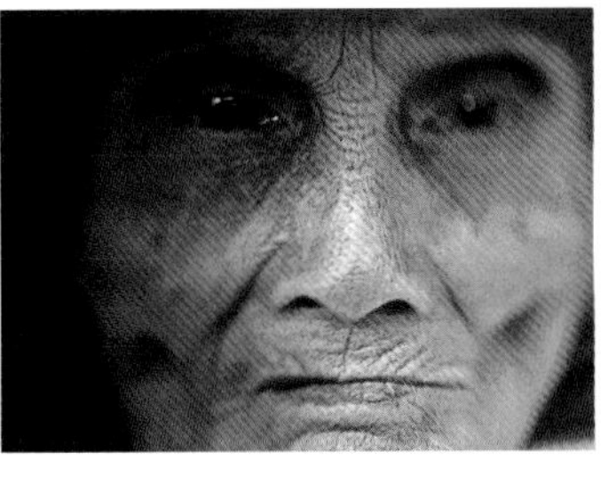

Individual

Directors
DELANEY
WHITEBLOOM

Art Directors
DELANEY
WHITEBLOOM

Copywriters
DELANEY
WHITEBLOOM

Producer
GARETH FRANCIS

Editor
DUNCAN SHEPHERD

Lighting Cameraman
STEVE KEITH-ROACH

Music Composers/Arrangers
ENIGMA

Record Company
VIRGIN RECORDS

Production Company
PALOMAR PICTURES

Client
VIRGIN RECORDS, GERMANY

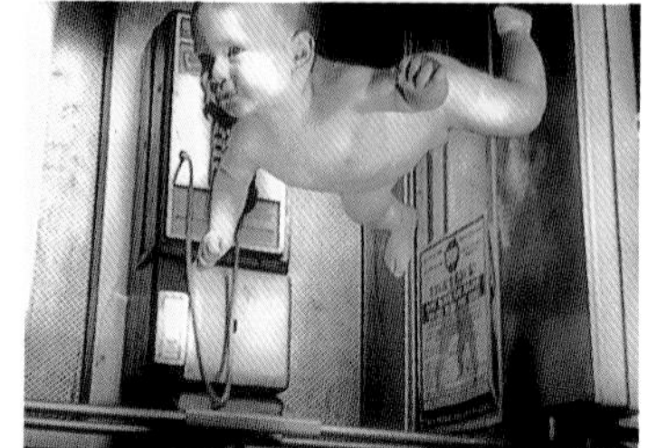

Individual

Director
SPIKE JONZE

Director of Photography
ARTURO SMITH

Art Director
REGAN JACKSON

Producer
DAWN ROSE

Music Composers/Arrangers
BEASTIE BOYS

Production Company
SATELLITE FILMS

Client
CAPITOL RECORDS

Direction

Director
MARK ROMANEK

Director of Photography
HARRIS SAVIDES

Art Director
TOM FODEN

Producer
KRISTA MONTAGNA

Executive Producer
LARRY PEREL

Editor
ROBERT DUFFY

Production Company
SATELLITE FILMS

Client
NOTHING RECORDS

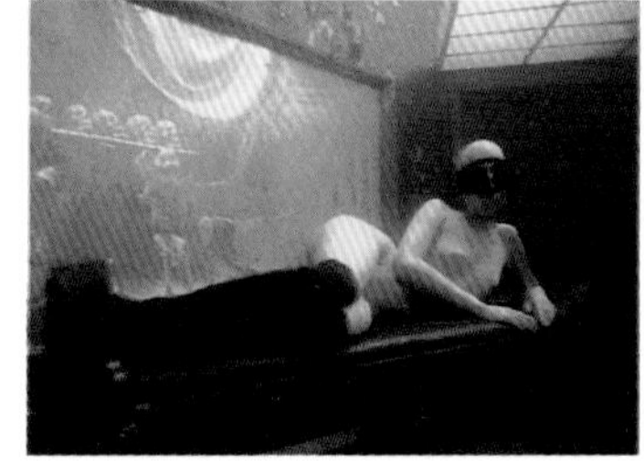

1995

STUDENT AWARDS

TYPOGRAPHY

FIRST PRIZE

STUDENT OF THE YEAR 1995

Student
SAM DAVY

Tutors
STEPHEN BLAND & SUSAN PEACE

College
UNIVERSITY OF NORTHUMBRIA

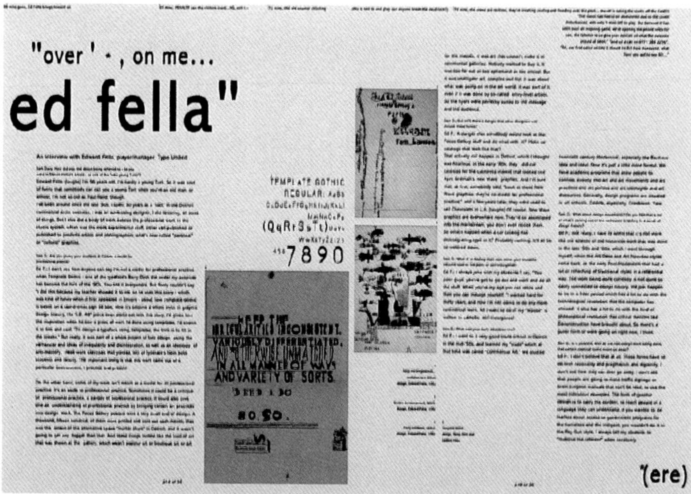

Sponsored by Real Time Studio

Brief set by Phil Jones: Real Time Studio,

Patrick Baglee: Scope

I was delighted by the enthusiasm, the careful research and the variety of solutions that I saw in students entries to this category. During my apprenticeship (like College only with less music and more beer) I set Manchester United match programmes in metal type, so the theme of the brief remains familiar to me (as my colleagues would tell you). Type and typography, however generated, need skill and concentration if they are to reach a high standard, not forgetting just that little bit of wry humour. All entries met these important criteria. My involvement with organisations like the Typographic Circle regularly throws me into the debate – about the merits of type when created by progressive technologies. As always, the answer is that it is as good as the operators are prepared to make it. I hope entrants continue to embrace new technologies (despite decreasing resources) and succeed in making it work for them. And finally; No!, Manchester United will NOT be buying Jan Tschichold – he moves much too slowly nowadays.

Phil Jones
Real Time Studio

SECOND PRIZE

Student
ED SULLIVAN

Tutor
DAVID HERBERT

College
DUNCAN OF JORDANSTONE UNIVERSITY

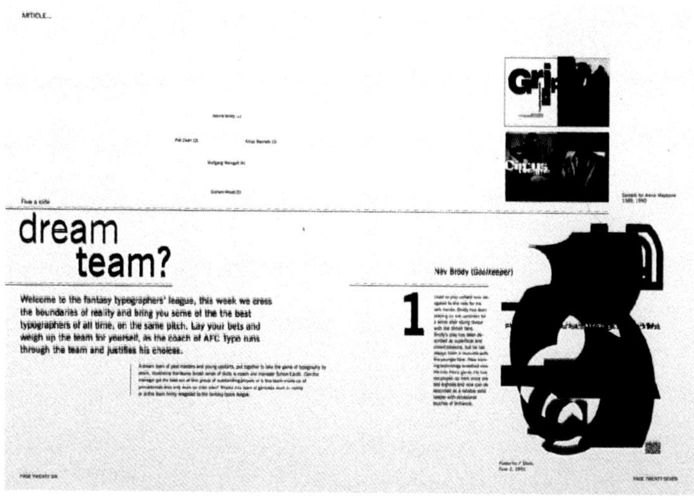

Sponsored by The Typographic Circle

Brief set by Patrick Baglee: Scope,

Phil Jones: Real Time Studio

Equal rights for people with cerebral palsy are still a long way off. Powerful images and clearly organised materials are vital if we are to get this message across. We need to change attitudes towards disability and empower people to do more, both in the community and at Government level to affect change for those who are denied even the most basic opportunities.

Entrants didn't shy away from bold statements, but equally, they managed to represent people with disabilities, their parents and carers, with dignity and respect. A prize is on its way to the entrant who bastardised the Scope logo in the most imaginative way.

Patrick Baglee Scope

EDITORIAL

FIRST PRIZE

Student
MATTHEW BAXTER

Tutors
STEPHEN BLAND & SUSAN PEACE

College
UNIVERSITY OF NORTHUMBRIA

SECOND PRIZE

Student
ANDREW PRITCHARD

Tutors
GERRY DOWNES & ELLEN MOORCRAFT

College
NORWICH SCHOOL OF ART & DESIGN

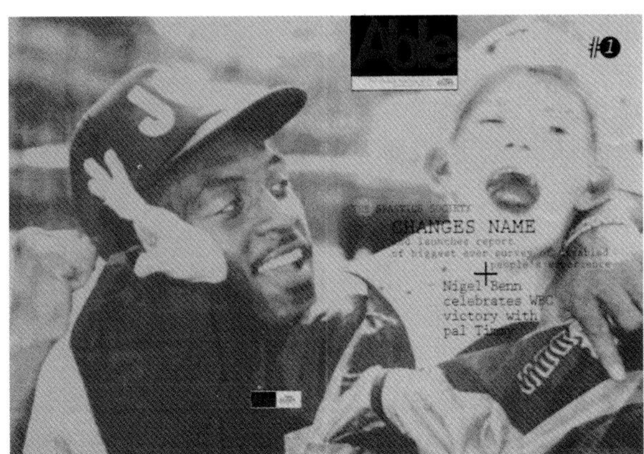

CORPORATE IDENTITY

FIRST PRIZE

Student
AMI VAN DINE

Tutors
MIKE LUXTON &
PHIL GIGGLE

College
BUCKINGHAMSHIRE
COLLEGE

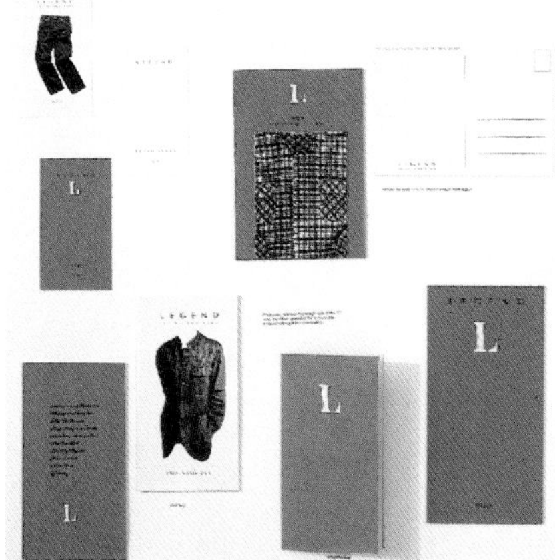

Sponsored by Pearce Signs

Brief set by Nicholas Pearce: Pearce Signs,

John Dunlop: Coley Porter Bell

In our first year as sponsors, we were delighted with both the quantity and particularly, the quality of entries. Students had clearly put a lot of thought and effort into their submissions which made our task as judges all the more difficult! We would like to have been able to award several more prizes but in the end our two winners emerged as outstanding. Congratulations to everyone who entered and better luck next year to those who did not win.

Nicholas Pearce
Pearce Signs

SECOND PRIZE

Student
DANIEL GRZONKA

Tutors
STEPHEN BLAND &
SUSAN PEACE

College
UNIVERSITY OF
NORTHUMBRIA

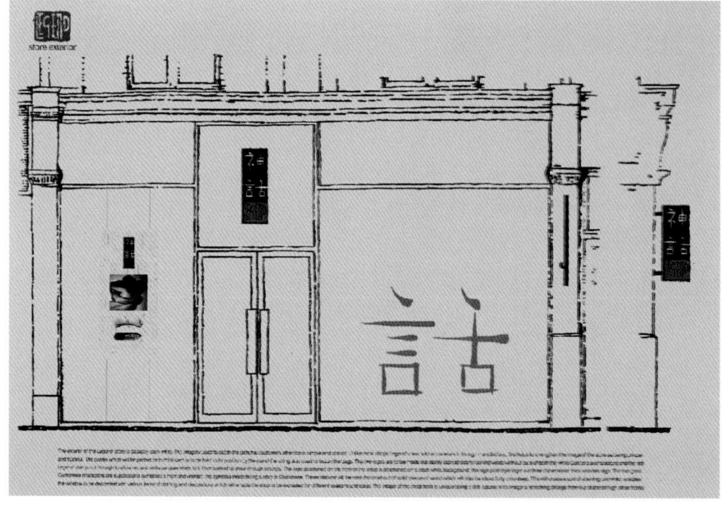

Sponsored by National Westminster Bank

Brief set by Graham Watson: Barle Bogle Hegarty,

Edward Pertwee: NatWest

NatWest is delighted to support the Student Awards for the second year.

It is increasingly difficult to create stand-out in a cluttered, ever expanding financial environment and the brief set was a real challenge.

The standard of work entered was exceptional, fresh/innovative ideas, real creative excellence.

Judging the award could not have been more rewarding as we agonised over the short-list. I hope the award will help some very talented individuals realise their full potential in an ad agency who I hope will someday work on the NatWest account.

Edward Pertwee
NatWest

TELEVISION ADVERTISING

FIRST PRIZE

Students
MAX MUNCK & ANDREW LLOYD-JONES

Tutor
JOHN GILLARD

College
SCHOOL OF COMMUNICATION ARTS

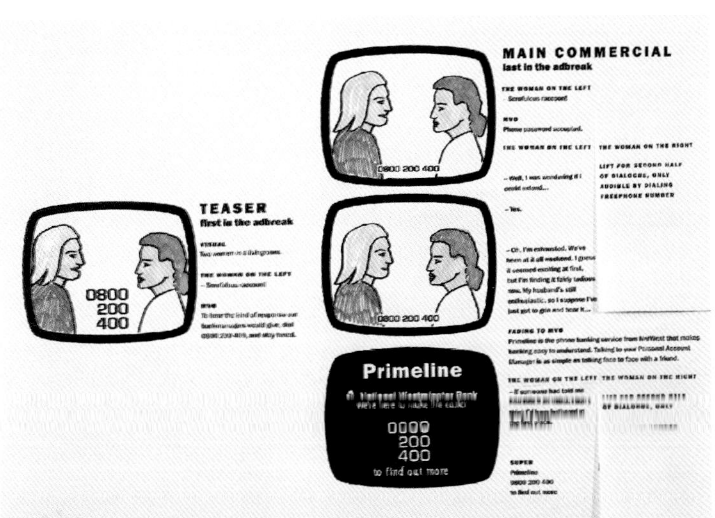

SECOND PRIZE

Student
AUSTIN CHARLESWORTH

Tutors
SUZIE HANNA & TERRY YETTON

College
NORWICH SCHOOL OF ART & DESIGN

BRAND IDENTITY

FIRST PRIZE

Student
STEVEN SPENCER

Tutors
PETER SMITH &
GILL SCOTT

College
RAVENSBOURNE
COLLEGE

Sponsored by The Burton Group

Brief set by Joanne Malster: Steven Sharp,

Nina Custerson: Dorothy Perkins

This was the Burton Group's first sponsorship of the D&AD Student Awards and we have found the involvement an interesting and rewarding experience as a fashion retailer.

The standard of work was outstanding.

It took a great deal of concentrated thought to keep the 'brief' requirements firmly in mind, whilst judging high standards of creative concepts.

The volume of entries and level of interest for the project was an added bonus. It has certainly been a very worthwhile partnership.

Nina Custerson
Dorothy Perkins

SECOND PRIZE

Student
ANGELA BAYNES

Tutors
MIKE LUXTON &
PHIL GIGGLE

College
BUCKINGHAMSHIRE
COLLEGE

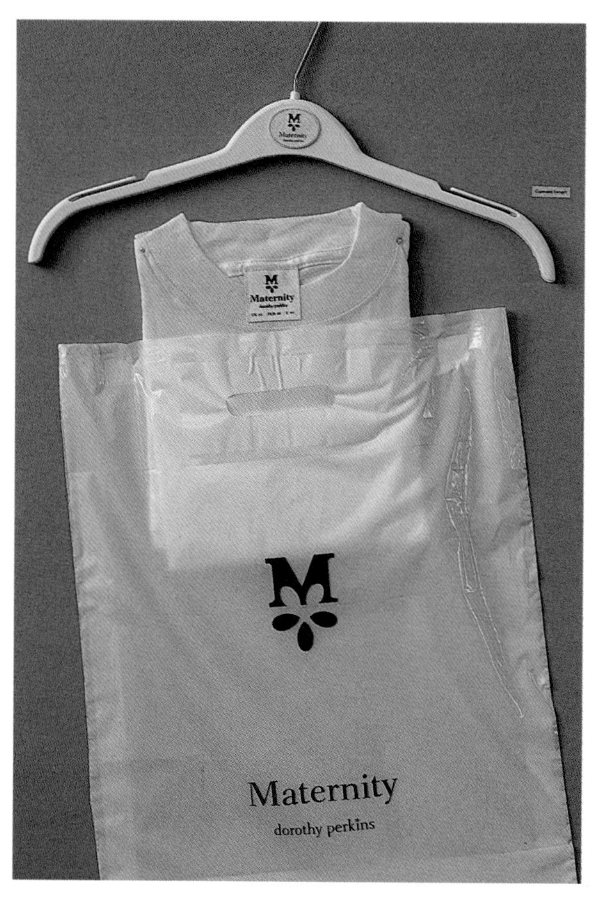

EXHIBITION DESIGN

FIRST PRIZE

Student
PEAKASH PATEL

Tutor
DAVID DALZIEL

College
NEWHAM COLLEGE

Sponsored by Philippe Wrigley Design Company

Brief set by Philippe Wrigley: Philippe Wrigley Design,

Paula Watson: Ericsson

It has been a great pleasure to be involved with the D&AD Student Awards. Its' influence has been immense in promoting young creativity towards a highly competitive market, increasing awareness to meet higher standards and stronger growth for our industries.

The exhibition entries although few, were of a very high standard in its creative response to a most difficult brief. Many of the students have developed some very interesting concepts that could have been winners. Unfortunately, some got so carried away that they neglected the brief or did not complete the project.

The overall winner was very impressive at all levels. The student had studied the brief carefully and developed a highly imaginary response. The design had been developed from the concept right through to the final presentation. The consideration to how people behave, the practical and comfortable issues, along with the visual communication stood out. This in conjunction with the excellent execution of the final design and presentation format has made this student a worthy winner to this category. The standard of work and presentation was very complete and highly professional.

POINT OF SALE

FIRST PRIZE

Students
MARIA HIPWELL &
ARLETTE DUNN

Tutor
JOHN FAIRBANKS

College
BUCKINGHAMSHIRE
COLLEGE

SECOND PRIZE

Student
TIM BREMNER

Tutors
STEPHEN BLAND &
SUSAN PEACE

College
UNIVERSITY OF
NORTHUMBRIA

*Sponsored by
Time Out*

*Brief set by Gill Auld,
Kirk Teasdale,
Jim Heinemann: Time Out*

It is sometimes said that there are no new ideas – only old ones re-invented. Yet it is true that in a fiercely competitive environment such as publishing, we rely on ideas to get noticed. The fusion between industry and education, such as that which happens during student awards, is vital to encourage and reward the kind of invention without limitations from which genuinely new ideas flow.

We were extremely impressed by the overall standard of all the work submitted in our category and spent much longer than anticipated discussing each one. In the end our winner was an unanimous and instant hit! We chose the winner because of the utter simplicity of the idea and the fact that it was useful, inexpensive, space-saving benefit to the outlet, produced with wit and humour.

In short, we could not have expected the brief to be met so perfectly.

*Gill Auld
Time Out*

Sponsored by Mercury Communications

Brief set by Axel Chaldecott & Ruth Lees: Howell Henry Chaldecott Lury & Partners

Creativity in radio advertising, if this year's entries are anything to go by, still suffers from the general malaise in this category of the regurgitation of tried and tested 'formulas' – the well known presenter route is obviously still a popular choice but entirely predictable and moving things nowhere. The main thing to remember about radio advertising is that 90% of it either irritates the hell out of the listener or remains background noise to be ignored – the challenge is to find a way of getting people's attention and retaining it before they can turn the sound down.

There are real opportunities in radio advertising however and the winners of this category have taken the challenge of doing something interesting by creating a new and different way of talking to the target market.

The winning team have answered the brief cleverly by playing surprising and entertaining games with the media, understanding its shortcomings and strengths and, importantly, exploiting fully the target market's psyche. By literally 'highjacking' radio programmes and duping phone-ins the idea creates a greater halo of publicity and noise around the campaign than a straightforward advertising idea can. It is a brave solution and a challenge to execute.

Ruth Lees
Howell Henry Chaldecott Lury & Partners

Mercury Minicall Live Radio

"Request Show"

Our caller gets onto request shows on stations like Kiss FM, Radio 1 etc, and once on air, asks the DJ to play "Hanging on the Telephone", by Blondie.
He says he would like to dedicate the song to his Mercury Minicall, because since buying it, he hasn't been hanging on the telephone at all.
His friends can contact him wherever he is, and he never misses out on anything...

"Agony Aunt"

Our caller is close to tears when he calls an agony-aunt slot on Talk Radio, Capital, etc, and begins a very sad story.
He tells how his friends just won't leave him alone...he says how nice and quiet his life used to be. He then begins crying, saying it's no good, he's [illegible]... he just can't [illegible] to his Mercury Minicall...that it won't stop beeping...how he is trapped in a world of non-stop socialising... What can he do?
If he gets a response, he then tries to sell his Minicall to listeners, asking them to call him on 0500 505 505, howling that he just can't take anymore...

RADIO ADVERTISING

FIRST PRIZE

Students
SIMON HARDY & STEVE WILLIAMS

Tutors
DAVE MORRIS & LYNDON MALLET

College
BUCKINGHAMSHIRE COLLEGE

TITLE: JULIA (3)

DJ: We've still not heard from or been able to trace Neil Freeman, so if you're listening Neil would you kindly get to a phone and call Julia now. She has some very important news for you.
Of course, if you'd had a Mercury Minicall, like Julia, she could have contacted you. Anytime of the day. Anywhere in the country and for only 20p.
But never mind, we hope you have a good time tonight, wherever you end up.

F.V.O To find out more about Mercury's Minicall, call 0500 505 505. And ask to speak to Julia.

SECOND PRIZE

Students
SIMON ROSEBLADE & GLENN GIBBINS

Tutor
LOU KLEIN

College
BUCKINGHAMSHIRE COLLEGE

STATIONERY DESIGN

FIRST PRIZE

Student
MARTIN LAWLESS

Tutors
STEPHEN BLAND &
SUSAN PEACE

College
UNIVERSITY OF
NORTHUMBRIA

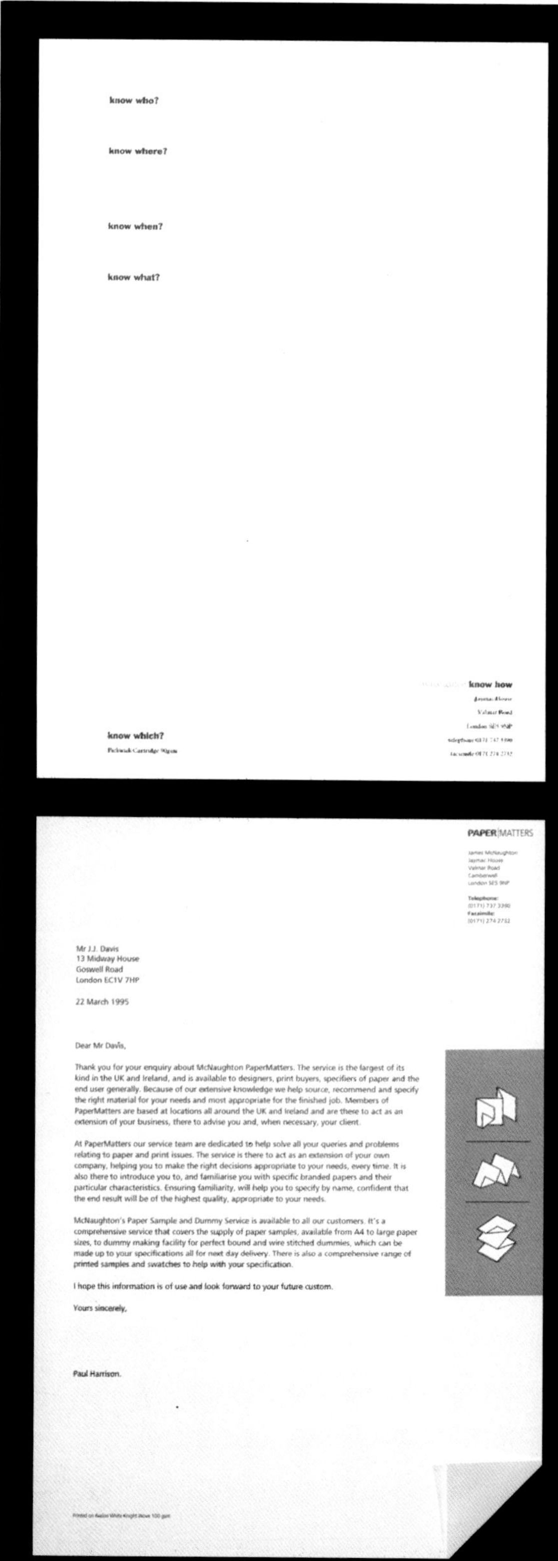

know who?

know where?

know when?

know what?

know how

know which?

PAPER|MATTERS

Telephone:
(0171) 737 3390
Facsimile:
(0171) 274 2732

Mr J.J. Davis
13 Midway House
Goswell Road
London EC1V 7HP

22 March 1995

Dear Mr Davis,

Thank you for your enquiry about McNaughton PaperMatters. The service is the largest of its kind in the UK and Ireland, and is available to designers, print buyers, specifiers of paper and the end user generally. Because of our extensive knowledge we help source, recommend and specify the right material for your needs and most appropriate for the finished job. Members of PaperMatters are based at locations all around the UK and Ireland and are there to act as an extension of your business, there to advise you and, when necessary, your client.

At PaperMatters our service team are dedicated to help solve all your queries and problems relating to paper and print issues. The service is there to act as an extension of your own company, helping you to make the right decisions appropriate to your needs, every time. It is also there to introduce you to, and familiarise you with specific branded papers and their particular characteristics. Ensuring familiarity, will help you to specify by name, confident that the end result will be of the highest quality, appropriate to your needs.

McNaughton's Paper Sample and Dummy Service is available to all our customers. It's a comprehensive service that covers the supply of paper samples, available from A4 to large paper sizes, to dummy making facility for perfect bound and wire stitched dummies, which can be made up to your specifications all for next day delivery. There is also a comprehensive range of printed samples and swatches to help with your specification.

I hope this information is of use and look forward to your future custom.

Yours sincerely,

Paul Harrison.

SECOND PRIZE

Student
JOHN DOWLING

Tutors
STEPHEN BLAND &
SUSAN PEACE

College
UNIVERSITY OF
NORTHUMBRIA

Sponsored by The James McNaughton Paper Group

Brief set by Michael Johnson: Johnson Banks,

Wendy Morrell: James McNaughton Paper Group,

Debbie Stacey: McNaughton Paper Advisory Service

The brief for the Paper Advisory service stationery was intentionally broad. It had both a lot of detail and a lot of holes. It was carefully written to allow someone to break through the brief to the other side.

It's fair to say that most struggled to do this. We saw of a lot of very literal reactions to the brief: a lot of paper made into everything from paper aeroplanes to letters, paper in piles, paper in boxes and then folded paper as, well, folded paper.

But the two winners shone through. The runner-up whilst, yes, using the dreaded folded paper, used it in such a tasteful, consistent and clean way that it defied belief that it was a student piece we were looking at.

But the winner did what I wanted. He read the brief, digested it, then threw it away. He thought of a great name, applied it brilliantly to stationery, and then designed one of the loopiest mailers I've seen for a long, long time.

Perfectly on, or off, brief, depending on how you look at it. And from my perspective, absolutely on. I'm only sorry that I'll be away and will not meet the two winners but I'd like to buy them both a big fat lunch when I get back.

Wendy Morrell
James McNaughton Paper Group,

DIRECT MAIL

*Sponsored by
Thrislington Cubicles*

*Brief set by
Patrick Wilson:
Thrislington Cubicles,*

Aziz Cami: The Partners

As usual the quality and original ideas provided by students was first class. In my view the winning work is outstanding. Both judges agreed on a clear winner which is unusal considering the overall standard.

It is the [illegible] [illegible] sponsored the Awards and the benefits it gives, not only to the students but the staff at Thrislington, will mean we will sponsor them for many years to come.

*Patrick Wilson
Thrislington Cubicles*

FIRST PRIZE

Student
STEPHEN CONCHIE

Tutor
BRYN JONES

College
UNIVERSITY
OF CENTRAL
LANCASHIRE

SECOND PRIZE

Student
JAMES MOUNTAIN

Tutor
JOHN FAIRBANKS

College
BUCKINGHAMSHIRE
COLLEGE

POSTERS

FIRST PRIZE

Students
KARIN WEIDEMA &
MARK RUDD

Tutor
JOHN GILLARD

College
SCHOOL OF
COMMUNICATION
ARTS

SECOND PRIZE

Student
ALISTAIR ROSS

Tutors
BARRIE TULLETT &
BOBBIE COLEMAN

College
EDINBURGH
COLLEGE OF ART

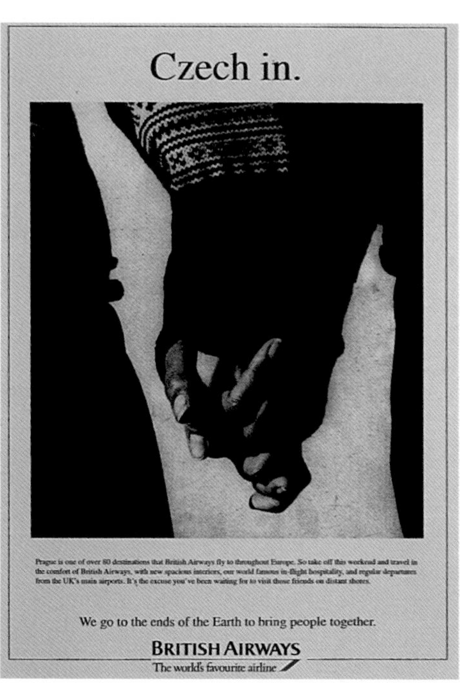

Sponsored by British Airways

Brief set by Mike Crump: British Airways

British Airways felt strongly enough to support the Student Awards with a live brief that was derived from a project set to its own advertising agency round about the same time. The brief was set as part of the airlines masterbrand 'repositioning' programme and the students were asked to bring a new approach to the companies advertising specifically looking at the poster element of a cross media campaign.

The response was as diverse as it was enthusiastic. The majority of entrants demonstrated a great deal of thought and innovation in their concepts, producing effective pieces of communication within the framework of the British Airways brand identity.

However, the winner had simply the best creative execution of the brief and had all the elements of a successful campaign. It was very easy to see how the concept could develop over a period of time and how it could naturally cut across into many of our international markets. Its message was very clear, bold and humorous, effectively answering the key message in the brief from the airlines repositioning statement of 'global and caring'.

Mike Crump
British Airways

Sponsored by Vauxhall

Brief set by Peter Stephenson-Wright: Lowe Howard-Spink,

John Deed. Vauxhall

Anyone involved in the real-life process of trying to brief and produce outstanding advertising under the pressures of time and resource that apply in the real world, can't fail to be seduced by the prospect of judging from hundreds of solutions, carefully developed over many months to get the most from the brief. In the event, we were not disappointed.

The range and finish of the submissions were immediately impressive. Fresh ideas were perhaps at something more of a premium – I hope I never have to read another variation of 'Vauxhall will build a car any colour you like as long as it's green.' And lots of entrants had apparently missed that injunction in our brief to avoid 'boy-racer' imagery.

But in the end, the winners stood out clearly from the rest. Simple thoughts married to visual analogies pared to the minimum. The first prize winner did all this slightly better than the second. Straightforward as that.

And we've commended another campaign that was a bit of a personal favourite but lacked that last bit of development to make the idea as clear in practice as it was in theory. But overall, if this is the kind of talent shortly to be entering our industry, the future looks bright. Roll on the next Millennium!

Peter Stephenson-Wright
Lowe Howard-Spink

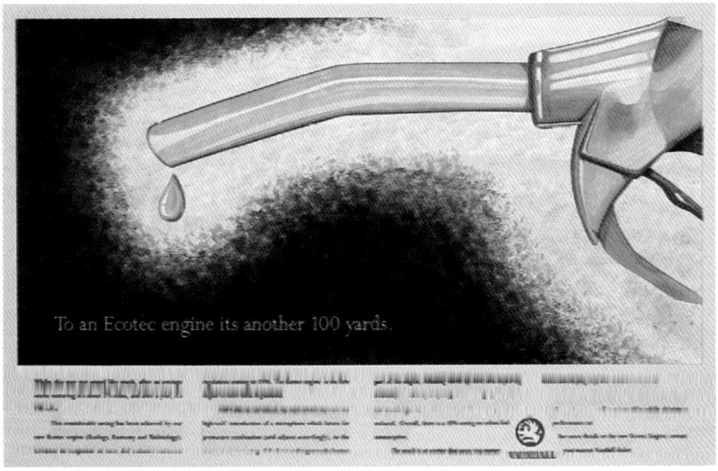

PRESS & MAGAZINE ADVERTISING

FIRST PRIZE

Students
MICHELLE POWER & SUSAN BYRNE

Tutor
DAVE MORRIS

College
BUCKINGHAMSHIRE COLLEGE

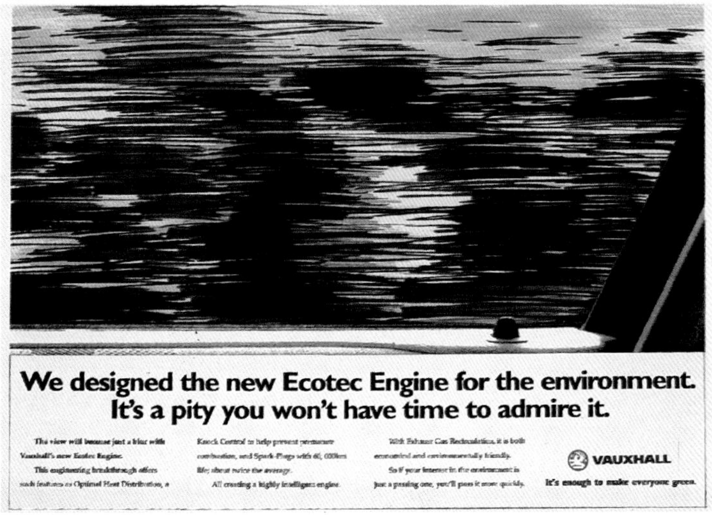

SECOND PRIZE

Students
ALEXANDRA HILL & KERRY FINLAY

Tutors
LINDA SINCLAIR & TONY TUCKER

College
UNIVERSITY OF CENTRAL LANCASHIRE

PHOTOGRAPHY

FIRST PRIZE

Student
KES JAMES

Tutors
JEAN BRAID &
LEE WIDOWS

College
KINGSTON
UNIVERSITY

SECOND PRIZE

Student
JONATHAN KITCHEN

Tutor
GEOFF CLARK

College
BLACKPOOL & THE
FYLDE COLLEGE

Sponsored by Benson & Hedges, Gallaher

Brief set by Billy Mawhinney: SPLintas

No client has done more to raise standards in photography than Gallahers. Their poster work has championed the cause of talented lensmen for many years now so I was delighted when they agreed to sponsor this category.

The high standard set by the sponsors was more than met by the 85 entries from students all over the country. Technically they were all superb so congratulations to the tutors who have obviously worked hard with their students to achieve this.

There was also a richness of ideas which made it difficult to narrow the field to a shortlist of 25 and even harder to make the final selection.

Well done to everyone who entered especially the winners, the future for clients who recognise the benefit of excellence in photography is looking good.

Billy Mawhinney
SPLintas

ILLUSTRATION

SECOND PRIZE

Student
ALISON GOULD

Tutors
MIKE LUXTON &
PHIL GIGGLE

College
BUCKINGHAMSHIRE
COLLEGE

Sponsored by EMI Classics

Brief set by Polly Miller: EMI Classics,

David Freeman: Sampson Tyrrell

EMI Classics sponsored the illustration category, and the entrants were judged by myself, along with David Freeman and Christopher Nurko from Sampson Tyrrell, our main design agency.

However, the work submitted was more predictable than we would have liked, and the judging process saw us rejecting a high percentage of the work at an early stage. Some of this was due to students not following the mandatory requirements of the brief, but mostly the rejected work was too limited in its approach. We would have liked to see more unexpected and innovative solutions come out of the brief, rather than the mimicking of current illustration trends.

EMI Classics looks forward to further sponsorship and support in design, illustration and photography with D&AD.

Polly Miller
EMI

PACKAGING

FIRST PRIZE

Student
HAYLEY JANE WALL

Tutors
STEPHEN BLAND &
SUSAN PEACE

College
UNIVERSITY OF
NORTHUMBRIA

Sponsored by Beck's

Brief set by Anthony Fawcett: Anthony Fawcett Sponsorship Consultants,

Rupert Hopkins: Barker & Ralston

SECOND PRIZE

Student
ANTHONY WILKS

Tutors
MIKE LUXTON &
PHIL GIGGLE

College
BUCKINGHAMSHIRE
COLLEGE

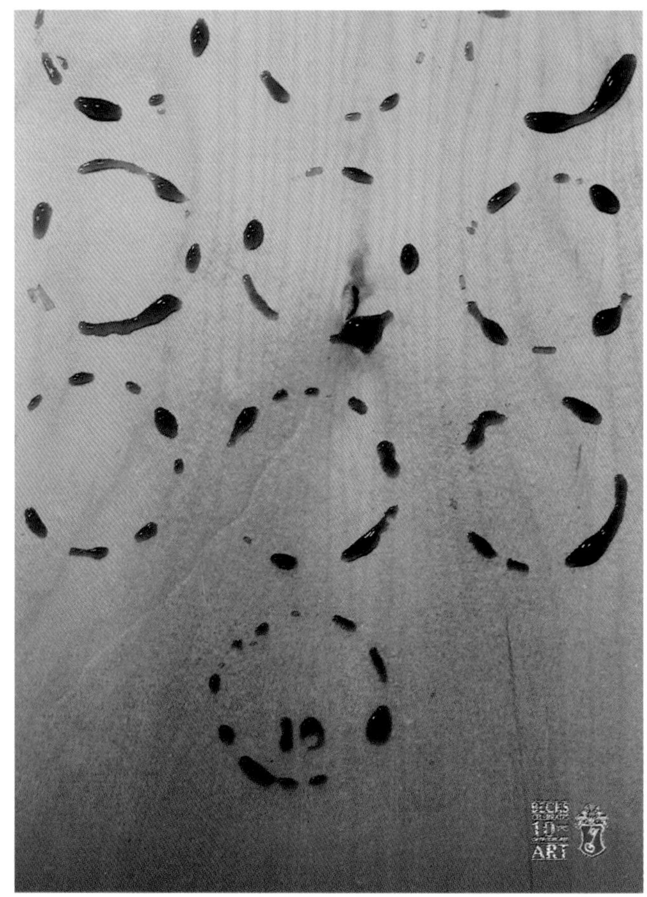

1995
D&AD MEMBERS

HOW TO BECOME A MEMBER

D&AD is supported by both individuals and companies and has a membership of over 1450 leading professionals.

FULL MEMBERSHIP

This is open to individuals whose work is judged to be of sufficiently high standard to be included in the D&AD Annual. Full Members run the Association, elect the Executive and form part of D&AD's constitution. Full Members are drawn from a range of disciplines including art directors, copywriters, designers, photographers, typographers and illustrators.

ASSOCIATE MEMBERSHIP

This is open to individuals, proposed by Full Members, who demonstrably support D&AD's aims and ideals - the promotion and encouragement of creative excellence - and who are responsible for and involved in, work of significant quality. Associate Members are often drawn from the client community but many others are involved in the management of creative projects - for example Marketing Managers or Account Handlers.

First and second prize-winners of the D&AD Student Awards are invited to join the Associate Membership scheme for one year at no charge.

INTERNATIONAL MEMBERSHIP

This is open to individuals, living overseas, who appreciate the value of creative excellence and want to keep in touch with developments in UK advertising and design work.

BENEFITS OF MEMBERSHIP

All members receive the following benefits:

- Free copies of the D&AD Annual and showreel which includes your work and your name in the credits
- A new quarterly newsletter and regular mailings updating you on important events and special offers
- Members' discounts on D&AD programmes including the President's Lectures and Festival of Excellence
- Invitations to Private Views and special events
- Regular special offers

For further information on Membership please contact the Membership Department on 0171 582 6487.

A

Scott Aal · *Copywriter*
David Abbott · *Copywriter*
Alan Aboud · *Art Director*
Marksteen Adamson · *European Creative Director*
Bela Adler · *Photographer*
Jim Aitchison · *Creative Director*
Stak Aivaliotis · *Film Director*
Roger Akerman · *Art Director*
Ahmad Munjed Al-Sharif · *Producer/Director*
Douglas Alexander · *Designer*
Roger Alexander · *Solicitor*
Julia Alldridge · *Designer*
David Allen · *Managing Director*
Robyn Alpert · *Executive Creative Director*
John Altman · *Composer*
Ethan Ames · *Graphic Designer*
Silas Amos · *Designer*
Mark Andrews · *Agency Producer*
Christopher Ang · *Managing Director*
Nicholas Angell · *Managing Director*
Geoffrey Appleton · *Illustrator*
Derek Apps · *Copywriter*
Robert Archer · *Graphic Designer*
Paul Arden · *Commericals Director*
Andy Arghyrou · *Art Director*
Morag Arman Addey · *Publisher*
Rosemary Arnold · *Art Director*
Tim Ashton · *Creative Director*
John Athorn · *Creative Director*
Will Atkinson · *Creative Director*
Maria Au Yeung · *Creative Director*
Gillian Auld · *Marketing Director*
Will Awdry · *Copywriter*

B

John Bacon · *Creative Director*
Scott Bain · *Art Director*
Andy Baker · *Modelmaker/Designer*
Jim Baker · *Director*
Mandy Baker · *Typographer*
Roger Baker · *Joint Managing Director*
Stewart Baker · *Art Director*
Jack Bankhead · *Photographer*
John Banks · *Chairman*
Brian Bansgrove · *Lighting Director*
Zafer Baran · *Photographer*
Daniel Barber · *Director*
Don Barclay · *Concept Creator/Art Director*
David Barker · *Copywriter*
Larry Barker · *Copywriter*
Mike Barker · *Art Director*
Will Barnett · *Copywriter*
Olea Barr · *Creative Director*
Jacci Barrett · *Producer*
Bob Barrie · *Art Director*
Tony Barry · *Copywriter*
Neil Barstow · *Photographer*
John Bartle · *Joint Chief Executive*
Shaun Bateman · *Copywriter*
Peter Bates · *Designer*
John Bateson · *Designer*
Ann Baxendale · *Art Director*
Matthew Baxter · *Junior Designer*
Tim Bayless · *Writer Director*
Flo Bayley · *Designer*
Angela Baynes · *Graphic Designer*
Richard Baynes · *Photographic Producer*
Robert Bean · *Managing Partner*
David Beard · *Designer*
Roger Beattie · *Copywriter*
Trevor Beattie · *Creative Director*
Ian Beck · *Illustrator*
Roger Beckett · *Copywriter*
John Bedford · *Creative Director*
Nick Bell · *Copywriter*
Peter Bell · *Managing Director*
Madeleine Bennett · *Designer*
Marc Bennett · *Art Director*
Keith Benton · *Producer*
Simon Bere · *Copywriter*
Bruce Beresford · *Designer*
James Best · *Chairman*
Gary Betts · *Art Director*
James Beveridge · *Designer*
Dave Beverley · *Art Director*
Paul Bevitt · *Photographer*
Anthony Biles · *Designer*
Lloyd Billing · *Sound Engineer*
Bob Bird · *Director of Public Relations*
Ian Bird · *Computer Animator*
John Blackburn · *Creative Director*
Murray Blacket · *Designer*
Stephen Blackman · *Director*
Bernadette Blair · *Designer/Course Director*
Anthony Blake · *Photographer*
Stuart Blake · *Copywriter*
Stephen Bland · *Principal Lecturer*
Nick Bleasel · *Copywriter*
Laurence Blume · *Copywriter*
Anthony Blurton · *Designer*
Hans Bockting · *Designer*
Tony Bodinetz · *Creative Director*
Wilton Boey · *Art Director*
Nigel Bogle · *Joint Chief Executive*
Mike Boles · *Copywriter*
Andrew Bone · *Design Director*
Bill Borders · *Director of Creative Services – Advertising*
Julia Bostock · *Creative Director*
Hein Botha · *Group Creative Director*
George Boyter · *Art Director*
Chris Bradley · *Designer*
James Bradley · *Managing Director*
Barry Brand · *Head of Typography*
Kevin Bratley · *Art Director*
Timothy Braybrooks · *Copywriter*
Paul Brazier · *Art Director*
Tim Bremner · *Designer*
John Br[illegible] · *Creative Director*
Paul Briginshaw · *Art Director*
Tony Brignull · *Copywriter*
Jane Brimblecombe · *TV Producer*
Paul Bringloe · *Copywriter*
John Brockliss · *Graphic Designer*
David Brook · *Marketing Director*
Mike Brooking · *Copywriter*
Sheila Broom · *Lecturer Graphic Design*
Newy Brothwell · *Art Director*
Bryan Brown · *Designer*
David Brown · *Copywriter*
David Brown · *Director*
Graham Brown · *Vice Chairman*
Ron Brown · *Art Director*
Warren Brown · *Art Director*
Mick Brownfield · *Illustrator*
Paul Browton · *Creative Director*
Gary Bryan · *Film Director/Photographer*
Andy Bryant · *Account Director*
David Buchanan · *Copywriter*
Alex Buckingham · *Photographer*
Stuart Buckley · *Art Director*
Frank Budgen · *Director*
Matthew Bull · *Creative Director*
Sheila Bull · *Copywriter*
Andy Bunday · *Art Director*
Terry Bunton · *Director*
Paul Burke · *Concept Creator*
Hugh Burkitt · *Chairman*
Rob Burleigh · *Copywriter*
Alan Burles · *Art Director*
Max Burt · *Board Account Director*
Jethro Burton · *Photographer*
Thomas Bury · *Managing Director*
Gaby Bush · *Executive Creative Director*
Richard Butler · *Deputy Chairman*
Ian Butterworth · *Art Director*
Graham Button · *Associate Creative Director*
Brian Byfield · *Director*
Stuart Byfield · *Creative Director*
James Bygrave · *Senior Editor*
Susan Byrne · *Art Director*

C

Adrian Caddy · *Deputy Creative Director*
Andrew Cade · *Creative Director*
Felix Calitz · *Creative Director*
Steve Callen · *Creative Director*
Aziz Cami · *Designer*
Joe Campbell · *Composer*
Maggie Campbell · *Head of TV*
Robert Campbell · *Copywriter*
Walter Campbell · *Art Director*
Tom Campion · *Copywriter*
Jon Canning · *Copywriter*
Graham Cappi · *Art Director*
Simon Carbery · *Copywriter*
Paul Cardwell · *Copywriter*
Richard Carman · *Copywriter*
Fiona Carpenter · *Art Director*
Jeremy Carr · *Art Director*
Cameron Carruthers · *Designer*
Rooney Carruthers · *Creative Director*
Peers Carter · *Copywriter*
Philip Carter · *Designer/Creative Director*
Terry Carter · *Creative Director*
Tom Carty · *Copywriter*
Ben Casey · *Designer*
Iain Cassie · *Director*
Neil Cassie · *Deputy Chairman*
Olivia Castelnau · *TV Producer*
Paul Catmur · *Copywriter*
Steve Cavalier · *Photographer*
Mario Cavalli · *Director*
Michael Cavers · *Creative Director*
Christopher Cawte · *Designer*
Justin Cernis · *Business Development Director*
Alison Davis Chaitham · *National Illustration Director*
Alan Chan · *Creative Director*
Theseus Chan · *Art Director*
Mark Chapman · *Director*
Andrew Chappin · *Art Director*
Nicolas Charavet · *Graphic Designer*
Charity Charity · *Copywriter*
Austin Charlesworth · [illegible]
Barry Chattington · *Director*
Mark Chaudoir · *Graphic Designer*
Andy Cheetham · *Creative Director*
Christopher Cheetham · *Photographer*
Steve Chetham · *Art Director*
Ian Chilvers · *Graphic Designer*
Ross Chowles · *Creative Director*
Andrew Christie · *Managing Director*
Jean Chu · *Graphic Design*
Paul Cilia La Corte · *Graphic Designer*
Alan Cinnamond · *Art Director*
John Claridge · *Photographer*
Bryan Clark · *Designer*
Curtis Clark · *Cinematographer*
Andy P Clarke · *Director*
John S Clarke · *Director*
Nicholas Clements · *Executive Business Director*
John Clifford · *Art Director*
Tom Climpson · *Art Director*
Martin Coates · *Marketing Director*
Phil Cockrell · *Copywriter*
Tim Coddington · *Film Producer*
John Coe · *Company Director*
Simon Coker · *Senior Designer*
Peter Collingwood · *Copywriter*
Damon Collins · *Art Director*
Kim Collins · *Company Director*
Mark Collis · *Copywriter*
Patrick Collister · *Copywriter*
Alan Colville · *Designer*
Terry Comer · *Senior Writer*
Stephen Conchie · *Designer*
Thomas Connaughton · *Copywriter*
Brian Connolly · *Art Director*
Philip Contomichalos · *Producer*
Gary Cook · *Creative Director*
Malcom Cook · *Marketing Manager*
Gary Cooke · *Designer*
Mark Cooke · *Creative Services Director*
Mary Cooke · *Director*
Roger Cooper · *Designer*
Stephen Cooper · *Account Director*
Mark Coppos · *Director*
Mike Cornish · *Managing Director*
David Corr · *Copywriter*
Michael Coulter · *Copywriter*
Michael Courthold · *Designer*
Keith Courtney · *Art Director*
Geoff Cousins · *Copywriter*
Jon Cousins · *Director*
Jason Coward · *Account Director*
Barry Cox · *Management Supervisor*
Tony Cox · *Creative Director*
Michael Cozens · *Director*
Andrew Cracknell · *Creative Director*
Jeremy Craigen · *Copywriter*
Robert Cramp · *Photographer/Film Director*
Mark Cramphorn · *Managing Partner*
Ricard Cresa · *Creative Director*
Allan Crew · *Creative Director*
Charles Crisp · *Head of TV*
Iain Crockart · *Graphic Designer*
Cecily Croke · *Copywriter*
Steve Cronan · *Creative Services Director*
Cyril Cronin · *Creative Director*
Peter Crossing · *Company Director*
Bruce Crouch · *Copywriter*
Peter Crowther · *Communications Manager*
Sean Cummins · *National Creative Director*
Karen Cunningham · *Producer*
Doug Currie · *Photographer*
Alan Curson · *Copywriter*
Philip G Czarnec · *Art Director*

D

Richard Daglish · *Managing Director*
Graham Daldry · *Copywriter*
Michael Darby · *Designer*
Peter Darrell · *Film Director*
Ashted Dastor · *Designer*
Peter Davenport · *Designer*
Ian David · *Art Director*
Andrew Davidson · *Illustrator*
Glynn Scott Davidson · *Art Director*
Tony Davidson · *Art Director*
Chris Davies · *Managing Director*
Gill Davies · *Graphic Designer*
[illegible] · *Managing Director*
Steve Davies · *Design Director*
Bill Davison · *Lecturer*
Janice Davison · *Graphic Designer*
Sam Davy · *Graphic Designer*
Gary Dawson · *Copywriter*
Neil Dawson · *Art Director*
Nigel Dawson · *Typographer*
Peter Dawson · *Creative Director*
Derek Day · *Director*
Michel de Boer · *Designer/Partner*
Will De L'Ecluse · *Designer*
Russell De Rozario · *Art Director*
Trevor De Silva · *Copywriter*
Gerard de Thame · *Director*
Lewin De Villers · *Creative Director*
John Dean · *Creative Director*
Richard Dean · *Film Technician*
Robert L Dean · *Sales Rep.*
Philip Dearman · *Copywriter*
Barry Delaney · *Copywriter*
Gregory Delaney · *Creative Director*
Paul Delaney · *Creative Director*
Simon Delaney · *Director*
Theo Delaney · *Film Director*
Tim Delaney · *Creative Director*
Penny Delmon · *Graphic Designer*
Mike Dempsey · *Art Director*
Rita Dempsey · *Copywriter*
Richard Dennison · *Art Director*
Michael Denny · *Graphic Designer*
Jonathan Dent · *Designer*
Mark Denton · *Creative Director*
Stephen Denton · *Copywriter*
Brian Denyer · *Design Consultant*
Michael Devito-French · *Art Director*
Martin Devlin · *Graphic Designer*
Shaun Dew · *Director*
Alan Dewhurst · *Executive Producer*
Dario Diaz · *Executive Vice President-Executive Creative Director*
Mark Dibsdall · *Account Director*
Chris Dickens · *Worldwide Media Director*
Ian Dickens · *Communications Director*
Nigel Dicker · *Art Director*
Simon Dicketts · *Creative Director*
Rachel Dinnis · *Graphic Designer*
Blackett Ditchburn · *Corporate Communications Manager*
Patricia Doherty · *Copywriter*
John Doig · *Creative Director, Advertising*
John Donnelly · *Copywriter*
Sheila Donovan · *Lecturer*
Michael Doran · *Photographer*
John Dowling · *Graphic Designer*
Terry Dowling · *Graphic Designer*
Nick Downes · *Art Director*
Jim Downie · *Creative Director*
Steve Dowson · *Designer*
Sean Doyle · *Copywriter*

Rick Dublin · *Director/Photographer*
Scott Duchon · *Copywriter*
Ian Ducker · *Art Director*
Bruce Duckworth · *Designer*
Malcolm Duffy · *Copywriter*
Belinda Duggan · *Design Director*
Gert Dumbar · *Designer*
Geoff Dunbar · *Director*
Arlette Dunn · *Art Director/Copywriter*
Iain Dunn · *Copywriter*
Paul Dunn · *Photographer*
Maire-Catherine Dupuy · *Creative Director*
Dave Dye · *Art Director*

E

Dave East · *Creative Director*
Helen East · *Tutor*
Antony Easton · *Art Director*
Paul Eastwood · *Creative Director*
Ged Edmondson · *Copywriter*
Garnet Edwards · *Art Director*
Steve Eichenbaum · *Creative Director*
Jonathan Ellery · *Creative Director*
Maggie Elsdon · *Executive Creative Director*
Dick Emery · *Director of Market Strategy*
Ruth Emslie · *Marketing Communications Consultant*
Vince Engel · *Associate Creative Director*
Peter Engelhardt · *Designer*
Simon Esterson · *Designer*
Trevor Evans · *Producer*
Michael Everett · *Copywriter*
Andy Ewan · *Graphic Designer*

F

Will Farquhar · *Copywriter*
Gerry Farrell · *Copywriter*
Mark Farrow · *Designer*
Neil Fazakerly · *Senior Writer*
Graham Featherstone · *Art Director*
Paul Fella · *Art Director*
Alan Field · *Designer*
Sandy Field · *Graphic Designer*
Paul Fielding · *Designer*
David Fincher · *Director*
Graham Fink · *Director*
Kerry Finlay · *Copywriter*
Nick Finney · *Designer*
Julia Fish · *Director of Corporate Communications*
Kate Fishenden · *Designer*
George Fisher · *Managing Director*
Paul Fishlock · *Copywriter*
Rodney Fitch · *Designer*
David Flack · *Director*
Alistair Fleming · *Designer*
Alan Fletcher · *Designer*
Howard Fletcher · *Copywriter*
Winston Fletcher · *Chairman*
Richard Flintham · *Art Director*
Adrian Flowers · *Photographer*
Bonnie Folster · *Creative Director*
Graham Ford · *Photographer*
Chris Forman · *Buying Controller*
Max Forsythe · *Photographer*
John Foster · *Art Director*
Nigel Foster · *Producer*
Richard Foster · *Copywriter*
Richard Foster · *Photographer*
Nancy Fowler · *Director*
Richard Fowler · *Creative Director*
Barry Fox · *Writer*
Joseph Fraine · *Copywriter*
Mike Frampton · *Creative Director*
Cliff Francis · *Copywriter*
Stephen Franks · *Graphic Designer*
Dominic Frary · *Graphic Designer*
Andrew Fraser · *Copywriter*
Brian Fraser · *Art Director*
Glen Fraser · *Account Director*
Paul Fraser · *Copywriter*
Mike Freedman · *Creative Director*
Cliff Freeman · *Chairman/Ex. Creative Director*
David Freeman · *Creative Director*
Eddy French · *Film Editor*
John French · *Design Director*
Jason Fretwell · *Copywriter*
Paula Friedland · *Photographer*
Vince Frost · *Art Director*
James Fryer · *Copywriter*
David Fudger · *Tutor*
Jane Fuller · *Producer*

G

Bill Gallacher · *Art Director*
Cara Gallardo · *Graphic Designer*
Charles Grandin Gallichan · *Advertising Health Education*
Martin Galton · *Head of Art*
Jasvir Garcha · *Typographer/Designer*
David Gardiner · *Photographers Agent*
Surrey Garland · *Copywriter*
Paul Garrett · *Art Director*
Peter Garrett · *Art Director*
Karina Garrick · *Designer/Stylist*
Malcolm Gaskin · *Creative Director*
Tiggy Gatfield · *Producer*
Peter Gatley · *Art Director*
Peter Gausis · *Art Director*
Paul Gay · *Art Director*
Harry Georgiades · *Art Director*
Lisa Gernon · *Group Director of Marketing*
Domini Gettins · *Copywriter*
Aftab Gharda · *Course Director*
Tony Gibber · *Producer*
Glenn Gibbins · *Art Director*
Ginger Gibbons · *Producer*
Steve Gibbons · *Designer*
Luke Gifford · *Graphic Designer*
Nick Gill · *Art Director*
Stuart Gill · *Art Director*
John Gillard · *Principal*
Michael Gilmour · *Managing Director*
Dexter Ginn · *Art Director*
Hans Gissinger · *Phototographer*
Marco Giusti · *Executive Producer*
Rolph Gobits · *Photographer*
Keith Goddard · *Director of Photography*
Peter Goddard · *Film Editor*
Lexi Godfrey · *Executive Producer*
Neil Godfrey · *Art Director*
Jo Godman · *Managing Director*
Peter Goldammer · *Copywriter/Creative Director*
Gerald H Goldberg · *Executive*
M Golding · *Creative Director*
Colin Goodhew · *Graphic Designer*
Mark Goodwin · *Copywriter*
Michael Gore · *Creative Director*
John Gorham · *Graphic Designer*
Bernard Gormley · *Director*
Jason Gormley · *Copywriter*
John Gorse · *Art Director*
Harmut Gottschalk · *Photographer*
Alison Gould · *Graphic Designer*
Carl Gover · *Executive Producer*
Neil Gower · *Illustrator*
Alasdair Graham · *Copywriter*
Gordon Graham · *Copywriter*
Heather Graham · *Marketing Director*
Kenneth Grange CBE RDI FCSD · *Product Designer*
Kes Gray · *Copywriter*
Antony Green · *Designer*
Deborah Green · *Commercial Production*
Malcolm Green · *Copywriter*
Simon Green · *Art Director*
Charles Greene · *Creative Director/General Manager*
Howard Greenhalgh · *Director*
Jon Greenhalgh · *Art Director*
Michael Greenlees · *Chairman*
Barry Greensted · *Copywriter*
Iain Greenway · *Senior Graphic Designer*
Eddy Greenwood · *Art Director*
Mark Greenwood · *Art Director*
Nicky Gregorowski · *TV Producer*
Laura Gregory · *Producer*
Richard Gregory · *Graphic Designer*
John Grey · *Design Consultant*
Michael Griffin · *Producer*
Julian Griffiths · *Director*
Kenneth Griffiths · *Photographer*
Oscar Grillo · *Animation Director*
Steven Grime · *Creative Director*
Ken Grimshaw · *Art Director*
Ian Grindle · *Designer*
Lol Grinter · *Graphic Designer*
Steven Grounds · *Copywriter*
Paul Grubb · *Creative Director*
Daniel Grzonka · *Graphic Designer*
Michael Guarini · *Coordinator, Creative Services*
Guy Gumm · *Art Director*

H

John Hackney · *Managing Director/Producer*
Karen Hagemann · *Art Director*
Bruce Haines · *Chief Executive Officer*
Jeremy Haines · *Creative Director*
Jan Hall · *European Chief Executive*
Jonathan Hall · *Art Director*
Michael Hall · *Producer*
Ralph Hall · *Photographer*
Robin Hall · *Designer*
Siggi Halling · *Copywriter*
Geoff Halpin · *Typographer*
Doug Hamilton · *Creative Director*
Garrick Hamm · *Designer*
Martin Handyside · *Creative Services Director*
Mike Hannett · *Art Director*
Mark Hanrahan · *Head of Television*
Wayne Hanson · *Art Director*
Bryan Harber · *Sales Director*
Tony Hardcastle · *Art Director*
George Hardie · *Designer/Illustrator/Lecturer*
Chips Hardy · *Copywriter*
Simon Hardy · *Copywriter*
Liz Harold · *Career Consultant*
Peter Harold · *Head of Art*
Shaw Harper · *Creative Director*
W G Harrington · *Joint Creative Partner*
John Harris · *Creative Director/Partner*
Robert Harris · *Art Director*
Tony Harris · *Creative Director*
David Harrison · *Copywriter*
Iain Harrison · *Copywriter*
Simon Harsent · *Photographer*
Michael Hart · *Photographer*
Dragana Hartley · *Deputy Managing Director*
Chris Hartwill · *Director*
Mark Harwood · *Photographer*
Marcus Haslam · *Creative Director*
Derrick Hass · *Art Director*
Lionel Hatch · *Graphic Designer*
Jackie Hathiramani · *Senior Copywriter*
Michael Hausberger · *Chairman/Creative Director*
Ric Hawkes · *Director (Film) & Photographer*
Ian Hay · *Designer*
Richard Haydon · *Art Director*
Sarah Hayes · *Senior Administrator*
Nigel Haynes · *Photographer*
Diana Hayward · *Film Producer*
John Heaps · *Chairman*
Tim Hearn · *Copywriter*
John Hegarty · *Creative Director*
Alexander Hemming · *Director*
David Henderson · *Copywriter*
Ian Henderson · *Creative Director*
Richard Henderson · *Design Director*
Cathy Heng · *Art Director*
Max Henry · *Executive Creative Director*
Susie Henry · *Copywriter*
Robert Ian Heron · *Copywriter*
Margie Hetherington · *Designer*
Andreas Heumann · *Photographer*
Jerry Hibbert · *Animator*
David Hieatt · *Copywriter*
Sue Higgs · *Copywriter*
Alexandra Hill · *Art Director*
Robert Hillier · *Senior Lecturer*
Robert Hinks · *Model Maker*
Maria Hipwell · *Art Director/Copywriter*
Paul Hiscock · *Designer*
Jamie Hobson · *Lecturer*
Lee Hoddy · *Designer*
Martin Hodges · *Head of Copy*
Derek Hodgetts · *Copywriter*
Paul Hodgkinson · *Creative Director*
Gillian Hodgson · *Graphic Designer*
Kenneth Hodgson · *Art Director*
Peter Hodgson · *Designer*
Kenneth Hoggins · *Art Director*
Paul Holden · *Graphic Designer*
Roger Holdsworth · *Copywriter*
Jerry Hollens · *Art Director*
Megan Hollister · *Producer*
Robert Holloway · *Senior Marketing Manager*
Adrian Holmes · *Creative Director*
David Holmes · *Art Director/Designer*
Tony Holmes · *Design Director*
Steve Hooper · *Joint Creative Director*
Jeff Hopfer · *Art Director*
Jonathan Hornby · *Account Director*
Geoff Horne · *Copywriter*
Sue Horner · *Designer*
Sarah Horry · *TV Producer*
Michael Horseman · *Art Director*
John Horton · *Art Director*
Niall Horton-Stephens · *Photographers Agent*
Keren House · *Graphic Designer*
Mark Howard · *Art Director*
Michael Howard · *Designer*
Stewart Howard · *Art Director*
Peter Howard-Williams · *Managing Director*
Joe Hoza · *Typographer*
Tom Hudson · *Copywriter*
David Hughes · *Art Director*
Graham Hughes · *Photographer*
Sophie Humphreys · *Producer*
Robin Hunnam · *Creative Director*
Barrie Hunt · *Creative Director*
John Hunt · *Creative Director*
Simon Hunt · *Art Director*
Andrew Hunter · *Managing Director*
Tif Hunter · *Photographer*
Nan Huntingford · *Head of Marketing*
Sam Hurford · *Art Director*
Mark Hurst · *Designer*
Chris Hutchinson · *Creative Director*
Craig Hutton · *Graphic Designer*
Ian Hutton · *Copywriter*
Charlene Hymers · *Office Manager/Film Production House*
Richard Hytner · *Managing Director*

I

Jon Iles · *Art Director*
Claudia Immig · *Art Director*
Susie Immurs · *Creative Director*
Christopher Impey · *Designer*
Charles Inge · *Art Director*
Darrell Ireland · *Graphic Designer*
Richard Irvine · *Copywriter*
Richard Irvine · *Commercial Writer*
Richard Irving · *Art Director*
Bob Isherwood · *Creative Director*
Paul Izard · *Designer*

J

Craig Jackson · *Copywriter*
Harry M. Jacobs, Jr. · *Chief Executive Officer*
David James · *Photographer*
Kes James · *Designer*
Liz James · *Graphic Designer*
Rob Janowski · *Copywriter*
David Jeffers · *Managing Director*
Frazer Jelleyman · *Art Director*
David Jenkins · *Copywriter*
Nina Jenkins · *Graphic Designer*
Tom Jenkins · *Copywriter/Creative Director*
David Jennings · *Copywriter*
Yoh Jinno · *Printing Director/Art Director/Author*
Jonathan John · *Copywriter*
Simon John · *Design Director*
Betty Johnson · *Creative Dept. Administrator - Advertising*
Michael Johnson · *Designer*
Richard Johnson · *Designer*
Stephen Johnson · *Creative Director*
Timothy Johnson · *Head of Art*
David Johnston · *Art Director*
Derek Johnston · *Graphic Designer*
Barrie Joll · *Director*
Christopher I H Jones · *Executive Vice President*
David Jones · *Director*

Ed Jones · *Copywriter*
Ivor Jones · *Copywriter*
Nigel Jones · *Head of Planning*
Paul Jones · *Advertising Executive*
Penny Jones · *Designer*
Phil Jones · *Managing Director*
Steve Jones · *Art Director*
Michael Joseph · *Photographer*
Jane Joyce · *TV Producer*
Gerry Judah · *Production Designer/ Art Director/Modelmaker*
Jerry Judge · *Managing Director*

K

Nadav Kander · *Photographer*
Charles H. Kane · *Advertising Writer*
Esther Kaposi · *Communication Consultant*
Vidhu Kapur · *Traffic Manager*
Michael Kaufman · *Editor*
Dieter Kaufmann · *National Creative Director/Executive Vice President*
George Kavanagh · *Photographer*
Tony Kaye · *Director*
Adam Kean · *Copywriter*
Thomas Keane · *Art Director*
Giles Keeble · *Executive Creative Director*
John Kelley · *Creative Director*
Steve Kelsey · *Designer*
Adrian Kemsley · *Art Director*
Matthew Kemsley · *Typographer*
Kiki Kendrick · *Art Director*
Malcolm Kennard · *Designer*
Roger Kennedy · *Graphic Designer*
Trevor Kennedy · *Art Director*
Miranda Kennett · *Director of Training*
Nigel Kent · *Typographer*
Lucinda Ker · *Producer*
David Kerr · *Producer*
Barry Kettlewell · *Designer*
Phoa Kia Boon · *Designer*
Paul Kilvington · *Design Director*
Jeff Kindleysides · *Designer*
Ashley King · *Art Director*
Jason King · *Art Director*
Paul King · *Design Director*
Barry Kinsman · *Director*
Rodney Kinsman · *Art Director*
Janice M Kirkpatrick · *Designer*
Jonathan Kitchen · *Photographer*
Robert Kitchen · *Creative Director*
Alan Kitching RDI AGI · *Graphic Designer/Letterpress Typographer*
Kevin Kneale · *Copywriter*
Jilly Knight · *Animator*
Andrew Knowles · *Design Partner*
Claus Koch · *Designer*
Jacques Koeweiden · *Designer*
Amy Krouse Rosenthal · *Copywriter*
Thomas Krygier · *Director*
Albert Kueh · *Graphic Designer*
Klaus Kuster · *Chief Creative officer*
Ray Kyte · *Designer*

L

Kate Lackie · *Designer*
Larry Lai · *Business Manager*
Christine Lalumia · *Deputy Director*
Jimmy Lam · *Chairman & Executive Creative Director*
Claire Lambert · *Managing Director*
David Lambert · *Photographers Agent*
Martin Lambie-Nairn · *Designer*
Max Landrak · *Art Director*
Stephen Landsberg · *Senior Vice President/Creative Director*
Joe Lang · *Managing Director*
Ben Langdon · *Managing Director*
Sean Langford · *Designer*
John Larkin · *Managing Director*
Barry Lategan · *Photographer*
Peter Lavery · *Photographer*
Martin Lawless · *Graphic Designer*
Rick Lawley · *Film Editor*
Peter Lawlor · *Composer*
Amanda Lawrence · *Designer*
Norman Lawrence · *Lecturer*
Bob Lawrie · *Graphic Designer*
Andy Lawson · *Art Director*
Lauryn Le Clere · *Production Designer*
Ronald Leagas · *Chairman*
Sandra Leamon · *Creative Group Head*
Simon Learman · *Copywriter*
Richard Learoyd · *Film Editor*
Harvey Lee · *Art Director*
Vernon Lee · *Creative Director*
Paul Leeves · *Creative Director*
Stephen Legate · *Typographer*
Stein Leikanger · *Film Director*
David Leite · *Vice President/Senior Copywriter*
Adrianne Leman · *Managing Director*
Mike Lescarbeau · *Copywriter*
Timothy Leslie-Smith · *Graphic Designer*
Claudia Lester · *Computer Animator*
Peter Levelle · *Film Director*
Barbara Levett · *Producer*
Janetta Lewin · *Art Director*
Adrienne Lewis · *Corporate Communications Executive*
Dennis Lewis · *Art Director*
John Lewis · *Copywriter*
Mary Lewis · *Designer*
Frank Lieberman · *Agency Producer*
Melanie Light · *Studio Manager*
Daniel Lim · *Copywriter*
Sing Lim · *Copywriter*
Graham Lincoln · *Creative Director*
Andrew Lindsay · *Creative Director*
Christine Lindsay · *TV Producer*
Gavin Lindsay · *Model Maker*
Tim Lindsay · *Managing Director*
Gyles Lingwood · *Designer*
Domenic Lippa · *Design Director*
Rami Lippa · *Designer*
Tony Liston · *Creative Director*
David Little · *Creative Director*
Marrianne Little · *Copywriter/ Art Director*
Mark Littler · *Graphic Designer*
Carla Lloyd · *Education*
John Lloyd · *Designer*
Andrew Lloyd-Jones · *Copywriter*
David Lock · *Designer*
Linda Loe · *Designer*
Ian Logan · *Designer*
John Londei · *Photographer*
Mike London · *Art Director*
Martin Loraine · *Copywriter*
Peter Lorimer · *Copywriter*
Fran Lovell · *Creative Group Head*
Di Lowe · *Copywriter*
Frank Lowe · *Chairman*
Chris Lower · *Creative Director*
James Lowther · *Creative Director*
Marketa Luskacova · *Photographer*
David Lyle · *Chief Executive*
Doug Lyon · *Art Director*

M

Andrea MacArthur · *Film Editor*
Andrew MacDonald · *Special Effects Director/Editor*
David MacGregor Barlow · *Creative Director*
Stuart Mackay · *Planning Director*
David Mackersey · *Art Director*
Jonathan Madden · *Typographer*
Farrokh J Maddon · *Senior Copywriter*
Shyam Madiraju · *Art Director/ Copywriter*
David Magee · *Designer*
Peter Maisey · *Art Director*
Tony Malcolm · *Copywriter*
Lyndon Mallet · *Creative Director*
Simon Mallinson · *Producer*
Michael Manwaring · *Deputy Chairman*
Alex Maranzano · *Designer*
Alfredo Marcantonio · *Copywriter*
Pearce Marchbank · *Designer*
Pedro Marin-Guzman · *Creative Director*
Giles Marking · *Director*
John Marles · *Director*
Colin Marr · *Creative Director*
John Marsh · *Designer*
Ann Marshall · *Designer*
Jill Marshall · *Account Director*
Chris Martin · *Copywriter*
Gary Martin · *Art Director*
Greg Martin · *Art Director*
Paul Martin · *Designer*
Peter Martin · *Creative Principal*
Steven Martyn · *Managing Director*
Peter Matthews · *Designer*
Peter Matthews · *Creative Director*
Billy Mawhinney · *Creative Director*
Miriam Mawle · *Vice President Research & Development*
David May · *Art Director*
Sigi Mayer · *Creative Director/ Graphic Designer*
Beryl McAlhone · *Writer*
Douglas McArthur · *Managing Director*
Ian McAteer · *Account Manager*
Brian McCabe · *Art Director*
Ros McClellan · *Agency Producer*
Alex McCuaig · *Managing Director*
Vincent McEvoy · *Art Director*
Ian McIlroy · *Design Director*
Lynne McIntosh · *Graphic Designer/ Typographer*
Peter McIntosh · *Film Director*
Gordon McIntyre · *Creative Director*
Andy McKay · *Head of Art*
Mike McKenna · *Copywriter*
Sarah Jane McKenzie · *Design Director*
Denise McKeon · *TV Producer*
Roger McKerr · *Account Planner*
Aird McKinstrie · *Designer*
Deanne McLean · , *Director of Creative Recruitment*
Andy McLeod · *Copywriter*
Brigid McMullen · *Designer*
Tony McTear · *Art Director*
Roy Meares · *Creative Director*
Lindsay Medalia · *Creative Director*
Paul Meijer · *Creative Director*
Gary Mellish · *Managing Director*
Richard Mellor · *Designer*
Tim Mellors · *Creative Director*
Jack Melville · *Creative Director*
Jeff Merrells · *Head of Typography*
John Merriman · *Art Director*
Janos Meszaros · *Consultant*
Suzanne Miao · *Journalist*
Isabelle Michiet · *Artistic Director*
Peter Middleton · *Marketing Director*
Alan Midgley · *Creative Director*
Marcia Mihotich · *Graphic Designer*
Ruan Milborrow · *Creative Director*
David Miles · *Partner*
Jeremy Miles · *Board Account Director*
Peter Mill · *Copywriter*
Brian Millar · *Copywriter*
Don Miller · *Art Director*
Gerry Miller · *Copywriter*
Kathy Miller · *Designer*
Polly Miller · *Art Director*
Robert Miller · *Photographer*
Rodney Miller · *Designer*
Greg Mills · *Producer*
Colin Millward · *Creative Director*
Howard Milton · *Designer*
Marcello Minale · *Designer*
Clare Mitchell · *Producer*
Peter Mitchell · *Managing Director*
Andrew Mockett · *Illustrator*
Maxwell Modray · *Director/ Cameraman*
Gerry Moira · *Creative Director*
John Montgomery · *Television Producer*
Bob Moore · *Associate Creative Director*
Craig Moore · *Creative Director*
Guy Moore · *Art Director*
Karen Morgan · *Graphic Designer*
Rebecca Morgan · *Account Handler*
Kevin Morley · *Chairman*
Wendy Morrell · *Marketing Manager*
Brian Morris · *Director*
Edward Morris · *Art Director*
Robert Morris · *Art Director*
Brian Morrow · *Director*
Alan Moseley · *Copywriter*
James Mountain · *Designer*
David Muir · *Advertising Executive*
Kim Mukerjee · *Copywriter*
Ken Mullen · *Copywriter*
Barry Munchick · *Director*
Max Munck · *Art Director/Copywriter*
Chris Munds · *Chairman*
Tony Muranka · *Advertising Creative Independent*
Michael Murphy · *Art Director*
Patricia Murphy · *Director*
Richard Murray · *Client Services Director*
Lorna Murrell · *Copywriter*
Robin Murtough · *Copywriter*
Nicholas Mustoe · *Managing Director*
Richard Myers · *Copywriter*

N

Minazali Nanji · *Graphic Designer*
Ovais Naqvi · *Advertising Executive*
Stephanie Nash · *Designer*
Bill Naylor · *Managing Director*
Quentin Newark · *Graphic Designer*
Frances Newell · *Creative Director*
Stuart Newman · *Art Director*
Ronald Newsham · *Managing Director*
David Newton · *Art Director*
Grant Nielson · *Creative Director*
Barbara Nokes · *Copywriter*
Roger Nokes · *Creative Director*
Brendon Norman-Ross · *Director (Commercials)*
Mehdi Norowzian · *Director*
Tilly Northedge · *Designer*
Jim Northover · *Designer*
Graeme Norways · *Art Director*
Tom Notman · *Art Director*

O

Nicholas O'Bryan-Tear · *Copywriter*
Lizzie O'Connell · *Agency Producer*
Joseph O'Connor · *International Sales*
John O'Donnell · *Copywriter*
Daniel O'Donoghue · *Joint Chief Executive Officer*
John O'Driscoll · *Art Director*
Gerard O'Dwyer · *Designer*
Seamus O'Farrell · *Account Director*
Sean O'Flynn · *Creative Director*
John O'Keefe · *Copywriter*
Kate O'Mulloy · *Agency Producer*
Brian O'Neill · *Creative Director*
Laurence O'Neill · *Creative Services Director*
Chris O'Shea · *Copywriter*
Michael O'Sullivan · *Art Director*
Bill Oberlander · *Creative Director*
Stephen Ohler · *International Creative Director*
Barbro Ohlson · *Art Director*
Jerry Oke · *Photographer*
Robert Oliver · *Art Director*
Mark Osborn · *Creative Services Director*
Mark Osborne · *Designer*
Rosemary Oxley · *Art Director*

P

Alan Page · *Copywriter*
John Pallant · *Copywriter*
Chris Palmer · *Creative Director*
David Palmer · *Company Director*
Lizzie Palmer · *Head of Marketing & Events*
Kim Papworth · *Copywriter*
Ronnie Paris · *Musician*
Malcolm Park · *Creative Director*
John Parker · *Photographer*
John Parker · *Photographer*
Nigel Parry · *Photographer*
Mike Parsons · *Photographer*
Nick Parton · *Art Director*
John Pasche · *Creative Director*
Gemini Patel · *Graphic Designer/ Illustrator*
Peakash Patel · *Graphic Designer*
Neil Patterson · *Creative Director*
Gerardo Pavone · *Executive Creative Director*
Derek Payne · *Copywriter*
Geoff Payne · *Film Editor*
Lyndy Payne · *Managing Director*
Arnold Pearce · *Producer*
David Pearce · *Designer*
Harry Pearce · *Design Director*
Jack Pearce · *Designer*
Mark Pearce · *Designer*
Alex Pearl · *Copywriter*
John Pearson · *Managing Director*
John Pearson-Taylor · *Designer*
Peter Pedersen · *Typographer/ Technical Director*

Nicholas Peers · *TV Producer*
Jeremy Pemberton · *Creative Director*
Simon Pemberton · *Designer*
Ricardo Perez · *President Creative Director*
Sean Perkins · *Designer*
Michael Peters · *Designer*
Richard Petersen · *Design Consultant/Lecturer*
David Petschack · *Typographer*
Tor Pettersen · *Designer*
Bob Pettis · *Partner*
Chrissie Phillips · *Producer*
Steve Philpott · *Marketing Director*
John Pickering · *Designer*
T Pinder · *Creative Director*
Joyce Pinto · *Portfolio Presentation*
Emanuele Pirella · *Chairman*
Donna Pittman · *Designer/Director*
Jane Pollard · *Design Manager*
Jeanna Polley · *Producer*
Nick Pollitt · *Designer*
Paolo Pollo · *Copywriter*
David Pollock · *Director*
Jay Pond-Jones · *Creative Director*
Russell Porcas · *Photographer*
Colin Porter · *Illustrator*
Robert Porter · *Copywriter*
Mark Posnett · *Creative Director*
Michael Potter · *Managing Director*
Chris Powell · *Chief Executive*
Michelle Power · *Copywriter*
John Powner · *Graphic Designer*
Keith Priest · *Designer*
Hamish Pringle · *Chairman*
Andrew Pritchard · *Editorial Designer*
Ann Pugsley · *Managing Director*
Tim Purvis · *Creative Director*
Trevor Purvis · *Creative Director*
David Puttnam · *Film Producer*

Q

Andrew Quinn · *Chief Executive*
Stephen Quinn · *Publishing Director*

R

M T Rainey · *Managing Partner*
Sonia Ralton · *Producer*
Russell Ramsey · *Art Director*
Harry Rankin · *Producer*
Malcolm Rasala · *Director*
Andy Ray · *Copywriter*
Tom Rayfield · *Creative Director*
Richard Reast · *European Account Director*
Carolyn Reed · *Designer*
Nigel Reed · *Copywriter*
Sharon Reed · *Managing Director*
Helena Rees · *Managing Director*
Steven Reeves · *Copywriter*
Mabelle Rennie · *Creative Director*
Jeremy Rewse-Davies · *Design Director*
Hugh Ribbans · *Graphic Designer*
Jill Richards · *Creative Director*
Mark Richards · *Film Editor*
Paul Richards · *Board Account Director*
Steven Richards · *Copywriter*
Darren Richardson · *Designer*
Martin Riddiford · *Designer*
Philip Ridge · *Product Development Manager*
Chris Ridley · *Photographer*
Tony Riggs · *Art Director*
Tim Riley · *Copywriter*
James Riswold · *Associate Creative Director/Partner*
Ian Ritchie · *Designer*
John Ritchie · *Deputy Chairman*
Mike Rix · *Typographer*
Francesco Rizzi · *Art Director*
Mark Roalfe · *Art Director*
Colin Robinson · *Designer*
Frederick Robinson · *Producer*
Mark Robinson · *New Business Director*
Michael Robinson · *Illustrator*
Stuart Robinson · *Art Director*
Paul Rodger · *Designer*
Simon Rodway · *Copywriter*
Justin Rogers · *Copywriter*
Tom Rogers · *Art Director*
Joe Roman · *Director/Designer*
Stephen Ronchetti · *Joint Managing Director*
Graham Rose · *Director*
Nigel Rose · *Creative Director*
Simon Roseblade · *Copywriter*
Peregrine Roskilly · *Illustrator*
Alistair Ross · *Art Director/Copywriter*
Helen Ross · *Creative Manager*
Michael Ross · *Art Director/Designer/Director*
David Rossiter · *Copywriter*
Tom Roth · *Creative Director*
Paul Rothwell · *TV Producer*
Andy Rott · *Art Director*
Robin Rout · *Art Director*
Adrian Rowbotham · *Director*
Lin Roworth-Stokes · *Managing Director*
Mark Rudd · *Copywriter*
John Rushton · *Director*
John Rushworth · *Designer*
Geoffrey Russell · *Marketing Controller*
Jonathan Russell · *Designer*
Michael C E Russell · *Photographer*
Peter Russell · *Copywriter*
Richard Russell · *Copywriter*
Matt Ryan · *Art Director*
Phil Rylance · *Art Director*
David Ryland · *Creative Director*
Michael Rylander · *Creative Director*

S

Eric Saarinen · *Director/Cameraman*
Charles Saddington · *Photographic Producer*
Anthony Sadler · *Composer*
Gaynor Sadler · *Composer*
Maurizio Sala · *Chief Creative Director*
John Salmon · *Creative Director*
Martin Sampson · *Director*
Gustavo Sanchez · *Associate Creative Director*
Madeleine Sanderson · *Producer*
Colin Sands · *Designer*
Jim Saunders · *Art Director*
Tiger Savage · *Art Director*
Murray Savidan · *Film Director*
Paolo Savignano · *Copywriter/Creative Director*
Clemens Schedler · *Principal*
Bob Schiffrar · *Copywriter*
Richard Schlagman · *Book Publisher*
Richard Scholey · *Designer*
Nick Schon · *Art Director*
Gerrit Schreurs · *Photographer*
Klaus Schultheis · *Art Director*
Graham Scott · *Design Director*
Kenneth Scott · *Creative Director*
Nicholas Scott · *Art Director*
Simon Scott · *Creative Director*
William Scott · *Art Director*
Luca Scotto Di Carlo · *Copywriter*
Pat Scovell · *Art Buyer*
Derek Seaward · *Photographer*
Richard Selbourne · *Copywriter*
Katy Sender · *Deputy Director*
Geoff Senior · *Photographer*
Geoffrey Seymour · *Director*
Richard Seymour · *Designer*
Bob Shannon · *Copywriter*
Harry Shaw · *Copywriter*
Jaspar Shelbourne · *Creative Director*
Robin Shenfield · *Facility Director*
Duncan Shepherd · *Editor*
Sarah Shepherd · *Designer*
Simon Sherwood · *Managing Director*
Allan Shiach · *Chairman*
Eddie Shieh · *Art Director*
Brian Shields · *Director*
Jono Shubitz · *Creative Director*
Paul Silburn · *Copywriter*
Peter Silk · *Graphic Designer*
Roland Sillem · *Art Director*
John Silver · *Copywriter*
Paul Simblett · *Creative Director*
Anthony Simonds-Gooding · *Chairman*
Sergio Simonetti · *Animator/Director*
Paul Simons · *Chairman*
Matt Simpkins · *Copywriter*
Loz Simpson · *Copywriter*
James Sinclair · *Copywriter*
Jeremy Sinclair · *Executive Creative Director*
Ros Sinclair · *Copywriter*
Indra Sinha · *Copywriter*
Ian Sizer · *Art Director*
Gabriele Skelton · *Career Consultant*
David Smart · *Head of Design*
Barry Smith · *Copywriter*
David Smith · *Director*
Geoff Smith · *Copywriter*
Jan Smith · *Marketing Director*
Jay Smith · *Designer*
John Smith · *Editor*
Markham Smith · *Copywriter*
Martin Smith · *Vice Chairman*
Paul Smith · *Art Director*
Richard Peter Smith · *Design Director*
Rick Smith · *Creative Director/Chairman*
Roy Smith · *Lighting Cameraman*
Willie Sonnenberg · *Chairman & Executive Creative Director*
John Sorrell · *Art Director*
Peter Souter · *Copywriter*
Georgia Spaccapietra · *Copywriter*
John Spearman · *Chief Executive*
Dorothy Speed · *Head of Marketing*
Stephen Spence · *Copywriter*
Charlie Spencer · *Music Composer*
Steven Spencer · *Graphic Designer*
David Sproxton · *Director*
Vince Squibb · *Art Director*
Bela Stamenkovita · *Creative Director*
Gerard Stamp · *Creative Director*
Michael Staniford · *Creative Director*
John Stanley · *Managing Director*
Kate Stanners · *Art Director*
Horst Stasny · *Photographer*
Jon Steel · *Partner/Planning Director*
Hillary S Steinberg · *Manager, Creative Library*
Kate Stephens · *Designer*
Mike Stephenson · *Director*
Paul Stephenson · *Design Manager*
Terence Stevens Prior · *Art Director*
David Stevenson · *Corporate Communications Manager*
Jeffrey Steventon · *Designer*
Brian Stewart · *Creative Director*
Anthony Stileman · *Designer/Art Director*
Nigel Stone · *Managing Director*
Graham Storey · *Art Director*
Celia Stothard · *Graphic Designer*
Mark Stothert · *Producer*
Tony Strong · *Copywriter*
David Stuart · *Designer*
John Stubbings · *Managing Director*
Jeremy Stubbs · *European Advertising Manager*
Barry Sugondo · *Copywriter*
Ed Sullivan · *Designer*
Frank Sully · *Art Director*
Sarah Summerbell · *Design Manager*
Kevin Summers · *Photographer*
James Surridge · *Designer*
Sian Sutherland · *Managing Partner*
Jeff Suthons · *Art Director*
Linda Sutton · *Art Director*
Rupert Sutton · *Copywriter/Creative Director*

T

Shen Guan Tan · *Executive Creative Director*
Clive Tanquerary · *Account Director*
Amanda Tatham · *Graphic Designer*
Brian Tattersfield · *Designer*
Alexandra Taylor · *Head of Art*
Brian Taylor · *Design Manager*
David Taylor · *Film Director*
Graham Taylor · *Creative Director*
Steven Taylor · *Art Director*
Philippa Tedder · *Producer*
Nancy Temkin · *Senior Partner, Creative Manager*
Keith Terry · *Art Director*
Genevieve Theseira · *Style Director*
Nick Thirkell · *Designer*
Allen Thomas · *Copywriter*
Andrew Thomas · *Designer*
Kevin Thomas · *Art Director*
Bill Thompson · *Art Director*
Mark Campbell Thompson · *Writer*
Martin Thompson · *Photographer*
Matt Thomson · *Typographer*
Sean Thompson · *Art Director*
Ross Thomson · *Creative Director*
Ross Thomson · *Creative Director*
John Thornton · *Director*
Mark Thrush · *Designer*
Vernon Tickell · *Managing Director*
Dan Tierney · *Photographer*
Richard Tilley · *Designer*
Sean Toal · *Copywriter*
Andre Toet · *Creative Director*
Alison Tomlin · *Designer*
Tony Tonkin · *Art Director*
Gary Topolewski · *Advertising/Creative Director*
Gordon Torr · *Creative Director*
Peter Townsend · *Creative Director*
John Townshend · *Copywriter*
Lynn Trickett · *Director/Designer*
Steve Trotter · *Creative Director*
John Trumper · *Sales Director/Marketing Director*
Mike Turnbull · *Managing Director*
David Turner · *Designer*
John Turner · *Exhibition Designer*
John Turner · *Photographer*
Joyce Turner · *Copywriter*
Dean Turney · *Copywriter*
Christopher Turrall · *Art Director*
Claire Tuthill · *Designer*
Glenn Tutssel · *Designer*
Paul Twivy · *Chief Executive*

V

Peter Van den Engel · *Art Director/Creative Director*
John Van Dyke · *Graphic Designer*
Jan Van Meel · *Creative Director*
Jan Van Mesdag · *Copywriter*
Ami Van Dine · *Designer*
Christopher Vane · *Designer*
Louise Vanstone · *Copywriter*
Andy Vargo · *Designer*
Judy Veal · *Designer*
Tony Veazey · *Copywriter*
Malcolm Venville · *Photographer*
Andrew Vere · *Company Director*
Pierre Vermeir · *Designer*
Jackie Vicary · *Creative Director*
Sian Vickers · *Art Director*
Cedric Vidler · *Creative Director European*
Mike Villiers-Stuart · *Producer/Director*
Suzanne Viner · *Creative Director*
Irene Von Treskow · *Illustrator*

W

Russell Wailes · *Art Director*
Christopher Waite · *Copywriter*
David Wakefield · *Typographer*
Alan Waldie · *Art Director*
Russell Waldron · *Art Director*
Mitch Walker · *Director*
Neil Walker · *Designer*
Robert Walker · *Photographer*
Hayley Jane Wall · *Graphic Designer*
Steven Wallington · *Typographer*
Jake Wallis · *Photographer*
Michael Wallis · *Graphic Designer*
Robert Wallis · *Head of Typography*
Bill Wallsgrove · *Creative Director*
Martyn Wallwork · *Designer*
Amanda Walsh · *Managing Director*
Baillie Walsh · *Film Director*
Martyn Walsh · *Art Director*
Michael Jeffrey Walsh · *Chairman*
Sam Walsh · *Broadcast Producer*
John Ward · *Planning Director*
Nigel Ward · *Studio Manager*
Richard Ward · *Designer*
Jamie Warde-Aldam · *Copywriter*
Simon Warden · *Typographer*
David Wardlaw · *Marketing Manger*
Peter Warren · *Director*
Rod Waskett · *Art Director*
Dave Waters · *Creative Director*
Eric Watson · *Director*
Graham Watson · *Art Director*
Chris Wauton · *Advertising*
Mary Wear · *Copywriter*
Brian Webb · *Designer*
Graham Webb · *Graphic Designer*
Peter Webb · *Photographer*
Mitch Webber · *Account Director*
John Webster · *Copywriter*

Geoff Weedon · *Creative Director*
Karin Weidema · *Art Director*
Ian Weil · *Film Editor*
Paul Weiland · *Director*
Paul Weinberger · *Creative Director*
Len Weinreich · *Creative Director*
Mark Welby · *Designer*
Nicholas Welch · *Creative Director*
Michael Wells · *Art Director*
Joanna Wenley · *Art Director*
Douglas Werby · *Director*
Michael Werkmeister · *Designer*
Paul West · *Art Director*
Ronnie West · *Producer*
Shaun Westgate · *Designer*
Sean Wetz · *Packaging Development Designer*
Ken Wheat · *Copywriter*
John Wheeler · *Managing Director*
Mandy Wheeler · *Managing Director*
David Wheldon · *Vice President, Director of Advertising*
David White · *Art Director/Copywriter*
Jane White · *Client Services Director*
Paul White · *Creative Director*
Paul White · *Creative Director*
Montgomery Whitebloom · *Director*
Pauline Whitehouse · *Registrar*
Mark Wickens · *Chairman*
Valerie Wickes · *Design Director*
Ian Wight · *Designer*
Robin Wight · *Chairman*
Scott Wild · *Copywriter*
Christopher Wilkins · *Creative Director*
Mark Wilkins · *Copywriter*
Anthony Wilks · *Graphic Designer*
Greg Willcox · *Editor*
Simon Willcox · *Film Editor*
Brian Williams · *Creative Director*
David Williams · *Copywriter*
Don Williams · *Creative Director*
Nancy Williams · *Designer*
Rodger Williams · *Creative Director*
Steve Williams · *Art Director*
Gary Willis · *Art Director*
Dennis Willison · *Art Director*
Mark Wilson · *Advertising Executive*
Patrick Wilson · *Managing Director*
Peter Windett · *Art Director*
Paul Windsor · *Photographer*
Guy Wingate · *Composer*
Guy Winston · *Creative Director*
Brian Wiseman · *Managing Director*
Mariann Wissa · *Art Director/ Visual Designer*
Mark Wnek · *Senior Copywriter*
Michael Wolf · *Designer*
Stephen Wolstenholme · *Typographer*
David Wombwell · *Creative Director*
Alan Wong · *Art Director*
Eddie Wong · *Art Director*
Margaret Wong · *Administrative Secretary*
Phillip Wong · *Designer*
Alistair Wood · *Copywriter*
John Wood · *Creative Director*
John Wood · *Sign Designer*
Lynne Wood · *Director*
Peter Wood · *Photographer*
David Woodall · *Art Director*
Graham Woodall · *Executive Creative Director*
Roger Woodburn · *Film Director*
Gary Woodward · *Art Director - Deputy C.D.*
Patrick Woodward · *Copywriter*
Nick Wootton · *Art Director*
Claire Worthington · *MD, Advertising Staff Consultants*
David Worthington · *Designer*
Nick Worthington · *Copywriter*
Susan Worthy · *Director*
Matthew Wurr · *Model Maker*

Y

Jimmy Yang · *Graphic Designer*
Clive Yaxley · *Art Director*
Ruth Yee · *Art Director*
Richard Yelland · *Copywriter*

Z

Bernie Zlotnick · *Advertising/ Sales Promotion*
Richard Zobel · *Chairman & CEO*
Debra Zuckerman · *Consultant Art Director*

INDEX

AGENCIES

AGENCY PRODUCERS

ANIMATORS

ARCHITECT

ART DIRECTORS

AUTHORS

CLIENTS

CONCEPT CREATORS

COPYWRITERS

CREATIVE DIRECTORS

DESIGN DIRECTORS

DESIGN GROUPS

DESIGN TEAMS

DESIGNERS

DIRECTORS OF PHOTOGRAPHY

DIRECTORS

EDITORS

GRAPHIC DESIGNERS

ILLUSTRATORS

INDUSTRIAL DESIGNERS

LIGHTING CAMERAMEN

MANUFACTURERS

MARKETING EXECUTIVES

MUSIC COMPOSERS/ ARRANGERS

OS & ELECTRONIC DESIGN

PHOTOGRAPHERS

PRODUCERS

PRODUCTION COMPANIES

PRODUCTION DESIGN ENGINEERS

RECORD COMPANIES

RECORDING ENGINEERS

RECORDING STUDIO

ROSTRUM CAMERAMEN

SCULPTORS

SET DESIGNERS

SOFTWARE DESIGNERS

SOUND DESIGNERS

SPECIAL EFFECTS

STYLISTS

TECHNICAL DESIGNERS

3D SUPERVISOR

TYPOGRAPHERS

CUDA PRODUCTS CORP.
This is
Mr. Tony Spelling
head neurosurgeon.
On average Tony will perform Brain Surgery 4 times a week.
Unlike Photographers, Designers, Art Directors, Copywriters and Film Makers
there are no award systems to commend Tony's line of work.
However, if he fails to deliver 100%, people die.
Congratulations
to all those people who received accolades and commendations in this year's D&AD,
for those who didn't, think of Tony and ask yourself, did you put in 100%?
SPONSORS OF D&AD
95.8 CAPITAL FM
LONDON

BEWARE WET PAINT
PHAIDON

Ian Berry
Living Apart
PHAIDON
Witty thinking in graphic design
Beryl McAlhone & David Stuart
A SMILE IN THE MIND
Foreword by Edward de Bono
Designed by The Partners
PHAIDON

John Welsh
Modern House
PHAIDON

E.H.GOMBRICH
THE STORY OF ART
PHAIDON

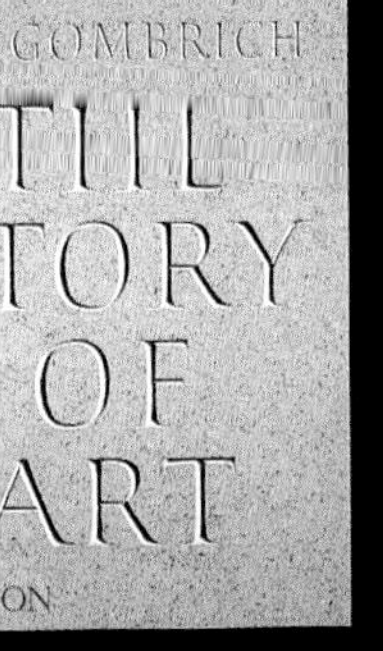

PHAIDON

H·A·MEEK
THE SYNAGOGUE
PHAIDON
THE ART BOOK
PHAIDON

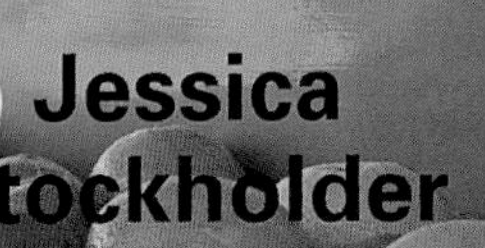
Jessica Stockholder
Edward Lucie-Smith
ARTODAY

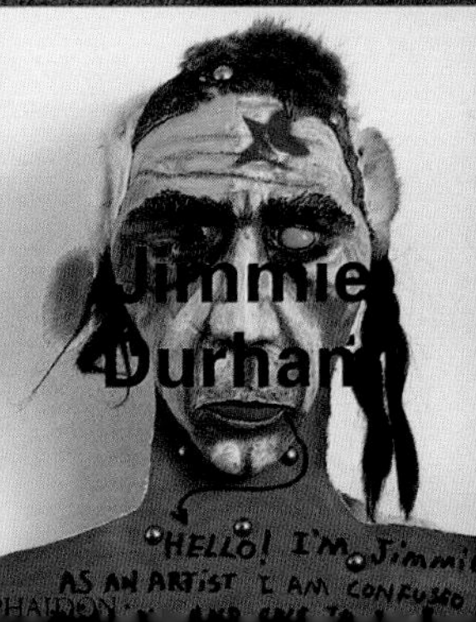
Jimmie Durham
HELLO! I'M Jimmie
AS AN ARTIST I AM CONFUSED